Where to Wear 2006

FASHION SHOPPING FROM A-Z

Fairchild & Gallagher

NEW YORK • LONDON

PUBLISHERS
Jill Fairchild, Gerri Gallagher & Julie Craik

SERIES COPY EDITOR
John Graham

SERIES DESIGN/PRODUCTION ARTIST
Jeff Baker & Cynthia Roberts
at BookMechanics

WRITER
Angela Gaimari

FACT CHECKER
H. Anna Suh

PREVIOUS EDITOR
Greg Zinman

COVER DESIGN
Richard Chapman

DISTRIBUTION, SALES AND MARKETING
The Julie Craik Consultancy

Where to Wear, New York, 2006 Edition

ISBN 0-9766877-0-4

Copyright © 2005 Fairchild & Gallagher

Manhattan maps © 2000 Eureka Cartography
Maps courtesy of Graphic Image, Inc.

Printed and bound in China.

Table of Contents

You can contact Where to Wear at our offices in
New York, London or Sydney as follows:

New York
666 Fifth Avenue
PMB 377
New York, NY 10103
tel 212-969-0138
toll-free 1-877-714-SHOP (7467)
fax 914-763-0056
e-mail usa@wheretowear.com

London
10 Cinnamon Row, Plantation Wharf
London SW11 3TW
tel 020 7801 1381
e-mail uk@wheretowear.com

Sydney
tel 0061 (02) 9361 3341
e-mail australia@wheretowear.com
www.wheretowear.com

Introduction

Dear New York Shopper,

Welcome to *Where to Wear*, the world's most detailed and authoritative directory of clothing and accessory stores. *Where to Wear* annually updates its collection of global guides, making your travels through the world's fashion cities a breeze. We pioneered in 1999 with *Where to Wear New York*, and we have since added London, Los Angeles, Paris, San Francisco, Italy (Florence, Milan and Rome), Las Vegas, Florida and Australia.

The 2006 edition of *Where to Wear New York* has all the information you'll need to look and feel great. We describe nearly 1,000 different clothing and accessories stores, ranging from the global celebrity names of Madison Avenue and SoHo to out-of-the-way treasure-houses. *Where to Wear* shows visitors where to begin and New Yorkers where to go next. If you want the best vintage value or the brightest bikini, you'll find them using *Where to Wear*.

Where to Wear is the only shopping guide written by a team of professional fashion journalists. We have our fingers on the pulse of the ever-changing fashion world. We've tromped through each and every store to discover what's fabulous, functional, frumpy, fancy or frightful in them this season. We tell you what the store and its merchandise are all about and who its target customer is, and we list the address, phone number and opening hours. We've marked those stores that merit special consideration with a star (★), and occasionally we have something sweet (or not so sweet) to say about the staff's helpfulness or attitude. Please let us know if you disagree.

And to make your life even simpler we have included ten pages of user-friendly maps and two separate indexes grouping the stores both by category and by location. Shopping has never been easier! In addition, you'll find the best addresses for beauty treatments, fitness studios, day spas, couture dry cleaners, shoe repair shops, specialty stores (for beads, ribbons, etc) and much else.

Life is not all shopping, of course, so you will also find a list of in-store restaurants and other delightful lunch spots. It's an eclectic list, chosen by our experts for your fun and convenience.

So rev up your credit card and get going, and make sure to keep *W2W* in your handbag, briefcase or backpack.

—Jill Fairchild, Gerri Gallagher & Julie Craik

p.s. We love feedback! Please e-mail us on

uk@wheretowear.com or usa@wheretowear.com

Jill Fairchild, daughter of fashion world legend and *W* magazine founder John Fairchild, worked as an intern at *Glamour* magazine, *GQ* and *Vogue*. Ms Fairchild has also worked for Ailes Communications, a television production company, and in the late Eighties she founded and ran her own accessories company.

Gerri Gallagher is a Condé Nast editor who has lived in Europe for 20 years. She was the managing editor of Fairchild Publication's *W Europe* from 1990 to 1993 and is currently associate editor of *Tatler* magazine in London.

Julie Craik, *Where to Wear* partner and director of sales, marketing and distribution has worked in publishing for 20 years. Before joining *Where to Wear* she was associate publisher of *Tatler* magazine and had previously worked for the National Magazine Company.

Where to Wear 2006

Best Picks

Size Conversion Chart

Glossary of Terms

Manhattan Overview Map

Best Picks *(marked ⭐ in the Directory)*

If money were no object...

37=1
Alexander McQueen
Asprey
Barneys
Balenciaga
Basso Furs
Bergdorf Goodman
Berluti
Bottega Veneta
Brioni
Burberry
Celine
Chanel
Chloé
Christian Louboutin
Comme des Garçons
Dolce & Gabbana
Domenico Vacca
Emanuel Ungaro
Eres
Gucci
Hermès
Hot Toddie
Jeffrey
Jimmy Choo
J.Mendel
Keni Valenti
Kirna Zabête
Linda Dresner
Louis Vuitton
Manolo Blahnik
Marc Jacobs
Marni
Massimo Bizzocchi
Michael Kors
Missoni
Oscar de la Renta
Prada
Pucci
Ralph Lauren
Resurrection Vintage
Seize sur Vingt (16/20)
Tod's
Vera Wang
Versace
Via Bus Stop
Yohji Yamamoto
YSL

Because we're worth it—for instant cheer on a rainy day...

Anthony Kirby
Anya Hindmarch
Azaleas
Bond 07
Borealis
Butik
Calypso

Cantaloup
Castor & Pollux
Catbird
Catriona MacKechnie
Christopher Fischer
Erica Tanov
Jamin Puech
Lace
La Petite Coquette
Le Corset
Lucien Pellat Finet
Lunettes et Chocolat
Malatesta
Marc by Marc Jacobs
Mayle
Me & Ro
Pucci
Selima Optique
Shop
Sleep
Some Odd Rubies
Tory by TRB
Tracy Feith

Show-stoppers—these stores have to be seen to be believed...

Alexander McQueen
An Earnest Cut & Sew
Asprey
Balenciaga
Bergdorf Goodman
Carlos Miele
Catherine Malandrino
Christian Dior
Diesel
Donna Karan
Duncan Quinn
Ellen Christine Millinery
Elizabeth Charles
Geminola
Girlshop
Henry Béguelin
Hermès
Jeffrey
Kirna Zabête
Louis Vuitton
Prada
Stella McCartney
Three Turtle Doves

Great style, fantastic prices...

30 Vandam
Abercrombie & Fitch
Amarcord Vintage Fashion
Beacon's Closet
Century 21
Darling
Edith & Daha

Hootie Couture
Ina
J.Crew
Operations
Pearl River Mart
Pippin
Slang Betty
Sorelle Firenze
Tokio 7

Pitter-patter of tiny feet...

Cadeau
La Layette
Liz Lange Maternity
Veronique Maternity

...and for the kids themselves

Baby Bird
Bombalulus
Bonpoint
Calypso Enfant
City Cricket
Gap Baby/Kids
G.C.William
Great Feet
Greenstones & Cie
Gymboree
Jacadi
Julian and Sara
Just for Tykes
Koh's Kids
Lilliput/SoHo Kids
Magic Windows
Morris Bros
Old Navy
Oilily
OshKosh B'Gosh
Peanutbutter & Jane
Peter Elliot (Kids)
Petit Bateau
Ralph Lauren Baby
Yoya
Z' Baby

Ever-reliable...

American Apparel
Ann Taylor
Anthropologie
Banana Republic
Barneys
Bergdorf Goodman
Brooks Brothers
Century 21
Coach
Earl Jean
Eileen Fisher
Gap
Henri Bendel
Intermix
James Perse

J.Crew
Jeffrey
Lord & Taylor
Old Navy

If we could take the whole shop home...

Albertine
Alife
Asprey
Elizabeth Charles
Frock
Girlshop
Henry Béguelin
Hermès
Jeffrey
Kirna Zabête
Marc Jacobs
Miu Miu
Puma
Rubin Chappelle
Some Odd Rubies
Tracy Feith
Via Bus Stop

Service with a smile—the most helpful people in town...

Addison on Madison
Bagutta Life
Blades Board and Skate
Brioni
Brooks Brothers
Catbird
Chanel
Christian Dior
Darling
Denimaxx
Eastern Mountain Sports
Elizabeth Charles
H.Herzfeld
Henri Bendel
Hervé Léger
Jane
Jeffrey
Keiko
Malia Mills
Operations
Paragon
Pookie & Sebastian
Ralph Lauren
Saint Laurie
Sleep
Swiss Army
Super Runners Shop
Turnbull & Asser
Yves Saint Laurent
 Rive Gauche

3

Clothing & Shoe Size Equivalents

Children's Clothing

American	3	4	5	6	6X
Continental	98	104	110	116	122
British	18	20	22	24	26

Children's Shoes

American	8	9	10	11	12	12	1	2	3
Continental	24	25	27	28	29	30	32	33	34
British	7	8	9	10	11	12	13	1	2

Ladies' Coats, Dresses, Skirts

American	3	5	7	9	11	12	13	14	15
Continental	36	38	38	40	40	42	42	44	44
British	8	10	11	12	13	14	15	16	17

Ladies' Blouses and Sweaters

American	10	12	14	16	18	20
Continental	38	40	42	44	46	48
British	32	34	36	38	40	42

Ladies' Hosiery

American	8	8.5	9	9.5	10	10.5
Continental	1	2	3	4	5	6
British	8	8.5	9	9.5	10	10.5

Ladies' Shoes

American	5	6	7	8	9	10
Continental	36	37	38	39	40	41
British	3.5	4.5	5.5	6.5	7.5	8.5

Men's Suits

American	34	36	38	40	42	44	46	48
Continental	44	46	48	50	52	54	56	58
British	34	36	38	40	42	44	46	48

Men's Shirts

American	14	15	15.5	16	16.5	17	17.5	18
Continental	37	38	39	41	42	43	44	45
British	14	15	15.5	16	16	17	17.5	18

Men's Shoes

American	7	8	9	10	11	12	13
Continental	39.5	41	42	43	44.5	46	47
British	6	7	8	9	10	11	12

Glossary of Terms

Avant-garde: forward-thinking or advanced. When referring to art or costume, sometimes implies erotic or startling. Derived from the French for "advance guard".

Bridge collection: a collection that is priced between designer and mass market.

Couture: French word used throughout fashion industry to describe the original styles, the ultimate in fine sewing and tailoring, made of expensive fabrics, by designers. The designs are shown in collections twice a year—spring/summer and fall/winter.

Custom-made/tailor-made, also called bespoke: garments made by tailor or couture house for an individual customer following couturier's original design. Done by either fitting a model form adjusted to the customer's measurements or by several personal fittings.

Diffusion line: a designer's second and less expensive collection.

Ensemble: an entire costume, including accessories, worn at one time. Two or more items of clothing designed and coordinated to be worn together.

Fashion trend: direction in which styles, colors and fabrics are moving. Trends may be influenced by political events, films, personalities, dramas, social and sporting events or indeed any human activity.

Faux: false or counterfeit, imitation: used in connection with gems, pearls and leathers. Faux fur (fake fur) is commonplace today, as is what is sometimes known as "pleather" (plastic leather). Artificial gems, especially pearls, are often made from a fine kind of glass known as "paste", and are accordingly sometimes called "paste" for short.

Haberdashery: a store that sells men's apparel and furnishings.

Knock-off: trade term for the copying of an item of apparel, e.g. a dress or a coat, in a lower price line. Similar to piracy.

Made-to-measure: clothing (dress, suit, shirt etc) made according to individual's measurement. No fittings required.

One-off: a unique, one-of-a-kind item that will not be found in any other store or produced again in the future, e.g. a customized denim skirt or a rare vintage cocktail dress. Can also refer to made-to-measure and couture garments designed for a particular person and/or event, such as a dress for the Oscars.

Prêt-à-porter: French term which literally means ready-to-wear, i.e. to take (or wear) straight out of the shop.

Ready-to-wear (rtw): apparel that is mass-produced in standard sizes. Records of the ready-to-wear industry tabulated in the U.S. Census of 1860 included hoop skirts, cloaks, and mantillas; from 1890 shirtwaists and wrappers were added; and, after 1930, dresses.

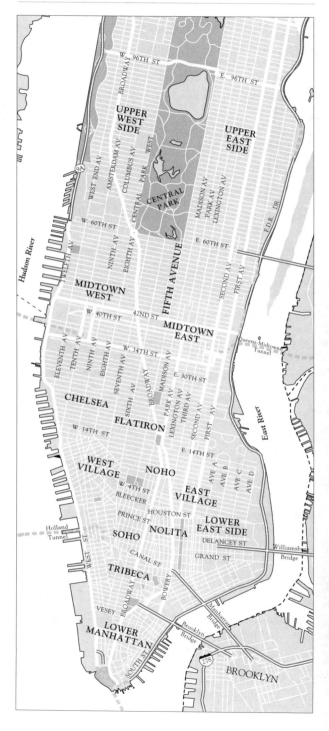

Alphabetical Store Directory

★ **30 Vandam**

Like being the only kid on your block with the flashiest new threads? Well, you aren't truly running with the in crowd if you haven't heard of 30 Vandam. This new SoHo boutique, practically a stone's throw from the Holland tunnel, showcases 50 handpicked designers that it foresees being the next batch of fashion big shots. Names like Colleen Quen Couture, Pure Ginger, Ashley Dearborn and Mle Hagen may not mean anything to you now, but remember: you saw it here first. *30vandam.com*

Expensive   *Amex/MC/V*

SoHo   **(212) 929-6454**
30 Vandam Street   btw Sixth/Varick
NYC 10013   Daily 12-8 (Sun 12-6)

★ **37=1**

Designer Jean Yu's clients are 'women who can discern the small and subtle nuances'. Maybe that's why most are willing to pay upwards of $350 for a pair of panties. Not that 37=1 is just lingerie, it's more like a couture atelier in the Vionnet mold. And although Yu's chic made-to-measure pieces and garter belts are worth the trip alone (most lingerie here has no elastic and is made from the most delicate silks, secured with subtle hooks), she also dreams up beautifully constructed silk dresses with a slightly decadent Twenties bent, which are now available in London at Dover Street Market, the new Commes des Garçons. In a word, extraordinary.

Luxury   *Amex/MC/V*

SoHo   **(212) 226-0067**
37 Crosby Street   btw Broome/Grand
NYC 10013   Tues-Sun 1-6 (and by appointment)

A Bathing Ape (BAPE)

Japanese fashion fanatics border on obsessive when it comes to their favorite couture designer, and strive to collect as much limited-edition merch as possible. A Bathing Ape is bringing this concept to the American hip-hop/skater demographic with the small quantity urban streetwear collections available at this split-level white and chrome enclave. Signature ape-infused print covers wallets and flip-flops, and the store's mantra 'Ape Shall Never Kill Ape' emblazons tees. Also available are baseball caps by Pharell Williams' Billionaire Boyz Club. Head upstairs for a wall of backlit cubbyholes, each displaying a single shoe— Foot Locker, this is not. *www.bape.com*

Moderate   *Amex/MC/V*

Soho   **(212) 925-0222**
91 Greene Street   btw Prince/Spring
NYC 10012   Daily 12-7 (Sun 12-6)

AB Apollo Braun

'I am one of the few designers who does not want to work with Gisele because I love to offer something new', says owner, fashion designer and former gossip cdolumnist Apollo Braun, gesturing to the walls papered with spreads from Paper and I-D magazines. To that end he's created a mecca for downtown hipsters in search of one-of-a-kind accessories and deconstructed T-shirts from his own line as well as other up-and-coming and mostly local designers. Britney Spears and Nicole Kidman and Björk have stopped by to pick up slogan shirts like 'I'm better naked' while browsing the leather, fur and rhinestone accessories. A biweekly rotation of local art is a new feature. Don't miss the $29 sale rack.   apollobraun.com

Moderate   *Amex/MC/V*

Lower East Side   **(212) 726-8075**
193 Orchard Street   at Houston
NYC 10002   Daily 12-10

★ Abercrombie & Fitch

Known for its risqué catalog, occasionally naughty logo T-shirts and fresh-faced, outdoorsy American style, Abercrombie & Fitch trades in affordable, sexy and athletic looks. Stamped with the ubiquitous A&F logo, the chain offers a wide selection of pants (cargo, denim and parachute), shorts (including the bright ones for surfers), tees, sweaters, knits and outerwear. Also on the agenda are a slew of accessories (from adjustable caps to belts and flip-flops), intimates, tanks, halter tops and swimsuits. The massive new flagship in midtown is a must-visit for frat guys and high-schoolers alike.   abercrombie.com

Affordable   *Amex/MC/V*

Lower Manhattan/Tribeca   **(212) 809-9000**
199 Water Street   at South Street Seaport
NYC 10038   Daily 10-7 (Sun 11-6)

Midtown   **n/a at press time**
720 Fifth Avenue   at 56th St
NYC 10019   n/a at press time

ABH Design

A lovely, quiet, space to take in exotic scarves, handcrafted jewelry and eccentric home accents. Owned by movie costume designer Aude Bronson Howard, ABH Designs specializes in custom napkins and tablecloths with specialty fabrics from India, Italy, Ireland and France. Jeweled flip-flops, pointy striped slippers, silk scarves and robes in rich greens and orange reveal a far eastern influence on Howard's goods, while quilted paisley jackets and floppy sunhats offer stylish updates on homey comfort. ABH Designs has a slew of celebrity/socialite clients (but they're too demure to name names) who swear by the store's candles, place mats, evening wraps, towels and everything an Upper East Side woman could possible need for herself or her glamorous home. A new garden out back offers respite from retail therapy.   abh-design.com

Expensive   *Amex/MC/V*

Upper East Side   **(212) 249-2276**
401 East 76th Street   at First Ave
NYC 10021   Mon-Sat 11-6:30

a. cheng ♀

A tour of duty at Tommy Hilfiger gave designer Alice Cheng the savvy—and commercial sense—she needed to open her own shop. Cheng's collection is pretty and delicate enough to appeal to the softer side of any professional. Best buys: her signature shirt dress as well as skirts, pants dressed up with decorative waistbands, jackets, silk print tops and feminine button-down shirts.   *achengshop.com*

Expensive   *Amex/MC/V*

East Village   **(212) 979-7324**
443 East 9th Street   btw First/Avenue A
NYC 10009   Daily 11:30-8 (Sat-Sun 11:30-7)

Active Wearhouse ♂♀

Hit up your inner hip-hop hottie—or at least just dress like one—at this store nestled in the heart of Broadway. Choose from the latest offerings in urban clothing, from beloved labels like Rocawear, Phat Farm and Babyphat. And don't forget to check out Active Wearhouse's larger-than-life collection of kicks from all the major sneaker brands like Puma, Nike and Adidas in the basement.   *activewearhousenyc.com*

Affordable   *Amex/MC/V*

SoHo   **(212) 965-2284**
514 Broadway   btw Broome/Spring
NYC 10012   Mon-Sat 9-9, Sun 10-8

Add accessories ♀

Stocking the wares of over 40 designers, this small accessories boutique is packed with hats, handbags, knockout costume jewelry, sandals and an abundance of wraps in a variety of styles—fur, velvet, mohair, etc. Check out satin evening purses, raffia totes, and fashionable day bags by Francesco Biasia and Carla Mancini. Hat styles include fancy dress numbers, adjustable straw boaters, madras caps and panamas by labels like Annabel Ingall and Amsterdam's Bronte. Jewelry includes Double Happiness and Alessi New York. Great for the races.   *addaccessories.com*

Affordable   *Amex/MC/V*

SoHo   **(212) 539-1439**
461 West Broadway   btw Houston/Prince
NYC 10012   Mon-Sat 11-8, Sun 12-7

☆ Addison on Madison ♂

No it's not on Madison any more because the lease ran out, but no matter—this is the place for the man who hates shopping. A far cry from the stuffy darkness and wood paneling of traditional men's departments, this bright, uncluttered office space will outfit you with your choice from a wide selection of Italian cotton and silk shirts made in

America. They provide on-site tailoring, custom sleeve lengths, and custom-made shirts. Short on time? Request a set of fabric swatches by mail. Accessories include Italian silk neckties, bow ties, pocket squares and cufflinks.

Affordable to moderate   *Amex/MC/V*

Midtown East   **(212) 308-2660**
29 West 57th Street (9th floor)   btw Fifth/Sixth Ave
NYC 10019   Mon-Fri 10-6

A Détacher

Owner/designer Monika Kowalska's collection, with its high-concept Japanese sensibility, is, in her words, 'art fashion for adults'. The result is a clean, minimalist line of constructed but feminine dresses, pants, skirts, blouses and more. Kowalska uses linear cuts (not form-fitting) and a basic seasonal color palette, as well as some prints. Head to the back of the shop for handbag designer Dillen's fantastic, Hermès-like leather accessories. Also amuse yourself with a quirky collection of housewares—everything in the store is for sale, you just have to ask…

Moderate   *Amex/MC/V*

Nolita   **(212) 625-3380**
262 Mott Street   btw Houston/Prince
NYC 10012   Tues-Sat 12-7, Sun 1-6

Adidas

With the coolest three stripes in the sports world, Adidas has had a firm hold on everyone from athletes to the style set for over 80 years. And it just keeps getting better. Its Originals store in SoHo befits the ideal Adidas consumer—garage-style layout with a DJ spinning in the back. Hipsters head here for the newly reinvented and super-hip Originals line. Shiny polyester tracksuits beloved by the artists and athletes alike, limited-edition sneakers, casualwear—the whole world of retro Adidas is here for you. Too cool for school.   *adidas.com*

Affordable   *Amex/MC/V*

SoHo   **(212) 777-2001**
136 Wooster Street   btw Houston/Prince
NYC 10012   Daily 11-7 (Sun 12-6)

Adidas Performance Store

This massive modern two-story sportswear store has a huge selection of workout gear for men, women and children. Check out Stella McCartney's designs made for Adidas: a floppy terry boxer's robe, off-the-shoulder workout tees with metallic lettering that could seamlessly go from the gym to a new-wave dance party, belted mesh ringer tanks, and gold lamé detailed sneakers. In the unlikely event that your guy doesn't also have an armful of gear to try on, he can busy himself at one of the X-Box stations or a computer game console and play away.   *adidas.com*

Affordable   *Amex/MC/V*

11

SoHo **(212) 529-0081**
610 Broadway at Houston
NYC 10012 Mon-Sat 10-10, Sun 11-7

Aerosoles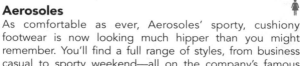

As comfortable as ever, Aerosoles' sporty, cushiony footwear is now looking much hipper than you might remember. You'll find a full range of styles, from business casual to sporty weekend—all on the company's famous orthopedically correct soles. Many knee-high winter boots, stiletto sandals, and loafers are under $60.   *aerosoles.com*

Affordable *Amex/MC/V*

Harlem **(212) 665-5353**
2913 Broadway btw 113/114th St
NYC 10025 Mon-Sat 9:30-8, Sun 11-7

Upper East Side **(212) 987-9483**
150 East 86th Street btw Lexington/Third Ave
NYC 10028 Mon-Fri 9-8, Sat 9-8, Sun 11-7

Upper East Side **(212) 751-6372**
1155 Second Avenue at 61st St
NYC 10021 Mon-Sat 9:30-8, Sun 12-6

Upper West Side **(212) 865-4934**
2649 Broadway btw 100/101st St
NYC 10025 Mon-Sat 9:30-8, Sun 11-7

Upper West Side **(212) 579-8659**
310 Columbus Avenue btw 74/75th St
NYC 10023 Mon-Sat 9:30-8, Sun 11-7

Midtown East **(212) 755-0683**
709 Lexington Avenue btw 57/58th St
NYC 10022 Mon-Sat 9-9, Sun 11-7

Midtown East **(212) 370-0094**
137 East 42nd Street btw Lexington/Third Ave
NYC 10017 Mon-Fri 8-8, Sat 10-8, Sun 11-6

Midtown West **(212) 563-0610**
36 West 34th Street btw Fifth/Sixth Ave
NYC 10001 Mon-Fri 8-9, Sat 9-9, Sun 11-7

Midtown West **(212) 307-6465**
1250 Avenue of the Americas at 50th St
NYC 10112 Mon-Fri 8-8, Sat 11-7, Sun 10-6

Flatiron **(646) 486-2826**
168 Fifth Avenue btw 21/22nd St
NYC 10010 Mon-Sat 9:30-8, Sun 11-6

NoHo **(212) 358-7855**
63 East 8th Street btw Broadway/University Place
NYC 10003 Mon-Sat 9:30-8, Sun 11-7

Lower Manhattan **(212) 577-9298**
18 John Street (lobby level) btw Broadway/Nassau
NYC 10038 Mon-Fri 9-7

Lower Manhattan **(212) 608-4980**
206 Front Street at South Street Seaport
NYC 10038 Mon-Wed 9:30-7, Thurs-Sat 10-8, Sun 11-7

Brooklyn   **(718) 230-1680**
100C Seventh Avenue
Park Slope 11215   Daily 10-8 (Sun 10-6)

Agent Provocateur

Welcome to the underworld. No one has given designer lingerie such a kick in the pants as Agent Provocateur, the masters of kinky chic. London's most exclusive lingerie label, started almost a decade ago by Vivienne Westwood's son Joe Corré and wife Serena Rees, perfectly marries shameless eroticism and naughty exhibitionism—which is probably why their little nothings are craved by every supermodel and superstar on the planet. This SoHo store is a chic retail bordello with a comely staff in baby-pink uniforms (think Fifties beautician/diner waitress/nurse)—a world of equally naughty, retro-inspired knickers. It's the perfect place to dispatch your boyfriend to pick up the signature lingerie (which also includes elegant silk and lace numbers), Swarovski-crystal-studded collars and cuffs, Forties peep-toe heels, or perhaps a bottle of AP's saucy fragrance. Sexy with a capital S.   *agentprovocateur.com*

Expensive   *Amex/MC/V*

SoHo   **(212) 965-0229**
133 Mercer Street   btw Prince/Spring
NYC 10012   Mon-Sat 11-7, Sun 12-6

agnès b.

Effortlessly stylish women have long shopped at agnès b. to snare some Parisian bon ton (fashionability without trendiness). The classic and clever ready-to-wear collection offers pants, jackets, sweaters, suits and skirts that are simple, chic and feminine—and some of the best T-shirts around.   *agnesb.net*

Expensive   *Amex/MC/V*

Upper East Side   **(212) 570-9333**
1063 Madison Avenue   btw 80/81st St
NYC 10028   Mon-Sat 11-7, Sun 12-6

Flatiron   **(212) 741-2585**
13 East 16th Street   btw Fifth Ave/Union Square West
NYC 10003   (opening hours as above)

SoHo   **(212) 925-4649**
103 Greene Street   btw Prince/Spring
NYC 10012   Daily 11-7

agnès b. homme

Agnès b. homme caters to the suave and preppy men of the world seeking classic looks with that particular Parisian edge. Choose from a ready-to-wear collection of suits, dress pants, shirts, khakis and jeans—all up, a one-stop foolproof wardrobe. It's clean-cut clothes with covetable French elegance. Sizes run small.   *agnesb.fr*

Expensive   *Amex/MC/V*

SoHo   **(212) 431-4339**
79 Greene Street   btw Spring/Broome
NYC 10012   Daily 11-7

★ Albertine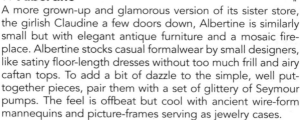

A more grown-up and glamorous version of its sister store, the girlish Claudine a few doors down, Albertine is similarly small but with elegant antique furniture and a mosaic fireplace. Albertine stocks casual formalwear by small designers, like satiny floor-length dresses without too much frill and airy caftan tops. To add a bit of dazzle to the simple, well put-together pieces, pair them with a set of glittery of Seymour pumps. The feel is offbeat but cool with ancient wire-form mannequins and picture-frames serving as jewelry cases.

Moderate to expensive   *Amex/MC/V*

West Village   **(212) 924-8515**
13 Christopher Street   btw Greenwich/Waverly Pl
NYC 10014   Daily 12-8 (Sun 12-7)

Aldo

Calling all twentysomethings: this is your funky footwear home. Shop for streety looks like Cher-worthy platforms, wedges, rubber or wooden soles, boots, sassy stilettos and sandals in bursts of raspberry pink, purple, blue and orange (black and white, too, if you insist). Affordably priced footwear with attitude to spare.   *aldoshoes.com*

Affordable   *Amex/MC/V*

Upper East Side   **(212) 828-3725**
157 East 86th Street   btw Lexington/Third Ave
NYC 10028   Mon-Wed 10-8, Thurs-Sat 10-9, Sun 12-7

Midtown East   **(212) 832-1692**
730 Lexington Avenue   btw 58/59th St
NYC 10022   Mon-Wed 10-8, Thurs-Sat 10-9, Sun 12-7

Midtown West   **(212) 594-6255**
15 West 34th Street   btw Fifth/Sixth Ave
NYC 10001   Mon-Sat 10-9, Sun 11-8

Flatiron   **(212) 229-9865**
97 Fifth Avenue   at 17th St
NYC 10003   Mon-Sat 10-9, Sun 11-8

NoHo   **(212) 982-0958**
700 Broadway   at East 4th St
NYC 10003   Mon-Sat 10-9, Sun 11-8

SoHo   **(212) 226-7974**
579 Broadway   btw Houston/Prince
NYC 10012   Mon-Wed 10-8, Thurs-Sat 10-9, Sun 11-7

Midtown East   **(212) 661-0208**
139 East 42nd Street (Chrysler Building)
NYC 10017   btw Lexington/Third Ave
                                 Mon-Sat 9-8, Sun 11-6

Midtown East   **(212) 586-6293**
1230 Sixth Avenue   at Rockefeller Center
NYC 10020   Mon-Fri 9-8, Sat 10-8, Sun 12-7

Upper West Side   **(212) 362-7976**
2345 Broadway   at 86th St
NYC 10024   Mon-Wed 10-8, Thurs-Sat 10-9, Sun 11-7

Directory

Alex

Alex helps women look fabulous with the least bit of effort. Casual chic has never looked or felt so good as with the super-soft, super-flattering tees by Majestic that you'll find here, and don't miss great shirts and dresses by C+C California and gotta-have-'em jeans by Paper Denim and Cloth. Find a few colorful pieces among the mainly neutral-toned color palette, and you'll be set for a stylish weekend.

Expensive   *Amex/MC/V*

Nolita   **(212) 343-0567**
268 Elizabeth Street   btw Houston/Prince
NYC 10012   Daily 11:30-7:30

★ Alexander McQueen

Fashion's dark prince, who once again stunned audiences with his runway homage—complete with dancing models—to *They Shoot Horses, Don't They?* has established himself as a bona-fide international brand, following backing by fashion powerhouse Gucci. After opening his first store in Tokyo, McQueen's New York outpost, in the über-fashionable Chelsea, is a deliberate trip into the recesses of his mind. 'It's supposed to be a spaceship environment, so everything hovers. It's very ethereal,' he says. The single-floor store showcases the majority of McQueen's women's collection: sinuous suits, sharp pants, his signature leather corsetry, death-defying shoes (six-inch stilettos) and logo sunglasses.   *alexandermcqueen.com*

Luxury   *Amex/MC/V*

Chelsea   **(212) 645-1797**
417 West 14th Street   btw Washington/Ninth Ave
NYC 10014   Mon-Sat 11-7, Sun 12:30-6

Alexandre de Paris

Having trouble finding a barrette? Well, this is the best option you will ever find in New York City. You'll find bows, banana clips, headbands, small veils, pins, scrunchies, combs—and all handmade to perfection. A private line of hairbrushes and mirrors is also available. Simply put, this Paris-based store will have your hair looking as beautiful as your ensemble.   *jovy-alexandredeparis.com*

Expensive   *Amex/MC/V*

Upper East Side   **(212) 717-2122**
971 Madison Avenue   btw 75/76th St
NYC 10021   Mon-Sat 10-7, Sun 12-5

Alexandros

Choose from a collection of quality avant-garde and classic fur coats—from sporty fox to luxurious chinchilla, mink, sable or lynx. Alongside the house label, they design and carry the luxe lines Ekso and Douglas Hannant. Other outerwear includes cashmere overcoats and reversibles. Alexandros also offers storage, cleaning and remodeling.

Luxury   *Amex/MC/V*

Midtown East   **(212) 702-0744**
5 East 59th Street (2nd floor)   btw Fifth/Madison Ave
NYC 10022   Mon-Fri 10-6, Sat 10-5
                                              (closed Saturdays in summer)

Chelsea   **(212) 967-1222**
213 West 28th Street   btw Seventh/Eighth Ave
NYC 10001   Mon-Sat 10-6
                                          (also Sundays, October-February)

Chelsea   **(212) 868-1043**
345 Seventh Avenue   btw 29/30th St
NYC 10001   Mon-Fri 9-6, Sat 9-2

Alfred Dunhill

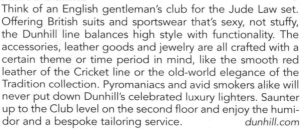

Think of an English gentleman's club for the Jude Law set. Offering British suits and sportswear that's sexy, not stuffy, the Dunhill line balances high style with functionality. The accessories, leather goods and jewelry are all crafted with a certain theme or time period in mind, like the smooth red leather of the Cricket line or the old-world elegance of the Tradition collection. Pyromaniacs and avid smokers alike will never put down Dunhill's celebrated luxury lighters. Saunter up to the Club level on the second floor and enjoy the humidor and a bespoke tailoring service.   *dunhill.com*

Expensive   *Amex/MC/V*

Midtown East   **(212) 753-9292**
711 Fifth Avenue   btw 55/56th St
NYC 10022   Mon-Sat 10-6:30 (Thurs 10-7)

Alicia Mugetti

Alicia Mugetti, who designs fancy duds for opera, theater and film, specializes in romantic damsel dresses designed in rich velvets and crushed satins. Find them in beautiful colors and feminine, floor-length silhouettes. It's lush fabrics and Renaissance looks—all very Knights of the Round Table (or the princesses they woo, anyway).   *aliciamugetti.com*

Expensive   *Amex/MC/V*

Upper East Side   **(212) 794-6186**
999 Madison Avenue   btw 77/78th St
NYC 10021   Mon-Sat 10-6

★ Alife

Get Alife! An eclectic, defiantly downtown mix of footwear, clothing, graffiti paraphernalia (i.e. loose, comfy hip-hop wear), design books and the ever-vital stuffed animals. Check out a skateboard designed by graffiti guru ESPO, Rogan jeans, local designer tees, silk-screened sweatshirts, shirts, industrial accessories and edgy shoes ranging from modern-looking sneaks by Ritefoot and Converse. Every two months they feature progressive installations by up-and-coming artists. As we went to press, Alife was due to relocate to a space right next door to their sneaker emporium Alife Rivington Club.   *alifenyc.com*

Expensive   *Amex/MC/V*

Lower East Side   **n/a at press time**
158 Rivington Street   btw Clinton/Suffolk
NYC 10002   Daily 12-7

Alife Rivington Club

Confirming the Lower East Side's new status as the sneaker capital of the world, along comes Alife Rivington Club, looking like a cross between a Savile Row tailor and Athlete's Foot. Find obscure and dead cool limited-edition sneakers back-lit and reverently displayed in cherrywood cases. Look out for classic retro Adidas and contemplate your next sneaker addition from the gorgeous Italian leather couch that lines an entire wall of the store. Of course, shoes this cool cost a bundle—think of it as the club's membership dues.   *rivingtonclub.com*

Expensive   *Amex/MC/V*

Lower East Side   **(212) 375-8128**
158 Rivington Street   btw Clinton/Suffolk
NYC 10002   Daily 12-7

Alixandre

Run by three generations of the Schulman family, Alixandre delivers honest, reliable and knowledgeable service as well as an outstanding selection of fur coats. Find top quality shearlings, broadtails, minks and sables from Oscar de la Renta. Alixandre also offers superior cleaning, storage, remodeling and alteration services. Appointments suggested between Memorial Day and Labor Day. *alixandrefurs.com*

Expensive   *Amex/MC/V*

Midtown West   **(212) 736-5550**
150 West 30th Street   btw Sixth/Seventh
NYC 10001   Mon-Fri 9-5, Sat 9-1:30
                                               (appointments suggested)

Allan & Suzi

The eccentric, self-proclaimed 'Home of Retro Fashion', Allan & Suzi sell new and vintage consignment garb from all the industry heavyweights (Gucci, Prada, Versace, Pucci, Cavalli, to name only a few) and relative newcomers like Zac Posen. Specializing in shoes, especially of the platform variety, and eveningwear, where the motto seems to be The More Sequins, The Better, owners Allan Pollack and Suzi Kandel are sure to please any Elton John or Vanna White in waiting. With trademark style, Kandel claims that the opening of a second location in New Jersey has set off New York's 'pilgrimage to Asbury Park'.   *allanandsuzi.net*

Expensive   *Amex/MC/V*

Upper West Side   **(212) 724-7445**
416 Amsterdam Avenue   at 80th St
NYC 10024   Mon-Sat 12-7, Sun 12-6

New Jersey (732) 988-7372
711 Cookman Avenue Asbury Park
NJ 07712 Thurs-Sat 11-5, Sun 12-5

Allen Edmonds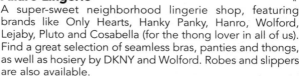

For over 75 years, the customer has come first at Allen Edmonds. Find over 200 styles of dress and corporate classics, from casual weekend shoes to fashion-forward lifestyle footwear. Great care has gone into obtaining the perfect balance between quality and price. *800-235-2348*
allenedmonds.com

Moderate *Amex/MC/V*

Midtown East (212) 308-8305
551 Madison Avenue btw 55/56th St
NYC 10022 Mon-Fri 9-7, Sat 9-6, Sun 12-5

Midtown East (212) 682-3144
24 East 44th Street btw Fifth/Madison Ave
NYC 10017 (opening hours as above)

Allure Lingerie

A super-sweet neighborhood lingerie shop, featuring brands like Only Hearts, Hanky Panky, Hanro, Wolford, Lejaby, Pluto and Cosabella (for the thong lover in all of us). Find a great selection of seamless bras, panties and thongs, as well as hosiery by DKNY and Wolford. Robes and slippers are also available.

Moderate *Amex/MC/V*

Upper East Side (212) 860-7871
1324 Lexington Avenue btw 88/89th St
NYC 10128 Mon-Fri 11-7, Sat 11-6

Alpana Bawa

Alpana Bawa's signature is vibrantly colored pieces with brave geometric and floral patterns. They also stock accessories in hand-embroidered wool, silk, cotton or nylon. Look for A by Alpana for equally vivid and adventurous casualwear. The Bawa line includes a collection of colorful cotton men's shirts, embellished with prints and embroidery, as well as jackets and pants favored by out-there actor types like Willem Dafoe. *alpanabawa.com*

Moderate *Amex/MC/V*

Lower East Side (212) 965-0559
181 Chrystie Street (fourth floor) at Rivington
NYC 10002 Mon-Sat 1-8, Sun 1-6

Alskling

Alskling, a small Swedish dress boutique who's name means 'darling' in its mother tongue, offers clothing for women and girls who prefer May flowers to April showers. In addition to their signature line of slip and sundresses in an array of prints from punchy polka dots to pretty posies, Alskling offers a variety of super-girly garments like camisole tops and flouncy skirts that make every day feel like spring has finally sprung. *alsklingsbutiken.se*

Moderate Amex/MC/V

Upper West Side (212) 787-7066
228 Columbus Avenue btw 70/71st St
NYC 10023 Daily 12-6

★ Amarcord Vintage Fashion 👫

This airy shop sells vintage clothing lovingly handpicked by owners Patti Bordoni and Marco Liotta. These passionate Italian expatriates collect many of their pieces direct from Europe through word-of-mouth and top-secret sources. Find both non-designer prized pieces, as well as winning looks by Cacharel, Gucci, Roberto Cavalli, you name it. Everything is in great condition (especially the classic handbags) and attractively priced. Unlike so many other vintage emporiums they only pick the best, and they color code them too. *amarcordvintagefashion.com*

Expensive Amex/MC/V

East Village (women only) (212) 614-7133
84 East 7th Street btw First/Second Ave
NYC 10003 Tues-Sun 12-7:30 (later in summer)

Williamsburg (718) 963-4001
223 Bedford Avenue btw North 4th/North 5th St
Brooklyn 11211 Daily 12-8 (later in summer)

★ American Apparel 👬

Sexy, simple, perfect. Surrounded by the photo exhibits, hip music and beautiful sales staff at American Apparel, you would never guess that this rising star of a company stands nearly alone in the garment industry in its commitment to socially-conscious manufacturing and labor practices. AA's 'sweatshop-free' goods are made in downtown L.A. with organic, pesticide-free materials; workers are paid competitive wages and have access to free English language classes held in the L.A. workshop. If the politics don't motivate you, the great fits, stylish colors and reasonable prices—qualities helping make the label a preferred choice for rock bands' tour tees—certainly will. Best bets are flattering basics like solid-colored tees, pants, sweats and skirts, most of which can be had for under $40. Also find comfy loungewear, hot underwear, trendy tanks, cute kids' clothing and a small selection of art and photography books for sale. If it sounds too good to be true, just get in line—you'll be glad you did. *americanapparelstore.com*

Affordable Amex/MC/V

NoHo (646) 383-2257
712 Broadway at Washington Place
NYC 10003 Mon-Thurs 10-9, Fri-Sat, 10-10, Sun 11-8

Lower East Side (212) 598-4600
183 East Houston Street at Orchard
NYC 10002 Mon-Sat 11-10, Sun 12-8

West Village (646) 336-6515
373 Sixth Avenue at Waverly Place
NYC 10014 Mon-Sat 11-9, Sun 11-8

SoHo   **(212) 226-4880**
121 Spring Street   at Greene
NYC 10012   Mon-Sat 10-9, Sun 11-8

Upper East Side   **(212) 772-7462**
1090 Third Avenue   btw 63/64th St
NYC 10021   Mon-Fri 10-9, Sat 10-10, Sun 11-8

Williamsburg   **(718) 218-0002**
104 North 6th Street btw Wythe/Berry   Mon-Thurs 11-10
Brooklyn 11211   Fri-Sat 11-1, Sun 11-9

Downtown Brooklyn   **(718) 855-4627**
112 Court Street   at State St
Brooklyn 11201   Mon-Thurs 10-10
    Fri-Sat 10-12, Sun 11-9

Amsale

Fed up with puffy wedding cake bridal gowns, Amsale Aberra took matters into her own hands—and designed her own. Today she is the leading vendor of couture bridal gowns in department stores, as well as the largest bridal salon on Madison Avenue. Known for timeless, classic elegance, the collection features both elaborate hand-beaded gowns with Swarovski crystals and simple column dresses. Prices run from $3,000 to approximately $15,000, with a six-month delivery. Don't miss the Evening collection, which glistens with glamour and sophistication. Looks include cocktail dresses, suits, satin coats, silk ballgowns, slinky long dresses and fabulous tuxedo jacket and pant ensembles.   amsale.com

Luxury   Amex/MC/V

Midtown East   **(212) 583-1700**
625 Madison Avenue (mezzanine)   btw 58/59th St
NYC 10022   Tues, Thurs 11-6, Wed 11-7
(by appointment only)   Fri 10-6, Sat 10-5

Amy Downs Hats at YU

Amy Downs is one of New York's most creative milliners; her style is deliberately and eclectically downtown. Shop for headwear with names like Twister or Happy Family, or choose from a collection of polar fleece and wool hats, straw sunhats, funky felts, fun fake furs, bold berets, wool ski hats and more.   yu-nyc.com

Moderate   Amex/MC/V

Lower East Side   **(212) 979-9370**
151 Ludlow Street   btw Stanton/Rivington
NYC 10002   Wed-Sat 12-7, Sun 12-6

★ An Earnest Cut & Sew

Like a field trip to a textile mill from the Industrial Revolution, Earnest Sewn Jeans' first freestanding shop is full of intimidating-looking machines that make custom jeans to your specifications. Fill out an order form indicating which kind of denim (from Italian Heavy Slub to

Japanese Black), then pick a fit, pocket, buttons and rivets (add $25 for 24kt gold). While you wait, lounge with a latte at the in-store café and soon enough you've got fresh jeans. They also do repairs for a reasonable fee. Smaller purchases can be made from the pebble-filled wood display case where leather and copper jewelry hang from jackknives. *earnestsewn.com*

Expensive	*Amex/MC/V*

Chelsea (212) 242-3414
821 Washington Street btw Little West 12/Gansevoort
NYC 10014 Mon-Tues by appointment
Wed-Sun 11-7 (Sat 11-8)

Andy's Chee Pees

A vintage store for style swingers in search of fun one-of-a-kind fashion hits. Find collectible denim, swing clothes from the Forties and Fifties, biker and bomber jackets, jeans, old police leather jackets, Hawaiian shirts, a complete line of unisex Dickies in bold, bright colors, party wigs, vintage jewelry and more. For the 18-35 crowd desperate for some nostalgia—or something eye-catching to wear to a costume party.

Affordable *Amex/MC/V*

NoHo (212) 420-5980
691 Broadway btw 3/4th St
NYC 10012 Mon-Sat 11-9, Sun 12-8

Angelo Lambrou

Celebrities from Goldie Hawn to Salma Hayek look to Angelo Lambrou for modern, sexy clothing. Inspired by art and design from all over the world, this Botswana native creates ethereal silk dresses and beaded tops that are both edgy and timeless. From couture bridal dresses to ready-to-wear evening attire, Lambrou's designs are bias-cut for a perfectly flattering fit. Lambrou himself puts shoppers at ease with his warm, gregarious personality. *angelolambrou.com*

Luxury *Amex/MC/V*

East Village (212) 460-9870
96 East 7th Street btw First/Avenue A
NYC 10009 Tues-Sat 1-8, Sun 1-7

Anik

Talk about a wide range of options—Anik has everything from careerwear to sportswear for both moms and daughters. The store's broad assortment includes Alice & Trixie dresses, Duca d'Andrea suits, Malika cashmere sweaters and Moncler baseball jackets. The best part of Anik is a sale section in the back of the Third Avenue shop, where you're bound to find something worth more than what you'll pay. Prices range from $40 for a Splendid tee to $500 silk dresses. *aniknyc.com*

Moderate to expensive *Amex/MC/V*

Upper East Side (212) 861-9840
1355 Third Avenue btw 77/78th St
NYC 10021 Mon-Sat 10:45-8, Sun 12-7

Upper East Side (212) 249-2417
1122 Madison Avenue btw 83/84th St
NYC 10028 Mon-Sat 10-8, Sun 11-7

Anna 👤

One of New York's best kept secrets, this is the kind of boutique that fashion-obsessed East Village girls wish they could keep to themselves. Sorry, we have to spread the love. Owner/designer Kathy Kemp sells her collection of addictive striped wrap dresses with ribbons and girlish double-layered skirts, plus carefully chosen, complementary vintage pieces in the sale bin (always $20). The look is feminine and fantastically offbeat. *annanyc.com*

Moderate *Amex/MC/V*

East Village (212) 358-0195
150 East 3rd Street at Avenue A
NYC 10009 Mon-Sat 1-8, Sun 1-7

Anna Sui 👤

Purple, purple everywhere. At the heart of every Anna Sui collection comes 'the celebration of the nouvelle hippy'. Her SoHo treasure trove is inspired by a myriad of decades, but the Sixties and Seventies are clearly the favorites. The store is decorated with vintage-style posters from bands such as 311, Foo Fighters and The Doors. Choose Sui's head-to-toe collection: dresses, skirts tossed with crocheted pieces, romantic blouses, chunky coats, sexy denim, patchwork and even dainty underwear. Devotees include Britney Spears, Madonna and all of Anna's many model friends. Accessories include fanciful decorative shoes, handbags, jewelry, cute-goth make-up, and fragrances. *annasui.com*

Expensive *Amex/MC/V*

SoHo (212) 941-8406
113 Greene Street btw Prince/Spring
NYC 10012 Mon-Sat 11:30-7, Sun 12-6

Anne Fontaine 👤

Brazil-born and Paris-based designer Anne Fontaine's New York boutiques are visions in white—white shelves, white carpet, white walls. Not that this should come as a surprise, as the designer's overwhelming obsession is perfecting the white shirt, with an occasional detour into seasonal colors. Fontaine displays roughly 100 variations on this wardrobe staple, using ruching, lace, flowers made of fabric, mother-of-pearl buttons, strong tailoring and a variety of materials—from stretchy cotton to poplin to organza appliqué—to turn plain into perfection. *annefontaine.com*

Expensive *Amex/MC/V*

SoHo **(212) 343-3154**
93 Greene Street btw Prince/Spring
NYC 10012 Mon-Sat 11-7, Sun 12-6

Fifth Avenue **(212) 489-1554**
610 Fifth Avenue btw 50/51st St
NYC 10020 Mon-Fri 10-7, Sat 11-6, Sun 12-5

Upper East Side **(212) 688-4362**
687 Madison Avenue at 62nd St
NYC 10021 Mon-Sat 10-6, Sun 12-5

Anne Klein ♀

Established and elegant, Anne Klein has been dressing women for more than 30 years. But the brand upped the ante of late, positioning itself as a fashion-oriented collection rather than simply a career-driven bridge line. Modern looks and clean-cut styles permeate the Anne Klein label—think simple pieces like silk jersey tops and taffeta pants—plus the sportier AK Anne Klein line. The signature lion's head logo is in evidence, both on accessories and in the store's dramatic decor. *anneklein.com*

Moderate *Amex/MC/V*

SoHo **(212) 965-9499**
417 West Broadway btw Prince/Spring
NYC 10012 Mon-Wed 10-7, Thurs-Sat 10-8, Sun 12-7

Annelore ♀

Frustrated by mass-produced clothing that can be seen on every fifth girl riding the subway, designer Juliana Cho has created a line of original, hand-sewn and impeccably tailored pieces for women. Cho employs a tailor, seamstresses and a cobbler to transform her handpicked European fabrics and leathers into timeless feminine pieces. The cuts are flawless, and include intricate details like hand-painted glass buttons. Annelore's limited-edition pieces have drawn a loyal following from clothes-horses like Helena Christensen and Gretchen Mol.

Moderate *Amex/MC/V*

West Village **(212) 255-5574**
636 Hudson Street at Horatio
NYC 10014 Tues-Sat 12-7, Sun 12-6

Annika Inez ♀

A fab little secret on the Upper East Side, Annika is a destination for chic beaded jewelry made by Swedish store owner Annika Salame, using vintage beads from the Thirties to the Seventies. The store is simple and uncluttered, all the better to display this small collection which also includes coconut-bead charm bracelets, acrylic-bead and cork cuffs, semi-precious necklaces, minimalist sterling silver earrings and Danish knitwear designers. Great for gifts—or just for spoiling yourself. *annikainez.com*

Affordable *Amex/MC/V*

Upper East Side　　　　　　　　**(212) 717-9644**
243 East 78th Street　　　　　　btw Second/Third Ave
NYC 10021　　　Mon-Wed 11-7, Thurs-Fri 12-8, Sat 11-6

⭐ **Ann Taylor**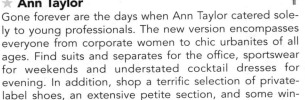

Gone forever are the days when Ann Taylor catered solely to young professionals. The new version encompasses everyone from corporate women to chic urbanites of all ages. Find suits and separates for the office, sportswear for weekends and understated cocktail dresses for evening. In addition, shop a terrific selection of private-label shoes, an extensive petite section, and some winning accessories.　　　　*800 677-0300　anntaylor.com*

Affordable　　　　　　　　　　　　*Amex/MC/V*

Upper East Side　　　　　　　　**(212) 988-8930**
1055 Madison Avenue　　　　　　　　　　at 80th St
NYC 10028　　　Mon-Fri 10-8, Sat 10-6, Sun 12-6

Upper East Side　　　　　　　　**(212) 832-9114**
645 Madison Avenue　　　　　　　　　　at 60th St
NYC 10022　　　Mon-Fri 10-8, Sat 10-7, Sun 12-6

Upper East Side　　　　　　　　**(212) 861-3392**
1320 Third Avenue　　　　　　　　　　at 75th St
NYC 10022　　　Mon-Fri 10-8, Sat 10-6, Sun 12-6

Upper West Side　　　　　　　　**(212) 721-3130**
2380 Broadway　　　　　　　　　　　at 87th St
NYC 10024　　　　　Mon-Sat 10-8, Sun 12-6

Upper West Side　　　　　　　　**(212) 873-7344**
2015-17 Broadway　　　　　　　　　　at 69th St
NYC 10023　　　　　Mon-Sat 10-8, Sun 12-6

Midtown East　　　　　　　　　**(212) 308-5333**
850 Third Avenue　　　　　　　　　　at 52nd St
NYC 10022　　　Mon-Fri 10-8, Sat 10-6, Sun 12-5

Midtown East　　　　　　　　　**(212) 949-0008**
330 Madison Avenue　　　　　　　　　at 43rd St
NYC 10017　　　Mon-Fri 9-8, Sat 11-6, Sun 12-5

Midtown West　　　　　　　　　**(212) 642-4340**
1166 Sixth Avenue　　　　　　　　　at 46th St
NYC 10036　　　Mon-Fri 9-8, Sat 10-7, Sun 12-6

Fifth Avenue　　　　　　　　　**(212) 922-3621**
575 Fifth Avenue　　　　　　　　btw 46/47th St
NYC 10017　　　Mon-Fri 10-8, Sat 10-7, Sun 11-6

Flatiron　　　　　　　　　　　**(212) 253-1445**
149 Fifth Avenue　　　　　　　　　　at 21st St
NYC 10010　　　　　Mon-Sat 10-8, Sun 12-6

Lower Manhattan　　　　　　　**(212) 945-1991**
225 Liberty Street　　　at 2 World Financial Center
NYC 10281　　　Mon-Fri 9-7, Sat 11-5, Sun 12-5

Lower Manhattan　　　　　　　**(212) 480-4100**
4 Fulton Street　　　　　　　at South Street Seaport
NYC 10038　　　　　Mon-Sat 10-8, Sun 11-7

Ann Taylor Loft

If you like to dress up with Ann Taylor during the week, then you'll probably enjoy relaxing in Ann Taylor Loft on weekends. Taylorphiles shop here for casual basics like sweater sets, pants, cotton and silk shirts, dresses—all up, laid-back and practical pieces at lower price points than the signature line. This year's collection includes a versatile array of accessories: sunglasses, necklaces, stockings, shoes and hats, as well as new items like watches and umbrellas. *anntaylorloft.com*

Moderate *Amex/MC/V*

Midtown West **(212) 244-8926**
35 West 34th Street btw Fifth/Sixth Ave
NYC 10001 Mon-Sat 10-8, Sun 11-7

Upper East Side **(212) 472-7281**
1492 Third Avenue at 84th St
NYC 10028 Mon-Sat 10-9, Sun 11-6

Midtown West **(212) 399-1078**
1290 Sixth Avenue at 52nd St
NYC 10104 Mon-Fri 9-9, Sat 10-8, Sun 11-6

Upper East Side **(212) 772-9952**
1155 Third Avenue at 68th St
NYC 10021 Mon-Sat 10-8, Sun 11-7

Midtown East **(212) 883-8766**
150 East 42nd Street at Lexington Ave
NYC 10017 Mon-Sat 9-9, Sun 11-6

Midtown East **(212) 308-1129**
488 Madison Avenue at 52nd St
NYC 10022 Mon-Fri 11-8, Sat 11-7, Sun 12-5

NoHo **(646) 602-1582**
770 Broadway btw 8/9th St
NYC 10003 Mon-Sat 10-9, Sun 12-6

SoHo **(212) 625-0427**
560 Broadway btw Prince/Spring
NYC 10012 Mon-Sat 10-8, Sun 12-6

Tribeca **(212) 809-1435**
2 Broadway btw Beaver/Stone
NYC 10004 Mon-Fri 8-7

★ Anthony T Kirby

Here we have the essential haberdashery for clients such as *Vanity Fair*'s Graydon Carter and his fashionable peers. Make an appointment with Anthony T for custom-made neckwear and debonair accessories. His new gray flannel trouser collection for men has garnered raves, and his canvas totes are perfect for getting around town or for a day off at the beach. Also find a selection of English bench-made shoes for men and women. *anthonytnewyork.com*

Expensive *Amex/MC/V*

(by appointment only) **(718) 783-2570**

⭐ Anthropologie

The grown-up sibling of Urban Outfitters, this massive store has a Parisian flea market feel and is packed with an eclectic selection of apparel and home furnishings aimed at a slightly more sophisticated customer. Labels include in-house designers Odille, Elevenses and Louie, as well as La Cosa, Nanette Lepore, Plenty, Ruth and Marimekko. There is also a vast selection of affordable housewares from antique-style tableware to luxurious provencal bath lotions and potions. *800-309-2500 anthropologie.com*

Moderate *Amex/MC/V*

SoHo **(212) 343-7070**
375 West Broadway | btw Spring/Broome
NYC 10012 | Daily 11-8 (Sun 11-6)

Flatiron **(212) 627-5885**
85 Fifth Avenue | at 16th St
NYC 10003 | Mon-Sat 10-8, Sun 11-7

⭐ Anya Hindmarch

This quirky London handbag designer turns out sophisticated and witty collections of Italian-crafted designs. Choose from classics in scratch-resistant, luxurious leathers, evening numbers in couture satins and velvets, and cotton or silk bags with playful, vintage photographic images of dogs, cats and ladies lying on the beach. Resort bags are printed with kitsch maps of the Hamptons or Mustique. Each bag carries (stamped or hand-sewn) a dainty bow logo. The fashion crowd are still carrying the personalized bags, complete with photos of their own choosing. Pay $190-$260 for print bags and $400-$1,400 for leather handbags. Small leather goods, jewelry, wallets, travel and make-up bags are also available. *anyahindmarch.com*

Moderate to expensive *Amex/MC/V*

Upper East Side **(212) 750-3974**
29 East 60th Street | btw Madison/Park Ave
NYC 10022 | Mon-Sat 10-7

SoHo **(212) 343-8147**
115 Greene Street | btw Prince/Spring
NYC 10012 | Mon-Sat 11-7, Sun 12-6

The Apartment

This hip space blazed a new trend through the retail scene: store as reality entertainment, where the customers (and occasionally models) play the role of performer/observer and the shop and merchandise become the stage and props. As one would expect, The Apartment's primary focus is on groovy furniture, kitchen equipment and bathroom fixtures; however, cutting-edge clothing and accessories from Trash A Porter, Alice Roi and the Apartment T-shirt line can be found among the housewares. *theapt.com*

Moderate *Amex/MC/V*

SoHo   **(212) 219-3661**
101 Crosby Street   btw Prince/Spring
NYC 10012   Wed-Sat 12-7, Sun 12-6
                   (Mon-Tues by appointment)

A.P.C.

A.P.C., an abbreviation for Atelier de Production et Creations, is a favorite among fashion insiders seeking urban basics that are cool without trying. Owner/designer Jean Touitou produces a trendy yet casual collection of lightweight dress shirts, comfy sweaters, cool sweatshirts, chinos, and outerwear along with some of the coolest jeans (approximately $120) around. Accessories include sunglasses, ties, bags, limited-edition tees, CDs and shoes. Staff are super-cool, but friendly.   *apc.fr*

Moderate   *Amex/MC/V*

SoHo   **(212) 966-9685**
131 Mercer Street   btw Prince/Spring
NYC 10012   Mon-Sat 11-7, Sun 12-6

April Cornell

The Canadian-based chain boutique April Cornell offers a selection of ultra-feminine clothing, accessories and housewares that can transform even the dreariest New York winter day into a romantic countryside getaway. In addition to their large variety of dresses, straw hats and silk sleepwear, April Cornell sells children's apparel for girls ages 2-12 including delicate matching floral-printed dresses for mother and daughters. Their popular housewares collection including tea sets, table linens and bedding that appears to have been lifted from a charming traditional country home in Provence or the Cotswolds.   *aprilcornell.com*

Moderate   *Amex/MC/V*

Upper West Side   **(212) 799-4342**
487 Columbus Avenue   btw 83/84th St
NYC 10024   Mon-Sat 10-8, Sun 12-6

Arche

A super-popular family-owned French company known for comfortable, spongy leather shoes in a myriad of colors and styles. They might not be terribly refined for the grown-ups but the thick rubber soles and clunky heels—printed with everything from Klimt paintings to zebras to American flags—continue to do it for younger customers.   *arche-shoes.com*

Moderate   *Amex/MC/V*

Upper East Side   **(212) 439-0700**
995 Madison Avenue   at 77th St
NYC 10021   Mon-Fri 10-7, Sat 10-6, Sun 12-5

Upper East Side   **(212) 838-1933**
1045 Third Avenue   btw 61/62nd St
NYC 10021   (opening hours as above)

Midtown West (212) 262-5488
128 West 57th Street btw Sixth/Seventh Ave
NYC 10019 (opening hours as above)

SoHo (646) 613-8700
123 Wooster Street btw Prince/Spring
NYC 10012 Mon-Sat 11-7, Sun 12-6

NoHo (212) 529-4808
10 Astor Place btw Broadway/Lafayette
NYC 10003 Mon-Fri 10-7, Sat 10-6, Sun 12-5

Arden B. ♀

Street sensibility pervades at this overly-lit SoHo spot where the stock is finally veering away from the peasant girl look: the latest styles are more creative and sophisticated, while still retaining their casual air. Fishnet fabrics and gauzy materials seem to be everywhere—you need to be young and/or have a great figure to pull off a lot of this stuff. Accessories like knit caps and huge belts thankfully distract one's eye from, depending on one's opinion, the either very now or very department-store decor. *ardenb.com*

Affordable *Amex/MC/V*

Upper East Side (212) 628 2003
1130 Third Avenue btw 66/67th St
NYC 10021 Mon-Sat 10-8, Sun 11-6

Flatiron (646) 638 0361
104 Fifth Avenue btw 15/16th St
NYC 10011 Mon-Sat 10-8, Sun 12-7

SoHo (212) 941-5697
532 Broadway btw Prince/Spring
NYC 10012 Mon-Sat 10-8, Sun 11-7

Arleen Bowman ♀

Arleen Bowman's line of casual sportswear features signature two-pocket shirts in perforated suede, linen, silk, cotton and velvet, plus relaxed skirts, pants and coats. In addition to her own line Arleen Bowman Chin Chin, you'll find traveling suits, sweaters, dresses, T-shirts, tops and jeans from Margaret O'Leary, Cambio, Neesh, Womyn, Hanky Panky, Johnny Was and Three Dots. Accessories include fabulous handbags, jewelry and shoes. *arleenbowmannewyork.com*

Expensive *Amex/MC/V*

West Village (212) 645-8740
353 Bleecker Street btw West 10th/Charles
NYC 10014 Mon-Sat 12-7, Sunday 1-6

Arthur Gluck Shirtmakers ♂♀

Lovely custom shirts are produced here. Choose a fabric from Gluck's stunning selection, ranging from solid broadcloth to Sea Island cotton to luxurious zendaline to silky crepe. With options like hand-sewn monograms, the shop's signature mother-of-pearl buttons, and nifty cufflinks, the possibilities for creating a unique shirt are end-

less. Orders are carefully prepared and take approximately one month. *shirtcreations.com*

Moderate *Amex/MC/V*

Midtown West **(212) 755-8165**
47 West 57th Street btw Fifth/Sixth Ave
NYC 10019 Mon-Thurs 8:30-5, Fri 8:30-2

Art Fiend Foundation

Art Fiend Foundation is a not-for-profit organization providing a carefully curated gallery/retail outlet for budding
designers like Miyako Nakamura, Susan Cianciolo, Tess
Giberson, Jodi Busby and Elisa Jiminez. Find select racks of
one-of-a-kind pieces, including clothes, accessories and
jewelry. Handmade treasures—from delicate skirts to tiny
detailed purses—are on display here, as are photographs,
paintings, books, and pretty much anything else that happens to catch the foundation's fancy. A great spot to indulge
in fashion's future. *artfiendfoundation.com*

Moderate *Amex/MC/V*

SoHo **(212) 420-1033**
123 Ludlow btw Rivington/Delancey
NYC 10002 Tues-Sun 1-7

Ascot Chang

One of New York's finest shirtmakers, Ascot Chang caters to
some of the world's nattiest dressers with custom-made
suits and overcoats as well. Choose from 2,000 luxurious
fabrics and know that your purchase will last forever. If your
wallet isn't quite that flush, Chang also features off-the-rack
shirts, sportcoats, blazers, pajamas and silk robes. Custom-
made suits start at $1,600, shirts at $90. *ascotchang.com*

Expensive *Amex/MC/V*

Midtown West **(212) 759-3333**
7 West 57th Street btw Fifth/Sixth Ave
NYC 10019 Mon-Sat 9:30-6

Ashley Tyler

Ms Tyler has designed for Ralph and Calvin, but you'd never
guess based on the free form of her own creations. Her
drapey, Tinkerbell-worthy jersey dresses are luxe and comfy,
and hang ever-so-perfectly on a range of body types. Color-
blocked and solid-colored dresses come in every shade
from muted earth tones to bold pinks and greens, and fas-
ten with wooden tusk clasps. A rusty birdcage sits at the
forefront of this Soho basement flagship/studio, which is
rather wood-nymphish itself, tree branches for racks and a
silky circus tent, also fashioned from twigs, serving as the fitting room. *ashleytyler.com*

Expensive *Amex/MC/V*

Soho **(212) 965-1110**
112 Greene Street btw Prince/Spring
NYC 10012 Mon-Fri 11-7, Sat-Sun 12-6

⭐ Asprey

This iconic English brand has given itself a makeover, marrying its long-standing aristocratic, high-quality standards with an updated rock 'n' roll sensibility. The often eclectic (and always luxurious) selection includes porcelain figures, leather board games, cufflinks, tableware, pens and watches. You'll chuckle at the novelty items, covet the jewelry and gasp at the prices—all in all, not a place to miss. *asprey.com*

Luxury   *Amex/MC/V*

Fifth Avenue   **(212) 688-1811**
725 Fifth Avenue   at 56th St
NYC 10022   Mon-Sat 10-6

Assets London

A bust of colorful Ibiza energy on the Upper West Side and Tribeca, Assets London carries top European designer labels such as Cacharel, Point Sud and Barbara Bui, all looks that the most label-conscious club-hopper dreams of being decked out in. Also find a large selection of sunglasses, stockings from top brands like Gucci and Dior and why-bother underthings from the likes of Cosabella. For bored boyfriends, there's a couch and a monitor playing catwalk videos (Gisele in a swimsuit should keep their interest).

Moderate   *Amex/MC/V*

Upper West Side   **(212) 874-8253**
464 Columbus Avenue   btw 82/83rd St
NYC 10024   Mon-Sat 11-8, Sun 12-7

Tribeca   **(212) 219-8777**
152 Franklin Street   btw Hudson/Varick
NYC 10013   Mon-Sat 10-7

Atelier New York

Packed with threads from hot designers such as Ann Demeulemeester, Rick Owen, Undercover, Raf Simons, Carol Christian Poell and Carpe Diem, Atelier New York comes off like the highest-fashion mini mall. The small store is filled with sleek and slender shirts, jackets and well-cut pants for those New Yorkers looking to distinguish themselves from the rest of the fashion crowd. *ateliernewyork.com*

Expensive   *Amex/MC/V*

SoHo   **(212) 941-8435**
125 Crosby Street   btw Prince/Houston
NYC 10012   Mon-Fri 11-7, Sat 12-7, Sun 12-6

A.Tempo

A super-girly store for that knockout party dress. A great selection features beaded and sequined evening dresses, flowing chiffon column dresses, and floor-length skirts paired with spaghetti-strap tops. Embellish your fancy outfit with coordinating accessories like beaded purses, jewelry, shawls and a ton of diamanté hair ornaments.

Moderate   *Amex/MC/V*

Upper West Side   **(212) 769-0368**
290 Columbus Avenue   btw 73/74th St
NYC 10023   Mon-Sat 11-8, Sun 12-7

A.Testoni

A footwear designer from Bologna, A.Testoni's high-quality leather shoes are the very epitome of understatement. For men, find handmade and bench-made dress shoes, tennis shoes, colorful loafers with multiple buckles and tougher-than-you-think mandals. For women, styles run from loafers and boots to pumps and eveningwear. Check out the A.Testoni version of a slingback—so smooth. Handbags, briefcases, scarves, ties, belts and luggage complete the offerings.   *877-testoni testoniusa.com*

Expensive   *Amex/MC/V*

Fifth Avenue   **(212) 223-0909**
665 Fifth Avenue   at 53rd St
NYC 10022   Mon-Fri 10-7, Sat 10-6:30, Sun 12-6

A.T.Harris Formalwear

A brilliant source for renting a tuxedo anytime, but especially for short notice and weddings, A.T.Harris takes the pain out of the penguin suit with its comfy space and speedy (but classy) service. You'll have the option of renting or buying at equally reasonable prices— expect to pay $145 to $200 for a 24-hour rental, including everything except shoes. Shirts and the necessary black-tie accoutrements are also available.   *atharris.com*

Moderate   *Amex/MC/V*

Midtown East   **(212) 682-6325**
11 East 44th Street   btw Fifth/Madison Ave
NYC 10017   Mon-Fri 9-6 (Thurs 9-7)
Sat (by appointment only) 10-5

The Athlete's Foot

It's a bonanza of sneakers for every sport on the planet—be it yoga, tennis, running, basketball or just plain walking around. You'll find every top brand here, including Adidas, New Balance, Nike and Reebok, as well as NBA gear, although don't expect the staff to be too knowledgeable about any product. Children's sizes vary from store to store.

Affordable to moderate   *Amex/MC/V*

Upper East Side   **(212) 426-7583**
233 East 86th Street   btw Second/Third Ave
NYC 10028   Daily 10-8 (Sun 10-6)

Atomic Passion

Don't mess with the folks at Atomic Passion, this legendary, kitsch-heavy vintage store. 'Buy or Die' reads their business card, which also boasts a skull and crossbones in case you didn't get the message. While the eclectic mix of clothing, which includes graphic tees, Fifties dresses, Western shirts and a huge amount of shoes, handbags and sunglasses may be daunting at first, patience rewards those shoppers with time to rummage through the store's many racks. If you can see beyond the endless strands of Christmas baubles and fake fruit on the ceiling, that is…

Moderate   *Amex/MC/V*

East Village   **(212) 533-0718**
430 East 9th Street   btw First/Avenue A
NYC 10009   Daily 1-8

Atrium

This marble store with denim-patched couches is an anomaly of button-downs, Seven and Miss Sixty jeans, Triple 5 Soul sweatshirts and J.Lo-style tube tops. The mix of trendy designs and streetwear includes an array of sunglasses, footwear and other accessories.   *atriumnyc.com*

Moderate   *Amex/MC/V*

NoHo   **(212) 473-9200**
644 Broadway   at Bleecker
NYC 10012   Mon-Sat 10-9, Sun 11-8

Avirex

Rappers and Red Baron wannabes get their sporty leather looks from Avirex. Since 1975, Jeff Clyman has been fashioning hides for sports legends, rock stars, actors and aviators (he's an official supplier to the U.S. Air Force). His selection of colorful collegiate jackets, motorcycle numbers, oversized baseball bombers, jeans and T-shirts (heavily logo'd with the Avirex name) are all sold here. Don't miss the encased model planes around the store.   *avirex.com*

Moderate   *Amex/MC/V*

SoHo   **(212) 254-4000**
652 Broadway   btw Bleecker/Bond
NYC 10012   Mon-Sat 11-7, Sun 12-6

Avitto

In the heart of SoHo, Avitto offers footwear styles that cover all the bases. Women can choose from mules, pumps, slingbacks, evening shoes and a large boot selection; fellas can browse business and casual shoes from sandals to $800 alligator lace-ups.   *avitto.com*

Moderate to expensive   *Amex/MC/V*

SoHo   **(212) 219-7501**
424 West Broadway   btw Prince/Spring
NYC 10012   Daily 10:30-8 (Sun 11-8)

A/X Armani Exchange

This emporium caters to the logo-conscious in search of casual basics with the essential Armani insignia. Find jeans, T-shirts, pants, sweaters, jackets and outerwear that are relaxed and hip—the denim skirts are especially cool. Think of it as an upmarket Euro version of Gap. Prices are surprisingly reasonable and quality is up to the lofty Armani standards, of course. *armaniexchange.com*

Moderate   *Amex/MC/V*

Fifth Avenue   **(212) 980-3037**
645 Fifth Avenue   at 51st St
NYC 10022   Mon-Sat 10-8, Sun 11-7

Flatiron   **(212) 254-7230**
129 Fifth Avenue   btw 19/20th St
NYC 10003   (opening hours as above)

SoHo   **(212) 431-6000**
568 Broadway   at Prince
NYC 10012   (opening hours as above)

Midtown West   **(212) 823-9321**
10 Columbus Circle   Time Warner Center
NYC 10019   Mon-Sat 10-9, Sun 11-7

★ Azaleas

Beach or bedroom, Azaleas has you covered. This adorable boutique stocks the cutest and flirtiest lingerie and swimwear around. The fabulous staff will help you navigate through the adorable goods, which range from super-flattering bikinis by Lisa Curran to coquettish underthings by Princesse Tam Tam. Other swimwear labels include Errol, Vix, and TNA. Lingerie runs the gamut from basic to stylish, functional to naughty, with brands such as Aubade, Underglam, Le Mystère and Fleur't. This is the place to shop for cheeky gifts such as Daniella Simon's 'Mommy-to-be' panties or 'Kiss the Bride' briefs. Also find a fantastically eclectic assortment of accessories such as costume jewelry, sachets, candles, and shoes.   *800-775-0540 azaleasnyc.com*

Expensive   *Amex/MC/V*

East Village   **(212) 253-5484**
223 East 10th Street   btw First/Second Ave
NYC 10003   Tues-Fri 1-8, Sat 12-8, Sun 1-6

B2Gear

Keith Lewis, community mentor and founder of Youth America, came up with a wonderful idea to get children more involved in their communities—have them build their own business. B2Gear is the result: one of cheapest and coolest places for teens to shop and buy gear from other teens. Fashion-forward youngsters manage and supply the store, stocking everything from Rasta-colored tights to denim, funky jewelry, and colorfully tagged tees. Every piece has been selected and promoted by teens who know what kids want to wear. Nothing is overpriced, and a student with 50 dollars can leave with at least three new outfits for school or play. *b2gear.com*

Affordable   *Amex/MC/V*

Fort Greene   **(718) 643-1860**
777 Fulton Street   btw South Oxford/South Portland
Brooklyn 11217   Daily 12-8

B8 Couture

The space itself is über-sleek and shiny with black lacquer walls, purple carpeting, sectional couches, a blinding chandelier, a big-screen broadcasting runway shows and a stereo pounding techno music. This young store has had a few conceptual facelifts since its inception. Originally unisex, B8 has already slashed the wild womenswear and is concentrating on the guys. On offer are European-designed over-embellished screenprinted muscle tees, jeans with copious amounts of zippers, leather jackets with patches and pockets that go beyond extraneous. The wares are borderline-Eurotrash, but with enough pizzazz it's possible to pull anything off with style.

Expensive   *Amex/MC/V*

West Village   **(866) 623-5545**
27 Little West 12th Street   at Ninth Ave
NYC 10014   Mon-Fri 11-7, Sat 11-8, Sun 12-5

★ Baby Bird

Baby Bird is the perfect boutique for Park Slope princes and princesses. Parents can establish street cred at an early age with rock 'n' roll tees for baby, showcasing bands like the Flaming Lips, the Sex Pistols and Bob. Super-soft blankets and too-cute toddler kimonos (wrapped in a sushi box) are also on offer. Baby Bird smartly built a fish tank right into the front counter, so kids can gape while mom and dad make purchases.   *shopbird.com*

Moderate   *Amex/MC/V*

Park Slope   **(718) 788-4506**
428 7th Avenue   btw 14/15th St
Brooklyn 11215   Mon-Sat 10:30-6:30, Sun 12-6

Baghouse

This is one-stop shopping for portage needs—a huge showroom filled floor to ceiling with travel bags. There are messenger bags, rucksacks, carryalls, pouches, handbags and wallets—everything from all-weather gear by Eagle Creek to luxury suitcase sets by Tumi. It's also a great place to pick up a briefcase.

Moderate   *Amex/MC/V*

NoHo   **(212) 260-0940**
797 Broadway   btw 10/11th St
NYC 10003   Mon-Sat 11-6:45, Sun 1-5:45

★ Bagutta Life

Moving from its former West Broadway location, Bagutta Life, a spacious SoHo boutique, boasts the crème de la crème of haute designers from both sides of the Atlantic. Snap up a D&G or John Galliano jacket. Adorn yourself in an Alaïa or Zac Posen evening dress. And if you just can't bring yourself to splurge on that decadent Dior must-have, pick up a bottle of the store's signature perfume and you will still feel like a European fashion forerunner. Temporarily closed for renovations at press time, the store was due to open in 2006. *baguttalife.com*

Expensive   Amex/MC/V

SoHo   **(212) 925-5216**
76 Greene Street   btw Broome/Spring
NYC 10012   n/a at press time

Bakers

In the tourist wasteland around the Empire State Building there are few clothing and shoe shops not aimed at the itinerants, but one of the oldest denizens is the shoe store Bakers. Suiting the area, its offerings are more mass than class, focusing on such labels as Steve Madden, Guess, Diesel and its own Bakers line. Designs range from ankle-wrap stilettos to sporty sneaker-pump boots—decent fashionable footwear at middle-market prices. *bakersshoes.com*

Moderate   Amex/MC/V

Midtown East   **(212) 279-7016**
358 Fifth Avenue   at 34th St
NYC 10001   Mon-Fri 9-8:30, Sat 9-9:30, Sun 11-7

Baldwin Formalwear

Tuxedos, black tie, white tie and tails, morning suits, shirts, neckwear, vests and cummerbunds—all a man's formalwear needs are met at Baldwin. And with class: Givenchy, Chaps Ralph Lauren, After Six, Charles Jourdan, Oscar de la Renta and Perry Ellis are just a few of the labels featured ($300 and up). Not ready to buy your own? Thousands of designer styles are available for rent ($100 and up), and you'll also find shoes by Frederico Leone. *nyctuxedos.com*

Moderate   Amex/MC/V

Midtown West   **(212) 867-4420**
1156 Avenue of the Americas (2nd floor)   at 45th St
NYC 10036   Mon-Fri 9-7, Sat 10-5

☆ Balenciaga

It's a bold move on Balenciaga's part: eschewing SoHo and the Upper East Side, they plant their flagship on Chelsea's Gallery Row. Pretentious? A bit, but with clothes this beautiful and strange they might as well be art. The space itself is a marvel of exposed distressed brick and concrete, with a flat video projection of Nicholas Ghesquière's current collection on one wall. As for the clothes, you'll feel your horizons expand as you inspect the meticulously constructed (but hot) aviator jackets, roomy drop-waist pants and shrunken knits. Superior chic, and definitely worth the out-of-the-way walk. *balenciaga.com*

Luxury   Amex/MC/V

Chelsea   **(212) 206-0872**
542 West 22nd Street   btw Tenth/Eleventh Ave
NYC 10011   Mon-Sat 11-7, Sun 12-5

Bally 👫

In 1850 Carl Franz Bally from Switzerland was inspired by the 'subtly decorated' shoes he saw on a business trip to Paris. A successful tradition lives on in the shoes, bags, sportswear and casualwear that bear his name. The designs are sleek, from striped-handle messenger bags to signature-print vinyl satchels, and the craftsmanship is high, from sun-dried, hand-applied leather flowers on bags to the fishermen-inspired leather-and-canvas-mesh footwear. A showroom at Fifth Avenue and 57th serves as their temporary store while the original location undergoes renovations, scheduled to be finished by early 2006.   *bally.com*

Expensive   *Amex/MC/V*

Midtown East   **(212) 751-9082**
628 Madison Avenue   at 59th St
NYC 10153   Mon-Fri 10-6:30 (Thurs 10-7)
                                    Sat 10-6, Sun 12-5

Bambini 👶

Every child should be so lucky to be all dressed up in a jaunty Bambini outfit. There is everything from casual and back-to-school basics to party and dress wear. Bambini is packed with Italian brand names featuring traditional looks in pants, dresses, shirts, sweaters, tees, rompers and more. Highlights include their private-label shoes and handknit sweaters. Be sure to check out their half-yearly sales, which are legendary among the buying-for-baby set. From newborn to size 8 (some boys' suits are available up to a size 12).

Moderate   *Amex/MC/V*

Upper East Side   **(212) 717-6742**
1088 Madison Avenue   btw 81/82nd St
NYC 10028   Mon-Sat 10-6, Sun 12-5

★ Banana Republic 👫

Ah, BR. Banana Republic had a fashion show in New York last year, signifying a greater fashion focus for the one-time adventure/safari store. While the prices are still affordable, the fabrics and looks have turned to luxurious touches like silk and eyelet lace dresses, bamboo-handled suede bags, mother-of-pearl earrings and lizard sandals. Banana Republic is right for work and the mix-and-match hi/low style remains immensely popular. Men will find textured, tea-dyed shirts, mock-croc loafers, slim suits and the quintessential khakis.   *bananarepublic.com*

Affordable   *Amex/MC/V*

Fifth Avenue   **(212) 974-2350**
626 Fifth Avenue   at 50th St
NYC 10022   Mon-Sat 10-8, Sun 11-7

Upper East Side   **(212) 570-2465**
1136 Madison Avenue   at 85th St
NYC 10028   Mon-Sat 10-7, Sun 12-6

Upper East Side	**(212) 288-4279**
1110 Third Avenue	at 65th St
NYC 10021	Mon-Sat 10-8, Sun 11-7
Upper East Side	**(212) 360-1296**
1529 Third Avenue	at 86th St
NYC 10128	Mon-Sat 10-9, Sun 11-7
Upper West Side	**(212) 787-2064**
2360 Broadway	at 86th St
NYC 10024	Mon-Sat 10-9, Sun 11-7
Upper West Side	**(212) 873-9048**
215 Columbus Avenue	btw 69/70th St
NYC 10023	Mon-Sat 10-9, Sun 11-7
Midtown East	**(212) 751-5570**
130 East 59th Street	at Lexington Ave
NYC 10022	Mon-Fri 9:30-8:30, Sat 10-7, Sun 11-7
Midtown East	**(212) 490-3127**
107 East 42nd Street	btw Vanderbilt/Lexington Ave
NYC 10017	Mon-Fri 8-9, Sat 10-8, Sun 11-6
Midtown West	**(212) 244-3060**
17 West 34th Street	btw Fifth/Sixth Aves
NYC 10001	Mon-Sat 10-9, Sun 11-8
Flatiron (M)	**(212) 366-4691**
114 Fifth Avenue	at 17th St
NYC 10011	Mon-Fri 10-9, Sat 10-8, Sun 11-7
Flatiron (W)	**(212) 366-4630**
89 Fifth Avenue	at 16th St
NYC 10009	Mon-Fri 10-9, Sat 11-8, Sun 11-7
Chelsea	**(212) 645-1032**
111 Eighth Avenue	btw 15/16th St
NYC 10011	Mon-Sat 10-8, Sun 12-7
West Village	**(212) 473-9570**
205 Bleecker Street	at Sixth Ave
NYC 10012	Mon-Sat 10-8, Sun 11-7
SoHo (W)	**(212) 925-0308**
550 Broadway	btw Prince/Spring
NYC 10012	(opening hours as above)
SoHo (M)	**(212) 334-3034**
528 Broadway	at Spring
NYC 10012	(opening hours as above)
Lower Manhattan	**(212) 962-1461**
200 Vesey Street	at World Financial Center
NYC 10285	Mon-Fri 8-7:30, Sat 10-6, Sun 12-5

Barami

Are you a corporate woman that lets her hair down immediately after the big meeting? If yes, you might want to consider Barami. They offer suits, co-ordinated tops, dresses and skirts at reasonable prices—linen suits for $180 or pleated skirts for $45, for example. They also carry denim and plenty of casualwear. Be sure to visit the scarf and accessory section. *barami.com*

Moderate MC/V

Midtown East
136 East 57th Street
NYC 10022

(212) 980-9333
at Lexington Ave
Mon-Fri 10-9, Sat 10-8, Sun 11-7

Midtown East
375 Lexington Avenue
NYC 10017

(212) 682-2550
at 41st St
Mon-Fri 9-7:30, Sat-Sun 11-6

Midtown West
485 Seventh Avenue
NYC 10018

(212) 967-2990
btw 36/37th St
Mon-Fri 9-7:30, Sat 9-6:30, Sun 12-6

Fifth Avenue
535 Fifth Avenue
NYC 10017

(212) 949-1000
at 45th St
Mon-Fri 9-8, Sat 10-7, Sun 11-6

Barbara Bui

French-Vietnamese designer Barbara Bui's clothes are best known for their rock 'n' roll attitude. Bui's forte is her extensive range of beautifully tailored pants, ranging from bootleg to man-tailored—'I always make at least three cuts of pants, for different bodies', she says—but you can also choose from a huge number of jackets, skirts, sweaters, dresses, form-fitted tees (shrink-wrapped—very groovy), outerwear and shoes. An enormous, minimalist shop serves as a backdrop for this cool Parisian designer's monochromatic ready-to-wear collection. Our tip: wait for the sales, when the pricey numbers are reduced by as much as 50%. *barbarabui.fr*

Luxury   *Amex/MC/V*

SoHo
115-117 Wooster Street
NYC 10012

(212) 625-1938
btw Prince/Spring
Mon-Sat 11-7, Sun 12-6

Barbara Feinman Millinery

Barbara Feinman's hats achieve that rare level of perfection that results from old-world craftsmanship and modern style. Beautiful fabrics (from straw to velvet) and attention to detail have made Feinman's toppers popular with award-winners like Marisa Tomei and Glenn Close. The lovely fedoras, bucket shapes, newsboys and cloches are all handmade in the back of the store. In addition to offering services like hand-blocking and custom fittings, the boutique also carries delicate jewelry and exquisite handbags. *barbarafeinmanmillinery.com*

Expensive   *MC/V*

East Village
66 East 7th Street
NYC 10003

(212) 358-7092
btw First/Second Ave
Mon-Sat 12:30-8, Sun 1-7

Barbara Shaum

Barbara Shaum is the haute sandal specialist, having whipped up beautiful woven versions for almost 50 years. But she has experienced something of a reinvention thanks to king of cool Calvin Klein, who once paired his men's collection with Shaum's gladiator or thong-style custom-made creations. Since then she's hit the big league, with her shoes on the fabulous feet of photographer and trendsetter Steven Meisel and designer Ralph Lauren. Prices run from $225 to $500. Belts are available, too.

Expensive   *Amex/MC/V*

East Village   **(212) 254-4250**
60 East 4th Street   btw Bowery/Second Ave
NYC 10003   Wed-Sat 1-6

Barbour by Peter Elliot

Since 1894, J. Barbour & Sons have focused on making clothes for those weekends out of town. Famous for their commitment to quality and durability, their name is synonymous with the best of country living. A men's stowaway flyweight quilted jacket is easily packed into a pocket, and womens' tailored equestrian jackets bring grace to a long ride. Lord James Percy's Northumberland line of shooting clothing, launched in fall 2004, is 'uncompromising in its fitness for purpose' and wearable in all seasons and for all disciplines (shooting and non-shooting alike). To the manor, Jeeves…   *barbour.com*

Expensive   *Amex/MC/V*

Upper East Side   **(212) 570-2600**
1047 Madison Avenue   btw 79/80th St
NYC 10021   Mon-Thurs 10-7, Fri 10-6:30
                                               Sat 10-6, Sun 12-5

★ Barneys New York

Oh, Barneys, hallowed be thy name. This too-chic-to-speak fashion emporium is God's gift to shopping. In addition to excellent beauty—check out the new Foundation level on the lower ground floor (get it?)—and accessories departments, it boasts seven more floors of perfectly edited and ultra-hip women's and menswear, from retro-sleek Proenza Schouler to conceptual Yohji Yamamoto. Young fashionistas head at light-speed to the seventh and eighth floor Co-op for the hippest denim, swimwear, shoes and accessories from such labels as Marc by Marc Jacobs, Theory, Libertine, James Perse, and Habitual. Other departments include outerwear; designer shoes (from Manolos to Chloe); lingerie; Barneys New York label; a maternity line, aptly named Procreation; a newborn and toddler section; and Chelsea Passage, a tabletop and gift department. Then there's a vintage section and a full-fledged luxury bridal salon that features over 60 unbelievably chic styles. In contrast, the men's store is an oasis of calm, where classic types can go for suits from the likes of Brioni, Ermenegildo Zegna, Hickey Freeman, Raf Simons, Dries Van Noten, Canali and Kiton; under the suits go Hamilton shirts, and below them Berluti shoes. Coolsters, meanwhile, can choose from Armani, Cloak, Trovata, Dior Homme, Dolce & Gabbana, and Prada. Other departments include men's furnishings, made-to-measure suits and dress shirts, designer shoes, sportswear, rainwear, outerwear, special sizes, casualwear, formalwear, shoes and, phew, accessories. If you are nearly dropping from shopping, find sustenance at Barneys' fabulous in-store restaurant Fred's, which is an in spot for fashionistas. And did we tell you about the twice yearly warehouse sales? Legendary.　　　　　　　　888-222-7639 barneys.com

Expensive　　　　　　　　　　　　　　　　　Amex/MC/V

Upper East Side　　　　　　　　　　**(212) 826-8900**
660 Madison Avenue　　　　　　　　　　　　at 61st St
NYC 10022　　　　　　　Mon-Fri 10-8, Sat 10-7, Sun 11-6

Barneys Co-op

This trio of trendy stores defines what it means to be fiercely stylish in America's fashion capital. Their selection of the chicest threads, shoes and accessories by the likes of Marc by Marc Jacobs, Diane von Furstenberg, Libertine, James Perse and Theory, not to mention the definitive selection of must-wear designer jeans (Habitual, Edun), makes visiting the Co-op a monthly, if not weekly, must. And with locations from funky Chelsea and SoHo to the sophisticated climes of the Upper West Side, there's always one nearby.　　barneys.com

Expensive　　　　　　　　　　　　　　　　　Amex/MC/V

Chelsea　　　　　　　　　　　　　**(212) 593-7800**
236 West 18th Street　　　　　　btw Seventh/Eighth Ave
NYC 10011　　　　　　　Mon-Fri 11-8, Sat 11-7, Sun 12-6

SoHo (women only)　　　　　　　　**(212) 965-9964**
116 Wooster Street　　　　　　　　　btw Prince/Spring
NYC 10012　　　　　　　　　　Mon-Sat 11-7, Sun 12-6

Upper West Side　　　　　　　　　**(646) 335-0978**
2139-2157 Broadway　　　　　　　　　btw 75/76th St
NYC 10023　　　　　Mon, Wed, Fri 10-8, Thurs 10-9
　　　　　　　　　　　　　　　　Sat 10-7, Sun 10-6

Barry Kieselstein-Cord

'We so often miss the beauty in things; my mission is to bring this into the world,' proclaims Barry Kieselstein-Cord. With bags featured on *Sex and the City* and jewelry worn by the Hollywood's biggest names, it's fair to say, 'mission accomplished'. From alligator earrings to diamond and platinum necklaces, you'll see why this is one of the largest designer-owned fine jewelry companies. Tom Hanks, Steven Spielberg, and Oprah are said to be Cord fans through and through, and his belts, opulent jewelry and leather-with-gold hardware handbags (examples of which are in the Louvre and the Metropolitan) are all more than ready for their close-ups. The new Madison Avenue store has a precious jewelry collection, with platinum and gold items, and offers an extensive selection of handbags in alligator and lizard.　　　　　　　　　　　kieselstein-cord.com

Luxury　　　　　　　　　　　　　　　　　Amex/MC/V

SoHo　　　　　　　　　　　　　　**(212) 529-9361**
132 Prince Street　　　　　btw Wooster/West Broadway
NYC 10012　　　　　　　　　　Mon-Sat 11-7, Sun 12-6

Upper East Side
810 Madison Avenue
NYC 10021

(212) 400-1482
at 68th St
Mon-Sat 10-6, Sun 12-5

Basic Basic

Guess what you'll find here? Assuming the name didn't give it away, you'd be right to say 'basic contemporary junior clothing'. Choose from a great selection of tops and jeans for tweens, as well as cute skirts, dresses and sweaters to complete the easy-breezy assortment. Labels include Petit Bateau, Three Dots, Juicy Couture and Mavi. *tee-zone.com*

Affordable   *Amex/MC/V*

NoHo
710 Broadway
NYC 10003

(212) 477-0267
btw Washington Place/4th St
Mon-Sat 11-8, Sun 12-7

★ Basso Furs

Step into this light and airy store and allow yourself to be enticed by the furrier-to-the-stars collection of perfect pelts. The store's natural woods and limestone floors show off Dennis Basso's sumptuous wares to their best effect, while his white-hot client list—Hillary Clinton, Elizabeth Taylor, Barbara Walters, Eartha Kitt, Star Jones and Patti LaBelle—makes the goods look even better. Basso's signature sable coats go for $25,000-$100,000, and his broadtail lamb suits run from $15,000-$25,000. *bassofurs.com*

Luxury   *Amex/MC/V*

Upper East Side
765 Madison Avenue
NYC 10021

(212) 794-4500
btw 65/66th St
Mon-Sat 10-6 (Thurs 10-7)
Sun 12-5 (in season)

Bati

This nice neighborhood boutique has carved out a niche for leather shoes. Carrying practical pumps, boots, flats and sandals in both trendy and conservative styles, Bati offers a variety of European designer brands including Enrico Antinori, Pura Lopez and Gola as well their own line. For the sporty shopper, Bati also sells a variety of fashion-forward sneakers by the likes of Goya and Royal Elastics.

Moderate to expensive   *Amex/MC/V*

Upper West Side
2151 Broadway
NYC 10024

(212) 362-0244
btw 75/76th St
Mon-Sat 11-8, Sun 12-7

BBL (Baby Blue Line)

Korean designer Eunjoo Lee adds a welcome touch of diversity to Nolita with her hip, sassy collection. Her design philosophy: cater to all body types and make clothes comfortable and easy to wear, from sportswear to informal but romantic eveningwear. Many of her dresses, skirts and tops incorporate custom-made screen prints and unusual fabrics like crinkled viscose and silk cotton viscose.

Although the clothes are well priced, the look probably won't appeal to everyone.

Moderate   *Amex/MC/V*

Nolita   **(212) 226-5866**
238 Mott Street   btw Prince/Spring
NYC 10012   Daily 12-7

BCBG Max Azria

Max Azria chose the name BCBG because it stands for 'bon chic, bon genre,' Parisian for 'good style, good attitude.' And that's the secret of BCBG Max Azria's phenomenal success: the perfect balance of classic style with chic, cute detailing. It's impossible not to find something that makes you look fabulous in here—from sexy separates and figure-hugging pants to floaty tops and beaded dresses. What Azria does so well is take the current trends and make them accessible—and desirable—to every cool girl in town. And what makes it all the better are price tags that allow those girls to get all dressed up and still have enough left over for somewhere to go. His higher-end runway line, BCBG Max Azria Collection, is also sold here. Accessories include shoes, handbags like killer evening clutches, eyewear, swimwear, denim, evening dresses, bridesmaid dresses and jewelry.   *bcbg.com*

Expensive   *Amex/MC/V*

Upper East Side   **(212) 717-4225**
770 Madison Avenue   at 66th St
NYC 10021   Mon-Sat 10-7 (Thurs 10-8), Sun 12-6

SoHo   **(212) 625-2723**
120 Wooster Street   btw Prince/Spring
NYC 10012   Mon-Sat 11-7, Sun 12-6

★ Beacon's Closet

What a well-edited vintage store should be. Having expanded beyond its name with two locations and plenty of floor-space, Beacon's Closet includes an array of clothes—from party dresses to Western shirts—and accessories (bags, jewelry, shoes) for men and women that are carefully arranged by color, article, style and size. Unlike many thrift shops, there aren't a lot of duds in here and the look is definitely on the hipster/artsy side of the fashion scale, but you still have to pay multiple visits to make the most out of the constantly changing stock. And if you have some hip duds that you've outgrown or simply grown tired of, Beacon's Closet buys clothes every day of the week (though it's much busier at weekends).   *beaconscloset.com*

Affordable   *Amex/MC/V*

Williamsburg   **(718) 486-0816**
88 North 11th Street   btw Berry/Wythe
Brooklyn 11211   Mon-Fri 12-9, Sat-Sun 11-8

Park Slope   **(718) 230-1630**
220 5th Avenue   btw President/Union
Brooklyn 11215   (opening hours as above)

Bebe

If you're a flaunt-it kinda girl, Bebe is the store for you. Its sexy pieces are heavy on the Lycra and are no doubt devilishly effective. Pants, skirts, dresses, navel-baring tops, tanks, tees and cute accessories make up the saucy collection. Only for the young, the brave…and Britney wannabes. *bebe.com*

Moderate *Amex/MC/V*

Upper East Side **(212) 935-2444**
1127 Third Avenue at 66th St
NYC 10021 Mon-Fri 10-8, Sat 10-7, Sun 11-6

Midtown East **(212) 588-9060**
805 Third Avenue at 50th St
NYC 10022 Mon-Fri 10-8, Sat 10-7, Sun 12-6

Flatiron **(212) 675-2323**
100 Fifth Avenue at 15th St
NYC 10011 Mon-Fri 10-8, Sat 10-7, Sun 11-6

Behrle

Since almost everyone is in need of a new leather bustier, Carla Behrle has moved her custom leather clothing store to bustling 34th Street, where steady clients and newcomers alike can access her creations more easily. Although she's dressed the derrieres of Jennifer Lopez, Chyna (the pro wrestler), LeAnn Rimes, U2 and Alicia Keys, you don't have to be a celebrity to purchase these wares. Leather pants are her forte—rocking it in every style from boot- and straight-leg to hip huggers and capris. Other sex-o-matic items include bustiers, jackets, skirts and shirts. Expect a week to a month for delivery of her custom-made pieces. *behrlenyc.com*

Expensive *Amex/MC/V*

Midtown West **(212) 279-5626**
440 West 34th Street btw Ninth/Tenth Ave
NYC 10001 (by appointment only)

Belgian Shoes

Belgian shoes are distinctive, handmade loafers ('more comfort than barefoot') that continue their fine tradition as Waspy status symbols with a cult following among the 'most leisurely members of the leisure class,' according to *GQ*. Founded by Henri Bendel, the store offers an incredible range, from linen and leather to positively quirky crushed velvet. If you feel the need for a royal crest or crown (no wardrobe is complete…), they will add one just for you. Once hooked, you may end up collecting every one of their 50-plus colors. Expect to wait six months to a year for special orders, depending on how special you are. *belgianshoes.com*

Expensive *Amex/MC/V*

Midtown East **(212) 755-7372**
110 East 55th Street btw Park/Lexington
NYC 10022 Mon-Fri 9-4:30

Benetton

Benetton is a truly global brand that sells rainbow-colored, energetic casual clothes for men and women. Best are the sweaters in every style and color imaginable but there is also a nifty line in work suits, A-line skirts, T-shirts, jeans, wool coats, awesome swimwear, shoes and accessories. Benetton gives true meaning to the term 'lifestyle' because these are clothes purpose-built for easy living.   *800-535-4491 benetton.com*

Moderate   *Amex/MC/V*

NoHo   **(212) 533-0230**
749 Broadway   at 8th St
NYC 10003   Mon-Thurs 10-9
Fri-Sat 10-9:30, Sun 12-8

Lower Manhattan   **(212) 509-3999**
10 Fulton St.   at South Street Seaport
NYC 10038   Mon-Sat 10-9, Sun 11-8

Fifth Avenue   **(212) 317-2501**
601 Fifth Avenue   btw 48/49th St
NYC 10017   Mon-Fri 10-7 (Thurs 10-8), Sun 11-6

Chelsea   **(646) 638-1086**
120 Seventh Avenue   at 17th St
NYC 10011   Mon-Sat 10-8, Sun 12-7

Ben Thylan Furs

Ben Thylan's extensive styles run the gamut from sporty to dressy. Its specialty: fur-lined or fur-trimmed water-repellent coats. These all-weather classics can be lined in any fur of your choosing, including mink, fox and sable. Cashmere, wool and camelhair coats are also available. Services include color and fashion consultations, as well as storage and cleaning.   *benthylanfurs.com*

Expensive   *Amex/MC/V*

Chelsea   **(212) 753-7700**
345 Seventh Avenue (5th floor)   btw Sixth/Seventh Ave
NYC 10001   Mon-Fri 9-5 (by appointment)

Beretta Gallery

Clothes, accessories and accoutrements that would make James Bond proud—they're all here at Beretta. Renowned the world over for its guns, Beretta also manufactures fine hunting, sporting and weekend wear. The tweeds, lodens and cashmeres displayed beside cases of sidearms make for a sophisticated, if explosive, atmosphere. This is classic sportswear fit for a king—or a globe-trotting secret agent.   *berettausa.com*

Expensive   *Amex/MC/V*

Upper East Side   **(212) 319-3235**
718 Madison Avenue   btw 63/64th St
NYC 10021   Mon-Sat 10-6

⭐ Bergdorf Goodman

Bergdorf's is the bee's knees in luxury retailing, from a first floor devoted to handbags, classic to adventurous jewelry and accessories, to six upper floors stocked with the chic to the edgy, including Armani, Dolce & Gabbana, Donna Karan, Michael Kors, Missoni, Oscar de la Renta, Valentino, Vera Wang, Chloé, Zac Posen, Comme des Garçons and Narciso Rodriguez. The 'New Level of Beauty' is a lower-level cosmetics planet featuring exclusive beauty and skin-care treatments, fragrances, spa products, and the Buff Spa nail salon (fantastic pedicures and somewhere to rest your shopping bags). Other departments include contemporary shoes, lingerie, eveningwear, sportswear, suits, bridal, custom, couture, outerwear and a genius gift and tabletop shop. The John Barrett Hair Salon, which delivers a great blow-out, and the Susan Ciminelli Day Spa are on the ninth floor. *800-964-8619 bergdorfgoodman.com*

Luxury *Amex/MC/V*

Fifth Avenue **(212) 753-7300**
754 Fifth Avenue at 58th St
NYC 10019 Mon-Sat 10-7 (Thurs 10-8), Sun 12-6

Bergdorf Goodman The Men's Store

Here is a huge, 45,000-square-foot emporium that still somehow manages to have the feeling of an intimate and exclusive gentleman's club. It might have something to do with the classic labels in stock: Turnbull & Asser, Charvet and Ferragamo shirts and ties and traditional suit collections by Oxxford, Canali, Hickey Freeman and Luciano Barbera. Not that they compromise cool: you'll also find Giorgio Armani, Jil Sander, Etro and the sex appeal of Gucci. Custom lines include Saint Andrews, Kiton, Domenico Spano and Oxxford. Mark the sales in your calendar now—they're fantastic. *800-964-8619*

Luxury *Amex/MC/V*

Fifth Avenue **(212) 339-3311**
745 Fifth Avenue at 58th St
NYC 10022 Mon-Sat 10-7 (Thurs 10-8), Sun 12-6

Berkley Girl

Berkley Girl is already prepping the next generation of New York style leaders with their pre-teen threads. The fun-filled store carries the latest from Puma, Betsey Johnson, Submarine and Lilly Pulitzer—all cute enough to satisfy Mom and fashionable enough to satisfy the young clotheshorse. Accessories such as grosgrain belts, baseball caps, diaries and books make great gifts. Pick up a fashionable laundry bag for tweens heading off to camp (or boarding school); friendly, welcoming staff. Watch for a new store on the corner of 74th and 2nd coming soon. *berkleygirl.com*

Expensive *Amex/MC/V*

Upper West Side   **(212) 877-4770**
410 Columbus Avenue   btw 79/80th St
NYC 10024   Mon-Fri 11-6:30, Sun 12-6

★ **Berluti**

Madame Olga Berluti, the world's only female bespoke shoemaker, has opened the first Stateside shop in her family's 110-year career of top-of-the-line shoemaking for men. Made-to-measure, with unique smooth and colorful Venetia leather, there's even an in-house colorist to help create the perfect depth and nuances. They offer classic designs, like the original court shoe from the late 1800s, as well as unique stitched designs with contrasting patches sewn on. Every shoe has a story: there's the pair she made for Andy Warhol, and then there are the ones with treads modeled after those of a 1930s Rolls Royce.   *berluti.com*

Luxury   *Amex/MC/V*

Upper East Side   **(212) 439-6400**
971 Madison Avenue   at 76th St
NYC 10021   Mon-Sat 10-6 (Thurs 10-7)

Bess

Find exquisite designs at this serene, sensual store. Her jewelry is too elegant to be trendy and too stylish to be classic, but has a harmonious sensibility that just might make it a favorite for years to come. Long, graceful earrings, glamorous cocktail rings and chunky necklaces are standouts. Prices run from $500 to $4,500—an easily justifiable level given the mesmerizing effects of the pieces.

Expensive   *Amex/MC/V*

Nolita   **(212) 260-6740**
259 Elizabeth Street   btw Houston/Prince
NYC 10012   Tues-Sun 12-7

Best of Scotland

And it is. A top-floor retreat that sells Scottish cashmere sweaters at terrific prices. They carry a full range of styles for men and women, from sizes 32 to 58, at prices which average an amazing 50% below retail. Crew necks priced at $450 uptown on Madison Avenue retail for around $225, so get in here fast. Delicious cashmere overcoats, lush scarves and mufflers are also available.   *cashmerenyc.com*

Moderate   *Amex/MC/V*

Fifth Avenue   **(212) 644-0415**
581 Fifth Avenue (penthouse)   btw 47/48th St
NYC 10017   Mon-Sat 10-6

Betsy Bunki Nini

A mouthful of a name, but worth the brouhaha, with labels like Piazza Sempione, Alberta Ferretti, Paul Smith and Rene Lezard. A pleasant mix of styles for the well put together Upper Eastsider.

Expensive   *Amex/MC/V*

Upper East Side (212) 744-6716
980 Lexington Avenue btw 71/72nd St
NYC 10021 Mon-Sat 10:30-6 (Thurs 10:30-7)

Betsey Johnson

Betsey Johnson's world is a fun, flirtatious and often completely far-out place to be. Johnson—who just celebrated her 62nd birthday and is best known for cartwheeling down the runway at the end of her shows—sells wild, sexy designs that have dazzled and shocked women for over 20 years. Her store is the perfect mirror for her worldview, with pink walls, flowered wallpaper and blue tile floors. The vibrant energy isn't limited to the decor, however, as the clothes are equally sensational: signature bias-cut slip dresses, sequined shrugs, lively sundresses, and knitted car coats are standouts. Prices are never outrageous because the merchandise is always under $700. Betsey's accessories—from the amazing shoes ($190) to the street-vendor jewelry (around $40)—will spice up any outfit. A must-stop for Madison Avenue shoppers. *betseyjohnson.com*

Expensive *Amex/MC/V*

Upper East Side (212) 734-1257
1060 Madison Avenue btw 80/81st St
NYC 10028 Mon-Sat 11-7, Sun 12-6

Upper East Side (212) 319-7699
251 East 60th Street btw Second/Third Ave
NYC 10022 Mon-Sat 11-7, Sun 12-7

Upper West Side (212) 362-3364
248 Columbus Avenue btw 71/72nd St
NYC 10023 Mon-Sat 11-7, Sun 12-7

SoHo (212) 995-5048
138 Wooster Street btw Houston/Prince
NYC 10012 Mon-Sat 11-7, Sun 12-6

Beverly Feldman Shoes

Her store's mantra is 'Too much is not enough.' Perhaps not, but it's still too much, which is undoubtedly the look for which Beverly strives. With a leopard and zebra interior, lip-shaped couch and rose petal chair, the shoes and bags fall right into place. Patent leather, big suede flowers, animal prints, rhinestones, gold lamé, sequins and Lucite heels make the accessories fit for RuPaul but more likely to be worn by an older lady looking to spice things up a bit. Desperate housewives will love the jewel and cheetah embellished dishwashing gloves and black satin potholders. *beverlyfeldmanshoes.com*

Moderate *Amex/MC/V*

Midtown West (212) 484-0000
7 West 56th Street at Fifth Ave
NYC 10019 Mon-Fri 10-7, Thurs 10-8, Sun 10-6

Big Drop

With an eclectic mix of young designers like Bella Freud, Karl Donoghue, Roberta Collina, Seven, Rubin Chappelle and Rebecca Taylor, Big Drop caters directly to the cool crowd. The accessories section is way underrated—be sure to check out the funky handbags. *bigdropnyc.com*

Expensive   *Amex/MC/V*

Upper East Side   **(212) 988-3344**
1321 Third Avenue   btw 75/76th St
NYC 10021   Mon-Sat 11-8, Sun 12-7

Upper East Side   **(212) 794-3200**
1044 Madison Avenue   btw 79/80th St
NYC 10021   Mon-Sat 10-7, Sun 11-6

SoHo   **(212) 966-4299**
174 Spring Street   btw Thompson/West Broadway
NYC 10012   Daily 11-8

SoHo   **(212) 226-9292**
425 West Broadway   btw Prince/Spring
NYC 10012   Daily 11-8

Billabong

Many young tourists plan pilgrimages to 1515 Broadway: a holy land of all things teen. Yes, it's MTV's address, and now also home to the Billabong flagship and conjoined Element skate shop. Beachwear rules at this mainstream surf shop with punky Polynesian-print board shorts for the dudes and skimpy string bikinis for the Betties. The clothes follow that same pattern: tiny crochet tank tops, hot pants and miniskirts in California colors for her, and baggy jeans and oversized logo tees for him. *billabong.com*

Affordable   *Amex/MC/V*

Midtown West   **(212) 840-0550**
1515 Broadway   btw 44/45th St
NYC 10036   Daily 9-midnight

Billy Martins

Ride 'em, cowboy, straight to Billy Martins. This Western-themed store is the best place around for hand-crafted cowboy boots and fancy belts. Urban cowgirls and buckaroos will also find everything from suede jackets and skirts to cowboy shirts, jewelry and belt buckles. These are high-priced statement pieces that will get you back to your Ponderosa in complete style. *800-888-8915 billymartin.com*

Expensive   *Amex/MC/V*

Upper East Side   **(212) 861-3100**
220 East 60th Street   btw Second/Third Ave
NYC 10022   Mon-Fri 11-7, Sat 11-6, Sun 12-5

Bio

Like to be the first to wear the Next Big Thing? Head to Bio, where you will find a rotating selection of up-and-coming labels, all on the brink of becoming fashion editor faves (and the store makes it easy for them: a short bio of each designer is included on the price tag of each item). Owner An Vu has a fabulous eye for equally fabulous pieces that are sure to start trends. A recent visit found incredible jeans by Kasil, and the chic look of Tom K Nguyen. By the time these items hit the glossy mag pages, you can be sure that Vu will be stocking new gear for you to drool over. *bio-nyc.com*

Expensive   *Amex/MC/V*

Nolita   **(212) 334-3006**
29 Prince Street   btw Elizabeth/Mott
NYC 10012   Daily 12-8 (Sun 12-7)

Bis Designer Resale

Keep an eagle eye on Bis because every other day this secondhand clothing and accessories store receives a delivery of designer merchandise straight from the bulging closets of well-dressed, well-heeled New Yorkers. Clever women head here for high-end European and American labels in tip-top condition—and at fabulous prices. It's not uncommon to spot an Armani beaded evening jacket for $300 (regular retail $1,500), an Hermès handbag for $900 ($2,600) or a Michael Kors cashmere sweater for $250 ($1,250). You'll also find the occasional vintage piece like a Pucci dress. *bisbiz.com*

Expensive   *Amex/MC/V*

Upper East Side   **(212) 396-2760**
1134 Madison Avenue (2nd floor)   btw 84/85th St
NYC 10028   Mon-Thurs 10-7, Fri-Sat 10-6, Sun 12-5
                                    (closed Sundays in summer)

★ Blades Board and Skate

In-line skating is still one of the hippest sports around and nowhere can you find the requisite cool accessories better than at Blades. The selection includes skates, skateboards, snowboards and ice skates (some locations), as well as the obligatory protective gear. Top it off with matching clothing and accessories and you're ready to roll. In-line skate rentals are $20 a day with a $200 deposit. Helpful staff. *blades.com*

Affordable   *Amex/MC/V*

Upper West Side   **(212) 787-3911**
120 West 72nd Street   btw Columbus/Amsterdam Ave
NYC 10023   Mon-Fri 10-8, Sun 10-7

NoHo   **(212) 477-7350**
659 Broadway   btw West 3rd/Bleecker
NYC 10012   Mon-Sat 10-9, Sun 11-7

Midtown   **(212) 563-2448**
901 Sixth Avenue (Level C2)   at 33rd St
NYC 10009   Mon-Sat 10-8, Sun 11-7

Blair Delmonico

Blair Delmonico incorporates Swarovski crystals into both her wedding and daywear collections for a sparkling finishing touch. The wedding collection has a wide range of looks for the bride and bridal party, while the daywear is well-suited for uptown ladies-who-lunch (almost everything's pink or pastel here)—or those who want look like they do. Look for a fabulous new store at Columbus Circle this fall, where they'll roll out a new line of Italian knits, cashmeres, sunglasses, and jet-set accessories. *blairdelmonico.com*

Expensive *Amex/MC/V*

Midtown West **(212) 246-6578**
10 Columbus Circle Time Warner Center
NYC 10019 Mon-Sat 10-9, Sun 11-6

Bloch

Just a hop, skip and a jump away from Lincoln Center, the 70-year-old Australian dancewear company Bloch has set up shop Stateside with this chic and modern Upper West Side flagship. With their specialty bodywear including leotards, dance pants, knitwear, and footwear for ballet, jazz, tap and even hip-hop, Bloch is sure to be a pointe well taken. *blochworld.com*

Affordable *Amex/MC/V*

Upper West Side **(212) 579-1960**
304 Columbus Avenue btw 74/75th St
NYC 10023 Mon-Sat 11-7, Sun 12-6

Bloomingdale's

The Bloomingdale's experience is a must for any New York visitor. After all, it would be a dull tourist who didn't want to glance at Harrods on their first-ever visit to London, or at Galeries Lafayette in Paris. Yes, a stop by Bloomies is essential, but make sure you're feeling high-energy, because it can be an exhausting adventure even for the most seasoned of shoppers—the crush of people extends well past the first floor and it's all too easy to get lost in the plus-size section when you're actually looking for shoes. But you must persist. Well into its 14th decade, the store continues to be a trendsetter, with innovative merchandising concepts and sales extravaganzas. Boulevard Four showcases the latest designer fashions for women by Armani, Calvin Klein, Chanel, Donna Karan, Ralph Lauren and others, while the contemporary selection boasts the best range in the city—Marc by Marc Jacobs, Trina Turk, and Theory. Men's fashions run from designer suits and formalwear to sports and casualwear from Joseph Abboud, Canali, Donna Karan, Hugo Boss and Kenneth Cole, as well as Bloomingdale's own private label. Also find one of the largest—and most intimidating—cosmetics floors and accessories departments around, as well as three floors of home furnishings and decorative accessories. An added plus are the outstanding service departments, which include personalized shopping, in-store TicketMaster, hotel delivery and a bridal registry. Shoppers suffering from low blood sugar or simply in need of some respite can choose from four in-house eateries. *800-777-0000 bloomingdales.com*

Affordable to expensive *Amex/MC/V*

Midtown East
1000 Third Ave
NYC 10022

(212) 705-2000
btw 59/60th St
Mon-Fri 10-8:30, Sat 10-7, Sun 11-7

Bloomingdale's SoHo

Bloomies gone downtown. Taking cues from the cult of Barneys Co-op, this downtown version of its East Side sister features the trusted trendsetters in casualwear from Juicy, Marc by Marc Jacobs, Habitual and Joie, to higher end up-and-comers like Derek Lam, Zac Posen and Matthew Williamson. The store even sells those gadgets that went from newfangled to can't-live-without in a flash, like Canon digital cameras, iPods and flat-screen TVs. Although the focus here is the women's clothes, fellows should be sure to check out the men's department in the lower level.

Moderate to expensive   *Amex/MC/V*

SoHo
504 Broadway
NYC 10012

(212) 729-5900
btw Spring/Broome
Mon-Fri 10-9, Sat 10-8, Sun 11-7

Blue

Greek-born designer Christina Kara sews custom cocktail dresses and bridalwear in this tiny East Village storefront. For the traditional bride, Kara has white floor-length ballgowns fit for a fairy princess. But she also has funkier looks reflecting the hip downtown clientele—think plunging necklines and organza adornments.

Moderate to expensive   *Amex/MC/V*

East Village
137 Avenue A
NYC 10009

(212) 228-7744
btw 8/9th St
Mon-Fri 12-7, Sat-Sun 12-5

Blue Bag

This is one of the cuter shops among the current crop of handbag boutiques in the neighborhood. Husband-and-wife team Marnie and Pascal Legrand run the design gamut from basic totes to whimsical one-offs to great looking wallets. Bags come in mixed patterns and colors in a variety of fabrics including silk, cotton and canvas. There is a constant stream of new arrivals and in summer they stock cool swimsuits, too.

Moderate   *Amex/MC/V*

Nolita
266 Elizabeth Street
NYC 10012

(212) 966-8566
btw Houston/Prince
Daily 11-7 (winter), 12-8 (summer)

Bohkee

A passage to India, more or less. Find handmade treasures at this lovely Upper East Side boutique. The Indian-inspired eveningwear is a standout, but don't miss the delicate jewelry, hand-embroidered blouses, and luscious pashminas. Friendly, welcoming sales staff.   *bohkee.com*

Moderate   *Amex/MC/V*

Upper East Side **(212) 319-0707**
1077 Third Avenue btw 63/64th St
NYC 10021 Mon-Sat 10:30-7:30

Bolton's

Easy-access shopping, all over Manhattan. Head here for a selection of wardrobe staples that includes business suits, blouses, sportswear, lingerie and accessories, all at discount prices. Buyer beware: there are rarely designer finds, but you'll find some good deals nonetheless.

Moderate *Amex/MC/V*

Upper East Side **(646) 672-9253**
175 East 96th Street btw Lexington/Third Ave
NYC 10128 Mon-Fri 10-8, Sat-Sun 10-7

Upper East Side **(212) 988-7212**
1402 Second Avenue at 75th St
NYC 10021 Mon-Fri 10-8, Sat-Sun 10-7

Upper East Side **(212) 223-3450**
787 Lexington Avenue btw 61/62nd St
NYC 10021 Mon-Fri 9:30-8:30, Sat 10-8, Sun 11-7

Upper East Side **(212) 722-4419**
1180 Madison Avenue at 86th St
NYC 10028 Mon-Fri 10-8, Sat 10-7, Sun 12-7

Upper East Side **(212) 639-9298**
1198 Third Avenue btw 69/70th St
NYC 10028 Mon-Fri 10-8, Sat-Sun 10-7

Upper West Side **(212) 362-7396**
181 Amsterdam Avenue at 68th St
NYC 10023 Mon-Fri 10-8, Sat 10-7, Sun 12-7

Midtown East **(646) 865-0898**
109 East 42nd Street btw Vanderbilt/Lexington Ave
NYC 10017 Mon-Fri 8-8, Sat-Sun 10-7

Midtown East **(212) 684-3750**
4 East 34th Street btw Fifth/Madison Ave
NYC 10016 Mon-Sat 9-7 (Wed-Thurs 9-8), Sun 11-7

Midtown East **(646) 865-0884**
485 Lexington Avenue at 46th St
NYC 10017 Mon-Fri 8-8, Sat-Sun 10-7

Midtown West **(212) 935-4431**
27 West 57th Street btw Fifth/Sixth Ave
NYC 10019 Mon-Fri 10-8, Sat 10-7, Sun 11-7

Midtown West **(212) 307-5089**
1700 Broadway at 54th St
NYC 10019 Mon-Fri 9-8, Sat-Sun 10-7

Lower Manhattan **(212) 385-3435**
52 Duane Street btw Lafayette/Elk
NYC 10007 Mon-Fri 8-7

Lower Manhattan **(212) 566-4621**
253 Broadway btw Murray/Warren
NYC 10007 Mon-Fri 8-7, Sat-Sun 10-7

★ Bombalulus

One of those great children's stores where it looks like kids were given free rein to design their own clothes. Boys explore the city wearing jackets and overalls decorated with familiar motifs like taxi cabs and fire trucks, while girls flutter about town in medieval-style princess dresses and butterfly wings. Bombalulus' flights of fancy are, for the most part, designed by the owner and priced appropriately for the seven and under clientele. *bombalulus.com*

Moderate   *Amex/MC/V*

West Village   **(212) 463-0897**
101 West 10th Street   btw Greenwich/Sixth Ave
NYC 10011   Daily 11-8 (Sun 11-7)

Bonaparte

Designer Junko Yoshioka, a former MaxMara designer, fell into bridal when she was preparing for her own wedding and realized the lack of options available to fashion-forward brides. Her modern, unfrilly couture bridal gowns promise a flattering cut and no poufiness, and are made of the finest French lace, organza, silk duchesse, chiffon or zibeline. Brides-to-be come to this simple white space that doubles as her studio, accented with fresh-cut flowers and light-catching crystals, for custom fittings and to design their dream gowns with Junko. Headwear is custom-ordered through hip veil-sters Bride's Head Revisited. *bonaparteny.com*

Luxury   *Amex/MC/V*

SoHo   **(212) 206-9302**
154 Spring Street (2nd Floor) btw West Broadway/Wooster
NYC 10003   Mon-Sat 9-6, by appointment

★ Bond 07 by Selima

A super-cool accessories wonderland where hip girls are spoiled for choice. One of a number of Selima Optique shops in the City, Bond 07 carries hats, handbags, vintage pieces and perfumes, plus clothing from European and cool downtown designer labels such as Cacharel, Puvlic, Tsumori Chisato, Alexandre Herchovitch, Ashish, Fancy Pony Land and Claudia Brown. Don't miss the groovy eyewear and pre-scription eyeglass service. *selimaoptique.com*

Expensive   *Amex/MC/V*

NoHo   **(212) 677-8487**
7 Bond Street   btw Broadway/Lafayette
NYC 10012   Daily 11-7 (Sun 12-7)

Bonne Nuit

Slightly hidden in bustling Lincoln Plaza, this crowded shop has the feel of a Left Bank pietà boutique. Delicate lingerie for women can evoke a Romantic sonnet or a rousing chanson, and is often finished with handmade details. Whether ladylike and pristine or vampy and risqué, there's something here for every trousseau. Unique children's pajamas will have them dreaming in French.

Moderate to expensive   *Amex/MC/V*

Upper West Side   **(212) 489-9730**
30 Lincoln Plaza   btw 62/63rd St
NYC 10023   Mon-Sat 10-9, Sun 12-7

Upper East Side   **(212) 472-7300**
1193 Lexington Avenue   at 81st St
NYC 10028   Mon-Sat 9-7, Sun 12-5

★ Bonpoint

If you're the type to play show-off with your child, the exclusive French Bonpoint is the store for you. Luxury fabrics, attention to detail and impeccable tailoring are the keys to its well-earned reputation for perfect fancy dress-up clothes—beautiful hand-smocked dresses, traditional blouses, shirts, pants, outerwear, swimwear and accessories, all at haute couture prices—maybe buy a size up, in case they outgrow of them in a month… Newborn to size 16 girls/12 boys. Could they make clothing for adults, please? *bonpoint.com*

Expensive   *Amex/MC/V*

Upper East Side   **(212) 722-7720**
1269 Madison Avenue   at 91st St
NYC 10128   Mon-Sat 10-6 (at both stores)

Upper East Side   **(212) 879-0900**
811 Madison Avenue   at 68th St
NYC 10021

★ Borealis

Beautiful jewelry lights up this minimalist space. The rotating selection features work by a variety of artists: find delicate treasures by Philip Crangi and Jeanine Payer presented alongside equally covetable pieces by lesser-known designers. While the shop might present the work of different artists, the overall aesthetic is always exquisite and elegant.

Expensive   *Amex/MC/V*

Nolita   **(917) 237-0152**
229 Elizabeth Street   btw Houston/Prince
NYC 10012   Mon-Sat 12-7, Sun 1-6

Borrelli

This Neapolitan shirtmaker carries over 3,000 fabrics, and is where ageing hunks Robert Redford and Harrison Ford find their smashingly elegant attire. There is a dashing selection of ready-to-wear suits, sportcoats, leathers, cashmeres and knits. For a more luxurious purchase, custom-order handmade shirts fitted with mother-of-pearl buttons. A full women's line is imminent.

Expensive   *Amex/MC/V*

Upper East Side   **(212) 644-9610**
16 East 60th Street   btw Madison/Fifth Ave
NYC 10022   Mon-Sat 10-7, Sun 12-6

★ Bottega Veneta

Bottega Veneta has long been one of the most glamorous accessories labels in the world, and creative director Tomas Maier is holding this Italian luxury liner steady on course, continuing to turn out gorgeous intrecciato (woven) leather DEL handbags, shoes and Venetian loafers. Accessories and some apparel occupy this huge, softly lit space like precious museum pieces. Men and women alike will enjoy Bottega's innovative designs that play off the suppleness of the materials, like convenient roll-up loafers and cute frog-shaped coin purses.   bottegaveneta.com

Expensive   *Amex/MC/V*

Fifth Avenue   **(212) 371-5511**
699 Fifth Avenue   btw 54/55th St
NYC 10022   Mon-Sat 10-6:30 (Thurs 10-7), Sun 12-5

Botticelli

Located in the bustling Midtown area, Botticelli stocks Italian leather of its own design. Find classic shoes for work, casual loafers for the weekend and water-resistant boots for city puddles or country marshes. Other styles include sandals, mules, slingbacks, fur-lined loafers and fashionable boots. Also look for Francesco Biasia bags—bella! Prices run up to $595.   botticellishoes.com

Expensive   *Amex/MC/V*

Fifth Avenue   **(212) 768-1430**
522 Fifth Avenue   btw 43/44th St
NYC 10036   Mon-Sat 10-7, Sun 12-6

Fifth Avenue   **(212) 586-7421**
666 Fifth Avenue   at 53rd St
NYC 10103   Mon-Sat 10-7, Sun 11-6

Fifth Avenue (W)   **(212) 582-6313**
620 Fifth Avenue   at Rockefeller Center
NYC 10020   Mon-Sat 10-7 (Thurs 10-8), Sun 11-6

Boucher Jewelry

Celebs including Laura Dern and Courteney Cox Arquette are among those who have discovered that designer Laura Mady's tiny store is a gem (she also supplies Neiman Marcus). Browse the unusual and beautiful selection of semi-precious stones including mother-of-pearl cuffs, Peruvian opal bracelets, blue topaz drop earrings and turquoise lariats.   boucherjewelry.com

Expensive   *Amex/MC/V*

West Village   **(212) 206-3775**
9 Ninth Avenue   btw Little West 12/13th St
NYC 10014   Mon-Sat 12-8, Sun 12-6

Boyd's Madison Avenue

One part high-end drugstore, one part small-scale department store, Boyd's is a one-of-kind shopping destination for luxe health and beauty products. Shop here for Mason-Pearson brushes, Manuel Canovas candles, the store's own Renoir cosmetics line and better known brands such as Clarins and Lancôme. Or just browse and find things you never knew you needed, like distortion-free make-up glasses. Also find children's toys, jewelry, lingerie and a full-service pharmacy. *800-683-2693 boydsnyc.com*

Moderate *Amex/MC/V*

Upper East Side **(212) 838-6558**
655 Madison Avenue btw 60/61st St
NYC 10021 Mon-Fri 9-8, Sat 10-7, Sun 11-6

Upper West Side **(212) 877-3307**
309 Columbus Avenue btw 74/75th St
NYC 10023 Daily 8:30-8 (Sat-Sun 10-8)

Midtown East **(212) 838-6558**
968 Third Avenue at 58th St
NYC 10022 Mon-Fri 9-8, Sat 10-7, Sun 11-6

Bra Smyth

We all know that buying a bra is never a funfest, but Bra Smyth makes it a little easier. Choose from over 1,500 styles with sizes that range from A to DDD cups. Custom fittings and alterations are their specialty. Also find a good selection of undergarments from Hanro, Lise Charmel, Aubade, Chantelle and Wacoal and swimwear by Karla Colletto and Domani. Alterations available on premises. *brasmyth.com*

Expensive *Amex/MC/V*

Upper East Side **(212) 772-9400**
905 Madison Avenue btw 72/73rd St
NYC 10021 Mon-Fri 10-7, Sat 10-6:30, Sun 12-5

Bric's

This first US location for the 50-year-old Italian luggage maker is a big, bright space with immaculately presented suitcases and handbags along shelf-lined walls. It looks ritzier than it is: a big (and pleasant) surprise comes upon checking the price tag. Modest price points make jet-set friendly matching luggage sets accessible to non-heiresses. Synthetic PVC that's been treated like leather to look like suede creates a formidable illusion and feel. Buttery Napa leather and croc-print stamped calfskin handbags and suitcases in seasonal colors are available in abundance. Your next (and last) gym tote will be their X-Bag, made of silken nylon with a rubberized liner. *brics.it*

Moderate *Amex/MC/V*

Midtown East **(212) 688-4490**
535 Madison Avenue at East 53rd St
NYC 10022 Mon-Fri 10-7, Sat 10-6, Sun 12-5

Bridal Atelier

The serene, quiet atmosphere of this bridal boutique will calm the even the most anxious bride. Set in a townhouse, the store offers elegant looks from Angel Sanchez, Rivini,

Monique Lhuillier and Peter Langner. Mother-of-the-bride styles are also available.

Expensive *Amex/MC/V*

Midtown East **(212) 319-6778**
127 East 56th Street (3rd floor) btw Park/Lexington Ave
NYC 10022 (by appointment only)

Brief Encounters

This boutique has a vast selection of European undergarments for all a foxy lady's lingerie lusts (gentlemen, you may come too, but by appointment only). Offering everything from sleepwear basics from Natori and The Cat's Pajamas to everyday necessities like bras, thongs, camisoles and slips by On Gossamer, DEL and Cosabella to sexy underpinnings by Lise Charme, Chantelle and Aubade, Brief Encounters have you (un)covered.

Moderate to expensive *Amex/MC/V*

Upper West Side **(212) 496-5649**
239 Columbus Avenue at 71st St
NYC 10023 Mon-Sat 11-7, Sun 12-6

★ Brioni

These gracious Italians have provided hand-tailored suits (off-the-rack or custom made), dress shirts, neckties, outerwear and sportswear to Donald Trump, Pierce Brosnan, Gary Cooper and Clark Gable. If you've yet to reach real estate mogul or movie star status, don't worry: everyone who sets foot in the store gets the royal treatment. Brioni's backbone lies in 11 on-premises tailors who it shares between its two men's locations. Guys wanting to enjoy the tranquility of Park Avenue Plaza should visit the 52nd Street store; power couples should head for 57th Street where the Four Seasons Hotel has looks for both men and women. Ladies looking for class and style to last a lifetime will appreciate the leather accessories, silk scarves, and blouses offsetting wool and cashmere suits. *brioni.it.com*

Luxury *Amex/MC/V*

Midtown East **(212) 376-5777**
57 & 67 East 57th Street btw Madison/Park Ave
NYC 10022 Mon-Sat 9:30-6

Midtown East **(212) 355-1940**
55 East 52nd Street btw Madison/Park Ave
NYC 10022 (opening hours as above)

Brooklyn Industries

From showing borough pride with a now-ubiquitous 'Brooklyn' hoodie, to finding that perfect esoteric graphic tee to go with your thick black-framed glasses, Brooklyn Industries will help you attain that I've-lived-in-Williamsburg-for-longer-than-two-months look you've been searching for. Plenty of cool tank tees and sexy print skirts are available for gals, as are '718' baseball tees for your Brooklyn toddler. Don't forget standard-issue WB accessories like messenger bags and trucker hats. *brooklynindustries.com*

Affordable *Amex/MC/V*

Williamsburg **(718) 486-6464**
162 Bedford Avenue at North 8th St
Brooklyn 11211 Mon-Fri 11-9, Sun 12-8:30

Park Slope **(718) 789-2764**
206 5th Avenue at Union St
Brooklyn 11217 Daily 11-9 (Sun 11-8:30)

SoHo **(212) 219-0862**
286 Lafayette Street btw Houston/Prince
NYC 10012 Mon-Sat 11-8, Sun 12-7:30

Carrol Gardens **(718) 596-3986**
100 Smith Street at Atlantic
NYC 11201 Mon-Sat 11-9, Sun 12-8:30

South Williamsburg (factory store) **(718) 596-3986**
100 Smith Street at Atlantic
NYC 11201 Daily 11-8 (Sun 12-8)

Brooklyn **(718) 218-9166**
184 Broadway at Broadway/Drakes
Brooklyn 11211 Daily 11-8 (Sun 12-8)

★ Brooks Brothers 👕👕👕

Brooks Brothers is so well known that its name has become an adjective, like 'he was so Brooks Brothers'. That said, the Establishment label has been subject to a series of makeovers in the last five years in an attempt to appeal to more than prep school and Ivy League types. Owner Claudio del Vecchio has now injected more of luxury flair. The Country Club men's collection, launched in 2003, incorporates luxe casual for a more sophisticated customer. It includes polos, sweaters, vests and blazers, but you'll still find basics such as suits, ties and non-iron shirts. Women have an entire department of classic suits, skirts, shirts, pants and jackets, as well as modern casualwear. The capri pants, cashmere sweater sets, T-shirts and dresses in hot, vibrant colors are a big hit. For boys over age 5, tradition dictates a trip to Brooks Brothers for that first pair of gray flannels and navy blazer. *brooksbrothers.com*

Moderate *Amex/MC/V*

Midtown East **(212) 682-8800**
346 Madison Avenue btw 44/45th St
NYC 10017 Mon-Sat 9-7 (Thurs 9-8), Sun 12-6

Fifth Avenue **(212) 261-9440**
666 Fifth Avenue btw 52/53rd St
NYC 10103 Mon-Fri 10-8, Sat 10-7, Sun 11-7

Bu and the Duck 👕

Cool name—Lord knows what it means—but Bu and the Duck sells fashionable trappings for your pampered child. Inspired by American styles of the Thirties, Susan Lane has created a clothing and toy collection that captures the innocence of children with wonderful crocheted sweaters from Peru and linen overalls. Accessories include Italian hand-made shoes and stuffed animals and hair accessories. From newborn to eight years.   *buandtheduck.com*

Expensive   *Amex/MC/V*

Tribeca   **(212) 431-9226**
106 Franklin Street   btw West Broadway/Church
NYC 10013   Mon-Sat 10-6, Sun 11-5

Buckler

The alternating clear and reflecting walls give a carnival house-of-mirrors sense of disorientation, accented by pillars with peeling paint and an uneven cement floor. It sounds dumpy, but it works well with the clothes' charming yet unrefined vibe, which works equally well with the oh-so-attractive men that make up Buckler's constituency. The graphic-printed toughie tees are rather Chelsea, while the sandblasted, scrubbed and raked jeans could easily fit a downtown boy. Hanging from the old-school wooden hangers labeled with a metal Buckler tag are frayed and reconstructed buttondown shirts perfect for a haphazard fashion plate of a man.   *bucklerjeans.com*

Moderate   *Amex/MC/V*

West Village   **(212) 255-1596**
13 Gansevoort Street   btw Eighth/Ninth Ave
NYC 10014   Tues-Sat 11-7, Sun 12-6

Buffalo Chips USA

A specialist in handmade custom Western clothes and one of Carson Kressley's fashion finds on *Queer Eye for the Straight Guy*. Look for rocker, cowboy and biker leathers and handmade sterling and gold belt buckles. Don't forget to check out their table of bargain boots marked down 50%.

Affordable   *Amex/MC/V*

SoHo   **(212) 625-8400**
355 West Broadway   btw Broome/Grand
NYC 10013   Mon-Sat 11-7, Sun 12-6

Built by Wendy

Downtown's indie girl Wendy Mullin set up shop to showcase her fun, hip and— even better—affordable clothes. This artsy lady is coolly confident with color and has just the right dose of retro chic: think cute corded canvas pants, funky blouses, edgy slogan T-shirts, plaid wool jackets and stripey tops. Mod girls, schoolgirls, cool girls…this is the place for you. Make sure you take a peek at the new men's collection, too: button-down shirts, slogan tees, and lightweight jeans with animal-print pocket lining.   *builtbywendy.com*

Moderate   *Amex/MC/V*

SoHo   **(212) 925-6538**
7 Centre Market Place   btw Broome/Grand
NYC 10013   Mon-Sat 12-7, Sun 1-6

Built by Wendy Outlet

Open only on weekends, this waterfront Williamsburg Wendy outpost sells her overstock jeans designed for Wrangler, farmer's daughter dresses, gingham tanks, basket-weave blouses, and hipster track jackets at reduced rates. The shop is small and out of the way, but worth the trip for too-cool-for-school girls on a budget.   *builtbywendy.com*

Affordable   *Amex/MC/V*

Williamsburg   **(718) 384-2282**
46 North 6th Street   btw Wythe/Kent Ave
Brooklyn 11211   Fri-Sun 12-7

★ Burberry

The British house of Burberry's signature plaid-lined trench coat (designed for 'safety on land, on air or afloat') has ruled the elements for over a century. But since its funky days—remember when the plaid became rampant everywhere from umbrellas to bikinis?—creative director Christopher Bailey has kept the tradition but added the cool. The massive Manhattan flagship is meant to showcase all that is the reborn Burberry: fantastic rainwear, of course, as well as beautiful leathers, trench-inspired dresses, great knits, better than ever accessories from bags to shoes and casualwear under the Burberry London and the more expensive Burberry Prorsum labels. For men, there are classic English suits, jackets and casualwear, plus butter-soft leathers and knits. Don't forget to browse Burberry's children's line for your tots—fantastic. The SoHo store has a younger, hipper edge, with hardwood floors and exposed ducting, and offers an edited-down selection of the collections.   *800-284-8480 burberry.com*

Expensive   *Amex/MC/V*

Midtown East   **(212) 407-7100**
9 East 57th Street   btw Fifth/Madison Ave
NYC 10022   Mon-Fri 9:30-7, Sat 9:30-6, Sun 12-6

SoHo   **(212) 925-9300**
131 Spring Street   btw Greene/Wooster
NYC 10012   Mon-Sat 11-7, Sun 12-6

Burlington Coat Factory

Burlington Coat Factory continues to grow as a chain, thanks to its unusual retail hybrid of off-price mass merchant and department store. Its motto says 'More than just great coats', so you'll also find career and sportswear, children's wear, maternity, plus sizes, shoes and baby furniture, all at discounted prices. But the coats are still the best reason to stop by.   *800-444-2628 burlingtoncoatfactory.com*

Affordable   *Amex/MC/V*

Chelsea   **(212) 229-1300**
707 Sixth Avenue   at 23rd St
NYC 10010   Mon-Sat 9-9, Sun 10-6

Butik

Supermodel Helena Christensen and fellow Dane Leif Sigersen have opened a multipurpose shop selling clothes by Danish designers, antique furniture, organic chocolates and flowers (Leif's a florist as well). It looks like a page out of *The Secret Garden* with rusty wire lawn chairs, chipped white-painted display cases, plants and flower arrangements galore. Very eclectic are the housewares, as are the clothes: vintage-inspired Baum and Pferdgarten wrap skirts speckled with daisies, carnation pink empire-waist Valley of the Dolls dresses by Melene Birger, Veronica Civa wooden bead necklaces and Camilla Staerk's witchy low boots.

Expensive   *Amex/MC/V*

West Village   **(212) 367-8014**
605 Hudson Street   at Eighth Ave
NYC 10014   Tues-Sat 11-7, Sun 12-6

Caché

More shopping mall than city chic, Caché is best for special-event eveningwear. Although it covers the latest trends, expect much of it to be manufactured in synthetic fabrics. Looks include spaghetti-strap dresses, tiny lacy tops and snug-fitting outfits perfect for club-hopping. A massive selection of coordinating jewelry rounds out the collection.   *800-788-cache cache.com*

Moderate   *Amex/MC/V*

Midtown East   **(212) 588-8719**
805 Third Avenue   btw 49/50th St
NYC 10022   Mon-Fri 10-7, Sat 10-6, Sun 12-6

Midtown West   **(212) 823-9693**
10 Columbus Circle   Time Warner Center
NYC 10019   Mon-Sat 10-9, Sun 11-7

★ Cadeau

Cadeau is an incredibly fashionable maternity brand. Why? Well, it might have to do with the fact that owners Emilia Fabricant and Chrissy Yu both worked at Barneys New York—for the beloved Co-op and as a women's designer buyer, respectively. 'The modern styles, manufactured in Italy, are about allowing a woman to be herself throughout her pregnancy without having to give up her sense of style,' Fabricant says. Hear, hear. A nice touch: the store is conveniently organized by pre-pregnancy size.   *cadeaumaternity.com*

Affordable   *Amex/MC/V*

Nolita   **(212) 674-5747**
254 Elizabeth Street   btw Houston/Prince
NYC 10012   Mon-Sat 11-7, Sun 12-6

Calliope

Calliope follows the neighborhood fashion recipe, mixing thrifty vintage, local indie designer pieces and a sprinkling of high-end accessories. Beyond the carved wood doorway, and between the periwinkle and green walls, lie a bevy of Williamsburg hip duds. The Sarah label uses cartoon details and unique fabrics to make things like cute little lederhosen with heart pockets. Sweet Guise for Girls incorporates boxing shorts' distinctive waistbands onto skirts and dresses. Caitlin Mociun makes flapper-style drop-waist dresses with subtle screenprinted designs that you must squint to discern. Great totes and belts, as well as lots of unworn resale designer shoes by Prada, Marc Jacobs, Louis Vuitton etc.

Moderate to expensive   *Amex/MC/V*

Williamsburg   **(718) 486-0697**
135 Grand Street   btw Berry/Bedford Ave
Brooklyn 11211   Tues-Sat 1-8, Sun 1-6

Calvin Klein

Where would we all be without our Calvins? Klein reinvented American casual and continues to set the trends in slickly minimalist city pieces that strike a perfect balance between uptown polish and downtown chic. With his precise cuts and monochromatic palette (you want black, you got it) Klein is the effortless master of cool. This is the best destination for sleek-chic suits, clingy knits, shirts, dresses, skirts, relaxed sweaters and beautifully basic eveningwear. Then there are the shoes, accessories, jeans, underwear and home furnishings. All up, Calvin Heaven.   *877-256-7373*

Moderate   *Amex/MC/V*

Upper East Side   **(212) 292-9000**
654 Madison Avenue   at 60th St
NYC 10021   Mon-Sat 10-6 (Thurs 10-7), Sun 12-6

Calvin Klein Underwear

You might not look like the chiseled models adorning his Times Square billboards, but Calvin Klein's underwear collection never fails to satisfy, or titillate—even when worn by mere mortals. Basic yet sexy, completely cool and comfortable, this underwear perfectly preps you for taking clothes off or putting them on. This spot marks the first Calvin Klein intimates-only boutique in the United States, and you'll love the delicate camisoles and bras in satin and lace, cotton boxers and T-shirts that you'll find here.

Moderate   *Amex/MC/V*

SoHo   **1-877-258-7646**
104 Prince Street   btw Greene/Mercer
NYC 10012   Mon 11-8, Tues-Sat 10-8, Sun 11-7

Calvin Tran

Formerly called Sac Boutique, this small two-story shop specializes in multitasking. Vietnamese-born Calvin Tran designs with utility in mind: many of his pieces can be worn two, three, even four different ways. Take his matte jersey dresses, for example, which can transform into ponchos or skirts, or tie-tops that can be rearranged as off-the-shoulder or halter numbers. And if you're looking for stay-the-same items, more conventional goods are to be found in Sac's classic wool coats and workplace-ready suits.

Moderate *Amex/MC/V*

SoHo **(212) 431-2576**
115 Grand Street btw Mercer/Broadway
NYC 10013 Mon-Sat 11-7, Sun 12-6

★ Calypso

From a life of growing up in the French Rivera and living in St Barths, the Hamptons and now New York City, it's easy to see where Calypso owner Christiane Celle has found inspiration for her luxurious boutiques. Never one to hide her love affair with West Indian whimsy, Celle's tropically inspired store caters to bohemians and other free spirits longing for luscious, bright, resort-ready clothing by a mixture of international designers. Bursts of pinks, blues, reds and oranges and ethnic prints dot the pleasant pastel-hued store in the form of silk sarongs, cashmere sweaters, filmy blouses, T-shirts, tiny tank tops and swimwear. And if the clothes don't immediately transport you into paradise, Mimosa, Calypso's signature scent (a blend of rose, mimosa and jasmine) will have you there in no time. *christianecelle.com*

Moderate to luxury *Amex/MC/V*

Chelsea **(646) 638-3000**
654 Hudson Street btw Gansevoort/13th St
NYC 10014 Mon-Sat 11-7, Sun 12-7

Upper East Side **(212) 535-4100**
935 Madison Avenue btw 74/75th St
NYC 10021 Mon-Fri 10-6, Sun 12-6

SoHo **(212) 274-0449**
424 Broome Street btw Crosby/Lafayette
NYC 10013 Mon-Sat 11-7, Sun 12-7

Nolita **(212) 965-0990**
280 Mott Street btw Houston/Prince
NYC 10012 Mon-Sat 11-7, Sun 12-7

Calypso Bijoux

The delicate jewelry found here provides the perfect complement to the tropical-chic outfit you picked up at nearby Calypso St Barths. Double-dipped gold and silver pieces by Heather Moria are standouts, but there are plenty of baubles here that are perfect for the beach—or for feeling like you're already there. *calypso-celle.com*

Expensive *Amex/MC/V*

Nolita **(212) 334-9730**
252 Mott Street btw East Houston/Prince
NYC 10012 Mon-Sat 11-7, Sun 12-7

SoHo (outlet store) **(212) 343-0450**
405 Broome Street btw Centre/Lafayette
NYC 10013 Daily 11-7

★ Calypso Enfant

A cuter-than-cute children's shop that carries top-of-the-line French clothing. Like the whimsical Calypso St Barths, which caters to adults, this is an outpost for spirited clothes in bursts of bright color, from bustle skirts and pants to embroidered shirts and cute accessories. You can even find your child an outfit that matches your own. For les enfants, find an adorable layette selection, irresistible sailor outfits, jumpers, pleated skirts, dresses, knits with matching hats, outerwear, shoes and accessories. Newborn to 12 years. *calypsostbarth.com*

Moderate   *Amex/MC/V*

Nolita   **(212) 966-3234**
426 Broome Street   btw Crosby/Lafayette
NYC 10012   Mon-Sat 11-7, Sun 12-7

Camouflage

Buy these labels and you won't want to camouflage them one bit: Helmut Lang, Paul Smith, Etro, Michael Kors and John Smedley, just for starters. Casual, younger clothing melds with more sophisticated pieces. Also find outerwear, cool cashmeres and accessories.

Expensive   *Amex/MC/V*

Chelsea   **(212) 741-9118**
139-141 Eighth Avenue   at 17th St
NYC 10011   Mon-Fri 12-7, Sat 11:30-6:30, Sun 12-6

Camper

Looking for ultra-hip, immediately recognizable shoes that are scratch-resistant and equipped with light rubber soles and special linings to absorb perspiration? Look no further than Camper. This defiantly quirky Spanish shoe company is on the road to world domination. Nothing here is standard, from the five gigantic fiberglass lamps that hang above a footwear runway to the company's lofty design mission: to develop shoes so pure that every step feels as though you're walking barefoot. No stilettos here, then. The coolest styles: sneakers that look like football boots in strong color combos of black and beige. *camper.com*

Moderate   *Amex/MC/V*

SoHo   **(212) 358-1841**
125 Prince Street   at Wooster
NYC 10012   Mon-Fri 11-8, Sat 12-8, Sun 12-6

★ Cantaloup

'Downtown comes Uptown' is the rallying cry at this pink-doored oasis. Hip neighborhood girls too tired to take the train are more than pleased to stay put, what with Cantaloup's collection of cashmere, Repetto flats, hard-to-find Luella Bartley bags, Woo tanks, hottest-hot pants by Da-nang and edgy tops and clingy dresses from Australian designers Sass & Bide and Scanlan & Theodore. Don't miss the display case nestled by the checkout counter, full of flirty bracelets and funky necklaces. *cantaloupnyc.com*

Expensive   *Amex/MC/V*

Upper East Side   **(212) 249-3566**
1036 Lexington Avenue   at 74th St
NYC 10021   Mon-Sat 11-7, Sun 12-6 (except July-August)

Upper East Side   **(212) 288-3569**
1359 Second Avenue   btw 71/72nd
NYC 10021   Mon-Sat 11-7 (Wed-Fri 11-8), Sun 12-6

Canyon Beachwear

For a little California style, head to this store and shop for bikinis, thongs, one-pieces, tankinis and everything in between, all in the best color selection around. European and American brands include Dolce & Gabbana, Bachata by Melissa Odabash, Pin Up, TNA, Vix, Salinas, Huit, Luce di Sole, Le Tarte, Anne Cole, Calvin Klein, Delfina and Domani. Sarongs, matching cover-ups, sandals, beach hats and totes and lotions complete the amazing range. Sizes run from 0 to 22. *canyonbeachwear.com*

Expensive   *Amex/MC/V*

Upper East Side   **(917) 432-0732**
1136 Third Avenue   btw 66/67th St
NYC 10021   Mon-Fri 10-8, Sat 10-7, Sun 11-6

Capezio

Shall we dance? Well, twirl your way to Capezio, which since 1887 has caressed the feet of legendary twinkle-toes like Anna Pavlova, Fred Astaire and Bob Fosse. Today the company has expanded its horizons to cover other dancewear, including leotards, leg warmers, leggings, tights, jazz pants and knits by pro makers like Danskin, City Lights, Marika, Baltog and, of course, Capezio. They're perfect for ballerinas of all sizes and skills. Footwear includes ballet slippers, tap, jazz and toe shoes. *capeziodance.com*

Moderate   *Amex/MC/V*

Upper East Side   **(212) 758-8833**
136 East 61st Street   btw Park/Lexington Ave
NYC 10021   Mon-Sat 10-6, Sun 12-5

Upper East Side   **(212) 348-7210**
1651 Third Avenue (3rd floor)   btw 92/93rd St
NYC 10028   Mon-Fri 9-6, Sat 9-4, Sun 9-1

Midtown West   **(212) 245-2130**
1650 Broadway (2nd floor)   at 51st St
NYC 10019   Mon-Fri 9:30-7, Sat 9:30-6:30, Sun 11:30-5

Midtown West   **(212) 586-5140**
1776 Broadway (2nd floor)   at 57th St
NYC 10019   Mon-Fri 10-7, Sat 10-6, Sun 12-5

★ Carlos Miele

Cutting corners in the best possible way, Sao Paolo's hottest fashion export opened his first store on the city's West Side recently, and it's a stunner. All pale green and gray curves, its Kubrick-meets-couture appearance makes it a cool place in its own right. Throw in Miele's multimedia art projects and his flamboyant, body-revealing clothes, and it feels like a very 21st-century kind of party. It's not all fun and games for Miele, though—he employs dressmakers from Rio's poorest favelas to help create the chiffon, silky satin, Lycra/linen and beaded crocheted looks (check out this year's abstract-print cape) that have won him an international fan base, not to mention raves from the likes of Britney and fellow country-woman Gisele. *carlosmiele.com.br*

Luxury   *Amex/MC/V*
Chelsea   **(646) 336-6642**
408 West 14th Street   btw Ninth/Tenth Ave
NYC 10014   Mon-Sat 11-7, Sun 12-6

Carolina Herrera

When one thinks of Carolina Herrera, so many great words come to mind: elegance, glamour, sophistication, refinement. Regardless of seasonal trends, one can always count on gorgeous silk gowns, soft leathers, lovely fur pieces, perfectly appropriate to-the-knee skirts and immaculately cut pants. Ascend the storybook staircase to the embellished, breathtaking, embroidered wedding gowns that will enhance any bride's silhouette, while elegant organza shawls, pleated and ruffled trains, silk flowers and covered buttons add the ideal finishing touches. Classic accessories include handbags, sunglasses and scarves. *carolinaherrera.com*

Luxury   *Amex/MC/V*
Upper East Side   **(212) 249-6552**
954 Madison Avenue   at 75th St
NYC 10021   Mon-Sat 10-6

Cashmere New York

Jet-setters buy up gorgeous Scottish and Italian sweaters here, all meeting the highest standards of quality and design. Choose from over 50 glorious shades in styles from basic turtlenecks and twinsets to dressier satin-trimmed and beaded sweaters. They also sell day and eveningwear ensembles like capri pants paired with a cashmere camisole or a taffeta long skirt worn with a lightweight silk/cashmere beaded top.

Expensive   *Amex/MC/V*
Upper East Side   **(212) 744-3500**
1100 Madison Avenue   btw 82/83rd St
NYC 10021   Mon-Sat 10-6

★ Castor & Pollux

A little-known jewel in the burgeoning Brooklyn style scene, Castor & Pollux offers subtle chic with an avant-garde twist. Think of Imitation of Christ's Tara Subkoff and fashion editor fave Chloe Sevigny on a non-celebrity budget, and you have the right idea. The store carries perfect summer tops and skirts from Mint and Anja Flint, Havaianas in every shade and sweatshirts and bags with Castor & Pollux's own logo, not to mention vintage and contemporary jewelry by local designers that will add panache to your outfit. A finishing touch: Italian leather bags in gold and silver that will get you noticed on and off Flatbush Avenue. *castorandpolluxstore.com*

Moderate   *Amex/MC/V*

North Flatbush   **(718) 398-4141**
67½ 6th Avenue   at Bergen
Brooklyn 11217   Tues-Sat 12-7, Sun 11-6

★ Catbird

A cute little shop off of Williamsburg's beaten path sells killer low-rise Jordache jeans with the Seventies wash and great pockets, Bardot and Shrimpton jeans by Ben Sherman, wild appliquéd handmade clothes by Fancy Ponyland, local designer Hannah Clark's silk and gold jewelry, Paper Fig's classically styled, solid gold seashells as picked up by Maggie Gyllenhaal, Vermillion vintage beaded convertible necklaces that can be worn long or doubled up, espadrilles from Spain, clogs from Sweden, DIY embroidery kits and iron-ons to jazz up your own clothes, and retro-styled multi-pocket leather wallets by La Tico. *catbirdnyc.com*

Moderate to expensive   *Amex/MC/V*

Williamsburg   **(718) 388-7688**
390 Metropolitan Avenue   at Havemeyer
Brooklyn 11211   Mon-Fri 1-9, Sat-Sun 12-8

★ Catherine Malandrino

Flirty feminine dresses that French designer Malandrino herself says 'float around the body, making a woman feel as if she is walking in a dream,' is this beloved downtown boutique's specialty. Curve-hugging cuts and luscious luxury materials make Malandrino's designs adored by celebrities and fashionistas worldwide. *catherinemalandrino.com*

Expensive   *Amex/MC/V*

SoHo   **(212) 925-6765**
468 Broome Street   at Greene
NYC 10013   Mon-Sat 11-7 (Thurs 11-8) Sun 12-6

Chelsea   **(212) 929-8710**
652 Hudson Street   at 13th St
NYC 10014   Mon-Fri 11-7, Sat 11-8, Sun 12-7

Cath Kidston

Interior designer Cath Kidston, known for her vintage-inspired housewares and accessories, brings her 10-year old Notting Hill (London) store Stateside with this Nolita flagship. Her famous prints, from large flowers to Western cowboy scenes reminiscent of Fifties Americana, appear on everything from oilcloth bags and purses to ironing boards and wallpaper. *cathkidston.com*

Moderate   *MC/V*

Nolita
201 Mulberry Street
NYC 10012

(212) 343-0223
btw Spring/Kenmare
Mon-Sat 11-7, Sun 12-6

Catimini

Does the image of your child outfitted head-to-toe in SpongeBob SquarePants regalia give you the willies? Catimini offers a welcome change from branding your child via Viacom. Flower prints and characters from French storybooks are the preferred ornamentation on clever tops (from $36), bottoms (from $42) and coats (from $93). Six months to 10 years. *catimini.com*

Affordable

Amex/MC/V

Upper East Side
1125 Madison Avenue
NYC 10028

(212) 987-0688
at 84nd St
Mon-Sat 10-6, Sun 11-5

★ Catriona MacKechnie

Between the fish-scale tiled wall and the colorful backlit enamel panels lie carefully selected brands of high-end lingerie. Big labels like Dolce & Gabbana and Cavalli are interspersed with indie undies by Alöe, Kharana satin and silk camis, Deborah Marquit nearly neon lace bras, and Damaris vintage-inspired underthings. Custom-made knickers from the British designer duo Strumpet & Pink go beyond your measurements and favorite color and get rather personal, incorporating your personal fantasies and stories into the design. Their Little Bow Peep crepe bloomers have a row of magenta satin bows down the back and a discreet strategically placed cut-out that dare not be referred to as 'crotchless'. *catrionamackechnie.com*

Expensive to luxury

Amex/MC/V

Chelsea
400 West 14th Street
NYC 10014

(212) 242-3200
at Ninth Ave
Mon-Sat 11-7:30, Sun 12-6

★ Celine

Celine is the ultimate brand for uptown girls. This French label perfected a classic rich American glamour under Michael Kors, and his successor Roberto Menichetti maintained the standards and kept the jetsetters coming. He too has moved on, and as we went to press Celine were about to name their new designer. Some things will probably not change, such as the popularity of the Boogie bag and the shoes that are the very avatar of globetrotting chic. We expect Celine to remain a byword for quality. *celine.com*

Luxury

Amex/MC/V

Upper East Side
667 Madison Avenue
NYC 10021

(212) 486-9700
at 61st St
Mon-Sat 10-6 (Thurs 10-7)

Central Park West

A West Side emporium of comfy duds and designer jeans. Everything in jersey: tees, skirts and even dresses are made of stretchy cotton, making CPW a hotspot for

moms-to-be with expanding bellies. They go for floral tees and swingy skirts by Ella Moss, sandals by Mella, top-quality tees by James Perse and T-Luxury. The massive denim selection includes Loom State, Serfontaine, Henry Duarte, True Religion, Chip & Pepper and Edun (the collaboration between Rogan and Mr and Mrs Bono of U2). The staff is small and very neighborhood-oriented. It's one of those places where everybody knows your name (and your dress size).

Moderate   *Amex/MC/V*

Upper West Side   **(212) 579-3737**
495 Amsterdam Avenue   at 84th St
NYC 10024   Mon-Fri 11-7:30, Sat 11-7, Sun 12-6

★ Century 21

Bargain hunters thank their lucky stars that Century 21 exists in such a high-priced city. Located at the edge of Ground Zero, Century 21, one of the city's cult retail destinations, came back strong after 9/11 with a refurbished interior, fresh inventory and the best prices anywhere. A polyglot mix of shoppers flocks here for heavily reduced designer clothing from Prada to Polo Sport. Check out Italian designer suits from $250 to $700, wedding dresses from $130 to $375, Polo sweaters from $40 to $70, designer outerwear from $300 to $750, and—yes!—Marc by Marc Jacobs denim and T-shirts for as little as $50. Other merchandise includes intimates, a great teens department, cosmetics, luggage, housewares, bed linens (Donna Karan, Ralph Lauren and more, all at fabulous prices), appliances and electronics. Take a deep breath and go nuts... *c21stores.com*

Affordable   *Amex/MC/V*

Lower Manhattan   **(212) 227-9092**
22 Cortland Street   btw Church/Broadway
NYC 10007   Mon-Fri 7:45-8 (Thurs 7:45-8:30)
                               Sat 10-8, Sun 11-7

Cesare Paciotti

Sex-o-matic! With their signature silver dagger logo stamped or affixed to much of their footwear, you'll never forget you're wearing a pair of Cesare Paciotti shoes. No one else will either, and that's the point. The collection showcases unapologetically sexy stiletto heels, pumps, flats and boots, with toes as pointed and sharp as the aforementioned dagger. For men, find a slightly tamer selection of shoes and boots better suited to artsy pursuits than to Wall Street.   *cesare-paciotti.com*

Luxury   *Amex/MC/V*

Upper East Side   **(212) 452-1222**
833 Madison Avenue   btw 69/70th St
NYC 10021   Mon-Sat 10-6

Champs

Whether it's golf, soccer, basketball, racket sports, running, billiards or the extremely athletic game of darts, Champs is happy to accommodate you. Find a large sneaker department for the whole family, as well as team logo'd jerseys and sweats. Best for boys and men.

800-991-6813 champssports.com

Affordable to moderate   *Amex/MC/V*

Harlem   **(212) 280-0296**
208 West 125th Street   at Seventh Ave
NYC 10027   Mon-Sat 10-8:30, Sun 11-7

Fifth Avenue   **(212) 239-3256**
1 West 34th Street   at Fifth Ave
NYC 10001   Mon-Sat 9-9, Sun 11-7

Midtown West   **(212) 354-2009**
5 Times Square   at Seventh Ave/42nd St
NYC 10036   Mon-Fri 8-12, Sun 10-12

★ Chanel

Coco would be proud. Chanel's guiding light lives on in this jewel box of a store, where you'll find signature pearls and perfect tweedy suits mixed in with a dash of Karl Lagerfeld's rock 'n' roll sensibility (see the patent leather thigh-highs). Two floors stocked with make-up, perfumes, camilla pins and classic tailoring should be more than enough for any style enthusiast. And if you're not feeling properly coddled by the more than helpful sales associates, just head upstairs to the five floors of the Frédéric Fekkai spa for a little more pampering.   *chanel.com*

Expensive   *Amex/MC/V*

Midtown East   **(212) 355-5050**
15 East 57th Street   btw Fifth/Madison Ave
NYC 10022   Mon-Wed, Fri 10-6:30
                                                    Thurs 10-7, Sat 10-6, Sun 12-5

Upper East Side   **(212) 535-5505**
737 Madison Avenue   at 64th St
NYC 10021   Mon-Sat 10-6

Upper East Side   **(212) 535-5828**
733 Madison Avenue   at 64th St
NYC 10021   (opening hours as above)

SoHo   **(212) 334-0055**
139 Spring Street   at Wooster
NYC 10012   Mon-Sat 11-7, Sun 12-6

Charles Nolan

This part-time politico and former Anne Klein designer has decided to fly solo with a shop showcasing his own designs, including not only casual chic womenswear but also furniture, housewares and whatever else he deems worthy. Back at AK, Charles kickstarted the lagging line by injecting it with mod inspired pieces and bright color that got them some attention and put them back on the runway. He continues to inspire with his rough-hewn, friendly and stylish Meatpacking shop.   *charlesnolan.com*

Moderate   *Amex/MC/V*

Meatpacking District
30 Gansevoort Street
NYC 10014

(212) 924-4888
btw Hudson/Ninth Ave
Mon-Wed 11:30-7:30
Thurs-Sat 11:30-8, Sun 12-6

Charles Tyrwhitt

This London shirtmaker—from Jermyn Street, unbelievably elegant home of shirtmakers—is perfect for the man who is sick of staid Brooks Brothers but isn't quite ready for zany Paul Smith. Classic spread-collared shirts in fine cotton poplin are paired with silk print ties to create a crisp business look. Women will be pleased with Tyrwhitt's added attention to womenswear with his cashmere sweaters, jersey knits and tastefully tailored shirts. Handmade English shoes and boots are available, and be sure to look for the store's monthly promotions—past offerings have included 'buy two handmade shirts, get one free'. Lester Hyman, Washington insider and political and legal éminence who worked with John Kennedy and was John Kerry's first political mentor, swears by Charles Tyrwhitt and regularly orders from them by mail: 'The fit is perfect, the style is classy, and the price is right.'   *ctshirts.com*

Affordable to moderate   *Amex/MC/V*

Midtown East
377 Madison Avenue
NYC 10017

(212) 286-8988
at 46th St
Mon-Fri 10-7:30 (Thurs 10-8)
Sat 10-6, Sun 12-5

Cheap Jack's

It's all about sheer volume here: 12,000 square feet and three levels of vintage clothes encompassing every decade since the Thirties. There are literally thousands of jeans, disco shirts, bell-bottoms, evening dresses, sportswear (including some Boy Scouts gear), concert tees and leather jackets. Head upstairs for handbags and a fairly impressive selection of hats—just try not to go blind in the Hawaiian shirt section.   *cheapjacks.com*

Affordable   *Amex/MC/V*

NoHo
841 Broadway btw 13/14th St
NYC 10003

(212) 777-9564
Mon-Sat 11-8
Sun 12-7

Che Che

Testimonials from satisfied customers adorn the façade of this brightly lit little glass box of a shop, and it's easy to see why: Che Che represents one Hong Kong family's full-on fascination with handbags. From elegant evening clutches to fanciful sacs with hand-painted mermaids or zebras, every item is a beguiling mix of whimsy and function. Summer totes with embroidered flowers and pocketbooks shaped like fish (complete with sequined leather scales) are also guaranteed attention-grabbers, whether you're strolling on the boardwalk or sidling up to the bar.   *chechenewyork.com*

Moderate   *Amex/MC/V*

Upper East Side   **(212) 249-0819**
1034a Lexington Avenue   btw 73/74th St
NYC 10021   Mon-Fri 10:30-6, Sat 11-5

Chelsea Girl

Owner Elisa Casas has got a Fifties thing going on, judging from this cult store which stocks a great range of sundresses in bright colors from the Twenties right through to the Seventies. Visited regularly by celeb vintage fans like Sheryl Crow, Hilary Swank, Winona Ryder and Debra Messing, Chelsea Girl houses such labels as Yves Saint Laurent, Gucci and Valentino. Accessorize your retro look with kitschy coordinated print shoes and handbags that Lucy Ricardo would love. Be warned: Fifties dresses are best on Fifties-size waists. Breathe in.   *chelsea-girl.com*

Affordable   *Amex/MC/V*

SoHo   **(212) 343-1658**
63 Thompson Street   btw Spring/Broome
NYC 10012   Daily 12-7

Cherry

If you're looking for that one killer piece to top off your wardrobe, then Cherry is your store. This vintage Village shop is stocked with one-of-a-kind finds from legends like Chanel, Hermès, Versace, Pucci and Dior. Used and new pieces, from the Fifties through the Eighties, are packed everywhere, AC/DC plays on the stereo, and everything from sunglasses to scarves can be found here. Cherry's well-edited apparel is appropriate for anyone who wishes they lived in another decade. The store separates itself from other vintage boutiques with its superior selection and a nifty assortment of shoes that features never-worn vintage footwear in several different sizes. Many a fashion girl has been known to spend a week's rent on that perfect pair of boho boots.   *cherryboutique.com*

Expensive   *Amex/MC/V*

West Village   **(212) 924-1410**
19 Eighth Avenue   btw West 12th/Jane
NYC 10014   Mon-Sat 12-8, Sun 12-7

West Village   **(212) 924-5188**
17 Eighth Avenue   at 12th St
NYC 10014   (opening hours as above)

★ Chloé

Chloé is experiencing yet another revival under the creative direction of Phoebe Philo. The girl has left rock chic behind and is following her free sprit. She looks to her past for inspiration: a fabulous (but never obvious) town-and-country aesthetic featuring mannish trousers, camel coats, cable knits with oversized buttons, conservative blouses, razor-cut pants and Fifties-femme dresses that give new meaning to the word filmy. Terrific shoes and terribly popular bags complete the insouciantly glamorous look.   *chloe.com*

Luxury   *Amex/MC/V*
Upper East Side   **(212) 717-8220**
850 Madison Avenue   at 70th St
NYC 10021   Mon-Sat 10-6

★ Christian Dior

Housed in the awesome glass tower designed for LVMH by award-winning architect Christian de Portzamparc, the Dior boutique is home to John Galliano's sexy (in a Hilton sisters kind of way) wear. Frosted glass offsets saddlebag purses and daringly low or high-cut dresses. Skin is always in here, as is shockingly tight denim. Dior's sweaty, lusty fashion shows are shown on the walls, and the fragrances, which promise to make others equally sweaty and lusty for you, are but an arm's reach away. The accessory-happy girl will appreciate Dior's stilettos, watches, purses, jewelry and fake tattoos (jeweled, and only $300-400). *dior.com*

Luxury   *Amex/MC/V*
Midtown East   **(212) 931-2950**
21 East 57th Street   btw Fifth/Madison Ave
NYC 10022   Mon-Fri 10-7, Sat 10-6, Sun 11-6

★ Christian Louboutin

Before setting up his own label, Christian Louboutin designed for Chanel, YSL and Charles Jourdan, so you know the man knows his footwear. Enter this boudoir-like boutique and you'll find yourself cooing over his line of shoes, all marked by the designer's signature red soles. 'Black soles are for widows, beige soles are for the Milanese, but red soles are for those who want to flirt and dance,' he says. Louboutin also celebrates offbeat detailing, which includes using silk fabrics from French tie manufacturers, dainty rose petals and even old postage stamps. Find mules, embroidered flats, gray-flannel spectator pumps, ponyskin boots and killer evening stilettos. His range of handbags is also wonderfully distinctive—and one you'll pay for.

Luxury   *Amex/MC/V*
Upper East Side   **(212) 396-1884**
941 Madison Avenue   btw 74/75th St
NYC 10021   Mon-Sat 10-6

West Village   **(212) 255-1910**
59 Horatio Street   at Greenwich
NYC 10014   Tues-Sat 11-7, Sun 12-6

Christie Brothers Furs

Normally the terms 'discount' and 'luxury' are not found in the same sentence, but Christie Brothers Furs is a wonderful exception to the rule. A discount retailer of luxury fur coats with a selection of mink, shearling and Russian sable, as well as cashmere and microfiber coats which can be custom-lined and fitted with the fur of your choosing, Christie

Brothers has an impressive selection. If you have an old fur in good condition, be sure to discuss trading it in against a new one. Storage facilities are available, too.

Moderate   *Amex/MC/V*

Chelsea   **(212) 736-6944**
150 West 30th Street (17th floor)   btw Sixth/Seventh Ave
NYC 10001   Mon-Fri 9-6, Sat 9-2
                                                          (and by appointment)

★ Christopher Fischer

He's known in high-end department stores and in the Hamptons as a cashmere guru, so who better to turn to for your sweaters and tees? They come in a spectrum of colors, and in sizes from XS to XL, and there are kids' clothes as well. The Italian leather bags and frilly embellished skirts complement the staple sweaters perfectly. Cashmere throws are a must-have for the jet set, as they are a dramatic improvement from scratchy airplane blankets. Bold African wood tables and benches not only make a lovely display for immaculately folded cashmeres, they're also part of his expanding furniture offerings.   *christopherfischer.com*

Expensive   *Amex/MC/V*

Soho   **(212) 965-9009**
80 Wooster Street   at Spring
NYC 10012   Mon-Sat 11-7, Sun 11-6

Christopher Totman

Christopher Totman melds cultures in his colorful Indian and Japanese-inspired prints, hand-loomed fabrics, circular crochets and alpaca knits. Tree-trunk table bases and a salt-water aquarium add to the natural feel of the store, which features shirts made from vintage kimonos. Also look for his trademark single-seam long skirt (the Luna skirt), gauze shirts, dresses, handknit pima cotton sweaters and more.   *christophertotman.com*

Expensive   *Amex/MC/V*

Nolita   **(212) 925-7495**
262 Mott Street   btw Houston/Prince
NYC 10012   Sun-Thurs 12-7, Fri-Sat 12-7:30

Chrome Hearts

Every item in this ultra-luxe lifestyle store is handmade, from the soft leather couches and armchairs to the ebony and sterling silver hangers...and it's all for sale. Like it? Buy it— Chrome Hearts will restock whatever you've taken off their hands, or racks, or floors. We don't know if they've purchased the fixtures, but one-name celeb shoppers like Britney, Cher, Justin, Mick and Julia have fallen for Chrome Hearts' leather motorcycle jackets and stretch pants, executive luggage, 22k gold and sterling silver jewelry and snazzy eyewear. Chrome Hearts' commitment to excellence means they have their own woodworking and silversmith workshops, and pretty much anything you settle on should last a lifetime.   *chromehearts.com*

Luxury   *Amex/MC/V*
Upper East Side   **(212) 327-0707**
159 East 64th Street   btw Lexington/Third Ave
NYC 10021   Mon-Sat 11-7

Chuckies

Not the swankiest name, but don't be fooled: this cool boutique features a fabulous range of footwear. Find high-style shoes from Jimmy Choo, Miu Miu, Marc Jacobs and Dolce & Gabbana, to name only a few. An excellent source for fun, funky and glamorous shoes that you won't find anywhere else.

Expensive to luxury   *Amex/MC/V*
Upper East Side   **(212) 593-9898**
1073 Third Avenue   btw 63/64th St
NYC 10021   Mon-Thurs 10:45-7:45
                                            Fri-Sat 10:45-7:30, Sun 12:30-7

Upper East Side   **(212) 249-2254**
1159 Madison Avenue   btw 85/86th St
NYC 10028   Mon-Thurs 10:45-7:45
                                            Fri-Sat 10:45-7:30, Sun 12:30-7

Church's English Shoes

When it comes to men's shoes, nobody does it better than the English (well, except for maybe the Italians), and Church's shoes are certainly among the best. For over 100 years they have been justly celebrated for classic, bench-made shoes. Now owned by growing fashion conglomerate Prada, Church's shoes continue to exhibit the fine materials and craftsmanship that made them famous. Find a variety of classic styles, including plain-toed oxfords, slip-ons, wingtips, loafers and moccasins. Two to three months' delivery for custom orders.   *churchshoes.com*

Expensive   *Amex/MC/V*
Upper East Side   **(212) 758-5200**
689 Madison Avenue   at 62nd St
NYC 10019   Mon-Sat 10-6, Sun 12-5

Citishoes

Citishoes is popular with Midtown executives, as well as tourists staying at neighboring hotels. Loyal fans of the following brands will be happy with the selection of dress shoes by Alden, Church's English Shoes, Allen Edmonds, Santoni, Cole Haan and Kenneth Cole. When the work day is over, slip into casual comfort shoes by Mephisto, Ecco, Sebago or Rockport. The assortment of wide-width shoes and a professional fitting service will pacify frustrated feet, while the Crookhorn belts and Byford trouser socks might make you pick up more than you stopped in for.   *citishoes.com*

Affordable   *Amex/MC/V*

Midtown East
445 Park Ave
NYC 10022

(212) 751-3200
btw 56/57th St
Mon-Fri 9:30-6:30, Sat 10:30-5:30

★ City Cricket

This adorable children's shop offers an exclusive selection of merchandise with a magical appeal. Find cute knitted sweaters and one-of-a-kind handmade blankets and quilts in unusual fabrics and playful designs, plus layettes and clothing for kids up to six years old. Other items include children's indoor and outdoor furniture like upholstered wing chairs, hand-painted tables and chairs, antique wicker and bent willow twig chairs. *citycricket.com*

Moderate   *Amex/MC/V*

West Village
215 West 10th Street
NYC 10014

(212) 242-2258
at Bleecker
Mon-Sat 11-7, Sun 12-5

Clarks/Bostonian

Men head here for the selection of affordable footwear, which runs from businesswear to weekend casual. The Bostonian label offers classic lace-ups and dressy loafers, while there are sporty looks from the likes of Kenneth Cole and casual styles from such labels as Timberland, Ecco and Clarks. Women can take a break from stilettos with more-stylish-than-you-might-imagine hiking sandals and moccasin-inspired loafers. *clarksusa.com*

Affordable   *Amex/MC/V*

Midtown East
363 Madison Avenue
NYC 10017

(212) 949-9545
at 45th St
Mon-Fri 9-7 (Thurs 9-8), Sat 10-6, Sun 12-6

Classic Kicks

You can definitely get your kicks at this stylish NoHo sneaker shop, where you don't have to be an O.G. to have access to one of the city's most complete collection of classic reissues and sportswear. Hipsters and hip-hoppers alike bond over the wide selection of fresh finds by the likes of Asics, Vans, Nike, Le Coq Sportif and Fred Perry. *classickicks.com*

Moderate   *Amex/MC/V*

NoHo
298 Elizabeth Street
NYC 10012

(212) 979-9514
btw Houston/Bleecker
Mon-Sat 12-7

Claudine

Hanging below rudimentary watercolor paintings on the simple white walls are softened versions of all the fiercest current trends, as interpreted by young NYC and L.A. designers. The clothes have that distinctive handmade look: slightly rough with exposed stitching and uneven hemlines. It's all very playful, young and bright, while totally eschewing any tartiness. Maximum unfussiness can be found in the threadbare silk-sreened tees and jersey wrap dresses. Birds are big here—with their likeness on mini-totes and flowy skirts. Silver and pearl twig and tusk jewelry hangs in built-in picture-frame cubbies.

Moderate   *Amex/MC/V*
West Village   **(212) 414-4234**
19 Christopher Street   btw Greenwich/Waverly Place
NYC 10014   Mon-Sat 12-8, Sun 12-7

Clea Colet

This elegant boutique offers one-on-one personalized service for brides-to-be. The luxurious atmosphere creates a comfortable setting in which to browse Clea Colet's collection of glamorous bridal and eveningwear. The stunning classic styles—which range from surprisingly come-hither columns to storybook gowns—are customized to each bride's personal style and fit. A truly memorable experience, as befitting your walk down the aisle.   *cleacolet.com*

Expensive   *Amex/MC/V*
Upper East Side   **(212) 396-4608**
589 Eighth Avenue (20th floor)   at 39th St
NYC 10018   Mon-Sat 11-6 (by appointment only)

Clifford Michael Design

The place to hit for special occasion dressing. If you're the bride, the mother-of-the-bride or just a guest, you can select your appropriate wedding attire here. When the invitation says 'black tie', doll yourself up in an elaborate gown, tuxedo, evening suit or sexy cocktail dress. Coordinating handbags and silk scarves are also available, as well as leathers and shearling outerwear.   *cliffordmichael.com*

Expensive   *Amex/MC/V*
Upper East Side   **(212) 888-7665**
45 East 60th Street   btw Madison/Park Ave
NYC 10022   Mon-Fri 10-6:30, Sat 10-6
              (appointments encouraged for gown fittings)

Club Monaco

Yes, you'd rather have designer labels in your closet but let's face it, you're about maxed out on your credit cards. So let this Canadian-based company owned by Ralph Lauren come to your rescue. Club Monaco's airy store has plenty of contemporary looks: neat halter top dresses, asymmetrical striped tops and pleated skirts for women; belted white jeans and poor man's Helmut Lang-style polos and button-downs for men. The clothes may not be quite runway-class, but they are cute and the prices make them nearly risk-free. Club Monaco also has accessories and cosmetics for women.   *clubmonaco.com*

Affordable   *Amex/MC/V*
Midtown West   **(212) 459-9863**
8 West 57th Street   btw Fifth/Sixth Ave
NYC 10019   Mon-Sat 10-9, Sun 11-7

Upper East Side
1111 Third Avenue
NYC 10021

(212) 355-2949
at 65th St
(opening hours as above)

Upper West Side
2376 Broadway
NYC 10024

(212) 579-2587
at 87th St
(opening hours as above)

Flatiron
160 Fifth Avenue
NYC 10010

(212) 352-0936
at 21st St
Mon-Sat 10-9, Sun 11-7

SoHo
121 Prince Street
NYC 10012

(212) 533-8930
btw Wooster/Greene
Mon-Sat 10-8, Sun 11-6

SoHo
520 Broadway
NYC 10012

(212) 941-1511
btw Spring/Broome
Mon-Sat 10-9, Sun 11-7

★ Coach 👫

Coach continues to grow as an accessories brand, and the fashion crowd is proud to carry their signature totes and prance around in their cool sandals and espadrilles. Shop for briefcases, handbags, travel bags and small leather goods, manufactured in clean, chic and functional shapes. The handbag collection includes shoulder bags, sleek clutches, cotton-twill travel totes and a collection of canvas bags trimmed in leather. There are also leather jackets, wallets, belts, gloves, shoes, watches and umbrellas.   *800-223-8647 coach.com*

Expensive   *Amex/MC/V*

Upper East Side
35 East 85th Street
NYC 10028

(212) 879-9391
at Madison Ave
Mon-Sat 10-8, Sun 11-6

Upper West Side
2321 Broadway
NYC 10024

(212) 799-1624
at 84th St
Mon-Sat 10-8, Sun 11-6

Midtown East
595 Madison Avenue
NYC 10022

(212) 754-0041
at 57th St
Mon-Sat 10-8, Sun 11-6

Midtown East
342 Madison Avenue
NYC 10017

(212) 599-4777
at 44th St
Mon-Fri 8:30-8, Sat 10-8, Sun 11-7

Midtown West
10 Columbus Circle
NYC 10019

(212) 581-4115
Time Warner Center
Mon-Sat 10-9, Sun 11-7

Fifth Avenue
620 Fifth Avenue
NYC 10020

(212) 245-4148
at 50th St
Mon-Sat 10-8, Sun 11-6

Flatiron
79 Fifth Avenue
NYC 10003

(212) 675-6403
at 16th St
Mon-Sat 10-8, Sun 11-6

SoHo
143 Prince Street
NYC 10012

(212) 473-6925
at West Broadway
Mon-Sat 10-8, Sun 11-6

Lower Manhattan
193 Front Street
NYC 10038

(212) 425-4350
at South Street Seaport
Mon-Sat 10-8, Sun 11-5

Cole Haan

Cole Haan delivers a brilliant footwear collection of modern classics that embrace fashion. Both sexes will find smart-looking loafers, snappy mules, driving moccasins, oxfords, sensible sandals and boots. Best buys are the fabulously comfortable sports shoes, developed with help from parent company Nike and equipped with its Nike Air technology. Coordinating accessories include classy handbags in all leathers, luggage, belts, socks and leather jackets. *800-488-2000 colehaan.com*

Expensive *Amex/MC/V*

Upper East Side
667 Madison Avenue
NYC 10021

(212) 421-8440
at 61st St
Mon-Sat 10-7 (Thurs 10-8), Sun 12-6

Fifth Avenue
620 Fifth Avenue
NYC 10020

(212) 765-9747
at 50th St
(opening hours as above)

Midtown West
10 Columbus Circle
NYC 10019

(212) 823-9420
Time Warner Center
Mon-Sat 10-9, Sun 11-7

★ Comme des Garçons

If you suffer from fashion's cruelest afflictions—avant-garditis and conspicuous consumption—get yourself to Comme des Garçons. Known for her high-concept designs, cult Japanese designer Rei Kawakubo's collection is long on intellectualism. Kawakubo founded Comme in 1969, and her clothes received international fame in the Eighties for their somber color palette and asymmetrical detailing. Enter the store through an aluminum tunnel into a parallel universe: an interior of white enamel-covered steel walls houses pieces from the basic to the absurd and textiles that are wondrous in color and quality. Be sure to check out Kawakubo's collaboration with English sportswear designer Fred Perry—hip tennis shirts with oversized buttons, giant zippers and funky colors that add a bit of flair to Perry's traditional stylings. Best accessory bets: her fabulous logo'd bags and wallets that look good on everyone. *commesdesgarcons.com*

Luxury *Amex/MC/V*

Chelsea
520 West 22nd Street
NYC 10011

(212) 604-9200
btw Tenth/Eleventh Ave
Tues-Sat 11-7, Sun 12-6

Constanca Basto

Carnival! Two Brazilian designers team up to get your feet noticed. One look at their glimmering, open-toed sultry pink sandals, or the patent-leather tricolor heels, and you'll know these shoes are not for the faint of heart or the unpedicured of toe. The orange and white striped boutique, replete with enormous gilt-framed, floor-to-ceiling mirrors, will make you feel like a south-of-the-equator Cinderella as you try on pair after pair of stunning slippers perfect for work or a night on the town. *constancabasto.com*

Expensive   *Amex/MC/V*

West Village   **(212) 645-3233**
573 Hudson Street   btw West 11th St/Bank
NYC 10014   Daily 11-7

Cose Belle

Designer Shannon McLean specializes in clean, simple designs made in luxury fabrics. Located in a penthouse showroom, Cose Belle features pants, dresses, sweaters and evening and bridal gowns. It's classic clothing with sporty elegance: you'll find everything from hip-huggers for $380 to bridal gowns starting at $2,500. *shannonmclean.com*

Expensive   *Amex/MC/V*

Upper East Side   **(212) 988-4210**
7 East 81st Street (4th floor)   btw Fifth/Madison Ave
NYC 10028   (Mon-Fri, by appointment only)

Costume National

Italian designer Ennio Capasa's aesthetic is a dark one: an androgynous world of lean, mean and sleek silhouettes where sexy black rules. Each collection is extremely edgy but always accessible and wearable. Capasa cuts a mean pair of pants, but the standouts are his sexy evening tops, often with cut-out backs or shoulders. This store is one of the best places in the city for a slick modern suit and killer leather pieces. Then there are his sinuous, earthy-toned shoes and kick-ass boots. *costumenational.com*

Expensive   *Amex/MC/V*

SoHo   **(212) 431-1530**
108 Wooster Street   btw Prince/Spring
NYC 10012   Mon-Sat 11-7, Sun 12-6

Couture by Jennifer Dule

Designer Jennifer Dule specializes in women's custom tailoring for 'after five', special occasion and bridal. Bring a photograph from a magazine and she'll copy it to a T or change it to your specifications. Pants average $475, suits start at $1,800. An elaborate satin evening gown with lavish detailing will run you $3,500 plus.

Luxury   *Amex/MC/V*

Flatiron   **(212) 727-8700**
89 Fifth Avenue (4th floor)   at 16th St
NYC 10003   (by appointment)

C.P.Shades

Simple, carefree and comfortable clothing designed with down-to-earth practicality, with everything guaranteed to withstand the rigors of wash and wear. All dresses, skirts, pants and separates are made in easy-care fabrics. If comfort is key, then C.P.Shades is a must. *cpshades.com*

Moderate *Amex/MC/V*

SoHo **(212) 226-4434**
154 Spring Street btw Wooster/West Broadway
NYC 10012 Mon-Sat 11-7, Sun 12-6

CPW

The Upper West Side's best destination for downtown duds is no doubt CPW (an abbreviation for, yes, Central Park West). This 15-year-old boutique, often compared to Barneys Co-Op or Fred Segal in Los Angeles, carries the hottest up-to-the-second brands for the relaxed, west coast clothing aesthetic of flirty skirts, tiny tees, shrunken blazers and vintage belts. CPW also sells the complete range of 'it' denim lines from the likes of Chip and Pepper, True Religion, Paper Denim & Cloth and Capital.

Expensive *Amex/MC/V*

Upper West Side **(212) 579-3737**
495 Amsterdam Avenue at 84th St
NYC 10024 Mon-Fri 11-7:30, Sat 11-7, Sun 12-6

C.Ronson

Charlotte Ronson, a member of the society pages' favorite family, opened this cooler-than-cool store three years ago to showcase her hip streetwear. She's best known for her wedge-heeled espadrilles and for her cheekily named Tooshies, an underwear line. Her designs include tank tops, T-shirts and tracksuit-inspired gear, and the store also boasts Shoshanna bikinis, neon lingerie by Deborah Marquit and jewelry by various designers. The store recently moved from a shared space to a new independent location. *cronson.com*

Affordable *Amex/MC/V*

Nolita **(212) 625-9074**
239 Mulberry Street btw Prince/Spring
NYC 10012 Daily 12-7

Crouch & Fitzgerald

Crouch & Fitzgerald have sold first-rate leather goods since 1839. Look for pony-hair business totes in pink, yellow, and lime green, patent-leather backpacks, business accessories and Longchamp luggage in pink and blue. Crouch & Fitzgerald offer handbags and luggage from Ghurka, as well as their own line of traditional English cases for men. Beautiful jewelry boxes, too. *crouchandfitzgerald.com*

Moderate *Amex/MC/V*

Midtown East **(212) 755-5888**
400 Madison Avenue btw 47/48th St
NYC 10017 Mon-Fri 9-7, Sat 10-6, Sun 11-5

Crunch

This hip gym chain has its own shop packed with the Crunch collection of fleece jackets, Lycra outfits, leggings, sweats, hats, unisex jazz pants, bodywear and sportswear, perfect for working out or just posing. *crunch.com*

Moderate *Amex/MC/V*

Upper West Side **(212) 875-1902**
162 West 83rd Street btw Columbus/Amsterdam Ave
NYC 10024 Mon-Thurs 5:30-11, Fri 5:30-10, Sat-Sun 8-9

Midtown East **(212) 758-3434**
1109 Second Avenue btw 58/59th St
NYC 10022 Mon-Thurs 5:30-11, Fri 5:30-10, Sat-Sun 8-9

Midtown West **(212) 869-7788**
144 West 38th Street btw Seventh Ave/Broadway
NYC 10018 Mon-Fri 5:30-10, Sat-Sun 8-6

Midtown West **(212) 594-8050**
555 West 42nd Street at Eleventh Ave
NYC 10036 Mon-Fri 6-10, Sat-Sun 9-7

East Village **(212) 475-2018**
54 East 13th Street btw Broadway/University Place
NYC 10003 Mon-Fri 6-10, Sat-Sun 8-8

West Village **(212) 366-3725**
152 Christopher Street at Greenwich
NYC 10014 Mon-Fri 6-11, Sat-Sun 8-9

NoHo **(212) 420-0507**
623 Broadway at Houston
NYC 10012 Mon-Fri 6-11, Sat-Sun 8-8

NoHo **(212) 614-0120**
404 Lafayette Street btw Astor Place/East 4th St
NYC 10003 Open 24/7 from Mon 5am to Sat 9pm
Sun 8-9

Lower Manhattan **(212) 269-1067**
25 Broadway at Morris
NYC 10004 Mon-Fri 5-9, Sat-Sun 8-5

Midtown East **(212) 545-9757**
554 Second Avenue at 31st St
NYC 10016 Mon-Fri 6-12, Sat-Sun 8-8

Crush

Beloved by tweens for their impressive selection of cute Paul Frank and goth-girl Emily the Strange accessories, as well as Betsey Johnson dresses for girls, Crush is also bound to seduce their older sisters with vintage booty in excellent condition, slightly naughty knickers and way cool concert tees—the sort you shouldn't wear if you're old enough to have gone to the show. Girls of all ages will swoon over dreamy handbags. *crushstore.com*

Moderate *Amex/MC/V*

Brooklyn **(718) 237-4994**
231 Smith Street btw Douglas/Butler
Brooklyn 11231 Wed-Thurs 3-9, Fri 3-11
Sat 12:30-11, Sun 12:30-7

Cynthia Rowley

Designer Cynthia Rowley's frilly, flirty clothes swing with unabashed girliness. Detailing emphasizes ruffles, ruching, eyelets and other retro touches and twists. Good girls will love her full-skirted dresses nipped at the waist, knits, tops with dainty detailing, print dresses and coats, while bad ones will go for her leather and sexier pieces. Rowley's frocks are guaranteed to bring out the coquette in every woman. Don't miss the purses, shoes and sunglasses and the rack of men's clothing in the back.   *cynthiarowley.com*

Expensive   *MC/V*

West Village   **(212) 242-3803**
376 Bleecker Street   btw Perry/Charles
NYC 10014   Mon-Sat 11-8:30, Sun 11-8

Daffy's

One of New York's largest, and loudest, discount chains, Daffy's carries clothing for the entire family with discounts up to 80% on sportswear, outerwear, workout apparel, underwear, accessories and shoes. If you're lucky, you might even come across a designer label like Tommy Hilfiger, Versace or Guess. Daffy's claim their prices are so low that 'you'll be tempted to haggle them up.'   *daffys.com*

Affordable   *Amex/MC/V*

Midtown East   **(212) 376-4477**
135 East 57th Street   btw Park/Lexington Ave
NYC 10022   Mon-Fri 10-8, Sat 10-7, Sun 11-6

Midtown East   **(212) 557-4422**
335 Madison Avenue   at 44th St
NYC 10017   Mon-Fri 8-8, Sat 10-6, Sun 12-6

Midtown West   **(212) 736-4477**
1311 Broadway   btw 33/34th St
NYC 10013   Mon-Fri 10-9, Sat 10-8, Sun 11-7

Flatiron   **(212) 529-4477**
111 Fifth Avenue   at 18th St
NYC 10003   Mon-Sat 10-9, Sun 12-7

SoHo   **(212) 334-7444**
462 Broadway   at Grand
NYC 10012   Mon-Sat 10-8, Sun 12-7

Midtown West   **(212) 294-4477**
1775 Broadway   at 57th St
NYC 10019   Mon-Fri 9-8:30, Sat 10-7, Sun 11-6

Lower Manhattan   **(212) 422-4477**
50 Broadway   at Exchange Place
NYC 10004   Mon-Fri 8-8, Sat 10-6, Sun 12-6

Dana Buchman

Dana Buchman offers what seem like two separate lines catering to the executive woman in search of a professional, polished look. A comfortably stylish collection of career-wear, suits and desk-to-dinner basics are jazzed up with surprises like floor-length chiffon graphic skirts and yellow leather jackets. Her casual line offers up chinoiserie tops and sherbet-cool colors in flavors from raspberry to lemon. A certain maritime influence pops up in navy blue and white sweaters and pants, while pinstripes seem to be a favorite print. Petite sizes also available. *danabuchman.com*

Moderate to expensive   *Amex/MC/V*

Midtown East   **(212) 319-3257**
65 East 57th Street   btw Madison/Park Ave
NYC 10022   Mon-Sat 10-6 (Thurs 10-8), Sun 12-5

D&G

For many, 'sexy' can't be spelled without the letters D and G. The bridge line of Dolce & Gabbana continues to exude sex appeal throughout the two floors of this store's sportswear, eveningwear and casualwear. Super-tight pants, sexy minis, distressed jeans, rugged furs, chiffon florals, lots of sheer lace, pencil-thin leathers, smart suits and VLBDs (very little black dresses) are the norm. The designers say the D&G woman 'takes incredible joy at dressing up aimed at perplexing, teasing, having fun and, of course, showing herself.' And how. Men aren't left out, though, and can choose from everything from classic Italian suits to screaming floral shirts, leather pants, jeans and logo'd T-shirts. Not for the timid. *dolcegabbana.it*

Expensive   *Amex/MC/V*

SoHo   **(212) 965-8000**
434 West Broadway   btw Prince/Spring
NYC 10012   Mon-Fri 11:30-7:30
                               (Thurs 11:30-8), Sat 11:30-8, Sun 11:30-7

Danskin

Danskin equals second skin. Check out their signature exercise, dance and activewear which include leotards, leggings, unitards, tanks, sweatpants and ballet and jazz shoes. But since you need clothes to wear on the way to ballet class, too, you can choose from Danskin's selection of fashionable streetwear such as short skirts, slim-fitted dresses and slinky tops. *danskin.com*

Moderate   *Amex/MC/V*

Upper West Side   **(212) 724-2992**
159 Columbus Avenue   btw 67/68th St
NYC 10023   Mon-Sat 9:30-9, Sun 11-7

Daphne

Daphne, a specialty boutique for larger-sized women, carries their own line of apparel crafted out of luxury fabrics such as silk, chiffon and cashmere that aim to flatter the figure. Carrying easy-to-coordinate separates and a sizeable selection of eclectic jewelry, including bohemian-style necklaces and chandelier earrings, Daphne sells clothing that any voluptuous diva is sure to love. *daphne1.com*

Moderate   *Amex/MC/V*

Upper West Side   **(212) 877-5073**
467 Amsterdam Avenue   btw 82/83rd St
NYC 10023   Mon-Sat 12-7, Sun 12-6

Darryl's ♀

Darryl's, an 18-year-old Upper West Side 'contemporary woman's boutique', offers day-to-day staples that aim to maximize the refined woman's wardrobe. Carrying mostly European labels like BCBG, Mica, Trina Turk, Tocca and Teen Flo, Darryl's offers a little bit of everything, from ready-for-work tailored suits to flirty dresses and casual knitwear.

Moderate   *Amex/MC/V*

Upper West Side   **(212) 874-6677**
492 Amsterdam Avenue   btw 83/84th St
NYC 10024   Mon-Fri 11-7, Sat 11-6, Sun 12-6

★ Darling ♀

Darling is oh-so dramatic and the girls are just loving it. Former Broadway costume designer Ann French Emonts Sherman has a flair for turning the spotlight on shoppers with her exquisite selection of grown-up-yet-flirty skirts, dresses, separates, jackets and fabulous lingerie. Pieces are a mix of Emonts Sherman's own designs and the talents of stylish friends such as Mary Green, as well as a vintage selection. A fun place to be a lady, Darling sweetens the shopping experience by offering wine and champagne on Thursday nights. Now that is sure to give shopaholics a buzz.

Moderate   *Amex/MC/V*

West Village   **(646) 336-6966**
1 Horatio Street   at Eighth Ave
NYC 10014   Mon-Sat 11-8 (Thurs 11-10), Sun 12-6

Davide Cenci ♀♂

Davide Cenci's mission statement is comfort, warmth, lightness and balance. That mission is met with the clean lines and subtle color palette that characterize the Cenci aesthetic. The ready-to-wear suits, sportswear, shirts, sweaters, outerwear and accessories, plus the custom-made designs, all display luxurious fabrics and impeccable tailoring. Expect to pay for such quality: made-to-measure suits start at $2,500.   *davidecenci.com*

Luxury   *Amex/MC/V*

Upper East Side   **(212) 628-5910**
801 Madison Avenue   btw 67/68th St
NYC 10021   Mon-Sat 10-6:30 (Thurs 10-7:30)

David Yurman ♂♀

Spread throughout his extensive line of fine jewelry is Yurman's signature 'cable': a tightly coiled, thin wrap-around chain that started with his popular solid silver coil bracelet. Also famous are the luxury watches he designs and makes in his factory in Switzerland. The vibrant stone jewelry (blue topaz rings, amethyst pendants) use his signature cushion cut, giving a soft edge to geometric-shaped gems. His line of bridal jewelry incorporates the cushion and the cable as well. His son Evan has taken over the men's: colorful cufflinks and other offbeat accessories.   *davidyurman.com*

Luxury *Amex/MC/V*

Upper East Side (212) 752-4255
729 Madison Avenue at 64th St
NYC 10021 Mon-Sat 10-6

DDC Lab 👫

DDC lab uses innovative methods to concoct seriously cool fashion-forward gear. One part pretty, one part hip, with a dash of high-tech utilitarianism, the goods range from leather-pleated minis to Teflon-treated jeans. Denim looks are the main attraction (including 18 new styles of jean), but great jackets and corduroys should not be missed. Complete your look with stylish tees and PF Flyers sneakers. The Chelsea store carries a higher end DDC line. *ddclab.com*

Expensive *Amex/MC/V*

West Village (212) 414-5801
427 West 14th Street btw Ninth/Tenth Ave
NYC 10014 Mon-Fri 11-7, Sun 12-6

Debra Rodman 👩

The large print wallpaper in this tiny store gives a sort of Alice in Wonderland feel. The minidresses are retro cut and made of fittingly kitschy prints: some look like they were meant to be curtains in Nana's parlor, others are plaids and stripes like they just don't make 'em anymore. Cutesy blazers and deconstructed military jackets with feminine details similarly have that artsy-crafty, one-of-a-kind look of handmade clothing. Pleated miniskirts with wide leather belts, paired with puff-sleeved blouses give a sexy-yet-wholesome Sixties secretary look. The shop carries choice pieces from Debra's Yogini line of workout gear with fun cutouts and embroidered flowers. *debrarodman.com*

Moderate *Amex/MC/V*

Nolita (212) 925-6553
49 Prince Street at Mulberry
NYC 10012 Daily 11-7:30

Deco Jewels 👩

Deco's Janice Berkson travels far and wide in search of Lucite handbags from the Forties and Fifties and lovingly restores them to pristine perfection. Collectable pieces, including vintage costume jewelry and cufflinks from the Twenties to the Sixties, round out the gorgeous assortment.

Moderate *Amex/MC/V*

SoHo (212) 253-1222
131 Thompson Street btw Prince/Houston
NYC 10012 Daily 12-7

Delfino 👫

Delfino's motto is that there's a bag for every outfit (only one?) and this stylish little shop houses a selection of all sizes and shapes in eye-popping colors and wild animal textures, as well as basic leathers. Labels include Longchamp,

Jack Gomme, Hervé Chapelier, Francesco Biasia, France's
Bronti Bay and Mandarina Duck.   delfinoshop.com

Expensive   *Amex/MC/V*

Midtown West   **(212) 956-0868**
56 West 50th Street   at Rockefeller Center
NYC 10021   Mon-Fri 10:30-8, Sat 10:30-7, Sun 12-6

Upper East Side   **(212) 517-5391**
1351A Third Avenue   btw 76/77th
NYC 10021   Mon-Fri 10:30-8, Sat 10:30-7:30, Sun 12-7

★ Denimaxx

Denimaxx's sales staff will spoil you with treats from their
coffee and wet bar as you frolic through three floors of fur
and leather outerwear, pants, shirts, skirts, accessories, hats,
purses and even housewares. Where else would you go for
a fur bathing suit, Mongolian lamb pillows or a $6,000 mink
bedspread? The store has even tried to accommodate animal lovers with its line of Bassoni Edwardo faux-fur coats. Be
on the watch for their sales, when they discount their goods
50-70%.   denimaxx.com

Moderate to luxury   *Amex/MC/V*

Midtown East   **(212) 207-4900**
444 Madison Avenue   btw 49/50th St
NYC 10022   Daily 10-6

Dernier Cri

Owner Stacia Valle, the former tour manager for Third Eye
Blind, has assembled an eclectic collection of clothes,
accessories and, basically, incredibly cool stuff from designers specializing in that very thing: rocking. The store's edgy
wears with a distinctly rebellious vibe are perfect for the
Chelsea's nearby clubs. Dernier Cri's independent spirit
embraces designers like Vivienne Westwood, Development,
Tsubi, Circle by Mara Hoffman and Grey Ant. Also find vintage issues of Rolling Stone, punk T-shirts, hats by Eugenia
Kim and bags by Not Rational—perfect accessories for
those looking to add an offbeat spin to their wardrobe.

Expensive   *Amex/MC/V*

Chelsea   **(212) 242-6061**
869 Washington Street   btw 13/14th St
NYC 10014   Mon-Sat 12-8, Sun 12:30-7:30

Designer Loft

Ah, your wedding day—a special day that you will remember forever, and Designer Loft is here to guarantee that the
memories will be happy ones. Brides-to-be will blush when
they see the delicious designs available here, including Maz
Chaoul, Ristarose, Kirstie Kelly, Gallit Levy, Jenny Packham,
and Atelier Aimee. Gowns for bridesmaids and the mother
of the bride are also drool-inducing. In addition to the lovely dresses, the Loft offers full wedding planner services, and
their trunk shows are not to be missed. Check out their new,

larger showroom, with separate bridesmaid and evening-wear areas. *designerloftnyc.com*

Expensive *Amex/MC/V*

Midtown West **(212) 944-9013**
226 West 37th Street (15th floor)   btw Seventh/Eighth Ave
NYC 10018 Tues, Wed, Sat 10-6,
Thurs-Fri 10-8 (by appointment only)

Design in Textiles by Mary Jaeger 👫

Melding her experience as a designer for Mary McFadden and Jack Mulqueen with her eight years in Japan studying textiles, Mary Jaeger brings a sprightly palette to her Zen-infused apparel and furnishings. Jaeger outfits clients in heavily dyed, shrunken wool shawls, capes and scarves, and makes shibori (a Japanese take on tie-dye) onesies for their children. Her home product line (which already features beautiful table runners fashioned from vintage kimonos) includes made-to-order ottomans and wall hangings. *maryjaeger.com*

Expensive *Amex/MC/V*

SoHo **(212) 941-5877**
51 Spring Street btw Lafayette/Mulberry
NYC 10012 Mon-Fri 12:30-6:30, Sat 12-7, Sun 12-5

Destination 👫

After a serious designer clothes fix at Jeffrey (just one block away), make this your, er, destination for hot new accessories, from hats and shoes to handbags and jewelry from a great selection of labels. Best is an eclectic mix of jewelry (from feminine, delicate pieces to hard-core punk) by Gilbert Gilbert and Serge Thoroval and stylish handbags from labels like Jacques LeCorre. *destinationny.net*

Moderate *Amex/MC/V*

Chelsea **(212) 727-2031**
32-36 Little West 12th Street btw Washington/Ninth Ave
NYC 10014 Mon-Fri 11-8, Sat-Sun 12-7

Detour 👤

Wonder where young girls are getting their hip, tight-fitting outfits? Look no further—Detour features a sexy, slinky and somewhat pricey assortment of tees, jeans, skirts, dresses, leather jackets and racy ensembles perfect for club-hopping—because that's what Detour girls do.

Affordable *Amex/MC/V*

SoHo **(212) 979-6315**
421 West Broadway at Prince
NYC 10012 Daily 11-8

Diana & Jeffries 👤

For the Charlotte York in all of us, there is Diana & Jeffries. Offering pretty patterned dresses and skirts by Tibi, trendy jeans by Juicy Couture and Joie, shrunken tweed blazers by Nanette Lepore and delicate tanks by Cosabella, Diana & Jeffries makes every day into a walk down Park Avenue.

Expensive   *Amex/MC/V*

Upper East Side   **(212) 831-0531**
1310 Madison Avenue   btw 92/93rd St
NYC 10128   Mon-Sat 11-7, Sun 1-7

Upper West Side   **(212) 874-2884**
2062 Broadway   btw 70/71st St
NYC 10023   Mon-Sat 11-8, Sun 1-7

Diana Kane   🕴

Like lingerie? Sheer, lacy sweet nothings abound at Diana
Kane, who sells Diane von Furstenberg's lingerie line
Boudoir as well as bedroom favorites like Cosabella. Even
the bathrobes are sexy here—they look and function like a
wrap dress, or even a small trench. Great selection of
camisoles, too.   *dianakane.com*

Moderate   *Amex/MC/V*

Park Slope   **(718) 638-6520**
229b 5th Avenue   btw Carroll/President
Brooklyn 11215   Mon 2-8, Tues-Sat 11-8, Sun 11-6

Diane T   🕴

Affluent Brooklynites need not travel over the bridge for
their designer duds. The front room of this bright and simple space concentrates on casual clothes: jeans from 7 for all
Mankind, cutesy Marc Jacobs dresses, Juicy Couture terry
cloth sweatpants, and Paul & Joe soft tees. Beyond the
French doors lie dressier selections like ruffled and embroidered Diane von Furstenberg skirts, Ulla Johnson frocks,
Calypso sundresses, vintagey tweed suits by Cacharel, and
Miguelina satin pieces. Don't miss the promising sale rack.

Expensive   *Amex/MC/V*

Cobble Hill   **(718) 923-5777**
174 Court Street   btw Amity/Congress
Brooklyn 11201   Tues-Fri 11-7:30, Sat 11-6:30, Sun 1-5

Diane von Furstenberg the Shop   🕴

This is your one-stop for fun, feminine and ultra-flattering
fashion. Though slightly off the beaten track, it's well worth
the trek: canopies suspended from the ceiling frame the
central mirrors while racks of light, versatile and utterly wearable pieces—flirty ruched tops, silk shirts, bias-cut georgette and matte jersey skirts, slim-fitting Ultrasuede pants
and jeans—line the walls. The wrap dress, von Furstenberg's
signature creation, is continuously released in fresh, unique
patterns to match the mood of each month's collection.
Priced around $300, the Wrap, like everything von
Furstenberg, is easy to fit, easy to wear and effortlessly chic.
The lingerie in the back also offers DvF's unparalleled patterns in the same basic, true-to-size cuts, and the new make-
up collection is as simple to select as it is to sport. *dvf.com*

Expensive   *Amex/MC/V*

West Village   **(646) 486-4800**
385 West 12th Street   btw Washington/West Side H'way
NYC 10014   Mon, Fri-Sat 11-6, Tues-Thurs 11-7, Sun 12-5

★ Diesel

At Diesel, there's a party going on and everyone's invited. DJs spin all day at this superstore, which feels more like a club than a shop. Skaters, snowboarders and downtown coolsters will find quirky sportswear in whacked-out colors, an awesome denim selection, including 18 new styles, and Diesel's fab collection of sneakers and bags carried by club kids everywhere. Denim alert: newly svelte Chanel designer Karl Lagerfeld has designed a limited-edition collection (available only at the Denim Gallery branch)—cut on the skinny side. *diesel.com*

Moderate *Amex/MC/V*

NoHo **(646) 336-8552**
1 Union Square West at 14th St
NYC 10003 Mon-Sat 11-9, Sun 11-8

Upper East Side **(212) 308-0055**
770 Lexington Avenue at 60th St
NYC 10021 Mon-Sat 10-8, Sun 12-6

SoHo (Denim Gallery) **(212) 966-5593**
68 Greene Street btw Spring/Broome
NYC 10012 Mon-Sat 11-7, Sun 12-6

Diesel Children's Boutique

Now moms and dads can turn their offspring into mini-hipsters. Babies and kids look as cool as their parents in Diesel label-emblazoned jumpers, track jackets, screenprinted tees, drawstring shorts, gas station shirts and, of course, denim jackets and jeans. The Seventies-inspired logo tees are doubly ironic on young ones born 30 years later. This high-traffic SoHo shop is more fun for grown-ups than kids: the walls are lined with dump trucks, trophies and other toys spray-painted in solid colors, serving as artwork rather than playthings. *diesel.com*

Affordable *Amex/MC/V*

SoHo **(212) 343-3863**
414-416 West Broadway btw Prince/Spring
NYC 10012 Mon-Sat 11-7, Sun 12-6

Dinosaur Designs

This Australian jewelry label launched Down Under in the late Eighties and quickly developed a cult following for its chunky resin jewelry—rings, bracelets and knockout strands of beads. Each piece is handmade in Australia. Beyond the resiny goods, the brand has expanded into strong silver pieces and housewares. Confident, colorful and cool. *dinosaurdesigns.com.au*

Moderate *Amex/MC/V*

Nolita **(212) 680-3523**
250 Mott Street btw Houston/Prince
NYC 10012 Mon-Sat 11-7, Sun 12-6

Dior Homme

Hedi Slimane's elegant but forward-looking designs for men have garnered accolades around the world, and it's easy to see why when you step into this sleek Fifth Avenue space. Everyone (women continue to sport Slimane's work) can dive into the beautifully tailored jackets and pant suits that he's known for, not to mention sleekly futuristic luggage, shoes, belts, must-have jeans, suits, accessories and sportswear. Throw in fragrances, eyewear, shoes, and singular items like an ultra-chic, black leather iPod case, and you have one-stop Euro-lifestyle shopping. *diorhomme.com*

Moderate to expensive   *Amex/MC/V*

Midtown East   **(212) 421-6009**
17 East 57th Street   btw Fifth/Madison Ave
NYC 10022   Mon-Fri 10-7, Sat 10-6, Sun 12-6

DKNY

Designer Donna Karan brings her spot-on vision to DKNY, her diffusion line of high-performance, affordable sportswear. The easy-to-wear clothes are infused with loads of personality, setting DKNY apart from like-minded brands. The color-coordinated collection of tops, pants, skirts, dresses and eveningwear is wonderfully fresh and fun, and distinguished by easy silhouettes and original details. Accessories include handbags and shoes. *dkny.com*

Expensive   *Amex/MC/V*

Upper East Side   **(212) 223-3569**
655 Madison Avenue   at 60th Street
NYC 10021   Mon-Sat 10-8, Sun 11-6

SoHo   **(646) 613-1100**
420 West Broadway   btw Prince/Spring
NYC 10012   Mon-Sat 11-8, Sun 12-7

D/L Cerney

Being trendy can be so exhausting—and no one understands that better than husband-and-wife team Duane Cerney and Linda St John. Their antidote: a collection of classic retro-inspired clothing featuring everything from simple gabardine shirts and straight skirts to fitted shift dresses and stretch pants. It's all in natural fabrics and hand-finished, right down to the last button and stitch. Great silhouettes and colors also distinguish these clothes, from the easy sheath dresses and well-cut pants to classic button-downs. Sometimes closed Monday and Tuesday—call to check.

Expensive   *MC/V*

East Village   **(212) 673-7033**
13 East 7th Street   btw Second/Third Ave
NYC 10003   Daily 12-8

Do Kham

Treasures from the Himalayas are beautifully displayed in this elegant shop, where you can choose from traditional

Tibetan styled dresses, skirts and tops plus a collection of richly brocaded, fur-trimmed silk hats. Check out the fabulous selection of ever-versatile pashmina shawls ($125 to $195) as well as plain or embroidered scarves, boas and handbags in a myriad of colors and fabrics.

Moderate   *Amex/MC/V*

SoHo   **(212) 966-2404**
51 Prince Street   btw Mulberry/Lafayette
NYC 10012   Daily 10-8

East Village   **(212) 358-1010**
304 East 5th Street   btw First/Second Ave
NYC 10003   Daily 12:30-7:30

★ Dolce & Gabbana

Agent provocateurs Domenico Dolce and Stefano Gabbana get sex. They really get it—and their saucy vision rules everywhere from the streets of Milan to the Hollywood red carpet. They are so in synch with what the stars want to wear that they have designed stage costumes for everyone from Madonna to Kylie Minogue, while their signature curvy, bra-strapped dresses have brought out the babe in Isabella Rossellini, Gwyneth Paltrow…every celebrity worth her *Vogue* cover. This flagship store, their largest in the world, serves up a gorgeously rich collection of men's and women's ready-to-wear as well as some couture pieces from pin-striped suits (another Dolce classic) to seductive leopard dresses. Not to mention their to-die-for accessories like silk ribbon belts and denim stilettos.   *dolcegabbana.it*

Expensive   *Amex/MC/V*

Upper East Side   **(212) 249-4100**
825 Madison Avenue   btw 68/69th St
NYC 10021   Mon-Sat 10-6 (Thurs 10-7), Sun 12-5

Domenico Spano

Calabria-born Domenico 'Mimmo' Spano has been creating extraordinary suits for tasteful gents for 'longer than he'd like to admit,' laughs a staffer. Such experience yields treasures, and these pieces will last a lifetime. The former director of custom tailoring at Bergdorf Goodman also provides a small tailoring service for women—think Katherine Hepburn's inimitable Thirties style and you've got it. This is one of the best places in the city for a wedding tuxedo, with the bespoke wool version starting at $4,200 and prices escalating, depending on threads per square inch, from there. Lack the patience (or funds) for bespoke suits but still admire the defined shoulders, tapered waists and unique color schemes that characterize Mimmo's work? He recently started his first ready-to-wear line, where his 'vintage with a modern twist' look will be made available to one and all.

Luxury   *Amex/MC/V*

Midtown East   **(212) 940-2676**
611 Fifth Avenue   at 50th St
NYC 10022   Mon-Sat 10-6 (Thurs 10-8)

★ Domenico Vacca

'The first authentic Italian boutique in the United States,' promises owner Domenico Vacca (the man behind Borrelli) of this chic slice of Milan in the heart of Midtown. Master tailor Cesare Attolini, whose father Vincenzo tailored suits for Clark Gable and the Duke of Windsor, provides movie-star glamour, while fine shirting by Finamore and handmade belts and shoes by Stefano Bi and Andrea D'Amico complete the dapper looks. Then there's the house's signature collection of refined classic separates and suiting, lovely V-neck sweaters and brightly colored ties—all perfect for your lunch next door at Harry Cipriani. *domenicovacca.com*

Luxury   *Amex/MC/V*

Midtown East   **(212) 759-6333**
781 Fifth Avenue   btw 59/60th St
NYC 10022   Mon-Sat 10-7, Sun 12-6

SoHo   **(212) 925-0010**
367 West Broadway   at Broome
NYC 10013   Mon-Sat 11-8, Sun 12-7

Upper East Side   **n/a at press time**
702 Madison Avenue   btw 62/63rd St
NYC 10021   n/a at press time

Donna Karan

Discover the Donna Karan worldview at this flagship store where the clothes and the decor project the designer's calmly chic aesthetic. Karan has always designed what she herself would like to wear—distinctive yet comfortable clothing—and that's the secret of her success. This modern, streamlined style can be found on three floors of men's and women's suits, great black jackets (great black everything, actually), cozy sweaters, smart khaki trench coats, leathers and outerwear, as well as modern eveningwear. Also find home accessories to outfit the total DK-inspired lifestyle. A serene bamboo garden in the back offers a respite to weary shoppers. *donnakaran.com*

Luxury   *Amex/MC/V*

Upper East Side   **(212) 861-1001**
819 Madison Avenue   btw 68/69th St
NYC 10021   Mon-Sat 10-6 (Thurs 10-7), Sun 12-5

Dooney & Burke

Dooney & Burke's flagship offers its extensive collection of handbags, leather goods and luggage. Find a variety of fabrics and shapes, from classic, durable leather goods to more colorful, recent additions, all emblazoned with the company's logo. Be sure to look past the fabulous bags and browse the men's and women's clothing lines, which feature cashmere sweaters, hats and gloves. Also find shoes, briefcases, phone cases and even a great-looking unisex watch. *800-347-5000 dooney.com*

Expensive   *Amex/MC/V*

Upper East Side
20 East 60th Street
NYC 10022

(212) 223-7444
btw Madison/Park Ave
Mon-Sat 10-6

Dosa

L.A.-based Dosa designer Christina Kim makes a lot of women very, very happy with clothes that have a chicly bohemian vibe. The loose, girlish pieces include silks in delicious rainbow colors, handwoven Khadi cotton, covetable cashmeres, Tibetan-inspired tops and long, wrap skirts.

Expensive   *Amex/MC/V*

SoHo
107 Thompson Street
NYC 10012

(212) 431-1733
btw Prince/Spring
Mon-Sat 12-7, Sun 12-6

Doyle & Doyle

Doyle and Doyle carry exquisite antique and estate jewelry that will seduce anyone—even those not in the market for an Art Deco diamond bracelet. Owned by two sisters from Massachusetts, the sleek space belies the friendly, welcoming service and charming atmosphere. Shop here for a range of items, from Belle Epoque engagement rings to Victorian brooches. They also carry accessories such as late 19th-century mesh purses, as well as more contemporary pieces. All the jewelry is in excellent condition and sparkles with a distinctive, unique feel. The best part? Reasonable prices, given the condition and provenance of the pieces.   *doyledoyle.com*

Expensive   *Amex/MC/V*

Lower East Side
189 Orchard Street
NYC 10002

(212) 677-9991
btw Stanton/Houston
Tues-Sun 1-7 (Thurs 1-8)

★ Duncan Quinn

It would take massive amounts of restraint not to make an Austin Powers reference right now. But a 'Groovy!' or 'Yeah, baby!' wouldn't even do justice to this menswear treasure chest, in which both the interior and the wares are very British, unabashedly retro, and bursting with colors not seen in suits since the swinging Sixties. Op-art patterned ties and dress shirts mixing magenta and plum sound gaudy, but are traditionally and expertly crafted so that they wear brilliantly on a bold and fashionable gent. The custom-fit suits are a touch more staid, with a cheeky touch of color in the form of subtle pinstripes.   *duncanquinn.com*

Expensive   *Amex/MC/V*

Nolita
8 Spring Street
NYC 10012

(212) 226-7030
btw Bowery/Elizabeth
Tues-Sun 12-8

Dusica Dusica

Dusica Dusica shoes run the footwear gamut from sensible to sexy. The Italian label provides sultry stilettos, pumps and impressive boots as well as more functional—though equally stylish—flats, sandals and loafers. *dusicadusica.com*

Expensive *Amex/MC/V*

SoHo **(212) 966-9099**
67 Prince Street at Crosby
NYC 10012 Daily 11-8 (Sun 12-7)

Duty Free Apparel

Feels like a border crossing, without the hassle. Duty Free Apparel offers a fix of high-style European labels at great prices. Owner Joel Soren finds the best from across the pond and brings them to Manhattanites willing to trek to this slightly out-of-the-way space in the Garment District. Find Prada, Gucci, Ferragamo and Armani—the best of the best—for prices slightly below retail, even for this season's styles and bags. No passport necessary. *dutyfreeapparel.com*

Expensive *Amex/MC/V*

Midtown **(212) 967-6548**
204 West 35th Street (2nd floor) btw Seventh/Eighth Ave
NYC 10001 Tues-Fri 10-6

Earl Jean

Earl Jean was the first of the hip, micro-jeans brands that now include Lucky and Seven and took on the Levi's and Diesels of the world. Devotees like Jennifer Aniston and Cameron Diaz swear by Earl creative director Suzanne Costas Freiwald's super-flattering, leg-lengthening cuts, and her fans grow daily. The look is ultra-sexy, hip bone-revealing jeans in dark denim, slim silhouettes and boot-leg cuts. Epitomizing this look is Earl Jean's most distinctive style #55. There's a world of other jean styles in fabrics like corduroy, chambray, leather and velvet, as well a collection of jean jackets, skirts and tops. Also check out Earl's accessory line of jewelry, handbags, boots and belts. And there's good news for guys: Earl's men's line flatters in the same way as the women's—it includes T-shirts, knits and outerwear, as well as denim in a variety of washes. *earljean.com*

Moderate *Amex/MC/V*

SoHo **(212) 226-8709**
160 Mercer Street btw Houston/Prince
NYC 10012 Mon-Sat 11-7, Sun 12-6

★ Eastern Mountain Sports

Whether your idea of a great outdoor adventure consists of hiking the Appalachian Trail or just up Fifth Avenue, Eastern Mountain Sports will outfit you for all your wilderness needs—as wild or wimpy as they may be. Specializing in clothing and equipment for mountaineering, backpacking, hiking, skiing and camping, EMS carries the leading nature-loving labels including Columbia, The North Face, Patagonia and their own in-house brand of apparel, gear and goods. *888-463-6367 ems.com*

Affordable to moderate *Amex/MC/V*

SoHo **(212) 966-8730**
591 Broadway btw Houston/Prince
NYC 10012 Mon-Fri 10-9, Sat 10-8, Sun 12-6

Upper West Side **(212) 397-4860**
20 West 61st Street at Broadway
NYC 10023 (opening hours as above)

East Side Kids

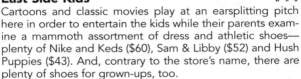

Cartoons and classic movies play at an earsplitting pitch here in order to entertain the kids while their parents examine a mammoth assortment of dress and athletic shoes—plenty of Nike and Keds ($60), Sam & Libby ($52) and Hush Puppies ($43). And, contrary to the store's name, there are plenty of shoes for grown-ups, too.

Affordable *Amex/MC/V*

Upper East Side **(212) 360-5000**
1298 Madison Avenue at 92nd St
NYC 10128 Mon-Fri 9:30-6, Sat 10-6

Easy Spirit

Easy Sprit Shoes have always emphasized comfort, and the brand commits to continuously advancing shoe construction by incorporating the latest technology. Styles range from career and fitness to fun and casual. It's footwear that protects your feet from shock—and your wallet, too. *easyspirit.com*

Affordable *Amex/MC/V*

Upper East Side **(212) 828-9593**
1518 Third Avenue btw 85/86th St
NYC 10028 Mon-Fri 10-8, Sat 10-7, Sun 11-6

Upper West Side **(212) 875-8146**
2251 Broadway at 81st St
NYC 10024 Mon-Sat 10-7:30, Sun 11-6

Midtown East **(212) 715-0152**
555 Madison Avenue btw 55/56th St
NYC 10022 Mon-Fri 9-7, Sat 10-6, Sun 12-5

Midtown West **(212) 398-2761**
1166 Sixth Avenue at 46th St
NYC 10036 Mon-Fri 9-7, Sat 10-6, Sun 12-5

SoHo **(212) 406-8159**
182 Broadway at John
NYC 10038 Mon-Wed 8-7, Thurs-Fri 8-8
Sat 11-6, Sun 12-5

Eddie Bauer

Classic style for classic Americans should be Eddie Bauer's motto. Originally a purveyor of innovative, rugged outdoor gear and apparel, Eddie Bauer, having been in business over 80 years, maintain their sporty yet understated style, providing men and women with perfectly preppy polos, wrinkle-resistant pleated khakis and ribbed Henleys, along with parkas, duffles and all the camping gear and gadgets you need for the perfect weekend getaway. *800-625-7935 eddiebauer.com*

Affordable   *Amex/MC/V*

Upper East Side   **(212) 737-0002**
1172 Third Avenue   at 68th St
NYC 10021   Mon-Sat 10-8, Sun 11-6

Upper West Side   **(212) 877-7629**
1960 Broadway   at 67th St
NYC 10023   Mon-Thurs 10-9, Fri-Sat 10-10, Sun 11-8

SoHo   **(212) 925-2179**
578 Broadway   btw Houston/Prince
NYC 10012   Mon-Thurs 10-8, Fri-Sat 10-9, Sun 11-7

★ Edith & Daha

There are precious beaded capelets and Bakelite accessories here, but the real draw is the massive selection of vintage leather shoes, belts and purses in all styles, sizes and
colors. The shoes are organized by size, and in every size: a
welcome exception for vintage shoes. After you've found
your perfect pair, find a slouchy, buttery leather purse in the
exact same shade, from basic brown to early-Eighties soft
red. Though there is a smattering of vintage Gucci and Dior
in the mix, most purses are no-name deadstock, which
keeps the prices low.

Affordable to moderate   *Amex/MC/V*

Lower East Side   **(212) 979-9992**
104 Rivington Street   btw Ludlow/Essex
NYC 10002   Daily 1-8 (Sat-Sun 12-8)

★ Eileen Fisher

Fisher's claim to fame: casual, maintenance-free clothing
that travels anywhere. There are jackets, skirts, pants with
elastic waistlines and T-shirts designed in a relaxed fit. A
solid, pretty color palette makes mixing and matching a
cinch.   *800-345-3362 eileenfisher.com*

Affordable   *Amex/MC/V*

Upper East Side   **(212) 879-7799**
1039 Madison Avenue   btw 79/80th St
NYC 10021   Mon-Sat 10-7, Sun 12-5

Upper West Side   **(212) 362-3000**
341 Columbus Avenue   btw 76/77th St
NYC 10024   Mon-Sat 10-7, Sun 12-6

Midtown East   **(212) 759-9888**
521 Madison Avenue   btw 53/54th St
NYC 10022   Mon-Sat 10-7, Sun 12-6

Flatiron   **(212) 924-4777**
166 Fifth Avenue   btw 21/22nd St
NYC 10003   Mon-Sat 10-7, Sun 12-6

SoHo   **(212) 431-4567**
395 West Broadway   btw Spring/Broome
NYC 10012   Mon-Thurs 11-7, Fri-Sat 11-8, Sun 12-6

East Village (outlet)   **(212) 529-5715**
314 East 9th Street   btw First/Second Ave
NYC 10003   Mon-Sat 12-8, Sun 12-7

Midtown West   **(212) 823-9575**
10 Columbus Circle   Time Warner Center
NYC 10019   Mon-Sat 10-9, Sun 11-7

Eisenberg & Eisenberg

For over a century this shop has been one of New York's sources for inexpensive formalwear. Don't let the unglamorous façade deter you from venturing inside, where you'll find suits, slacks, sportcoats, blazers, shirts, men's furnishings and a full range of tuxedos. Pay an average price of $375 for suits and from $190 to $650 for tuxedos. Extra for alterations, which are done in the store.   *eisenbergandeisenberg.com*

Moderate   *Amex/MC/V*

Chelsea   **(212) 627-1290**
16 West 17th Street   btw Fifth/Sixth Ave
NYC 10011   Mon-Wed, Fri 9-5:45, Tues 9-5:30
Thurs 9-6:45, Sat 9-5, Sun 11:30-4 (except in summer)

Elaine Arsenault

This jaunty accessories store recalls the equally jaunty aesthetic of Kate Spade in a range of clever totes in various shapes with leather handles, each efficiently displayed like art on the wall. Perfect for taking to Sunday brunch, they come in a variety of prints and are handmade in the store. Also available: make-up bags and clutches.   *elainearsenault.com*

Moderate   *Amex/MC/V*

East Village   **(212) 228-3251**
305 East 9th Street   btw First/Second Ave
NYC 10003   Mon-Sat 12-7, Sun 12-6

Eleni Lambros

Consider Eleni Lambros your fashion fairy godmother. She has created couture bridal and eveningwear for over 12 years, and recently launched a ready-to-wear bridal gown collection, which she shows exclusively in a SoHo showroom every bit as decadent as its custom counterpart. From hand-stitched beadwork using Swarovski crystals, to feather trim and braided silk piping, Lambros's creations would make even Cinderella jealous.   *elenilambros.com*

Luxury   *Amex/MC/V*

SoHo   **(212) 226-1167**
591 Broadway   btw Houston/Prince
NYC 10012   (by appointment only)

Elie Tahari

Tahari had runaway success with his Theory sportswear line, and has now refocused attention on his eponymous label. Having cultivated a following at Bergdorf's, Tahari has opened his own beautifully minimalist flagship in SoHo. Sexy, modern, clean pieces are his signature—like his flirty tennis dresses, buckled asymmetrical minis, tweedy skirts, and beautiful double-face wool coats for fall. Tahari's looks are refined, a little glamorous, and great for everything from turning heads at the office to making friends at cocktail hour.   *elietahari.com*

Expensive *Amex/MC/V*

SoHo **(212) 334-4441**
417 West Broadway btw Spring/Prince
NYC 10012 Mon-Sat 11-8, Sun 12-6

★ Elizabeth Charles

Redheaded Aussie Elizabeth heads down under twice yearly for Fashion Week, where she handpicks the best designers from Oz and New Zealand to stock in her cozy enclave. Many of the cult designers are available Stateside through her shop alone. The store doesn't have a definite theme, but rather an array of styles ranging from frilly strapless dresses to sailor shorts. Karen Walker's high-waisted jeans with butt-enhancing pockets have been snatched up by the likes of J-Lo and Kate Hudson. Walk through a small garden to get to the fitting room, and sip on a latte made from beans imported from, you guessed it, Australia. *elizabeth-charles.com*

Moderate to expensive *Amex/MC/V*

Chelsea **(212) 243-3201**
639½ Hudson Street at Ninth Ave
NYC 10014 Tues-Sat 12-7:30 (Thurs 12-9)

Ellen

Local fashion designers shop at Ellen Koenigsberg's teeny vintage boutique because, the proprietor promises, 'every piece is special'. Eschewing label snobbery in favor of whatever catches her eye, Ellen stocks her limited space with great shoes and hats from the Sixties. Familiar names do crop up, however, in her stash of Pucci shorts in turquoise and yellow, Geoffrey Beene dresses, and the occasional Courrèges floral skirt.

Expensive *Amex/MC/V*

Lower East Side **(212) 471-0080**
122 Ludlow Street btw Rivington/Delancey
NYC 10002 Daily 1-7 (closed Tuesday)

★ Ellen Christine Millinery

Whether it's a major fashion mag in need of authentic vintage leopardprint hats for a shoot, or a customer craving an extravagant number for the Kentucky Derby, they come to Ellen to draw from her arsenal of over 1,000 hats from the Forties right on back to Victorian times. She recreates these hats the old-fashioned, labor-intensive way, using their original designs and with antique materials whenever possible. Also for sale are capes, boleros and stoles as well as the vintage lamps and hatboxes that make the tiny shop feel like grandma's attic.

Moderate to luxury *Amex/MC/V*

Chelsea **(212) 242-2457**
255 West 18th Street btw Seventh/Eighth Ave
NYC 10011 Tues-Sat 11-7, Sun 1-6
(Mon by appointment only)

Elleven Up　👤

A simple space on the top floor of a building on this fashionable street, Elleven Up forgoes the bells and whistles to offer a unique service to women with larger feet. Stocking sizes 11 to 13, this shop carries basic loafers, heels and flats, along with a smattering of wilder styles. Brands represented include Anne Klein New York, Thierry Rabotin, Stuart Weitzman, Cole Haan, Delman and Claudia Chiuti. While the selection here wouldn't make a size eight shoe junkie jealous, big-footed ladies have never had so many choices. The staff are very concerned about fit and will ensure you needn't ever again wear shoes that pinch your toes.

Moderate　　　　　　　　　　　　　　　*Amex/MC/V*
Midtown East　　　　　　　　　　　**(212) 757-2154**
12 West 57th Street (suite 1005)　　　　　at Fifth Ave
NYC 10019　　　　　　　　　　　　　Mon-Sat 11-6

★ Emanuel Ungaro　👤

Ungaro is every girl's guilty pleasure. 'Pink is the institutional color for Ungaro,' says the man himself, and it's more than obvious when you walk into this brilliantly rose-toned store. Ungaro gave up the ready-to-wear reins at his house five years ago to his former design assistant Giambattista Valli, who has started to hit his stride. This store is the perfect showcase for the company's deliciously feminine pieces: flirty dresses in the signature silk jersey, or with floral prints that are regularly sported by seductive celebs like Jennifer Lopez and Cameron Diaz as well as the model set, who often dress the romantic pieces down by wearing them over jeans. Accessories include fabulously flirty shoes (some in, yes, pink), belts, bags and evening shawls.　*emanuelungaro.com*

Luxury　　　　　　　　　　　　　　　*Amex/MC/V*
Upper East Side　　　　　　　　　**(212) 249-4090**
792 Madison Avenue　　　　　　　　　　at 67th St
NYC 10021　　　　　　　　　　　　　Mon-Sat 10-6

Emporio Armani　👨👩

Bridging the gap between the perfect Armani power suit and the euro-styled jeans and tees of Armani Exchange is Emporio Armani, where you'll find younger, sportier takes on the restrained elegance of Armani's pant suits, beaded dresses for evenings out, clean lines and fluid cuts. The palette is refined, and the details minimalist—no Hawaiian shirts here. For men, Emporio offers exquisite pinstripe dress shirts and more affordable versions of the classic Armani jackets, pants and suits. Women can head upstairs to try on sporty Italian designs like—and only Armani could make this beautiful—a $500 nylon dress with plastic straps.　*emporioarmani.com*

Expensive　　　　　　　　　　　　　*Amex/MC/V*
Midtown East　　　　　　　　　　　**(212) 317-0800**
601 Madison Avenue　　　　　　　　　btw 57/58th St
NYC 10022　　　　　　　　　　Mon-Sat 10-7, Sun 12-6

SoHo
410 West Broadway
NYC 10012

(646) 613-8099
at Spring
Mon-Sat 11-7, Sun 12-6

Encore

The idea of the consignment shop began with Encore when it opened in 1954 as a place for uptown ladies to unload last season's digs for cold hard cash. The shop is like taking a trip down memory lane, with all the purchases you never got around to—until now, that is. You'll find Donna Karan dresses, Jil Sander suits, Tod's bags, as well as items from luxe labels like Yohji Yamamoto, Prada, Chloé and Fendi—all deeply discounted from original prices. You, too, can get in on the action by selling your unwanted threads on Tuesdays through Saturdays from 10:30-5. *encoresale.com*

Moderate   *Amex/MC/V*

Upper East Side   **(212) 879-2850**
1132 Madison Avenue (2nd floor)   btw 84/85th St
NYC 10028   Mon-Fri 10:30-6:30 (Thurs 10:30-7:30)
           Sat 10:30-6, Sun 12-6 (closed Sundays June-August)

Enerla Lingerie

For more than 20 years this East Village shop has been keeping the girls happy with its sexy, romantic lingerie and great basics. The range runs from naughty to nice, and includes sleepwear, robes, foundations, bustiers, swimwear and hosiery from labels like Le Mystère, Claire Pettibone, Chiarugi, Orablu, Eberjey, Mary Green and the ubiquitous Cosabella. Fun accessories, too: don't miss Enerla's massage oils and marabou bedroom slippers.

Expensive   *Amex/MC/V*

East Village   **(212) 473-2454**
48½ East 7th Street   btw First/Second Ave
NYC 10003   Daily 12-8

Entre Nous

Just between us—or as the French say, entre nous—this shop is one of New York's best kept secrets. It's a sophisticated showcase of luxury European labels—Luciano Barbera's complete collection of pants, classic blazers, cashmeres and tailored shirts; sportswear by Agnona; evening dresses and gowns by Sylvia Heisel.

Expensive   *Amex/MC/V*

Upper East Side   **(212) 249-2225**
1124 Third Avenue   btw 65/66th St
NYC 10021   Mon-Fri 10-6, Sat 10-5

Enzo Angiolini

Enzo Angiolini is Nine West's better footwear division. Find up-to-the-minute styles that include basic comfort flats, tailored loafers, trendy sandals, platforms, boots and more. It's about fashion-forward shoes that look expensive but aren't.

Moderate   *Amex/MC/V*

Midtown East　　　　　　　　　**(212) 339-8921**
551 Madison Avenue　　　　　　　　　　at 55th St
NYC 10022　　Mon-Fri 9:30-7:30, Sat 10-6:30, Sun 12-5:30

Midtown West　　　　　　　　　**(212) 695-8903**
901 Sixth Avenue　　　at Manhattan Mall, btw 32/33rd St
NYC 10001　　　　　　　　　　Mon-Sat 10-8, Sun 11-6

Equinox

Forgot your gym bag at home again? With Equinox gym's 13 Manhattan locations, you have no excuse to skip your workout. This shop carries a colorful selection of sportswear including sweatpants, sports bras and spandex numbers from Champion, Fred Perry, Puma and Smith's Basic Tees. They also have the famous Adidas sports sandals, perfect for communal showering. Pick up a pair of Cosabella panties individually wrapped in a small packet in case you forgot those, too. The website lists info for all 13 locations. *equinoxfitness.com*

Affordable　　　　　　　　　　　　　*Amex/MC/V*

Midtown East　　　　　　　　　**(212) 953-2499**
420 Lexington Avenue　　　　　　　　at East 44th St
NYC 10070　　　　　　　　Mon-Thurs 8-9, Fri 8-8

Eredi Pisan

Made from the finest textiles and traditionally tailored, this Roman suitmaker's first US location has fared well with diplomats from the nearby UN and businessmen with international taste. Besides suits, they sell cashmere sweaters, brightly colored silk ties, and dress shirts for women.　　*eredipisan.it*

Expensive　　　　　　　　　　　　　*Amex/MC/V*

Midtown East　　　　　　　　　**(212) 418-9630**
520 Madison Avenue　　　　　　　　btw 53/54th St
NYC 10022　　　　Mon-Fri 10-7, Sat 11-6, Sun 12-6

★ Eres

With boutiques in Paris, Palm Beach and Manhattan, Eres' luxury lingerie draws a sleek-chic clientele (Vogue adores it) with its high-quality everyday basics and fabulous, perfect-fitting bra styles. Manufactured in trademark skin tones and featherweight fabrics (trying 'le soufflé' is a must), Eres' natural silhouettes can easily pass for custom lingerie, but at lower prices—panties are $65-$90 and bras $140-$190. Their swimwear is second to none: bikinis, thankfully, are sold as separates, with racy styles like deep V-necks and low-cut backs, and sexy, boy-leg shorts paired with string tops. Pareos and cover-up dresses are also on show, not to mention a seductive line of garter belts, bustiers, pantyhose and tights.　　　　　　　　　　　　*eresparis.com*

Moderate to expensive　　　　　　　　*Amex/MC/V*

Midtown East　　　　　　　　　**(212) 223-3550**
621 Madison Avenue　　　　　　　　btw 58/59th St
NYC 10022　　　　　　　　　　　Mon-Sat 10-6

SoHo   **(212) 431-7300**
98 Wooster Street   at Greene
NYC 10012   Mon-Sat 11-7, Sun 12-6

★ Erica Tanov

This large, clean space is the perfect backdrop for Erica Tanov's collection of sophisticated womenswear, bed linens, baby clothes, lingerie and accessories defined by elegant fabrics, classic styling and careful attention to detail. Her pieces are complemented by knitwear from John Smedley and Brooklyn Handknits, dresses by Megan Park and lingerie by La Cosa. Children can be turned out in Erica Tanov and I Golfini della Nonna's collection of cheerful printed rompers, bloomers and smocks.   *ericatanov.com*

Moderate to expensive   *Amex/MC/V*

Nolita   **(212) 334-8020**
204 Elizabeth Street   btw Prince/Spring
NYC 10012   Mon-Sat 11-7, Sun 12-6

Eric Shoes

Why ruin your Choos chasing the perfect shoes all over town? Eric Shoes supplies you with all the downtown soles you'll ever need uptown, with brands like Miu Miu, Vanessa Noel, Cynthia Rowley and Mark Swartz, as well as their own label. The store also carries a considerable number of bridal shoes. Prices range from $95-$325.

Moderate   *Amex/MC/V*

Upper East Side   **(212) 289-5762**
1222 Madison Avenue   at 88th St
NYC 10128   Mon-Fri 10-7, Sat 10-6, Sun 12-6
    (except in summer)

Upper East Side   **(212) 288-8250**
1333 Third Avenue   btw 76/77th St
NYC 10021   Mon-Fri 10-7:30 (Thurs 10-8)
    Sat 10-6:30, Sun 12-6

Ermenegildo Zegna

Zegna is, simply, a byword for luxury menswear. Their classic suits range from high-powered tailored styles to deconstructed modern versions at an average price of $1,840 (and much more for custom). Shirts, ties, sportswear, outerwear, shoes and accessories are also available. A first-ever women's line, Agnona, is now in the Zegna boutique. It features hand-finished tailored jackets and knitwear in fine Italian fabrics.   *zegna.com*

Luxury   *Amex/MC/V*

Fifth Avenue   **(212) 421-4488**
663 Fifth Avenue   btw 52/53rd St
NYC 10022   Mon-Sat 10-6 (Thurs 10-7), Sun 12-6

Escada

German fashion house Escada will color you happy. Opulent fabrics, vibrant prints and lots of embroidery are the trademarks of their three collections: Escada Couture, Escada Ready-to-Wear and Escada Sport. This is the place to find that lime-green skirt suit you've always dreamed of. Looks range from wool suits to glitzy sequined eveningwear. The boutique also offers the Badgley Mischka Bridal and Atelier collections, plus the usual head-turning accessories, handbags, scarves and shoes. *escada.com*

Expensive   *Amex/MC/V*

Fifth Avenue   **(212) 755-2200**
715 Fifth Avenue   at 56th St
NYC 10022   Mon-Sat 10-6 (Thurs 10-7), Sun 12-5

Eskandar
Half-British, half-Persian designer Eskandar's NYC installment of his London-based line of high-end hippie clothes is housed in a massive space with white brick walls, pillars, and pleasant track lighting. Affluent earth muffins will love the yoga-friendly ecru tunics and flowy pants in linen, cashmere and other natural fabrics. The accessories are equally crunchy: necklaces made of African beads and Brazilian seeds and bone bracelets. Decorate your boho pad with vintage furniture from around the world and earthy European housewares. He also has his own all-natural bath line using ingredients like black tea or ginger blossom. *eskandar.com*

Luxury   *Amex/MC/V*

SoHo   **(212) 533-4200**
33 East 10th Street   btw University/Broadway
NYC 10003   Mon-Sat 10:30-7

Esprit
Your favorite sweet 'n' sexy clothing line offers simple casuals with a nice fit, exquisite eveningwear, sportswear, sleepwear, outerwear, shoes, accessories, watches, glasses and great classics for home. They have a great selection of bikinis, too, so you can stock up and be ready for summer's rays. *esprit.com*

Moderate   *Amex/MC/V*

Flatiron   **(212) 651-2121**
110 Fifth Avenue   at 16th St
NYC 10011   Mon-Fri 10-9, Sat 10-8, Sun 10-7

Midtown West   **(212) 823-9922**
10 Columbus Circle   Time Warner Center
NYC 10019   Mon-Sat 10-9, Sun 11-7

Etro
A luxe Italian label that's perfect for seasoning your wardrobe with color, pattern and texture. Find four floors of ready-to-wear, home furnishings, shoes, accessories, luggage and fragrances, as well as a custom atelier for both men and women. Boldly patterned clothing is distinguished by expert craftsmanship for a look that is both classic in tailoring and rich in design. Stripes and paisleys adorn silks and cashmeres

that pair beautifully with sleek pants, jackets and suits. A great place for acquiring urbane uptown style. *etro.it*

Expensive   *Amex/MC/V*

Upper East Side   **(212) 317-9096**
720 Madison Avenue   btw 63/64th St
NYC 10021   Mon-Sat 10-6

Eugenia Kim

Walk into milliner Eugenia Kim's Rubik's Cube-colored shop to see firsthand her collectible, cool hats that are flaunted at awards shows everywhere by 'look at me!' celebrities like Jennifer Lopez and Nicole Kidman, not to mention the requisite socialites and downtown hipsters. Standouts include simple-chic leather caps, floppy hippy hats with gold chain bands, felt cloches, and fur numbers from rabbit trooper hats and berets to fox toques. Shoes and a couture service (for those who simply can't bear to have the same newsboy as the next celeb) complete the offerings. Prices run from $120 to $500, and you'd be well advised to make an appointment. *eugeniakim.com*

Expensive   *Amex/MC/V*

East Village   **(212) 673-9787**
203 East 4th Street   btw Avenue A/B
NYC 10009   Mon-Fri 9-7, Sat-Sun 12-7

Express

This division of the giant fashion conglomerate The Limited is great for younger shoppers who are making the transition from campus to workplace—and who aren't exactly loaded. Dresses, pants, skirts, T-shirts and quick-hit accessories all match the latest color forecasts and trends—from hippy to clubby to relaxed sweats. More than one glam actress-about-town swears by their thongs. In 2001 Express joined forces with its brother store Structure, so men's trendy casual clothes and accessories are now available alongside women's in Express stores. *877-657-2292 expressfashion.com*

Affordable   *Amex/MC/V*

Upper West Side (W)   **(212) 580-5833**
321 Columbus Avenue   at 75th St
NYC 10023   Mon-Fri 8:30-9, Sat 9-9, Sun 11-7

Midtown East   **(212) 421-7246**
722-728 Lexington Avenue   at 58th St
NYC 10022   Mon-Sat 8:30-9, Sun 11-7

Midtown East (W)   **(212) 644-4453**
477 Madison Avenue   at 51st St
NYC 10021   Mon-Sat 8:30-9, Sun 10-7

Midtown West (W)   **(212) 629-6838**
7 West 34th Street   btw Fifth/Sixth Ave
NYC 10001   Mon-Sat 8:30-9, Sun 11-7

Midtown West   **(212) 971-3280**
901 Sixth Avenue   at Manhattan Mall, btw 32/33rd St
NYC 10001   Mon-Sat 9-9, Sun 11-7

Flatiron (W)
130 Fifth Avenue
NYC 10011

(212) 633-9414
at 18th St
Mon-Sat 8:30-9, Sun 11-7

SoHo
584 Broadway
NYC 10012

(212) 625-0313
btw Houston/Prince
Mon-Sat 9:30-9, Sun 11-7

Lower Manhattan
89 South Street
NYC 10038

(212) 693-0096
at South Street Seaport
Mon-Sat 10-9, Sun 11-8

Eye Candy

Eye Candy is a shining jewel of a store, literally…the cute retro baubles in here are bright enough to cause cornea damage. It's also one of the city's top destinations for primo vintage and new accessories, including diamanté and beaded jewelry, hats, sunglasses, a great collection of shoes, and lots of bags (everything from Sixties Gucci to colorful Mexican straw). Owner Ron Caldwell can often be found trying on groovy shades and asking customers for their opinions. The wares aren't cheap, but they're distinctive enough to be worth it.

Moderate to expensive   *Amex/MC/V*

NoHo
329 Lafayette Street
NYC 10012

(212) 343-4275
btw Bleecker/Houston
Daily 12-8

Fabulous Fanny's

A hit with costume designers and vintage aficionados, Fabulous Fanny's antique glasses and 'optical oddities', as they call them, mix the quirky with the cool. Indeed, the carefully organized store lives up to its slogan—'If you have to wear them, make it fun.' Fabulous Fanny's is owned by a pair of serious collectors who outfit many Broadway productions and movies (note the frames in *The Royal Tenenbaums*, for example). They also offer a host of repair services for the old frames you already own. There's an equally great collection of men's and women's vintage clothes, as well as a line of handmade costume jewelry reconfigured from antique and vintage pieces. *fabulousfannys.com*

Expensive   *Amex/MC/V*

East Village
335 East 9th Street
NYC 10003

(212) 533-0637
btw First/Second Ave
Daily 12-8

Façonnable

The perfect shop for the well-dressed man has taken up residence in a 21,000-square-foot Rockefeller Center location. It's Façonnable heaven. No wardrobe is complete without a Façonnable tie or spread-collar shirt. Suits come in classic silhouettes, the sportswear is perfect for weekends and the outerwear is a must, including a wide selection of beautiful topcoats as well as the classic parka. It's a stylish French version of Ralph Lauren. Logophobes beware: the Façonnable insignia is everywhere you look. The store also has womenswear and lots of accessories.   *nordstrom.com/faconnable*

Expensive   *Amex/MC/V*

Fifth Avenue   **(212) 319-0111**
636 Fifth Avenue   at 51st St
NYC 10022   Mon-Sat 10-8, Sun 12-6

Fame

A pioneering retail effort in the garment district that has fashionistas housed in the glam magazine offices close by especially thankful. They pop into this big, airy space on their lunch breaks to rifle through a groovy sportswear collection including Sharagano, Allen B, Joe's Jeans, Jill Stuart Jeans and the edgy pieces from L.A. label Haley Bob. And where the fashionistas go for a style fix, the curious should definitely follow.   *fameny.com*

Moderate to expensive   *Amex/MC/V*

Midtown West   **(212) 730-4806**
512 Seventh Avenue   btw 37/38th St
NYC 10018   Mon-Fri 8:30-7:30, Sun 12-6

The Family Jewels

Have you been searching for a poodle skirt, vintage Pucci or a pair of rounded-toe pumps? This store has a wide range of quirky and fabulous finds for the serious collector. Women will love the Fifties flare dresses reminiscent of many a Doris Day flick, while fellas will enjoy combing through myriad Western shirts, corduroy jackets and striped pants. If you need a breather, take a seat on the couch and check out the record collection in the back. The perfect place to complete any look under the sun.   *familyjewelsnyc.com*

Moderate to expensive   *Amex/MC/V*

Chelsea   **(212) 633-6020**
130 West 23rd Street   btw Sixth/Seventh Ave
NYC 10011   Daily 11-7

Fendi

Fendi is the ideal stop for any Roman Goddess. The premier Italian fur and handbag dealer for four generations, Fendi is festooned with gilded objects, only some of which are for sale. The opulent furs in mink and sable practically cry out 'caress me!'—but be prepared to lay out up to $200,000 for the opportunity to do so. It's no wonder J.Lo commands the spotlight with her Fendi furs and glistening bags. This season, keep an eye out for the Vanity bag, a new baguette that follows in the tradition of Silvia Venturni Fendi's 1997 landmark design.   *fendi.com*

Luxury   *Amex/MC/V*

Midtown East   **(212) 767-0100**
677 Fifth Avenue   btw 53/54th St
NYC 10019   Mon-Fri 10-6:30, Sat 10-6, Sun 12-6

Upper East Side   **(212) 734-8910**
755 Madison Avenue   btw 65/66th St
NYC 10021   Mon-Sat 10-6 (Thurs 10-7)

Fila

Fila is pulling itself up by the shoestrings by opening a New York City flagship. Specializing in tennis and running sneakers, as well as tennis whites, the shop sells all sorts of workout gear for on and off the court. Filativa is the women's lifestyle line, featuring yoga clothes and stylized sneaks.   *fila.com*

Affordable   *Amex/MC/V*

Midtown East   **n/a at press time**
340 Madison Avenue   at 43rd St
NYC 10017   n/a at press time

Filene's Basement

One of the country's oldest and most famous discount stores, Filene's has provided higher-end goods at a fraction of the cost since 1908. If you're lucky, you can find a pair of coveted Seven jeans, or an entire outfit by Valentino, Donna Karan, Arnold Scassi or Liz Claiborne. As at all discounters, the selection is a little hit or miss, but the store also sells bath products, shoes, clothing, and has a small section for perfume.   *filenesbasement.com*

Affordable   *Amex/MC/V*

Chelsea   **(212) 620-3100**
620 Sixth Avenue   at 18th St
NYC 10011   Mon-Sat 9:30-9, Sun 11-7

Upper West Side   **(212) 873-8000**
2222 Broadway   at 79th St
NYC 10024   Mon-Sat 9:30-9, Sun 11-7

Find Outlet

Imagine the world's smallest sample sale that nevertheless stocks labels like Nili Lotan, Twinkle and Mint. This adorable, well-kept store doesn't have an enormous selection but they do carry Cosabella thongs at $12 a pop, which is significantly less than what you'll pay elsewhere. Everything is always 50-70% off retail, and customers can receive e-mails about weekly arrivals, so get added to their list, quick.   *findoutlet.com*

Affordable to moderate   *Amex/MC/V*

Chelsea   **(212) 243-3177**
361 West 17th Street   btw Eighth/Ninth Ave
NYC 10011   Thurs-Sun 12-7

Nolita   **(212) 226-5167**
229 Mott Street   btw Prince/Spring
NYC 10012   Daily 12-7

Fisch for the Hip

Anyone in search of a vintage Hermès handbag in perfect condition (and that would be, like, everyone) should hurry down to Fisch for the Hip, a luxe consignment shop. In addition to stocking three display cases with said posh handbags and Louis Vuitton luggage, owner Terin Fischer brings in the best of the best from labels like Gucci, Celine, Helmut

Lang, Prada and Dolce & Gabbana. The merchandise is in mint condition and half the price of retail. Also find shoes by Manolo Blahnik, Prada and Chanel. *fischforthehip.com*

Expensive   *Amex/MC/V*

Chelsea   **(212) 633-9053**
153 West 18th Street   btw Sixth/Seventh Ave
NYC 10011   Daily 12-7 (Sun 12-6)

Flight 001

This must be the coolest travel store in New York and maybe anywhere, for that matter. It's all very *Wallpaper**, with snappy travel gear in cool colors that takes its design straight from the mid-century style celebrated in that interior/travel magazine. From digital watches (which display multiple time zones) to guide books, passport holders, perfectly-proportioned nylon carry-ons, teddy bears that double as in-flight pillows, and de-stress kits, these products are perfect for passengers who insist on being prepared and pampered. The coolest thing? Gift-wrapping is sealed with a sticker that looks like a boarding pass. Book a trip to Flight 001 immediately. *flight001.com*

Moderate   *Amex/MC/V*

West Village   **(212) 691-1001**
96 Greenwich Avenue   btw West 12th St/Jane
NYC 10011   Mon-Fri 11-8:30, Sat 11-8, Sun 12-6

Flirt

Brooklyn loves its own, and Flirt shows its pride by showcasing the work of local designers. Tired of 'Brooklyn' and '718' shirts? With feminine and, you guessed it, flirty dresses just right for a stroll through Prospect Park or a night out on Smith Street, this store provides the perfect alternative to the standard-issue alterna-gear you see in most Brooklyn hoods. Every item in the store is one of a kind, custom is available, and you'll find some steals in Flirt's rummage bin. *flirtbrooklyn.com*

Affordable   *Amex/MC/V*

Cobble Hill   **(718) 858-7931**
252 Smith Street   btw Douglas/Degraw
Brooklyn 11231   Tues-Sat 12-8, Sun 12-6

Park Slope   **(718) 783-0364**
93 Fifth Avenue   btw Warren/Baltic
Brooklyn 11217   Tues-Sat 12-8, Sun 12-6

Flying A

Flying A differentiates itself from its peers by offering distinctive styles at affordable prices. The store provides cool sportswear from labels like Fred Perry, brashly colorful T-shirts from Custo Barcelona, girly shirts and skirts from Imperio, folksy tops from Ella Moss and easy-wearing accessories from Sequoia and Loop. They also sell a range of vintage clothes, and with a little digging you can find some choice items. *flyinga.net*

Affordable   *Amex/MC/V*

SoHo (212) 965-9090
169 Spring Street btw West Broadway/Thompson
NYC 10012 Mon-Thurs 11-7, Fri-Sat 11-8, Sun 12-7

FM Allen

FM Allen was, according to store lore, 'one of the best great white hunters and safari guides in Africa'. The goods and services bearing his name now tempt gridlocked New Yorkers seeking safari consultants and gear for trips to South Africa, Botswana, Zimbabwe, Kenya and Tanzania. FM Allen offers high quality leather and canvas bush luggage, along with intriguing antique campaign furniture like an elegant early-20th-century English iron-bound leather traveling trunk with leather loop handles. Allen's 'world's best' hot-weather performance clothing has outfitted the likes of Elle Macpherson, Liv Tyler and jungle-lover Tom Selleck. *fmallen.com*

Luxury *Amex/MC/V*

Upper East Side (212) 737-4374
962 Madison Avenue btw 75/76th St
NYC 10021 Mon-Sat 10-6

Fogal

You can never have enough saucy stockings—so head here for one of the best labels around (alongside Wolford). It's famous for its fabulous colors—at last count, over 80 tempting shades—from sophisticated to downright saucy. They have everything from sheer ($25) and opaque hose ($29.50) to patterned and textured styles like Flamenco, a fishnet, or Petit Points, a sheer style with dots. If you really want to indulge yourself, there are always Fogal's fabulous cashmere-silk tights, which will set you back a mere $295. But think of the joy they'll give you. Other items include luxurious bodysuits in cashmere/silk blends and lingerie. For men, socks and hosiery. Good personalized service. *fogal.com*

Expensive *Amex/MC/V*

Midtown East (212) 355-3254
510 Madison Avenue at 53rd St
NYC 10022 Mon-Sat 10-6:30

Foley + Corinna

With so many celebrity fans—Gwyneth, Cameron, Liv, Britney (to first-name but a few)—it's hard to believe that this amazing shop is still one of New York's best kept secrets. Co-owned by Dana Foley and Anna Corinna, the store sells Foley's original designs and Corinna's vintage finds. But you will have to look at labels to tell the difference—Foley's creations are so individual they could be vintage and Corinna's treasures are in such great condition they could be brand new. Find anything and everything from sexy chiffon tops to cowboy boots to stylish trench coats Audrey would have loved. There is really no reason to shop anywhere else. Hurry in, before the secret is out… *foleyandcorinna.com*

Moderate to expensive *Amex/MC/V*

Lower East Side
114 Stanton Street
NYC 10002

(212) 529-2338
btw Ludlow/Essex
Sun-Mon 12-7, Tues-Sat 1-8

Foley + Corinna Men 👤

Dana Foley and Anna Corinna know cool. The latest proof is presented by their new men's shop (around the corner from their original boutique), where vintage tees, leather jackets, hip scarves, hats, wallets and a small selection of home furnishings (old-school video games and classy bar sets) rule the roost. A whole hipster lifestyle awaits you—and all you have to do is visit one store. *foleyandcorinna.com*

Moderate to expensive   *Amex/MC/V*

Lower East Side
143 Ludlow Street
NYC 10002

(212) 529-5043
btw Stanton/Rivington
Mon-Fri 1-8, Sat-Sun 12-8

Foot Locker 👤👤

Foot Locker sells athletic wear and footwear for the entire family. There are workout clothes for fitness and basketball and shoes suitable for running, tennis, basketball or cross-training from such brands as Nike, Reebok, Adidas, Fila and New Balance.   *800-991-6681 footlocker.com*

Affordable to moderate   *Amex/MC/V*

Upper East Side
159 East 86th Street
NYC 10028

(212) 348-8652
btw Lexington/Third Ave
Mon-Sat 10-9, Sun 11-6

Upper East Side
1911-13 Third Avenue
NYC 10029

(212) 828-3871
at 106th St
Mon-Sat 10-8, Sun 11-6

Upper West Side
1530 Broadway
NYC 10036

(212) 869-4983
btw 44/45th St
Mon-Thurs 9-11, Fri-Sun 9-12

Harlem
268 West 125th Street
NYC 10027

(212) 316-1667
at Eighth Ave
Mon-Fri 9-9, Sat 10-9, Sun 11-6

Midtown East
150 East 42nd Street
NYC 10017

(212) 856-9411
btw Lexington/Third Ave
Mon-Sat 9-9, Sun 11-7

Midtown West
120 West 34th Street
NYC 10001

(212) 629-4419
btw Sixth/Seventh Ave
Mon-Sat 8-9, Sun 11-8

Midtown West
901 Sixth Ave
NYC 10001

(212) 268-7146
at Manhattan Mall, btw 32/33rd St
Mon-Sat 10-8, Sun 11-6

Midtown West
43 West 34th Street
NYC 10001

(212) 971-9449
btw Fifth/Sixth Ave
Mon-Fri 8-9, Sat 9-9, Sun 11-7

Midtown West
120 West 34th Street
NYC 10001

(212) 629-4419
btw Fifth/Sixth Ave
Mon-Sat 8-9, Sun 11-7

East Village
252 First Avenue
NYC 10009

(212) 254-9187
at 15th St
Mon-Sat 10-9, Sun 11-7

East Village
58 West 14th Street
NYC 10011

(212) 255-6481
at Sixth Ave
Mon-Sat 9-8, Sun 11-6

Lower East Side
94 Delancey Street
NYC 10002

(212) 533-8608
btw Ludlow/Orchard
Mon-Sat 10-8, Sun 11-6

NoHo
734 Broadway
NYC 10003

(212) 995-0381
at 8th St
Mon-Sat 9-9, Sun 11-7

SoHo
523 Broadway
NYC 10012

(212) 965-0493
btw Spring/Broome
Mon-Sat 10-9, Sun 11-7

Lower Manhattan
55 Fulton Street
NYC 10038

(212) 791-5530
at Gold
Mon-Fri 9-8, Sat 10-7, Sun 11-7

Lower Manhattan
89 South Street
NYC 10038

(212) 608-3640
at South Street Seaport
Mon-Sat 10-9, Sun 11-8

Forever 21

Chocolate gelato on your white top? Buy a tee for $5. Tragically under-embellished for an impromptu date? Add metal fringe earrings and a beaded satin sash belt to sparkle up your work clothes. For those in need of emergency clothing replacement, in financial straits, or craving just a dose of cheap thrills, Forever 21 serves as an even lower-budget H&M. Get formidable adaptations of runway trends for little more than a tenner. You won't be fooling anyone, but you can put that extra dough towards some real deal designer duds.

Affordable   *MC/V*

SoHo
40 East 14th Street
NYC 10003

(212) 228-0598
at Fifth Ave
Mon-Fri 9-9:30, Sat-Sun 10-9:30

Midtown West
50 West 34th Street
NYC 10001

(212) 564 2346
btw Fifth/Sixth Ave
Mon-Fri 9-9:30, Sat 10-9:30, Sun 11-8

Forman's

This is the place for sportswear, separates and outerwear at terrific discounted prices. Forman's also has extensive petite and plus-size departments, and the merchandise changes constantly. Labels include Jones New York, Evan Picone, Ralph Lauren, Kasper and Liz Claiborne. Prices drop even lower during end-of-season sales.

Affordable to moderate   *Amex/MC/V*

Fifth Avenue
560 Fifth Avenue
NYC 10017

(212) 719-1000
at 46th St
Mon-Thurs 8-8, Fri 8-5:30, Sun 10-6

Directory

Lower East Side
82 Orchard Street
NYC 10002

(212) 228-2500
btw Broome/Grand
Sun-Wed 9-6, Thurs 9-7, Fri 9-4

Forreal

While Forreal Basics targets twentysomethings and teens, Forreal appeals to women in search of dressier looks with a selection of slim-fitted pants, sexy knits, jackets, sweaters and T-shirts from such labels as Juicy Couture, Michael Stars and Petit Bateau. Free delivery in Manhattan.

Moderate   *Amex/MC/V*

Upper East Side
1335 Third Avenue
NYC 10021

(212) 734-2105
btw 76/77th St
Mon-Sat 11-7, Sun 12-6

Forreal Basics

Mothers bring their teenage daughters here for the hip assortment of jeans and casual basics, but get sucked in to the vortex and end up buying something for themselves as well. The denim selection includes Diesel, Miss Sixty, Mavi and Buffalo, and there is an abundance of fitted tees from labels like Michael Stars, Three Dots and Petit Bateau. Don't visit after school on a weekday, however, as you'll fear for you life when those teens and moms start fighting over Petit Bateau tanks, James Perse tees and AG jeans. Agoraphobes, take heart: Forreal offers free delivery in Manhattan.

Moderate   *Amex/MC/V*

Upper East Side
1375 Third Avenue
NYC 10021

(212) 396-0563
btw 78/79th St
Mon-Sat 11-7, Sun 12-6

Fortuna

The first shop to take Williamsburg shopping off the Bedford Avenue hipster highway was Fortuna. Starting as a choosy vintage shop, Fortuna moved towards local designers making everything from tote bags to stationery. The main draw are the Madame Fortuna necklaces, made of the owner's seemingly endless collection of darling charms and unique chains. She makes multistrand numbers, as well as charm necklaces themed after various goddesses. We found one based on the goddess of the sea that was like a treasure chest of nautical goodies: a seahorse, a shell with a pearl inside and a ceramic flower delicately dangling from a rusty chain.   *fortunasalon.com*

Affordable to moderate   *Amex/MC/V*

Williamsburg
370 Metropolitan Avenue
Brooklyn 11211

(718) 486-2682
at Havemeyer
Tues-Fri 2-9, Sat 1-9, Sun 12-9

Forward

As in 'fashion-forward'. A combination workshop, showroom and retail space for emerging NYC designers, Forward offers handcrafted ballet slippers by La Voleuse, fun tropical print bags and clutches from Alyssa Graves, 'preppy and trashy' jersey shirts by Dina Magnes, and rockin' tops by Phyl Casual Couture. This is the fifth group of young designers the space has sponsored since opening last spring—the inventory changes with each new group, so get what you can while you can. *forwardnyc.com*

Expensive *Amex/MC/V*

Nolita **(646) 264-3233**
72 Orchard Street btw Broome/Grand
NYC 10002 Daily 12-7

Fossil

'The American classic, original and genuine,' the nearly 50-year-old Fossil trumpets from the window of this huge colorful store, the first to sell clothing and accessories from the company best known for its funky watches. As far as Fossil gear is concerned, think Quiksilver with a Fifties retro edge. There is a huge range of activewear, including walls of Hawaiian shirts, cheeky tees for the chicks and a signature jeans collection. Great for gifts are, of course, the watches, each one coming in a Fifties tin that the customer chooses. *fossil.com*

Moderate *Amex/MC/V*

SoHo **(212) 274-9579**
541 Broadway btw Prince/Spring
NYC 10012 Mon-Fri 10-8, Sat-Sun 11-9

Flatiron **(212) 243-7296**
103 Fifth Avenue at 17th St
NYC 10003 Mon-Sat 10-8, Sun 11-7

Midtown East **(212) 997-3978**
530 Fifth Avenue btw 44/45th St
NYC 10036 Mon-Fri 9:30-8, Sat 10-8, Sun 11-7

Fragments

This jewelry supermarket is a hit with celebrities ranging from Sienna Miller to Axl Rose as well as common folk. The cheaper 'fashion jewelry' at the front of the store is a lot of silver and semi-precious stones; the glittery gold and diamonds are towards the back. There are over 50 designers represented and the array is impressive. Let's say you need a coral and turquoise bauble to go along with a particular sundress. Pop into Fragments and you'll undoubtedly find dangly spiderweb earrings or a multi-strand necklace that fits the bill and doesn't necessarily break the bank. *fragments.com*

Moderate to luxury *Amex/MC/V*

Soho **(212) 334-9588**
116 Prince Street at Greene
NYC 10012 Mon-Sat 11-7, Sun 12-6

Upper East Side **(212) 537-5000**
997 Madison Avenue btw 76/77th St
NYC 10021 Mon-Sat 10-6

Frank Shattuck

Don't let the frequently changing store locations keep you from a Frank Shattuck creation. Frank takes over where his mentor Henry Stewart, one of New York's most distinguished old-world tailors, left off. Each suit is handmade from start to finish, from construction and drafting to the final three-hour pressing process. The handiwork is well worth $5,000, plus the expense of the cloth—expect to wear it for a lifetime.

Luxury   *Amex/MC/V*

Midtown East   **(212) 636-9120**
510 Madison Avenue (suite 600)   at 53rd St
NYC 10022   (by appointment)

Frank Stella

Since opening the original Columbus Avenue store in 1976, Frank Stella has been selling updated, no-nonsense classics that range from professional business suits to casual sportswear. He offers many prominent menswear names: Ben Sherman, Ted Baker, Alexander Julian, Tommy Bahama, Nat Nast and more.

Affordable   *Amex/MC/V*

Upper West Side   **(212) 877-5566**
440 Columbus Avenue   at 81st St
NYC 10024   Mon-Fri 11-8, Sat-Sun 11-6

Upper East Side   **(212) 744-5662**
1326 Third Avenue   btw 75/76th St
NYC 10021   Mon-Fri 11-8, Sat 11-6, Sun 12-6

Midtown   **(212) 957-1600**
921 Seventh Avenue   at 58th St
NYC 10019   Mon-Fri 10-7, Sat 10-6, Sun 12-5

Fratelli Rossetti

Italian icon Fratelli Rossetti began making shoes for cyclists and skaters half a century ago and later introduced the first brown loafer to the fashion world. His design mission statement: quality, elegance, comfort and practicality. The classic loafers and lace-ups are best suited for daytime wear. Prices run from $185 to $575 (for leather boots). You'll also find colorful leather bags, belts, and motorcycle jackets.   *rossetti.it*

Moderate   *Amex/MC/V*

Midtown East   **(212) 888-5107**
625 Madison Avenue   at 58th St
NYC 10022   Mon-Fri 10-6:30 (Thurs 10-7)
                                           Sat 10-6, Sun 12-5

Fred Leighton

Fancy a palm-sized rose made entirely of diamonds? Well, if it's 'rare collectible jewels' that you're in the market for, Fred Leighton is the place to be. Huge brooches, jumbo chokers, engagement rings bigger than Jupiter's moons—they're all here in Leighton's impossibly stately showroom, where the pieces are impeccably crafted, ornate in design, and guaranteed to engender envy in all those who lay eyes on them. You'll find Leighton's creations on the pages of fashion magazines (he's a fave of top fashion stylists), on the red carpet at movie premieres and, if you've got the money to spend, on your very lucky fingers and wrists. Bodyguards not included. *fredleighton.com*

Luxury   *Amex/MC/V*

Upper East Side   **(212) 288-1872**
773 Madison Avenue   at 66th St
NYC 10021   Mon-Sat 11-5 (closed Saturday in summer)

French Connection

A British company known for sportswear geared toward an under-30 crowd—and for its controversial FCUK logo and advertising campaign. Think Banana Republic or Express with a British edge—suits, jeans, logo'd T-shirts, casualwear, plus accessories and a burgeoning beauty line. Colors lean toward the discreet rather than the adventurous. *frenchconnection.com*

Moderate   *Amex/MC/V*

Midtown West   **(212) 262-6623**
1270 Sixth Avenue   at 51st St
NYC 10020   Mon-Fri 9-9, Sat 10-8, Sun 10-7

NoHo   **(212) 473-4699**
700 Broadway   btw Astor Place/4th St
NYC 10003   Mon-Sat 10-9, Sun 11-8

SoHo   **(212) 219-1197**
435 West Broadway   at Prince
NYC 10012   Mon-Thurs 10-9, Fri-Sat 10-10, Sun 11-8

French Sole

If there is a season to shop at French Sole, it will be because flats are back. The store is the size of a rich woman's closet, crammed floor to ceiling with flats, indeed with any kind of flat you can imagine: silver, gold, croc-embossed, quilted, velvet, patent-leather, and ballet shoes. Many designs are the store's own brand, but you'll also see numbers from Delman, Bruno Magli, and Lauretta Reiss. Accessories include satin ribbon wristlets, beaded baguettes, plastic flip-flops and umbrellas. *frenchsoleshoes.com*

Moderate   *Amex/MC/V*

Upper East Side   **(212) 737-2859**
985 Lexington Avenue   btw 71/72nd St
NYC 10021   Mon-Fri 10-7, Sat 11-6, Sun 12-5

Frida's Closet

Frida Kahlo was a great artist and she doesn't make for a shabby fashion icon, either. Long Mexican peasant skirts, soft feminine blouses and tons of jewelry were signature looks that Kahlo used on canvas and in life, and designer/owner of Frida's Closet, Sandra Paez, is claiming the painter's fashion sensibility as her own. Paez's gorgeous dresses and blouses are custom-made right here in the boutique, and she imports jewelry and handbags direct from Mexico. *fridascloset.com*

Moderate *Amex/MC/V*

Carroll Gardens **(718) 855-0311**
296 Smith Street btw Union/Sackett
Brooklyn 11231 Wed-Fri 2-8, Sat 12-8, Sun 12-6

★ Frock

The divas who kept their clothes this pristine from the Studio 54 era mustn't have been partying too hard, but rather keeping their composure and maintaining these fab duds for future generations. Vintage designer resaler Frock carries Halston toga dresses, big Balenciaga sunglasses, Maud Frizoni sky-high heels, Carlos Falchi bags and Charles Jourdan wedges, to name only a few. Ossie Clark, designer of choice for British invasion bands and their groupies/wives, serves as a major inspiration for the store and one of the featured labels. The staff are friendly and helpful, and obviously in love with the over-the-top glamour of high-end disco fashion. *frocknyc.com*

Moderate to expensive *Amex/MC/V*

Lower East Side **(212) 594-5380**
148 Orchard Street btw Stanton/Rivington
NYC 10002 Daily 12-7

Furla

For less-is-more accessories head to Furla, where you will find the sleek lines, shiny materials, and classic sophistication that one expects from an Italian brand. Find chic, understated handbags designed with crisp, structured lines and minimal hardware. The stylish, minimalist look also characterizes Furla's belts, sunglasses, coin purses and wallets. Quality on par with Prada, but without the jet-setter price tags. *furla.com*

Expensive *Amex/MC/V*

Upper East Side **(212) 755-8986**
727 Madison Avenue btw 63/64th St
NYC 10021 Mon-Sat 10-7

Midtown East **(212) 980-3208**
598 Madison Avenue at 57th St
NYC 10022 Mon-Sat 10-7, Sun 12-6

The Fur Salon @ Saks Fifth Avenue

Just what you would expect from the iconic department store—high quality designer furs that will last a lifetime. The Fur Salon provides both classic and trendy styles in fur coats, jackets and accessories. Service is also top-notch. End of the season sales are the time to pick up next year's luxury sable or mink.

Expensive *Amex/MC/V*

Fifth Avenue **(212) 940-4465**
611 Fifth Avenue at 49th St
NYC 10022 Mon-Sat 10-7 (Thurs 10-8), Sun 12-6

Gabay's Outlet

An East Village treasure, Gabay's offers high-end designer fashions at steeply discounted prices. While shoes and handbags are the main attraction, fabulous designer duds can often be scored, too. A recent visit turned up Manolos, Christan Louboutin, Tod's and Chanel shoes with prices far below what these treads go for uptown. As with many outlets, the shopping here is often hit or miss, but those who love high style and good deal (and who doesn't?) check in regularly for new shipments. Excellent staff. *gabaysoutlet.com*

Moderate   *Amex/MC/V*

East Village   **(212) 254-3180**
225 First Avenue   btw 13/14th St
NYC 10003   Mon-Sat 10-7, Sun 11-7

Gallery of Wearable Art

Although the term 'wearable art' may conjure up nightmarish visions of hemp caftans, the one-of-a-kind goods at this boutique are of a decidedly more sumptuous nature. Popular with celebrities such as Whoopi Goldberg and Julie Taymore, the apparel features antique textiles and ornate embroidery. Housed in the ground floor of a brownstone, the gallery is the perfect atmosphere in which to purchase a richly decorated 'art coat', costume jewelry, bridalwear, daywear, furs and accessories. Rare vintage finds and a new Wearable Art fragrance complete the eclectic offerings. *galleryofwearableart.com*

Expensive   *Amex/MC/V*

Upper East Side   **(212) 570-2252**
34 East 67th Street   btw Madison/Park Ave
NYC 10021   Tues-Sat 10-6

Galo

A veteran of Madison Avenue, established shoe label Galo offers a collection of loafers, flats, pumps, sandals and boots. For children (toddler to size 5) there are styles from casual and contemporary basics to dress-up. Prices range from moderate to expensive. The handbag selection includes leather clutches, straw totes and shoulder bags. *galoshoes.com*

Moderate to expensive   *Amex/MC/V*

Upper East Side   **(212) 288-3448**
1296 Third Avenue   btw 74/75th St
NYC 10021   Mon-Sat 10-7, Sun 12:30-5:30

Upper East Side   **(212) 744-7936**
895 Madison Avenue   at 72nd St
NYC 10021   (opening hours as above)

Upper East Side   **(212) 832-3922**
825 Lexington Avenue   at 63rd St
NYC 10021   (opening hours as above,
but closed Sundays in summer)

Gamine

Walk into this jewel box of a boutique and be darn near over-stimulated by its ultra-feminine collection with an ethnic edge, from flirty daytime dresses by Nanette Lepore to informal eveningwear made up of sari prints, beading and embroidery. Fabulous handbags and colored stone jewelry complete the collection.

Moderate   *Amex/MC/V*

Upper East Side   **(212) 472-6918**
1322 Third Avenue   btw 75/76th St
NYC 10021   Mon-Sat 11-7

Gant

Gant has traditionally specialized in men's and boys' classic American sportswear. Three floors are devoted to casual basics in categories called 'Ivy University', 'Navigator', 'Key West', 'Park Avenue', 'Adventure' and 'Sport'. Check out jeans, khakis, fleece outfits, rugby shirts, sweatpants, knits, outerwear and polo shirts in all colors. Fleece outerwear is a best bet. A women's line was about to be introduced at the Fifth Avenue store as went to press and will feature rugby sweaters, twinsets, trench coats and flared skirts. *gant.com*

Moderate   *Amex/MC/V*

Fifth Avenue   **(212) 813-9170**
645 Fifth Avenue   btw 51/52nd St
NYC 10022   Mon-Sat 10-8, Sun 11-7

SoHo (M)   **(212) 431-9610**
77 Wooster Street   btw Spring/Broome
NYC 10012   Mon-Sat 11-7, Sun 12-6

☆ Gap

While its fashion can be hit-and-miss, Gap remains the source of super staples for everyone, not to mention the unbelievable sales. Fit yourself out with casual weekendwear like khakis for the professional, cool denims and cute T-shirts for twentysomethings and a complete uniform for teenagers. Choose from racks and racks of jeans—from dark to dirty denim—shirts, sweaters, T-shirts, belts and accessories (which have gotten better thanks to former Marc Jacobs designer Emma Hill), all at some of the best prices in town. The GapBody collection features intimates and sleepwear, as well as bath and body products. Try out Gap's new stress-free khakis for men and women which are wrinkle and spill resistant—apparently, they're able to repel coffee, food and oil stains.   *800-427-7895 gap.com*

Affordable   *Amex/MC/V*

Upper East Side   **(212) 794-5781**
1511 Third Avenue   at 85th St
NYC 10028   Mon-Sat 10-9, Sun 10-8

Upper East Side   **(212) 472-4555**
1131-1149 Third Avenue   at 66th St
NYC 10021   Mon-Sat 10-8, Sun 11-7

Upper West Side
2373 Broadway
NYC 10024

(212) 873-1244
at 86th St
Mon-Sat 10-9, Sun 11-8

Upper West Side
1988 Broadway
NYC 10023

(212) 721-5304
at 67th St
Mon-Sat 10-9, Sun 11-8

Midtown East
734 Lexington Avenue
NYC 10022

(212) 751-1543
btw 58/59th St
Mon-Fri 8-9, Sat 10-8, Sun 11-6

Midtown East
657 Third Avenue
NYC 10017

(212) 697-3590
at 42nd St
Mon-Fri 9-8, Sat 9-7, Sun 10-6

Midtown West
250 West 57th Street
NYC 10019

(212) 956-3142
btw Broadway/Eighth Ave
Mon-Thurs 8:30-8:30, Fri 8:30-9
Sat 10-8, Sun 11-7

Midtown West
1212 Sixth Avenue
NYC 10036

(212) 764-0285
btw 47/48th St
Mon-Fri 8-8, Sat 10-8, Sun 11-6

Midtown West
1466 Broadway
NYC 10036

(212) 382-4500
at 42nd St
Mon- Fri 9-9, Sat 10-9, Sun 11-8

Midtown West
60 West 34th Street
NYC 10001

(212) 760-1268
at Broadway
Mon-Fri 9-9:30, Sat 10-9:30, Sun 10-8

Fifth Avenue
680 Fifth Avenue
NYC 10019

(212) 977-7023
at 54th St
Mon-Fri 10-8, Sat 9-8, Sun 11-7

Flatiron
122 Fifth Avenue
NYC 10011

(917) 408-5580
at 18th St
Mon-Fri 10-9, Sat 10-8, Sun 11-7

Chelsea
277 West 23rd Street
NYC 10011

(646) 336-0802
btw Seventh/Eighth Ave
Mon-Sat 10-9, Sun 12-8

East Village (M)
750 Broadway
NYC 10003

(212) 674-1877
at 8th St
Mon-Sat 10-9, Sun 12-8

East Village (W)
1 Astor Place
NYC 10003

(212) 253-0145
at Broadway
Mon-Sat 10-9, Sun 12-8

Lower Manhattan
225 Liberty Street
NYC 10281

(212) 945-4090
btw West Side Highway/South End Ave
Mon-Fri 8:30-7:30, Sat 11-5, Sun 12-5

★ Gap Kids & Baby Gap 🚹

The ultimate destination for moderately priced—and just trendy enough—children's jeans, T-shirts, overalls, shirts, pants, sweatshirts, sweaters, dresses, pajamas, shoes and accessories. From outdoor play clothes to back-to-school basics, Gap has it all, with great prices and some of the cutest designs around. From newborn to 13 years. *gap.com*

Affordable   *Amex/MC/V*

Upper East Side (K/B)
1535 Third Avenue
NYC 10028
(212) 423-0033
at 87th St
Daily 10-8

Upper East Side (B)
1131-49 Third Avenue
NYC 10021
(212) 472-4555
at 66th St
Mon-Sat 10-8, Sun 11-7

Upper West Side (K)
2300 Broadway
NYC 10024
(212) 873-2044
at 83rd St
Mon-Sat 10-8, Sun 11-7

Upper West Side (K)
1988 Broadway
NYC 10023
(212) 721-5119
at 67th St
Mon-Sat 10-9, Sun 11-8

Midtown East (K)
545 Madison Avenue
NYC 10022
(212) 980-2570
at 55th St
Mon-Sat 10-7, Sun 11-6

Midtown East (K)
657 Third Avenue
NYC 10017
(212) 697-3590
at 42nd St
Mon-Fri 9-8, Sat 9-7, Sun 10-6

Midtown West (K)
250 West 57th Street
NYC 10019
(212) 315-2250
btw Broadway/Eighth Ave
Mon-Thurs 8:30-8:30, Fri 8:30-9
Sat 10-8, Sun 11-7

Midtown West (K/B)
1466 Broadway
NYC 10036
(212) 302-1266
at 42nd St
Mon-Wed, Sat 9-9, Thurs 9-9:30
Fri 9-10, Sun 11-8

Midtown West (K)
1212 Sixth Avenue
NYC 10036
(212) 764-0285
btw 47/48th St
Mon-Fri 8-8, Sat 10-8, Sun 11-6

Midtown West (K/B)
60 West 34th Street
NYC 10001
(212) 760-1268
at Broadway
Mon-Fri 9-9:30, Sat 10-9:30, Sun 10-8

Fifth Avenue (K/B)
680 Fifth Avenue
NYC 10019
(212) 977-7023
at 54th St
Mon-Fri 10-8, Sat 9-8, Sun 11-7

Flatiron (K/B)
122 Fifth Avenue
NYC 10011
(917) 408-5580
at 18th St
Mon-Fri 10-9, Sat 10-8, Sun 11-7

Lower Manhattan/Tribeca
11 Fulton Street
NYC 10038
(212) 374-1051
at John
Mon-Sat 10-9, Sun 11-8

Garde Robe 👤👤👤

No walk-in-closet, you say? Space is hard to come by in New York City, but Garde Robe is here to help. This sophisticated service dry-cleans and stores your precious, out-of-season or occasional pieces in their climate-controlled, high-security facility. Don't fear: this is no ordinary storage locker—Garde Robe will photograph each piece so you can view your closet online and request same-day delivery of any one piece, any given day. And if you're lucky enough to have plenty of hanger-space at home, Garde Robe can organize your closet, provide personal shopping and tailoring services, and even help you pack for a trip. Fees start at $225 a month. *garderobeonline.com*

Expensive   *Amex/MC/V*

P.O. Box 746   **(212) 255-3047**
NYC 10159   (by appointment)

Gas Bijoux

Fashion girls have been known to make cooing noises while looking in the window of this divine jewelry store in Nolita. The handmade pieces imported from the South of France perfectly mix bohemia with cool—check out how the sales staff dress down their intricately beaded earrings with slouchy jeans and T-shirts. Too-chic-to-speak, and not ridiculously expensive either.

Moderate to expensive   *Amex/MC/V*

Nolita   **(212) 334-7290**
238 Mott Street   btw Prince/Spring
NYC 10012   Mon-Fri 12-8, Sat-Sun 12-7

★ G.C.William

This hip boutique keeps Manhattan's younger uptown crowd outfitted with downtown styles from brands like Puma, Miss Sixty and Juicy Couture. Find great tees from James Perse and Petit Bateau, as well as the de rigueur denim selection. *gcwilliam.com*

Expensive   *Amex/MC/V*

Upper East Side   **(212) 396-3400**
1137 Madison Avenue   btw 84/85th St
NYC 10029   Daily 10-6:30 Sun 12-5
                                    (sometimes closed on Sundays)

Upper West Side   **(212) 873-2314**
111 West 72nd Street   btw Amsterdam/Columbus Ave
NYC 10023   Mon-Sat 11-7:30, Sun 12-6

★ Geminola

British interior designer Lorraine Kirke's new store will transport you back a century, and make you feel as if you're the belle of the ball. Kirke's West Village shop sells feminine pieces made from reworked and mostly re-dyed vintage and antique fabrics. The lace, silk, tulle and cotton numbers feature a distinctive mix of textures on dresses, tops, skirts, petticoats, slips, gowns, pjs, handbags, bedding, curtains and linens. The store spans a fascinating gap between 1800s decadence and 1950s prom dresses, all updated and redesigned for this year. Also find C+C Brazilian bathing suits, jewelry by Tom Binns and a host of other surprises too sweet to skip over. *geminola.com*

Expensive   *Amex/MC/V*

West Village   **(212) 675-1994**
41 Perry Street   btw Seventh Ave South/West 4th St
NYC 10014   Tues-Sun 12:30-7

Geox

Practicality is an important factor when buying shoes, but you don't want to be seen walking around in Nan's orthopedics, either. Take a break from the Louboutin skyscrapers and ease into a comfortable yet chic pair of Geox kicks, perfect for a long day schlepping the city from boutique to boutique. The smartly designed Italian dress shoes for men and women at this new Midtown flagship are available in various shades of leather with low-key accoutrements like metal buckles or stitching, but the real kicker is in the soles: tiny microholes (aka vents) draw moisture out and let fresh air in, while keeping undesirables out. Refreshing!   geox.com

Moderate   *Amex/MC/V*

Midtown East   **(212) 319-4243**
595 Madison Avenue   at 57th St
NYC 10022   Mon-Fri 10-6, Sat 10-7, Sun 11-5

Gerry's

An easy-access clothing store nestled amongst West Village restaurants, Gerry's carries a hip collection of menswear from American and European designers. A variety of Brit-style checked shirts by Ted Baker dominates the racks, and you'll also find sweatshirts by Blue Marlin, sweaters by Nicole Farhi, jeans by Armani, and other threads from Ben Sherman, Henry Cotton's and Masons. If you're feeling a little sportier, Gerry's is a fine spot for Fred Perry tracksuits as well as for cool sneakers by Puma and Camper.

Expensive   *Amex/MC/V*

West Village   **(212) 691-0636**
353 Bleecker Street   btw West 10th/Charles
NYC 10014   Mon-Sat 11-8, Sun 12-6

Chelsea   **(212) 243-9141**
110 Eighth Avenue   btw 15/16th St
NYC 10011   Mon-Fri 11-8, Sat 11-9, Sun 12-6

Chelsea (W)   **(212) 691-2188**
112 Eighth Avenue   btw 15/16th St
NYC 10011   (opening hours as above)

Gerry Cosby & Co

Pay attention, sports fans: Gerry Cosby & Co is a great source for pro-level equipment and clothing for your basketball, baseball, hockey and football needs. Shop here for NFL, NBA or NHL jerseys and souvenirs from your favorite team.   cosbysports.com

Affordable   *Amex/MC/V*

Midtown West   **(212) 563-6464**
3 Penn Plaza   at Madison Square Garden
NYC 10001   Mon-Fri 9:30-7:30, Sat 9:30-6, Sun 12-5

Ghost

Float away into British designer Tanya Sarne's world. Ghost is best known for soft, loosely feminine designs in vibrant colors and manufactured in special crinkly rayons which are wrinkle-resistant and machine washable. Sarne's line of light, interchangeable clothing, which some devotees buy in bulk every season, is based on essential pieces like slip dresses, camis and pants that are always available in several colors. Check out their denim line and a sale rack (usually to be found to the far right of the store), offering steals at 30-70% off.   *ghost.co.uk*

Expensive   *Amex/MC/V*

NoHo   **(646) 602-2891**
28 Bond Street   btw Bowery/Lafayette
NYC 10012   Mon-Sat 11-7, Sun 12-5

Ghurka

Classic, expertly handcrafted handbags, luggage and accessories perfect for your next African safari. Choose from the exotic Savanna collection of bags in alligator, zebra print or water buffalo—all trimmed with sterling silver accents—or the durable leather-trimmed twill travel bags and handbags (now in new colors such as yellow check and pastel canvas). Be sure to slip your feet into Ghurka's popular moccasins, too.   *800-587-1584 ghurka.com*

Luxury   *Amex/MC/V*

Midtown East   **(212) 826-8300**
683 Madison Avenue   btw 61/62nd St
NYC 10022   Mon-Sat 10-6 (Thurs 10-7), Sun 12-6

Gianfranco Ferré

Season after season this Italian designer celebrates his über-glam and high-drama muse: the supremely confident woman, unafraid to wear Ferré's deliberately sharp, structured pieces that walk a line between fashion and architecture (he was trained as the latter). Now she can luxuriate in his huge new flagship, where she'll find that Ferré is a master at mixing extremes: hard with soft, tough with feminine. He loves a corset, fur and angular jackets. He is best for sleek pinstriped suits, beautifully detailed blouses, leather pants, fur-lined biker jackets and coats. For evening, Ferré's siren (think Sharon Stone in full diva mode) will conquer all in a clingy cut-out jersey dress. For men, find a slick collection of suits and sportswear.   *gianfrancoferre.com*

Expensive   *Amex/MC/V*

Upper East Side   **(212) 717-5430**
870 Madison Avenue   btw 70/71st St
NYC 10021   Mon-Sat 10-6

Gi Gi

Gi Gi is Girlie with a capital G. Its collection of sportswear pieces has a deliberately feminine edge, just like the pistachio-colored walls. There are lots of pretty prints, ruffles and flowy chiffons in dresses, blouses and skirts from such labels as Rebecca Beeson, Blue Cult, Myth & Ritual and its own Gi Gi line.

Moderate   *Amex/MC/V*

Nolita   **(212) 274-1570**
217 Mulberry Street   btw Prince/Spring
NYC 10012   Mon-Sat 12-7, Sun 12-6

Upper East Side   **n/a at press time**
1173 Second Avenue   at 62nd St
NYC 10021   n/a at press time

Giordano's

Women with small feet, rejoice. This store is devoted exclusively to otherwise hard-to-find shoe sizes 4 to 5½. The great
selection includes Charles Jourdan, Via Spiga and Stuart
Weitzman.   *petiteshoes.com*

Expensive   *Amex/MC/V*

Upper East Side   **(212) 688-7195**
1150 Second Avenue   btw 60/61st St
NYC 10021   Mon-Fri 11-7, Sat 11-6

Giorgio Armani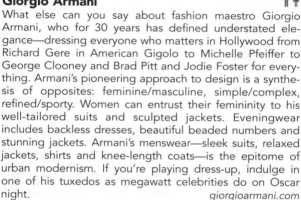

What else can you say about fashion maestro Giorgio
Armani, who for 30 years has defined understated elegance—dressing everyone who matters in Hollywood from
Richard Gere in American Gigolo to Michelle Pfeiffer to
George Clooney and Brad Pitt and Jodie Foster for everything. Armani's pioneering approach to design is a synthe-
sis of opposites: feminine/masculine, simple/complex,
refined/sporty. Women can entrust their femininity to his
well-tailored suits and sculpted jackets. Eveningwear
includes backless dresses, beautiful beaded numbers and
stunning jackets. Armani's menswear—sleek suits, relaxed
jackets, shirts and knee-length coats—is the epitome of
urban modernism. If you're playing dress-up, indulge in
one of his tuxedos as megawatt celebrities do on Oscar
night.   *giorgioarmani.com*

Luxury   *Amex/MC/V*

Upper East Side   **(212) 988-9191**
760 Madison Avenue   at 65th St
NYC 10021   Mon-Sat 10-6 (Thurs 10-7)

Giraudon

Giraudon's footwear is fit for everyone who digs a chunky
rubber sole. Two lines designed by Alain Guy Giraudon
feature everything from rugged boots and sporty loafers
with lug soles to leather-soled dressy lace-ups and slip-
ons.   *800-278-1552 giraudonnewyork.com*

Moderate   *MC/V*

Chelsea   **(212) 633-0999**
152 Eighth Avenue   btw 17/18th St
NYC 10011   Mon-Sat 11:30-11, Sun 1-7

Girl Cat

This fabulous new addition to Elizabeth Street displays
beautifully unique accessories. Handbags are a standout,

like the exquisitely patterned clutches and sturdy leather shoulder bags inspired by Art Nouveau. Girl Cat also carries great shoes, cufflinks for men, and a small but lovely selection of home accessories. Reasonable prices mean you have no excuse not to check out this lovely, whimsical store.

girlcatnyc.com

Moderate   Amex/MC/V

Nolita   **(212) 219-1647**
167 Elizabeth Street   btw Spring/Kenmare
NYC 10012   Sun-Mon 11:30-7:30

Girlprops.com

Although the SoHo branch of this shop is below street level, its zebra-striped interior sucks you right into this 'inexpensive—we never say cheap' (the motto on the canopy entrance) accessory shop. It's packed to the rafters with an over-stimulating collection of camouflage belts, rhinestone jewelry, leather spiked bracelets, handbags, tiaras, sunglasses, beaded bracelets, turquoise and coral jewelry, dangly earrings, purple wigs and boas, all fabulously affordable and disposable.

girlprops.com

Affordable   Amex/MC/V

East Village   **(212) 533-3159**
33 East 8th Street   btw Broadway/University Place
NYC 10003   Sun-Wed 12-7, Thurs 12-8, Fri-Sat 12-9

SoHo   **(212) 505-7615**
153 Prince Street   at West Broadway
NYC 10013   Mon-Wed 9-8, Thurs 9-9
                                              Fri-Sat 9-10, Sun 10-8

★ Girlshop

In a city as renowned for chic shops as New York, shopping online for indie label clothes has never been necessary. Why point and click when you can just hop in a taxi and see the goods up close? Besides, what looks fab on a website might fizzle on your person. Hence the opening of a real live shop housing girlshop.com's wares. Experience sensory overload with the metallic pineapple wallpaper, glittery rounded couches, giant mod chandelier and, most importantly, the tightly packed racks full of colorful, unique and fabulous clothes by small designers.

girlshop.com

Expensive   Amex/MC/V

West Village   **(212) 255-4985**
819 Washington Street   btw Ninth/Tenth Ave
NYC 10014   Mon-Wed 11-7, Thurs-Sat 11-8, Sun 12-7

Giuseppe Zanotti Design

Giuseppe Zanotti is best known for his jewel-encrusted, high-heeled sandals and stilettos that often feature embroidery, jewel and stone embellishments—which, all up, equals very sexy shoes. The look-at-me designs include closed-toe pumps with mother-of-pearl heels; thigh-high, super-pointy stiletto boots in embroidered leather with encrusted rubies; two- and three-band open-toed flirty sandals, and classic crocodile pumps and slingbacks. Prices run from $395 to $1,700.   *giuseppe-zanotti-design.com*

Expensive   *Amex/MC/V*

Upper East Side   **(212) 650-0455**
806 Madison Avenue   btw 67/68th St
NYC 10021   Mon-Sat 10-6

Givenchy   👫

The house that Audrey Hepburn built has undergone some renovations, but Givenchy still is the place to go for sleek sophistication. Designer Julien Macdonald has been providing ultra-feminine looks with plenty of wool, silk and tweed, all of which nestle comfortably alongside updated *Breakfast at Tiffany's* icons like the classic belted trench and a dizzying number of variations on the little black dress, many of which catch the light with embedded crystal.   *givenchy.com*

Luxury   *Amex/MC/V*

Upper East Side   **(212) 688-4338**
710 Madison Avenue   at 63rd St
NYC 10021   Mon-Sat 10-6 (Thurs 10-7)

The Good, The Bad and The Ugly   🚺

Skateboarding, music, graffiti, hip-hop, art, the can-can... all are inspirations for designer Judi Rosen, the owner of this fun, East Village-cute shop. As with all the cool stores these days, Rosen is inspired by vintage; her quirky pieces cover the gamut from bright-colored dresses (she's a brights fanatic) to sweatshirts to adjustable garters. Basically, the downtown girl can find it all here. That and the rainbow striped legwarmers she always wanted...   *goodbaduglynyc.com*

Moderate   *Amex/MC/V*

East Village   **(212) 473-3769**
437 East 9th Street   btw First/Avenue A
NYC 10002   Daily 12:30-8

The Gown Company   🚺

Any bride feeling a bit overwhelmed should make The Gown Company her first and only stop. Find dresses for the big day from a range of top American and European designers, such as Lazaro, Peter Langner and Amy Michelson. Or, save big in the store's sample room, which sells discontinued styles and excess inventory from those same top designers at prices from $1,000 to $1,800. Find accessories in the branch across the street, and ask about the Gown Co's couture services, custom tailoring, alterations and full-service specialty dry cleaning. The personal attention is consistent throughout the store, and the relaxed atmosphere will put anyone with wedding-day jitters at ease.   *thegowncompany.com*

Expensive   *Amex/MC/V*

East Village   **(212) 979-9000**
333 East 9th Street   btw First/Second Ave
NYC 10003   Tues-Fri 12-7, Sat 10-5 (by appointment only)

Granny-Made

This shop specializes in handknits from Italy, England and the U.S. Mothers can choose from a cute-as-pie collection of children's novelty sweaters featuring appliqués, sweet embroideries, animals and floral motifs. For adults, there is a similar selection by labels like Christine Foley, Roni Bis, Susan Bristol and English Weather. Accessories include socks, hats and scarves. *granny-made.com*

Moderate   *Amex/MC/V*

Upper West Side   **(212) 496-1222**
381 Amsterdam Avenue   btw 78/79th St
NYC 10024   Mon-Fri 10:30-7, Sat 10-6, Sun 12:30-5:30

☆ Great Feet

Fashionable feet for kids, featuring brands like Converse, Naturalino, Stride Rite, Elefanten and Primigi. From cute to hipster, any youngster would look ready for recess in these shoes. Sizes range from newborn to 6. *striderite.com*

Affordable   *Amex/MC/V*

Upper East Side   **(212) 249-0551**
1241 Lexington Avenue   at 84th St
NYC 10029   Mon-Sat 9:30-6 (Thurs-Fri 9:30-8), Sun 11-5

☆ Greenstones & Cie

Outfitting children from baby-bottle to lunchbox, Greenstones offer both posh and practical European and American children clothing for fashion-forward kids ages 0-12. In additional to their tiny threads from designers such as Petit Bateau, Jean Bourget and Deux par Deux, Greenstones also carry a large selection of shoes for every occasion, including the Upper West Side favorite and oh-so-cute Kidadorable rain galoshes, ribbons and hair ties galore.

Moderate to expensive   *Amex/MC/V*

Upper West Side   **(212) 580-4322**
442 Columbus Avenue   btw 81/82nd St
NYC 10024   Mon-Sat 10-7, Sun 12-6

Upper East Side   **(212) 427-1665**
1184 Madison Avenue   btw 86/87th St
NYC 10128   Mon-Sat 10-6:30

☆ Gucci

Shoppers should keep an eye on this space to see what happens now that Tom Ford, long-time creative director of Gucci, has left the company. Only Pilates-honed physiques need shop here among the store's hard angles, low benches, chrome and ubiquitous mirrors (all the better for checking yourself out). The looks may be severe, but the ambiance is top-notch, with private dressing-rooms and champagne service. For the logo hounds, please note that double G everything—fragrances, jewelry, bags—is available here. *gucci.com*

Luxury   *Amex/MC/V*

Upper East Side
840 Madison Avenue
NYC 10021

(212) 717-2619
btw 69/70th St
Mon-Sat 10-6 (Thurs 10-7), Sun 12-5

Midtown East
685 Fifth Avenue
NYC 10022

(212) 826-2600
at 54th St
Mon-Wed, Fri 10-6:30
Thurs, Sat 10-7, Sun 12-6

Guess?

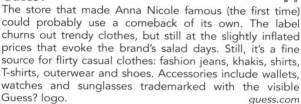

The store that made Anna Nicole famous (the first time) could probably use a comeback of its own. The label churns out trendy clothes, but still at the slightly inflated prices that evoke the brand's salad days. Still, it's a fine source for flirty casual clothes: fashion jeans, khakis, shirts, T-shirts, outerwear and shoes. Accessories include wallets, watches and sunglasses trademarked with the visible Guess? logo. *guess.com*

Moderate   *Amex/MC/V*

SoHo
537 Broadway
NYC 10012

(212) 226-9545
btw Prince/Spring
Mon-Sat 10-9, Sun 11-7

Lower Manhattan
23 Fulton Street
NYC 10038

(212) 385-0533
at South Street Seaport
Mon-Sat 10-9, Sun 11-8

Gureje

Hailing from Nigeria, Jimi Gureje brings a stylish African sensibility to Brooklyn. Combining African tailoring and tie-dye techniques, Gureje's long denim and cotton dresses for women are natural and cool, while his button-down shirt/jackets for men have a pleasant retro feel. Sexy, comfortable clothes with cross-cultural appeal. *gureje.com*

Moderate   *Amex/MC/V*

Clinton Hill
886 Pacific Street
Brooklyn 11238

(718) 857-2522
at Washington
Mon-Sat 12-10, Sun 2-8

★ Gymboree

Gymboree is so big that they offer their own Visa. The store sells great kids' clothes like raglan sweaters, French-inspired outfits complete with berets, and motocross tees for boys. Affordable prices in fun categories from newborn to 'kid boy/girl', plus gifts and toys. *gymboree.com*

Affordable   *Amex/MC/V*

Upper East Side
1120 Madison Avenue
NYC 10028

(212) 717-6702
btw 83/84th St
Mon-Sat 10-7, Sun 12-6

Upper East Side
1332 Third Avenue
NYC 10021

(212) 517-5548
at 76th St
Mon-Sat 10-7, Sun 11-6

Upper East Side
1049 Third Avenue
NYC 10021

(212) 688-4044
at 62nd St
Mon-Sat 10-7, Sun 11-6

Upper West Side (212) 595-9071
2271 Broadway btw 81/82nd St
NYC 10024 Mon-Fri 10-9, Sat 10-8, Sun 11-6

Upper West Side (212) 595-7662
2015 Broadway at 69th St
NYC 10023 Mon-Fri 10-8, Sat 10-7, Sun 11-6

Hable Construction

This jaunty textile company is named after Katharine and Susan Hable's grandfather's road construction business, and their accessories are indeed more than roadworthy. Aiming to 'fuse fabric, art and utility,' their collection of signature print fabrics is turned into colorful canvas totes and baskets, while exaggerated floral designs appear on indispensable shoe bags and cute shoe inserts—perfect for keeping your Jimmy Choos in tip-top order. A great gift stop. hableconstruction.com

Moderate Amex/MC/V

Nolita (212) 343-8504
230 Elizabeth Street btw Prince/Houston
NYC 10012 Mon-Sat 11-7, Sun 12-5

H&M (Hennes & Mauritz)

First things first: H&M rules. This rapidly expanding Swedish retailer continues to break land-speed records by turning out trendy clothes (with many items taking their cues straight from the catwalk) at incredibly low prices. Shop their 35,000-square-foot store on Fifth Avenue and be wowed by the constantly changing inventory. Coats and clubby tops and inexpensive swimwear are H&M's stock in trade. The clothes aren't built to last but at these prices, who cares? Look for kids' clothes (they'll grow out of them soon anyway), at the Broadway and Seventh Avenue locations. hm.com

Affordable Amex/MC/V

Fifth Avenue (212) 489-0390
640 Fifth Avenue at 51st St
NYC 10019 Mon-Fri 10-8, Sat 10-9, Sun 11-7

Midtown West (646) 473-1165
1328 Broadway at 34th St
NYC 10001 Mon-Sat 10-9, Sun 11-8

SoHo (212) 343-2722
588 Broadway btw Prince/Spring
NYC 10012 (opening hours as above)

SoHo (212) 965-8975
515 Broadway btw Spring/Broome
NYC 10015 Mon-Sat 10-9, Sun 11-8

Harlem (212) 665-8300
125 West 125th Street at Lenox Ave
NYC 10027 Mon-Sat 10-8, Sun 11-7

Midtown West (212) 643-6955
435 Seventh Avenue at 34th Street
NYC 10001 Mon-Sat 10-9, Sun 11-7

Midtown West   **(212) 935-6781**
731 Lexington Avenue   btw 58/59th St
NYC 10005   Mon-Sat 10-9, Sun 11-6

Handmade NYC

As the name would have it, you'll find handmade personal and home accessories in this lovely small store. Beautiful jewelry by Erica Rosenfeld, Maya Brenner and Kristina Larson (to name a few) mesmerizes, while home accessories like ceramics, hand-blown glass pieces, pillows, bowls and wall hangings will provoke many an 'ooh' and 'aah'. Special orders are available, although chances are you will find the perfect something for yourself the first time stick your head in for a visit.   *handmadenyc.com*

Expensive   *Amex/MC/V*

West Village   **(212) 924-6410**
150 West 10th Street   btw Greenwich/Seventh Ave
NYC 10014   Mon-Fri 11:30-7:30, Sat 11-7, Sun 11-6

Hans Koch

Koch's passion for color drives all his designs in handcrafted, one-of-a-kind belts, handbags and jewelry. Belts are simple and versatile. His handbag styles, all of which are classic looking, but different, range from soft to constructed.

Moderate   *Amex/MC/V*

SoHo   **(212) 226-5385**
174 Prince Street   btw Sullivan/Thompson
NYC 10012   Mon-Thurs 12-8, Fri-Sat 12-9, Sun 1-8

Harry Rothman's

A great source for well-priced men's clothing, Rothman's offers discounts of 20-40% on brand names like Canali, Joseph Abboud, Ben Sherman, Kenneth Cole and Hugo Boss. Also find a selection of shirts, ties, underwear, sport jackets, outerwear and shoes.   *rothmansny.com*

Affordable   *Amex/MC/V*

Flatiron   **(212) 777-7400**
200 Park Avenue South   at 17th St
NYC 10003   Mon-Fri 10-7 (Thurs 10-8)
                          Sat 9:30-6, Sun 12-6

Harry's Shoes

On any given weekend day Harry's is abuzz with families who appreciate the store's enormous selection and full-service approach to shoe buying. While this isn't the spot for sexy stilettos or thigh-high leather boots, Harry's has just about everything else, including sensible styles by Clarks, Rockport and Birkenstock, kids' shoes by Stride Rite and Elefanten, athletic shoes by Puma and New Balance and men's dress shoes by Johnston & Murphy, Cole Haan and Bruno Magli. Those in need of larger or wider sizes will be especially pleased with the extensive offerings available here.   *harrys-shoes.com*

Moderate   *Amex/MC/V*

Upper West Side
2299 Broadway
NYC 10024

(212) 874-2035
at 83rd St
Mon, Thurs 10-7:45
Tues, Wed, Fri, Sat 10-6:45, Sun 11-6

Harry Winston

Gems that shine like the sun are the norm at jeweler-to-the-stars (he's dressed more Oscar winners, presenters and nominees than anyone else, ever) Harry Winston's midtown emporium. Once you pass through the heavy iron gates at this Fifth Avenue palace, you'll swoon at the sight of flawlessly cut diamonds, rubies and emeralds adorning watches, rings, tiaras, cufflinks and earrings. If you think you have what it takes to accessorize like Faye Dunaway, Sting, Gwen Stefani, Helena Christensen or any other celeb worth their weight in bling, be prepared to pay half a million dollars for the privilege. Looking like red-carpet royalty comes at a price. *harrywinston.com*

Luxury   *Amex/MC/V*

Fifth Avenue
718 Fifth Avenue
NYC 10019

(212) 245-2000
at 56th St
Mon-Sat 10-6

The Hat Shop

Enter this tiny milliner and check out up to 30 talented New York designers, including Brenda Lynn, Eric Javits, Jennifer Hoertz and Jennifer Ouellette. Owner Linda Pagan will help you pick out the perfect hat to match your personal style or any occasion. This whimsical world of toppers guarantees the perfect fit for every head and is pretty much a one-stop shop for styles from classic straw boaters to wide-brimmed show stoppers.

Moderate   *Amex/MC/V*

SoHo
120 Thompson Street
NYC 10012

(212) 219-1445
btw Prince/Spring
Mon-Sat 12-7, Sun 1-6

Helen Mariën

The fabulously chic bags at Helen Mariën are displayed as works of art, and it suits them. Mariën creates each bag by hand, mostly from lamb, silk and Ultrasuede. Choose from a variety of materials, designs, and 'flavors'. Names for her signature handbags include the Sunday Brunch tote or the Saturday on the Subway shopper. Accessories include belts and jewelry, featuring neckline-adjustable necklaces with magnetic clasps. Modern designs, and superior quality and craftsmanship, set this label apart from the rest. *helenmarien.com*

Expensive   *Amex/MC/V*

Nolita
250 Mott Street
NYC 10012

(212) 680-1911
btw Prince/Houston
Mon-Sat 11:30-7, Sun 11:30-6

Helen Yarmak

After wrapping Russians in sable and chinchilla, this theoretical-mathematician-turned-fur-designer now dresses celebrity clients like Melanie Griffith and Goldie Hawn. Yarmak's trademarks are her unique pelt processing, which leaves her furs virtually weightless. Find over 350 different pieces, including a line of reversibles, a one-size-fits-all collection (there's regular sizing, too) and a kneaded line for the softest possible feel. You'll find mink, fox, rabbit, chinchilla and, of course, sable, at prices from $500 to $150,000. Accessories include knit fox scarves, decadent fur-lined handbags and jewelry. *helenyarmak.com*

Luxury   *Amex/MC/V*

Fifth Avenue   **(212) 245-0777**
730 Fifth Avenue (23th floor)   btw 56/57th St
NYC 10019   Mon-Fri 10-6 (by appointment)

Hello Sari

Find the best in authentic Indian and Pakistani apparel, from beaded and embroidered dresses to cashmere shawls, scarves, saris, mirrored sandals and embroidered shoes. Pair these items with what's already in your wardrobe for a fresh, idiosyncratic look that will have others asking 'Where did you find that?' Best bet: the shalwar kameez, a Pakistani open-front dress with side slits worn over pants (popularized by Jemima Khan).

Moderate   *Amex/MC/V*

Lower East Side   **(212) 274-0791**
261 Broome Street   btw Allen/Orchard
NYC 10002   Mon, Thurs 12-5, Tues-Wed, Fri-Sun 12-6

★ Henri Bendel

Bendel's—fashion lovers use only the last name when addressing their favorite store—is prized by clothes-horses far and wide for its coolly eclectic inventory. One of the store's best features is its manageable size, which makes it perfect for a quick pop in or lunchtime visit. The cosmetics and accessories areas are compact and easy to get around, while the clothing departments are small, well edited and well staffed. Bendel's is the perfect spot to check out new dresses from Collette Dinnigan, Matthew Williamson, Missoni, Michael Kors, and Heatherette; jeans by Chip & Pepper, Rock & Republic, Joe's Jeans, SaltWorks, Paper Denim Cloth, True Religion; and designs by Lilly Pulitzer, Pout, Sue Wong, Rick Owens, Matthew Williamson and Anna Molinari. The sweater collection is so phenomenal that it warranted additional floor space. Bendel's also boasts a Street of Shops, exclusive in-store boutiques for Femmegems Design-Your-Own Gemstone Jewelry, Diane von Furstenberg and Bendel's La Lingerie. Hats, hosiery, casualwear and outerwear departments round out the amazing assortment—while their activewear section (featuring Christy Turlington's Nuala label and Yohji Yamamoto's Y-3) is a hit with sporty types equally concerned with sweat and style. This is a department store that literally outfits you from head to toe—one of New York's top hair stylists, Frederic Fekkai will be opening on the fourth floor in February 2006.

800-423-6335 henribendel.com

Expensive   *Amex/MC/V*

Fifth Avenue   **(212) 247-1100**
712 Fifth Avenue   at 56th St
NYC 10019   Mon-Sat 10-8, Sun 12-7

☆ Henry Beguelin
This luxury leather shop on the ground floor of the Gansevoort Hotel sells bags, shoes and jackets that are equal parts boho and home-on-the-range. Many of the hand-tooled leather pieces made by artisans on the Italian islands of Elba and Vigevano are one-of-a kind. The look is luxurious but sturdy—with hearty leather bags and sandals that will stand up to miles and miles of trail. Silver and 18kt gold tusk jewelry by Caroline Roumeguere, a Parisian by way of Kenya, go perfectly with the ornate but rough-hewn vibe of the shop. The high-end Santa Fe interior has leather floors and a horsehair checkout counter.   *henrybeguelin.com*

Expensive   *Amex/MC/V*

Chelsea   **(212) 647-8415**
18 Ninth Avenue   at West 13th St
NYC 10014   Mon-Sat 11-7, Sun 12-5

Henry Lehr
Henry Lehr carries a fabulous denim selection by the hottest labels in town: Juicy, Paper Denim & Cloth, Seven, Rogan and AG Jeans. Prices run from $97 to $220. The newly consolidated store also features T-shirts in an abundance of styles by Jet, Three Dots, Michael Stars, Great Wall of China, Christina Lear and others. A good source for basic, casual tops at reasonable prices. Other items include jean jackets, button-down shirts and hip belts.

Moderate   *Amex/MC/V*

Nolita   **(212) 219-9801**
11 Prince Street   btw Elizabeth/Bowery
NYC 10012   Daily 11-7

Nolita   **(212) 274-9921**
9 Prince Street   btw Elizabeth/Bowery
NYC 10012   Daily 11-7

☆ Hermès
Hermès is the first and last word in classic French accessories. Socialites, celebrities, and the merely very wealthy all flock to this five-story, 20,000-square-foot space to indulge in the brand's distinctive neckties, scarves, handbags, fra-

grances and leather goods. The lengthy waiting list for the iconic Kelly and Birkin bags seen dangling from many much-photographed arms is a testament to their timeless appeal—they may run $5,000, but they'll last forever. The clothing selection, designed by the deliberately obscure Martin Margiela, provides a world of luxury basics from chic shirts to unbelievably luxe cashmere sweaters. You'll drop a bundle for a slice of this thoroughbred luxury, but it's still a better btw than a punt at the races. *hermes.com*

Luxury   *Amex/MC/V*

Upper East Side   **(212) 751-3181**
691 Madison Avenue   at 62nd St
NYC 10021   Mon-Sat 10-6 (Thurs 10-7)

☆ Hervé Léger

Shop in sexy style at Hervé Léger's New York store. On the first floor you'll find a lounge with a large sofa and chairs—the perfect spot for sipping champagne between fittings in the nicely appointed dressing-rooms. On the second level you'll goggle at Leger's famous 'bandage' wrap dresses, delicate silk jersey evening gowns and structured leather tops that leave little to the imagination. Working out certainly seems to be a requirement for wearing these clothes. Perfume, body lotions and shower gels are also available.

Expensive   *Amex/MC/V*

Upper East Side   **(212) 794-7124**
744 Madison Avenue   btw 64/65th St
NYC 10021   Mon-Sat 10-6, Sun 12-5

☆ H.Herzfeld

Step in here and you'll find everything the well-heeled gentleman needs: tailored suits, shirts, neckwear, sweaters, sportswear, underwear, pajamas and accessories—all with a classic English flair. Although the suits are generally custom-made, you will also find a good selection off-the-rack. Hickey Freeman suits are priced from $1,000 to $2,000; custom starts at $2,500. The knowledgeable and courteous staff may well suggest you top everything off with a stylish Borsalino hat . *herzfeldonline.com*

Luxury   *Amex/MC/V*

Midtown East   **(212) 753-6756**
118 East 57th Street   at Park Ave
NYC 10022   Mon-Sat 9-6

Hickey Freeman

One of America's premier names in men's tailored clothing, Hickey has been clothing the great and the good for decades—from Colin Powell to numerous chief executives—and is conveniently located next to another iconic American clothier, Brooks Brothers. Suits, jackets and pants in luxurious fabrics and classic cuts are the Hickey Freeman trademark. A perfect place for a father to take his son for his first suit—they can bond over the Bobby Jones golf line.   *hickeyfreeman.com*

Expensive   Amex/MC/V

Fifth Avenue   **(212) 586-6481**
666 Fifth Avenue   btw 52/53rd St
NYC 10103   Mon-Sat 10-7, Sun 12-6

Highway
Highway (formerly known as Hiponica) accessorizes downtown hipsters and uptown girls with everything from fabulous handbags for summer to scarves and hats in winter. Japanese owner Jem Filippi is a design perfectionist, and her handbag line is fun, functional and notable for its out-there colors. Most items are unisex, so guys can share in the fun. Simple shapes in calfskin and nylon show off playful details like vintage fabrics for linings and leather trimmings; other accessories include glass-trimmed leather wallets, amusing change purses and fancy fabric briefcases.

Moderate   Amex/MC/V

Nolita   **(212) 966-4388**
238 Mott Street   btw Prince/Spring
NYC 10012   Daily 12-7

Himalayan Crafts
A serene haven from neighborhood hustle and bustle, Himalayan Crafts has been purveying quality artisanal clothes and accessories since 1975. Dharma bums questing for authenticity will dig the trousers in rich silks and linen and the wine- and sea-colored wooly sweaters, slippers and coats. While they do stock plenty of low and moderately priced items, this is not the spot for cheap ethnic novelty—you'll have to go downtown for that.   *himalayancraft.com*

Moderate to expensive   Amex/MC/V

Upper West Side   **(212) 787-8500**
2007 Broadway   btw 68/69th St
NYC 10023   Mon-Fri 11-7:30, Sat 11-7, Sun 12-6

Hogan
Tired of trudging around town in your battered Nikes? Head for Hogan, sister store to Tod's and the purveyor of a new breed of walking/comfort shoes. Peruse their spacious, minimalist store for rubber soles designed in fabulous solid colors or canvas—these sneakers are hip and edgy. Also check out their sporty, structured handbags in richly hued leather, canvas and suede. All the bags have been designed to be paired with the shoes.   *hogancatalog.com*

Moderate   Amex/MC/V

SoHo   **(212) 343-7905**
134 Spring Street   btw Greene/Wooster
NYC 10012   Mon-Sat 11-7, Sun 12-6

Hollywould

This shop conjures up a Fifties Hollywood cabana, what with its periwinkle-striped fabric and wicker poolside stools festooned with striped cushions. A fab collection of coordinating shoes and handbags offers looks like chocolate-brown pumps with matching suede shopper's totes. Hollywould's cabana collection includes a number of wicker-handled bags and an array of gorgeous ballet slippers in every color from bronze to electric blue.   *ilovehollywould.com*

Expensive   *Amex/MC/V*

Nolita   **(212) 343-8344**
198 Elizabeth Street   btw Prince/Spring
NYC 10012   Mon-Sat 11:30-7, Sun 12-5

Hoofbeats

A delightful miniature store, Hoofbeats has developed a notable following of admirers among au courant shoppers looking for not-so-common gifts. You'll find personalized hooded bath towels ($29), robes ($53), bibs ($25) and mobiles ($45). Small and sweet.

Affordable   *Amex/MC/V*

Upper East Side   **(212) 517-2633**
232 East 78th Street   btw Second/Third Ave
NYC 10021   Mon-Fri 11-6 (Tues, Thurs 11-7)

★ Hootie Couture

Alison Houtte has been collecting vintage clothing for over 10 years, and her boutique is filled with yesteryear's inexpensive fashion finds. Look for classic floral print dresses or a vintage straw cowboy hat, or dare to wear a pastel lingerie gown as a sweet summer slip dress. New stock arrives daily, so there is always something to add to your wardrobe.   *hootiecouture.com*

Affordable   *MC/V*

Park Slope   **(718) 857-1977**
321 Flatbush Avenue   at 7th Ave
Brooklyn 11217   Daily 11-8

Hotel Venus

Owned by cult stylist Patricia Field (of *Sex and the City* fame), Hotel Venus takes the same deliberately faddish approach as her eponymous downtown store. Shop a daring and colorful selection of vinyl bustiers, sheer fitted shirts, leather halter tops, microminis, hard-core rubberized patent-leather outfits, funky clubwear, boas, lingerie, shoes and accessories from labels like Clutch, Lip Service and, of course, Patricia Field. It's worth a trip just to experience the amusing sales staff. For the camp and fearless.   *patriciafield.com*

Moderate   *Amex/MC/V*

SoHo (212) 966-4066
382 West Broadway btw Broome/Spring
NYC 10012 Daily 11-8

★ Hot Toddie †

Looking for something to make your child stand out during recess? This family-owned children's clothier in Fort Greene stocks hip lines for toddlers such as Petit Bateau, Armani, Diesel and Dolce & Gabbana. Custom-made Rolling Stones and Pink Floyd tour shirts sized for the littlest of rockers are available, too. Hot Toddie hopes that youngsters can learn that it's never too early to be too cool for school. *hottoddieonline.com*

Moderate *Amex/MC/V*

Fort Greene (718) 858-7292
741 Fulton Street btw South Portland/South Elliot
Brooklyn 11217 Tues-Sun 11-6

Housing Works ††††

Pretty is as pretty does and no one does it more beautifully than Housing Works. Uptowners who lunch and Midtown hipsters with heart purge their wardrobes by dropping off last year's treasures and this season's impulse buys at one of these chock-a-block thrift shops (store credit for taxi receipts up to $10). Proceeds go toward helping homeless New Yorkers living with HIV and Aids, and the take from all those serendipitous Marc Jacobs and Diane von Furstenberg finds totals over $3m annually. Go early in the day and, if you're lucky enough, you may even spy some do-good designer over-stock. *housingworks.org*

Affordable *Amex/MC/V*

Upper West Side (212) 579-7566
306 Columbus Avenue btw 74/75th St
NYC 10023 Mon-Fri 11-7, Sat 10-6, Sun 12-5

Upper East Side (212) 772-8461
202 East 77th Street btw Second/Third Ave
NYC 10021 Mon-Fri 11-7, Sun 12-5

Midtown East (212) 529-5955
157 East 23rd Street btw Lexington/Third Ave
NYC 10010 Mon-Sat 10-6, Sun 12-5

Chelsea (212) 366-0820
143 West 17th Street btw Sixth/Seventh Ave
NYC 10011 (opening hours as above)

Hugo Boss ††

Having already conquered Europe, this German label landed in New York with a massive four-floor, naturally lit store featuring clean, modern classics for him and her. Such a wealth of floorspace means plenty of room for menswear, accessories, bridge label Hugo and the fitted line Red Label. The Boss man will find a full selection of tailored suits, jackets, pants, shirts, classic trenches, ties, shoes and grooming products. He can also dress down in Boss Sport or play the game in Boss Golf. Boss woman will find a variety of looks, from ultra-tailored blazers and coats to shiny glam evening-wear and vintage-inspired prints. *hugoboss.com*

Expensive *Amex/MC/V*

Fifth Avenue **(212) 485-1800**
717 Fifth Avenue at 56th St
NYC 10022 Mon-Fri 10-7 (Thurs 10-8)
Sat 10-6, Sun 12-6

Hugo Hugo Boss

Young style-conscious men and women shop Boss's bridge line for unusual and unconventional clothes that won't stretch the wallet. The clothes range from trendy suits and separates in quality fabrics to bubble skirts…think of the hipsters bouncing around in the fragrance ads and you've pretty much got it. *hugoboss.com*

Expensive *Amex/MC/V*

SoHo **(212) 965-1300**
132 Greene Street btw Houston/Prince
NYC 10012 Mon-Sat 11-7, Sun 12-6

Huminska

A milliner who is tired of making hats, Miss Huminska designs dresses, tops and skirts—all with unique designs and described by her as classics with a twist. This allows her to pursue her love affair with fabrics, but among the accessories you'll still find hats (old habits are hard to break) and a sprinkling of bags. *huminska.com*

Expensive *Amex/MC/V*

East Village **(212) 677-3458**
315 East 9th Street btw First/Second Ave
NYC 10003 Mon-Fri 1-8, Sat 12-8, Sun 12:30-6:30

Hunting World

Going on a safari? Then your first stop should be Hunting World. Outfit yourself in the latest safari jackets, pants, vests, silk scarves, hats and shoes. Don't forget to check out their signature travel bags, which range from carryall shoulder bags to canvas duffles. What better way to carry your new gear while stalking big game? *huntingworld.com*

Moderate *Amex/MC/V*

SoHo **(212) 431-0086**
118 Greene Street btw Prince/Spring
NYC 10022 Mon-Sat 11-7, Sun 12-6

Ibiza/Ibiza Kidz

Part hippy-chic boutique for adults filled with long flowing dresses in fun prints and accessories incorporating turquoise and leather; part children's boutique, largely filled with European designers. Be sure to check out the tiny little boots and hats.

Moderate   *Amex/MC/V*
West Village   **(212) 533-4614**
46 University Place   btw 9/10th St
NYC 10003   Mon-Sat 11-8, Sun 12:30-6:30

ICB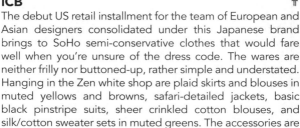

The debut US retail installment for the team of European and Asian designers consolidated under this Japanese brand brings to SoHo semi-conservative clothes that would fare well when you're unsure of the dress code. The wares are neither frilly nor buttoned-up, rather simple and understated. Hanging in the Zen white shop are plaid skirts and blouses in muted yellows and browns, safari-detailed jackets, basic black pinstripe suits, sheer crinkled cotton blouses, and silk/cotton sweater sets in muted greens. The accessories are similarly demure: nothing too clunky or blingy.

Expensive   *Amex/MC/V*
SoHo   **(212) 274-1255**
159 Mercer Street   btw West Houston/Prince
NYC 10012   Mon-Sat 11-7, Sun 12-6

If

A SoHo purveyor of avant-garde clothing and accessories, with ready-to-wear from such inspired designers as Comme des Garçons, Ivan Grundahl, Marc Le Bihan, Martin Margiela, Junya Watanabe, Dries Van Noten and Veronique Branquinho. The sales staff are notoriously unfriendly yet knowledgeable, but the truly fashionable consumer neither needs nor wants help in choosing outfits here. Shoes, hats, handbags and accessories are also available.

Expensive   *Amex/MC/V*
SoHo   **(212) 334-4964**
94 Grand Street   btw Mercer/Greene
NYC 10013   Mon-Sat 11-7, Sun 12-6:30

i heart

This high-ceilinged warehouse space, embellished with a purposefully cheesy neon sign and nu-wave soundtrack, sells cutesy Japanese-inspired duds with just a touch of early-Nineties Eurotrash that is oddly appealing. Puffy pastel running shorts and silk-screened Ivana Helsinki hoodies are the perfect cure for Juicy Couture overload. Chic teens will love the skater tees, Sonia Rykiel minidresses and Spring & Clifton minisweaters emblazoned with hearts. If the imaginative Ziggy Stardust-inspired tops by United Bamboo on the regular racks aren't funky enough, check the rejects on the sale rack: too weird for words.   *iheartnyc.com*

Moderate   *Amex/MC/V*
Nolita   **(212) 219-9265**
262 Mott Street   btw Prince/Houston
NYC 10012   Mon-Sat 12-8, Sun 12-7

Il Bisonte

Come here for durable, handcrafted leather goods embossed with a bison logo and perfect for weekends. The leather may be undyed, vegetable-dyed (which makes things look richer as they age) or colored (black, tan, green, red, brown), and it may have brass and nickel hardware—these are the defining elements of Il Bisonte designs. Choose from a plethora of styles, colors and textures. The store stocks a complete line of handbags, small leather goods, briefcases, agendas and luggage. *ilbisonte.com*

Moderate   *Amex/MC/V*

SoHo   **(212) 966-8773**
120 Sullivan Street   btw Prince/Spring
NYC 10012   Sun-Mon 12-6, Tues-Sat 12-6:30

★ Ina

Ina's mission: 'To select only what's in fashion from those who are in fashion, for those who want to be in fashion.' This is a truly amazing consignment shop where the fashion cognoscenti part with their designer clothes—including Prada, Gucci, James Perse, Louis Vuitton, Marc Jacobs—and the rest of the fashion cognoscenti scoop them up. Handbags, scarves and shoes by Blahnik, Gucci, Chanel and Hermès round out the brilliantly edited assortment. Ina's secret recipe: her wares are in pristine condition and her prices can't be beat. But as with any consignment store, it takes some digging—or repeated visits—to find the true gems. *inanyc.com*

Moderate to expensive   *Amex/MC/V*

SoHo   **(212) 941-4757**
101 Thompson Street   btw Prince/Spring
NYC 10012   Sun-Thurs 12-7, Fri-Sat 12-8

Nolita   **(212) 334-9048**
21 Prince Street   btw Mott/Elizabeth
NYC 10012   (opening hours as above)

Nolita (M)   **(212) 334-2210**
262 Mott Street   btw Houston/Prince
NYC 10012   (opening hours as above)

Upper East Side   **(212) 249-0014**
208 East 73rd Street   btw Second/Third Ave
NYC 10021   Mon-Sat 12-7, Sun 12-6

Infinity

Maybe they call it Infinity because the piles of T-shirts, pants, skirts and other clothing for tween girls seem like they go on forever. Looks run from bathing suits to strapless dance dresses. You'll also find silly string, temporary hair color, a girl's 'first glitter roll-on deodorant', camp keepsake boxes and soaps in watermelon, peach or lime. Any brand of the moment can be found at Infinity, including Juicy Couture, Miss Sixty and Triple 5 Soul. Prices range from $30-$150. *infinitynyc.com*

Affordable   *Amex/MC/V*

Upper East Side   **(212) 517-4232**
1116 Madison Avenue   at 83rd St
NYC 10028   Mon-Sat 10-6

In God We Trust

Like a little country store picked up by a twister and
dropped haphazardly in hipster Williamsburg, this woodsy
log cabin of a boutique carries local designers' offbeat casualwear. Men's two-piece suits by Yoko Devereux are fashioned entirely of sweatshirt material, while women's designer Judi Rosen makes Jetson's-style space girl dresses in
heavy cotton knit. The aesthetic is part campfire Americana
(earth tones, puff sleeves, plaids and patchwork) part
Japanese surrealist (asymmetrical hemlines and oddly cut
dresses). House label bracelets and necklaces dangle rusty
charms like anchors and hearts. To give your folksy guy a
touch of suave, check out the charm jewelry line's counterpart cufflinks.   *ingodwetrustnyc.com*

Moderate   *Amex/MC/V*
Williamsburg   **(718) 388-2012**
135 Wythe Avenue   btw North 7th/North 8th St
Brooklyn 11211   Tues-Sun 1-8

Institut

Institut's party-like atmosphere, colorful interior and selection of trendy European and American designers draw
young New Yorkers to its urban street fashions. The clothes
are organized by color and arranged against the store's glittering pink walls. Find an assortment of body-hugging
pants, leathers, jackets, slinky knits, fitted tops, skirts and
accessories that include fun jewelry. Remember that this is
hip fashion, not high fashion (although it's priced more
toward the latter).

Expensive   *Amex/MC/Visa*
SoHo   **(212) 431-5521**
97 Spring Street   btw Mercer/Broadway
NYC 10012   Daily 11-8

★ Intermix

Ask any dedicated Madison Avenue shopper what her
favorite store is, and chances are good that she'll say
Intermix. Their bright window displays are like a cosmic
force pulling you into the store. Intermix buyers do a brilliant
job of bringing you the hottest designers every season, such
as Blumarine and C & C California. The accessories include
goodies from Marc by Marc Jacobs, Michael Kors and Stella
McCartney heels. Everything is conveniently organized by
color, so there is no time wasted if you need a pink dress,
right now. Prices range from $45 Minnetonka moccasins to
$2,500 Chloé dresses.   *intermixonline.com*

Expensive   *Amex/MC/V*
Upper East Side   **(212) 249-7858**
1003 Madison Avenue   btw 77/78th St
NYC 10021   Mon-Sat 10-7, Sun 12-6

Upper West Side
210 Columbus Avenue
NYC 10023

(212) 769-9116
at 69th St
Mon-Sat 11-8, Sun 12-6

Flatiron
125 Fifth Avenue
NYC 10003

(212) 533-9720
btw 19/20th St
Mon-Sat 11-8 (Thurs, Fri 11-8:30), Sun 12-7

West Village
365 Bleecker Street
NYC 10014

(212) 929-7180
at Charles
Mon-Sat 11-7:30 (Fri 11-8:30), Sun 12-6:30

SoHo
98 Prince Street
NYC 10012

n/a at press time
at Mercer
n/a at press time

Iramo 👨👩

Here's an innovative concept in retailing: when you want to open another hip-hop shoe store in the same neighborhood with exactly the same merchandise but want to stay original, simply spell the name of your first store backwards and, voilà, you've created a totally 'new' store. If this makes no sense to you, go to Omari and read all about Iramo. That, and check out the street-cool shoes.

Moderate

Amex/MC/V

SoHo
89 Spring Street
NYC 10012

(212) 334-9159
btw Mercer/West Broadway
Daily 11-7:30 (Sun 11-7:30)

Isa 👨👩

Hands-down, this is one of Brooklyn's brightest shopping highlights. This raw, minimalist store highlights underground labels like Rogan, Noah and Blessed. Politically minded silk-screened tees, Martin Margiela frocks and the latest Nike Trainers all share shelf space in a celebration of street-savvy, hi-lo fashion.

Moderate

Amex/MC/V

Williamsburg
88 North 6th Street
Brooklyn 11211

(718) 387-3363
at Wythe
Mon-Fri 1-9, Sat 12-10, Sun 1-7

Issey Miyake 👨👩

Mr Miyake's work is more museum-quality than trendy. A landmark cast-iron building (designed by Frank Gehry, no less), an interior of undulating titanium forms that curve throughout, and the sheer strength of Miyake's aesthetic make for a unique shopping experience. The Japanese designer has shown nearly 100 collections and won almost every fashion award in existence. Long admired for his inno-vation, Miyake has boiled and melded both natural fibers and synthetic to create groundbreaking fabrics. He has long experimented with pleated fabrics of all kinds…wrinkles have never looked so good. Many of the looks are reveal-ingly sheer and require serious underpinnings. Fabulous bags and accessories in interesting colors and patterns

143

include heavy cotton beach bags with brilliant color stitching and mirroring. *isseymiyake.com*

Expensive   *Amex/MC/V*

Tribeca   **(212) 226-0100**
119 Hudson Street   at North Moore
NYC 10013   Mon-Sat 11-7, Sun 12-6

Upper East Side   **(212) 439-7822**
992 Madison Avenue   at 77th St
NYC 10021   Mon-Fri 10-6, Sat 11-6
                              Sun 12-5 (except in July and August)

It's a Mod, Mod World

Feeling down on a rainy Sunday? We dare you to hang onto a bad mood after coming out of this accessories and gifts paradise loaded with completely unnecessary kitsch must-haves. Highlights include a full range of plastic jewelry, including those wafer-thin stackable colored bracelets. Also look for leopard-print light-switch plates, tons of T-shirts and lamps made of plastic dolls and toasters. *modworldnyc.com*

Affordable   *Amex/MC/V*

East Village   **(212) 460-8004**
85 First Avenue   btw 5/6th St
NYC 10003   Mon-Thurs 12-10, Fri-Sat 12-11, Sun 12-8

★ Jacadi

Since the Seventies, Jacadi has been educating children with tasteful, refined clothes. Items are neatly displayed according to size, color and style and include back-to-school basics, casual play clothes, shoes and accessories; looks range from adorable smocked dresses to embroidered and appliquéd overalls. Jacadi has a great sweater and blouse selection, as well as a layette department that sells everything from bumpers to towels. Newborn to age 12. Great sales, too. *jacadiusa.com*

Moderate   *Amex/MC/V*

Upper East Side   **(212) 369-1616**
1296 Madison Avenue   at 92nd St
NYC 10128   Mon-Sat 10-6 (Thurs 10-7), Sun 12-5

Upper East Side   **(212) 535-3200**
787 Madison Avenue   at 67th St
NYC 10021   (opening hours as above)

Upper East Side   **(212) 717-9292**
1260 Third Avenue   at 72nd St
NYC 10021   (opening hours as above)

Upper West Side   **(212) 246-2753**
1841 Broadway   at 60th St
NYC 10023   (opening hours as above)

Jack Gomme

C'est tout génial at this bright and modern Parisian accessory boutique in very eurocentric Nolita. Boasting a selection of colorful leather and polyester goods with the perfect mix of unmistakably French charm and wit, Jack Gomme sells basic bags that still pack a punch with unexpected details like colorful contrasting handles and graphic prints featuring caricatures of the company's designers Paul Droulers and Sophie Renier. Don't forget to check out the small selection of distinctly French clothing, complete with a navy and white striped boat shirt a la Pablo Picasso. *jackgomme.com*

Moderate   *Amex/MC/V*

Nolita   **(212) 925-6414**
252 Elizabeth Street   btw Houston/Prince
NYC 10012   Mon-Sat 11-7, Sun 12-6

Jack Rogers

Former Chanel mannequin turned designer custom-makes stiff, structured tops and ball gowns with puff sleeves and exaggerated details like big bows or roses that are perfect for mothers of the bride or groom, or for the Kentucky Derby. Satin-faced organza and other fabrics in solid, bold colors fill a basket of swatches; there's bound to be a perfect match for the bridesmaids' dresses. The space itself is cramped, and lined with glamorous black and white photographs of Jackie and her rich and famous friends.   *jackierogers.com*

Luxury   *Amex/MC/V*

Upper East Side   **(212) 535-0140**
1034½ Lexington Avenue   at 74th St
NYC 10021   Mon-Sat 10-6

Jack Silver Formal Wear

The formalwear 'choice of the stars', Jack Silver has dressed the best in television soap operas, films and major network television shows. Rent or buy, this is the place to find what you need for that black-tie event or gala evening. Labels include Oscar de la Renta, Pierre Cardin, After Six and, of course, Ralph Lauren. Black-tie accessories like shirts, bow ties, cummerbunds, suspenders and shoes are available as well. While you'll find that rentals are in stock, if you plan to purchase you must place your order in advance.   *jacksilverformalwear.com*

Expensive   *Amex/MC/V*

Midtown West   **(212) 582-0202**
1780 Broadway (suite 303)   btw 57/58th St
NYC 10019   Mon-Fri 9-6, Sat 10-3

Jack Spade

Since 1993 female fashionistas have bought handbags from accessories diva Kate Spade. Good news, gentlemen, it's your turn. Husband Andy Spade has created a collection of snappy, efficient travel bags, day bags, informal briefcases, totes, messenger bags, computer bags, bankers' envelopes and wallets. They fall under the semi-eponymous Jack Spade label and in fabrications like canvas, nylon, worsted wools and water-repellent, waxed cotton canvas. Lots of extra amenities like pockets for cellphones and pens. Bags start at $150.   *jackspade.com*

Moderate   *Amex/MC/V*
SoHo   **(212) 625-1820**
56 Greene Street   btw Spring/Broome
NYC 10012   Mon-Sat 11-7, Sun 12-6

Jaime Mascaro   👤

Jaime Mascaro took over the entire boutique when Kerquelen closed, with impressive results. To cater to SoHo foot traffic Mascaro changes merchandise at least monthly, so there's always a fresh selection of slingbacks, wooden-heeled sandals and satin round-toe flats. *jaimemascaro.com*

Moderate to expensive   *Amex/MC/V*
SoHo   **(212) 965-8910**
430 West Broadway   btw Prince/Spring
NYC 10012   Mon-Thurs 11-7, Fri-Sun 11-8

★ James Perse   👫

For those of us tired of American Apparel's tawdry ads, there's a new Los Angeles luxury cotton loungewear store in town. 'T-shirt king' James Perse makes the best tees and casual separates of ridiculously soft cotton jersey. Never underestimate the power of a T-shirt: a perfectly cut, expertly worn tee can be the sexiest addition to your wardrobe since the little black dress. James Perse's first NYC shop sells his expanded line of outerwear, including dresses, jackets, pants and so forth, made of washed fabrics. *jamesperse.com*

Moderate   *Amex/MC/V*
Chelsea   **(212) 620-9991**
411 Bleecker Street   at West 11th St
NYC 10014   Mon-Fri 11-7, Sat 11-8, Sun 12-5

★ Jamin Puech   👤

A sophisticated bohemian handbag shop catering to sophisticated bohemian handbag addicts. Intricate beading, exotic feathers and soft, slouchy shapes give these handbags vintage appeal. Find leather and straw bags, delicate knits, organza floral bags and peacock-trimmed and beaded purses. Each handbag is beautifully made and detailed to perfection.   *jaminpuech.com*

Expensive   *Amex/MC/V*
Nolita   **(212) 431-5200**
247 Elizabeth Street   btw Houston/Prince
NYC 10012   Mon-Sat 12-8, Sun 12-6

★ Jane   👤

This petite boutique has been dressing stylish East Side ladies in sophisticated European separates for the past 17 years. Designs range from casual to evening, with an emphasis on luxurious fabrics and chic styling. Poule Vasseur, Blumarine, Philosophy di Alberta Ferretti, Orla Kiely and Les Copains are just a few labels from the eclectic collection. Super-friendly staff will assist you in searching through the overstuffed racks.

Expensive   *Amex/MC/V*

Upper East Side　　　　　**(212) 772-7710**
1025 Lexington Avenue　　　btw 73/74th St
NYC 10021　　　Mon-Sat 10-6 (closed Saturdays in summer)

Jared M

Jared Margolis recently launched Jared M, a high-end, made-to-measure menswear line for Big & Tall clientele. The shop's one-on-one image consultation is a definite plus, and hoops stars like Allan Houston and Kurt Thomas of the NY Knicks are already noted as fans. Livin' large, indeed.　　　　　　　　　　　　　　　*jaredm.com*

Expensive　　　　　　　　　　　　*Amex/MC/V*

Midtown West　　　　　　**(212) 868-1400**
252 West 37th Street (suite 1201)　btw Seventh/Eighth Ave
NYC 10001　　　　　　　　Mon-Fri 9:30-5:30
　　　　　　　(appointments highly recommended)

Jay Kos

Shopping at Jay Kos is like shopping at your own personal club. An intimate atmosphere of beautifully displayed merchandise makes you want to buy it all—classic Italian suits (ready-made or custom), tweed shooting jackets, all-weather coats (including Macintosh jackets and Austrian loden coats), silk-lined cashmere sweaters from Scotland, handmade shirts from one of the oldest workshops in Italy, and English corduroys. In addition, find furnishings and accessories that include fabulous English cufflinks, Swaine Adeney & Brigg umbrellas and hats from Borsalino and James Lock & Co. Kos's appeal is based on traditional styling, luxury fabrics and pure elegance. Expensive—but worth it.　　Mothers can also enjoy having their son on the best-dressed list by stopping at the adjoining Lexington Avenue Jay Kos boys store (ages 3-14).

Luxury　　　　　　　　　　　　*Amex/MC/V*

Upper East Side　　　　　**(212) 327-2382**
986 Lexington Avenue　　　　btw 71/72nd St
NYC 10021　　　　　Mon-Thurs 10-7, Fri-Sat 10-6

Midtown East　　　　　　**(212) 319-2770**
475 Park Avenue　　　　　　btw 57/58th St
NYC 10022　　　　　Mon-Thurs 10-7, Fri-Sat 10-6

★ J.Crew

The preppies over at J. Crew have really livened things up. Where standby sweaters and chinos used to be their specialty, they now offer more creative and colorful pieces with daring embellishments: glittering beaded sweaters, novelty puffy skirts, Egyptian cotton printed cardigans, or belts made of men's ties, for example. The clothes are younger and flirtier with more retro influence than the staid classic looks of the past. Still on offer are simple shift dresses in linen, cotton or wool and classic button-down shirts. J.Crew also sell their own line of dress-up and bridalwear.　　　　　*800-562-0258　jcrew.com*

Affordable　　　　　　　　　　　*Amex/MC/V*

Fifth Avenue
30 Rockefeller Center
NYC 10022

(212) 765-4227
at 50th St
Mon-Sat 10-8, Sun 11-7

Flatiron
91 Fifth Avenue
NYC 10003

(212) 255-4848
btw 16/17th St
(opening hours as above)

SoHo
99 Prince Street
NYC 10012

(212) 966-2739
at Mercer
(opening hours as above)

Lower Manhattan
203 Front Street
NYC 10038

(212) 385-3500
at South Street Seaport
Mon-Sat 10-9, Sun 11-8

Midtown East
347 Madison Avenue
NYC 10017

(212) 949-0570
at 45th St
Mon-Fri 10-7 (Thurs 10-8)
Sat 10-6, Sun 12-6

Midtown West
10 Columbus Circle
NYC 10019

(212) 823-9302
Time Warner Center
Mon-Sat 10-9, Sun 11-7

Jean Paul Gaultier 👤👤

For serious fashion that's a whole lot of fun, take a gander around Jean Paul Gaultier's flagship store. The iconoclastic French designer has for years managed to marry chic and camp like no other: where else could you find his typically ethnic-printed layered pieces alongside snowglobes filled with JPG fragrance, or his striped sailors' T-shirts next to camouflage gym boots? Also, in this surprisingly minimalist store, you will find sunglasses, boxer shorts and cheeky ties emblazoned with the designer's name. Buy up big and make like Cate Blanchett and Nicole Kidman, famous fans of Gaultier's divine couture. *jeanpaulgaultier.com*

Luxury *Amex/MC/V*

Upper East Side
759 Madison Avenue
NYC 10021

(212) 249-0235
btw 65/66th St
Mon-Sat 10-6

The Jean Shop 👤👤

Jeans in every color, wash, and distress imaginable are strewn atop each other in this rough wooden shop with a definite country-western vibe. The California-based line also makes jean and leather jackets, rawhide belts with metal buckles, soft hooded sweatshirts and tees in no-nonsense colors. Look for the light-up pig, and mosey on in for everything you need to be a Chelsea cowboy.

Expensive *Amex/MC/V*

Chelsea
435 West 14th Street
NYC 10014

(212) 366-JEAN
btw Ninth/Tenth Ave
Mon-Sat 11-7, Sun 12-5

★ Jeffrey

The Chelsea is now fashion central thanks largely to the pioneering efforts of Jeffrey Kalinsky, the impresario of this 18,000-square-foot multi-designer emporium. Kalinsky's unique ability to cull the highlights from each designer's collection sets this mini department store apart from the competition. He has chosen the best pieces from luxe labels like Jil Sander, Helmut Lang, Narciso Rodriguez, Dior, as well as Hedi Slimane's Dior Homme line that women covet as much as men. The best thing about Jeffrey is his fabulous—and dangerously expensive—shoe selection: Gucci, Christian Louboutin, Robert Clergerie, Yves Saint Laurent, Manolo Blahnik and Prada…order a pair of shoes over the phone and have them delivered the same day. The store also has the chicest home furnishings, including objets d'art that also serve as tables. Wonderful.

Luxury	*Amex/MC/V*
Chelsea	**(212) 206-1272**
449 West 14th Street	btw 9/10th St
NYC 10014	Mon-Fri 10:30-8
	Sat 10:30-7, Sun 12:30-6

Jenne Maag

Texan-born designer Jenne Maag has been making her signature fitted stretch pants for the past 15 years, way before they were the thing. Her boutique carries her line, which comes in matching groups (depending on the season: pants, jackets, halter tops and shirtdresses). Manufactured in her trademark Tarallo fabric, a polyester/Lycra blend similar to what Prada uses, Maag's designs feature classic cuts and form-fitted shapes and always have a bit of stretch. 'I try to make clothes that fit any shape, from skinny minis to fuller figures, and that make women feel and look great,' she says, which must be why women flock here for her expert tailoring. Sizes run P, S, M and L. Expect to spend between $100 and $400. *jennemaag.com*

Moderate	*Amex/MC/V*
Nolita	**(212) 625-1700**
29 Spring Street	at Mott
NYC 10012	Mon-Sat 11-7, Sun 12-6

Jill Anderson

The North Dakota-born designer is a whiz at turning out comfortable clothes with offbeat detail. Design is a kind of yoga, says Anderson, 'where the space of calm contentment feeds my imagination'. Clean lines and unusual up-to-the-minute fabrics give a modern sensibility to her feminine dresses, including her signature widow dress (loose-fitting, long-sleeved and below-the-knee), skirts, jackets, easy-wearing lace tops and coats. Bonus: free alterations and great sales. *jillanderson.com*

Expensive	*Amex/MC/V*

East Village   **(212) 253-1747**
331 East 9th Street   btw First/Second Ave
NYC 10003   Daily 12-8

Jill Stuart

Jill Stuart gets what New York women want to wear: a combination of tasteful and approachable clothes with a deft mix of femininity and urban edge (her perfect-fit jeans are a must). Delicate fabrics and beautiful patterns permeate her collection of dresses, skirts, jackets, cashmeres and tops. Not to be missed is Stuart's basement vintage boutique, a decadent setting housing armoires stuffed with floral print dresses and dramatic, bias-cut evening gowns.   *jillstuart.com*

Expensive   *Amex/MC/V*

SoHo   **(212) 343-2300**
100 Greene Street   btw Prince/Spring
NYC 10012   Mon-Sat 11-7, Sun 12-6

Jil Sander

Jil Sander's myriad devotees are unconsolable (or pretend to be) now that she appears to have left the brand for good, but majority owner Prada have appointed Raf Simons as the new designer and express great confidence in him and the brand's future. We have to reserve judgement, since his first collections will not be until early 2006, but the black and white store is a fine space in which to show off that perfect skirt or structured shirt. Before Sander's departure her clothes evoked a simpler, quiet luxury amidst the neighborhood's loud logo madness.   *jilsander.com*

Expensive   *Amex/MC/V*

Midtown East   **(212) 838-6100**
11 East 57th Street   btw Fifth/Madison Ave
NYC 10022   Mon-Sat 10-6 (Thurs 10-7)

★ Jimmy Choo

When Madonna searched for the perfect shoes for her wedding and when George W. Bush's daughters Barbara and Jenna twinkle-toed their way to the inaugural ball, which brand did they choo-se? Jimmy Choo, whose shoes have graced the feet of London and New York It-girls (not to mention a movie star or two) for the past 10 years. A rival to Manolo Blahnik, Choo causes women to throw logic to the wind and pay up to $1,200 for Tamara Mellon's creations. Narrow toes, high heels and serious femininity define the collection of delicate pumps, slingbacks, demure gingham kitten heels, reptile-skin boots, fanciful stilettos (adorned with fur or seashells), slinky sandals with crystal embroidered straps and towering gold ankle-wrap stilettos.   *jimmychoo.com*

Luxury   *Amex/MC/V*

Fifth Avenue   **(212) 593-0800**
645 Fifth Avenue   at 51st St
NYC 10022   Mon-Sat 10-6 (Thurs 10-7), Sun 12-5

Upper East Side
716 Madison Avenue
NYC 10021

(212) 759-7078
at 63rd St
Mon-Sat 10-6, Sun 12-5

Jim Smiley Vintage

'Through the clothing I learn all about history,' says vintage guru Jim Smiley. A second-floor eyrie of exquisite frocks and accessories spanning the Victorian era through the Sixties (many of which are unworn and sporting their original tags), this a shop dedicated to the finest garments of the past. Smiley, who moved his shop from New Orleans to New York two years ago, boasts a client list that includes the Museum of Fine Arts in Boston, movie production houses and A-list actresses who stop by for extraordinary pieces by Dior, Adrian, Trigères and McCardell. While you have to ask to touch some of the rarer dresses, feel free to caress less expensive items like breezy sundresses and embroidered kimonos. *jimsmileyvintageclothing.com*

Expensive *Amex/MC/V*

Chelsea
128 West 23rd Street
NYC 10011

(212) 741-1195
btw Sixth/Seventh Ave
Mon-Sat 11-7, Sun 12:30-5

Jivamukti Yoga

The longtime haven of downtown model types seeking inner peace, or at least a body like student Christy Turlington's. The boutique carries an ever-widening selection of yoga pants and tops adorned with Hindu deities, instructional videos, incense sticks and beauty products, including the center's own line of vegan, cruelty-free bath and body treats. Om shanti. *jivamuktiyoga.com*

Moderate *Amex/MC/V*

East Village
404 Lafayette Street
(3rd floor)
NYC 10003

(212) 353-0214
btw Astor Place/East 4th St
Mon-Fri 11:30-7
Sat-Sun 9:30-6

J.Lindeberg

The uncommon combination of fashion and golf is what makes Swedish designer Lindeberg tick and his passions coalesce into a contemporary sportswear collection showcased here. This 2,200-square-foot two-level space, equipped with marigold Formica fixtures, houses fashion-forward men's clothing from leathers and three-piece pin-striped suits to staples like black and khaki pants and button-down shirts. Lindeberg's ultra-hip On Course golf collection is appropriate either on and off the links. Women's fashions are sexy and form-fitted, while golf attire for the fellows is preppy chic. *jlindeberg.com*

Expensive *Amex/MC/V*

SoHo
126 Spring Street
NYC 10012

(212) 625-9403
at Greene
Mon-Sat 11-7, Sun 12-6

J.McLaughlin   👨👩

For over 25 years J.McLaughlin has been putting its mark on classic American sportswear. Men and women shop here for a casual, comfortable wardrobe that's appropriate for a relaxed work atmosphere or weekend living. The clothes combine tradition and preppy cool in khakis, corduroys, polo shirts, cable sweaters, button-down shirts and quilted jackets. Accessories include silk headbands and knots, Lucite cufflinks, grosgrain ribbon belts, and handbags.   *jmclaughlin.com*

Moderate to expensive   *Amex/MC/V*

Upper East Side   **(212) 369-4830**
1311 Madison Avenue   btw 92/93rd St
NYC 10128   Mon, Fri 10-6, Tues-Thurs 10-7
                                          Sat 11-6, Sun 12-6

⭐ J.Mendel   👩

PETA activists beware: Fur is in 365 days a year here. This gorgeous fur salon offers the finest ready-to-wear furs and accessories available in mink, chinchilla, sable, fisher and fox, as well as cashmere overcoats and leather handbags. Regular clients include Jennifer Lopez and many Upper East Side It-girls, most of whom are on a first-name basis with the pleasant, accommodating sales staff.   *jmendel.com*

Luxury   *Amex/MC/V*

Upper East Side   **(212) 832-5830**
723 Madison Avenue   btw 63/64th St
NYC 10021   Mon-Sat 10-6

J.M.Weston   👨👩

The handmade shoes offered at this French footwear retailer are classically stylish, and their handstitching ensures they'll last a lifetime. For a slice of this luxury, you'll have to pay anywhere from $400 to $5,000. The company also offers a collection of shoes designed by fashion footwear darling Michel Perry. More good news—you can return your worn shoes and, for a nominal fee, have them resoled and rebuilt. This bright, airy store also sells women's loafers and lace-up golf shoes. Warm sales staff, too.   *jmweston.com*

Expensive   *Amex/MC/V*

Upper East Side   **(212) 535-2100**
812 Madison Avenue   at 68th St
NYC 10021   Mon-Fri 9:30-6, Sat 10-6

John Anthony   👩

Ooh very expensive, but so worth it. John Anthony is the affluent lady's stop for the grandest custom-made attire. High couture and gorgeous gowns can accompany you home—if you have at least $10,000 to spend.

Luxury   *Amex/MC/V*

Midtown West   **(212) 245-6069**
130 West 57th Street (suite 11b)   btw Sixth/Seventh Ave
NYC 10019   (by appointment only)

John Fluevog Shoes

Fluevog's shoes may be the wildest footgear in Gotham. With their 6-inch platform heels, they 'will keep you above the urban trash,' says Fluevog (like Patrick Cox, another Canadian shoe maestro). Serious club-hoppers and teen types will find everything from platforms to pedal-pushers, from hand-carved wooden clogs for women to pastel-colored motorcycle boots for men (or women, why not?). Favorites of hip-hoppers Black Eyed Peas, the shoes in general are well made, but you might need both youth and guts to strut the streets in these chunky numbers.   fluevog.com

Moderate   *Amex/MC/V*

Nolita   **(212) 431-4484**
250 Mulberry Street   at Prince
NYC 10012   Mon-Fri 11-7, Sat 11-8, Sun 12-6

John Lobb

Since 1850 John Lobb's handmade shoes have been caressing the feet of distinguished gentlemen and reassuring them with their motto 'Some things are forever'. Now Britain's venerable shoemaker has crossed the pond and is open for business with a selection of straight-cap oxfords, loafers, buckle shoes, Jodhpur boots, evening slip-ons and classic moccasins. Beautiful craftsmanship and traditional styling define the Lobb label. Pay an average price of $900, while custom-made starts at $4,200.

Expensive to luxury   *Amex/MC/V*

Upper East Side   **(212) 888-9797**
680 Madison Avenue   btw 61/62nd St
NYC 10021   Mon-Sat 10-6

Johnson

Straightforward attire with a bit of a downtown edge.This small, cozy boutique features Kim Johnson's keyhole dresses, corduroy pants and bow-trim tops. The look is classic with a twist, and you'll find a range of accessories from wrist bags to winter hats.   johnsonshop.com

Expensive   *Amex/MC/V*

Lower East Side   **(646) 602-8668**
179 Orchard Street   btw Stanton/Houston
NYC 10002   Tues-Fri 1-7, Sat 12:30-8, Sun 1-6

Johnston & Murphy

This American men's footwear retailer has satisfied its customers since 1850 with a full range of styles, from dress and formal to casual and weekend. Johnston & Murphy offer matching accessories, quality shoe care products (including sweet-smelling cedarwood foot trees), and a small casual sportswear selection for the conservative dresser looking to kick back.   *800-424-2854 johnstonmurphy.com*

Moderate   *Amex/MC/V*

153

Midtown East   **(212) 697-9375**
345 Madison Avenue   btw 44/45th St
NYC 10017   Mon-Fri 9-7, Sat 10-6, Sun 12-5

Midtown East   **(212) 527-2342**
520 Madison Avenue   at 54th St
NYC 10022   Mon-Fri 9-7, Sat 10-7, Sun 12-6

John Varvatos

After tours of duty with Calvin Klein and Ralph Lauren, John Varvatos stepped out on his own with this exclusive men's shop. Who is his customer? According to the man himself, 'there's the modern guy who shops at Prada and Gucci, the classic Armani customer and then the guy in the middle—the Varvatos customer, a modern man who wants to look elegant but with a relaxed feel.' Choose from a selection of sophisticated wool suits, luxurious cashmeres, bulky knits, wide-legged pants, shearlings and pea-coats. So we ask again, who is his customer? Dylan McDermott from *The Practice* is seen wearing Varvatos in court and Eric McCormick flaunts his designs in *Will & Grace*. Very cool is his collaboration with Converse on designer sneakers, sported by the likes of Jimmy Fallon and Tobey Maguire.   *johnvarvatos.com*

Moderate   *Amex/MC/V*

SoHo   **(212) 965-0700**
122 Spring Street   btw Houston/Prince
NYC 10012   Mon-Sat 11-7, Sun 12-6

Jonathan Adler

Fashion hounds who favor Jonathan Adler's stylish home accessories—like his signature porcelain aorta vases, or his handmade Beekman sofas—can now take a piece of his to go, thanks to the introduction of a line of luxe handbags. Adler's store is known for its beautiful lighting designs, dinnerware, pottery and furniture (including chic dog beds), and his new purses and totes are marked by the same clean and simple lines (no logos, mercifully) and made of the most supple, luxurious materials. Beautiful.   *jonathanadler.com*

Expensive   *Amex/MC/V*

SoHo   **(212) 941-8950**
47 Greene Street   btw Broome/Grand
NYC 10013   Mon-Sat 11-7, Sun 12-6

Upper East Side   **(212) 772-2410**
1097 Madison Avenue   at 83rd St
NYC 10028   Mon-Sat 10-6, Sun 12-5

Joseph

London retailer Joseph Ettedgui has his customers coming back for more by sticking to what he knows best: keeping to the same basic styles, especially his cult pants, which return every season with updated fabrics, colors and textures. Think Banana Republic or Club Monaco, and then add a few digits to the price tag. Joseph is all about modern separates in easy-to-wear shapes, including pants, shirts, jackets, leathers, knitwear and shearlings, as well as

the one drop-dead gorgeous, high-end piece he introduces into each collection.

Expensive *Amex/MC/V*

SoHo **(212) 343-7071**
106 Greene Street btw Prince/Spring
NYC 10012 Mon-Sat 11-7:30, Sun 12-7

Upper East Side **(212) 570-0077**
816 Madison Avenue btw 68/69th St
NYC 10021 Mon-Sat 10-6:30, Sun 12-6

Joseph A. Bank
A Baltimore retailer featuring tailored career clothing for
the conservative dresser. In keeping with its traditional
origins, Bank offers a comfortable shopping environment
for a complete selection of suits, sportswear, sportswear,
ties and underwear, as well as a Cole Haan shoe department. Even better: every spring Bank invites you to trade
in an old suit for up to $200 credit towards a new suit
(ranging from $300 to $1,600)—now, if only Prada did
that... *800-285-2265 josabank.com*

Moderate *Amex/MC/V*

Midtown East **(212) 370-0600**
366 Madison Avenue at 46th St
NYC 10017 Mon-Sat 9-8, Sun 12-6

Joyce Leslie
Joyce Leslie's clothes are like Kleenex: so necessary the
day you acquire them, but ultimately disposable. Long
patronized by NYU students on a budget for the cheap, if
slightly slutty, lingerie section in the basement that also
houses a wide selection of sequined bikinis. Upstairs, it
may be worth weeding through a sea of polyester halter
tops for hipster staples such as basic cotton blouses with
Avril Lavignesque ties, plus some surprisingly cute denim
jackets. *joyceleslie.com*

Moderate *Amex/MC/V*

West Village **(212) 505-5419**
20 University Place at Eighth St
NYC 10019 Mon-Wed 10-9, Thurs-Sat 10-10, Sun 11-8

J.Press
One of the oldest menswear shops in New York, J.Press
prides itself on its selection of traditional suits, sportswear,
formalwear, outerwear and accessories, all in good taste at
reasonable prices. A great shop for young career guys. Suit
prices start at $350. *jpressonline.com*

Moderate to expensive *Amex/MC/V*

Midtown East **(212) 687-7642**
7 East 44th Street btw Fifth/Madison Ave
NYC 10017 Mon-Sat 9-6

Judith Leiber
Accessories legend Judith Leiber has over 500 bags for
evening or daytime, from a classic alligator style to an elab-

orately detailed design for fancy nights out. But true Leiber aficionados shop here for her rhinestone evening bags and tiny jewel-encrusted minaudières. These bags are often seen in the clutches of society types, including Nancy Reagan, oh, and avant-garde darlings like Bjork. See? Versatile. *judithleiber.com*

Expensive   *Amex/MC/V*

Upper East Side   **(212) 223-2999**
680 Madison Avenue   at 61st St
NYC 10022   Mon-Sat 10-6

★ Julian and Sara

A cozy shop stocked with children's clothing lines imported from France and Italy. Find back-to-school basics, play clothes and accessories handpicked from top labels like Lili Gaufrette, Mona Lisa, Kenzo, Petit Bateau, Clayeux, Mini Man and Elsy. Sizes are aimed mostly at infants, but range from newborn through pre-teen. *julianandsara.com*

Expensive   *Amex/MC/V*

SoHo   **(212) 226-1989**
103 Mercer Street   btw Prince/Spring
NYC 10012   Mon-Fri 11-7, Sat-Sun 11:30-6

Julie Artisan's Gallery

Since 1973 this artisan's gallery has showcased techniques like weaving, handpainting, stitching, quilting and knitting. Each piece is a lovingly crafted work of art, either one-of-a-kind or sold in limited editions. Women shop here for loomed and handwoven knitted jackets, colorful sweaters, hand-dyed and painted shirts and more from such labels as Tim Harding and Linda Mendelson. Also find Bakelite and Modernist vintage jewelry, as well as some decorative home accessories. For mature customers into arty dressing, this is your spiritual home. *julieartisans.com*

Expensive   *Amex/MC/V*

Upper East Side   **(212) 717-5959**
762 Madison Avenue   btw 65/66th St
NYC 10021   Mon-Sat 11-6

Jungle Planet

It's a jungle in here, with a thicket of goods spanning the world over, from Nepal to little ol' Gotham. Jungle Planet's global selection of Mandarin dresses, shirts, T-shirts, hand-crafted blazers, scarves, beaded handbags, jewelry, rings and pendants is fun, feminine and full of international flair.

Moderate   *MC/V*

West Village   **(212) 989-5447**
175 West 4th Street   btw Sixth/Seventh Ave
NYC 10014   Mon-Thurs 12-9, Fri 12-10
                                          Sat 12-11, Sun 12-8

Juno

This footwear emporium is all about color—purples, fuchsias, greens and yellows. For shoe addicts who absolutely must have the very latest styles, from casual to sporty to evening, Juno has sexy pumps, boots (a fantastic and well-priced selection—especially in winter), slides and sandals. Men can choose from Prada-esque sneaker/dress shoes, boots and sandals. Great children's shoes, too. 'Buy one pair, get one free,' sales happen frequently, so don't miss out. *junoshoes.com*

Moderate   *Amex/MC/V*

SoHo   **(212) 625-2560**
543 Broadway   btw Prince/Spring
NYC 10012   Mon-Sat 10:30-9, Sun 11-8

Jussara Lee

This über-hot Brazilian designer known for her custom-made sportswear and eveningwear has opened a super-cool glass and concrete boutique-cum-art-gallery in the Chelsea. You'll find Lee's usual assortment of minimalist sheer chiffon dresses and skirts, but people really visit the store for her coats and near-perfect pants. There's a surprise around every corner, including some gorgeous faux-fur wraps and power suits. And if you can't find what you're looking for, get it custom-made for the same price you'd pay if it was on the racks. *caipirinha.com/jussara*

Expensive   *Amex/MC/V*

West Village   **(212) 242-4128**
11 Little West 12th Street   btw Ninth Ave/Washington
NYC 10014   Mon-Sat 11-7, Sun 12-6

★ Just for Tykes

This full-service, high-end children's store sells all the practical essentials and little goodies you'll need for your little ones: clothing, furniture (including cribs), bedding, baby gear, accessories and lots of toys. Drop off your kids in the play space so you can peruse the store quickly, sans distractions. Whether shopping for a new family or the perfect nursery gift, the knowledgeable staff are on hand to make your shopping experience a little easier. *justfortykes.com*

Expensive   *Amex/MC/V*

SoHo   **(212) 274-9121**
83 Mercer Street   btw Spring/Broome
NYC 10012   Mon-Fri 10-6, Sat 11-7, Sun 12-6

Jutta Neumann

Hippies and fashion editors (her work has been featured in *Vogue* and *Elle*), two seemingly incompatible groups, nevertheless share a love for Jutta Neumann's traditional craftsmanship and bohemian-chic sandals. Using a variety of skins (cow, calf, suede, snake, stingray, python, alligator), as well as a surfeit of colors (turquoise, bright yellow, orange and traditional browns and blacks, Neumann will create a one-of-a-kind pair just for you. While in the shop, she will also design a handbag to match, or make a coordinating belt or wristband. Everything is lovingly constructed to your specifications. Custom sandals cost around $250 with a five-to-seven week delivery period.   *juttaneumann-newyork.com*

Expensive   *Amex/MC/V*

Lower East Side   **(212) 982-7048**
158 Allen Street   btw Stanton/Rivington
NYC 10002   Mon-Sat 12-8

Karin Alexis   ♂

What to do when you've searched high and low and you simply cannot find a decent wardrobe for your newborn? Well, Karin Alexis solved the problem by starting her own line. Reproducing vintage fabric finds, she pairs them with cozy fleece for jackets and 100% cotton flannel for trousers and rompers. The result is an adorable, durable kids' collection with vintage charm and modern practicality. Because Karin's muse is her son, this is one of the few places where the boys actually have more choices—but there's plenty for little girls, too.   *karinalexis.com*

Moderate   *Amex/MC/V*

Upper West Side   **(212) 769-9550**
490 Amsterdam Avenue   btw 83/84th St
NYC 10024   Mon-Sat 10:30-6, Sun 12-5

Kate Spade   ♀

Fashionistas call her the 'purse queen', and former accessories editor Spade lives up to the name with her classically styled handbags in bold, jaunty colors. Each season she reinvents her signature pieces in fashionable fabrics like glossy satin nylons, silks, bouclé wools, canvas and leathers. Looks run from practical shoulder and tote bags to silk and satin evening bags bright as jellybeans. Spade's accessories include lots of shoes, sunglasses, raincoats, pajamas, fragrances and even home goods and etiquette books.   *katespade.com*

Expensive   *Amex/MC/V*

SoHo   **(212) 274-1991**
454 Broome Street   at Mercer
NYC 10013   Mon-Sat 11-7, Sun 12-6

Kavanagh's Designer Resale Shop   ♀

Owner Mary Kavanagh, former director of personal shopping at Bergdorf Goodman, sells pre-owned but pristine, high-end, designer clothing. Her specialty is Chanel suits priced under $1,200, but you can also find Armani, Ungaro, Jil Sander and Prada. Handbag and shoe labels include Fendi, Hermès, Gucci, Chanel, Tod's and Manolo Blahnik. During the winter, look for sable fur coats from J.Mendel.

Luxury   *Amex/MC/V*

Midtown East   **(212) 702-0152**
146 East 49th Street   btw Lexington/Third Ave
NYC 10017   Tues-Fri 11-6, Sat 11-4

Kazuyo Nakano

Cameron Diaz is said to be one of the many who love the glossy Italian leather of Japanese designer Nakano's feminine yet functional bags. This season finds Nakano flirting with zestier earth tones, large chain-linked straps, tassels, flower adornment and a sexier, sleeker look (yes, that is a cracked-silver finish on that fresh-faced purse) Be sure to slide up to Nakano's new soft-leather Sheila line and her popular Amanda bags. *kazuyonakano.com*

Moderate *Amex/MC/V*

Nolita **(212) 941-7093**
117 Crosby Street btw Houston/Prince
NYC 10012 Daily 12-7

K.C.Thompson New York

Jewels, glorious jewels, and a fab store in which to buy them. Designer Kristen Thompson dreamed up a space (in a former nail salon) that she sees as a 'pampered women's dressing-room'. Think vanity mirrors where indulgent customers can try on such pieces as large, vintage-inspired flower earrings, or chunky-chic semi-precious necklaces featuring stones like cornelian, turquoise and coin pearls. Each piece has an 18kt gold butterfly clasp. Expect to pay from $1,000 to $5,000 for her jewels—and spend hours more at the mirror at home admiring them. *kcthompsonny.com*

Expensive *Amex/MC/V*

Upper East Side **(212) 396-0974**
987 Madison Avenue (the Carlyle Hotel) btw 76/77th St
NYC 10021 Mon-Fri 10-6, Sat 12-5

KD Dance

Get footloose! KD stands for Kate and David, but it could easily stand for Knitwear and Dance, as that's exactly what you'll find here. Their specialty is dance, fitness and fashion knitwear that moves from yoga and Pilates straight to the streets, all without breaking a sweat. Find great looking tops, cardigans, tanks, yoga pants and stretch cotton/Lycra workout clothes alongside new items like ponchos and shawls. Better yet, almost all items are machine washable. Men and children have to do their shopping online. *kddance.com*

Moderate *Amex/MC/V*

NoHo **(212) 533-1037**
339 Lafayette Street at Bleecker
NYC 10012 Mon-Sat 12-8, Sun 2-6

★ Keiko

Have you ever wondered where those sexy swimsuits featured in fashion magazines come from? And how do they get such a perfect fit? Well, the answer is Keiko's, which offers a collection of bathing attire in mouth-watering colors. Prices start at $110, and alterations will cost you more. Suits seen in the pages of *Maxim* and *Sports*

Illustrated can be mix-matched and paired off with the hottest durable bags and hats. New shady stripes, artsy appliqués and a tantalizing mesh are perfect for draping over basic separates. Customized suits start at $250, and are available for men, women (including more supportive designs) and children (only samples are showcased, ask for assistance). keikonewyork.com

Moderate Amex/MC/V

SoHo (212) 226-6051
62 Greene Street btw Spring/Broome
NYC 10012 Mon-Sat 12-6, Sun 1-6

Kelly Christy

This eponymous boutique sells chic toppers with a flair for the dramatic: Christy describes her aesthetic as classic with a twist. A switch to a showroom/studio means that shopping is now by appointment only; watch the website or call for the address. Each design highlights her unique use of trim, leather and ribbon on fedoras, boleros, cloches, berets and boaters. Choose off-the-rack or made-to-measure. kellychristyhats.com

Expensive Amex/MC/V

Nolita (212) 965-0686
by appointment only

★ Keni Valenti

Located in the heart of the garment district, this four-room showroom boasts one of the foremost collections of vintage fashions from the Twenties to the Eighties, including beautiful designer dresses, couture eveningwear, shoes, handbags and jewelry. From choice pieces by American sportswear legends like John Kloss and Clovis Ruffin to heavy hitters like Yves Saint Laurent, Halston, Geoffrey Beene, Alaïa and Courrèges, it's all in impeccable condition. Former Fiorucci designer Valenti has also designed his own line, called KV, featuring bias-cut silk jersey evening dresses and luncheon-bound gabardine suits, that the model crew and downtown hipster Chloe Sevigny have been buying up bigtime. Expect to pay high couture designer prices for a little slice of vintage luxury. Also expect to look amazing. kenivalenti.com

Expensive Amex/MC/V

Midtown West (212) 967-7147
247 West 30th Street (5th`floor) btw Seventh/Eighth Ave
NYC 10001 Mon-Fri 10-6 (by appointment)

Kenneth Cole

Socially conscious Kenneth Cole is doing his best to inform minds while covering bodies in clean lines. He started by selling shoes out of a trailer and created a $300 million footwear empire, and he has since become a major force in men's and womenswear. His hallmark: clean, urban functionality at incredible value, and ads that spark political and health awareness. Both sexes can shop for fashionable sportswear, shiny jeans, embracing knits, tailored shirts and coats in buttery leather and shearling. In footwear, find a broad range of styles from career and dress shoes to trendy and casual basics. Accessories include handbags, scarves and sunglasses. Smart designs at smart prices. *800-536-2653 kennethcole.com*

Moderate   *Amex/MC/V*

Fifth Avenue (Rockefeller Center)   **(212) 373-5800**
610 Fifth Avenue   at 49th Street
NYC 10020   Mon-Sat 10-8, Sun 11-6

Midtown East (Grand Central Station) **(212) 949-8079**
107 East 42nd Street   at Park Ave
NYC 10017   Mon-Fri 8-9, Sat 10-8, Sun 10-7

Midtown East   **(212) 688-1670**
130 East 57th Street   at Lexington Ave
NYC 10022   Mon-Sat 10-8, Sun 11-7

Flatiron   **(212) 675-2550**
95 Fifth Avenue   at 17th St
NYC 10003   Mon-Sat 10-8, Sun 11-7

SoHo   **(212) 965-0283**
597 Broadway   at Prince
NYC 10012   Mon-Sat 10-8, Sun 11-7

Upper West Side   **(212) 873-2061**
353 Columbus Avenue   btw 76/77th St
NYC 10024   Mon-Sat 10-8, Sun 11-7

Kids Foot Locker

It has exactly what you expect: a large selection of children's athletic wear, from baseball jerseys and tennis outfits to top-of-the-line sneakers. Brand names include Adidas, Nike and Reebok. From infants to size 6. *footlocker.com*

Affordable   *Amex/MC/V*

Midtown West   **(212) 465-9041**
120 West 34th Street   btw Sixth/Seventh Ave
NYC 10001   Mon-Sat 9-9, Sun 9-8

Kinnu

Enter a world of Indian color, fabric and design. Handwoven, iridescent silks and cross-dyed cottons made up into kurta-styled tunics, dresses, asymmetrical wraps and drawstring pants define the collection. Gold brocade trim on hems and cuffs, intricate embroidery, mirror-work and hand-dyeing exemplify the elaborate workmanship that goes into each design. Decorative items like quilted bedspreads, wall-hangings and artwork also available.

Moderate to expensive   *Amex/MC/V*

Nolita   **(212) 334-4775**
43 Spring Street   btw Mulberry/Mott
NYC 10012   Daily 11:30-7

★ Kirna Zabête

Owners Sarah Easley (nicknamed Kirna) and Beth Buccini (nicknamed Zabête) have created a 5,000-square-foot two-level mini department store dedicated to goth, glam, girly but, most importantly, high fashion. The savvy duo buy an eclectic mix of the hottest designers from London, Paris, Belgium and New York, including Bruce, Martine Sitbon, A.F.Vandevorst, DEL, Cacharel, lots of Chloé, Wink and Balenciaga. The lower level is home to funky-chic and sporty looks featuring knits, T-shirts with ironic messages, lingerie, shoes, hats and handbags. Other goodies include lotions and potions, a candy section and a pet section. Accessories include huge numbers of handbags, hats, lingerie and pretty shoes. *kirnazabete.com*

Expensive   *Amex/MC/V*

SoHo   **(212) 941-9656**
96 Greene Street   btw Prince/Spring
NYC 10012   Mon-Sat 11-7, Sun 12-6

Kiton

With shops around the world proudly carrying Kiton's exquisitely tailored men's suits, why not go straight to the source? Can't make it out to Italy with your gent before your sister's wedding? Head midtown to the Kiton shop, and get him fitted for a custom suit. What makes it special and luxurious is that one craftsman makes the entire garment in his workshop, rather than having the sleeves made in Bangalore and the lining sewn in by an apprentice, and so forth. Each suit is a laborious creation, and the Kiton craftsmen take great pride in their work.

Expensive to luxury   *Amex/MC/V*

Midtown East   **(212) 813-0272**
4 East 54th Street   btw Fifth/Madison Ave
NYC 10022   Mon-Fri 10-7, Sat 11-6, Sun 12-5

Kleinfeld

The baron of designer bridalwear. It used to be a trek to Kleinfeld's, but their new location in Chelsea makes this legendary destination more important than ever for blushing brides-to-be and their entourages. Find over 1,000 gowns in stock at all times from labels including Badgley Mischka, Christian Lacroix and Oscar de la Renta. *kleinfeldbridal.com*

Expensive   *Amex/MC/V*

Chelsea   **(212) 352-2180**
110 West 20th Street   at Sixth Ave
NYC 10011   Tues, Thurs 12:30-9:30, Fri 10-6
              Sat 9:30-6, Sun 10-6 (by appointment only)

Klurk

Klurk's owner Brian Chik is a former desk clerk-turned-designer whose line of casual menswear is best for the young and adventurous. The collection combines cool urban streetwear with ironic collegiate styles—high-necked sweaters, knits with inside-out seams, funky patterned golf-like pants, dress pants with nylon waistbands and button-down cashmere shirts. Accessories include watches, clever key chains, a few bags and refined wallets.

Moderate　　　　　　　　　　　　*Amex/MC/V*

Nolita　　　　　　　　　　　　**(212) 966-3617**
360 Broome Street　　　　　btw Mott/Elizabeth
NYC 10012　　　　　　　　　Sun-Fri 1-7 (closed Tues)

★ Koh's Kids

Grace Koh's shop offers hip, offbeat clothing for children (newborn to age 10). Dresses, jackets, shirts and all sorts of dressy and casual attire from American and European labels like Confetti, Flapdoodles, Cherry Tree, Zutano and Petit Bateau are available here; don't miss Koh's handknitted sweaters, either. The shelves of this small store sparkle with seasonal items like snow suits and gloves for winter frolics and shorts, bathing suits and sun hats for those summer beach dates. You'll also find fun toys, shoes and accessories (including hair ornaments and jewelry).

Moderate　　　　　　　　　　　　*Amex/MC/V*

Tribeca　　　　　　　　　　　　**(212) 791-6915**
311 Greenwich Street　　　　btw Chambers/Reade
NYC 10013　　　　　　　　　Mon-Sat 10-7, Sun 11-5

Krizia

Krizia designer Mariuccia Mandelli believes clothing is our second skin, so her ready-to-wear designs are body-conscious and comfortable. The collection runs the gamut from a glam $8,000 dress to a simple T-shirt. Other items include sculpted black crepe suits, pants, stretch cashmere twinsets, separates and coats. Her best offering, though, is luxury knitwear, from cling-to-the-body dresses to form-fitted sweaters. Eveningwear includes glamorous beaded chiffon gowns and slinky, black jersey dresses. Fellini fans will purr with delight when they see her signature animal-print sweaters. Her men's fashions border on avant-garde. *krizia.it*

Expensive　　　　　　　　　　　*Amex/MC/V*

Upper East Side　　　　　　　**(212) 879-1211**
769 Madison Avenue　　　　　btw 65/66th St
NYC 10021　　　　　　　　　Mon-Sat 10-6

Label

Store owner Laura Whitcomb was doing Adidas dresses back in 1993 when Hollywood had yet to discover tracksuits, and her funky sportswear boutique is still ahead of the curve with tough yet sexy knitwear for skater chic. Staples like full-length skirts and sweatshirts are given surprise twists like asymmetrical cuts, slashes and zippered collars. Instead of baggy pants, Whitcomb offers full-length skirts with lots of pockets—and major attitude. Also a small selection of menswear.　　　　　　　　　　　*labelnyc.com*

Moderate　　　　　　　　　　　*Amex/MC/V*

Nolita　　　　　　　　　　　　**(212) 966-7736**
265 Lafayette Street　　　　btw Prince/Spring
NYC 10012　　　　　　　　　Daily 12-7

★ Lace

Chintzy flowered wallpaper, a phony fireplace and a gilded display case make Lace resemble a caricature of grandma's living room, though the shoes on offer are hardly orthopedic. Being the only Stateside shop to sell Vivienne Westwood shoes, you must come here to pick up her famous witchy open-toe gladiator stilettos. Glam rock shoe designer Terry de Havilland made shoes for Bowie and Mick, and now sells his metallic croc-skin platform heels, peep-toes, and ankle-strap wedges to downtown girls. Also available are lovelies by Gaspard Yurkievich, Venera Arapu, Johanna Ho, Sonia Rykiel, Camilla Staerk and Moschino Cheap & Chic. *lacenyc.com*

Expensive   *Amex/MC/V*

Nolita   **(212) 941-0528**
223 Mott Street   btw Prince/Spring
NYC 10012   Tues-Sat 12-7:30, Sun 12-6

Lacoste

That little alligator never seems to go out of fashion. Women who love preppy French style tumble over their tennis nets for sexy, striped open-necked tees, pleated minis and beach hats, while men will be immune to unforced errors in those iconic polos and cooler-than-K-Swiss sneaks. Luxuriating in its Fifth Avenue digs, Lacoste tops off its fresh-from-the-Riviera wear with watches, sunglasses and even perfumes. In other words, it's superior sporty gear for people who wouldn't be caught dead breaking a sweat. *800-4-LACOSTE lacoste.com*

Expensive   *Amex/MC/V*

Fifth Avenue   **(212) 459-2300**
608 Fifth Avenue   at 49th St
NYC 10022   Mon-Sat 10-8, Sun 11-6

SoHo   **(212) 226-5019**
134 Prince Street   btw Wooster/West Broadway
NYC 10012   Mon-Thurs 11-7, Fri-Sun 11-8

Midtown East   **(212) 750-8115**
575 Madison Avenue   at 57th St
NYC 10022   Mon-Fri 10-7 (Thurs 10-8)
                                         Sat 10-6, Sun 12-5

LaCrasia Gloves

In 1973 belt-designer and FIT graduate LaCrasia Lome Duchein had a vision: to reclaim the fame of gloves and bring them back as a women's wardrobe staple. Now, with partner and master glovemaker Jay Ruckel, LaCrasia has brought her dream to life, creating over 60,000 gloves a year for rich and famous folks from the White House to Broadway to Hollywood: Jackie Kennedy, Donna Karan, Michael Jackson, Madonna, Angelica, Gwyneth and Uma are but a few well-known clients. The store sells everything from lacy fingerless styles, white debutante gloves, snakeskin numbers, leather driving gloves and much more. Guess who made Brittany's white leather opera gloves? *wegloveyou.com*

Moderate *Amex/MC/V*

Midtown West **(212) 803-1600**
15 West 28th Street (suite 401) btw Fifth/Broadway
NYC 10001 Mon-Fri 10-5 (Sat by appointment)

Lady Foot Locker

Strictly for the gals, Lady Foot Locker offers a great choice of shoes and athletic apparel for running, tennis, basketball and cross-training. Find all the big names: Nike, Reebok, Adidas, Fila and New Balance. *800-877-5239 ladyfootlocker.com*

Affordable *Amex/MC/V*

Midtown West **(212) 629-4626**
120 West 34th Street at Sixth Ave
NYC 10120 Mon-Fri 8-9, Sat 9-9, Sun 10-8

LAI

LAI specializes in leather, focusing on bags but spanning out into a full range of accessories from belts and wallets to tape measures and business card holders. Lizard, python, alligator, crocodile, ostrich and more can be natural and neutral or wildly dyed to your specifications. Lovely and inventive clutches in mauve, coral, pistachio and other pleasing hues are available structured, slouchy, asymmetrical or classically cut. For the stylish 18-holer in your life, pick up a custom leather golf bag, or the more reasonably priced tee cozies. *luxuryaccessories.com*

Luxury *Amex/MC/V*

Upper East Side **(212) 794-3874**
35 East 65th Street btw Madison/Park Ave
NYC 10021 Mon-Fri 10-6, Sat 12-6 (except in summer)

Laila Rowe

It's accessories galore at this busy SoHo boutique and its many branches. Rowe's trendy costume jewelry, handbags and scarves are a great way to update your wardrobe without putting out for an entire new ensemble. The pieces are of-the-moment, but inexpensive enough that you won't kick yourself for following the trend when it passes. Great deals (two scarves for $30) and lots of choice. *lailarowe.com*

Affordable *Amex/MC/V*

SoHo **(212) 966-9210**
424 West Broadway btw Spring/Prince
NYC 10012 Daily 11-8

Flatiron **(212) 242-0364**
2 West 14th Street at Fifth Ave
NYC 10011 (opening hours as above)

Upper East Side **(212) 980-5535**
1031 Third Avenue at 61st St
NYC 10021 (opening hours as above)

Flatiron
600 Sixth Ave
NYC 10011

(212) 647-0002
btw 17/18th St
(opening hours as above)

SoHo
199 Prince Street
NYC 10012

(212) 473-9703
btw Sullivan/McDougal
(opening hours as above)

Midtown East
8 East 42nd Street
NYC 10017

(212) 949-2276
at Fifth Ave
(opening hours as above)

East Village
55C East 8th Street
NYC 10003

(212) 677-1808
btw Mercer/University
(opening hours as above)

West Village
649 Broadway
NYC 10012

(212) 673-6456
at Bleecker
(opening hours as above)

Upper West Side
2190 Broadway
NYC 10023

(212) 579-3045
at 78th St
(opening hours as above)

Upper West Side
253 Columbus Avenue
NYC 10023

(212) 579 5254
at 72nd St
(opening hours as above)

Laina Jane Lingerie

Slipping into a sound and sexy number is made easy in Laina Jane's great selection of nighties and pajamas from labels like Arianne and Hanky Panky. This is also an excellent West Village destination for some of the top makers of bras and panties such as Eberjay, Le Mystère, Cosabella and Gemma. Hosiery and a small selection of swimwear also available.   *lainajane.com*

Moderate to expensive   *Amex/MC/V*

Upper West Side
416 Amsterdam Avenue
NYC 10024

(212) 875-9168
at 80th St
Daily 11-7

West Village
45 Christopher Street
NYC 10014

(212) 807-8077
btw Sixth/Seventh Ave
Sun-Wed 11:30-7:30, Thurs-Sat 11:30-8

★ La Layette et Plus

Attention all doting grandmothers. Exquisite, old-world charm infuses this tiny store, which offers luxurious European children's clothing and a complete layette selection. Appointments are encouraged to ensure customers receive exclusive attention while being shown a large array of receiving blankets, christening gowns, bibs, crib linens and more. Also find luxurious gifts like porcelain piggy banks and satin hangers. Each item is prettier than the next.   *lalayette.com*

Expensive   *Amex/MC/V*

Upper East Side
170 East 61st Street
NYC 10021

(212) 688-7072
btw Lexington/Third Ave
Mon-Fri 11-6, Sat 11-5
(closed Saturdays in summer)

Lana Marks

Handbag aficionados shop here for Lana Marks' exotic skins like alligator, ostrich and lizard. Designs are classic and fashionable and colors run from black to vivid pink. True opulence comes in the form of Lana's $25,000 Cleopatra clutch which is embellished with yellow sapphires. Be sure to ask for assistance if you are interested in trying on a bag, as many items are understandably under heavy guard. Don't miss the skinny belts and the limited selection of men's accessories. *lanamarks.com*

Luxury   *Amex/MC/V*

Midtown East   **(212) 355-6135**
645 Madison Avenue   btw 59/60th St
NYC 10022   Mon-Fri 9-6:30 (Thurs 9-7), Sat 9-6

Lane Bryant

A name synonymous with plus sizes, but this does not mean that Lane Bryant ain't sexy. Absolutely not—it's getting positively racy: think a curvier Victoria's Secret and you've got it. Size 14-28s will find everything from a fabulous assortment of jeans to sexy intimate apparel, all moderately priced. Although it's quite a trek to visit their only Manhattan store, located in Harlem, it's well worth the trip. The line has embroidered tunics ($49), denim (from $34.50) and special occasion wear from $80. Fabulous knows no size, honey. *lanebryant.com*

Affordable   *Amex/MC/V*

Harlem   **(212) 678-0546**
222 West 125th Street   btw Seventh/Eighth Ave
NYC 10027   Mon-Sat 10-8, Sun 12-5

Midtown West   **(212) 594-2115**
7 West 34th Street   btw Fifth/Sixth Ave
NYC 10001   Mon-Sat 10-9, Sun 11-6

La Perla

Totally gorgeous, fiendishly expensive—the caviar of lingerie. A legendary label of feminine intimates that run from tasteful and elegant to seductive and sexy, La Perla also features a fashion line of bustiers and bodysuits with built-in bra cups, as well as swimwear and sleepwear. Be prepared to pay up to a few hundred dollars for a single item. *laperla.com*

Luxury   *Amex/MC/V*

Upper East Side   **(212) 570-0050**
777 Madison Avenue   btw 66/67th St
NYC 10021   Mon-Sat 10-6 (Thurs 10-6:30), Sun 12-5

SoHo   **(212) 219-0999**
93 Greene Street   btw Prince/Spring
NYC 10012   Mon-Sat 11-7, Sun 12-6

Chelsea   **(212) 242-6662**
425 West 14th Street   btw Ninth/Tenth Ave
NYC 10014   Mon-Sat 11-7, Sun 12-6

★ La Petite Coquette

In business for 25 years, La Petite Coquette remains the in-place for high-end sexy lingerie. Just ask regulars like Julianne Moore, Liv Tyler, Cindy Crawford and Sarah Jessica Parker. Once you've seen the storefront windows, it's impossible to resist stepping into a space that feels more like a boudoir than a shop, with its sweet vanilla smell and hand-painted pin-ups on the wall. There's an incredible selection of private-label silk intimates in a multitude of colors and looks that range from alluring corsets and garters to flirty nighties and feminine basics. Besides the bedroom attire, be sure to check out the swimwear, a new jewelry collection and a small men's collection. Labels include La Perla, Lise Charmel, Ravage, Damaris, Dolce & Gabbana, Andres Sarda, Cotton Club, Naory and Aubade, and prices run from $38 to $1,800. One of the best lingerie shops in the city. *thelittleflirt.com*

Expensive   *Amex/MC/V*

NoHo   **(212) 473-2478**
51 University Place   btw 9/10th St
NYC 10003   Mon-Sat 11-7 (Thurs 11-8), Sun 12-6

Lara Hélène Bridal Atelier

Sisters Lara and Hélène have opened a big, bright, glamorous bridal shop showcasing unique dresses by several international exclusive designers. Their clientele ranges from fashion-savvy young brides, to women getting remarried who have already done the big white princess gown thing and want something different. Though the shop is not cheap, they work with brides-to-be on a budget to best make their dream dress. They also offer custom veils, tiaras and hair combs refashioned from vintage pieces. Instead of flowers, quirky brides might like to carry custom bouquets made of wire and crystals. They also offer custom mother-of-the-bride and evening gowns. *larahelene.com*

Luxury   *Amex/MC/V*

Upper East Side   **(212) 452-3273**
13 East 69th Street   Fifth/Madison Ave
NYC 10021   Mon-Sat 11-6, by appointment

Laundry by Shelli Segal

Although she continues to supply major department stores, Segal also has her own store for her softly shaped, reasonably priced pieces, from ruffled dresses and floral shirts to cashmere tops and drawstring pants. A Segal design is feminine, elegantly understated and easy-to-wear. *laundrybyshellisegal.com*

Moderate   *Amex/MC/V*

SoHo   **(212) 334-9433**
97 Wooster Street   btw Prince/Spring
NYC 10012   Mon-Sat 11-7, Sun 12-6

The Leather and Suede Workshop

It's a skins game for owner/tailor Ron Shahar, the go-to man for all your leather needs. Choose from suede, cowhide, leather, and snakeskin in a multitude of colors on, well, pretty much everything: pants, jackets, long and short skirts, dresses, shirts, coats, belts and even hats. Pants start at $595, jackets at $795. Shahar will custom tailor a micromini or a pair of black leather pants that will fit like a glove.

Expensive   *Amex/MC/V*

Midtown East   **(212) 688-1946**
107 East 59th Street   btw Park/Lexington Ave
NYC 10022   Mon-Fri 10-7, Sat 11-7
Sun 11:30-6:30 (except in summer)

The Leather Man

Okay, so bondage, handcuffs and Crispo masks aren't your thing. How about a pair of five-pocket jeans in motorcycle-weight leather to shake things up a bit? Well, The Leather Man offers custom-fit leather pants, vests and boots that run the gamut from biker to rock star to rough trade. Prices for pants start at $395.   *theleatherman.com*

Expensive   *Amex/MC/V*

West Village   **(212) 243-5339**
111 Christopher Street   btw Bleecker/Hudson
NYC 10014   Mon-Sat 12-10, Sun 12-8

Le Chateau

Trendy and ultimately disposable clubwear for teens and twentysomethings who need something cheap for a night out. Hoochie-mama tube tops in bright prints, tight flared bottoms and serious Seventies wedge platforms sit alongside fun accessories, including a wide selection of fake hair.   *le-chateau.com*

Affordable   *Amex/MC/V*

NoHo   **(212) 674-5560**
704 Broadway   btw Washington Place/West 4th St
NYC 10003   Daily 10-9 (Sun 11-7)

Midtown West   **(212) 967-0025**
34 West 34th Street   btw Fifth/Sixth Ave
NYC 10001   Mon-Sat 10-9, Sun 11-7

★ Le Corset

Ah, le corset! The seductive tool for breathless ladies that has the same (if slightly more forgiving) allure now as it did centuries ago. Owner Selima Salaun is an expert at spotting new trends in lingerie and provides a fabulously enticing selection of new and vintage lingerie that runs from flirty to retro to unabashedly sexy. There are satin and silk corsets, feminine camisoles, demi-cup bras that accentuate cleavage, bodysuits, lacy panties, chemises, garter belts and more from labels that include Selima (Le Corset's house design), Carine Gilson, Khurana, Chantal Thomass, Blumarine, Collette Dinnigan and Roberto Cavalli.

Moderate   *Amex/MC/V*

SoHo   **(212) 334-4936**
80 Thompson Street   btw Spring/Broome
NYC 10012   Mon-Fri 11-7, Sat 11-8, Sun 12-7

Lederer

In a world dominated by fleeting fashions and trends, this Paris-based bag and accessory maker is only interested in timelessness. Lederer has satisfied five generations of customers and is still going strong. The prices are terrific and the quality and workmanship impressive. Shop for classics like hand-woven leathers, bamboo-handled structured bags, steel or wood-framed investment banker briefcases and their exclusive Angelica bag. Luggage, small leather goods and desk accessories, hunting clothes and Barbour outerwear are also available. There is even a repair shop on the premises.   *888-537-6921 ledererdeparis.com*

Luxury   *Amex/MC/V*

Midtown East   **(212) 355-5515**
457 Madison Avenue   at 51st St
NYC 10022   Mon-Sat 9:30-6

Lee Anderson

A haven for the more serious minded New York woman, who orders from Anderson's couture collection of classic suits, separates, daywear and eveningwear. Choose from off-the-rack or order custom-made.

Expensive   *Amex/MC/V*

Upper East Side   **(212) 772-2463**
23 East 67th Street   btw Fifth/Madison Ave
NYC 10021   Mon-Fri 10-6, Sat 11-6 (except in summer)

Legacy

Vintage-inspired clothing without the musty smell or wear and tear of the real thing. Dresses, skirts, blouses, pants and more by a number of underground European designers who all have a retro feel and a distinctive look.   *legacy-nyc.com*

Moderate   *Amex/MC/V*

SoHo   **(212) 966-4827**
109 Thompson Street   btw Prince/Spring
NYC 10012   Daily 12-7

Leggiadro

If you missed out on the resortwear collections at department stores and boutiques, head to this Upper East Side store where sun-ready styles are in season 365 days a year. Clothing and swimwear by Sugar and Leggiadro are perfect for warm-weather destinations from St Tropez to Palm Beach. Expect lots of prints, bright colors and complementary accessories.   *leggiadro.com*

Expensive   *Amex/MC/V*

Upper East Side   **(212) 753-5050**
680 Madison Avenue   btw 61/62nd St
NYC 10021   Daily 10:30-6

Legs Beautiful

Pretty much what it says—lots of legwear to make the most of your gams. The fabulous hosiery selection includes brand names like DKNY, CK, Hue and Hanes, but there is also sexy lingerie, bodysuits, stretch tops, amusing socks, tights, and flip-flops. Now, if only there were one on every street corner. *1-866-243-1113 legsbeautiful.com*

Affordable   *Amex/MC/V*

Midtown East   **(212) 949-2270**
200 Park Avenue   at 45th St
NYC 10166   Mon-Fri 7:30-8

Leonard Logsdail

Once a Savile Row tailor, Leonard Logsdail now provides New York bankers, diplomats and high-powered lawyers with his British bespoke tailoring. He takes your measurements, cuts his paper pattern and then ships your order to London to be hand-stitched. Made-to-measure suits of the finest pedigree start at $2,700, custom suits at $4,400. Time is indeed money: expect to wait six to eight weeks for delivery.

Luxury   *Amex/MC/V*

Midtown East   **(212) 752-5030**
9 East 53rd Street (4th floor)   btw Fifth/Madison Ave
NYC 10022   Mon-Fri 8-5 (or by appointment)

Les Copains

This chicly decorated boutique offers a winning mix of classic and avant-garde looks, from suits and tweeds to stylish sweaters and superb coats—highlights include beautiful cashmere pants and great knitwear. Browse the Blue label for more casual finds and Trend for those young pieces perfect for spicing up your wardrobe.

Expensive   *Amex/MC/V*

Upper East Side   **(212) 327-3014**
807 Madison Avenue   btw 67/68th St
NYC 10021   Mon-Sat 10-6

Les Petits Chapelais

Packed with whimsical children's clothing, including hand-loomed sweaters, dresses in vintage fabrics, handknit tops, T-shirts, hats and accessories. Wicker baskets, complete with three-piece baby sets (chenille blanket, hat, and toy), make wonderful baby shower gifts. *lespetitschapelais.com*

Moderate to expensive   *Amex/MC/V*

SoHo   **(212) 505-1927**
142 Sullivan Street   btw Houston/Prince
NYC 10012   Sun-Mon 1-6, Tues-Sat 12-7

LeSportSac

LeSportSac continues to get better and better. With a more fashion-forward client in mind, LeSportSac take their bags well into the new millennium with modern shapes that reflect a girl-on-the-go lifestyle. The whitewashed walls, glass tables and friendly staff allow the ultra-person-ality bags—totes, weekend duffles, cosmetic clutches and handbags, all double-stitched on the inside and machine washable—to hog the spotlight. The price points are mostly under $100, with nothing over $200. With cute names like Rainbow Spectator and Classic Hobo, everyone is bound to find a style that reflects his or her personality.

800-486-BAGS   *lesportsac.com*

Moderate   *Amex/MC/V*

Upper East Side   **(212) 988-6200**
1065 Madison Avenue   btw 80/81st St
NYC 10028   Mon-Fri 10-7, Sat 10-6, Sun 12-5

SoHo   **(212) 625-2626**
176 Spring Street   btw West Broadway/Thompson
NYC 10012   Mon-Sat 11-7, Sun 12-6

Lester's

A nondescript store that features a good selection of back-to-school basics, casual play clothes and trendy sportswear for hard-to-please juniors from brand names like Juicy, Hard Tail and Quiksilver. There are also full-service layette and shoe departments, as well as accessories. From newborn to size 16 and juniors.

Affordable   *Amex/MC/V*

Upper East Side   **(212) 734-9292**
1534 Second Avenue   at 80th St
NYC 10021   Mon-Fri 10-7 (Thurs 10-8), Sat 10-6, Sun 12-5

Liana

This stylish uptown store nods to the trends while keeping things classic with a sizeable selection of casual basics, including sweater sets by Easel, White and Warren, and 525, tanks and tees by Michael Star and pants by Chaiken and Theory. And with the Upper West Side's largest selection of little black dresses, Liana has an ample selection of formal-wear, suits, and other tasteful party attire from the likes of Shin Choi, Tahari, Nanette Lepore and Trina Turk.

Expensive   *Amex/MC/V*

Upper West Side   **(212) 873-8746**
324 Columbus Avenue   btw 75/76th St
NYC 10023   Mon-Sat 11-7, Sun 1-6

Liberty House

Originally conceived in 1968 as a co-op that donated prof-its to the civil rights movement, Liberty House is still known for its large and varied selection of independent designers who work with natural fibers. While there is no shortage of ethnic-inspired prints, they also cram lots of pared-down, urban sophisticate tees, dresses and trousers into this packed, busy space. Check it out for unique jewelry and accessories and charming children's pjs.

Moderate   *Amex/MC/V*

Upper West Side
2466 Broadway
NYC 10024

(212) 799-7640
at 91st St
Tues-Sat 10-6:45 (Mon, Thurs 10-7:45)
Sun 12-6

Upper West Side
2878a Broadway
NYC 10025

(212) 932-1950
at 112th St
Mon-Sat 10-6:45, Sun 12-5:45

★ Lilliput/SoHo Kids

Inspired by the Lilliputians in *Gulliver's Travels*, this store carries a soup-to-nuts collection of children's clothing ideal for play, school and dress-up. For boys, choose from jeans, khakis, dress shirts, sweaters, T-shirts and windbreakers, while girls will find looks running from adorable print dresses to cool, fashionable leather jeans paired with a hip top. And for babies, they've got it all, from onesies in washable silks and cashmeres to a basic Petit Bateau undershirt. Labels include Lili Gaufrette, Marcel & Leon, I Golfini della Nonna, and Diesel. Shoes, hats, pajamas, bags and toys round out the assortment. From newborn to 18 years old. *lilliputsoho.com*

Moderate *Amex/MC/V*

SoHo
265 Lafayette Street
NYC 10012

(212) 965-9567
btw Prince/Spring
Sun-Mon 12-6, Tues-Sat 11-7

SoHo
240 Lafayette Street
NYC 10012

(212) 965-9201
btw Prince/Spring
(opening hours as above)

Lily

Imagine that the queen of Palm Beach chic and American design legend Lilly Pulitzer had a daughter who opened her own shop in Brooklyn, and you'll have some idea of what awaits you at Lily. Perhaps younger and hipper (though no less colorful) than Mrs Pulitzer's famous wares, these current takes on sportswear perfectly combine cheekiness with Brooklyn cool. Michael Stars tees and underwear are available, as are cute tops by Free People and Hanky Panky. A neighborhood favorite, Lily is great place to snag a little out-of-the-way style. *lilybrooklyn.com*

Affordable *Amex/MC/V*

Cobble Hill
209 Court Street
Brooklyn 11201

(718) 858-6261
btw Warren/Wyckoff
Mon-Sat 11-7, Sun 12-6

★ Linda Dresner

Linda Dresner is a legend in fashion-forward retailing, and she continues to lead the pack with her elite collection of cutting-edge designers. John Galliano, Yohji Yamamoto, Martin Margiela, Dries Van Noten, Chloé and Jil Sander have a regular spot in the store, while hot newcomers such as Gregory Parkinson and Clu have also been put into the rotation. High-end shopping for drop-dead chic designer

173

pieces, from knockout evening gowns to urbane suits, in an equally chic retail space. There is a limited range of shoes and accessories. *lindadresner.com*

Luxury   *Amex/MC/V*

Midtown East   **(212) 308-3177**
484 Park Avenue   btw 58/59th St
NYC 10022   Mon-Sat 10-6

Linda's

Sexy sophistication is this lingerie superstore's specialty, offering underpinnings from over 100 lingerie labels including favorites like On Gossamer, Swan and, of course, Cosabella, and slinky shirts and loungewear by Le Cosa and James Perse to name only a few. Add in a whole bottom floor devoted to gorgeous swimwear, and you'll see that Linda's makes undressing an art.

Moderate   *Amex/MC/V*

SoHo   **(212) 777-8677**
462 West Broadway   btw Prince/Houston
NYC 10012   Daily 11-8

Upper East Side   **(212) 751-2727**
828 Lexington Avenue   btw 63/64 St
NYC 10021   Mon, Tues 10-7, Wed-Fri 10-8
                                                      Sat 11-7, Sun 12-5

Lingerie on Lex

Don't be turned off by the less-than-creative name—this charming store features upscale American and European intimate apparel brands like Hanro, Cosabella and La Perla, to name but a few purveyors of sweet nothings. Customers will appreciate the large variety and good organization. Custom-made pieces are also available.

Expensive   *Amex/MC/V*

Upper East Side   **(212) 755-3312**
831 Lexington Avenue   btw 63/64th St
NYC 10021   Mon-Fri 10-7, Sat 11-6, Sun 12-5

Lingo

Lingo's teal and red trim facade is hard to miss, as are its fanciful floral window displays. Inside you'll find a heady cross-section of NY fashion: one-of-a-kind handmade, hand-embroidered shoulder bags, dangly silver earrings with semi-precious stones, sassy silk-screened T-shirts and leather clutches in bright colors. Owner Shin Yee Man keeps things current (and wildly eclectic) by featuring a number of different designers, many of whom moonlight as artists and musicians. *lingonyc.com*

Moderate   *Amex/MC/V*

Chelsea   **(212) 929-4676**
257 West 19th Street   btw Seventh/Eighth Ave
NYC 10011   Tues-Sun 1-8

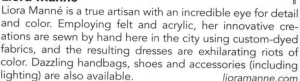

Liora Manné

Liora Manné is a true artisan with an incredible eye for detail and color. Employing felt and acrylic, her innovative creations are sewn by hand here in the city using custom-dyed fabrics, and the resulting dresses are exhilarating riots of color. Dazzling handbags, shoes and accessories (including lighting) are also available. *lioramanne.com*

Moderate   *Amex/MC/V*

SoHo   **(212) 965-0302**
91 Grand Street   btw Mercer/Greene
NYC 10013   Mon-Sat 11-7, Sun 12-6

Lisa Shaub

A quaint milliner, Lisa Shaub crafts hats with the hand of a surgeon and the eye of an artist. She hews these special toppers with straw, felt, fleece and wool in classic styles, often in shapes reminiscent of the Twenties and Thirties. Her shop is filled with fedoras, sophisticated cowboy hats, soft porkpies, boaters, wide-brimmed panamas, berets and cotton toppers for babies. Hats aren't the whole story, however, as she also caters to those seeking one-of-a-kind evening bags, floral scarves, hand-dyed sarongs, or beach bags brimming in straw and fancy feather headpieces. Custom hats are also available—call for a private appointment. *lisashaub.com*

Moderate   *Amex/MC/V*

Nolita   **(212) 965-9176**
232 Mulberry   btw Prince/Spring
NYC 10012   Wed 12-5, Thurs-Sat 12-7, Sun 1-6

Little Eric Shoes

Fancy some fancy footwear for your kids? Check out this exclusive collection of Italian footwear: casual basics, back-to-school essentials, formal dress shoes and high fashion styles for teenagers. The sales staff claim these shoes will outwear your child. Kids will enjoy the toys inside and the colorful train set painted along the store's ceiling. A good source for all ages, especially for your baby's first walking shoes.

Expensive   *Amex/MC/V*

Upper East Side   **(212) 717-1513**
1118 Madison Avenue   btw 83/84th St
NYC 10028   Mon-Sat 10-6, Sun 12-6

★ Liz Lange Maternity

A former *Vogue* editor, Liz Lange is the reigning queen of maternity chic (no longer an oxymoron) and her stylish store offers one-stop shopping for sportswear, eveningwear and activewear. Her secret: easy, chic clothing you would wear even if you weren't pregnant. Looks include capri pants, cashmere twinsets, sexy halter tops, A-line dresses, shifts, tunics, denim and spaghetti-strap evening dresses. Model mothers like Brooke Shields and Elle Macpherson have compared Lange's designs to Michael Kors and Calvin Klein. *lizlange.com*

Expensive *Amex/MC/V*

Upper East Side **(212) 879-2191**
958 Madison Avenue btw 75/76th St
NYC 10021 Mon-Fri 10-7, Sat 10-6, Sun 12-5

Loehmann's

Canny shoppers make this mounting legend their first stop when looking for top brand names at knockout prices. The selection includes men's and women's clothes, a petite section, accessories and shoes but the main attraction is without a doubt the Back Room, a department stocked with designer labels like Calvin Klein, Donna Karan and Armani. A chic Moschino trench for $100? Yes, it is possible here. By the way, if you're not satisfied, Loehmann's has a 14-day, get-your-money-back return policy. *loehmanns.com*

Moderate *Amex/MC/V*

Chelsea **(212) 352-0856**
101 Seventh Avenue btw 16/17th St
NYC 10011 Mon-Sat 9-9, Sun 11-7

Loftworks @ Lafayette

Designed to give folks a marvelous place to shop for designer clothing at discounted prices, Loftworks @ Lafayette draws shoppers to Lower Manhattan for great buys. The large stock includes formal business attire, designer sportswear and casualwear from Hugo Boss, Armani, DKNY, Fendi, Dolce & Gabbana, Calvin Klein, Prada and many others—all at slashed down prices. Many of the best bargains can be found on the lower level, where Loftworks keep their close-out items. *loftworkslafayette.com*

Affordable *Amex/MC/V*

Tribeca **(212) 343-8088**
100 Lafayette Street btw White/Walker
NYC 10013 Mon-Fri 10-7, Sat 11-7, Sun 12-6

Longchamp

Longchamp's nylon totes are ubiquitous on the Upper East Side these days, and with good reason. The bags are light, durable, and come in a panoply of colors. Other covetable items at this venerable French boutique include elegant structured handbags in leather, suede and, yes, nylon. Trendier pieces, such as hobo bags, provide some visual punch to Longchamp's otherwise graceful and understated collection. The company's sophisticated sensibility also appears in its briefcases, luggage, raincoats, belts, scarves and gloves. *longchamp.com*

Expensive *Amex/MC/V*

Upper East Side **(212) 223-1500**
713 Madison Avenue at 63rd St
NYC 10021 Mon-Sat 10-7

Lord & Taylor

After extensive remodeling, this behemoth department store looks better than ever. The makeover makes it easy to navigate between departments—all of which remain true to the store's mission of providing conservative and affordable clothing for sensible people. The selection is a melting-pot of classic fashion designers like Ralph Lauren, Donna Karan and Calvin Klein. Known for special occasion formalwear and hard-to-find shoe styles, Lord & Taylor also boasts extensive petite, career and sportswear sections. Other departments include cosmetics, accessories, children's, men's, lingerie, outerwear and large sizes. *lordandtaylor.com*

Moderate   *Amex/MC/V*

Midtown   **(212) 391-3344**
424 Fifth Avenue   at 39th Street
NYC 10018   Mon-Fri 10-8:30, Sat 10-7, Sun 11-7

Lord of The Fleas

While having little to do with a flea market or the William Golding book of a similar title, this cleverly named boutique sells tight tiny tops, super-short skirts, sassy logo tees and other funky items for juniors, teenagers or anyone willing to show a little skin. If you want to feed the action heroine within by wearing Superwoman skivvies, you're sure to find the perfect piece at Lord of the Fleas.

Affordable   *Amex/MC/V*

Upper West Side   **(212) 875-8815**
2142 Broadway   btw 75/76th St
NYC 10023   Daily 11-8

East Village   **(212) 260-9130**
305 East 9th Street   btw First/Second Ave
NYC 10009   Mon-Sat 12-8, Sun 12-7

Loro Piana

Apparently the higher a goat climbs, the finer its cashmere (impress your friends with this fact). Which means that Loro Piana's goats must have been climbing Everest. The collection features elegant knitwear, outerwear, pants, shirts and jackets in sumptuous fabrics like cashmere, silk and superfine wool. In addition, there is a luxurious assortment of cashmere shawls, scarves, stoles and capes in mouthwatering shades. Prices are sky-high, but then again, so were the goats...

Luxury   *Amex/MC/V*

Upper East Side   **(212) 980-7961**
821 Madison Avenue   btw 68/69th St
NYC 10021   Mon-Sat 10-6 (Thurs 10-7)

Lost Art

Have a rock star inside you just screaming to get out? Well, follow the lead of Britney Spears, Aerosmith's Steven Tyler and designer Anna Sui and turn to Lost Art's Jordan Betten for rock 'n' roll leather looks in cow, deer, elk, snake, croc and alligator. Intricate handcrafted details include antique beading, unique closures, stones, feathers and fur. Each creation is a one-of-a-kind artwork. Best bet: his whip-stitched lace-up leather pants. Kinky.   *lostartnyc.com*

Expensive   *Amex/MC/V*

Chelsea   **(212) 594-5450**
515 West 29th Street   btw Tenth/Eleventh Ave
NYC 10001   Mon-Fri 10-5 (by appointment)

⭐ Louis Vuitton

The mere utterance of the name Louis Vuitton conjures up an image of international chic. The often-imitated but never replicated luggage and clothing line, designed by the omnipresent designer of the decade Marc Jacobs, is legendary in its own time. From the classic monogrammed luggage sets that are said to last forever to the limited-edition bags-cum-art-objects, it's clear why people love those little interlocking LVs. Jacob's immensely stylish ready-to-wear collection for Vuitton is here for the taking, too. The new Fifth Avenue flagship is enormous, but for south-of-14th-Street style-seekers, the SoHo branch is also well stocked.   *800-847-2956 vuitton.com*

Expensive to luxury   *Amex/MC/V*

Fifth Avenue   **(212) 758-8877**
1 East 57th Street   at Fifth Ave
NYC 10022   Mon-Sat 10-7, Thurs 10-8, Sun 12-6

SoHo   **(212) 274-9090**
116 Greene Street   btw Prince/Spring
NYC 10012   Mon-Sat 11-7, Sun 12-6

The Lounge

This SoHo boutique sets the scene with a collection of label-loving, super-trendy streetwear from Von Dutch, James Perse, Roberto Cavalli, D&G and Rock and Republic. Complete with a café in the back and a DJ booth spinning (you can buy hot club mixes from Buddha Bar and the Hotel Costes), The Lounge is a fashion destination for those who love the nightlife.

Expensive   *Amex/MC/V*

SoHo   **(212) 226-7585**
593 Broadway   btw Prince/Houston
NYC 10012   Mon-Thurs 10-9, Fri-Sat 10-10, Sun 12-8

Love Saves the Day

The sign on the door says 'Unattended children will be sold as slaves.' but this crowded labyrinth of cheeky kitsch memorabilia is irresistible to kids and adults alike. Remember the G.I.Joe lunchboxes, Kiss dolls, and Pee Wee Herman collectibles? They're all here. You'll also find vintage clothes and shoes, mostly random pieces like wedding dresses from the Sixties. Some are a bit worse for wear, but you could get lucky—after all, this is where Rosanna Arquette got Madonna's pyramid jacket in *Desperately Seeking Susan*.

Affordable to moderate   *Amex/MC/V*

East Village   **(212) 228-3802**
119 Second Avenue   at 7th St
NYC 10003   Daily 1-8

Love Shine

Describing itself as the 'one-stop shop for bags, muffs and all kinds of stuff,' this crazy East Village store has eclectic ethnic gifts to suit every taste. Examples include pink fake-fur hand warmers with plastic flowers ($40), totes adorned with sequined Mexican masks or skull and crossbones, kitschy ashtrays and more skull and crossbones on car-ryalls.   *loveshinenyc.com*

Affordable   *Amex/MC/V*

East Village   **(212) 387-0935**
543½ East 6th Street   btw Avenue A/B
NYC 10009   Daily 1-8

Williamsburg   **(718) 302-2913**
249 Grand Street   btw Driggs/Roebling
Brooklyn 11211   Sun-Thurs 12-8, Fri-Sat 12-11

Luca Luca

Designer Luca Orlandi is a brave man—he's long been known for his bold approach to fashion, involving a strong use of color and bright, eye-popping patterns. And he has range: his silk/linen suits are perfect for an elegant dinner date, while his club-worthy tops look great with jeans. Luca Luca's accessories include t-strap sandals and chain-link leather purses. The store's white walls let the clothes take center stage, from dress suits, bias-cut pleated leather jackets and dresses, to cashmeres, suede shirtdresses, strapless eveningwear and perfectly polished outfits for the lunching set.   *lucaluca.com*

Expensive   *Amex/MC/V*

Upper East Side   **(212) 288-9285**
1011 Madison Avenue   at 78th St
NYC 10011   Mon-Sat 10-6:30 (Thurs 10-8), Sun 12-5

Upper East Side   **(212) 753-2444**
690 Madison Avenue   at 62nd St
NYC 10021   (opening hours as above)

★ Lucien Pellat-Finet

The sweaters on offer from this self-proclaimed 'King Kong of cashmere' are luxurious and come in a range of mouth-watering colors, but they have a decidedly down-town twist. Find the entire irreverent collection (this season's Gangs collection features 'I Hemp NY' sweatshirts, long-sleeved tees with bats, skull and bones bikinis and boss motorcycle jackets) in this exquisitely renovated 19th-century townhouse. Looks for kids eschew the scari-er prints in favor of ladybugs and sea creatures. Be sure to see the eclectic interior designs, including vintage Florence Knoll furniture, and inquire about made-to-measure clothing.   *lucienpellat-finet.com*

Luxury   *Amex/MC/V*

West Village   **(212) 255-8560**
14 Christopher Street   btw Sixth/Seventh Ave
NYC 10014   Mon-Sat 11-7, Sun 1-5 (except in summer)

Lucky Brand

In the beginning there was Levi's; now there's Lucky Brand, a Californian company that features a floor-to-ceiling selection of jeans, loungewear and everything in between. Pay an average of $70 for a pair of jeans. 'Lucky You' and a four-leaf clover logo mark the lining of every pair. Will they bring you good luck? Who knows…   *luckybrandjeans.com*

Affordable   *Amex/MC/V*

Upper West Side   **(212) 579-1760**
216 Columbus Avenue   at 70th St
NYC 10023   Mon-Sat 10-8, Sun 11-7

Upper East Side   **(646) 422-1192**
1151 Third Avenue   at 67th St
NYC 10021   Mon-Fri 10-8, Sat 10-7, Sun 11-7

Flatiron   **(917) 606-1418**
172 Fifth Avenue   at 22nd St
NYC 10010   Mon-Sat 10-8 (Wed-Fri 10-9), Sun 11-7

SoHo   **(212) 625-0707**
38 Greene Street   at Grand
NYC 10013   Mon-Sat 11-8, Sun 11-6

Lucy Barnes

Lucy Barnes creates romantic clothing for ladies who demand eclectic elegance. The label offers intricately embroidered and beaded leathers, tailored pants with vintage buttons, lace ruffled tops, and floral chiffon gathered skirts. And the luxurious details are often handcrafted—from crocheting, appliqué, patchwork and knitting, all of which help turn each piece into a treasured possession.   *lucybarnes.biz*

Expensive   *Amex/MC/V*

Chelsea   **(212) 255-9502**
320 West 14th Street   btw Eighth/Ninth Ave
NYC 10014   Mon-Sat 11-7, Sun 12-6

Lulu Guinness

Lulu Guinness handbags are a favorite among celebs like Madonna and Liz Hurley for their whimsical sensibility, and she has proven as widely popular in the States as in her native Great Britain. Instead of logos, find adorable prints (stilettos, dalmatians, gloved hands) and fascinating bags (one comes in the shape of an old rotary phone dial) and cosmetic cases in her new West Village digs. Irreverent and fun.   *luluguinness.com*

Expensive   *Amex/MC/V*

West Village   **(212) 367-2120**
394 Bleecker Street   btw 11th/Perry
NYC 10014   Mon-Sat 11-7, Sun 12-6

★ Lunettes et Chocolat

Designer chocolate, sunglasses and prescription eyeglasses—why didn't someone think of it sooner? French purveyor of eclectic eyewear Selima Salaun's spin-off (her main store is at 59 Wooster Street in SoHo) houses a selection of styles from Selima Optique, plus vintage shades by Givenchy, Missoni and St Tropez. This is the perfect pit stop for a marathon shopping session. Grab a gourmet Aztec hot chocolate from the counterperson dressed as Charlie Chaplin at the Cacao bar, and browse the shelves of vintage bags and accessories—you'll find everything from sequined coin purses to chocolate Cuban cigars at $8.50 each.

selimaoptique.com

Expensive	*Amex/MC/V*
Nolita	**(212) 334-8484**
25 Prince Street	btw Mott/Elizabeth
NYC 10012	Mon-Sat 12-8, Sun 12-7

Lyell

Selling half bona fide vintage, half convincing reproductions by Lyell's house designer, the mode is very 1930s with modestly cut blouses in tiny flower-print silk, mauve and gray cropped velvet jackets, and lacy slips and sheer dresses that were made for each other. Vintage selections are choosy and well edited: Maud Frizon heels, a small and precious jewelry collection, and a rack of white blouses in sheers, lace, eyelet and embroidered linen. The tiny room is lined in dainty wallpaper with a mosaic tiled floor and antique light fixtures: very fitting for the wares on offer.

Moderate	*Amex/MC/V*
Nolita	**(212) 966-8484**
173 Elizabeth Street	at Delancey
NYC 10012	Daily 12-7

Lynn Park NY

Downtown darling designer Lynn Park runs this eponymous boutique, specializing in cutting-edge fashion both from herself and a great edit of young designers. She offers a complete collection of individual clothes: roughed up denim, pop-colored dresses embellished with paillettes and roses, cute frilly miniskirts and ruched, customized tops and shirts. Alongside her own funky label, she also stocks coats by Chan Paul, and hip tops from Mimi Turner and Ouise. The menswear follows the same hip aesthetic, but focuses on slouchy-cool denim by Park. A line of fearless accessories completes the cooler-than-cool collection.

Expensive	*Amex/MC/V*
SoHo	**(212) 965-5133**
51 Wooster Street	at Broome
NYC 10012	Daily 12-6 (Sun 12-5)

m0851

Formerly called Rugby North America, this friendly, two-floor store does what the Canadians (see Club Monaco) do so well—chic basics for Americans. Leather is a focus here, from a huge range of coats and jackets (the mens' are a standout) to matching accessories like sleek handbags, briefcases and purses all stamped with the subtle Rugby logo. But look out for the brilliant selection of high-quality viscose T-shirts, polo shirts and simple cotton skirts, in a rainbow of colors and all at easy-access prices.   *m0851.com*

Moderate   *Amex/MC/V*

SoHo   **(212) 431-3069**
106 Wooster Street   btw Prince/Spring
NYC 10012   Mon-Sat 11-8, Sun 12-6

Upper East Side   **(212) 988-1313**
748 Madison Avenue   btw 64/65th St
NYC 10021   Mon-Sat 10-6, Sun 11-5

Macy's

Macy's has just about everything under the sun—which pretty much makes it a parallel universe. There are extensive men's, women's and children's departments, home furnishings and cosmetics, and places to grab a bite to eat. The end result: the world's largest (and at times messiest) department store, packed to the rafters with aggressive, bargain-hunting shoppers. While designer labels are scarce, you'll find a decent selection of labels like Jones New York, Polo Ralph Lauren and Tommy Hilfiger, and there's a great range of jeans from classic labels like Calvin Klein. For the feet, there's everything from sneakers to dress-up shoes. Another bonus is the vast array of services Macy's provides, such as an International Visitors Center, hair salons, restaurants, post office and jewelry appraising.   *800-431-9644 macys.com*

Affordable to expensive   *Amex/MC/V*

Midtown West   **(212) 695-4400**
Broadway at Herald Square   btw Broadway/34th St
NYC 10001   Mon-Sat 10-9, Sun 11-7

Maggie Norris Couture

Maggie Norris knows fashion better than most, having working for Ralph Lauren for 14 years. Her stunning collection is wildly romantic, using fabrics taken from old tapestries and Parisian textile archives, and is marked by intricate beading and vintage Lesage embroidery. You'll gasp when you see breathtaking pieces like her exquisite long evening gowns (for at least $10,000), bespoke shirts and amazing jackets. Private appointments are available at the Midtown Studio.   *maggienorriscouture.com*

Luxury   *Amex/MC/V*

Midtown West   **(212) 239-3433**
494 Eighth Avenue (suite 1505)   at 35th St
NYC 10001   (by appointment)

Fifth Avenue   **(212) 872-8957**
754 Fifth Avenue   at Bergdorf Goodman
NYC 10019   Mon-Sat 10-7 (Thurs 10-8), Sun 12-6

Magic Shoes

Magic it's not, but you might stumble upon some lucky kicks at this cramped Village store crammed with Doc Martens, cowboy boots, and Converse of every conceivable make (including many hard-to-find or discontinued models). Finding a spot to actually try anything on is a challenge, however, especially if another customer happens to be in Magic Shoes at the same time.

Moderate *Amex/MC/V*

West Village
178 Bleecker Street
NYC 10012

(212) 673-1633
btw MacDougal/Sullivan
Daily 12-8

★ Magic Windows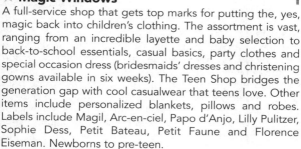

A full-service shop that gets top marks for putting the, yes, magic back into children's clothing. The assortment is vast, ranging from an incredible layette and baby selection to back-to-school essentials, casual basics, party clothes and special occasion dress (bridesmaids' dresses and christening gowns available in six weeks). The Teen Shop bridges the generation gap with cool casualwear that teens love. Other items include personalized blankets, pillows and robes. Labels include Magil, Arc-en-ciel, Papo d'Anjo, Lilly Pulitzer, Sophie Dess, Petit Bateau, Petit Faune and Florence Eiseman. Newborns to pre-teen.

Expensive *Amex/MC/V*

Upper East Side
1186 Madison Avenue
NYC 10028

(212) 289-0028
btw 86/87th St
Mon-Sat 10-6, Sun 11-5 (except in summer)

Make 10

Make 10 keeps in step with footwear trends by featuring casual and funky shoes, sandals, and boots from brands like Franco Sarte, Nine West, Anne Klein and Enzo. make10.com

Affordable *Amex/MC/V*

West Village
49 West 8th Street
NYC 10011

(212) 254-1132
btw Fifth/Sixth Ave
Mon-Sat 11-8, Sun 12-6

Fifth Avenue
366 Fifth Avenue
NYC 10001

(212) 868-1202
btw 34/35th St
Mon-Fri 10-7:30, Sat 11-7, Sun 12-6

Upper East Side
1227 Third Avenue
NYC 10021

(212) 472-2775
btw 70/71st St
Mon-Fri 11-7:30 (Thurs 11-8), Sat 11-6, Sun 12-6

Midtown West
1386 Sixth Avenue
NYC 10019

(212) 956-4739
btw 56/57th Street
Mon-Fri 10-7, Sat 11-6, Sun 12-6

Midtown West
44 West 39th Street
NYC 10018

(212) 391-2926
btw Fifth/Sixth Ave
Mon-Fri 10-6:30

Makie

👫👤

There is nothing like the joy of a great pair of pajamas. So head to this tiny SoHo store for your happy hit: it's packed with nightwear, including classic-styled pajamas, nightshirts and unisex bathrobes made in France by Bains-Plus. There are solid looks embellished with contrasting piping, jacquards, checks, stripes and florals in top-quality cottons and with the vital elasticized waists. Prices start at $140. Buy kids' pjs for $70 (2-12 years), as well as rompers and cute handmade dresses. Also look out for canvas totes, vintage buttons and other goodies.

Moderate   *Amex/MC/V*

SoHo   **(212) 625-3930**
109 Thompson Street   btw Prince/Spring
NYC 10012   Mon-Sat 12-7

Makola

👤

Venetian designer Ilaria Makola brings New Yorkers the romance and energy of her native country with a collection of ultra-feminine and boldly colored day and evening dresses. Choose from luxurious silks and whimsical, cotton print dresses styled with dainty (code for diet) waistlines and full petticoat skirts. The end result: romantic looks reminiscent of the Fifties. Coordinating accessories include shoes, handbags, jackets and hats. Very Doris Day.

Expensive   *Amex/MC/V*

Upper East Side   **(212) 772-2272**
1045 Madison Avenue   btw 79/80th St
NYC 10021   Tues-Sat 10-6

★ Malia Mills

👤

Hawaii native Malia Mills believes that all women are beautiful just the way they are—hence her dream bikinis to fit every cut and curve from AA to DD, including maternity. *Vogue* credited Malia with starting a 'veritable body image revolution,' and when you visit this comfy dressing lounge of a store you are applauded for your individuality. A flirty bandeau shows off a small bust, the V-neck 'Sophia' compliments a DD cup, and the cinch bottoms make any hips look like Marilyn Monroe's. For that perfect honeymoon, you can have custom bottoms designed with Swarovski crystals spelling out 'Just Married'.   maliamills.com

Expensive   *Amex/MC/V*

Nolita   **(212) 625-2311**
199 Mulberry Street   btw Spring/Kenmare
NYC 10012   Mon-Sat 12-7, Sun 12-6

Upper East Side   **(212) 517-7485**
1031 Lexington Avenue   at 74th St
NYC 10021   Mon-Sat 12-7

Upper West Side   **(212) 874-7200**
220 Columbus Avenue   at 70th St
NYC 10023   Mon-Sat 12-7, Sun 12-6

Malo

Malo are the kings of cashmere—theirs coming from the rugged Mongolian goat, which is the world's best source for the material. This is a New York staple for luxury knitwear: crewnecks, cardigans, V-necks, turtlenecks, twinsets and cablestitch pullovers. A ready-to-wear line of coats, jackets and pants fills out the cashmere collection, while Malo's home collection includes pajamas, robes, slippers, pillows and blankets. Items in other fabrics stay true to the brand's luxurious-yet-casual aesthetic. Look for accessories such as raincoats and surprisingly chic handbags. *malo.it*

Luxury   *Amex/MC/V*

Upper East Side   **(212) 396-4721**
814 Madison Avenue   at 68th St
NYC 10021   Mon-Sat 10-6

Manhattan Portage

Hard-wearing nylon messenger bags are what made this groovy brand's name, and this store carries a full selection of the cult carryalls in a rainbow of bright, colors (from $18 to $105). The line also includes one-strap backpacks, DJ bags for records and the odd-sounding (but very functional) 'urban support system' which is basically a laptop bag-style tote. *manhattanportage.com*

Affordable   *Amex/MC/V*

East Village   **(212) 995-5490**
333 East 9th Street   btw First/Second Ave
NYC 10003   Mon-Sat 12-8, Sun 12-7

SoHo   **(212) 226-4557**
301 West Broadway   btw Canal/Grand
NYC 10013   Daily 11-7

Manhattan Saddlery

Formerly known as Copperfields, New York's oldest saddlery shop has been catering to English riders since 1912. There is a complete selection of riding attire (ages 4 to adult) and equipment for you and your favorite equine friend, fitted and custom riding boots, accessories, gifts and toys, as well as top-of-the line saddles.

Expensive   *Amex/MC/V*

Flatiron   **(212) 673-1400**
117 East 24th Street   btw Park/Lexington Ave
NYC 10010   Mon-Sat 10-6 (Thurs 10-7)

Mankind

The modern male won't get far in this city looking like a cave dweller. Gentlemen, cast off your practically prehistoric pieces and update your look to the 21st century by wandering over to Mankind. This men's boutique sells the latest in cool casual essential, from Filippa K sailor striped knits and argyle sweaters by Pringle of Scotland to Nicole Farhi leather sandals and bags and accessories by Il Parcel and

Ant Industries. If you've taken care of your clothes, that's one less thing to think about when you're on the hunt.

Expensive *Amex/MC/V*

SoHo **(212) 966-5146**
8 Greene Street btw Grand/Canal
NYC 10013 Mon-Sat 12-6

★ Manolo Blahnik

Forced to choose between their husbands or their Blahniks, many women might well choose the latter: fans include Faye Dunaway, Madonna, Donatella Versace, Diane von Furstenberg and every fashion magazine editor in the business. The sultan of the stiletto, Blahnik designs the ultimate in sexy footwear. Each style is feminine, seductive and fabulously comfortable—and achieving this in a pair of sky-high heels is no mean feat. There are more demure offerings, from mules, glittery evening slippers, strappy sandals and chic loafers, and your wedding day will be sadly incomplete without a knockout pair of Manolo's bridal shoes. Prices typically run from $445 to approximately $1,000.

Expensive *Amex/MC/V*

Midtown West **(212) 582-3007**
31 West 54th Street btw Fifth/Sixth Ave
NYC 10019 Mon-Fri 10:30-6, Sat 10:30-5:30

★ Marc Jacobs

Marc Jacobs is the king of New York fashion right now, as well as one of the world's most influential designers. From the Grunge collection 10 years ago to his retro-luxe collections favored by sophisticated downtowners (and every model worth her *Vogue* cover), he can do no fashion wrong. He was the first big-name designer to hit Bleecker Street in the West Village and now everyone else has followed. Visit Jacobs for luxe cashmere sweaters, swingy party dresses and cartoon-cute shoes that all the Hollywood girls like Sofia Coppola wear. His Marc by Marc Jacobs line, a cheaper version of the luxe label, has been a phenomenal success—style mavens everywhere confess an addiction to his faded, creased jeans, tweedy pants and Sixties-inspired striped shirts. Accessories include his already-classic handbags (around $900), leather goods, and those lovely, lovely shoes (from $250 to $1,000). *marcjacobs.com*

Luxury *Amex/MC/V*

SoHo **(212) 343-1490**
163 Mercer Street btw Houston/Prince
NYC 10012 Mon-Sat 11-7, Sun 12-6

West Village **(212) 924-6126**
385 Bleecker Street at Perry
NYC 10014 Mon-Sat 12-8, Sun 12-7

★ Marc by Marc Jacobs

Ladies love cool Jacobs. Italian leather shoes ($400-$700) and bags ($500-$1,500) are the center of attention in his

Bleecker street store, although there is also a limited selection of scarves and perfume. Jacobs' long-time-coming collection of impeccable home furnishings and stunning jewelry point to the designer setting his sights on a larger kingdom than the fashion world he already commands.

Expensive   *Amex/MC/V*

West Village   **(212) 924-0026**
403 Bleecker Street   at Perry
NYC 10014   Mon-Sat 12-8, Sun 12-7

Mare

Chic shoes on the cutting edge of Italian style can be found at Mare. A sophisticated little shop, Mare offers classic, trendy and very funky footware designs at reasonable prices.

Moderate   *Amex/MC/V*

SoHo   **(212) 343-1110**
426 West Broadway   btw Prince/Spring
NYC 10012   Mon-Fri 11-8, Sat 11-7, Sun 12-7

Mariko

Fancy a bit of glitz? Some costume jewelry to leave the other girls in the dust? Head to this boutique, where the walls drip with beads and baubles and more beads. Paste diamonds and turquoise are popular here, but look out also for a range of chic silk shirts in jewel-like colors. A tip: put on your sunglasses before entering.

Affordable   *Amex/MC/V*

Upper East Side   **(212) 472-1176**
998 Madison Avenue   btw 77/78th St
NYC 10021   Mon-Sat 10-6

Marina Rinaldi

This is the place to shop for upscale, plus-sized fashions (sizes from 10-22). Marina Rinaldi is the sister company of Italian brand MaxMara and shares its sleek look. Find classic, figure-flattering styles in a chic pared-down aesthetic. Neutral colors and wearable fabrics are evident in the high-quality collection that includes everything from outerwear to pants, blouses, sweaters and a small shoe selection.

Expensive   *Amex/MC/V*

Upper East Side   **(212) 734-4333**
800 Madison Avenue   btw 67/68th St
NYC 10021   Mon-Sat 10-6 (Thurs 10-7)

Marmalade

We hear Sarah Jessica Parker is a fan of this vintage store that stocks pieces from the Seventies and Eighties. Find fabulous handbags, cocktail dresses, tees, great slouchy boots and lots of lace everything, including some Stevie Nicks-worthy dresses. Most pieces are under $400. The result? Eighties trash-glam girl meets downtown fashionista.   *marmaladevintage.com*

Moderate to expensive   *Amex/MC/V*

Lower East Side
172 Ludlow Street
NYC 10002

(212) 473-8070
btw Houston/Stanton
Daily 12-9

★ Marni 👗

Peppered with chic Italian flavor, pure whites, sharp colors and busy prints, Consuela Castiglioni's designs hang from large silver arcs in Marni—a fabulous shop for girls desiring seemingly effortless beauty. Featured are creatively cut pieces that use vintage fabrics to spice up modern styles. Classy jackets, coats and tops (including lovely blouses with puffy three-quarter sleeves) decorated with rainbows and polka dots hang beside breezy skirts. Exquisitely patterned shoes, glorious sunglasses and lovely bags complete Marni's girly-with-an-edge look.

Expensive   *Amex/MC/V*
SoHo   **(212) 343-3912**
161 Mercer Street   btw Houston/Prince
NYC 10012   Mon-Sat 11-7, Sun 12-6

Marsha D.D. 🧒

If you want a trip to the suburban mall without the car journey, walk over to Marsha D.D. The store features everything teens love: clothes, jewelry and plenty of swag like trucker hats, pencils and mouse pads. The store carries lines like Paul Frank as well as more underground labels like Junk Food. For boys, the clothes are of the surf/skate variety, featuring labels like Quiksilver and The North Face. From 7 to 16 years.

Affordable   *Amex/MC/V*
Upper East Side   **(212) 831-2422**
1574 Third Avenue   btw 88/89th St
NYC 10128   Mon-Sat 10-6

Martier 👗

At Martier you get two shops rolled into one: upstairs is filled with fashion-forward clothing, while downstairs boasts an abundance of sexy lingerie plus some swimwear. Typical fare includes sexy leather pants, body-hugging tops and print dresses by labels like Anti-Flirt, Vertigo, Parameter, Pinera, Sharagano and Ferré. Downstairs is home to a colorful selection of saucy intimates by La Perla, Lise Charmel and Malizia. Helpful sales staff.

Expensive   *Amex/MC/V*
Upper East Side   **(212) 758-5370**
1010 Third Avenue   at 60th St
NYC 10022   Mon-Sat 10-7:30, Sun 10-6

Upper East Side   **(212) 750-2633**
827 Lexington Avenue   btw 63/64th St
NYC 10024   Daily 10:30-7:30

Martinez Valero 👗

A convenient neighborhood shoe shop featuring trendy styles at attractive prices. Shop a selection from classic to trendy and looks that will complement any outfit, whether it's satin evening pumps, boots or summer sandals. Prices run from $125 to $265 for boots.

Moderate   *Amex/MC/V*

Upper East Side   **(212) 753-1822**
1029 Third Avenue   at 61st St
NYC 10021   Mon-Sat 11-7 (Thurs 11-8), Sun 12-6

Mary Adams

Because you can-can! Feel like you've stepped into the heart of the Moulin Rouge when you walk through the door of this boutique. The ruffled, lacy dresses would be perfect for a walk through the Left Bank, or to spice up your modern-day Manhattan wardrobe. Her Victorian-inspired designs are festooned with lace, peplums and ruffles and include elaborate corsets, skirts with full petticoats, iridescent silk ballgowns and unconventional wedding dresses. Custom orders also available.   *maryadamsthedress.com*

Expensive   *Amex/MC/V*

Lower East Side   **(212) 473-0237**
138 Ludlow Street   btw Stanton/Rivington
NYC 10002   Wed-Sat 1-6, Sun 1-5

Mary Efron

Mary Efron is noted for her 'fine and rare antique wearables' from the turn of the century to the Fifties, including silk and embroidered Chinese jackets, dresses from the Twenties and evening and special occasion wear. The beaded, jeweled and painted handbags available here are particularly eye-catching. Museum-quality fashion at your fingertips.

Moderate   *Amex/MC/V*

Upper East Side   **(212) 288-8809**
308 East 78th Street   at Second Ave
NYC 10021   Mon-Sat 1-7 (or by appointment)

Mason's Tennis Mart

Mason's is the oldest and most respected tennis retailer in the city. Athletic apparel, including cute tennis dresses, warm-ups, sweaters and shirts, comes from top-of-the-line labels like Polo, Fila, Nike, Adidas and Kaelin. Equipment brands include Babolat, Wilson, Volkl, Head and Prince. Great children's department. Same day stringing for rackets.   *masonstennis.com*

Moderate to expensive   *Amex/MC/V*

Midtown East   **(212) 755-5805**
56 East 53rd Street   btw Madison/Park Ave
NYC 10022   Mon-Fri 10-7, Sat 10-6, Sun 11-5

★ Massimo Bizzocchi

Italian eccentric Massimo Bizzocchi has brought his line, as well as some family-run Italian artisan lines, to his sleek New York flagship. His handcrafted suits are made by Martin Greenfield in Brooklyn, featuring two-tone lining and built-

Medici

Enter a world of accessories on the Upper West Side, where techno music plays backdrop to a collection of trendy shoes on the Medici label, the youthful CJ Bis by Charles Jourdan, and everything else besides from fringed bags, hats for the races, belts, even birthday cards. Best for men's shoes and summer sandals.

Moderate   *Amex/MC/V*

Upper West Side   **(212) 712-9342**
420 Columbus Avenue   btw 80/81st St
NYC 10023   Daily 10-8

Chelsea   **(212) 604-0888**
24 West 23rd Street   btw Fifth/Sixth Ave
NYC 10010   Mon-Sat 10-8, Sun 10-7

Meg

If you're tired of paying posh uptown prices, get down to Meghan Kinney's East Village store which specializes in polished, multi-purpose sportswear that can be custom-fitted. Separates are key: match pants with a double-knit wool jersey and work it with a jacket or coat. Each season Kinney introduces a new blend of fabric and texture combinations into her dominantly neutral color palette.   *megshops.com*

Expensive   *Amex/MC/V*

East Village   **(212) 260-6329**
312 East 9th Street   btw First/Second Ave
NYC 10003   Mon-Sat 12-8, Sun 12-6

Memes s

This flava-ful shop sells 'fresh baked gear' to men seeking cool, urban streetwear. Limited-edition clothing from underground brands Mad Anthony and 10 Deep are found alongside more standard fare from Adidas and Nike. Memes' core collection is made up of hip-hop staples like fatigue, track, and nylon pants, lots of denim, hoodies, coats, jackets, funky footwear, as well as a sprinkling of collectibles, sunglasses and CDs.   *memes-nyc.com*

Moderate   *Amex/MC/V*

NoHo   **(212) 420-9955**
3 Great Jones Street   btw Lafayette/Broadway
NYC 10012   Mon-Sat 11-7, Sun 12-6

Men's Wearhouse

With the addition of names like Armani and Valentino to their regular offerings of Canali, Kenneth Cole Reaction, Oscar De La Renta, Donna Karan and more, Men's Wearhouse can lay claim to having New York's widest selection of suit brands and prices. In addition to the office-ready duds, shop here for outerwear, dress shirts, tuxedos, accessories, casual sportswear, underwear, socks and ties (for print-lovers only, as ties in solid colors are curiously lacking), all for about 25% less than you'd pay elsewhere. Add a complete shoe department with labels such as Florsheim, Bostonian, Cole Haan and Bacco Bucci, tuxedo rentals, a courteous staff and lifetime free pressing on suits, and who can resist? *800-776-7848 menswearhouse.com*

Moderate to luxury   *Amex/MC/V*

Midtown East   **(212) 856-9008**
380 Madison Avenue   at 46th St
NYC 10017   Mon-Sat 10-8, Sun 10-6

Chelsea   **(212) 243-3517**
655 Sixth Avenue   at 20th St
NYC 10010   Mon-Fri 9:30-9, Sat 9:30-8, Sun 10-6

Lower Manhattan   **(212) 233-0675**
115 Broadway at Cedar
NYC 10006   Mon-Fri 8.30-7:30, Sat 10-6, Sun 11-6

Midtown   **(212) 299-0142**
350 Fifth Avenue   at 34th St (Empire State Building)
NYC 10118   Mon-Sat 9-9, Sun 10-6

Metropolis

A skip away from NYU, Metropolis is a late-night destination for student hipsters seeking to forget that dull lecture with a shopping hit. It's all quick-fix fashion, with sparkly T-shirts, retro overcoats, multi-pocketed cargos (for your lecture notes, see) and cool denims. Owner Christine Colligan says she plans to open 24/7, so if you need a pair of fuchsia platform maryjanes at 2am, you know where to go.

Affordable   *Amex/MC/V*

East Village   **(212) 358-0795**
43 Third Avenue   btw 9/10th St
NYC 10003   Daily 12-10

MEXX

Like H&M, only much better. Based in Holland and popular throughout Europe, Mexx has planted its flag on U.S. soil for the first time, offering up its mix of essentials (tees, sweaters, jeans, polos, skirts), sophisticates, sportswear and swimsuits for both sexes. It's more expensive than its European department-store brethren, but the clothes are better made and won't disintegrate weeks after they're purchased. Committed to one-stop shopping, Mexx also offers a kids' line, a shoe line, a cosmetics line, a jewelry line, bags and watches. Word of Mexx's wares spread quickly: the opening of the SoHo flagship this year has NYC hipsters lined up for hours.   *mexx.com*

Affordable   *Amex/MC/V*

Fifth Avenue   **(212) 956-6506**
650 Fifth Avenue   at 52nd St
NYC 10019   Mon-Wed 10-8, Thurs-Sat 10-9, Sun 11-7

SoHo   **1 877 MEXX USA**
500 Broadway   btw Prince/Spring
NYC 10012   Mon-Thurs 10-8, Fri-Sat 10-9, Sun 10-7

Medici

Enter a world of accessories on the Upper West Side, where techno music plays backdrop to a collection of trendy shoes on the Medici label, the youthful CJ Bis by Charles Jourdan, and everything else besides from fringed bags, hats for the races, belts, even birthday cards. Best for men's shoes and summer sandals.

Moderate   *Amex/MC/V*

Upper West Side   **(212) 712-9342**
420 Columbus Avenue   btw 80/81st St
NYC 10023   Daily 10-8

Chelsea   **(212) 604-0888**
24 West 23rd Street   btw Fifth/Sixth Ave
NYC 10010   Mon-Sat 10-8, Sun 10-7

Meg

If you're tired of paying posh uptown prices, get down to Meghan Kinney's East Village store which specializes in polished, multi-purpose sportswear that can be custom-fitted. Separates are key: match pants with a double-knit wool jersey and work it with a jacket or coat. Each season Kinney introduces a new blend of fabric and texture combinations into her dominantly neutral color palette. *megshops.com*

Expensive   *Amex/MC/V*

East Village   **(212) 260-6329**
312 East 9th Street   btw First/Second Ave
NYC 10003   Mon-Sat 12-8, Sun 12-6

Memes

This flava-ful shop sells 'fresh baked gear' to men seeking cool, urban streetwear. Limited-edition clothing from underground brands Mad Anthony and 10 Deep are found alongside more standard fare from Adidas and Nike. Memes' core collection is made up of hip-hop staples like fatigue, track, and nylon pants, lots of denim, hoodies, coats, jackets, funky footwear, as well as a sprinkling of collectibles, sunglasses and CDs. *memes-nyc.com*

Moderate   *Amex/MC/V*

NoHo   **(212) 420-9955**
3 Great Jones Street   btw Lafayette/Broadway
NYC 10012   Mon-Sat 11-7, Sun 12-6

Men's Wearhouse

With the addition of names like Armani and Valentino to their regular offerings of Canali, Kenneth Cole Reaction, Oscar De La Renta, Donna Karan and more, Men's Wearhouse can lay claim to having New York's widest selection of suit brands and prices. In addition to the office-ready duds, shop here for outerwear, dress shirts, tuxedos, accessories, casual sportswear, underwear, socks and ties (for print-lovers only, as ties in solid colors are curiously lacking), all for about 25% less than you'd pay elsewhere. Add a complete shoe department with labels such as Florsheim,

Bostonian, Cole Haan and Bacco Bucci, tuxedo rentals, a courteous staff and lifetime free pressing on suits, and who can resist? *800-776-7848 menswearhouse.com*

Moderate to luxury *Amex/MC/V*

Midtown East **(212) 856-9008**
380 Madison Avenue at 46th St
NYC 10017 Mon-Sat 10-8, Sun 10-6

Chelsea **(212) 243-3517**
655 Sixth Avenue at 20th St
NYC 10010 Mon-Fri 9:30-9, Sat 9:30-8, Sun 10-6

Lower Manhattan **(212) 233-0675**
115 Broadway at Cedar
NYC 10006 Mon-Fri 8.30-7:30, Sat 10-6, Sun 11-6

Midtown **(212) 299-0142**
350 Fifth Avenue at 34th St (Empire State Building)
NYC 10118 Mon-Sat 9-9, Sun 10-6

Metropolis

A skip away from NYU, Metropolis is a late-night destination for student hipsters seeking to forget that dull lecture with a shopping hit. It's all quick-fix fashion, with sparkly T-shirts, retro overcoats, multi-pocketed cargos (for your lecture notes, see) and cool denims. Owner Christine Colligan says she plans to open 24/7, so if you need a pair of fuchsia platform maryjanes at 2am, you know where to go.

Affordable *Amex/MC/V*

East Village **(212) 358-0795**
43 Third Avenue btw 9/10th St
NYC 10003 Daily 12-10

MEXX

Like H&M, only much better. Based in Germany and popular throughout Europe, Mexx has planted its flag on U.S. soil for the first time, offering up its mix of essentials (tees, sweaters, jeans, polos, skirts), sophisticates, sportswear and swimsuits for both sexes. It's more expensive than its European department-store brethren, but the clothes are better made and won't disintegrate weeks after they're purchased. Committed to one-stop shopping, Mexx also offers a kids' line, a shoe line, a cosmetics line, a jewelry line, bags and watches. Word of Mexx's wares spread quickly: the opening of the Union Square flagship last year had NYC hipsters lined up for hours to be cast for the store's inaugural ad campaign. *mexx.com*

Affordable *Amex/MC/V*

Fifth Avenue **(212) 956-6506**
650 Fifth Avenue at 52nd St
NYC 10019 Mon-Wed 10-8, Thurs-Sat 10-9, Sun 11-7

SoHo **1 877 MEXX USA**
500 Broadway btw Prince/Spring
NYC 10012 Mon-Thurs 10-8, Fri-Sat 10-9, Sun 10-7

Miao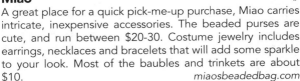

A great place for a quick pick-me-up purchase, Miao carries intricate, inexpensive accessories. The beaded purses are cute, and run between $20-30. Costume jewelry includes earrings, necklaces and bracelets that will add some sparkle to your look. Most of the baubles and trinkets are about $10.

Affordable

Lower Manhattan
176 Hester Street
NYC 10012

miaosbeadedbag.com

Amex/MC/V

(212) 965-9082
btw Mott/Mulberry
Daily 10:30-12:30

Michael K

Is it a shop, or a party? Lighting plays an important role in Michael K, where an illuminated yellow-brick road (of sorts) allows customers to navigate the fashion and lifestyle products displayed in a disco/nightclub manner. The store takes an ultra-futuristic approach (flat-screen TVs, metal rails, strangely shiny walls) and showcases a DJ booth (with fog machines, natch), creating a theme park atmosphere seemingly more intent on exciting its customers than persuading them to make a purchase. Once you're done being dazzled, though, you'll find a host of shoes and gear by names such as Ben Sherman, Polo Jeans, Nike, Puma, The North Face, Adidas and Lacoste, all set up as a slew of mini boutiques. Get your groove, er, shop, on.

Moderate

SoHo
512 Broadway
NYC 10012

Amex/MC/V

(212) 625-9491
btw Spring/Broome
Mon-Sat 9-9, Sun 10-8

★ Michael Kors

Michael Kors exemplifies what American designers do best: chic, soigné sportswear. This translates into both sleek urban clothes and posh country classics with patterns in plaids and tweeds, cozy cashmeres and fabulous shearlings, as well as eveningwear and a healthy dose of fur. His menswear line is the epitome of sporty luxury with its boot-cut pants, slick blazers, suits in cashmere and merino wool, knits and outerwear. The store reflects the lifestyle that Kors seeks to embody, with its dark wood floors, elegant flowers and minimalist decor. Make sure to check out his underrated accessories, including leather handbags and boots.

Luxury

Upper East Side
974 Madison Avenue
NYC 10021

michaelkors.com

Amex/MC/V

(212) 452-4658
at 76th St
Mon-Sat 10-6

Michael's The Consignment Shop for Women

For 45 years Michael's has set the pace in the consignment industry by stocking the ultimate in pre-owned couture clothing and bridalwear. Brides-to-be can select from magnificent dresses by Vera Wang, Arnold Scassi or Dior while non-brides (or bride wannabes) can select from designer frocks and accessories by fashion powerhouses like Prada, Gucci, Manolo Blahnik, Galliano and Hermès. You'll love the great prices, not to mention the thrill of the hunt. *michaelsconsignment.com*

Moderate   *Amex/MC/V*

Upper East Side   **(212) 737-7273**
1041 Madison Avenue (2nd floor)   btw 79/80th St
NYC 10021   Mon-Sat 9:30-6 (Thurs 9:30-8)
                                     (closed Saturdays in summer)

Michelle Roth Design Studio

In this private design studio, Michelle Roth, who provides limited appointments together with her brother Henry Roth, will consult lucky ladies for a wedding of their dreams. For the discerning bride who wants to enter an amusement park of wedding gowns, Michelle Roth holds a signature that is highly sophisticated, chic and completely personalized. Her designs have a contemporary feel, dramatic yet not over-embellished, and available only in her salon. 'No other experience will get you closer to your wedding than this one,' says Michelle. We couldn't agree more. *michelleroth.com*

Expensive   *Amex/MC/V*

Midtown West   **(212) 245-3390**
24 West 57th Street (suite 203)   btw Fifth/Sixth Ave
NYC 10019   (by appointment only)

Mika Inatome

For the non-traditional bride, this Tribeca store run by Japanese designer Mika Inatome specializes in slim, form-fitted gowns rather than a romantic—dare we say puffy?—dress. Styles include fashionable column dresses (plain or embroidered), gowns dolled up with magnificent silk chiffon trains, detachable side sarongs, sheath and fringe, and other designs trimmed in lace, pearl and sterling-silver beading. Prices start at $1,700. *mikainatome.com*

Expensive   *Amex/MC/V*

Tribeca   **(212) 966-7777**
93 Reade Street (2nd floor)   btw Church/West Broadway
NYC 10013   (by appointment)

Miks

Sure to please both you and Mom, sweet, smart designs are the rule at this Japanese ex-pat's small and friendly boutique. Find work basics with a twist of cute such as flowered button-downs, bow-trim sweaters and striped skirts. The designs are refreshingly conventional with a whimsical edge.

Moderate   *Amex/MC/V*

Lower East Side   **(212) 505-1982**
100 Stanton Street   btw Ludlow/Orchard
NYC 10002   Daily 12-730

Mimi Maternity

Don't think being pregnant means having to wear stuff that looks more like your grandma's muumuus than your favorite little black dress. Mimi Maternity offers sophisticated clothing that highlights rather than hides your beautiful body, from fitted tops, A-line skirts and tailored jeans to yoga gear and pant suits, to meet your desire for both style and comfort. *mimimaternity.com*

Affordable   *Amex/MC/V*

Midtown East   **(212) 697-0482**
360 Madison Avenue   at 45th St
NYC 10017   Mon-Fri 10-7 (Thurs 10-8)
                                          Sat 10-6, Sun 12-6

Upper East Side   **(212) 832-2667**
1021 Third Avenue   btw 60/61st St
NYC 10021   Mon-Fri 10-7 (Thurs 10-8)
                                          Sat 10-6, Sun 11-6

Upper West Side   **(212) 721-1999**
2005 Broadway   btw 68/69th St
NYC 10023   Mon-Thurs 10-8, Fri-Sat 10-7, Sun 12-6

Minette by Blue Bag

Minette is a treasure trove of wonderfully girly accessories from France. High-turnover merchandise that arrives every 15 days makes shopping here a truly excellent adventure. Find fabulous jewelry, great belts, scarves, wallets, hand-crocheted make-up bags that double as evening clutches, a few hats and hair accessories, as well as bathing suits, sandals and sarongs during the summer months. Prices range from $75 to $350.

Moderate   *Amex/MC/V*

Nolita   **(212) 334-7290**
238 Mott Street   btw Prince/Spring
NYC 10012   Daily 12-8 (Sun 12-7)

Min-K

Tokyo pop percolates on the iPod at this tiny East Village outpost of Asian fashion. Two racks, one on each side of the narrow store, showcase sharp designs from Japan and Korea. Downtown professionals and trendsetters looking to show off (or show some skin) help themselves to flirty dresses and graphic tees. Fun without being flashy, Min-K shows that a little bit of Shibuya-ku can go a long way.

Moderate to expensive   *Amex/MC/V*

SoHo   **(212) 219-2834**
219 Mott Street   btw Spring/Prince
NYC 10012   Daily 11-7:30

Missbehave

The decor at Missbehave—yearbooks, a chalkboard and desk—brings to mind many a naughty schoolday's reverie. Why not stay after class to treat yourself to under-the-radar, super-girly fashions from Leroy's Girl, Kitten and Kim White, or a sweatshirt from Megami Boogie that reads 'I'm in heaven with my boyfriend'? The stylish clothes are sexy, fun, and you won't have to worry about looking good in detention. *missbehavenyc.com*

Expensive *Amex/MC/V*

Lower East Side **(212) 254-9222**
231 Eldridge Street btw Stanton/Houston
NYC 10002 Tues-Sun 12-7

Miss Sixty

Tight, low-ridin', slinky jeans (with plenty of details) punchy sweaters, fiery miniskirts and a multitude of adventurous blouses and halter tops is what you encounter on a Miss Sixty visit. Girlie styles from every era—from the modish Sixties and laid back Seventies to the punk glam of the Eighties—are explored here, with the emphasis on fun, fun, fun. There are hot swimming pieces for the beach, a slew of accessories (including fine sunglasses) and flirty shoes galore. Be sure to check out the netted heels, ribbon-adorned sandals and funky sneakers. *misssixty.com*

Moderate *Amex/MC/V*

SoHo **(212) 334-9772**
386 West Broadway btw Spring/Broome
NYC 10012 Mon-Thurs 11-7, Fri-Sat 11-8, Sun 11-6

★ Missoni

For half a century the Missoni family has ruled the fashion world with their distinctive sexy, slinky, stripey knitwear. Angela Missoni is mad for wild, geometric patterns and sharp-edged graphics in bold color combinations...you won't find basic black here. Missoni has turned knitwear into a complete line of women's ready-to-wear that includes pants, halter dresses, skirts, sweaters and swimwear. The style crowd are crazy for the super-long, boho fringed scarves (approx $260), a true fashion classic. The store now features a large home collection as well, with dinnerware, pillows and blankets not available in most department stores, thus giving shoppers one more reason to visit Missoni's only U.S. store. Prices range from $165 for a scarf to $17,000 for a three-quarter-length fur coat. *missoni.it*

Expensive *Amex/MC/V*

Upper East Side **(212) 517-9339**
1009 Madison Avenue at 78th St
NYC 10021 Mon-Sat 10-6

★ Miu Miu

Miu Miu is Prada's cute, playful and slightly mad little sister—a girl who wears floral platform shoes, ragged minidresses and handbags that look like a prop from *Sesame Street*. Uptown girls and downtown hipsters (who can afford the label—this second line sadly comes with first line prices) come here for V-neck cardigans, shrunken sweaters, and vintage-inspired tweeds with a hint of sparkle. You'll also find washed-leather jackets, long-line maxi coats, and slim calf-length dresses. Miu Miu's shoes and fashionable handbags will have you one step ahead of the fashion meter—witness the ever-present crowd of hipper-than-hip Japanese tourists snapping up multiple pairs of girly cartoon shoes.   miumiu.com

Expensive   *Amex/MC/V*

Upper East Side   **(212) 249-9660**
831 Madison Avenue   btw 69/70th St
NYC 10021   Mon-Sat 10-6 (Thurs 10-7)

SoHo   **(212) 334-5156**
100 Prince Street   btw Greene/Mercer
NYC 10012   Daily 11-7

Mixona

This cool Nolita lingerie shop's name is a composite of Korean symbols: mi, beauty; xo, play of opposites; and na, me. Which basically just means that it's a haven for bedroom eyes looking for those intricately patterned bra and panties or camisole brimming in lacy stitches. Unlike Victoria's Secret on nearby Broadway, there's nothing pink or prissy about this shop. Dressing-rooms draped in crimson red silk are spacious enough for husbands/boyfriends to get a private viewing—ooh, saucy. Mixona runs the label gamut, from bold (Undressed, Andres Sarda, Christina Stott) to powdery sweet (Siren, Grazia'Iliani, Kristina Ti). Everyday basics by legends like Hanro and La Cosa, silk sleepwear and daywear are also available. Great sales.   mixona.com

Affordable   *Amex/MC/V*

Nolita   **(646) 613-0100**
262 Mott Street   btw Houston/Prince
NYC 10012   Mon-Sat 11:30-7:30, Sun 11:30-8

Modell's

Play ball, indeed. Athletes and armchair quarterbacks 'gotta go to Mo's' for everything from basketballs and Mets jerseys to Levi's and running watches. One of America's oldest sporting goods chains, Modell's stocks gear for nearly every kind of recreation, on or off the court, including camping, fishing and swimming. Always a big draw: a huge selection of brand-name sneakers at low prices.   *800-275-6633 modells.com*

Affordable   *Amex/MC/V*

Midtown East   **(212) 661-4242**
51 East 42nd Street   at Vanderbilt Ave
NYC 10017   Mon-Fri 8-9, Sat 9-7, Sun 10-6

Harlem   **(212) 280-9100**
300 West 125th Street   at St Nicholas Blvd
NYC 10027   Mon-Thurs 9-8, Fri-Sat 9-8:30, Sun 11-7

Lower Manhattan   **(212) 732-8484**
55 Chambers Street   at Broadway
NYC 10007   Mon-Fri 8:30-7:30, Sat 10-6, Sun 11-5

Lower Manhattan (212) 566-3711
200 Broadway btw Fulton/John
NYC 10038 (opening hours as above)

Midtown (Herald Square) (212) 244-4544
1293 Broadway btw 33/34th St
NYC 10001 Mon-Sat 9-9, Sun 11-7

Midtown West (212) 764-7030
234 West 42nd Street btw Seventh/Eighth Ave
NYC 10036 Mon-Thurs 8-12, Fri-Sat 8-1, Sun 10-10

Upper East Side (212) 996-3800
1535 Third Avenue at 86th St
NYC 10028 Mon-Sat 9:30-9, Sun 10:30-7:30

MoMo FaLana 👤

Sex and the City fans saw MoMo FaLana's vintage-inspired, hippy-chic apparel on the tube, and the brand is unwavering in its commitment to taking 'modern-day urban fantasies and making them real'. Now that may or may not be true, but MoMo hand-dyed dresses, embroidered brocade jackets and form-fitting silk tops and skirts certainly will help make your waking hours dreamy. momofalana.com

Expensive *Amex/MC/V*

East Village (212) 979-9595
43 Avenue A at 3rd St
NYC 10009 Sun-Wed 12-8, Thurs-Sat 12-9

Mom's Night Out 👤

Mom's Night Out caters to expectant mothers, offering an intimate shopping environment filled with glamorous eveningwear and allow you to rent, buy or custom-order. Tricia Shiland started Mom's Night Out because of the lack of sophisticated eveningwear for the woman with child. You'll find that neither store skimps on variety, offering up a multitude of styles, colors and sizes. You'll find bridal, cocktail dresses and evening gowns, as well as accessories—all at reasonable prices. momsnightout.com

Moderate *Amex/MC/V*

Upper East Side (212) 744-6667
147 East 72nd Street (2nd floor) btw Lexington/Third Ave
NYC 10021 Tues-Wed 11-5 (by appointment only)

Montmartre 👤

These ultimate uptown girl clothing stores dictate Upper West Side style with their selection of C&C California and Michael Star tanks and tees, Milly, Anna Sui, Tibi and Nanette Lepore delicate dresses; plus, the current crop of Seven and Joe's Jeans will keep any girl fashionable every day of the week. The new Shops at Columbus Circle location in the Time Warner Center has a huge selection of work-ready pumps, weekend-off Mella terrycloth flip-flops and plenty of other girly goodies. montmartrenyc.com

Moderate to expensive *Amex/MC/V*

Upper West Side
2212 Broadway
NYC 10024

(212) 875-8430
btw 78/79th St
Mon-Sat 11-8, Sun 11-7

Midtown West
10 Columbus Circle
NYC 10019

(212) 823-9821
Time Warner Center
Mon-Sat 10-9, Sun 11-7

Upper East Side
1157 Madison Avenue
NYC 10028

(212) 988-8962
btw 85/86th St
Mon-Sat 11-7, Sun 12-6

Lower Manhattan
World Financial Center
NYC 10281

(212) 945-7858
by West Side Highway/Liberty
Mon-Sat 11-7, Sun 12-5

Moreschi 👤👩

With an international following at its back, this high-quality Italian footwear brand made a significant step in expanding its consumer base with the opening of its first store in the U.S. in late 2002. While Moreschi offers leather jackets, accessories and, more recently, women's footwear, men's shoes are still the company's true strength. They offer a variety of styles from loafers (from $375) to the Rolls-Royce of footwear, alligator-skin shoes (note the $3,200 price tag). With its handstitching, leather soles and meticulous detailing, Moreschi is sure to please those with an eye for a finely shod foot.   *moreschishoes.com*

Expensive to luxury   *Amex/MC/V*

Midtown East
515 Madison Avenue
NYC 10022

(212) 644-4199
at 53rd Street
Mon-Fri 10-7, Sat 10-6, Sun 12-5

Morgane Le Fay 👩

Argentinian designer Liliana Casabal expertly translates fantasy into wearable reality with her softly feminine, clean designs in fabrics from silk charmeuse to dreamy chiffon and organza. The collection includes elegant dresses, slacks, coats, cashmeres and the creamiest ecru wedding gowns. This is the perfect place to shop for refined romantic clothing.   *morganelefay.com*

Expensive   *Amex/MC/V*

Upper East Side
746 Madison Avenue
NYC 10021

(212) 879-9700
btw 64/65th St
Mon-Sat 10-6, Sun 12-5

SoHo
67 Wooster Street
NYC 10012

(212) 219-7672
btw Spring/Broome
Daily 11-7

★ Morris Bros 👤

This place is such an Upper West Side institution that you half expect to see little Franny and Zooey buying their outfits for It's a Wise Child here. Specializing in clothes for summer camp and back-to-school, they keep up with the times with Paul Frank accessories and Saturday togs by Levi's,

Dickies and Juicy Couture. Faithful customers love the full-service approach of the staff and the convenience of being able to pick up everything a kid needs—from baseball caps to backpacks to bobby socks. *morrisbrosnyc.com*

Affordable   *Amex/MC/V*

Upper West Side   **(212) 724-9000**
2322 Broadway   at 84th St
NYC 10024   Mon-Sat 9:30-6:30, Sun 12-5:30

Motherhood Maternity

An affordable alternative to the pricier Manhattan maternity boutiques, Motherhood Maternity has everything from suits, casualwear and intimates to jeans, accessories and some swimwear. They also carry a few topical products for expectant mothers, such as anti-stretch mark creams and oils. The styles tend to be very practical, though the newest collection has stepped up the fashion quotient with bright colors and more sophisticated patterns.   *motherhood.com*

Affordable   *Amex/MC/V*

Midtown West   **(212) 564- 3548**
901 Sixth Avenue   at Manhattan Mall, btw 32/33rd St
NYC 10001   Mon-Sat 10-8, Sun 11-6

Midtown West (outlet)   **(212) 399-9840**
16 West 57th Street (3rd floor)   btw Fifth/Sixth Ave
NYC 10019   Mon-Wed 10-7, Thurs 10-8
                                              Fri-Sat 10-6, Sun 12-6

Chelsea   **(212) 741-3488**
641 Sixth Avenue   at 20th Street
NYC 10011   Mon-Sat 10-7 Sun 11-6

Midtown West   **(212) 695-9106**
36 West 34th Street (2nd floor)   btw Fifth/Sixth Ave
NYC 10001   Mon-Sat 10-9, Sun 11-6

Harlem   **(212) 987-8808**
163 East 125th Street   btw Lexington/Third Ave
NYC 10035   Mon-Sat 10-8, Sun 11-6

Myla

Rawer and more esoteric than fellow Briton Agent Provocateur, Myla sells not only lingerie but a range of 'Sex Life Accessories'. Not as deliciously naughty as the London branch, the small and rather unremarkable space lacks a discreet curtain that might make UES ladies a little more comfortable handling aerodynamic sex toys. The lingerie is demure for the most part, with lots of black satin and sheer ruffling, some pretty-in-pink numbers with cutesy bows, satin-tie undies and innocent flowered teddies. Saucier are the Marabou and feather-trim thongs, and the black pasties for when a bra offers too much coverage.   *myla.com*

Expensive   *Amex/MC/V*

Upper East Side   **(212) 570-1590**
20 East 69th Street   at Madison Ave
NYC 10021   Mon-Fri 10-5

MZ Wallace

A collection of tote and travel bags in durable materials like leather, Cordura nylon, burlap and printed, laminated cottons. These simply shaped weekend bags come in combinations like navy, floral print and sequins. The creator's goal: 'to create cool bags that have a chic and groovy look.' Good. *mzwallace.com*

Moderate *Amex/MC/V*

SoHo **(212) 431-8252**
93 Crosby Street btw Prince/Spring
NYC 10012 Mon-Sat 11-7, Sun 12-6

Nalu NYC

Hang ten! Look past the boards at this beach-bum paradise to find some great warm-weather gear that's fashionable enough to wear around town. Come here for Brazilian bikinis, trunks by Billabong and Wet Suit, Havaianas sandals, surf wax, hats and eye-catching sunglasses. *nalunyc.com*

Moderate *Amex/MC/V*

West Village **(212) 675-7873**
10 Little West 12th Street btw Seventh Ave/Washington
NYC 10014 Daily 12-10

Nancy & Co

This is one of those hipper-than-traditional neighborhood stores catering to Upper East Side women who want to be fashionable without stepping over the line into trendy. Nothing at all wrong with that, and at Nancy and Co you'll find dresses, cashmere sweaters and the perfect accessories to augment your personal style. Choose from Three Dots tees, Shin Choi silk shells and Jeanne Maag separates.

Moderate *Amex/MC/V*

Upper East Side **(212) 427-0770**
1242 Madison Avenue at 89th St
NYC 10128 Mon-Fri 10-7, Sat 10-6:30

Nancy Geist

Nancy Geist is one quirky lady—witness her signature shoes in a rainbow of colors and featuring unusual heels that possess an uncompromising femininity. Find leather boots, mules, denim espadrilles with appliqués, strappy sandals, baby-doll flats and evening shoes in looks from flirty to city. Prices run from $185 to $600. *nancygeist.com*

Moderate to expensive *Amex/MC/V*

SoHo **(212) 925-7192**
107 Spring Street at Mercer
NYC 10012 Mon-Sat 11-7, Sun 12-6

Nanette Lepore

Nanette Lepore's clothes have been known to inspire cat fights between rock stars. So there you have it, this is one party-girl label. Her pieces are fabulously sexy and feminine and fearless in color and pattern—all up, it's glam girl meets gypsy. Lepore's SoHo store carries lots of flirty dresses, corsets and suits in luxe fabrics. Accessories include her coveted handbags and select shoe designers. Wonderful sales help. *nanettelepore.com*

Expensive   *Amex/MC/V*

SoHo   **(212) 219-8265**
423 Broome Street   btw Lafayette/Crosby
NYC 10012   Mon-Sat 11-7, Sun 12-6

Natalie & Friends

Resembling a crayon box, the jam-packed colorful Natalie & Friends is a chic boutique for little ones. On the racks are bejeweled vintage rock tees, animal prints, colorblock dresses, sequin dress shoes and other loud pieces befitting a miniature Donatella Versace. There are also more demure, ballerina-inspired tiered pink skirts for little princesses and hippie-preppie hybrids by Bella Ami, an Anthropologie company. Jackie Chan's boys line features dragon-emblazoned jeans and tees. Claude makes Hawaiian shirts and Harley-Davidson tees for badass little boys. Natalie's showroom wholesales the best in kids' clothes to many major department stores, but this shop showcases her mother lode of cute collections. *natalieandfriends.com*

Moderate to expensive   *Amex/MC/V*

Midtown East   **(212) 759-9077**
205 East 60th Street   at Third Ave
NYC 10022   Mon-Tues 10-7, Wed-Fri 10-8
                                          Sat 11-8, Sun 11-7

Naturalizer

Nip into Naturalizer when your Manolos begin to blister or a subway grate claims the heel of your Jimmy Choos, and waltz out in cushiony comfort. Long recognized for their range of sizes, excellent value and, most of all, wearability, Naturalizer have never exactly been considered fashion-forward. Lately they've been trying to vamp up their image and they're making great strides with strappy sandals, classic pumps and, of course, durable flats for those long city treks. You'll probably never spot these babies in the pages of Italian Vogue, but when it comes to attractive practicality they've got it in spades. *naturalizeronline.com*

Affordable   *Amex/MC/V*

Midtown East   **(212) 759-3094**
712 Lexington Avenue   btw 57/58th St
NYC 10022   Mon-Sat 9-9, Sun 10-7

Neda

Neda is Persian for 'message', and the point this recently opened store is trying to get across has something to do with embracing a personal style. Culling little-known designers from the Tri-State area, Neda features tops and dresses that are at once edgy and feminine, Western and

Middle Eastern, with hand-painted details and contrasting fabrics such as linen and leather. Fabulous ballet flats and leather sandals in matching colors are a real find.

Moderate   *Amex/MC/V*

Park Slope   **(718) 965-0990/(646) 234-8752**
413A 7th Avenue   btw 13/14th St
Brooklyn 11215   Mon-Sat 12-7:30, Sun 12-6

Nellie M Boutique

From the outside Nellie M looks like it should have a sign on the outside that says '$10 or less', but once inside you real-ize Nellie M is great treat for Upper Eastsiders who do not want to make the trek to the 59th Street department stores. Nellie M features everything from established designers like Anna Sui, Chaiken and Nanette Lepore to fresh labels like Beth Bowley, Jessie Della Femina and Milly. There is also a serious jeans wall (Seven, Citizens of Humanity) in the back of the store that rivals the Co-op.   *nelliem.com*

Expensive   *Amex/MC/V*

Upper East Side   **(212) 996-4410**
1309 Lexington Avenue   at 88th St
NYC 10128   Mon-Fri 10-8, Sat 11-8, Sun 11-7

Net-a-Porter

You won't find this shop on any street, not even Madison Avenue or Fifth—it's fashion's unmissable virtual boutique, created by a gang of brilliant alumnae from that stylish and unique London magazine *Tatler*. The original concept was to create an online magazine with fashion features just like the glossies, but which visitors could buy from (see Gisele in a stunning Missoni bikini, double-click and it's yours). Its founder and managing director, Natalie Massenet (born in L.A., raised in Paris, lives in London), is famous for once find-ing three Hermès Kelly bags in an L.A. thrift store for $10 each, and her idea has been a similar serendipitous triumph (backed by good old-fashioned hard work). Click on runway reporter, bikini boutique, pretty woman, editor's favorites, most wanted, jewel colors, gift shop, sale section (key in your sizes) or The Salon for designer collections. Find out why Jennifer, Gwyneth and Gwen love Maharishi snopants, or who loves Juicy, or what's the next big thing. But why should we tell you any more? This is a fashion superstore which you can browse with your coffee cup—no need even to get dressed, let alone leave home. It's a one-stop shop for those who prefer logging on to trekking about and, like we said, unmissable.   *net-a-porter.com*

New & Almost New

If you have been searching for this snazzy consignment shop on Mercer, you are on the wrong block—they now have a new home on Elizabeth and a whole new batch of goodies to be snatched up. The rule is: if you see something you fancy, make that purchase, because timing is everything and the pieces are quick to go. Try your luck: dig for designer treasure, like Miu Miu shoes or a Chanel handbag, and there's a good chance that you'll go home happy.

Affordable   *Amex/MC/V*

SoHo   **(212) 226-6677**
166 Elizabeth Street   btw Spring/Kenmare
NYC 10012   Mon-Sat 12-6:30

New Balance New York

Originally a brand primarily targeting runners, New Balance has expanded to offer an impressive selection of quality footwear for running, cross-training, hiking, walking, tennis, golf, basketball…and just sitting around looking cool. The NB apparel line runs from basic shorts and tank tops to microfiber jackets and pants that offer performance, fit and a little fashion too. Men's casual shoes and children's sneakers are also available, as well as assorted paraphernalia which runners are bound to appreciate.   *1-866-521-NBNY*
newbalancenewyork.com

Affordable to moderate   *Amex/MC/V*

Midtown East   **(212) 421-4444**
821 Third Avenue   btw 50/51st St
NYC 10022   Mon-Fri 9-7, Sat 10-6, Sun 12-5

Midtown West   **(212) 997-9112**
51 West 42nd Street   btw Fifth/Sixth Ave
NYC 10036   Mon-Fri 9-7, Sat 10-6, Sun 11-5

Midtown West   **(212) 398-2449**
745 Seventh Avenue   at 49th St
NYC 10019   Mon-Fri 10-8, Sat 10-6, Sun 12-6

New York Golf Center

Fore! From the driving range to the clubhouse, NYGC has the city's largest selection of equipment for novices and pros. Featuring clubs and clothes from labels like Callaway, Taylor Made, Ping, Nike, Polo, Greg Norman and Titleist, you'll find what you need for smooth swinging on the links. Rainwear, socks, shoes, golf bags, balls, books and accessories are available, and be sure to inquire about lessons.   *nygolfcenter.com*

Moderate   *Amex/MC/V*

Midtown West   **(212) 564-2255**
131 West 35th Street   btw Seventh Ave/Broadway
NYC 10001   Mon-Fri 10-8, Sat 10-7, Sun 11-6

The New York Look

What does it mean to be fashionable in New York? Local chain store The New York Look is determined to answer that question by providing the latest trends in womenswear including Three Dots and Michael Star tops, Citizens of Humanity and Joe's Jeans, Teen Tahari and Theory workwear among other sophisticated small brands. And with a great selection of shoes and costume jewelry from little labels, The New York Look is sure to keep you looking sharp from head to toe.

Moderate to expensive   *Amex/MC/V*

Upper West Side　　　　　　　　**(212) 765-4758**
30 Lincoln Plaza　　　　　　　　　　btw 62/63rd St
NYC 10023　　Mon-Thurs 10-9, Fri 10-8, Sat 11-9, Sun 12-7

Upper West Side　　　　　　　　**(212) 362-8650**
2030 Broadway　　　　　　　　　　btw 69/70th St
NYC 10023　　　　　　　　Mon-Sat 10-9, Sun 12-7

Midtown West　　　　　　　　　**(212) 382-2760**
570 Seventh Avenue　　　　　　　　at 41st St
NYC 10018　　　　　　　　　　　　Mon-Sat 9-7

Fifth Avenue　　　　　　　　　　**(212) 557-0909**
551 Fifth Avenue　　　　　　　　　　at 45th St
NYC 10176　　　　　　　Mon-Sat 9-8, Sun 10-8

SoHo　　　　　　　　　　　　　**(212) 598-9988**
468 West Broadway　　　　　　　btw Houston/Prince
NYC 10012　　　Mon-Fri 10-8, Sat 10:30-8, Sun 12-8

New York Om Yoga　　　　　　　👤👤

Find yoga pants, tops, shoes, mats and more at this small boutique inside Om Yoga studio. All the apparel is from their own label, and is made by American Apparel and Alternative Apparel—sweatshop-free companies—so you can do your Downward Dog without worrying about unfair labor practices.　　　　　　　　　*omyoga.com*

Moderate　　　　　　　　　　　　*Amex/MC/V*

Union Square　　　　　　　　　**(212) 254-9642**
826 Broadway (6th floor)　　　　　　at 12th St
NYC 10003　　　Mon-Fri 7-9, Sat 9-7, Sun 10-7

Nicole Farhi　　　　　　　　　👤👤

British designer Nicole Farhi calls her clothes 'constant friends', but you could also call them instant classics. This three-floor, 16,000-square-foot flagship offers just that with men's and women's ready-to-wear and a home collection. Find racks of pant suits, embroidered skirts, brilliant chunky cashmeres and plenty of leather and suede, as well as classic (but never dull) shoes and accessories. Grab a bite downstairs at Nicole's, her sleek modern restaurant.　　*nicolefarhi.com*

Expensive　　　　　　　　　　　*Amex/MC/V*

Upper East Side　　　　　　　　**(212) 223-8811**
10 East 60th Street　　　　　btw Fifth/Madison Ave
NYC 10021　　Mon-Fri 10-6 (Thurs 10-7), Sat 11-6, Sun 12-5

Chelsea　　　　　　　　　　　　**(646) 638-0115**
75 Ninth Avenue　　　　　　　　　　at 16th St
NYC 10011　　　Mon-Fri 9-8, Sat 10-8, Sun 10-6

Nicole Miller　　　　　　　　　👤👤

Nicole Miller, from bridalwear to sportswear, has something that appeals to every woman. Designs are an impressive combination of sophistication and whimsy. The formal silk dresses and casual day ensembles will charm with their classic silhouettes and modern details. Look here for solids, prints, basics and eveningwear. Also find an ever-changing line of men's ties, featuring her famously tongue-in-cheek prints. Bridal by appointment.　　　　*nicolemiller.com*

Nine West

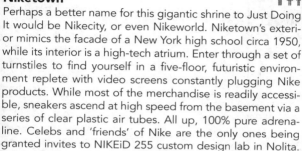

Expensive   Amex/MC/V

Upper East Side
780 Madison Avenue
NYC 10021

(212) 288-9779
btw 66/67th St
Mon-Fri 10-7, Sat 10-6, Sun 12-5

Niketown

Perhaps a better name for this gigantic shrine to Just Doing It would be Nikecity, or even Nikeworld. Niketown's exterior mimics the facade of a New York high school circa 1950, while its interior is a high-tech atrium. Enter through a set of turnstiles to find yourself in a five-floor, futuristic environment replete with video screens constantly plugging Nike products. While most of the merchandise is readily accessible, sneakers ascend at high speed from the basement via a series of clear plastic air tubes. All up, 100% pure adrenaline. Celebs and 'friends' of Nike are the only ones being granted invites to NIKEiD 255 custom design lab in Nolita. Put yourself on the waiting list at nikeid.com.

800-806-6453 nike.com/niketown.com/nikeid.com

Moderate   Amex/MC/V

Midtown East
6 East 57th Street
NYC 10022

(212) 891-6453
btw Fifth/Madison Ave
Mon-Sat 10-8, Sun 11-7

Nine West

This footwear behemoth claims to sell two pair of shoes per second. Nine West carries it all at the most affordable prices in town (even though the service can be downright terrible), from classic flats and loafers to trendy platforms and boots. Keep an eye open, because every so often you'll find a pair of heels that looks like they came straight from Gucci (fool your friends). Accessories include handbags, leather goods, sunglasses and jewelry, as well as a slick outerwear collection in leathers, nylons and shearlings.

800-260-2227 ninewest.com

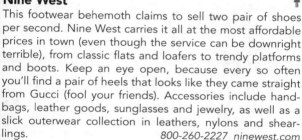

Affordable   Amex/MC/V

Upper West Side
2305 Broadway
NYC 10024

(212) 799-7610
btw 83/84th St
Mon-Fri 10-8, Sat 10-9, Sun 11-6

Midtown East
341 Madison Avenue
NYC 10017

(212) 370-9107
at 44th St
Mon-Fri 8-8, Sat 10-6, Sun 12-5

Midtown East
750 Lexington Avenue
NYC 10022

(212) 486-8094
btw 58/59th St
Mon-Sat 10-8, Sun 11-6

Midtown East
757 Third Avenue
NYC 10017

(212) 371-4597
btw 47/48th St
Mon-Fri 9-8, Sat 10-6, Sun 12-5

Midtown East
425 Lexington Avenue
NYC 10017

(212) 949-0037
btw 43/44th St
Mon-Fri 10-8, Sat 10-6, Sun 12-5

Midtown West
21 West 34th Street
NYC 10018
(212) 594-0781
btw Fifth/Sixth Ave
Mon-Fri 10-8, Sat 10-7, Sun 10-6

Midtown West
901 Sixth Avenue
NYC 10001
(212) 564-0063
at Manhattan Mall, btw 32/33rd St
Mon-Sat 10-8, Sun 11-6

Fifth Avenue
675 Fifth Avenue
NYC 10022
(212) 319-6893
at 53rd St
Mon-Sat 10-7, Sun 12-6

Flatiron
115 Fifth Avenue
NYC 10003
(212) 777-1752
at 19th St
Mon-Sat 10-8, Sun 11-7

SoHo
577 Broadway
NYC 10012
(212) 941-1597
at Prince
Mon-Sat 10-8, Sun 11-7

Lower Manhattan
179 Broadway
NYC 10007
(212) 346-0903
btw Day/Maiden Lane
Daily 8-7

Lower Manhattan
2 Broadway
NYC 10004
(212) 968-1521
btw Beaver/Whitehall
Mon-Fri 8-7

Nocturne

Nocturne imports 100% batiste cotton sleepwear from Brazil with handmade embroideries and lace. You'll find embellished pajamas, feminine nightshirts, luxurious robes worthy of a femme fatale and comfy nightgowns. Adorable children's slippers and cosmetic bags are also available.

Moderate   *Amex/MC/V*

Upper East Side
1744 First Avenue
NYC 10028
(212) 427-8282
btw 90/91st St
Mon-Sat 10-6

Nom de Guerre

The only thing harder to find than the subtle, minimalist clothes by Nom de Guerre is the store itself. Only the most fashion-hungry know that the black gate and green stairs on the southeast corner of Broadway and Bleecker lead to this below-ground, brick-and-cement shop (though we hear a sign may be in the works). As the name suggests, the shop is characterized by utilitarian, military-inspired clothing in rough, heavy fabrics and dark colors, with a few loud tees ($35-$85) thrown in the mix. Labels include esoteric favorites such as Rogan, Noah, United Bamboo and Habitual, Japan's A Bathing Ape and vintage Nikes.

Expensive   *Amex/MC/V*

NoHo
640 Broadway
NYC 10012
(212) 253-2891
at Bleecker
Mon-Sat 12-8, Sun 12-7

Noriko Maeda

Noriko Maeda's aesthetic is ladylike elegance and she achieves it through her superior tailoring of wool, cashmere and silk. In her new design studio, she does only custom-order jobs, another high-end aspect to the brand. There are gorgeous Russian sable stoles ($3,200) with matching sable-trimmed gloves ($430), and you can nibble from the complimentary tray of chocolate truffles and kisses while you think everything over. Sizes run small.

Luxury   *Amex/MC/V*
Midtown East   **(212) 715-0990**
598 Madison Avenue   btw 57/58th St
NYC 10022   (by appointment)

Norma Kamali

Norma Kamali provides a superb line of polo jerseys in bright colors that are washable, quick to dry and wrinkle-free. She has been having a resurrection of late, and now sells as many cult vintage pieces as new (singer Mandy Moore is a fan). Her seen-in-Sports Illustrated swimwear moves easily from poolside straight to resort lunch, while her everyday pieces like reversible slip dresses, wide-legged or pencil pants and sleeveless tees sit snugly along-side glamorous eveningwear and vintage bridal. One of the first designers to mix vintage with new, Kamali is complete-ly of the moment. Her staff is so dedicated to customer sat-isfaction that they have a 'shop like a celebrity' system, allowing customers to try before they buy—including bathing suits.   *normakamalicollection.com*

Moderate   *Amex/MC/V*
Midtown West   **(212) 957-9797**
11 West 56th Street   btw Fifth/Sixth Ave
NYC 10019   Mon-Sat 10-6

Nort 235

A special place for sneaker freaks, Nort sells limited-edition kicks that you can't find anywhere else, like exclusive offer-ings of Nike series that have die-hard enthusiasts lined up around the block. The selection is always hot, and your feet will inspire your friends' envy.

Expensive   *MC/V*
Lower East Side   **(212) 777-6102**
235 Eldridge Street   btw East Houston/Stanton
NYC 10002   Mon-Sat 12-7, Sun 12-6

Objets du Desir

Four jewelers—three Swiss and one Japanese—combined forces to open the quaint Objets du Desir gallery. Featuring one-of-a-kind as well as limited-edition pieces, they have set out to provide contemporary rings, bracelets and necklaces in a variety of materials (leather, rubber, bronze, silver, gold) and at a number of different price points (from $50 to $3,000). As might be expected with four creators, the col-lection is eclectic, but there's an indisputable charm to the boutique's variety, where fanciful insect and plant forms studded with large gems are balanced by simple designs with black and white pearls.   *objetsdudesir.com*

Moderate to expensive   *Amex/MC/V*

Nolita   **(212) 334-9727**
241 Mulberry Street   btw Prince/Spring
NYC 10012   Tues-Sat 12-7, Sun 12-6

Off Broadway

You just have to stand up and take notice when you hear Barbra belting out 'People' on the overhead system at this outrageous emporium staffed with would-be divas in fabulous head dress. Off Broadway caters to the woman who 'gets a kick out of sculpture and loves making an entrance', with dramatic suits, dresses and accessories in bold colors and realistic sizes for ladies of a certain age. Make no mistake, while Off Broadway is sure to tickle a costume designer's fancy, the clothes here are made and priced for the genuine article. At 30 years, it's the longest running show on the West Side.

Moderate to expensive   *Amex/MC/V*

Upper West Side   **(212) 724-6713**
139 West 72nd Street   btw Amsterdam/Columbus Ave
NYC 10023   Mon-Fri 10:30-8, Sat 10:30-7, Sun 1-7

★ Oilily

For the Peter Pan in all of us, Oilily is the perfect blend of youthful style and sophisticated silhouettes. The adult line was created for all the hip moms who want to wear their kids' clothes. But don't expect to find children's clothes sized for adults; the Oilily children's aesthetic translates into a bohemian-chic adult look that will appeal to women with or without kids. Find the company's signature prints and bright colors on skirts, dresses, pants, tops and even shoes. As for the famous and funky kids' clothes, prints again adorn almost all the pieces. From dresses to shoes, everything is decorated with energetic, youthful designs that look terrific on kids from newborn to 12 years old.   *oililyusa.com*

Expensive   *Amex/MC/V*

Upper East Side   **(212) 628-0100**
820 Madison Avenue   btw 68/69th St
NYC 10021   Mon-Sat 10-6, Sun 12-5

Old Navy Clothing Company

Old Navy is the best. Weighing in at 100,000 square feet per location, it is a retail behemoth that gives shoppers maximum buying power for casual clothing that pays perfect homage to designer trends—put it this way, Marc Jacobs would freak out in here. Kids, teens, adults, mothers-to-be and the plus-size set love shopping here for reliable, hip and affordable basics. The store is packed with essentials like jeans, T-shirts, swimwear, shorts, sweatshirts, sweaters and jackets. Best buys: the ribbed tanks for about 10 bucks.   *800-653-6289 oldnavy.com*

Affordable   *Amex/MC/V*

Midtown West   **(212) 594-0049**
150 West 34th Street   btw Sixth/Seventh Ave
NYC 10001   Mon-Sat 9-10, Sun 10-8

Chelsea	(212) 645-0663
610 Sixth Avenue	at 18th St
NYC 10011	Mon-Sat 9-9:30, Sun 10-8

SoHo	(212) 226-0865
503 Broadway	btw Spring/Broome
NYC 10012	Mon-Sat 9-9:30, Sun 10-8

Harlem	(212) 531-1544
300 West 125th Street	at Manhattan Ave
NYC 10027	Mon-Sat 9-9:30, Sun 10-8

Olive & Bette's 👗

Best friends and self-proclaimed 'It Girls of the Upper West Side', Olive and Bette opened this series of cheeky boutiques packed with trendy designer staples in order to 'save the world from fashion don'ts'. And just how do they do that? By providing flirtatious females with walls of neatly piled Michael Star and James Perse tanks and tees, rows of Dr. Scholl sandals and Tamara Henriquez rain boots, and racks of Alice & Olivia and Theory pants. And for the on-the-go-girl who just can't get enough must-haves, Olive and Bette even have a monthly e-newsletter. What more could an It Girl want? *oliveandbettes.com*

Moderate to expensive   *Amex/MC/V*

Upper West Side	(212) 579-2178
252 Columbus Avenue	btw 71/72nd St
NYC 10023	Mon-Sat 11-7 Sun 12-6

West Village/NoHo	212 712 0473
384 Bleecker Street	at Perry
NYC 10004	Mon-Sat 12-8, Sun 12-6

SoHo	(646) 613-8772
158 Spring Street	btw Wooster/West Broadway
NYC 10012	Mon-Fri 11-7, Sun 12-6

Upper East Side	(212) 717-9655
1070 Madison Avenue	btw 81/82nd St
NYC 10021	Mon-Sat 10-7, Sun 12-6

Only Hearts 👗

Helena Stuart opened her Columbus Avenue boutique in 1978 and has created an internationally recognized home for the hopeless romantic. A mecca for all things heart-shaped, from bath beads and paperweights to antiques and candles, Only Hearts sells gifts and intimate apparel for those who want every day to be Valentine's. The store's signature 'inner outwear', a selection of sweet and flirty camisoles, teddies, lace tanks and sexy underwear is so cute that you may be tempted to take them out of the bedroom and into your everyday wardrobe. *onlyhearts.com*

Moderate   *Amex/MC/V*

Upper West Side	(212) 724-5608
386 Columbus Avenue	btw 78/79th St
NYC 10024	Mon-Sat 11-7, Sun 12-7

Nolita	(212) 431-3694
230 Mott Street	btw Prince/Spring
NYC 10012	Mon-Sat 11-7, Sun 12-7

Onward SoHo

This huge store (well, for SoHo) sells its own ICB brand, featuring pared-down contemporary career and sportswear (similar to Theory) such as relaxed suits, knits, shirts and pants in muted colors, as well as handbags. Look out for the new denim line. *icb-brand.com*

Moderate   *Amex/MC/V*

SoHo   **(212) 274-1255**
159 Mercer Street   btw Prince/Houston
NYC 10012   Mon-Sat 11-7, Sun 12-6

The Open Door Gallery

Painter-turned-fashion-designer Madani views her work as art, and it looks like it too: movement and color play vital roles in her designs. She uses silks, linens, cottons and interesting prints and mixes them together to create individual pieces finished with raw, zigzagged edges. Her dresses often call for wrapping yourself sarong style. Feminine, flowing and festive, Madani will alter any piece to your exact measurements. Don't miss the unusual array of accessories and jewelry.

Expensive   *Amex/MC/V*

East Village   **(212) 982-7859**
77 East 4th Street   btw Second/Bowery
NYC 10003   Tues-Sun 1-8

Opening Ceremony

Now this is a cool idea for a boutique: dedicate each year or season to elegant, hard-to-find fashions from a different international hotspot. Started by two Berkeley grads, Opening Ceremony kicked things off last year by selling wares from Hong Kong, before moving on to the sunny glories of Brazil's Sao Paolo. They are now showcasing bold designs from the U.K., but the house line (designed by Humberto Leon) is another reason to visit—the unisex collection is filled with smart separates, blazers, coats and more. *openingceremony.com*

Expensive   *Amex/MC/V*

SoHo   **(212) 219-2688**
35 Howard Street   btw Broadway/Lafayette
NYC 10013   Mon-Sat 11-8, Sun 12-7

★ Operations

Who says work sucks? Owned by three gorgeous guys, Operations sells authentic workwear from around the world, handpicked for stylishness, like Refrigewear meat-packers' jackets in lime green, or multi-pocketed Portuguese masonry pants. Then there's the restyled workwear that is altered: either the fit is changed, or it's embellished with contrast stitching, or otherwise changed to be made more fashionable, like the British commando sweaters with asymmetrical leather patches on the elbows

and shoulders. Every garment has its back story document-
ed on its tag. The shop itself is work-inspired as well: pul-
ley system racks, meat locker dressing rooms, and hydraulic
lift bench tables. *operationswear.com*

Affordable to moderate *Amex/MC/V*

SoHo (212) 334-4950
60 Mercer Street at Broome
NYC 10003 Mon-Sat 11-8, Sun 12-7

Original Leather

If you're looking to complete your Matrix look, Original
Leather is your place. Selling mostly their own label, you'll
find leather blazers, trenches, skirts, five-pocket 'jeans' as
well as a home collection. Fabrics range from suede, fur and
shearling to exotic skins—if you can't find it here, you're not
going to find it anywhere. *originalleather.com*

Moderate *Amex/MC/V*

SoHo (212) 219-8210
176 Spring Street btw Thompson/West Broadway
NYC 10012 Mon-Sat 11-7:30, Sun 12-7:30

The Original Levi's Store

The king of the jeans business, Levi's is rising to the challenge of hip brands like Earl and Seven with limited-edition
ranges like the twisty Type 1 and the Superlow jeans for girls
who still think belly-button flashing is vital. Of course, there
is a huge range of 501s and other classic styles, plus casual
basics and accessories. *levis.com*

Moderate *Amex/MC/V*

Midtown East (212) 826-5957
750 Lexington Avenue btw 59/60th St
NYC 10022 Mon-Sat 10-8, Sun 11-6

SoHo (646) 613-1847
536 Broadway btw Prince/Spring
NYC 10012 Mon-Sat 10-8, Sun 11-7

Orva

A full-service department store for the price-conscious
woman. You could arrive naked (not that we'd advise that)
and leave fully dressed in its selection of designer and
brand-name sportswear, lingerie, activewear, juniors,
hosiery, accessories and shoe department. Labels like Juicy
Couture, Von Dutch, Kenneth Cole, Diesel and Calvin Klein
are 10-30% below retail prices.

Moderate *Amex/MC/V*

Upper East Side (212) 369-3448
155 East 86th Street btw Lexington/Third Ave
NYC 10028 Mon-Sat 10-9, Sun 10-8

Upper East Side (shoes & accessories only) (212) 838-3441
782 Lexington Avenue btw 60/61st St
NYC 10021 Mon-Thurs 10-8:30, Fri-Sat 10-9, Sun 11-7

★ Oscar de la Renta

Catering to ladies with taste, this shop feels like a chic tropical boutique with various shades of white, a large back mirror framed with white ceramic palm tree inlays, carved white chairs with chocolate satin cushions, and marble tables covered in opulent floral arrangements. Look towards the back at the flatscreen broadcast of Oscar's latest runway endeavors. A small elevated parlor showcases the famous streamlined gowns and fancy party dresses. Wearable on any given UES day are his amazing skirt suits, flouncy ruffly blouses, simple shell dresses, mod op-art prints in forgotten color combos like lime-green, lemon-yellow and brown paisleys.   oscardelarenta.com

Luxury   *Amex/MC/V*

Upper East Side   **(212) 288-5810**
772 Madison Avenue   at 66th St
NYC 10021   Mon-Sat 10-6

★ OshKosh B'Gosh

Childrenswear icon OshKosh's claim to fame: the bib overall, originally worn by farmers and railroad workers in the 1900s, and today worn by toddlers and children worldwide—in smaller sizes, of course. Parents flock here for durable, well-styled clothes that scream pure Americana. It offers everyday essentials like jeans, overalls, corduroys, T-shirts, activewear, swimwear, shoes and accessories, all color-coordinated with the OshKosh B'Gosh logo. Newborn to size 16.   *800-282-4674 oshkoshbgosh.com*

Affordable   *Amex/MC/V*

Fifth Avenue   **(212) 827-0098**
586 Fifth Avenue   at 47th St
NYC 10036   Mon-Fri 10-7, Sat 11-6, Sun 11-5

Otte

Think of it as an alternative to Scoop—same idea (diverse mix of designers), but not everything in the store costs an arm and a leg. Look for Rebecca Taylor, Paper Denim Cloth and Mint among others. Try on a sexy little tank by Fred Segal or check out the necklaces and bracelets, many of which run less than $100 at the West Village outpost (the Williamsburg store is the original). Perfect to weather recessions.

Expensive   *Amex/MC/V*

West Village   **(212) 229-9424**
121 Greenwich Avenue   at 13th St
NYC 10014   Mon-Sat 12-8, Sun 12-6

Williamsburg   **(718) 302-3007**
132 North 5th Street   at Bedford Ave
Brooklyn 11211   Mon-Sat 12-8, Sun 12-6

Ottiva

Here's a genius concept in retailing: when you want to open another trendy shoe store in the same neighborhood selling the same stuff but still want to be 'new', what should you do? Spell the name of your first store backwards, of course. If this makes no sense to you, go to Avitto and read all about Ottiva (Omari and Iramo suffer from the same syndrome). The salespeople may be sick of explaining the whole thing, but you'll still see a very nice selection of leather shoes imported from Italy here, along with some rugged footwear and some trendier numbers and a smattering of handbags and briefcases.

Moderate *Amex/MC/V*

SoHo
192 Spring Street
NYC 10012

(212) 625-0348
btw Thompson/Sullivan
Daily 11-8

Otto Tootsi Plohound

It's a strange name, and no one knows what it means, but when they see these shoes, no one really cares. This is a fabulous footwear store that straddles the divide between downtown and designer perfectly. Alongside Cynthia Rowley, Nancy Nancy, Miu Miu, and Prada Sport, you'll find their own label, Otto, that dilutes the trends into super-affordable and distinctive shoes. They have fantastic sales too. A must-visit store for any shoe shopper.

Affordable to expensive *Amex/MC/V*

Midtown East
38 East 57th Street
NYC 10022

(212) 231-3199
btw Madison/Park Ave
Mon-Wed 11-7:30
Thurs-Fri 11-8, Sat 11-7, Sun 12-6

Flatiron
137 Fifth Avenue
NYC 10010

(212) 460-8650
btw 20/21st St
Mon-Fri 11:30-7:30, Sat 11-8, Sun 12-7

SoHo
413 West Broadway
NYC 10012

(212) 925-8931
btw Prince/Spring
Mon-Fri 11:30-8, Sat 11-8, Sun 12-7

SoHo
273 Lafayette Street
NYC 10012

(212) 431-7299
btw Houston/Prince
(opening hours as above)

Outlet 7

Fashion editors in the know seek out high-end designer Showroom Seven's East Village outpost where you can snag last season's designer pieces at wholesale prices. The selection constantly changes, but look for Imitation of Christ dresses, handbags by Orla Kiely, and fun duds by Charlotte and Nikka in the current crop.

Expensive *Amex/MC/V*

East Village
117 East 7th Street
NYC 10009

(212) 529-0766
btw First/Avenue A
Tues-Thurs 1-8, Fri-Sat 12-9, Sun 12-8

Oxxford Couture Collection

Creative director Jack Simpson, a lover of the classic strong-shouldered American silhouette and a former co-designer of the basketball uniforms for UNC and the Charlotte Hornets, helms this made-to-measure showroom which operates (both literally and figuratively) 'one step above' the classic Oxxford menswear on the ground floor. Fashion-oriented fellas excited by the idea of Sherlock Holmes hitting the runway can rummage through tweedy fabrics for the ultimate fall suit. The tailoring is exquisite, the looks timeless. *theoxxfordstore.com*

Luxury	*Amex/MC/V*
Midtown East	**(212) 593-0230**
36 East 57th Street	btw Madison/Park Ave
NYC 10022	Daily 10-6 (by appointment)

Pan American Phoenix

A rare find on the Upper East Side, this cute little store imports the best goods from Mexico. Look for colorful skirts and peasants blouses to satisfy Frida Kahlo or a fashion-forward clientele. The embroidered dresses and gorgeous scarves are winners, too. Also find silver, jewelry, handbags and a great housewares collection. The best part? Prices so reasonable that you might be tempted to break for the border yourself. *panamphoenix.com*

Moderate	*Amex/MC/V*
Upper East Side	**(212) 570-0300**
857 Lexington Avenue	btw 64/65th St
NYC 10021	Mon-Fri 10:30-6:30, Sat 11-6

★ Paragon Sporting Goods

This is truly a sporting goods store for the Noughties: over 100,000 square feet devoted to clothes and gear for every sport imaginable, from racket sports, water sports, skiing and hiking to golf, camping, fitness and fishing. The selection is enormous, but the store is so well organized it makes shopping easy and pleasurable. You might take up a new hobby just to suit yourself in the perfect gear. *800-961-3030*

paragonsports.com

Moderate	*Amex/MC/V*
Chelsea	**(212) 255-8036**
867 Broadway	at 18th St
NYC 10003	Mon-Sat 10-8, Sun 11:30-7

Parke & Ronen

Body-conscious but forgiving—that's a winning combination, and one this design team works in streamlined sportswear geared toward a younger (and trim, they only forgive so much) customer. In addition to casual pants and shirts, look for knits, vests, scarves and hats as well as a selection of Frank and Daniel belts, bags and sunglasses from a variety of European designers. *parkeandronen.com*

Expensive	*Amex/MC/V*
Chelsea	**(212) 989-4245**
176 Ninth Avenue	btw 20/21st St
NYC 10011	Mon-Sat 12-8, Sun 1-6

Patagonia

Patagonia brings an environmentally minded, West Coast attitude to the rough and tough Big Apple. This means cozy fleece pullovers made from recycled plastic bottles, polos and pants made from organic cotton that is grown without the use of any harmful chemicals, and outdoor clothes for every activity from yoga to Alpine mountaineering. Putting consciousness back into cool clothing, the store has a small selection of guides, nature photography, books and novels by the likes of Thoreau and Krakauer, and is happy to provide you with eco-literature at the checkout. A visit to Patagonia makes for a truly fulfilling experience for the mind, body and spirit.   *800-638-6464 patagonia.com*

Moderate   *Amex/MC/V*

Upper West Side   **(917) 441-0011**
426 Columbus Avenue   btw 80/81st St
NYC 10024   Mon-Sat 10-7, Sun 11-6

SoHo   **(212) 343-1776**
101 Wooster Street   btw Prince/Spring
NYC 10012   Mon-Sat 11-7 (Thurs 11-8), Sun 12-6

Pat Areias

Upon entering this Madison Avenue belt store, face right and select from over 500 hanging belt straps in skins like calf, alligator, crocodile, lizard and ostrich, or horsehair. Decide on a color, from standard neutrals to bold brights and soft pastels. Then admire the sterling-silver buckles in the glass display case. Match a belt strap with a buckle, and voilà—you've just designed your own belt. Straps run from $70 to $450, while buckles go from $100 to $6,000 for an 18kt gold and diamond number.   *patareias.com*

Expensive   *Amex/MC/V*

Upper East Side   **(212) 717-7200**
966 Madison Avenue   btw 75/76th St
NYC 10021   Mon-Sat 10-6, Sun 11-5

Patina

A quaint vintage clothing shop, Patina offers a wide choice of vintage clothing, handbags and other goodies like ceramics, decorative glass and period costume jewelry. There are beaded sweater sets, dresses, skirts and handbags from the Forties through the Seventies, all in good condition. As with all vintage shops, timing is everything—repeat visits may be necessary to snag something truly special.   *patinavintage.com*

Moderate   *Amex/MC/V*

SoHo   **(212) 625-3375**
451 Broome Street   btw Broadway/Mercer
NYC 10012   Mon-Sat 12-7, Sun 1-6

Paul & Shark

This Italian retailer of yachting attire for, one suspects, the permanently land-locked, fuses urban and nautical influences. The two-level shop sells chic men's and women's sportswear, from sweaters, shirts and warm-up suits to swimwear, lightweight boating jackets, winter-weight coats and a line of polar fleece. It's all specifically fashioned for outdoor living and, best of all, is water-resistant. Some pieces are more hi-tech (don't miss jackets with an interior thermometer that adjusts temperature) than others, but they're all made to withstand the elements—just in case you do get a chance to hit the high seas. Also find golf apparel and boating shoes for men. *paulshark.it*

Expensive   *Amex/MC/V*

Upper East Side   **(212) 452-9868**
772 Madison Avenue   btw 66/67th St
NYC 10021   Mon-Sat 10-6 (Thurs 10-6:30), Sun 12-5

Paul Frank Industries
California designer Paul Frank is a cheeky monkey. Well, sort of. His cartoon chimpanzee Julius has become cult amongst equally cheeky fashion girls who like a bit of kitsch with their cool. Think the Hello Kitty of America. This downtown store carries the full Paul Frank range, from furniture to women's and menswear to handbags and wallets. He recently introduced eyewear too, so, to be franked, this is your place. *paulfrank.com*

Moderate   *Amex/MC/V*

Nolita   **(212) 965-5079**
195 Mulberry Street   at Kenmare
NYC 10013   Daily 11-7

Paul Smith
One of Britain's most successful designers, and knighted by the Queen to boot, Sir Paul Smith keeps his customers coming back for more. What distinguishes a Paul Smith design: a bold approach to fabric, pattern and color with traditional Old World styling. His classic pieces are never stuffy (more warm and clever, really), and his striped shirts are a must for both sexes. Shop a collection of English tailored menswear that includes suits, at an average price of $1,200, dress and casual shirts, sport jackets and outerwear. Accessories include watches, cufflinks and eyewear. *paulsmith.co.uk*

Expensive   *Amex/MC/V*

Flatiron   **(212) 627-9770**
108 Fifth Avenue   at 16th St
NYC 10011   Mon-Sat 11-7 (Thurs 11-8)

Paul Stuart
With its no-nonsense collection of suits, furnishings, shirts, sportswear and outerwear, as well as English bench-made shoes and accessories, this is the label of choice for high-powered bankers, lawyers, and stockbrokers ready and willing to drop a bundle to look their business best. Corporate men and women will find plenty of straightforward designs

to seal the deal. Whether you choose off the rack or opt for made-to-measure, Paul Stuart is a great source for traditional clothing.   *800-678-8278 paulstuart.com*

Luxury   *Amex/MC/V*

Midtown East   **(212) 682-0320**
Madison Avenue   at 45th St
NYC 10017   Mon-Fri 8-6:30 (Thurs 8-7), Sat 9-6
                                                 Sun 12-5 (except in summer)

Peacock NYC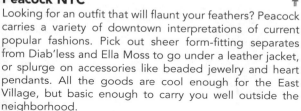

Looking for an outfit that will flaunt your feathers? Peacock carries a variety of downtown interpretations of current popular fashions. Pick out sheer form-fitting separates from Diab'less and Ella Moss to go under a leather jacket, or splurge on accessories like beaded jewelry and heart pendants. All the goods are cool enough for the East Village, but basic enough to carry you well outside the neighborhood.

Expensive   *Amex/MC/V*

East Village   **(212) 260-1809**
440 East 9th Street   btw First/Avenue A
NYC 10009   Daily 12-8

A Pea in the Pod

At this flagship store women no longer have to fret about putting together the perfect pregnancy wardrobe. It's 3,300 square feet of selling space offering A Pea in the Pod's private label as well as designs from the maternity lines of Nicole Miller, La Perla, Seven and Three Dots. Check out the Yanuk jeans, complete with extra maternity fabric (yes!), and items from Chaiken, the Vince collection, Shoshanna shifts and Lilly Pulitzer swimwear. The clothes are attractive, comfortable and versatile.   *apeainthepod.com*

Moderate   *Amex/MC/V*

Upper East Side   **(212) 988-8039**
860 Madison Avenue   at 70th St
NYC 10021   Mon-Fri 10-7, Sat 10-6, Sun 12-6

★ Peanutbutter & Jane

Anyone looking for cute and cool childrenswear should head for Peanutbutter & Jane, which carries baby and toddler clothes as well as big kids' sizes up to girls 12/14 and boys 10. The big kids will get a kick out of the printed jeans, beaded tops, surfer shorts, stylish hats and costume shoes. Labels include Ave. Blu, Corky + Co, Cotton Caboodle, Flowers by Zoe, Lipstik, Petit Bateau, Submarine and Wes and Willy. Sadly, no peanut butter sandwich with purchase.

Moderate   *Amex/MC/V*

West Village   **(212) 620-7952**
617 Hudson Street   btw Jane/West 12th St
NYC 10014   Mon-Fri 10:30-7, Sat 10-7, Sun 11-6

★ Pearl River Mart

They may have moved to new digs—to Broadway from their seedy former location next to the Canal Street subway station—and added a cascading waterfall, but the low prices on everything Asian-inspired remain. You'll find silk jacquard-quilted jackets in bright colors retailing for $80, Japanese silk blouses with hook (or 'frog') closures for $39.50, and a wide assortment of pajamas and kimonos. Check out the housewares section for bamboo blinds and room dividers, ceramics and traditional china, or pick up a rooster alarm clock or dragon-print duvet. There are also green tea beauty products. *pearlriver.com*

Affordable *(cash only)*

SoHo **(212) 431-4770**
477 Broadway btw Broome/Grand
NYC 10013 Daily 10-7

Peggy Pardon

Vintage clothes are inherently trendy, hence the oodles of shops in this city consisting entirely of polyester and crinoline from days of yore. Peggy Pardon's is a bit pickier. The collection is capped at the 1940s, and spans back to Edwardian times. Wearing her wares to a costume party would be a crime: they're pristine and gorgeous enough to don non-ironically. Herbert Sondheim liquid satin dresses, wearable fringe-free flapper dresses, ornate eyelet lawn dresses from the Victorian era, and Edwardian silk blouses with gold leaf are a few of the treasures she stocks. There's lots of lingerie to be worn in one's boudoir or under one of the sheer dresses. *peggypardon.com*

Expensive *Amex/MC/V*

Lower East Side **(212) 529-3686**
153 Ludlow Street btw Stanton/Rivington
NYC 10002 Mon-Fri 1-8, Sat-Sun 12-8

Pelle Via Roma

Want a great bag without a label? Owned by Max Fiorentino, this shop offers a similar selection of handbags and luggage crafted in the Florentine style. The classic designs are in supple and exotic skins like lamb, calf, alligator, lizard and deer, and feature shapes like the Fendi baguette, the Hermès bucket bag and Tod's and Pradaesque designs. Prices run from $70 to $900. Also shop an enormous selection of pashmina shawls retailing at $88.

Expensive *Amex/MC/V*

Upper East Side **(212) 327-3553**
1322 Third Avenue btw 75/76th St
NYC 10021 Mon-Fri 10-8, Sat 11-7, Sun 12-6

Upper East Side **(212) 717-5444**
234 East 75th Street btw Second/Third Ave
NYC 10021 Mon-Fri 10-8, Sat 11-7, Sun 12-6

Peter Elliot

An exemplary example of what a men's store should be, this small, dark wood-paneled space gives a nod to Savile Row days of yore. The store stocks business-ready Kiton suits, classic polo shirts, casual knits, dandy Peter Elliot blazers accented by ribbon belts, and Paul Smith polka-dot ties. For a store that is the size of most New York apartments, the service is exquisite, with tailors and sales help available at your beck and call, thanks to a 24-hour emergency line, a delivery service and free alterations.

Expensive   *Amex/MC/V*

Upper East Side   **(212) 570-2300**
1070 Madison Avenue   at 81st St
NYC 10028   Mon-Fri 10-7, Sat 10-6
                                  Sun 12-5 (except in summer)

Upper East Side   **(212) 570-2301**
997 Lexington Avenue   at 72nd St
NYC 10021   Mon-Thurs 10-7, Fri 10-6:30
                                            Sat 10-6, Sun 12-5

Peter Elliot Blue

'I'll bet I can build a store on the central theme of navy blazers,' is the thought Elliot Rabin had in mind when he opened Peter Elliot Blue. Another high-end boutique has been added to the empire, and with one theme in mind....blue, naturally. The store stocks at least 10 variations on the navy blazer, from a classic three-button to a very of-the-moment velvet. Everything else in the shop (khakis, corduroys, slacks) co-ordinates with or complements the jacket. Though beware, items are available in very limited styles and for a single season. Belts, for example, are offered strictly in alligator and shell cordovan, and are priced up to $1,000. You may be surrounded by it, but you sure won't be blue here.

Expensive   *Amex/MC/V*

Upper East Side   **(212) 570-2301**
997 Lexington Avenue   at 72nd St
NYC 10021   Mon-Thurs 10-7, Fri 10-6:30, Sun 12-5

★ Peter Elliot (kids)

If you want your child to be the chicest kid at his private school, this is your store. Specializing in old-fashioned, well-made clothes, including exquisite French, Italian and English labels as well as their own private line, this is the perfect place to find a seersucker suit from Hickey Freeman or a party dress from Piccano Piccana. Other labels include Due Sorelle, Pears & Bears, Kule, Marie Chantal, Euro Kids and Corgi Cashmere of England. Special amenities include a play area for kids, a changing area for babies, and a photo gallery starring their youthful customers. From 2 to 12 years old.

Moderate to expensive   *Amex/MC/V*

Upper East Side
1067 Madison Avenue
NYC 10028

(212) 570-5747
btw 80/81st St
Mon-Sat 10-6, Sun 12-5

Peter Elliot (women)

Fusing masculine tailoring with feminine styling, PE Women offers a great selection of high-end European labels with a chic edge. Highlights include a luxurious Jill Michelle car coat with matching skirt that would be perfect for both town and country; suits and handsome blazers by Isaia and Kiton; hacking jackets by Belvest; traditional men's shirts adapted for women; four-ply cashmere sweater sets from Scotland; double-faced cashmere coats with luxe chinchilla collars and chic alligator shoes.

Expensive   *Amex/MC/V*

Upper East Side
1071 Madison Avenue
NYC 10028

(212) 570-1551
at 81st St
Mon-Sat 10-6 (Thurs 10-7), Sun 12-5

Peter Fox Shoes

Seen on-screen in *Harry Potter* and *Chicago*, Peter Fox shoes are known to be glamorous, practical and comfortable. This is a full-service store specializing in classic styles from Italian leather to satin. Brides-to-be can choose from an extensive selection of bridal shoes. *peterfoxshoes.com*

Expensive   *Amex/MC/V*

SoHo
105 Thompson Street
NYC 10012

(212) 431-7426
btw Spring/Prince
Mon-Sat 11-7, Sun 12-6

Peter Hermann

Hundreds of designer bags are on offer at Peter Hermann. Find a brilliant variety of briefcases, luggage, handbags, knapsacks, totes and wallets from labels like Orla Kiely, Jamin Puech and Strenesse. The shop is also the exclusive U.S. retailer of the entire line of Mandarina Duck bags. Sleek eyewear by British spectacle specialists Cutler & Gross is also available.

Moderate to Expensive   *Amex/MC/V*

SoHo
118 Thompson Street
NYC 10012

(212) 966-9050
btw Spring/Prince
Mon-Sat 12-7, Sun 1-6

★ Petit Bateau

Created in 1893 and with over 140 boutiques worldwide, Petit Bateau has been making the best T-shirts in the world (at least for children) for quite some time. This 3,000-square-foot shop has three sections: Les Bébés for 0-24 months, Les Petits for 2-8 year olds and Les Grands for tweens to adults. Find casual daywear, loungewear, sleepwear, underwear and plenty of those classic tees in soft muted colors—

each one coming in its own cute lemon-colored box. Prices run from $10 to $150. Petit Bateau's perfume and body products are also available. *petitbateau.com*

Moderate · *Amex/MC/V*

Upper East Side · **(212) 988-8884**
1094 Madison Avenue · at 82nd St
NYC 10028 · Mon-Fri 10-7, Sat 10-6, Sun 11-5

Petit Peton

This upscale shoe store, nominated by both *Vogue* and *Elle* magazines as one of the top three in the U.S., is a sexy shoe lover's dream come true. Find a collection of high fashion footwear from top designers such as Gianfranco Ferré, Casadei, DSquared, Roberto Cavalli and Giuseppe Zanotti. And don't miss the designer sunglasses. *petitpeton.com*

Expensive · *Amex/MC/V*

NoHo · **(212) 677-3730**
27 West 8th Street · btw Fifth/Sixth Ave
NYC 10011 · Mon-Fri 11-9:30, Sat 11-9, Sun 12-9

Phat Farm

Impresario Russell Simmons's 'Classic American Flava' label offered the rap and hip-hop lifestyle full force, and has delighted its aficionados.. The store becamee known for its denim-based collection, lots of knits and velour, T-shirts, sweatshirts and pants and the signature argyle pieces. Not to mention Simmons's wife Kimora's hot collection for women, Baby Phat, a sassy, sexy mix of oriental and hip-hop style. Alicia Keys, Britney Spears and Destiny's Child are all fans. *phatfarm.com*

Moderate · *Amex/MC/V*

SoHo · **(212) 533-7428**
129 Prince Street · btw West Broadway/Wooster
NYC 10012 · Mon-Sat 11-7, Sun 12-8

Phi

With a mirror-like black wall to your left, dark gray Grecian pillars in an off-center row, and bright sunlight emanating from the back wall's windows and skylights, Phi's effect is museum-like and breathtaking. Then there are the clothes: medieval princess dresses comprised of corset bodices and tulle layered skirts, as well as crinoline skirts with chiffon, perfect for a glamour goth. Intricately cut, texturally layered pieces crafted from luxe fabrics hang from racks suspended on almost invisible wires hanging from the high ceiling, all in neutral colors so as not to overwhelm. *phicollection.com*

Luxury · *Amex/MC/V*

Soho · **(212) 966-0076**
71 Greene Street · btw Spring/Broome
NYC 10012 · Mon-Sat 11-7, Sun 12-6

Philosophy di Alberta Ferretti

Her silhouette is romantic without being cloying, wearable without being basic. Her ethereal dresses are perfection, often understated in design and color and distinguished by intricate, weightless folds, smocking and embroidery. Looks run from frothy chiffon skirts and pearly satin tops to velvet dresses and wool coats, all marked by a delicate femininity. *philosophy.it*

Expensive   *Amex/MC/V*

SoHo   **(212) 460-5500**
452 West Broadway   btw Houston/Prince
NYC 10012   Mon-Sat 11-7, Sun 12-6

Piccione

Is Italy the true home of custom tailoring? A visit to Signor Piccione's workshop will most likely convince you it is. He will graciously make a suit, sportcoat or pair of slacks for men, or a pant and jacket ensemble for women. Choose a fabric from the finest mills such as Zegna, Loro Piana, Holland & Sherry and Scabel. Suits prices start at $3,000 with delivery in five weeks. In addition, Piccione also sells ready-made shirts, cashmere knitwear and ties.

Expensive   *Amex/MC/V*

Midtown East   **(212) 421-2820**
116 East 57th Street (2nd floor)   btw Park/Lexington Ave
NYC 10022   Mon-Sat 10-6

Pieces

The celebrity stylists, trendsetters, and husband and wife fashion duo that run Pieces both have a sharp sense of style and an uncanny knack for what's hip before you do. Picking through colored designs by Petro Zilla, distressed denim pieces by Evisu and underground Parisian imports, you may find yourself shopping beside a local Brooklyn celebrity. Pieces has also been known to carry street-cult classics by such designers as Cedella Marley and the original Not Rational bag. Want to stay a sartorial step ahead? Just let yourself fall to Pieces.

Moderate   *Amex/MC/V*

Clinton Hill   **(718) 857-7211**
671 Vanderbilt Avenue   at Park Place
Brooklyn 11238   Mon 12-6, Tues-Thurs 11-7
                                            Fri-Sat 11-8, Sun 11-6

Pilar Rossi

For some extra bells and whistles on your big day, check out Pilar Rossi's frilly collection of bridalwear, evening gowns and dressy suits for special occasions. Choose off-the-rack or custom-order your own. Sequins, beads and embroidery are the norm, but subtler, high-glamour styles can also be found. A gown will run at least $3,000, but you will be brilliantly decked out on the way to the altar.   *pilarrossi.com*

Luxury   *Amex/MC/V*
Upper East Side   **(212) 288-2469**
784 Madison Avenue   btw 66/67th St
NYC 10021   Mon-Sat 10-6:30

★ **Pippin**

There are a couple of cases with real Victorian cameos, gold and pearls, but aside from that all the costume and estate jewelry that catches your fancy, like medallions, multi-strand beaded necklaces, chain belts, sweater clips or brooches will be exactly the price you'd be willing to pay, sometimes less. A set of skinny drawers from an old newsroom is filled with jewelry divided into categories like $5 clip-on earrings and $10 cufflinks. Pick up non-wearable accessories like cigarette holders, fancy pens, vintage compacts and other vanity table fodder. Add panache to a cardigan by sewing on vintage Bakelite buttons; make basic heels sparkly with shoe clips.

Affordable   *Amex/MC/V*
Lower East Side   **(212) 505-5159**
72 Orchard Street   btw Broome/Grand
NYC 10002   Tues-Wed, Fri 12-6, Thurs, Sat 12-7, Sun 11-6

Pipsqueak

Showcasing an international roster of clothing from Portugal, France, Italy, England and Japan, this Nolita boutique provides the new breed of fashionistas with some of the cutest children's clothing on the planet. From T-shirts and playsuits with cheeky slogans such as 'Enjoy Milk,' 'Hell Raiser' and 'Mommy's new man,' to dapper leather loafers by Start-Rite and mod polka-dot bibs by Baroni, Pipsqueak makes each of its petit patrons the coolest kid on their block—even if they don't know it yet. *pipsqueakforkids.com*

Affordable   *Amex/MC/V*
Nolita   **(212) 226-8824**
248 Mott Street   btw Prince/Houston
NYC 10012   Tues-Sat 11-6

Planet Kids

As the name suggests, Planet Kids has just about everything under the sun for little ones. Parents of babies (under age 3) should head to the East Side store for basics and play clothes from Carter's, Zutano, and OshKosh; those with older children will find a better selection at the West Side location. No one's going to stop you on the street and ask you where you bought these outfits, but they're durable, machine-washable classics that will probably be the first thing you reach for on an ordinary day.   *planetkidsny.com*
Affordable   *Amex/MC/V*

Upper West Side   **(212) 864-8705**
2688 Broadway   at 103rd St
NYC 10025   Mon-Tues 9:30-7:30
                                  Wed-Sat 9:30-8, Sun 11-6

Upper East Side   **(212) 426-2040**
247 East 86th Street   btw Third/Fourth Ave
NYC 10028   (opening hours as above)

Pleats Please, Issey Miyake

Issey Miyake's women's line is practical, light as a feather, hard to wrinkle and perfect to travel with. Inspired by dance (Miyake's perennial source of inspiration) and international influences (from Africa to the Far East), Pleats Please is bursting with smooth, permanently pleated polyester pieces (dresses, pants, T-shirts and coats) primal in shape and painted in mouth-watering colors. Long-lasting, durable and lovely, Pleats Please offers clothing to accompany women for decades.   *pleatsplease.com*

Moderate   *Amex/MC/V*

SoHo   **(212) 226-3600**
128 Wooster Street   at Prince
NYC 10012   Mon-Sat 11-7, Sun 12-6

Plum

Owned and operated by a veteran TV wardrobe stylist and a Stella McCartney alum, Plum strives to bring exclusive designers at a reasonable price. Denmark's Designers Remix takes themes and runs with them, like the cute-overload puff-sleeve gingham blouses with cinched waists. Fellow Danes Lundgren & Windinge make casual and soft drapey tops and skirts that are slightly more embellished and whimsical than the norm. The LES hipster aesthetic is firmly in place with frumpy Eighties schoolteacher blouses that look best when paired with a miniskirt and a shag haircut. Anyone can wear light blue jeans by Indigo Hand, or darker jeans by Grass.   *plumstyle.com*

Moderate   *Amex/MC/V*

Lower East Side   **(212) 529-1030**
124 Ludlow Street   btw Rivington/Delancey
NYC 10002   Mon-Sat 1-8, Sun 1-7

Polo Ralph Lauren

Dressier looks may rule at Ralph's mansion, but his Sport and Black labels take center stage at this location. You'll find the look for just about any recreational lifestyle here, whether you're running, cycling, swimming, skiing or simply sipping cocktails at the club. Polo Golf features the ultimate in classic golfing attire, while Polo Tennis caters to both player and spectator with its selection of chic net-ready duds. Interspersed throughout is Lauren's all-American sportswear, which includes fabulous suedes and leathers, cashmere sweaters, shirts, jackets, chinos, shoes and some vintage pieces. Be sure to see the beautifully embroidered

jackets and pants, and note that the staff are incredibly helpful if you should have any questions.   *polo.com*

Expensive   *Amex/MC/V*

Upper East Side   **(212) 434-8000**
888 Madison Avenue   at 72nd St
NYC 10021   Mon-Wed 10-7, Thurs 10-8
                                           Fri-Sat 10-6, Sun 12-6

West Village   **(646) 638-0684**
381 Bleecker Street   btw Perry/Charles
NYC 10014   Mon-Fri 12-8, Sat-Sun 11-7

SoHo   **(212) 625-1660**
379 West Broadway   btw Spring/Broome
NYC 10012   Mon-Sat 11-7, Sun 12-6

★ **Pookie & Sebastian**
A groovy little store in an unexpected location that sells a
collection of girly (but not too girly) casual pieces. Pink roses
welcome you into a world of paisley and print tops that sit
oh-so-prettily next to Seven jeans, Cosabella lingerie, NY-
style T-shirts and an ingenious shelf filled with a rainbow of
well-made tube tops for a great value $28. Staff are cheerful
and friendly—must be the roses… *pookieandsebastian.com*

Moderate   *Amex/MC/V*

Upper East Side   **(212) 861-0550**
1488 Second Avenue   btw 77/78th St
NYC 10021   Mon-Sat 11-9 Sun 12-7

Midtown East   **(212) 951-7110**
541 Third Avenue   at 36th St
NYC 10017   Mon-Sat 11-9, Sun 12-7

Upper West Side   **(212) 580-5844**
322 Columbus Avenue   at 75th St
NYC 10023   Mon-Wed 11-7:30
                        Thurs 11-8:30, Fri-Sat 11-9, Sun 12-7:30

Poppy
This sweet new Nolita shop offers a bouquet of girly goods
by the finest in ultra-feminine fashions. Selections such as
Mint sequined tops, pretty Velvet pastel tanks and tees, not
to mention the shimmery slinky imports from Australian
designer and Hollywood It-girl favorite Sass & Bride, make
Poppy a simply intoxicating find.

Expensive   *Amex/MC/V*

Nolita   **(212) 219-8934**
281 Mott Street   btw Houston/Prince
NYC 10012   Mon-Wed 12-7, Thurs-Sat 12-8

Porthault
Long recognized for luxurious bed, bath and tabletop linens,
Porthault is also the happy home of a small, enticing sleepwear department for men and women. Nighties, as they
should be, are feminine and romantic, while nightshirts and

robes are available in all the Porthault prints. Childrenswear goes from twelve months to six years. *d-porthault.com*

Expensive *Amex/MC/V*

Upper East Side **(212) 688-1660**
18 East 69th Street btw Fifth/Madison Ave
NYC 10021 Mon-Fri 10-6, Sat 10-5:30

Powers Court Tennis

Tennis is in the name, and tennis is what they do. They have the clothes, the footwear, the rackets, the accessories…and all at the lowest prices in town. Brand names include Price, Wilson, and Head. Same-day service on racket restringing. *nyctennisproshop.com*

Affordable *Amex/MC/V*

Chelsea **(212) 691-3888**
132 1/2 West 24th Street btw Sixth/Seventh Ave
NYC 10011 Mon-Fri 9-6

★ Prada

Even if you can't afford anything in there, you have to check out Italian powerhouse Prada's monolithic, conceptual super-store on Broadway. Designed by avant-garde architect Rem Koolhaas, Miuccia Prada's store aims to transcend basic style constructs. It succeeds grandly, with esoteric murals on the walls and a shoe display area that turns into seating for lectures. She also provides a select range of vintage Prada pieces…remember the 'geek chic' wallpaper jackets and 'bourgeoise' chiffon blouses? You can buy them again here. Not to mention the latest beautiful, intelligent Prada clothes—dip-dyed cable knits, buttonless cardigans, nylon handbags, urbane wedges and printed skirts—that have made this label legendary. *prada.com*

Luxury *Amex/MC/V*

Upper East Side **(212) 327-4200**
841 Madison Avenue at 70th St
NYC 10021 Mon-Sat 10-6 (Thurs 10-7)

SoHo **(212) 334-8888**
575 Broadway at Prince
NYC 10012 Mon-Sat 11-7, Sun 12-6

Midtown East (shoes only) **(212) 308-2332**
45 East 57th Street btw Madison/Park Ave
NYC 10022 Mon-Sat 10-6 (Thurs 10-7), Sun 12-6

Fifth Avenue **(212) 664-0010**
724 Fifth Avenue btw 56/57th St
NYC 10019 (opening hours as above)

Precision

A neighborhood boutique packed with trendy New York, L.A. and European brands. Labels like Theory, Language, Michael Stars, Juicy Couture, Poleci and Earl offer bold and funky styles for the rich and the beautiful (as long as they are a size 10 or under). Accessories include hats and girly bags.

Expensive *Amex/MC/V*

Midtown East **(212) 683-8812**
522 Third Avenue at 35th Street
NYC 10016 Mon-Fri 11:30-8, Sat 11-7, Sun 11-6:30

Upper East Side **(212) 879-4272**
1310 Third Avenue at 75th St
NYC 10021 Mon-Fri 11-8, Sat 11-7, Sun 12-6

Upper East Side **(212) 585 2125**
1295 Third Avenue at 74th St
NYC 10021 Mon-Fri 11-8, Sat 11-7, Sun 12-6:30

Upper East Side **(212) 752-7170**
1019 Third Avenue at 60th St
NYC 10021 Mon-Fri 11-8, Sat 11-7, Sun 11-6

Premium Goods

When in need of the latest and greatest in sneakers, try Premium Goods. Premium Goods rewards kicks enthusiasts with the highest grade of sneakers, stocking limited editions of classic Nikes and Adidas imported from Europe and Japan. Preserved in glass casings, the shoes become museum-ready exhibits: trainers that aren't for sport so much as they are to be seen, on or off your feet. *premiumgoods.net*

Moderate *Amex/MC/V*

Park Slope **(718) 369-7477**
347 Fifth Avenue btw 4/5th St
Brooklyn 11215 Daily 1-7

Princeton Ski Shop

Avid skiers, snowboarders and skaters schuss here to scoop up snow-worthy threads from labels like Bogner, Columbia, Obermayer and Burton. The equipment is from equally top-of-the-line manufacturers. *princetonski.com*

Expensive *Amex/MC/V*

Flatiron **(212) 228-4400**
21 East 22nd Street btw Broadway/Park Ave South
NYC 10010 Mon-Fri 10-8, Sat 10-6, Sun 12-6

Project 159

The youung enthusiastic staff here and at the sister shop Project 234 love to gush about their selection of independent and up-and-coming designers. A premiere Buddhist Punk stockist, Project carries an array of distressed Rolling Stones tanks fit for a withered roadie and also a downtown fashionista. Remade Members Only jackets and stretch lace tanks by Bilingual, as well as the rainbow-colored leather in the Spanish shoe line Fluxa, add to the must-have factor. The bright, colorful wares in the jewelry case include shell paillette necklaces and earrings from Amsterdam, as well as rope necklaces with big wooden beads. Vintage electric colored pumps and slouch boots round out the hipster look. *project159.com*

Moderate *Amex/MC/V*

West Village **(212) 929-4959**
159 Seventh Avenue South btw Perry/Waverly
NYC 10014 Mon-Sat 12-8, Sun 1-8

Nolita (Project 234)
234 Mulberry Street
NYC 10012

n/a at press time
btw Prince/Spring
Mon-Sat 12-8, Sun 1-8

★ Pucci

Pucci has a rich tradition—movie stars on holiday, the luxe resort life—which it retains with its distinctive, knockout printed pieces. Since 1949, Pucci has been famous for its colorful and graphic prints derived from abstract drawings. Now that designer Julio Espada has been replaced by color king Christian Lacroix, expect even more technicolor brilliance. Whoever is at the helm, Pucci's tradition is fabulous enough to make its clothes and accessories eternally desirable. Find a series of dresses, from mini shirtdresses to Sixties shifts, skirts, pants, swimsuits (some of the best around) and accessories.   *pucci.com*

Expensive   *Amex/MC/V*

Fifth Avenue
701 Fifth Avenue
NYC 10022

(212) 230-1135
btw 54/55th St
Mon- Sdat 10-6:30, Sun 12-5

Upper East Side
24 East 64th Street
NYC 10021

(212) 752-4777
btw Fifth/Madison Ave
Mon-Sat 10-6

★ The Puma Store

Not just for jocks anymore, the Puma Store is stocking Nuala: a stylish workout line by 90's supermodel and yoga fanatic Christy Turlington. Other higher-end brands on offer are Neil Barrett's 96 Hours and Japanese line Mihara. Along with Puma's classic cool sneaks, they're now selling Phillip Starck's new designs. Still available are are the cute tennis dresses, simple tees (with current and retro themes), tanks, cover-ups, running pants, athletic skirts, shorts, airy mesh pieces and a wide selection of rugged bags you know and love. The new Meatpacking location is big and bright with inventive rotating displays.   *puma.com*

Affordable   *Amex/MC/V/Dis*

SoHo
521 Broadway
NYC 10012

(212) 334-7861
btw Spring/Broome
Mon-Sat 10-8, Sun 11-7

Chelsea
421 West 14th Street
NYC 10014

(212) 206-0109
btw Ninth/Tenth Ave
Mon-Sat 11-7, Sun 12-6

Purdy Girl

Girly-girls flock to this apparel and accessories boutique for cute, feminine sundresses by designers including Nanette Lepore, plus shimmery off-the-shoulder numbers and ruffled miniskirts. Corinne Purdy handpicks the merchandise, which might include candy-cane-colored striped handbags, flowered flip-flops and a great selection of intimates by brands such as Loveletters Lingerie, with cheeky tank tops that say 'Naughty' and 'Cranky'.   *purdygirlnyc.com*

Moderate   *Amex/MC/V*

West Village   **(212) 529-8385**
220 Thompson Street   btw Bleecker/West 3rd St
NYC 10012   Sun-Thurs 11-8, Fri-Sat 11-11

West Village   **(646) 654-6751**
540 LaGuardia Place   at Bleecker
NYC 10012   Daily 11-8

Upper West Side   **n/a at press time**
464 Columbus Avenue   at 82nd St
NYC 10024   n/a at press time

Push

Owner Karen Karch caters to a hip Nolita crowd with looks that can be layered together for day or big pieces that can stand alone for a big night out. The displays are a mix of semi-precious pieces like a red draped coral necklace or turquoise drop earrings, as well as gold and silver tiaras with diamonds. Also check out the black or blue onyx cross pendants on ribbon—very Madonna.   *karenkarch.com*

Expensive   *Amex/MC/V*

Nolita   **(212) 965-9699**
240 Mulberry Street   btw Prince/Spring
NYC 10012   Mon-Sat 12-7, Sun 1-6

Quiksilver

Giant video screens depicting surfer girls and skate dudes enjoying the great outdoors frame this Times Square flagship for gnarly young-person threads. Inside you'll find another large screen, as well as Quiksilver logo tees, bathing suits, very large shorts and hooded sweatshirts. Tourists who would rather catch a wave or launch an Ollie than be in Midtown will find much to love here.   *quiksilver.com*

Affordable   *Amex/MC/V*

Midtown West   **(212) 840-8111**
3 Times Square   at 42nd St/Seventh Ave
NYC 10036   Daily 9:30-12

SoHo   **(212) 334-4500**
109 Spring Street   btw Mercer/Greene
NYC 10012   Sun-Thurs 11-8, Fri-Sat 11-9

Rafé New York

When celebs are snapping up your beauteous bags, you know you're onto a good thing. Cameron Diaz bought a Rafé multicolored wooden bead bag, Sandra Bullock a lacquered straw tote, and Kristen Davis a, well, Kristen bag. Rafé specializes in simple shapes in sleek leathers, including totes, messenger bags, briefcases with vacchetta trim, and evening purse knockouts in a rainbow of fabrics. As if that wasn't enough, Rafé also stocks a winning collection of shoes and jewelry.   *rafe.com*

Expensive   *Amex/MC/V*

NoHo   **(212) 780-9739**
1 Bleecker Street   at Bowery
NYC 10012   Daily 12-7

Rags A Go Go

Situated alongside many under par used-clothing stores, this vintage emporium distinguishes itself by the sheer mass of choice, spanning the Fifties to the Nineties, and by its bargain basement prices. They have everything, from sport jerseys, shoes, jackets and dresses to an entire wall of vintage jeans, as well as unusual accessories like Seventies watchbands. They also offer rentals for up to four days.

Affordable   *MC/V*

West Village   **(646) 486-4011**
218 West 14th Street   btw Seventh/Eighth Ave
NYC 10011   Mon-Sat 11-7, Sun 12-6

★ Ralph Lauren

'The romance, the beauty, the world of Ralph Lauren' say the fragrance advertisements, and don't we all want a piece of it. Ralph Lauren is the king of the American fashion establishment, who has earned his title over the past 35 years by delivering a luxe interpretation of classic American sportswear. His clothes embody the aspirational American lifestyle, one of leisure, privilege…and polo. And Ralph is on form—following a highly imitated prairie-themed collection he segued effortlessly into Victoriana, all the while retaining the quintessential Lauren look. Think Penelope Cruz in an evening dress in the rain, and dream… As for men, Ralph is your man. He has cultivated the preppy look for years, and it works a charm. Enter Lauren's anglophile world, where you'll find everything from ready-to-wear and Oscar-caliber eveningwear to sports and casualwear. Looks include tissue-thin leathers and suedes, luxurious cashmeres paired with tweed jackets, checked ponchos and strapless evening gowns.   *polo.com*

Luxury   *Amex/MC/V*

Upper East Side   **(212) 434-8000**
888 Madison Avenue   at 72nd St
NYC 10021   Mon-Wed 10-7, Thurs 10-8, Fri-Sat 10-6
                                                  Sun 12-6

SoHo   **(212) 625-1660**
381 West Broadway   btw Broome/Spring
NYC 10012   Mon-Sat 11-7, Sun 12-6

West Village   **(212) 645-5513**
380 Bleecker Street   btw Charles/Perry
NYC 10014   Mon-Fri 12-8, Sat-Sun 11-7

★ Ralph Lauren Baby

A testament to the idea of branding from birth, this outlet for pint-size versions of Ralph Lauren staples—like incredibly soft cashmere sweaters and sturdy polos—retains the trademark deep wood and white walls of its parent flagship store up the block. Outfitting newborns through size 4, the collection also includes such kid-centric items as cuddly crib blankets and 'Sunday best' girls' dresses in navy with matching white stockings.   *polo.com*

Luxury   *Amex/MC/V*
Upper East Side   **(212) 434-8099**
872 Madison Avenue   btw 71/72nd St
NYC 10021   Mon-Sat 10-6, Sun 12-5

Rampage

Seasonal, but fun. Rampage tackles the latest trends and packages them in affordable ensembles for youthful shoppers. Flying off the racks as soon as they are hung, Rampage pieces are constantly refreshed according to popular taste. Pleated minis, clingy sweaters (like a ribbed, off-the-shoulder zippered number), stretch cord cargos, jeans (with sashes) and puckered tops—the selection is huge, basic and delicious. Handbags and hats top off that new (for now) look.   *rampagestores.com*

Affordable   *Amex/MC/V*
SoHo   **(212) 995-9569**
127 Prince Street   at Wooster
NYC 10012   Mon-Wed 9-7, Thurs-Sat 9-9, Sun 9-8

Rapax

A good neighborhood shoe store that carries a large selection of fashionable classics, including simply styled flats, mules, sandals and evening pumps by Rapax, Roberto Peruzzini and Nadine.

Moderate   *MC/V*
Upper East Side   **(212) 734-5171**
1100 Madison Avenue   btw 82/83rd St
NYC 10028   Mon-Sat 10-7, Sun 12-6

R by 45rpm

An extremely trendy shop, R by 45rpm is home to one of the hottest Japanese jean collections around. Noted for wickedly detailed clothes (skirts, jackets, T-shirts, accessories) and hand-stressed denim, this place has great atmosphere and beautiful decor (floor-to-ceiling columns made from Japanese chestnut trees). It's the ultimate destination for denim fanatics who want their jeans aged just so, because each pair is worn-in by hand and then personally stamped on the inside pocket by the employee who 'distressed' it. Prices range from $150-$1,300.   *rby45rpm.com*

Expensive   *Amex/MC/V*
SoHo   **(917) 237-0045**
169 Mercer Street   at Houston
NYC 10012   Mon-Sat 11-7, Sun 12-7

Really Great Things

This pair of sleek sophisticated boutiques challenges the notion of what it means to be chic on the Upper West Side, and there isn't even a Nanette Lepore blazer or Michael Star tee in sight. Instead of relying on the trends, season in season out, owner Ryan Zentner searches Europe for 'the next Tom Ford' by choosing avant-garde accoutrements from up-

and-coming designers like Annette Goertz from Germany and Annette Rostel from France. Really Great Things also has a selection of really great leather shoes, both from their own line and lesser known labels like All Mine, Cydwoq and Grey Mer. And they provide a special event clothing service, regularly relied on by their large celeb clientele.

Expensive   *MC/V*

Upper West Side   **(212) 787-5354**
284 Columbus Avenue   btw 73/74th St
NYC 10023   Mon-Sat 11-7, Sun 1-6

Upper West Side   **(212) 787-5868**
300 Columbus Avenue   at 74th St
NYC 10023   (opening hours as above)

Rebecca & Drew Manufacturing

Nothing ruins a sleek office look like a busting open button-down shirt. Finally find your perfect fit at Rebecca & Drew, where shirts are made according to bra size, ranging from 32A to 38DD. Pick your size, sleeve length and fabric (a range of colors and prints) and get a custom 100% cotton wardrobe staple.   *rebeccaanddrew.com*

Moderate   *Amex/MC/V*

West Village   **(212) 647-8904**
342 West 13th Street   at Hudson
NYC 10014   Mon-Fri 11-7, Sat 11-8, Sun 12-7

Rebecca Taylor

Delicate and edgy without losing their feminine quality, New Zealand designer Taylor's clothes include silk skirts, sheer shirts and form-fitting dresses that enhance the women who wear them. Taylor's passion for the smallest detail keeps celebrities like Cameron Diaz, Anna Paquin, Ashley Judd and Minnie Driver coming back for more. Also find a collection of wallets and shoes. The beautiful courtyard in the back makes this a lovely place to shop.   *rebeccataylor.com*

Expensive   *Amex/MC/V*

SoHo   **(212) 966-0406**
260 Mott Street   btw Houston/Prince
NYC 10012   Mon-Sat 11-7, Sun 12-7

Redberi

Add something sweet to your wardrobe. Redberi sells fun, frisky clothing that includes frilly bikinis, cozy loungewear, sexy fitted tees by James Perse, traditional moccasins and Lulu Guinness handbags. A welcome fashion addition to Flatbush Avenue.

Affordable   *Amex/MC/V*

Park Slope   **(718) 622-1964**
339 Flatbush Avenue   btw Park/Prospect
Brooklyn 11217   Tues-Fri 12-8, Sat 11-8, Sun 11-7

DUMBO (BlueBeri)   **(718) 422-7724**
143 Front Street   btw Pearl/Jay
Brooklyn 11201   (opening hours as above)

Red Wong

Owner Suzy Wong never has a dull retail moment. Her Red Wong line is big on dresses—in colorful silk styles, with charmeuse cowl-neck and bateau-neck designs. Her super-short one-shoulder blousons and bias-cut dresses are truly lovely, and custom-made designs are also available. In addition, find beautiful chiffon coats alongside knits and chunky sweaters by Zoli and Smith & Home, lingerie from Juana De Arco and reconstructed vintage by Hillary Moore. There are some carefully chosen vintage accessories and a small but nice selection of shoes.

Expensive   *Amex/MC/V*

Nolita   **(212) 625-1638**
181 Mulberry Street   btw Kenmare/Broome
NYC 10012   Mon-Sat 12-8, Sun 12-6

Reebok

Here is a large, futuristic showplace for Reebok's fitness, tennis, running and cycling gear. The clothes are practical, good-looking and well priced. Reebok's sneaker selection is outstanding, even for kids.   *reebok.com*

Affordable   *Amex/MC/V*

Upper West Side   **(212) 595-1480**
160 Columbus Avenue   btw 67/68th St
NYC 10023   Mon-Sat 10-7:30, Sun 12-5:30

Reem Acra

You know you're in for something special when the frosted glass wall slides back to reveal a row of stunning bridal designs and eye-popping eveningwear. Pink strapless bejeweled gowns fit for a princess and a Deco-inspired, beaded, plunging crepe gown (with matching headband) out of a Fitzgerald novel are outdone only by wedding dresses that mix Empire waists with daring black embroidery or crystal and silver-accented Chantilly lace. The A-line cuts that have to be seen to be believed, and Acra's tiaras and hair jewels add to the fantasy. Plan ahead though, because these couture creations can only be viewed by appointment.   *reemacra.com*

Luxury   *Amex/MC/V*

Upper East Side   **(212) 308-8760**
14 East 60th Street   btw Fifth/Madison Ave
NYC 10022   Tues-Sat 10-6, Thurs 11-7
                    (bridal collection by appointment only)

Reiss

The first US location of the ubiquitous UK chain takes the form of a massive Soho shop, replete with brick walls and a high ceiling from which clear plastic tubing makes up a stunning light fixture, as well as a divider between the men's and women's sections. Reiss is more expensive than H&M and more esoteric than Club Monaco, and can provide a formidable suit for a first job interview. There's a lot to pick from and it's all very young and fun, with easy embellishments (sequins or a ruffle for her, contrast stitching or military details for him) on staple pieces that make fashion fun for the novice. *reiss.co.uk*

Moderate   *Amex/MC/V*

SoHo   **(212) 925-5707**
387 West Broadway   btw Spring/Broome
NYC 10012   Mon-Wed 11-8, Thurs-Sat 10-8, Sun 11-7

Reminiscence
A big draw for younger types who want a bit of retro grooviness in their wardrobe. Find fun and affordable Hawaiian T-shirts, baggy tie-string overalls, tube tops, halter tops, bike jackets, wrap skirts, vintage lingerie and boas, as well as military-style clothing. Accessories include handbags, body glitter, bikini headbands, Betty Boop lunch boxes and more. *reminiscence.com*

Affordable   *Amex/MC/V*

Chelsea   **(212) 243-2292**
50 West 23rd Street   btw Fifth/Sixth Ave
NYC 10010   Mon-Sat 11-7:30, Sun 12-7

René Collections
Iconic designer handbags get knocked off in style at this shop, which carries all shapes, sizes and colors at great prices. From an Hermès Kelly bag to Gucci's Hobo, it's hard to tell the copies from the originals. Costume jewelry and belts also available.

Moderate   *Amex/MC/V*

Upper East Side   **(212) 987-4558**
1325 Madison Avenue   btw 93/94th St
NYC 10128   Mon-Sat 9:30-6:30, Sun 12-6

Upper East Side   **(212) 327-3912**
1007 Madison Avenue   btw 77/78th St
NYC 10021   Mon-Sat 9:30-6:30, Sun 12-5

René Mancini
Refined, elegant shoes that are meticulously crafted in France. A signature Mancini design comes with perfect cap toes and delicate small heels, although he also gets adventurous with, for instance, clear plastic stilettos. Although expensive, they are worth every dollar. It's best to stock up during the semi-annual sales. *renemancini.fr*

Luxury   *Amex/MC/V*

Midtown East   **(212) 308-7644**
470 Park Avenue   at 58th St
NYC 10022   Mon-Sat 9:30-6

Replay
Replay's location in SoHo offers casual threads bearing the Italian company's label, including T-shirts, jeans, khakis, underwear and shoes. Not trendy, but fashionable enough to be current and you can find all sorts of sports-

wear and durable outdoor clothing for everyone in the family.

replay.it

Moderate   *Amex/MC/V*

SoHo   **(212) 673-6300**
109 Prince Street   at Greene
NYC 10012   Mon-Sat 11-7, Sun 11-6

★ Resurrection Vintage

In a city teeming with vintage clothing stores, Resurrection is one of the best. It's packed with well-chosen, mint-condition clothing from the Sixties to the Eighties, edited to reflect the current movements in fashion (which, of course, often looks backward for inspiration). It's a retro designer universe from Sixties Courrèges to Seventies Cacharel and Chloé, to Valentino, Yves Saint Laurent, Pucci, Ferragamo, Gucci...you name it. This is the store where the designers shop—Chloé's Phoebe Philo has been known to pick up Chloé originals here.

resurrectionvintage.com

Expensive   *Amex/MC/V*

Nolita   **(212) 625-1374**
217 Mott Street   btw Prince/Spring
NYC 10009   Mon-Sat 11-7, Sun 12-7

Richard Metzger

This designer has made it his mission to dress plus-size women sumptuously with body-conscious, sexy designs, and a lot of plus-size women are very grateful. By appointment only, he will show you his looks for the season (everything from tailored casual to drop-dead-entrance-making eveningwear) and tailor them just for your body. With curvaceous celebrity devotees such as Oprah Winfrey, Queen Latifah and Emme, Metzger is well on his way to being the couturier for plus-size women.

Expensive   *Amex/MC/V*

Midtown West   **877-METZGER**
325 West 38th Street (suite 1504)   btw Eighth/Ninth Ave
NYC 10018   (by appointment only)

Ricky's

This is possibly the world's best one-stop shop for sexy costumes and kitscherie. Whether tramping up for the office Halloween party or vamping up for a night on the town, Ricky's has your number with wild wigs, a psychedelic rainbow of make-up and nail polish colors and novelty hosiery that would make the naughtiest nurse blush crimson. Complete your alter ego's ensemble with the unlimited array of funky bags, costume jewelry and hair and body accessories.

rickys-nyc.com

Affordable   *Amex/MC/V*

Upper West Side   **(212) 769-3678**
112 West 72nd Street   btw Broadway/Columbus Ave
NYC 10024   Mon-Thurs 9-9, Fri 9-10, Sat 10-9, Sun 10-8

Upper East Side   **(212) 879-8361**
1189 First Avenue   at 64th St
NYC 10021   Mon-Thurs 9-9, Fri-Sat 9-10, Sun 10-10

Midtown West   **(212) 957-8343**
988 Eighth Avenue   at 58th St
NYC 10019   Mon-Fri 9-9, Sat 10-8

Fifth Avenue   **(212) 949-7230**
509 Fifth Avenue   btw 42/43rd St
NYC 10017   Mon-Fri 9-8, Sat 10-8, Sun 11-7

Chelsea   **(212) 206-0234**
267 West 23rd Street   btw Seventh/Eighth Ave
NYC 10011   Mon-Sat 9-11, Sun 10-10

West Village   **(212) 924-3401**
466 Sixth Avenue   btw 11/12th St
NYC 10011   Mon-Fri 8-11, Sat 9-11, Sun 10-10

NoHo   **(212) 254-5247**
44 East 8th Street   at Greene
NYC 10003   Mon-Fri 10-9, Sat 10-10, Sun 10-9

SoHo   **(212) 226-5552**
590 Broadway   btw Houston/Prince
NYC 10012   Mon-Thurs 9-9, Fri 9-10, Sat 10-10, Sun 10-9

Upper East Side   **(212) 737-7723**
1380 Third Avenue   btw 78/79th St
NYC 10021   Mon-Fri 9-10, Sat-Sun 10-10

Upper East Side   **(212) 452-4628**
1372 First Avenue   btw 73/74th St
NYC 10021   Daily 11-8

Midtown West   **n/a at press time**
332 West 57th Street   at Columbus Circle
NYC 10019   n/a at press time

Midtown West   **(212) 245-1265**
728 Ninth Avenue   btw 49/50th St
NYC 10019   Mon-Fri 10-9, Sat 10-10, Sun 11-8

Midtown West   **(212) 768-1175**
1412 Broadway   btw 39/40th St
NYC 10018   Mon-Fri 9-8, Sat 10-7, Sun 11-7

Midtown East   **(212) 481-6701**
383 Fifth Avenue   btw 34/35th St
NYC 10016   Mon-Fri 9-8, Sat 10-7, Sun 11-7

Stuyvesant   **(212) 253-7114**
278 Third Avenue   at 22nd St
NYC 10010   Mon-Sat 9-10, Sun 10-9

East Village   **(212) 691-7930**
7 East 14th Street   btw Fifth/University
NYC 10003   Mon-Sat 9-10, Sun 10-10

East Village   **(212) 674-9640**
111 Third Avenue   at 13th St
NYC 10003   Mon-Sat 9-10, Sun 10-10

SoHo   **(212) 925-6750**
235 Mulberry Street   btw Prince/Spring
NYC 10012   Daily 11-8

Ripplu

A firm bod without surgery—or a life in the gym? 'Yeah right, whatever', you say. Well, speak to the folks at Ripplu, who will fit you with a series of custom bras and panties that will lift and reshape those critical anatomical parts. If you find this hard to believe, just look at the sales helps' hour-glass figures (incidentally, they are also courteous and help-ful). Bra sizes run from 30A to 40G. Custom fittings and free alterations are available, too. *ripplu.com*

Expensive *Amex/MC/V*

Fifth Avenue **(212) 599-2223**
575 Fifth Avenue (2nd floor) btw 46/47th St
NYC 10017 Mon-Sat 11-7

Ritz Furs

Foxy ladies come here for new and 'gently' pre-owned furs. For years, Ritz has been a destination for a fine selection of used mink, lynx, fox, sable and more—all of which the store expertly restores to like-new condition. In addition, find shearlings, fur-trimmed and lined outerwear, fur hats and stoles. An attentive, polite sales staff and great prices are the keys to Ritz's 70 successful years in the biz. *ritzfurs.com*

Moderate *Amex/MC/V*

Midtown West **(212) 265-4559**
107 West 57th Street btw Sixth/Seventh Ave
NYC 10019 Mon-Sat 9-6

Robert Clergerie

Fashionistas crave Clergerie's footwear for his chic combina-tion of comfort and style. Heels, ballet slippers, and loafers are fashionable and easy to wear. Trendier numbers can be found in the selection of boots and sandals. All designs come in great colors and serious quality leathers, and there is a small selection for men. *robertclergerie.com*

Expensive *Amex/MC/V*

Upper East Side **(212) 207-8600**
681 Madison Avenue btw 61/62nd St
NYC 10021 Mon-Sat 10-6 (Thurs 10-7)
Sun 12-5 (except in summer)

Roberta Freymann

Chic retailer (and former hand-knitter) Roberta Freymann sells 'a little bit of everything'. This translates to a fabulous-ly eclectic range of ethnic-inspired women's and children's clothing and home accessories. Freymann travels the world to source clothing and fabrics from India, Argentina, Bolivia, Vietnam and Thailand. She will take home furnishing fabric from Thailand, for example, and fashion it into an elegant ready-to-wear collection of separates. Her focus is on dis-tinctive eveningwear in jewel-like colors. These clothes are a trip worth taking.

Moderate to expensive *MC/V*

Upper East Side
153 East 70th Street
NYC 10021

(212) 794-2031
at Lexington Ave
Mon-Sat 10-6

Roberto Cavalli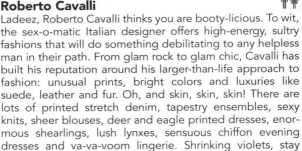

Ladeez, Roberto Cavalli thinks you are booty-licious. To wit, the sex-o-matic Italian designer offers high-energy, sultry fashions that will do something debilitating to any helpless man in their path. From glam rock to glam chic, Cavalli has built his reputation around his larger-than-life approach to fashion: unusual prints, bright colors and luxuries like suede, leather and fur. Oh, and skin, skin, skin! There are lots of printed stretch denim, tapestry ensembles, sexy knits, sheer blouses, deer and eagle printed dresses, enormous shearlings, lush lynxes, sensuous chiffon evening dresses and va-va-voom lingerie. Shrinking violets, stay home. *robertocavalli.com*

Luxury   *Amex/MC/V*

Upper East Side
711 Madison Avenue
NYC 10021

(212) 755-7722
at 63rd St
Mon-Sat 10-6 (Thurs 10-7), Sun 12-5

Robert Talbott

A fashionable California-based shirt shop that allows you to choose from 40 ready-made styles or custom-order from a selection of over 200 fabric swatches. Dress shirts are tailored in a full cut and made in top quality cottons and broadcloths. Ties, cufflinks, cummerbunds and pocket squares make perfect accessories. Shirt prices average $150. And don't miss the lovely women's shirts, sweaters and outerwear. *roberttalbott.com*

Expensive   *Amex/MC/V*

Upper East Side
680 Madison Avenue
NYC 10021

(212) 751-1200
btw 61/62nd St
Mon-Fri 10-6, Sat 10-5

Roberto Vascon

What do you do when you've searched the city for a handbag and cannot find one that is perfectly 'you'? Custom-order one, of course. Brazilian leather designer Roberto Vascon has got all your handbag fantasies covered, working with 30 shapes and around 200 different hides from ostrich to pony. And with your creation completed in a matter of weeks, you can take your name off that long waiting list for the bag of the moment that'll be so last season before you even lay your hands on it. *robertovascon.com*

Luxury   *Amex/MC/V*

Upper West Side
140 West 72nd Street
NYC 10023

(212) 787-9050
btw Broadway/Columbus Ave
Mon-Sat 11-7, Sun 1-6

Rochester Big & Tall Clothing

Welcome to America's number one source for the discriminating man in need of larger and lengthier sizes. This is a full-service shop running the gamut from underwear to designer suits with labels like Zegna, Canali, Donna Karan and Versace. Sportswear, casual and activewear and accessories complete the collection. Shoes are by Allen Edmonds, Cole Haan and Ferragamo.

800-282-8200 rochesterclothing.com

Moderate to expensive   *Amex/MC/V*

Midtown West   **(212) 247-7500**
1301 Sixth Avenue   at 52nd St
NYC 10019   Mon-Sat 9:30-6:30, Sun 12-5

Rockport

Rockport's mission is 'to make the world more comfortable', and they do. Their comfy hiking boots look rugged but feel splendid, and the same goes for their sneakers, loafers, sandals, lace-ups, sturdy pumps and trendy golf shoes. Foot-soothing massage products and sprays are also available to ease your precious tootsies.   rockport.com

Moderate   *Amex/MC/V*

Upper West Side   **(212) 579-1301**
160 Columbus Avenue   btw 67/68th St
NYC 10023   Mon-Sat 10-8, Sun 12-6

Rosa Custom Ties

Globetrotting executives visit Rosa's while in New York to custom-order luxurious cravats. Choose from over 5,000 Italian silk prints, stripes, wovens and solids, then wait two weeks for your tie to be hand-stitched and interlined to perfection. Prices range from $95 to $125. No minimum order required.

Moderate   *Amex/MC/V*

Midtown West   **(212) 245-2191**
30 West 57th Street (6th floor)   btw Fifth/Sixth Ave
NYC 10019   Mon-Fri 9:30-5:30
                                    (Saturdays by appointment)

Roslyn

Style-savvy uptowners who demand the sophistication of always-in-vogue virtuoso Steven Alan's SoHo boutique but don't want to brave the subway to the bottom of the island finally have a shop in their hood: Roslyn, an accessories store on the Upper West Side run by, you guessed it, Alan's mother of the same name. Proving that good taste is in the genes, this specialty shop is the stop for the latest in hip hats, from cloches to berets and back again. Not to mention handbags in all imaginable shapes, sizes and shades by the likes of Cammie Hill, Un Après Midi de Chien and Hervé Chapelier, plus a huge selection of new and re-worked antique diamond and semi-precious stone jewelry.

Expensive   *Amex/MC/V*

Upper West Side   **(212) 496-5050**
276 Columbus Avenue   at 73rd St
NYC 10023   Daily 11-7

★ Rubin Chappelle

Enter through a hallway lined with clear plastic tubing and a row of mannequins enticing you with the grown-up glam wares to come in Austrian Sonja Rubin and Ohioan Kip Chappelle's converted meat locker. The original dingy green, gray and brown walls remain, but the goods are clean, sleek and modern. Pod-like white half-pipes fashioned into racks hang a choice selection of pieces in complementary colors: carnation sheer blouses beside taupe shorts; dusty rose crumpled leather jackets and ecru wrap dresses. A futuristic Jackie O would buy her sweaters and slacks here, as the designs are classic with unique detailed collars and cuffs that are stylish but decidedly unflashy.   *rubinchappelle.com*

Expensive to luxury   *Amex/MC/V*

Chelsea   **(212) 647-8636**
410 West 14th Street   btw Ninth/Tenth Ave
NYC 10014   Mon-Fri 11-7, Sun 12-6

Ruehl

Any precocious young Abercrombie junkie worth her logo tee has probably racked up a few points on her A&F credit card buying clothes from Ruehl's sportswear line: a more grown-up label designed for the massive chain. After they've thrown their mortarboards up in the air on graduation day, it's quite possibly time to move onwards and upwards and adopt a more refined style. At press time, Ruehl had plans for a 600-square-foot townhouse-themed shop selling only handbags, at considerably higher price points ($268-$1098). Housed in a former antique shop and guarded by a wrought-iron gate, the vibe is bound to be quite different from the mall.

Expensive

West Village   n/a at press time
370 Bleecker Street   btw Charles/Perry
NYC 10014   n/a at press time

Rue St Denis

A longtime East Village staple—Jennifer Esposito and Drea de Matteo are regulars—this shop is revered for the quality of its merchandise, including unused European vintage from the Forties to the Eighties. Everything is clean and well organized—vintage jeans including Levi's 501s and Jordaches in one section; shirts, sports T-shirts and slacks in the room marked 'Vintage'. And its assortment of men's and women's restored leather jackets is unbeatable—everything from leather bombers to zippered black Eighties numbers and belted trench coats. Check out their new vintage furniture showroom for classic modern pieces, all the better to put your 'new' threads into context.

ruestdenis.com or *vintagenyc.com*

Moderate   *Amex/MC/V*

East Village   **(212) 260-3388**
170 Avenue B   btw 10/11th St
NYC 10009   Daily 12-8 (Sat-Sun 12-7:30)

Runway

Personalized and attentive service is the watchword at Runway, a boutique that celebrates the beauty of all ages with a collection of lifestyle-friendly separates in tactile techno fabrics that are appropriate for work, cocktails or dinner. *runwayconnection.com*

Moderate   *Amex/MC/V*

Flatiron   **(212) 807-1708**
12 West 23rd Street   btw Fifth/Sixth Ave
NYC 10010   Mon-Fri 12-8, Sat 12-7, Sun 12-6

SoHo   **(212) 925-9817**
450 Broome Street   at Mercer
NYC 10013   Daily 11-7

Saada

Downtown goes uptown at this groovy Upper East Side boutique. Its eclectic collection of pieces from up-and-coming designers is well worth checking out. You'll find cute dresses, pants, tops and accessories like fun hats and cool handbags from some of the hottest labels in town, including Tracey Reese, Nanette Lepore, Paper Denim & Cloth jeans and Pierre Urbach bags.

Moderate   *Amex/MC/V*

Upper East Side   **(212) 223-3505**
1159 Second Avenue   btw 60/61st St
NYC 10021   Mon-Fri 10-8, Sat 11-7, Sun 12-6

Sacco

Sacco is a footwear chain that makes the girls happy, because there truly is something for everyone. There are mules, pumps, loafers, maryjanes, platforms, slingbacks, sandals, great boots and more from such labels as Cynthia Rowley, Audley, Lisa Nading and Sacco's own line. The average price is $175 and they have great sales, too. Also, check out a jaunty selection of handbags, from floral prints to basic black. *saccoshoes.com*

Moderate   *Amex/MC/V*

Flatiron   **(212) 243-2070**
14 East 17th Street   btw Fifth/Union Square West
NYC 10003   Mon-Fri 11-8, Sat 11-7, Sun 12-7

Upper West Side   **(212) 799-5229**
324 Columbus Avenue   btw 75/76th St
NYC 10023   (opening hours as above)

Chelsea   **(212) 675-5180**
94 Seventh Avenue   btw 15/16th St
NYC 10011   (opening hours as above)

SoHo   **(212) 925-8010**
111 Thompson Street   btw Prince/Spring
NYC 10012   (opening hours as above)

Midtown East   **(212) 207-3151**
118 East 59th Street   btw Park/Lexington Ave
NYC 10022   (opening hours as above)

Saeyoung Vu Couture

Brides-to-be sashay across the hardwood floor in simple, strapless gowns in shades of white satin, organza and linen. The plain-looking store is lined with a rainbow of colored taffetas in flatteringly cut basic shapes. Another option is to mix-and-match: pick two colors for the girls instead of one (i.e. turquoise top with violet skirt, and so forth). Also on offer are accessories: silk flower corsages and tiny purses to match the dresses. Bridesmaids and flower girls will be able (and may even want) to wear their get-ups again after the big day. *vucouture.com*

Expensive to luxury   *Amex/MC/V*

Nolita   **(212) 925-6505**
214 Mulberry Street   btw Prince/Spring
NYC 10012 Tues-Sat 11-7, Sun 12-5 (by appointment only)

St John

Power dressing lives on at St John. This knitwear company sells head to-toe outfits perfect for executives, ladies who lunch, and more than a few politicians. St John's signature Santana fabric is wrinkle-resistant (and thus ideal for travel, to lunch or that political meeting), and they're not shy of color and other decorative touches like shiny buttons, silk flowers, paillettes and serious sequins. Looks include suits and elegant chiffon evening pants, classic black jackets with colorful underpinnings, sporty leathers and long knit gowns dusted with crystals and sequins. Also find a full range of accessories. Sizes from 2 to 16. Suits start at $1,200, evening couture at $3,000. *stjohnknits.com*

Expensive   *Amex/MC/V*

Fifth Avenue   **(212) 755-5252**
665 Fifth Avenue   at 53rd St
NYC 10022   Mon-Sat 10-6 (Thurs 10-7), Sun 12-6

★ Saint Laurie Merchant Tailors

A reliable supplier of traditional made-to-measure suits since 1913, jackets and shirts for the man about town. Choose from a great selection of fabrics and let Saint Laurie's tailors get to work with their 3D body-scanner, which ensures the accuracy of all measurements. Custom suits start at $1,200, dress shirts at $175. The super-attentive staff make shopping here a pleasure. Need more convincing? Hollywood heavyweights such as Al Pacino, John Goodman and Steve Buscemi will be happy to put in a good word. This fourth-generation family store recently started offering more contemporary styles, creating a rare combination of hipster cool and custom tailoring. *saintlaurie.com*

Luxury   *Amex/MC/V*

Midtown West   **(212) 643-1916**
22 West 32nd Street (5th floor)   btw Broadway/Fifth Ave
NYC 10001   Mon-Fri 9-6, Sat 9-5:30

Saks Fifth Avenue

Set in a gorgeous landmark building, this icon of New York fashion is in the midst of a five-year renovation to improve display and augment the selection of designer labels. There's no reason to wait for the plaster to dry, however: Saks remains an au courant stop for any serious shopper. Cosmetics, handbags, hosiery and accessories occupy the frenzied main floor, but women's fashions take center stage over four floors devoted to ready-to-wear, eveningwear and sportswear from a stellar line-up of designers: Gucci, Dolce & Gabbana, Burberry, Escada, Marc Jacobs, Carlos Miele, Blumarine, Elie Tahari, Michael Kors, Prada and more. Don't miss out on the lingerie, the extensive shoe department, especially the new boutique from the famous Sixties shoe designer Roger Vivier, the newly opened full-service bridal department including the Monique Lhuillier boutique, the wonderful selection of furs and plenty of clothes for kids. Men have two complete floors devoted to American and European designers, which include suits by Armani and Zegna, casualwear by Hugo Boss and John Varvatos and exquisite Ferragamo ties. Factor in a café, exclusive beauty treatments at the Elizabeth Arden Spa and the complete La Mer line of anti-ageing wonder creams, and you'll understand why Saks makes for the perfect all-in-one shopping experience.   *800-345-3454 saksfifthavenue.com*

Moderate to expensive   *Amex/MC/V*

Fifth Avenue   **(212) 753-4000**
611 Fifth Avenue   at 50th St
NYC 10022   Mon-Sat 10-7 (Thurs 10-8), Sun 12-6

Salvatore Ferragamo

Ferragamo's expansion of the Fifth Avenue flagship store allows more room than ever for luxurious suits, scarves, dresses, sportswear and home furnishings. But it's the little things, like the standard-setting ties (note the little animal prints and the über-rich colors) and those unbelievably well-made shoes (from the snappiest stilettos to the coolest sneakers) that make return shoppers out of discerning businessmen and fashionable women alike. Fashion influence is strongest in the rich, whimsical neckwear (buy up those ties!) and the shoes, which run from business and formal to casual and sporty.   *ferragamo.com*

Expensive   *Amex/MC/V*

Fifth Avenue   **(212) 759-3822**
661 Fifth Avenue   btw 52/53rd St
NYC 10022   Mon-Sat 10-7 (Thurs 10-8), Sun 12-6

Sample

This tiny boutique carries a signature collection of knitwear in special yarns from Italy. There is a good color range featuring silk/cotton/rayon blends in sensuous designs, including half-turtlenecks, ruffle-edged cardigans, roll-neck tops and zip-front cardigans perfect over Sample's own zip-up skirts. Also available: great oversized printed totes and semi-precious and precious jewelry. *samplestudio.com*

Expensive   *Amex/MC/V*

Nolita   **(212) 431-7866**
268 Elizabeth Street   btw Houston/Prince
NYC 10012   Daily 12-7

Samuel's Hats

Specializing in lids by top designers, including dainty church-worthy numbers by Jack McConnell, an array of Kangols and Philip Treacy's fabulous collection, Samuel's Hats leaves hat lovers drooling. Sophisticated ladies can find the dressiest crimson styles around in the Red Hats collection, or a picnic-ready straw crowner by Scala. They also have wonderful hatboxes that are perfect for travel and storage.   *samuelshats.com*

Expensive   *Amex/MC/V*

Lower Manhattan   **(212) 513-7322**
74 Nassau Street   btw Fulton/John
NYC 10038   Mon-Fri 9-7, Sat 10-5

Santoni

Santoni will supply you with those $4,800 crocodile shoes you've been looking for. This is a small and intimate store with friendly service, specializing in men and women's fine shoes, for Wall Streeter or soccer mom. The intoxicating smell whisks you inside to peruse the woven leather loafers, driving moccasins and boat shoes.   *santonishoesusa.com*

Luxury   *Amex/MC/V*

Upper East Side   **(212) 794-3820**
864 Madison Avenue   btw 70/71st St
NYC 10021   Mon-Sat 10-6

Scandinavian Ski Shop

A convenient Midtown source for ski and winter sports apparel and equipment by Bogner, Helly Hansen, Obermeyer, RLX and Killy. When the snow melts, Scandinavian's incredibly knowledgeable staff outfits the customers with gear for tennis, hiking and competition swimming.   *skishop.com*

Moderate   *Amex/MC/V*

Midtown West   **(212) 757-8524**
16 East 55th Street   btw Fifth/Madison Ave
NYC 10022   Daily 10-6

Scarpe Diem

Deep in the jungle of chains and children's stores that make up the Upper West Side, Scarpe Diem can only be a blessing to the neighborhood's hip young singles. The racks on the wall are neatly lined with sexy, urban shoes and bags from the likes of Kazuyo Nakano, Orla Kiely, Mitzi Baker. Prices and styles are well suited to high-earners who spend most of their salaries on rent.

Expensive Amex/MC/V

Upper West Side **(212) 362-5070**
2286 Broadway btw 82/83rd St
NYC 10024 Sun-Mon 11-8, Tues-Fri 11-10, Sat 10-10

Scoop

Scoop makes trends—everyone else just follows. After all, this was the first store in town to stock the famous Marc by Marc Jacobs line. The four NYC locations continue to carry cult classics such as Juicy, Seven and Theory while keeping their eye on the trends from coast to coast, including new acquisitions from California label C&C California. The jeans collection alone is worth the trip—they stock the most up-to-date and extensive collection of designer jeans around, including, but never limited to, Joe's and Paper Denim & Cloth. As we went to press, Scoop's first kids' store had just opened next to the women only store in the West Village. *scoopnyc.com*

Moderate to expensive *Amex/MC/V*

Upper East Side (men & women) **(212) 535-5577**
1275 Third Avenue btw 73/74th St
NYC 10021 Mon-Fri 11-8, Sat 11-7, Sun 12-6

West Village (men only) **(212) 929-1244**
873 Washington Street at 14th St
NYC 10014 (opening hours as above)

SoHo **(212) 925-2886**
532 Broadway btw Prince/Spring
NYC 10012 Mon-Sat 11-8, Sun 12-7

Chelsea (women only) **(212) 929-1244**
873 Washington Street btw 13/14th St
NYC 10014 Mon-Fri 11-8, Sat 11-7, Sun 12-6

Scott Mallory

When ready-to-wear belts just aren't posh enough, Scott Mallory can handcraft a belt to your specifications. With straps of alligator, crocodile, stingray, ostrich, water moccasin or farm-raised leather, that can be dyed any color and cut from skinny to wide, and buckles ranging from plain and simple to ornate starbursts of pavé diamonds, sapphires, and other jewels inlayed in 18kt white, yellow or rose gold, these belts are truly decadent. Buy a few straps to add mix-and-match capability to your investment. His belts are only available at the sparsely decorated retail store, as they don't wholesale so as to ensure complete exclusivity.

Luxury *Amex/MC/V*

Soho **(212) 226-4400**
155 Spring Street btw West Broadway/Wooster
NYC 10012 Tues-Sun 11-7

Screaming Mimi's

Although this store already had a cult following among downtown cognoscenti, the women of Sex and the City made it famous. Carrie and Co were often decked out in vintage garb (from the Forties to the Eighties) from Mimi's. Although the clothing is from previous eras, the collection is refreshingly well edited. Come here to rifle through girly dresses (including some real finds by Pucci and Yves Saint Laurent), vintage bustiers, skirts, tops, assorted shoes and an array of accessories. Girls don't get to have all the fun, though—the store stocks a nice selection of men's duds from days past, too. *screamingmimis.com*

Moderate *Amex/MC/V*

NoHo **(212) 677-6464**
382 Lafayette Street btw 4th/Great Jones
NYC 10003 Mon-Sat 12-8, Sun 1-7

Sean

Upper-crust menswear with a look that is Ralph Lauren meets agnès b. Find designer Emil Lafaurie's collection of well-made wool suits, silk ties, fabulous shirts in solid shades, cotton and corduroy pants, casual painter's jackets and Italian parkas. All up, just cool enough. *seanstore.com*

Moderate *Amex/MC/V*

Upper West Side **(212) 769-1489**
224 Columbus Avenue btw 70/71st St
NYC 10023 Mon-Sat 11-8, Sun 12-7

SoHo **(212) 598-5980**
132 Thompson Street btw Houston/Prince
NYC 10012 Mon-Sat 11-7, Sun 12-6

Sean John

Simple suits and printed dress shirts can turn any thug into a formidable date for your college roommate's wedding, while cream-colored linen suits channel St Barths via the Bronx. Of course, extraordinary sportswear is plentiful: track suits, basketball jerseys, baseball hats and logo-emblazoned sweat pants surely make up most of Sean John's best-sellers. Pair a golf hat with a pink terry polo shirt (for him, mind you) for a hip-hop on the links look. A rainbow of silk ties splayed around a table surrounded by tall palm plants forges a classy feel. Always a multitasker: also on offer are candles, a grooming line, belts, watches and iPod covers. *seanjohn.com*

Affordable *Amex/MC/V*

Midtown East **(212) 220-2633**
475 Fifth Avenue at East 41st St
NYC 10017 Mon-Sat 10-7 (Thurs 10-8), Sun 10-6

Searle

Searle doesn't just make fantastic shearlings, cashmeres, trench coats and Moncler goose down jackets, though they're certainly nothing to sniff at. They've beefed up their own sportswear line, adding frilly halter dresses, accordion skirts, and a generous dose of sequins. In addition they carry labels like Shoshanna, M Missoni and Trina Turk. Then there are the bags: leather clutches by Lauren Merkin and Moyna, saddlebags by Andrea Brueckner, bowler bags by Botkier and Carlos Falchi's doctor bags. The shoes: strappy sandals, ballet flats and glam heels by Hollywould and Sigerson Morrison. The service: stupendous. *searlenyc.com*

Expensive   *Amex/MC/V*

Upper East Side (W)   **(212) 988-7318**
1124 Madison Avenue   at 84th St
NYC 10028   Mon-Fri 10-8, Sat 10-7, Sun 12-6:30

Upper East Side (W)   **(212) 717-4022**
1035 Madison Avenue   at 79th St
NYC 10021   (opening hours as above)

Upper East Side   **(212) 750-5153**
635 Madison Avenue   at 60th St
NYC 10022   Mon-Fri 10-8, Sat 10-6, Sun 12-6

Upper East Side   **(212) 628-6665**
805 Madison Avenue   btw 67/68th St
NYC 10021   Mon-Fri 10-8, Sat 10-7, Sun 12-6:30

Upper East Side   **(212) 717-5200**
1296 Third Avenue   at 74th St
NYC 10021   (opening hours as above)

Upper East Side (W)   **(212) 838-5990**
1051 Third Avenue   at 62nd St
NYC 10021   Mon-Fri 10-8, Sat 10-7, Sun 12-6

Flatiron   **(212) 924-4330**
156 Fifth Avenue   at 20th St
NYC 10010   Mon-Fri 11-8, Sat 11-7, Sun 12-6

Seigo

Tie one on. Seigo sells limited-edition, 100% handmade silk ties using the same mills that manufacture Japan's traditional kimonos. The selection ranges from intricately colored ties to simple patterned ones, plus a large assortment of bow ties in vibrant colors. Bow ties start at $50, neckties at $80.

Affordable   *Amex/MC/V*

Upper East Side   **(212) 987-0191**
1248 Madison Avenue   btw 89/90th St
NYC 10128   Mon-Fri 9:30-6:30, Sat 10-6:30
                                                     Sun 11:30-5:30

★ Seize sur Vingt (16/20)

Luxury ready-to-wear and custom-made clothes for both sexes, and now children too. Choose from their specialty, impeccably tailored Italian cotton shirts, cashmere sweaters, pants, jackets and suits, as well as handmade boxers—ooh, fancy!—and accessories. While Seize sur Vingt has given itself the French school grade of 16/20 (equivalent to an A-), we'll give them a 20/20. Great men's-styled collar shirts for women, too.   *16sur20.com*

Expensive   *Amex/MC/V*

Nolita   **(212) 343-0476**
243 Elizabeth Street   btw Houston/Prince
NYC 10012   Mon-Sat 11-7, Sun 12-6

Selia Yang ♀

Finally, a beaded gown that says elegance, not high-school prom. Find this, as well as safely feminine fashions like dresses in simple hourglass silhouettes, skirts, shirts and knits that are perfect for cocktails at this high-end boutique. Yang's favorite fabrics are silk organza and beaded satin. Great coordinating accessories include handbags, tiaras and jewelry. The bridal boutique is next door at #328, (212) 254-9073.   *seliayang.com*

Luxury   *Amex/MC/V*

East Village   **(212) 254-8980**
324 East 9th Street   btw First/Second Ave
NYC 10003   Tues-Fri 12-7, Sat-Sun 12-6

★ Selima Optique ♀

Want to see the world through rose-tinted glasses? Check out the destination of choice for celebrities desperately seeking eyewear. French optician Selima Salaun's flagship New York store (she also has locations in Paris and Beverly Hills) showcases hundreds of styles in every shape and color imaginable, including the rhinestone-encased variety favored by P.Diddy. Cat's eye, aviator, Jackie O…you name it, she's got it. For the biggest selection of specs, head for the Madison Avenue and SoHo stores. Others have more limited offerings, but also stock clothing, since we all know that a new pair of glasses is a great occasion for additions to one's wardrobe.   *selimaoptique.com*

Moderate to expensive   *Amex/MC/V*

Upper East Side   **(212) 988-6690**
899 Madison Avenue   btw 72/73rd St
NYC 10028   Mon-Sat 10:30-7, Sun 12-6

SoHo   **(212) 343-9490**
59 Wooster Street   btw Spring/Broome
NYC 10012   Mon-Sat 11-8, Sun 12-7

East Village   **(212) 677-8487**
7 Bond Street   btw Broadway/Lafayette
NYC 10003   Mon-Sat 11-7, Sun 12-7

East Village   **(212) 260-2495**
84 East 7th Street   btw First/Second Ave
NYC 10003   Daily 12-7

Selma and Sid ♀

Adorable clothes made for grown women. This small, friendly store sells innocent, whimsical styles—think lots of polka dots, stripes and candy-colored hues. Sound too sugary? The fresh-looking handbags are the perfect complement to any New York woman's otherwise all-black wardrobe.   *selmaandsid.com*

Expensive   *Amex/MC/V*

Upper East Side   **(212) 486-1992**
220 East 60th Street   btw Second/Third Ave
NYC 10022   Mon-Fri 11-7:30, Sat 11-6:30

Selvedge

Art meets cutting-edge fashion at this tiny Levi's-owned boutique whose red floors and minimalism make it look like a SoHo gallery. They are deliberately elusive (they don't want just anyone to have it), but here you will find Levi's Vintage, Premium and Red collections, many indeed displayed like art on the walls. Most of the merchandise is limited-edition and notable for its special wash or conceptual cut.

Moderate   *Amex/MC/V*

Nolita   **(212) 219-0994**
250 Mulberry Street   btw Prince/Spring
NYC 10012   Mon-Sat 11-7, Sun 12-6

Seven New York

Seven is one of the most progressive stores in New York, and helped establish the Lower East Side as a vital fashion destination. Then it moved up to the next rung on the ladder, SoHo. Its mission statement is 'a perfect combination of art and fashion where one foot is in retailing and the other in the art world'. Cult bags from As Four are stocked next to Tess Giberson's handmade arty T-shirts and Bernard Willhelm sweaters. Then there's Preen, the feminine designer with an edge, and Marjan Pejoski's eclectic designs—she did Björk's swan dress for the Oscars.   sevennewyork.com

Expensive   *Amex/MC/V*

SoHo   **n/a at press time**
110 Mercer Street   Prince/Spring
NYC 10012   n/a at press time

Shack Inc

Of all the shops that have migrated south from retail-choked SoHo to laid-back Tribeca, Shack is a highlight. Designer J.Morgan Puett takes her inspiration from nature, history and daily events to create unisex clothing that women will 'feel utterly at ease in'. Most of her clothing is made in the shop and her fabrics of choice are silk, linen and cotton gauze in soft shades. On offer: coordinating separates like dresses, skirts, shirts, drawstring pants, tops and easy-wearing jackets.   shackinc.com

Moderate   *Amex/MC/V*

Tribeca   **(212) 267-8004**
137 West Broadway   btw Thomas/Duane
NYC 10013   Mon-Sat 11-6

Shanghai Tang

Despite its moody, mysterious decor, there is a blaze of brilliant color from Tang's Asian-inspired fashions and accessories. Everyone should experience this vibrant fusion of East meets West at least once. Shop a full range of Shanghai Tang's signature silky clothing, accessories and home products (great oriental lamps), from traditional Mao jackets and long cheongsam dresses to modern reproductions in lush velvets, silks, linens and printed cottons. Best bet: their silk Coolie and Tang jackets. Custom also available. *shanghaitang.com*

Expensive   *MC/V*

Upper East Side   **(212) 888-0111**
714 Madison Avenue   btw 63/64th St
NYC 10021   Mon-Sat 10-6, Sun 12-6

Sharagano

Wondering where to get those hotpants you love so much? Well, fear not, the flashy Sharagano will have your booty (barely) covered. This is a flaunt-it kind of store, for sassy girls who must have the very latest in clothing trends from military to denim to peasant to prints…and who will probably ditch them tomorrow. Find dresses, frilly blouses, sweaters, pants and coats—but dominant is their range of super-tight jeans. Good prices.   *sharagano.com*

Moderate   *Amex/MC/V*

SoHo   **(212) 941-7086**
529 Broadway   btw Prince/Spring
NYC 10012   Mon-Sat 11-8, Sun 11-7

Shelly Steffee

Sleek, pared down, with playful details, newcomer Shelly Steffee's line comes across like a mix of Costume National and Chloé—think structured leather, jersey dresses, silky skirts, motorcycle boots and heavily seamed coats. All in all, a winning combination that indicates Shelly Steffee will soon stand for a style all her own.   *shellysteffee.com*

Expensive   *Amex/MC/V*

West Village   **(917) 408-0408**
34 Gansevoort Street   at Hudson
NYC 10014   Mon-Sat 12-9, Sun 12-6

Shen

If you like a layer or two or three in your look, get yourself to Shen immediately. Sample their gossamer-weight chiffon pieces, stretch gabardine pants, jersey jackets with coordinating round-neck tops, silk skirts, tunic tops, comfortable pants and sweaters. FYI: They make it a rule not to carry dresses. We don't know why.

Moderate   *Amex/MC/V*

Upper East Side   **(212) 717-1185**
1005 Madison Avenue   btw 77/78th St
NYC 10021   Mon-Fri 10-6:30, Sat 10-6

Upper East Side   **(212) 249-2895**
990 Lexington Avenue   at 72nd St
NYC 10021   Mon-Fri 10-6:30, Sat 10-6

Upper West Side   **(212) 875-0153**
311 Columbus Avenue   btw 74/75th St
NYC 10023   Mon-Sat 10:30-6:30, Sun 12-6

Shin Choi

Practical and pretty, Korean designer Shin Choi's basics are sophisticated, classic and available for bridge prices. Adorable ribbed skirts with ribbons, silk chiffon trimmed tops, satin skirts, sheath dresses and three-quarter length jackets are staples of her smart, lovely collection. Strong separates in black and white are intermingled with Choi's brilliant color scheme. Spring lines are filled with fresh pink, mauve, light blue and flowery prints while the winter line warms up in shades of plum, chocolate, red and rose. Quality fabrics, clean lines, and all-around wearability define Choi's timeless and tasteful designs. *shinchoi.com*

Moderate   *Amex/MC/V*

SoHo   **(212) 625-9202**
119 Mercer Street   btw Prince/Spring
NYC 10012   Mon-Sat 11-7

The Shirt Store

The stars of Thoroughly Modern Millie got their stage shirts here, so why shouldn't you? At least you'll know a shirt will last through a song-and-dance number (so important). Request off-the-rack, made-to-measure or custom. Each shirt is finely tailored in Sea Island cotton and reasonably priced (from $55 to $110). Request any alteration, whether adding a pocket or shortening a sleeve. Custom shirts run from $120 to $300 with a six-to-eight-week delivery. Ties, cufflinks and suspenders are also available.

800-buy-a-shirt shirtstore.com

Moderate   *Amex/MC/V*

Midtown East   **(212) 557-8040**
51 East 44th Street   at Vanderbilt Ave
NYC 10017   Mon-Fri 8-6:30, Sat 10-5

Shoe

Men are particular fans of this store for L.A. designer Balouzin's Cydwoq collection, a line of deconstructed, handmade shoes that combine form, function and pure comfort. It also carries an assortment of select footwear labels with styles that include dainty mules, pumps, boots and sandals, especially great beaded sandals. Complement your feet with Shoe's accessory collection of totes and leather handbags, beaded evening purses and kidskin gloves in luscious colors, available at their sister store, Bag, just down the street at Shoe's old location, 197 Mulberry Street.

Moderate   *Amex/MC/V*

Nolita   **(212) 925-1735**
247 Mulberry Street   btw Prince/Spring
NYC 10012   Daily 12-7

The Shoe Box

You'll find a great selection of popular shoe brands at this clean, unimposing shop—from mid-priced, unfussy, casual shoes by Cole Haan, Stuart Weitzman, Lilly Pulitzer and Giuseppe Zanotti to snappy dress-up numbers from Chloé, D&G, Emilio Pucci, Ernesto Esposito, Givenchy, Jill Sander, Lambertson Truex, Kate Spade, Kors, Marc Jacobs and Sigerson Morrison. This is a footwear shop for grandmothers, their granddaughters, and everyone in between. *theshoeboxonline.com*

Expensive   *Amex/MC/V*

Upper East Side   **(212) 535-9615**
1349 Third Avenue   at 77th St
NYC 10021   10-8, Sat 10-7, Sun 12-7

Shoofly

A stylish, well-priced footwear store for your small fry. Find European labels like Aster, Mod 8, Minibel, Venetinni and Babybotte, newborn to size 9. Great accessories like wild-print tights, summer and winter hats, jewelry and cute beaded and faux-fur bags. *shooflynyc.com*

Moderate   *Amex/MC/V*

Tribeca   **(212) 406-3270**
42 Hudson Street   btw Thomas/Duane
NYC 10013   Mon-Sat 10-7, Sun 12-6

★ Shop

The clothes at Shop are as cool as the sales staff's attitude, so instead of waiting for a friendly hello just dive right into the great selection. Find trendy pieces from designers such as Development and Mint, hip-hugging jeans, cute skirts, T-shirts, separates and select vintage pieces. Also find Eberjey underwear and the ubiquitous Juicy Couture.

Expensive   *Amex/MC/V*

Lower East Side   **(212) 375-0304**
105 Stanton Street   at Ludlow
NYC 10002   Daily 12-7

Sigerson Morrison (shoes)

Many swear that shoes make the outfit, and Sigerson Morrison's always steal the show. Dazzling colors, metallic and suede textures, all sorts of heel and toe designs—these shoes are knockouts. Although Morrison's shoes are highly fashionable, they are never seasonal (i.e. they don't date—yes!). Be sure to check out the Belle collection, a more affordable line. *sigersonmorrison.com*

Expensive   *Amex/MC/V*

Nolita   **(212) 219-3893**
28 Prince Street   btw Mott/Elizabeth
NYC 10012   Mon-Sat 11-7, Sun 12-6

Sigerson Morrison (handbags)

Here is Sigerson Morrison's gorgeously fashionable and cunningly functional handbag store. Styles include ideal boxy day totes, triangular-shaped bags with metal handles, canvas beach totes and the popular hobo bags. Prices run from $160 to $700.

Expensive   *Amex/MC/V*
Nolita   **(212) 941-5239**
242 Mott Street   btw Houston/Prince
NYC 10012   Mon-Sat 11-7, Sun 12-6

Sisley

This is Benetton's higher-end label, packed with up-to-date basics and fun pieces for a fashion fix. They've added a new NoHo location, where you'll find suits, dresses, pants, sweaters, tops and outerwear that give you a head-to-toe look. While the clothes are hardly as saucy as Sisley's naughty advertising would have you believe, the prices are still hot enough to excite anyone.   *sisley.com*

Moderate   *Amex/MC/V*
Midtown West   **(212) 823-9567**
10 Columbus Circle   Time Warner Center
NYC 10019   Mon-Sat 10-9, Sun 12-6

Fifth Avenue   **(212) 420-5700**
133 Fifth Avenue   at 20th St
NYC 10013   Mon-Sat 10-8, Sun 11-7

NoHo/West Village (M)   **(212) 979-2537**
753 Broadway   at 8th St
NYC 10003   Mon-Thurs 10-9 Fri-Sat 10-9:30, Sun 12-8

Skechers USA

This California-based company, born by the water in Manhattan Beach, sells easy breezy footwear for the easy breezy crowd. Choose from a selection of men's, women's and children's shoes loaded with hip-hop attitude and ranging from utility rugged to casual basics, sport joggers and sneakers.   *800-shoe-411 skechers.com*

Affordable   *Amex/MC/V*
Midtown East   **(212) 869-9550**
3 Times Square   at 42nd/Seventh Avenue
NYC 10036   Mon-Thurs 9-11, Fri-Sat 9-12

Midtown West   **(646) 473-0490**
140 West 34th Street   btw Sixth/Seventh Ave
NYC 10011   Mon-Sat 9-10, Sun 11-8

Flatiron   **(212) 627-9420**
150 Fifth Avenue   btw 19/20th St
NYC 10011   Mon-Sat 10-8, Sun 11-6

SoHo   **(212) 431-8803**
530 Broadway   at Spring
NYC 10012   Mon-Thurs 10-8, Fri-Sat 10-10, Sun 11-8

★ Slang Betty

An excellent stop for rockers and bohemians alike, Slang Betty serves up vintage gear with plenty of attitude. Accessories like silver jewelry and watches are located in the front; clothes, like colorful wrap dresses and printed skirts with travel scenarios, are filed in the back. The latter are similar to last year's Prada collection, but cost half as much. Don't miss the collection of funky tights and colorful socks that add the perfect twist to any dull wardrobe.

Affordable   *Amex/MC/V*

Park Slope   **(718) 638-1725**
172 5th Avenue   btw Lincoln/Berkeley
Brooklyn 11217   Wed-Sun 12-7:30

★ Sleep

Resembling a vintage boudoir with huge-mirrored antique vanity tables, brass beds, hatboxes, hankies, and ornate perfume bottles, Sleep is a haven for the domesticated glamour kitten with a love for all things luxe. On offer are underthings in rich smooth satin with contrast stitching, and pale sheers trimmed with lace provided by French (naturally), British and U.S. labels (Huit, Fleur T, I.D. Sarrieri, and Passion Bait). Little touches like Egyptian cotton sheets by Signoria Firenze and pomegranate candles by Kai will cozy up your personal space, or opt for a dramatic change with special-ordered Polynesian/floral wallpaper from Osborne & Little.   *sleepbrooklyn.com*

Moderate   *Amex/MC/V*

Williamsburg   **(718) 384-3211**
110 North Sixth Street   at Berry
Brooklyn 11211   Tues-Sun 12-8

Small Change

Having recently relocated to a much larger space, this well-edited boutique specializing in beautiful European kids' clothing for parents with decidedly uptown tastes is better than ever. Brands carried here include Lacoste, Simonetta, Ralph Lauren and adorable Lili Gaufrette (just as cute for boys as it is for girls). The store's window display showcases bright accessories housed in old apothecary jars.

Moderate   *Amex/MC/V*

Upper East Side   **(212) 772-6455**
1196 Lexington Avenue   btw 80/81st St
NYC 10021   Mon-Fri 10-5:30, Sat 10-4:45

Soda Fine

Refurbishing vintage duds with handmade details, Soda Fine brings whimsy to fashion lovers. Owned by two young female entrepreneurs and featuring clothes, accessories and even a few fanzines, Soda Fine is host to several local designers and artists. Pretty vintage beaded clutches lie next to fabric satchels made by talented new designer Roxy Marj, while the innovative apparel from Feral Child employs traditional sewing techniques and fabric treatments to make must-see pieces.   *sodafine.com*

Affordable   *Amex/MC/V*

Clinton Hill   **(718) 230-3060**
246 DeKalb Avenue   btw Clermont/Vanderbilt
Brooklyn 11205   Tues-Sat 12-8, Sun 1-6

SoHo Baby

Dorothy Shu grew so frustrated buying clothes for her baby, she decided to take matters into her own hands. Her store is brimming with layettes, casual clothing, special occasion dresses, flotation swimsuits, sleepwear, raincoats and accessories, all fit for newborn to 8 years. Along with the best in babywear from Jean Bourget, Berlingot, Alphabets and Baby Steps is a collection of stuffed animals, framed pictures and all the bedding baby needs. Gift baskets are also available.

Moderate *Amex/MC/V*

Nolita **(212) 625-8538**
251 Elizabeth Street btw Houston/Prince
NYC 10012 Mon-Sat 11-7, Sun 12-6

SoHo Woman

Exquisite fabrics in simple silhouettes for sizes 10 through 28, including 100% cotton, linen, matte jersey, wool, crepe and silks. There are mandarin-styled tops in great colors, washable silks by URU and year-round merchandise from labels like Coco and Juan. A good source for easy-to-wear clothing perfect for travel.

Moderate *Amex/MC/V*

Midtown West **(212) 391-7263**
32 West 40th Street btw Fifth/Sixth Ave
NYC 10018 Mon-Fri 11-7, Sat 12-5

Sol

Sexy swimwear from Brazil (and it's not just thongs) fills this tiny SoHo boutique. Find all you need for the beach including suits, coverups, tops, skirts and dresses. Labels include Rio-ready Rosa Chá, Linda de Morrer and Havaianas. *solnewyork.com*

Expensive *Amex/MC/V*

Nolita **(212) 966-0002**
6 Prince Street btw Bowery/Elizabeth
NYC 10012 Mon-Sat 11-7, Sun 12-6

★ Some Odd Rubies

Not content with being just another vintage boutique on the Lower East Side, Some Odd Rubies' owners Summer Phoenix (actress and Joaquin's sister) and Odessa Whitmire go that extra style mile by customizing slightly worn cotton dresses, T-shirts or cast-off sweaters with new hems, new cuts, new seams or even a new ribbon—utterly transforming each to your exact specifications. Their small shop also stocks newer designers and a little jewelry, and has homey touches like a leafy terrace and a couch for weary trend-hunters (or their weary boyfriends). *someoddrubies.com*

Expensive *Amex/MC/V*

Lower East Side **(212) 353-1736**
151 Ludlow Street btw Stanton/Rivington
NYC 10002 Mon-Fri 1-8, Sat-Sun 12-8

Sonia Rykiel

Sonia Rykiel is known as the queen of knits and she has never strayed from her quintessentially luxe French style. Also known for her use of fluid jersey, wide trousers and black hose, Rykiel's tiny hotpants, hound's-tooth check jackets and flirty lace dresses will delight style seekers. Chic is evidently a family affair, as Rykiel's daughter Nathalie has created a line called Modern Vintage which reissues versions of Rykiel classics. And don't forget Mama Rykiel's superlative accessories, include punky bags with multicolored cats-eye snaps, satin caps and fabulous satin shoes with a rhinestone heel.   *soniarykiel.com*

Luxury   *Amex/MC/V*

Upper East Side   **(212) 396-3060**
849 Madison Avenue   btw 70/71st St
NYC 10021   Mon-Sat 10-6

★ Sorelle Firenze

Sorelle Firenze is Italian for 'sisters of Florence,' and is a fitting name for a store owned and operated by—you guessed it—two Italian sisters, Barbara and Monica Abbatemaggio. They sell a sexy, feminine line designed by themselves and their mother back in Florence. Along with treasures like delicate bikinis, silk and cashmere sweaters, flared dresses, stylish jewelry and hot denim, you'll find clothes from small, independent designers, including the fresh, angular designs of Heike Jarrick. Their retail store is now closed, but a new private showroom will open downtown in early 2006, offering custom tailoring and styling, as well as bridal designs. Call or check the website for contact information.   *sorellefirenze.com*

Expensive   *Amex/MC/V*

n/a at press time   **(212) 528-7816**

Space Kiddets

Everything for hip children or, should we say, hip parents who want their child to be the belle of the blackboard. It's all about jeans, print lace dresses and kid-and-teen-friendly labels like Juicy, Paul Frank, Riley, Diesel and Lili Gaufrette.   *spacekiddets.com*

Moderate   *Amex/MC/V*

Flatiron   **(212) 420-9878**
46 East 21st Street   btw Broadway/Park Ave South
NYC 10010   Mon-Sat 10:30-6 (Wed-Thurs 10:30-7)

Spatial Etc

The only shop in the Brooklyn Handknit mini-chain that's actually located in Brooklyn, and it's named otherwise! The inventory goes beyond their famous house-brand cashmere wraps, sweaters and throws to include Jack Spade bags, Tocca candles and bath goodies, Campers, Wendy Mink jewelry, as well as random leather goods and colorful housewares. While the soft sweaters are just the ticket in the

Hamptons, here they are given a Williamsburg slant when paired with the funky clothes: op-art skirts and dresses, graphic screenprinted tanks, big straw hats and colorful canvas totes. *brooklynhandknit.com*

Moderate   *Amex/MC/V*

Williamsburg   **(718) 599-7962**
135 Bedford Avenue   btw North 5/6th St
Brooklyn 11211   Mon-Sat 11-9, Sun 12-8

West Village   **(212) 206-0180**
19 Christopher Street   at Gay
NYC 10014   Mon-Sat 12-8, Sun 12-6

Spence-Chapin Thrift Shops

If you're looking for posh designer cast-offs that make you feel good about you, Spence-Chapin should be one of your first stops. The well-heeled like to unload their gently used (so gently used, in fact, that the staff sometimes have to remove the original price tag) goodies here so that the proceeds can benefit the Spence-Chapin Adoption Services. Go early on Mondays and Fridays to take advantage of newly reduced prices. *spence-chapin.org*

Affordable   *Amex/MC/V*

Upper East Side   **(212) 426-7643**
1850 Second Avenue   btw 95/96th St
NYC 10128   Mon-Sat 10-5, Sun 12-5

Upper East Side   **(212) 737-8448**
1473 Third Avenue   btw 83/84th St
NYC 10128   Mon-Fri 11-6:15, Sat 11-5:15, Sun 12-4:30

Sports Authority

Sports Authority caters to everyone's sports needs with apparel and equipment for skiing, skating, rollerblading, biking, tennis and football and more. *sportsauthority.com*

Affordable   *Amex/MC/V*

Midtown East   **(212) 355-9725**
845 Third Avenue   at 51st St
NYC 10022   Mon-Fri 9-8, Sat 10-7, Sun 11-6

Midtown West   **(212) 355-6430**
57 West 57th Street   at Sixth Ave
NYC 10019   Mon-Sat 9-8, Sun 11-7

Chelsea   **(212) 929-8971**
636 Sixth Avenue   at 19th St
NYC 10001   Mon-Fri 9:30-8, Sat 10-8, Sun 10-7

Spring Flowers

A large selection of European kids' clothes, including Burberry, Cacharel, G.C by Detomasso, Magil and Petit Bateau for boys, girls and layette. Plenty of dresses for birthday parties and church suits for boys. Spring Flowers is how you remember childhood—sweet, innocent and charming. *springflowerschildren.com*

Expensive   *Amex/MC/V*

Upper East Side
905 Madison Avenue
NYC 10021

(212) 717-8182
btw 72/73rd St
Mon-Sat 10-7

Midtown East
538 Madison Avenue
NYC 10022

(212) 207-4606
at 54/55th St
Mon-Sat 10-7

Upper East Side
1050 Third Avenue
NYC 10021

(212) 758-2669
at 62nd St
Mon-Sat 10-6

Stackhouse

Two of the better streetwear stores on this streetwear block of Lafayette Street, Stackhouse's separate women's and men's locations have an easy access selection of hip clothes for, er, hip-hoppers. Hummel track jackets, hoodies and 2K T-shirts are offered among sneakers (such as Etnies), shoes and bags. Other brands such as Obey and Mato are also represented on the racks. An assortment of accessories, including bandanas and jewelry, is here as well, ready to add a bit of bling to any outfit.

Moderate   *Amex/MC/V*

SoHo (M)
276 Lafayette Street
NYC 10012

(212) 925-6931
btw Houston/Prince
Mon-Sat 11:30-7:30, Sun 11:30-6:30

SoHo (W)
325 Lafayette Street
NYC 10012

(212) 219-3115
btw Houston/Bleecker
Mon-Sat 11:30-7:30, Sun 11:30-6:30

★ Stella McCartney

Stella McCartney shot out of nowhere to head Chloé eight years ago, and quickly quintupled its sales with her cheeky rock 'n' roll aesthetic—remember those naughty slogan T-shirts and diamanté sunglasses? Stella continues to cultivate her strength by tailoring suits and spaghetti-strapped numbers to accentuate the most beautiful parts of the female form, and remains current by making delicate pieces that highlight rather than hug the figure. She still loves a wacky T-shirt, but has added sculpted jackets, no-mess mules, and wonderful leg-elongating jeans. In keeping with her vegetarian principles, the store sells accessories made from non-leather materials—which is ironic in a neighborhood synonymous with meat.   *stellamccartney.com*

Luxury   *Amex/MC/V*

Chelsea
429 West 14th Street
NYC 10014

(212) 255-1556
btw Washington/Ninth Ave
Mon-Sat 11-7, Sun 12:30-6

Stephane Kélian

An elite footwear designer who made his glossy reputation in the Eighties, Stephane Kélian is the master of handwoven leather shoes. His slick collection includes platforms, wedges, boots, open-toed slings, two-tone woven pumps, sandals and loafers. Best bets: stretch leather knee-length boots, sandals and perfect black stilettos. His comfort line, a sneaker/loafer hybrid, is available in textured leathers and suedes.

Expensive   *Amex/MC/V*

Upper East Side   **(212) 980-1919**
717 Madison Avenue   btw 63/64th St
NYC 10021   Mon-Sat 10-6 (Thurs 10-7)

Steven Alan

Steven Alan carries progressive fashion at its best—for women who love edgy up 'n' coming designers. The store carries the coolest labels around, like A.P.C, United Bamboo and 6 by Martin Margiela, Rogan, Trovata, Clu, Park Vogel, Wyeth, Development and Mayle, plus the Steven Alan house label. It's a serious fashion destination for serious fashion lovers—or not so serious: check out their naughty slogan tanks.   *stevenalan.com*

Expensive   *Amex/MC/V*

Tribeca (M)   **(212) 343-0692**
103 Franklin Street   btw West Broadway/Church
NYC 10013   Daily 11:30-7 (Thurs 12-8)

Upper West Side   **(212) 595-8451**
465 Amsterdam Avenue   at 82nd St
NYC 10024   Mon-Sat 11:30-7, Sun 12-6

Steve Madden

Over-the-top, right-price shoes for young hipsters in search of the latest trends. If Madden is going to feature, say, leopard one season, he'll do 10 times more of it than anyone else. The collection includes platform-based styles like open-backed mules, platform boots, bumped-toe mary-janes, high wooden-stacked sandals (a summer staple) and sneakers.   *800-747-6233 stevemadden.com*

Affordable   *Amex/MC/V*

Upper East Side   **(212) 426-0538**
150 East 86th Street   btw Lexington/Third Ave
NYC 10028   Mon-Thurs 10-8:30, Fri-Sat 10-9, Sun 11-7:30

Upper West Side   **(212) 799-4221**
2315 Broadway   btw 83/84th St
NYC 10024   Mon-Thurs 10-8:30, Fri-Sat 10-9, Sun 11-7

Midtown West   **(212) 736-3283**
41 West 34th Street   btw Fifth/Sixth Ave
NYC 10001   Mon-Sat 10-9, Sun 11-7

SoHo   **(212) 343-1800**
540 Broadway   btw Prince/Spring
NYC 10012   Mon-Thurs 10-8:30, Fri-Sat 10-9
                                                    Sun 11-7:30

Steven

Steven (formerly David Aaron, still the higher end line designed by the Steve Madden team) will satisfy anyone in search of Prada looks without Prada prices, with stilettos, flats, mules, driving moccasins, fun sandals, slip-ons and boots. Pay anywhere from $79 to $149 and have everyone think you're wearing designer when you're not.

stevemadden.com

Moderate	*Amex/MC/V*
SoHo	**(212) 431-6022**
529 Broadway	at Spring
NYC 10012	Mon-Sat 10-9, Sun 12-8

Stuart Weitzman ♀

Women shop at this sensible store knowing that Weitzman has a shoe for every foot, small or large (sizes 4 to 12), narrow or wide (from AAAA to C). Styles run from casual, slip-on mules, wood-stacked heel slides and sporty golf shoes to dress pumps, spindly boots (OK, not so sensible), crystal sandals and made-to-order rhinestone pumps. Walking down the aisle soon? Choose from over 40 bridal shoes. Rest assured that your Stuart Weitzman shoes are constructed with care: the brand boasts 80 craftsmen who will work on each pair of shoes over the six to seven weeks it takes to make them. The Madison Avenue store was closed for part of 2005 for renovations, with a new store at the Time Warner Center filling the void.

stuartweitzman.com

Expensive	*Amex/MC/V*
Midtown East	**(212) 750-2555**
625 Madison Avenue	btw 58/59th St
NYC 10022	n/a at press time
Midtown West	**(212) 823-9560**
10 Columbus Circle	Time Warner Center
NYC 10019	Mon-Sat 10-9, Sun 11-7

Stussy ♂

In 1980 Sean Stussy was surfing California's Laguna Beach and selling his T-shirts to his surf buddies. Today, he runs an empire that covers the globe, selling streetwise clothing like checked shirts, tees, sweatshirts and caps, all covered with Stussy's scrawling signature logo. Head to this coolly minimalist store—complete with graffiti wall—and also check out Head Porter's line of industrial-strength nylon bags including backpacks, messenger bags and briefcases, located on the second floor.

stussy.com

Expensive	*Amex/MC/V*
SoHo	**(212) 995-8787**
140 Wooster Street	btw Houston/Prince
NYC 10012	Mon-Thurs 12-7, Fri-Sat 11-7, Sun 12-6

Suarez Handbags ♀

Since 1938 the Suarez family has been selling fine Italian-made shoes, and handbags by designers like Roberta di Camerino and Desmo. Belts, scarves and small leather goods are also available.

suarezny.com

Moderate	*Amex/MC/V*

Midtown East　　　　　　　**(212) 753-3758**
450 Park Avenue　　　　　　　at 57th St
NYC 10022　　　　　　　　　　Mon-Sat 10-6

★ Super Runners Shop 👫

The best specialized running shop in Manhattan sells shoes, clothing and accessories from brand names like Nike, New Balance, Asics, Adidas, In Sport and Moving Comfort for the super-athletic and super-chic alike. The staff are all runners, too, so you'll get firsthand advice while you browse. Try Saucony's Shadow 6000 for a splash of color to compliment your laps around Prospect Park, or look super-cute while huffing and puffing around The Jackie Onassis Reservoir in new Asics DS Trainers. The store also offers watches by Timex and Nike.　　　　　　　*superrunnersshop.com*

Moderate　　　　　　　　　*Amex/MC/V*

Upper East Side　　　　　　**(212) 369-6010**
1337 Lexington Avenue　　　　at 89th St
NYC 10028　　Mon-Fri 10-7 (Thurs 10-9), Sat 10-6, Sun 12-5

Upper East Side　　　　　　**(212) 249-2133**
1244 Third Avenue　　　　　　btw 71/72nd St
NYC 10021　　　　　　　　　　(opening hours as above)

Upper West Side　　　　　　**(212) 787-7665**
360 Amsterdam Avenue　　　　btw 77/78th St
NYC 10024　　Mon-Fri 10-7 (Thurs 10-9), Sat 10-6, Sun 11-5

Midtown East　　　　　　　**(646) 487-1120**
Grand Central Terminal　　　　main concourse
NYC 10017　　　　　　Mon-Fri 8-8, Sat 10-6, Sun 12-5

Supreme 🧍

Urban skaters love Supreme for its video wall sporting tricky skateboard maneuvers, racks overflowing with logo-driven threads, sneakers (Gravis, Axion) and skateboards and wheels. There's a slew of brands here, along with Supreme's own line of clothing and accessories, including Rookie, Lakai and DC. Perfect for the pro-skater, DJ dude or athletic hipster in your life.

Moderate　　　　　　　　　*Amex/MC/V*

Nolita　　　　　　　　　　**(212) 966-7799**
274 Lafayette Street　　　　　btw Houston/Prince
NYC 10012　　　　　　　　　Mon-Sat 11-7, Sun 12-6

Suzanne Couture Millinery 🧍

Squeeze into this tiny millinery shop stuffed with every hat imaginable. It's a great source for fancy dress or special occasion hats, like her natural straw Cannes number. If you're off to the Saratoga races, visit Suzanne for a memorable topper. Her bridal range is also excellent.　　*suzannemillinery.com*

Expensive　　　　　　　　　*Amex/MC/V*

Upper East Side　　　　　　**(212) 593-3232**
27 East 61st Street　　　　　　btw Madison/Park Ave
NYC 10021　　　　Mon-Sat 10-6 (and by appointment)

Suzette Sundae

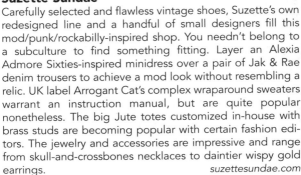

Carefully selected and flawless vintage shoes, Suzette's own redesigned line and a handful of small designers fill this mod/punk/rockabilly-inspired shop. You needn't belong to a subculture to find something fitting. Layer an Alexia Admore Sixties-inspired minidress over a pair of Jak & Rae denim trousers to achieve a mod look without resembling a relic. UK label Arrogant Cat's complex wraparound sweaters warrant an instruction manual, but are quite popular nonetheless. The big Jute totes customized in-house with brass studs are becoming popular with certain fashion editors. The jewelry and accessories are impressive and range from skull-and-crossbones necklaces to daintier wispy gold earrings. *suzettesundae.com*

Moderate   *Amex/MC/V*

East Village   **(212) 777-7870**
182 Avenue B   btw 11/12th St
NYC 10009   Tues-Sat 12-8, Sun 1-7

★ Swiss Army

You might not think it, but this store carries much more than all-in-one blade/screwdriver/scissors/toothpick utility tools. In addition to those world-famous knives, Swiss Army features a range of menswear, from good-looking, high-performance sportswear to simple blazers and jackets. Casual, everyday pieces such as button-down shirts and rough and tumble trousers offer a winning combination of function and fashion. But the real attraction in this large, airy store are the accessories. Find durable luggage, high-tech writing utensils, watches and, of course, a multitude of signature Swiss Army knives in a range of colors and options.

Expensive   *Amex/MC/V*

SoHo   **(212) 965-5714**
136 Prince Street   btw West Broadway/Wooster
NYC 10012   Mon-Sat 11-7, Sun 12-6

Tahir

Low-priced vintage makes for a quick turnover at Tahir, so expect new goodies each time you stop in. Run by an FIT grad with her finger on the pulse of the local designer scene, the boutique is stocked with choice pieces made by hip young things from the city. To Tie For makes tanks and skirts out of dad's favorite gift, and Christina Jean takes old pumps and handpaints them with colorful patterns. For the guys, local designers James and 1Aeon make killer graffiti tees. The shop's back patio plays host to mellow fashion party cookouts/sales. *tahirboutique.com*

Affordable   *Amex/MC/V*

East Village   **(212) 253-2121**
412 East 9th Street   btw First/Avenue A
NYC 10009   Mon-Sat 12-8, Sun 1-7

Takashimaya

What a breathtaking break from Fifth Avenue's stifling, nose-in-the-air, pristine path—Takashimaya is a clean, minimalist piece of Tokyo on Fifth Avenue. There are wonderful clothes here, exotic but wearable, the sort you'll never find anywhere else, and much more besides. The first floor includes a floral boutique, while the upper levels include a travel shop that sells everything from totes and carry-ons to rainwear and travel journals. Explore the store's exquisite home collection of unique tabletop items and giftware, and be sure to stop by the sixth floor for Takashimaya's unrivalled beauty and skincare department, featuring an array of treatments and essences from around the world.

Expensive   *Amex/MC/V*

Fifth Avenue   **(212) 350-0100**
693 Fifth Avenue   btw 54/55th St
NYC 10022   Mon-Sat 10-7, Sun 12-5

Tani

Long an unassuming fixture on the Upper West Side, Tani has had an interior facelift and the result is a clean, bright store that effectively showcases a great, colorful selection of shoes. There's everything from chunky and funky to sleek and feminine from such labels as Kors, Cynthia Rowley, Via Spiga, BCBG, Donald Pliner and more.

Moderate   *Amex/MC/V*

Upper West Side   **(212) 873-4361**
2020 Broadway   btw 69/70th St
NYC 10023   Mon-Fri 10-8, Sat-12-7:30, Sun 12-7

Upper West Side   **(212) 595-1338**
131 West 72nd Street   btw Broadway/Columbus
NYC 10023   Mon-Sat 10-7:30, Sun 12-7

T.Anthony

In 1946 T.Anthony's collection of sophisticated luggage catered to the world's social elite, including the Duke and Duchess of Windsor. The tradition continues today with briefcases, handbags, small leather goods, desk sets, photo albums, jewelry boxes and, of course, the signature leather and canvas luggage. Up there in the prestige stakes with the estimable Louis Vuitton.   tanthony.com

Expensive   *Amex/MC/V*

Midtown East   **(212) 750-9797**
445 Park Avenue   at 56th St
NYC 10022   Mon-Fri 9:30-6, Sat 10-5

Talbots

Talbots was founded in 1947 in a 17th-century colonial frame house in Hingham, Massachusetts. Who knew? Their mail-order business and nationwide chain of stores took off, and these days you'll find great career and casual clothing like preppy knits, pant suits, and comfy dresses that never

go out of style (in certain circles, at least). Classics such as five-pocket jeans ($68) and wrinkle-resistant cotton shirts ($58) can be found all year round. Reliability can be a woman's best friend. *800-992-9010 talbots.com*

Moderate *Amex/MC/V*

Upper East Side **(212) 988-8585**
1251 Third Avenue at 72nd St
NYC 10021 Mon-Fri 10-8, Sat 10-7, Sun 12-6

Upper West Side **(212) 875-8754**
2289-2291 Broadway btw 82/83rd St
NYC 10024 Mon-Fri 10-9, Sat 10-8, Sun 12-6

Lower Manhattan **(212) 425-0166**
189-191 Front Street at South Street Seaport
NYC 10038 Mon-Sat 10-8, Sun 11-6

Midtown East **(212) 838-8811**
525 Madison Avenue btw 53/54th St
NYC 10022 Mon-Fri 10-7, Sat 10-6, Sun 12-5

Talbot Kids

Talbots Kids caters to your wee ones' everyday needs. Unlike the conservative women's collection, Talbot's children's looks are pure fun, and include pants, dresses, blazers, ties, skirts, dress shirts, T-shirts, sweatshirts, sleepwear and even underwear. And their prices aren't too bad, either. With all the cutesy kids' boutiques in this neighborhood charging $50 for a T-shirt, Talbot Kids is a welcome break, providing real kiddie clothes that don't have to be treated as if they were precious artifacts. *talbots.com*

Moderate *Amex/MC/V*

Upper East Side **(212) 570-1630**
1523 Second Avenue at 79th St
NYC 10021 Mon-Sat 9:30-7 (Thurs 9:30-8), Sun 12-5

Midtown East **(212) 758-4152**
527 Madison Avenue at 54th St
NYC 10022 Mon-Fri 10-7, Sat 10-6, Sun 12-5

Tanino Crisci

Tanino Crisci offers conservative, handmade shoes in a range of styles from alligator pumps to loafers, from boots to classic wing-tips. Top-of-the-line leathers and expert craftsmanship set Tanino Crisci apart from other cobblers (and justify the prices). Jackets, ties, belts and wallets are also available. *taninocrisci.com*

Expensive *Amex/MC/V*

Upper East Side **(212) 535-1014**
795 Madison Avenue btw 67/68th St
NYC 10021 Mon-Sat 10-6

Taryn Rose

Designer Taryn Rose is an L.A.-based, shoe-crazed orthopedic surgeon. Her shoes are conservative enough for the office but fashion-forward enough to set you apart from the other worker drones, and all models are designed with acute attention to comfort. 877-440-7613 tarynrose.com

Luxury   *Amex/MC/V*

Midtown East   **(212) 753-3939**
30 East 60th Street   btw Madison/Park Ave
NYC 10022   Mon-Sat 10-6

Ted Baker London

Ted Baker shirts are a favorite of youthful British guys everywhere who swear by their relaxed cut and cool colors. Some have been known to claim that donning a Ted Baker shirt is like wearing lingerie (not that they would know, we hope). Manufactured in high-tech fabrics, these silky, soft shirts come long and short-sleeved in adventurous shades like lavender, pink and yellow. Contemporary-styled suits, knitwear and pants are also available. Baker's Endurance line includes wrinkle-free wool suits ideal for travel, water-repellent tuxedos, and Minted, which includes suits lined with anti-bacterial fabric.   *tedbaker.co.uk*

Moderate   *Amex/MC/V*

SoHo   **(212) 343-8989**
107 Grand Street   btw Mercer/Broadway
NYC 10012   Mon-Sat 11:30-7, Sun 12-6

Tees.com

Ever had a hankering for a customized iron-on T-shirt? We thought so, so head to this boutique filled with a mix of local designers including Bouncy Wear, Itsus and Glamhead. The perfect spot to find tees with slogans like 'Jesus is My Homeboy', 'Drama Queen' and 'Touch My Monkey'—or use your imagination to create a one-of-a-kind heat transfer.   *tees.com*

Affordable   *Amex/MC/V*

East Village   **(212) 254-5400**
147 Avenue A   btw 9/10th St
NYC 10009   Sun-Wed 12-8, Thurs-Sat 12-10

Temperley

London fashion phenom Alice Temperley brings some Old World charm to her Stateside store, decking the halls with vintage furniture from Italy and France, romantic columns and floor-to-ceiling windows. Loved by the likes of Renée Zellweger, Elizabeth Hurley and J.Lo, Temperley is known for her delicate sequined chiffon and silk tops and cashmere knits, while beading and Egyptian prints mark her undeniably chic ready-to-wear collection, which includes grand wool coats (with interesting straps and edging).   *temperleylondon.com*

Expensive   *Amex/MC/V*

SoHo   **(212) 219-2929**
453 Broome Street (2nd floor)   at Mercer
NYC 10013   Mon-Fri 10-6, Thurs 10-9
                                              Sat 11-6 (or by appointment)

T'Frisson

Upper East Side straight-laced elegance can be found downtown at this SoHo shop. This large black and white space with copious track lighting holds crepe evening gowns by Tufi Duek, tweed suits with tassel fringe by Iodice, bouclé suits by Ungaro Fuscia, Julien Macdonald's deep v-neck dresses, Vera Wang cocktail dresses, and sequin and pearl shell tops by Gai Mattiolo. The dressing-room waiting area is equipped with a black leather sofa conversation pit and a tacky fake aquarium presented via videoscreen. *tfrisson.com*

Luxury   *Amex/MC/V*

SoHo   **(212) 219-2215**
77 Greene Street   btw Broome/Spring
NYC 10012   Mon-Sat 12-7, Sun 12-6

TG-170

Shop at TG-170 to be the first to know tomorrow's trends. A neighborhood mainstay, this LES store has been supporting downtown designers since 1992. Fashion followers come here to be the first to wear new collections by under-the-radar labels like Lauren Moffitt and Stretsis. Note the assortment of sturdy Freitag messenger bags ringing the upper shelves, perfect for carting off tomorrow's styles today. *tg170.com*

Expensive   *Amex/MC/V*

Lower East Side   **(212) 995-8660**
170 Ludlow Street   btw East Houston/Stanton
NYC 10002   Daily 12-8

Theory

World famous for their straight-cut tailored pants that are casual enough for a stroll in the park but dressy enough for a night out on the town, Theory has mastered classic looks with understated chic. Their signature combination of soft and slightly stretchy sumptuous textiles lends an easy elegance to their mix-and-match wardrobe staples, from cotton button-downs, cashmere sweaters, jersey tanks and tees to basic blazers. *theory.com*

Moderate   *Amex/MC/V*

Upper West Side   **(212) 362-3676**
230 Columbus Avenue   btw 70/71st St
NYC 10023   Mon-Fri 10-7, Sat 11-7, Sun 12-6

Chelsea   **n/a at press time**
40 Gansevoort Street   at Hudson
NYC 10014   n/a at press time

Thom Browne

Former J.Crew heartthrob and Club Monaco designer Thom Browne has opened his own studio where he takes men's tailoring back to more elegant times. His inspiration lies in the Sixties: fitted and structured suits and button-down collars. Men will look more dapper than ever in custom-tailored suits by Thom.

Luxury   *Amex/MC/V*

West Village   **(212) 633-1197**
17 Little West 12th Street   btw 9th/Washington
NYC 10014   Mon-Sat 10-6, by appointment only

Thomas Pink

Don't be deceived by the brand's historically masculine image—LVMH-owned Thomas Pink has let the ladies in. Reap the benefits of Thomas Pink's traditional British shirt-making skills, utilizing quality fabrics, wonderful patterns and an extraordinary selection of colors. Ready-made shirts start at $140; pay $12 for sleeve alterations or monogramming. Dandy-friendly accessories include ties, cashmere sweaters, cufflinks, suspenders, pocket squares and scarves.   *thomaspink.com*

Expensive   *Amex/MC/V*

Midtown East   **(212) 838-1928**
520 Madison Avenue   at 53rd St
NYC 10022   Mon-Fri 10-7 (Thurs 10-8)
     Sat 10-6, Sun 12-6

Midtown West   **(212) 840-9663**
1155 Sixth Avenue   at 44th St
NYC 10036   Mon-Fri 10-7 (Thurs 10-8)
     Sat 10-6, Sun 12-5

Midtown West   **(212) 823-9650**
10 Columbus Circle   Time Warner Center
NYC 10019   Mon-Sat 10-9, Sun 11-6

Thread

Even if you never get to be a bride, you'd be thrilled to be a bridesmaid dressed by Thread. Eschewing the dowdy, the frumpy and everything taffeta in favor of hip colorful numbers in organza, duchesse satin, bengaline and chiffon, these wedding outfits could easily double as cocktail dresses. You'll hear rock 'n' roll in Thread's light and airy showroom while the fit-and-color-conscious staff do a great deal to defuse tying-the-knot jitters. Delivery takes 10-12 weeks and don't miss Thread's cute little extras, like 'Just Married' panties and bikinis.   *threaddesign.com*

Moderate   *Amex/MC/V*

Chelsea   **(212) 414-8844**
26 West 17th Street (suite 301)   btw Fifth/Sixth Ave
NYC 10011   Mon-Sat 10:30-6, Sat 10:30-4:30
     (by appointment)

★ Three Turtle Doves

In a space that feels like a cabin of a pirate ship, with nautical ropes, seahorses and shell wind chimes, it's the clothes that are the real buried treasure. Pick up a stylish swashbuckler hat or a mesh veiled cap with peacock feathers by

Cha Cha's House of Ill Repute Millinery. Sunbleached wooden display cases filled with black sand show off Reverie jewelry: a Brooklyn line of remade vintage pieces such as a broken chandelier-turned-necklace. Brianna Stone makes hers of wooden beads and coffee beans for an accessory pickme-up. The shop's owner's boyfriend can meld your keys together to form a clever but utilitarian non-jangling star.

Expensive   *Amex/MC/V*

East Village   **(212) 529-3288**
201 East 2nd Street   btw Avenue A/B
NYC 10009   Tues-Sun 2-9

Tibetan Arts & Crafts

This tiny boutique encapsulates the distinctive charm of Tibetan style. Best pieces include raw silk shirts at around $75 (a favorite of Cameron Diaz), reversible pashmina scarves and shawls in a dazzling array of colors, silk shirts ($38 for short sleeves, $60 for long), antique patched and brocaded bags at a mere $12, beaded slippers at $18-28, plus traditional ceremonial hats and jewelry.

Affordable   *Amex/MC/V*

West Village   **(212) 260-5880**
197 Bleecker Street   btw Sixth/MacDougal
NYC 10012   Mon-Fri 11-9, Sat-Sun 10-10

Tibet Bazaar

Begin your search for enlightenment at Tibet Bazaar, a specialty boutique offering unique clothing, with beaded fabrics, accessories and gifts direct from the Himalayas. Adorn yourself in luxurious apparel from slippers to jackets and faux fur-trimmed hats. Or choose from their wide variety of ritual items including singing bowls, CD recordings of Tibetan mantras and, of course, incense.

Moderate   *Amex/MC/V*

Upper West Side   **(212) 595-8487**
473 Amsterdam Avenue   btw 82/83rd St
NYC 10024   Daily 10-7

Timberland

Although Timberland made its reputation on its functional, outdoor footwear and accessories, lately the brand has gained popularity as a ubiquitous urban style. But whether you choose to wear their shoes on the street or in the country, rest assured that they will withstand the elements and the rigors of time. Styles run from casual shoes to rugged boots and include hiking boots, driving moccasins, boating shoes and weatherbucks. Men's outdoor apparel is also available. Children's from size 5 toddler and up.   *timberland.com*

Moderate   *Amex/MC/V*

Upper East Side   **(212) 754-0434**
709 Madison Avenue   at 63rd St
NYC 10021   Mon-Fri 9:30-7, Sat 10-6, Sun 12-6

Tina Tang

Tina Tang left a successful career at an investment bank to pursue a dream of designing jewelry. Two stores later, each filled with precious metals and stones, from chandelier earrings and monogram necklaces to custom-made charm bracelets and hair clips, Tina Tang's dream has become a glittering reality. Choose from an array of pieces made with gold, sterling silver, freshwater pearls and semi-precious stones. Check out the new Tina Tang Too store on Greenwich for higher-end pieces in gold and precious stones.   *tinatang.com*

Affordable   *Amex/MC/V*

Nolita   **(212) 226-3369**
230 Mulberry Street   btw Prince/Spring
NYC 10012   Mon-Sat 12-7, Sun 12-6

West Village   **(212) 645-6890**
49 Greenwich Avenue   btw Charles/Perry
NYC 10014   Mon-Sat 12-8, Sun 12-7

West Village (Tina Tang Too)   **(212) 645-3124**
48 Greenwich Avenue   btw Charles/Perry
NYC 10014   Mon-Sat 12-8, Sun 12-6

Tip Top Kids

If your tiny tots demand the snazziest sneakers in the schoolyard, this shoe store is sure to put them in tip-top shape. With their large selection of casual and athletic shoes for infants and children (up to size 7), Tip Top Kids will keep your little ones' toes covered in smart styles from in demand brands such as Ecco, Ugg, Diesel, Puma, Adidas and Converse.

Moderate to expensive   *Amex/MC/V*

Upper West Side   **(212) 874-1004**
149 West 72nd Street   btw Amsterdam/Columbus Ave
NYC 10023   Mon-Sat 9:30-6:45 (Thurs 9:30-7:45)
                                                                    Sun 12-5

T.J.Maxx

Off-price merchandise for the entire family, as well as a large selection of accessories for home, bed and bath. If you're lucky, you might find a designer name like Polo, DKNY or Tahari.   *tjmaxx.com*

Affordable   *Amex/MC/V*

Chelsea   **(212) 229-0875**
620 Sixth Avenue   btw 18/19th St
NYC 10011   Mon-Sat 9:30-9, Sun 11-7

★ Tod's

Tod's shoes enjoy a cult following among Hollywood actresses and society types who swear by their signature pebble driving shoes—available in a rainbow of colors—priced around $325. Other guaranteed chic styles include smart-looking mules, classic loafers, stylish pumps and sexy black boots with contrasting heels. Check out the status-symbol bags, as well as new sporty leather jackets that you're sure to see on the red carpet.

800-457-TODS todsonline.com

Luxury *Amex/MC/V*
Midtown East **(212) 644-5945**
650 Madison Avenue btw 59/60th St
NYC 10022 Mon-Sat 10-6 (Thurs 10-7), Sun 12-5

Togs

Urban streetwear and European chic are happily married in Togs's collection of imported Italian clothing. Contemporary separates, tops, knitwear, leather pants and a large selection of jeans are all surprisingly affordable. Low-key labels include Anima, Cristina Gavioli and Blu Sand. Perfect for the resort.

Moderate *Amex/MC/V*
SoHo **(917) 237-1882**
68 Spring Street btw Crosby/Lafayette
NYC 10012 Mon-Sat 11-8, Sun 11-7:30

★ Tokio 7

Don't let this consignment shop's dingy interior deter you, because you'll find everything here from old-school vintage to this season's hand-me-downs. Recent sightings include a studded Chloé dress, Ungaro pants and scores of Marc by Marc Jacobs—all under $100 dollars. Never-been-worn items garner higher prices, but all the pieces are covetable and, most importantly, attainable. The ever-rotating selection is worth checking out often.

Moderate to expensive *Amex/MC/V*
East Village **(212) 353-8443**
64 East 7th Street btw First/Second Ave
NYC 10003 Mon-Sat 12-8:30, Sun 12-8

Tokyo Joe

A cramped, overstocked consignment shop featuring hip designer labels at accessible prices. The merchandise changes each day, so scoop something up when you see it because it ain't gonna be there tomorrow. The goods include designer clothing, shoes, bags and accessories by labels like Gucci, Marc Jacobs, Prada, Comme des Garçons, Miu Miu and Donna Karan. Items are generally in good condition and the prices can't be beat. Current season shoes from top designers have been known to turn up, worn only once.

Moderate *Amex/MC/V*
East Village **(212) 473-0724**
334 East 11th Street btw First/Second Ave
NYC 10003 Daily 12-9

Tommy Hilfiger

The American idol of fashion designers, Tommy Hilfiger is known for his bold line of sportswear and legion of celebrity endorsers (including David Bowie, who lives nearby). Tommy Hilfiger's three-floor, 11,000-square-foot specialty store in SoHo caters to ladies and lads with sportswear, denim (emphasis on juniors) and accessories. Striped polos for preppy looks, worker-washed utility jeans for blue-collar kids, stitched denim jackets for the rockers and the jeans and tees that will carry you from street to club to beach. *tommyhilfiger.com*

Moderate *Amex/MC/V*

SoHo **(917) 237-0983**
372 West Broadway btw Spring/Broome
NYC 10012 Mon-Fri 11-7, Sat 11-8, Sun 12-6

★ Tory by TRB

Seen throughout the Hamptons and in countless fashion editorial spreads, Tory's designs have been draped over all the who's-who in Manhattan, the surrounding resort towns and beyond to L.A., where chic west-coasters were sick of NYC girls getting all the glam before they got their own branch. Behind the bright orange doors of this Nolita hideaway lies a high-end haven for those who believe that more really is more. Society girl around town turned style surveyor, Tory Burch's namesake label is clothing fit for a weekend in the Hamptons or some playtime in Palm Beach. Lush cashmere crewnecks, ever-popular espadrilles and, of course, her famous tunics are all available in Tory's signature 4T Op-art. Fabulous. *toryltd.com*

Moderate to expensive *Amex/MC/V*

Nolita **(212) 334-3000**
257 Elizabeth Street btw Prince/Houston
NYC 10012 Mon-Sat 11-8, Sun 12-6

★ Tracy Feith

Hot Australian surfer-dude-turned-designer Tracy Feith is one smart man. Not only does he know what the girls want to wear, he knows what their boyfriends want them to wear, too. His collection of romantic corset tops, pretty silk skirts, dolled-up dresses, fancy fabric totes and sultry printed pants will help any missy snag second glances. One peek into this island resort of a shop will have girls dreaming up steamy tropical encounters. *tracyfeith.com*

Moderate *Amex/MC/V*

Nolita **(212) 334-3097**
209 Mulberry Street btw Spring/Kenmare
NYC 10012 Mon-Sat 11-7, Sun 12-7

Training Camp

'Footwear is my addiction; the only thing I like more than footwear is my wife,' says Udi Avshalom. Now that is love. Training Camp followers like P. Diddy shop here for the latest in brand-name sneakers. Prices run from $30 to $160.

Affordable *Amex/MC/V*

Midtown West **(212) 840-7842**
25 West 45th Street btw Fifth/Sixth Ave
NYC 10036 Mon-Sat 9-8 (Fri 9-8:30), Sun 10-6

Midtown West   **(212) 921-4430**
1079 Sixth Avenue   at 41st St
NYC 10036   Mon-Sat 9-8 (Fri-Sat 9-8:30), Sun 10-6:30

Transit

One-stop shopping for sneaker enthusiasts (and those who just need a great pair of kicks). This two-floor emporium offers a healthy selection of New Balance, Nike, Puma, Adidas, Fred Perry and more, in a wide range of styles, colors and sizes. Chances are the large selection will satisfy any shoe connoisseur, but the staff are happy to order a specific item if they don't have it in stock.

Expensive   *Amex/MC/V*

NoHo   **(212) 358-8726**
265 Broadway   at Bond
NYC 10012   Mon-Sat 9-9, Sun 10-8

Trash and Vaudeville

Trash and Vaudeville, the destination of choice for punk gear for decades, is actually two stores in one. The upstairs Vaudeville is full of rock T-shirts, skirt/tie combos, apron-front pants, safety-pinned tops and plaids reminiscent of Vivienne Westwood. There's also an amazing selection of shoes from Doc Martens to spiked stilettos, some in hard-to-find sizes. The Trash underground is dedicated to goth: the front section has piercing jewelry, studded bracelets and belts and vintage lunchboxes, while the back is packed with fetish gear (think PVC corsets and rubber dresses).

Moderate   *Amex/MC/V*

East Village   **(212) 982-3590**
4 St Mark's Place   btw Second/Third Ave
NYC 10003   Mon-Thurs 12-8, Fri 11:30-8:30
                            Sat 11:30-9, Sun 1-7:30

Triple Five Soul

Sweet street style is Triple Five Soul's stock in trade. It's all about pairing low-rise jeans with a hot terry tank to help you get down on the dance floor later on. Just step to Triple Five Soul's selection of cargos, logo-heavy hoodies, shirts, tanks (screaming such important messages as 'Brooklyn' and 'Survival'), and record cases (for DJs and wannabes) for hip-hop wear par excellence.   *triple5soul.com*

Moderate   *Amex/MC/V*

Nolita   **(212) 431-2404**
290 Lafayette Street   btw Houston/Prince
NYC 10012   Daily 11-7

Tristan & America

A Canadian import that caters to the young professional woman and man in search of career and casual clothing at reasonable prices. Styles are simple, classic and sporty and include an ample selection of suits. Women's jackets run $100-$150 and skirts average $88.   *tristan-america.com*

Affordable   *Amex/MC/V*

Midtown West (212) 246-2354
1230 Sixth Avenue at 49th St
NYC 10020 Mon-Sat 10-8, Sun 12-6

Tse

The revolution continues at Tse, formerly Tse Cashmere. The luxe label is obviously best known for its cashmere and brief design stints by London conceptualist Hussein Chalayan and Annette Ishida who had been with the company for years. Keep an eye on the new lines for their next incarnation. *tsecashmere.com*

Luxury *Amex/MC/V*

Upper East Side (212) 472-7790
827 Madison Avenue at 69th St
NYC 10021 Mon-Sat 10-6 (Thurs 10-7)

Tsubi

When did dressing like an Eighties surf rat become so expensive? Australian cult line Tsubi somehow pulls off Spicoli-chic with washed out gray jeans complete with rips for $250 and threadbare logo tees for half that. The men's selection mirrors the women's, only in slightly larger sizes. Picture yourself leaning against an old clunker of a station wagon with surfboards on the roof rack, donning a baggy glitter tank sweater and cigarette-leg stretch jeans in pink or turquoise. Flashy unisex accessories include aviator sunglasses and rough leather bracelets. The small space is a perfect parallel to the clothes: perfectly shabby in a high rent neighborhood. *tsubi.com*

Expensive *Amex/MC/V*

Nolita (212) 334-4690
219C Mulberry Street btw Prince/Spring
NYC 10012 Mon-Sat 12-8, Sun 12-6

Tumi

Specializing in bags that will last just about forever, Tumi offers everything from purses, briefcases, and messenger bags to garment bags, full-sized luggage and golf bags. While some pieces are offered in leather, most are constructed in the highly durable woven nylon for which Tumi is famous. *800-322-8864 tumi.com*

Expensive *Amex/MC/V*

Midtown East (212) 973-0015
64 Grand Central Terminal (Lexington Passage)
NYC 10017 Mon-Fri 8-7:45, Sat 10-7:45, Sun 11-5:45

Midtown East (212) 813-0545
520 Madison Avenue at 54th St
NYC 10022 Mon-Sat 10-7, Sun 11-6

Midtown West (212) 245-7460
53 West 49th Street btw Fifth/Sixth Ave
NYC 10112 Mon-Sat 10-7, Sun 11-6

SoHo (646) 613-9101
102 Prince Street btw Mercer/Greene
NYC 10012 Mon-Sat 10-7, Sun 12-6

Midtown West
10 Columbus Circle
NYC 10019

(212) 823-9390
Time Warner Center
Mon-Sat 10-9, Sun 11-7

Tupli

Have an image in your mind of the perfect shoe, but can't seem to find it anywhere, or worse, finally find it, but not in your size? If you can dream it, Tupli can make it. This custom shoe atelier will work with you to design your perfect shoe, be it plain and proper or imaginative and unique. Start with a sketch and move onto custom measuring and fitting, choose a heel style and height and a material, and in three to four weeks you will pick up a handcrafted pair of completely you shoes. The service is particularly popular among brides, when everything needs to be just so.

Luxury   *Amex/MC/V*

Upper East Side
780 Madison Avenue (2nd floor)
NYC 10021

(212) 472 2576
btw 66/67th St
by appointment only

★ Turnbull & Asser

Turnbull & Asser has dressed England's aristocrats, moguls and movie stars since 1855. This New York outpost of London's finest haberdasher offers traditional suits, formalwear, sportswear, outerwear, sleepwear and accessories for both men and women. The best reason to shop here remains the bespoke shirt selection, which boasts over 600 fabrics and styles from bold stripes to checks to patterns. Rely on the remarkably friendly and helpful service to help you find the perfect fit.   *877-887-6285 turnbullandasser.com*

Luxury   *Amex/MC/V*

Midtown East
42 East 57th Street
NYC 10022

(212) 752-5700
btw Madison/Park Ave
Mon-Fri 10-6:30, Sat 9:30-6

Union

This small men's boutique is select, edgy and on the verge. Filled with the latest in street and skate clothing by cool, visionary designers (Duffer of St George, Goodenough, Pam, Gimme 5), this place has its collective finger on the pulse of hip NYC. Be sure to check out the T-shirts by local artists, sweaters, jackets, jeans and graphic pieces.

Moderate   *Amex/MC/V*

SoHo
172 Spring Street
NYC 10012

(212) 226-8493
btw Thompson/West Broadway
Mon-Thurs 11-7, Fri-Sat 11-7:30, Sun 12-6

Unis

Best known for making very cool (but never fey) looks for men—think softer-than-expected military jackets, slim Sixties trenches, classic jeans—former DKNY designer Eunice Lee (the store's name is a play on 'unisex' and her first name) started making clothes for women last year. The results? Well, now Lee ranks Kirsten Dunst and Maggie Gyllenhaal as fans alongside regular customers Mos Def and the Chemical Brothers. Hipsters delight in the silks and chiffons lending sexy texture to tops with plunging necklines, and applaud cargos with belted ankles and tight motorcycle jackets, demonstrating the feminine flipside to Lee's traditional male styles. *unisnewyork.com*

Moderate   *Amex/MC/V*

Nolita   **(212) 431-5533**
226 Elizabeth Street   btw Houston/Prince
NYC 10013   Daily 11-8

Unisa

Unisa offers simple, fashionable footwear at truly fabulous prices (almost everything is under $165). The shoes tend to stay on the safer side of current trends, but are cute enough to keep you walking in style. Find colorful sandals, feminine stilettos, and neutral mules, loafers and slingbacks, all under the Unisa label. Handbags, which run from $75 to $185, appeal to both those in and outside of Madison Avenue tax brackets. *unisa.com*

Affordable   *Amex/MC/V*

Upper East Side   **(212) 753-7474**
701 Madison Avenue   btw 62/63rd St
NYC 10021   Mon-Sat 10-6:30, Sun 12-5

United Nude Terra Plana

An offshoot of the Terra Plana footwear line, United Nude features ultra-modern sandals (available in 2½ and 3½-inch heels), with an open toe and an open space where you'd normally find a wedge. The brainchild of Dutch architect Rem D. Koolhaas, nephew of even more famous Rem Koolhaas (who designed the Prada flagship store), the not-quite wedges are modeled after Mies van der Rohe's iconic Barcelona chair. These exquisitely minimalist shoes deserve to be placed on a pedestal, and look even cooler spinning atop the turntables in the boutique's window. Over a dozen variations, in suede and leather, prints and solid colors, and a new closed-toe model, can be found inside. *unitednude.com* or *terraplana.com*

Moderate   *Amex/MC/V*

Nolita   **(212) 274-9000**
260 Elizabeth Street   btw Houston/Prince
NYC 10012   Mon-Sat 11-7, Sun 12-6

Untitled

Regardless of the store's sign, you find plenty of major-name designers here. Downstairs, peruse the array of sexy, tight-fitting sportswear for women, featuring labels like Juicy Couture and Follies, an excellent selection of denim and hats by Philip Treacy. Scoot upstairs to see how Untitled ups the men's fashion ante with Moschino, Class by Cavalli, Dirk Bikkemberg and Jean Paul Gaultier. Everything you need to cover you from head to toe can be found here—even a small shoe selection.

Expensive *Amex/MC/V*

West Village
26 West Eighth Street
NYC 10011

(212) 505-9725
btw Fifth/Sixth Ave
Mon-Sat 11:30-9, Sun 12-9

Urban Outfitters

Urban Outfitters is the perfect location for a quick fashion fix. Its collegiate-cool clothing and cute pick-me-up accessories (let alone its funky housewares and CD collection) make it worth a pilgrimage. Fast becoming an American classic, the labels here include Bulldog, Lux, Bella Dahl, Lee, Free People, Mooks and Urban Outfitters themselves. Tip 1: if something you like is a little pricey, wait a week or so—it will go on sale for sure. Tip 2: buy, buy, buy the cool printed tank tops—often as low as $4.99. *urbn.com*

Affordable *Amex/MC/V*

Upper West Side
2081 Broadway
NYC 10023

(212) 579-3912
at 72nd St
Mon-Thurs 11-9, Fri-Sat 11-10, Sun 11-8

Chelsea
526 Sixth Avenue
NYC 10011

(646) 638-1646
at 14th St
Mon-Fri 10-9, Sat 10-10, Sun 11-8

East Village
162 Second Avenue
NYC 10002

(212) 375-1277
btw 10/11th St
Mon-Sat 11-10, Sun 11-9

West Village
374 Sixth Avenue
NYC 10011

(212) 677-9350
btw Waverly/Washington Place
Mon-Sat 10-10, Sun 11-8

NoHo
628 Broadway
NYC 10012

(212) 475-0009
btw Bleecker/Houston
Mon-Sat 10-10, Sun 12-8

Midtown East
999 Third Avenue
NYC 10022

(212) 308-1518
btw 59/60th St
Mon-Wed 10-9, Thurs-Sat 10-10, Sun 11-8

Utowa

It means 'universal unity' in Japanese, and Utowa's ideal customer is looking for 'physical and spiritual balance focusing on health and the health of the environment'. If that's you, head on down. The store lets 'the feelings of the season' dictate current design of their products, like army-inspired shirt-jackets and chic button-front minis infused with a trace of Far East style. Utowa also carries a lovely array of beauty products and funky jewelry. *utowa.com*

Moderate *Amex/MC/V*

Chelsea
17 West 18th Street
NYC 10011

(212) 929-4800
btw Fifth/Sixth Ave
Mon-Fri 11-7, Sat 11-6, Sun 12-6
(except in July and August)

Valentino

Valentino is the master of old-school glamour that even the new girls want to wear. He is king of meticulous detailing and beautiful embroidery that is never ostentatious, yet remains fabulously luxurious. And his favorite color? Racy red, of course. For day, Valentino women will find beautiful suits, ruffled and pleated silk shirts paired with simple black pants, mink-edged cashmere cardigans, delicate lace blouses worn with long tweed skirts and saucy leathers. Eveningwear is Oscar-caliber and ranges from black crepe column dresses to jewel-encrusted evening gowns. Men will find smart-looking suits, shirts and Oscar night tuxedos. Prices are over the top, but that's Valentino—and we wouldn't have him any other way.   *valentino.com*

Luxury   *Amex/MC/V*

Upper East Side   **(212) 772-6969**
747 Madison Avenue   at 65th St
NYC 10021   Mon-Sat 10-6 (Thurs 10-7)

Vanessa Noel Boutique

Some call her the 'Queen of Brides' as she stocks a wide selection of bridal heels including her signature Bell shoe, a demure kitten heel with a v-cut front and a darling bow. Also appealing to brides is the comfort factor: she fancies herself a non-overexposed version Jimmy Choo or Manolo Blahnik and, as a woman fully understanding the plight of a night in four-inch heels, makes shoes that stay bearably wearable all night. As a former architect, she designed her shop, which is modern and sleek steel and feminine at once, with plum satin stools and geometric displays.   *vanessanoel.com*

Luxury   *Amex/MC/V*

Upper East Side   **(212) 906-0055**
158 East 64th Street   btw Lexington/Third Ave
NYC 10021   Mon-Sat 10-6

Varda

Italian handmade shoes in one-width sizing and classic designs that make the transition from day to evening as easy as one-two-three. Although the sales staff claim the neutral-colored shoes will fit narrow or wide feet, you will have to be the judge. Prices run from $200 to $550.

Moderate to expensive   *Amex/MC/V*

Upper East Side   **(212) 472-7552**
786 Madison Avenue   btw 66/67th St
NYC 10021   Mon-Sat 10-6:30

Upper West Side   **(212) 873-6910**
2080 Broadway   btw 71/72nd St
NYC 10023   Mon-Sat 10-7:30, Sun 12-7

SoHo   **(212) 941-4990**
147 Spring Street   btw West Broadway/Wooster
NYC 10012   Daily 11-7

SoHo **(212) 343-9575**
118 Spring Street btw Greene/Mercer
NYC 10012 Daily 11-7

Variazioni 👧

Fashionistas who crave the look of Cameron Diaz and Britney Spears will love this chain store for the huge selection of sassy skirts, skimpy tops, hip-hugging jeans and bold accessories from the likes of Diane von Furstenberg, Anna Argiolera, Red Engine and Von Dutch. And with their large and frequently rotating selection of sales items with up to 50% mark downs, Variazioni is sure to keep every girl happy, even those who don't have Justin Timberlake backing the bill. Cameron has her own money, surely?

Moderate *Amex/MC/V*

Upper East Side **(212) 744-9200**
1376 Third Avenue at 78th Street
NYC Mon-Sat 11-8, Sun 12-7

Upper West Side **(212) 595-1760**
2389 Broadway btw 87/88th St
NYC 10024 Mon-Sat 10-8, Sun 11-7

Upper West Side **(212) 595-8800**
2395 Broadway at 88th St
NYC 10024 Daily 10-8

VBH Gallery 👨

The enormous Warhol hanging in the foyer will be the first thing to catch your eye at this new Rome-based emporium of leather goods, 20th-century collectible furnishings and myriad objets d'art, but it certainly won't be the last. Housed in a magnificent three-story engraved concrete building (it used to be a bank), the luxe interior is nearly as impressive as the Whitney Museum down the street. The basement level is even more refined, featuring evening bags and fine jewelry, including signature 18k white gold bands and 'spider orchid' earrings in 18kt white gold with white diamond pavé for $74,000.

Luxury *Amex/MC/V*

Upper East Side **(212) 717-9800**
940 Madison Avenue btw 74/75th St
NYC 10021 Mon-Fri 10:30-7, Sat 10:30-6

★Vera Wang Bridal Salon 👨

Vera Wang has revolutionized the wedding dress, and that has made her collections renowned throughout the world. This heavenly salon will have the bride even more luminous than usual—just ask customers like Sharon Stone and Karenna Gore. Sheer elegance, sophisticated styling and beautiful craftsmanship define a Wang design, from the simple to the elaborate. Also find gorgeous eveningwear, like long beaded column dresses, bias-cut chiffon gowns with hand-sewn details and the perfect amount of beading and ruffles—just like her wedding dresses. Wang also has a complete ready-to-wear collection, featuring skirts and trousers with tidy, narrow waistbands, delicate blouses, chiffon tops, and fine cashmere sweaters. Be sure to check out her new forward-looking jewelry line, too. The flagship salon, located next to the Carlyle Hotel, is truly focused on the individual's needs—a welcome respite for anyone experiencing wedding-bell butterflies. *verawang.com*

Luxury *Amex/MC/V*

Upper East Side **(212) 628-3400**
991 Madison Avenue at 77th St
NYC 10021 Mon-Sat 9:30-6 (Thurs 10:30-7)
(by appointment)

★ Vera Wang Maids on Madison

Across the street from Wang's bridal salon is this store dedicated entirely to bridesmaids. 'The entire bridal party should be as beautiful as the bride,' Wang says. The whole wedding world is here, from dresses, skirts, separates and camisoles, to blouses and sweaters in wonderful shades of champagne, lilac, maize, soft pink and navy. You'll want your friends to get married over and over again.

Luxury *Amex/MC/V*

Upper East Side **(212) 628-9898**
980 Madison Avenue (3rd floor) btw 76/77th St
NYC 10021 Mon-Fri 10-6 (Thurs 11-7), Sat 9-4
(by appointment only)

★ Veronique Maternity

Veronique's expectant-mommy mission: 'To design clothes like the ones you're used to wearing when you're not pregnant.' Now there's an idea. The exclusive collections are imported from Paris and Milan and emphasize comfort, fit and fashionability. Looks include flat-front pants and Ultrasuede jackets by labels like Chaiken and Cadeau. Expensive, but worth it. *veroniquematernity.com*

Expensive *Amex/MC/V*

Upper East Side **(212) 831-7800**
1321 Madison Avenue at 93rd St
NYC 10021 Mon-Thurs 10-7, Fri-Sat 10-6, Sun 12-5
(except in July and August)

★ Versace

Viva Versace! Flashy and fearless, the Milanese label—from Gianni to Donatella—takes sex by the horns (or was that the heels?). The powerhouse that is Versace continues to fuse the worlds of fashion, royalty and music, earning Donatella the sobriquet 'rock 'n' roll designer'. These clothes are for vixens (or Elizabeth Hurley) who want to feel young, sexy and be noticed—kinetic, kaleidoscope prints, biker leathers and skinny silhouettes. Find ready-to-wear, sportswear, glam-slam couture, racy eveningwear, a collection of home furnishings fit for Cleopatra, and a world of accessories (Medusa-head bathrobe, anyone?). Sin is in. *versace.com*

Luxury *Amex/MC/V*

Fifth Avenue **(212) 317-0224**
647 Fifth Avenue btw 51/52nd St
NYC 10022 Mon-Sat 10-6:30, Sun 12-6

Vertigo and Friends/Magaschoni

These two connecting shops, carrying mostly the namesake labels, are ideal for mother-daughter shopping teams. Vertigo carries more mature clothes, including suits, while retaining a funky edge; Magaschoni is trendier and younger with lots of cashmere. Both brands provide luxurious adaptations of current trends. The space itself is particularly lovely, with bright sparkling chandeliers, fitting rooms lined with flowered wallpaper, sconces and velvet stools, and huge antique looking glasses. Also available are Antik Denim, fine jewelry by Michelle Lynn of Great Neck, and affordable 100% cotton hoodies and tank tops.

Moderate to expensive *Amex/MC/V*
Midtown East **(212) 935-7071**
36 East 60th Street btw Park/Madison Ave
NYC 10022 Mon-Sat 10:30-6:30

Verve Shoes

A West Village accessories shop that includes extras from Cynthia Rowley, Kazuyo Nakano, Santi, Lola, Nancy Nancy and IXOS. There are over 125 different lines in this tiny shop, from handbag and hat styles to sunglasses, jewelry and watches. Handbags include leather day bags and beaded purses, while the hat selection stretches all the way from the street to the beach.

Expensive *Amex/MC/V*
West Village **(212) 675-6693**
338 Bleecker Street btw Christopher/West 10th St
NYC 10014 Mon-Sat 11-8, Sun 12-6

★ Via Bus Stop

The first US branch of this Japanese emporium is a veritable supermarket of esoteric designers from around the globe. In this massive two-story shop, divided by tall gray drapes, you'll find Viktor & Rolf jackets fastened by sailor knots, Hussein Chalayan cropped blazers and pajama top dresses, Johanna Ho asymmetrical shrug capelets in dusty-colored soft knit, ornate beaded and ruffled pieces by Easton Pearson, and Bernhard Willheim's paisley brass-buttoned minidresses and bizarre cutout patterned stretch pants. The baubles are completely over the top, too: a necklace/bracelet/belt hybrid made of a cotton strap studded with daubs of bright plastic and necklaces with cartoonish dangling charms. *viabusstop.com*

Luxury *Amex/MC/V*
SoHo **(212) 343-8810**
172 Mercer Street at East Houston
NYC 10012 Mon-Sat 11-7, Sun 12-6

Via Spiga

Offering just about every shoe for every occasion, this Italian footwear company steps from knee-high suede boots with very high heels to the most sensible of slip-ons. Lucite slingbacks and open-toed pastel polka-dot numbers rest easily alongside more modest beige clogs and espadrilles. Via Spiga also offers a small sampling of men's shoes, as well as watches, sunglasses and playful bags with bow-tie handles. *viaspiga.com*

Moderate *Amex/MC/V*

Upper East Side **(212) 871-9955**
692 Madison Avenue btw 62/63rd St
NYC 10021 Mon-Sat 10-7, Sun 12-6

SoHo **(212) 431-7007**
390 West Broadway btw Spring/Broome
NYC 10013 Mon-Sat 11-7, Sun 12-6

Vice

This hip outpost, an offshoot of the Canadian music magazine of the same name, carries a mix of American and British designers for men and women. Look for unique one-offs like ruffled tank sundresses, zippered minidresses and windbreakers with shark designs on the back by You Must Create (YMC), and tops by Putsch. Also very cool athletic-inspired looks, like a pink tracksuit skirt with ruffles and 'Religion' stitched on the side. *viceland.com*

Moderate *Amex/MC/V*

Nolita **(212) 219-7788**
252 Lafayette Street btw Prince/Spring
NYC 10012 Mon-Sat 12-7, Sun 12-6

Victoria Keen

By handpainting and silk-screening vibrant, abstract, psychedelic patterns onto her clothing, accessories, and home furnishings, Victoria Keen extends her craft into wearable art. Tops, skirts, dresses, bags, sofas, chairs—each piece is unique and made from fine fabrics. Explore the store's three levels, with home furnishings in the basement and an art gallery in the sub-basement. Coming soon: menswear. *victoriakeen.com*

Moderate *Amex/MC/V*

Nolita **(212) 473-1412**
357 Lafayette Street btw Bond/Bleecker
NYC 10012 Daily 11-8

Victoria's Secret

All you can see is curves, don't you know. Well, Gisele's curves mostly, but there's hope here for the rest of us mortals too. Kudos to this lingerie power brand, which markets romance and allure at totally reasonable prices. Find short, sexy, baby-doll teddies, racy black garters and stockings, bustiers, lots of bras (plain or lacy and embellished), the best seamless thongs and sleepwear and slinky accessories in bright colors and soft feminine prints. Visit the new mega-mega store on Herald Square and thank God Victoria shared her secret. *800-888-1500 victoriassecret.com*

Affordable   *Amex/MC/V*

Upper East Side   **(212) 717-7035**
1240 Third Avenue   at 72nd St
NYC 10021   Mon-Sat 10-8, Sun 12-6

Upper East Side   **(646) 672-9183**
165 East 86th Street   btw Lexington/Third Ave
NYC 10028   Mon-Sat 10-9, Sun 11-7

Upper West Side   **(646) 505-2280**
1981 Broadway   at 67th St
NYC 10023   (opening hours as above)

Midtown East   **(212) 758-5592**
34 East 57th Street   btw Madison/Park Ave
NYC 10022   Mon-Sat 10-8, Sun 12-7

Midtown West   **(646) 473-0950**
901 Sixth Avenue   btw 32/33rd St
NYC 10001   Mon-Sat 10-8, Sun 11-6

Herald Square   **(212) 356-8380**
1328 Broadway   at 35th St
NYC 10001   Mon-Sat 10-9, Sun 11-7

Flatiron   **(212) 477-4118**
115 Fifth Avenue   btw 19/20th St
NYC 10011   Mon-Sat 10-8, Sun 12-6

SoHo   **(212) 274-9519**
565 Broadway   at Prince
NYC 10012   Mon-Sat 10-9, Sun 11-7

Lower Manhattan   **(212) 962-8122**
19 Fulton Street   Pier 17, South Street Seaport
NYC 10038   Mon-Sat 10-9, Sun 11-8

Vilebrequin   ♂♂

Who knew you could make an entire store around men's swimsuits? This French store sells cute father-son swim trunks in snappy prints like butterflies and pears—perfect for that Kodak moment. Suits come in four lengths with a variety of manly accessories such as towels, sarongs, sunglasses and baseball hats. From classic drawstring styles to surfer trunks, you and your little buddy will own the beaches. Pay $75-125 for men's or boys. From six months to adult. *vilebrequin.com*

Moderate to expensive   *Amex/MC/V*

Upper East Side   **(212) 650-0353**
1070 Madison Avenue   at 82nd St
NYC 10028   Mon-Sat 10-7, Sun 10-6

SoHo   **(212) 431-0673**
436 West Broadway   btw Prince/Spring
NYC 10012   Mon-Sat 11-8, Sun 11-7

Village Scandal

Hedda Hopper rising? Perhaps not, but vintage addicts will love the selection of retro pieces at this cool East Village store. Boxes of hats are artfully arranged along the top shelves—from pleather rain hats in a floppy old-school Hollywood style to currently trendy newsboys and bucket caps. Though it's really a hat store, there is also a fab selection of look-at-me handbags. The best bits? It's open until midnight, and it offers 10% off to students. Scandalous.

Moderate   *Amex/MC/V*

East Village   **(212) 460-9358**
19 East 7th Street   btw Second/Third Ave
NYC 10003   Mon-Thurs 12-12, Fri-Sat 12-1:30, Sun 1-12

Vincent and Edgar

There is Lobb, there is Cleverley—and then there is Vincent and Edgar. V & E is New York's finest custom-made shoe establishment. Shoemaker Roman Vaingauz can labor for 40 hours to produce a single pair of his bespoke shoes. Men's shoes start at $2,700 and women's at $2,100, with an additional $675 for a pair of wooden shoe lasts. Five to six months for delivery.

Luxury   *Amex/MC/V*

Upper East Side   **(212) 753-3461**
972 Lexington Avenue   at 71st St
NYC 10021   Mon-Fri 10-5 (by appointment only)

Vincent Nicolosi

A high-end tailor of classic bespoke suits for chairman-of-the-board types. Expect six-to-eight-week delivery, but they will rush an order if necessary. What they will not do is quote you prices over the phone—it's better that you make an appointment, and see for yourself.

Luxury   *(cash only)*

Midtown East   **(212) 486-6214**
510 Madison Avenue   at 53rd St
NYC 10022   Mon-Fri 10-6, Sat 10-5

Vitraux

Better than your average bling. Vitraux by Alejandra's jewelry designs are sold in high-end department stores like Bendel's and Saks, and pictures of celebs like Beyoncé and Christina wearing her pieces line the walls of this SoHo boutique. It's easy to understand the appeal of pieces like her turquoise and sterling-silver lariat choker—it's elegant, full of color, and brimming with personality and versatility...jewelry that perfectly complements any outfit, no matter how casual or dressy.   *877-388-2907 vitrauxstore.com*

Expensive   *Amex/MC/V*

SoHo   **(212) 925-8259**
72 Thompson Street   btw Spring/Broome
NYC 10012   Sun-Wed 11-7, Thurs-Sat 10:30-7:30

Vivienne Tam

New York style stalwart Vivienne Tam says her pieces take on a new feeling with each person. 'Once I put an idea on cloth, that cloth becomes a garment,' she says, 'and when somebody wears it, the garment comes to life.' She applies her signature arty, crafty, East-meets-West style to her collection of sheer floral dresses, embroidered skirts, jackets, printed nylon mesh tops and separates, many with delicate beading (reminiscent of Chinese art) and embroidery. *viviennetam.com*

Moderate   *Amex/MC/V*

SoHo   **(212) 966-2398**
99 Greene Street   btw Prince/Spring
NYC 10012   Mon-Fri 12-7, Sat 12-7:30, Sun 12-6:30

Viv Pickle

DIY design at its best—you dream up the handbag, they do all the work, and everything is under $100. At Viv Pickle, choose a shape, pick out fabric, handle and lining, and the staff will custom-create your handbag on the premises. You can be as creative or conservative as you like—the look is all your own. If you can't make it to the store, shop online or gather all your friends and have a Pickle Party in your own home. Really. *vivpickle.com*

Moderate   *Amex/MC/V*

West Village   **(212) 924-0444**
238 West 10th Street   at Bleecker/Hudson
NYC 10014   Wed-Sun 12-7

Vlada

Vlada has done stints at both Donna Karan and Chanel, but her own clothing passions have a vintage bent—from the Sixties to the Eighties, especially. For rock 'n' roll style (especially of the Studio 54 bent) start here, where the eclectic items range from sheer ponchos (think Halston) to the hipster-requisite military-inspired jackets. Also find flowing jersey dresses, silk-screened tops and a great shoe selection.

Expensive   *Amex/MC/V*

Lower East Side   **(212) 387-7767**
101 Stanton Street   at Ludlow
NYC 10002   Mon-Sat 12-8, Sun 12-7

Walter Steiger

Walter Steiger is one of the founding members of the shoe establishment: in a word, quality. Known for unusual heel shapes, Steiger offers a range of feminine styles, including sexy stilettos, mid-heeled pumps, platforms, sandals, loafers and even a treaded walking shoe (best, though, are their two-toned golf shoes). Men's shoes feature pointy or round-toed loafers and sleek sneakers. *walter-steiger.com*

Expensive   *Amex/MC/V*

Midtown East
417 Park Avenue
NYC 10022

(212) 826-7171
at 55th St
Mon-Sat 10-6

Warehouse 🕴

Trendy and seasonal, Warehouse is Britain's street label known for hot gear for the 18-35 crowd (leaning more towards the younger end, though). Stylish and very 'today', but not necessarily 'next week', the store is filled with basic tops, jeans, skirts, jackets, pants, suits and fun accessories.

Moderate   *Amex/MC/V*

SoHo
581 Broadway
NYC 10012

(212) 941-0910
btw Houston/Prince
Mon-Wed 10-8, Thurs-Sat 10-9, Sun 11-7

Warren Edwards 🕴

Great, stylish footwear from hand-stitched suede loafers and buttery leather boots to glamorous evening pumps and comfortable, plush moccasins. All the looks are feminine and attractive and the sales staff are pleasant. *warrenedwards.com*

Expensive   *Amex/MC/V*

Upper East Side
107 East 60th Street
NYC 10022

(212) 223-4374
btw Park/Lexington Ave
Mon-Sat 10-5:45

Watts 🕴

Watts specializes in contemporary and vintage apparel and accessories for men. Already host to labels such as Ben Sherman, Fred Perry and Penguin, Watts earns even more cool points by decorating their shop with Seventies memorabilia like lunchboxes. At Watts, dressing up doesn't mean taking oneself too seriously. Mixing chic sportswear with outlandish ties (check out the cravat decorated with a picture of an Uzi), Watts presents preppy looks with a laugh. *wattsonsmith.com*

Moderate   *Amex/MC/V*

Cobble Hill
248 Smith Street
Brooklyn 11231

(718) 596-2359
btw Douglass/Degraw
Tues-Sat 12-7, Sun 12-6

Western Spirit 🕴🕴🕴

Yee Haw! One does not need to be a Texan to dress like a cowboy, as the staff at New York's largest western store would be the first to tell you. Rustle up some gear—boots and moccasins galore, sharp hats, belt buckles and pearl-buttoned shirts are just some of the items to be found here. Men, women, and children can troll through three stories of clothing from Montana, Stetson, Akubra, Renegade and Charlie 1 Horse. Saddle up. *westernspiritnyc.com*

Moderate   *Amex/MC/V*

SoHo
395 Broadway
486 Broadway
NYC 10013

(212) 343-1476
at Walker
at Broome
Daily 10:30-7:30

East Village   **(212) 353-1186**
803 Broadway   at 11th St
NYC 10003   Daily 10:30-7:30

Midtown East   **(212) 688-5565**
686 Lexington Avenue   at 56th St
NYC 10022   Daily 10:30-7:30

Wet Seal

This California-based clothing company markets inexpensive, ultra-hip clothing for the junior set, and now that the store's layout has been overhauled it is easier to shop for everything from jeans, T-shirts and clubwear to underwear, sleepwear and accessories. Wet seal also carries plenty of sexy, tight-fitting little numbers for girls looking to grin-and-bare it.   *wetseal.com*

Affordable   *Amex/MC/V*

NoHo   **(212) 253-2470**
670 Broadway   at Bond
NYC 10012   Mon-Sat 10-9, Sun 12-7

Midtown West   **(212) 216-0622**
901 Sixth Avenue   at Herald Square
NYC 10001   Mon-Sat 10-8, Sun 11-6

What Comes Around Goes Around

…and indeed it does, about every five years. This vintage boutique sells its recycled wares to stylists, celebs and fashionistas citywide. The collection includes everything from Victorian tops to Thirties ballgowns, Sixties Pucci, Seventies Cacharel…you get the idea. Also head here for Hawaiian shirts, retro shoes and must-have military jackets. Sales staff are knowledgeable and eager to please.   *nyvintage.com*

Moderate   *Amex/MC/V*

SoHo   **(212) 343-9303**
351 West Broadway   btw Broome/Grand
NYC 10013   Mon-Sat 11-8, Sun 12-7

Whiskey Dust

Willie Nelson plays softly in this emporium with a huge selection of just about everything western (apart from whiskey and a poker game): bandanas, badges, barrels, belts, bolo ties, boots, buckles, bull whips—not to mention cowboy clothes not starting with 'b' are available for sale, or even rent. 'Go west without leaving New York' is Whiskey Dust's promise, and with an impressive collection of T-shirts, chaps and holsters, you'll be the John Wayne of the West Village, cowboy.   *whiskeydust.com*

Moderate   *Amex/MC/V*

West Village   **(212) 691-5576**
526 Hudson Street   btw West 10th/Charles
NYC 10014   Mon-Sat 12:30-7, Sun 1-6

The Wicker Garden

If you ever have a craving to see a perfectly decorated nursery, indulge it with a trip to Pamela Scurry's Wicker Garden.

You'll find spotless white wicker bookcases and hampers, crystal-knobbed, handpainted dressers, and sterling-silver frames and crocheted pillows for those shoppers carrying a black Amex. Rocking gliders start at $1,195, with matching ottomans for $650, and you can have custom upholstery made from 1,000 different fabrics. Don't miss the beautifully kitschy handpainted, nearly seven-feet-tall dollhouse armoire, which retails for $3,950 and seems straight out of Mommy Dearest. And what's all this to do with a fashion directory? They also have the most adorable children's clothes.

Luxury   *Amex/MC/V*

Upper East Side   **(212) 410-7001**
1300 Madison Avenue   btw 92/93rd St
NYC 10128   Mon-Sat 10-6

William Fioravanti

Descended from a long line of Neapolitan tailors, Fioravanti sets the standard for custom-made clothes. He has a waiting list just to get an appointment, but once you've got a foot in the door you're in for a sartorial treat. Choose from luxurious English and Italian fabrics and customize a suit, shirt or topcoat. Suits start at $5,000, and you should expect a two-month delivery.   *williamfioravanti.com*

Luxury   *Amex/MC/V*

Midtown West   **(212) 355-1540**
45 West 57th Street   btw Fifth/Sixth Avenue
NYC 10019   Mon-Fri 9-5 (by appointment)

Wolford Boutique

Long considered the Rolls-Royce of hosiery, Wolford is the ultimate provider of novelty hose, sheers, thigh-highs, opaques and knee-highs in colors running from cute to kinky. For the silkiest sheers, ask for the Aura 5 Collection and for a great run-resistant microfiber hose ask for their best-selling Individual 10. It's also the place for killer bodysuits, swimwear and, surprisingly, men's socks. *wolford.com*

Luxury   *Amex/MC/V*

Upper East Side   **(212) 327-1000**
996 Madison Avenue   btw 77/78th St
NYC 10021   Mon-Sat 10-6

Midtown East   **(212) 688-4850**
619 Madison Avenue   btw 58/59th St
NYC 10022   Mon-Sat 10-6

SoHo   **(212) 343-0808**
122 Greene Street   at Prince
NYC 10012   Mon-Sat 11-7, Sun 12-6

Work In Progress

Regardless of its name, Work In Progress seems to have reached its goal of stocking its shelves with every hot little number a sexy girl could desire. Boasting a large jean section, tasty skirts, fabulous tops and hip T-shirts, the clothing selection is fierce and varied. Hip-hop and dance beats blare as young shoppers sort through all the hot gear, which includes a wide selection of Miss Sixty apparel. Shoes are displayed in the middle of the shop, surrounded by a cheeky selection of accessories, books, gifts and other fun goodies. *wipsoho.com*

Moderate *Amex/MC/V*

SoHo **(212) 343-2577**
513 Broadway btw Broome/Spring
NYC 10012 Mon-Sat 10-9, Sun 11-8

SoHo **(212) 334-4380**
481 Broadway btw Broome/Grand
NYC 10012 Mon-Sat 10-9, Sun 11-8

The World of Golf

This small store sells an enormous volume of golf equipment, including top names like Callaway, Cobra, Ping and Taylor Made. The new downtown branch offers an even larger stock of equipment, plus a broad choice of designer golf apparel by Polo, Burberry, Nike and more. Friendly and knowledgeable staff. *800-499-7491 theworldofgolf.com*

Moderate *Amex/MC/V*

Midtown East **(212) 755-9398**
147 East 47th Street btw Lexington/Third Ave
NYC 10017 Mon-Sat 9-7, Sun 11-5

X Girl

Kim Gordon of Sonic Youth fame knows a thing or two about clothes for riot grrrrls. She started this streetwear line for trendy rockers, who feast on Gordon's groovy selection of T-shirts, snazzy pants, swimwear, embroidered tops and glorious accessories like studded vinyl belts. Be sure to pick up the newest addition to X Girl's inventory—too-cute Me, Myself & I pieces by German designer Katrin Wiens. *xgirlusa.com*

Moderate *Amex/MC/V*

Nolita **(212) 343-2457**
265 Lafayette Street btw Prince/Spring
NYC 10012 Mon-Sat 12-7, Sun 12-6

Y & Kei Water The Earth

Yes, it is a spectacularly odd name, but these designers' intentions are pure; if not exactly watering the earth, they do a fine job of dressing its inhabitants. The husband and wife team of Y (Hanii Y) and Kei (Gene Kei) spirit up feminine pieces like ruffled shirts with tulle detail in all colors from lemon to black, also deconstructed denim jeans, shoes and boho belts. Best bets in this bright, airy store are the pant suits, knockout flapper dresses and accessories. *yandkei.com*

Expensive *Amex/MC/V*

SoHo **(212) 477-7778**
125 Greene Street btw Prince/Spring
NYC 10012 Mon-Sat 11-7, Sun 12-6

Yaso

Turkish owner Janan Tomko is very proactive, launching the careers of many design talents from Europe and L.A.. The large selection here includes labels like Punch, Michael Stars, Belgium's Just in Case, Twin Set, Catalaque, Krista Larson and the Yaso Pazo vintage private label. Then there are the absolutely, positively vital dog carriers for your pooch by Emre NY.

Expensive   *Amex/MC/V*

SoHo   **(212) 941-8506**
62 Grand Street   btw West Broadway/Wooster
NYC 10012   Daily 11-7

Yellow Rat Bastard

Since causing an animal rights frenzy when it opened in 1996 by placing scurrying rats in the display window, this men's boutique has morphed into an urban legend that now houses a women's collection, dormwear and a quarterly magazine. YRB's key to longevity is its innate sense of what's right now, which means that cargo pants by Liv-N-Large and crocheted skullcaps can be found next to smart dress shirts by Ben Sherman.   *yellowratbastard.com*

Amex/MC/V   *Affordable*

SoHo   **(212) 334-2150**
478 Broadway   btw Broome/Grand
NYC 10013   Daily 10-8:30 (Sun 10-7:30)

Yigal Azrouel

Theatrical lighting, black-gray concrete floors, deep red brick walls and a single Victorian-style antique couch create the dramatic effect in Azrouel's store, all the better to high-light the Israel-born, French-Moroccan designer's gauzy flo-ral skirts, sexy clingy tops in dusty pinks, electric blues and yellows and stop-in-your tracks eveningwear. Azrouel has managed to attract downtown types while catering to a more mature crowd who won't flinch at the site of a $300 shirt. The store also has a few candles, bath beads and room sprays to add to the allure.   *yigal-azrouel.com*

Luxury   *Amex/MC/V*

Chelsea   **(212) 929 7525**
408 West 14th Street   at Ninth Ave
NYC 10014   Mon-Sat 11-7, Sun 12:30-6

★ Yohji Yamamoto

Yohji Yamamoto's designs are complex (he frequently uses tricky draping, ruching and folding), his color palette strong and stark, and his collections inventive, never trendy. Known for his sexy gabardine suits and sharp dress-es, Yamamoto has also been innovative with sportswear (those polyester jogging pants are wonderful), pairing dressed-down designs with more sophisticated pieces. Loose-fitting yet wildly creative, his new collection for men demands attention with its integration of historical and modern looks (the emperor's new clothes apparently include leather), while the women's line uses layers, angles and roomy twists and turns with fabric to create truly breathtaking clothes. *yohjiyamamoto.co.jp*

Expensive *Amex/MC/V*

SoHo **(212) 966-9066**
103 Grand Street at Mercer
NYC 10013 Mon-Sat 11-7, Sun 12-6

Young's Hat Corner

Gentlemen (and younger), look no further than Young's Hat Corner for casual and dressy styles. This shop has plenty of haberdashery history under its belt, having catered to male hat lovers since 1890, and offers a grand selection of fancy toppers, English caps, baseball and straw hats. A warning: call on Friday afternoon to make sure they'll be open on Saturday. *hats-capsonline.com*

Moderate *Amex/MC/V*

Lower Manhattan **(212) 964-5693**
139 Nassau Street at Beekman
NYC 10038 Mon-Fri 9-5:30, Sat 10:30-3:30

★ Yoya

Only the best for baby at this tiny West Village boutique: kid-friendly organic bath products, extra-soft North African blankets that can be worn as a wrap by Mom, Yoya's own cool crocheted sweaters, boys' check shirts and India-inspired embroidered pullover tops. Brands include European designers like Quincy, Petit Bateau and Bonpoint. The two fashionable matrons who own and run Yoya even had the forethought to provide a sliding-panel changing-room with a diaper table in the back. For older children, check out the sister store, Yoyamart, which has clothes for the 2-12 set, as well as gadgets and toys cool enough for the hip young things in this neighborhood. *yoyashop.com*

Moderate *Amex/MC/V*

West Village **(646) 336-6844**
636 Hudson Street at Horatio
NYC 10014 Mon-Sat 11-7

West Village **(212) 242-5511**
15 Gansevoort (Yoyamart) at Hudson
NYC 10014 Mon-Sat 11-7 Sun 12-6

★ Yves Saint Laurent Rive Gauche

Dozens of surprisingly friendly black-suited staff are ready to serve at the sleekest YSL store, where you'll find chic sunglasses, perfumes, watches and handbags amidst two floors of Stefano Pilati's dazzling designs. Shiny black walls and shelves show off chic gear for fashion-forward guys, while au courant women take notice of clean lines and classic silhouettes. *ysl.com*

Luxury *Amex/MC/V*

Midtown East
3 East 57th Street
NYC 10022

(212) 980-2970
btw Fifth/Madison Ave
Mon-Fri 10-7, Sat 10-6, Sun 12-5

Upper East Side
855 Madison Avenue
NYC 10021

(212) 988-3821
btw 70/71st St
Mon-Sat 10-6
(Thurs 10-7)

Yvone Christa

Hollywood's It-girls are big fans of the cool handbags and ethnic-inspired jewelry from this girly, white-curtained store. Bags come in all shapes, colors, sizes and textures—the tapestry sewing bags are particularly cute—but are primarily for evening; priced from $50 to $500. There also is a vast selection of delicate, flirty jewelry for L.A. babes (or their East Coast sisters). *yvonechrista.com*

Moderate   *Amex/MC/V*

SoHo
107 Mercer Street
NYC 10012

(212) 965-1001
btw Prince/Spring
Mon-Sat 12-7, Sun 12-6

Zabari

Zabari will take a trend and run with it—translation, it's perfect for teenagers. This bright, cavernous store stocks all the latest looks, from capri pants and skimpy tops to slip dresses, jeans and jackets. Zabari's bright fabrics look great from a distance but feel a leetle flimsy up close. Best buys are their hip, colorful knickers and fun handbags. Labels include Alice & Trixie, Zabari, Plenty and Anna Kuan.   *zabari.com*

Affordable   *Amex/MC/V*

SoHo
506 Broadway
NYC 10012

(212) 431-7502
btw Spring/Broome
Daily 11-8

SoHo
542 Broadway
NYC 10012

(212) 966-4470
btw Prince/Spring
Daily 11-8

Zan

These spacious boutiques with their stark white shop fittings and diverse collections including suiting, sportswear, leather pieces and formalwear, would be right at home in an upscale suburban mall. Flirty pieces by Cynthia Steffe, Trina Turk and Cultura attract the younger, time-share set, while women with more classic tastes appreciate the well-made, affordable careerwear by French label Tehen.

Moderate   *Amex/MC/V*

Midtown West
1666 Broadway
NYC 10019

(212) 582-5580
btw 51/52nd St
Mon-Sat 9:30-9, Sun 11-7

Upper West Side
2394 Broadway
NYC 10024

(212) 877-4853
btw 87/88th St
Mon-Sat 10-8:30, Sun 11-6:30

Zara

This super-cool Spanish chain is taking over the globe with strikingly accurate interpretations of current designer looks. Find everything from Marc Jacobs-inspired tops and skirts to near-replications of Chanel's tweed suits and bags. Young professionals head here for smart suits, basic shirts, sweaters and coats (some for a bargain $160) for work, while clubbier types can indulge themselves with colored Lycra halters and super-tight jeans. The company has recently added footwear: Prada Sport-meets-Diesel sneaks for men and strappy *Sex and the City* stilettos for women; the quality of materials and construction, however, leaves something to be desired. *zara.com*

Moderate *Amex/MC/V*

Midtown East **(212) 754-1120**
750 Lexington Avenue at 59th St
NYC 10022 Mon-Sat 10-8, Sun 12-7

Midtown West **(212) 868-6551**
39 West 34th Street btw Fifth/Sixth Ave
NYC 10001 Mon-Sat 10-8:30, Sun 12-7

Fifth Avenue **(212) 371-2555**
689 Fifth Avenue at 54th St
NYC 10022 Mon-Sat 10-8, Sun 11-7

Flatiron **(212) 741-0555**
101 Fifth Avenue btw 17/18th St
NYC 10003 Mon-Sat 10-8, Sun 10-7

SoHo **(212) 343-1725**
580 Broadway at Prince
NYC 10012 Mon-Sat 10-8, Sun 12-7

★ Z'baby

The sign behind the cash register says 'Your husband called... he said buy anything you want', and you'll want to when you see the European and domestic duds from Magill B. Kids, Valeria Blue, Blumarine and D&G. Just as cool for boys as it's cute for girls. *zbabycompany.com*

Moderate *Amex/MC/V*

Upper East Side **(212) 472-2229**
996 Lexington Avenue at 72nd St
NYC 10021 Mon-Sat 10-7, Sun 11:30-5

Upper West Side **(212) 579-2229**
100 West 72nd Street at Columbus Ave
NYC 10023 Mon-Sat 10:30-7:30, Sun 11-6

Zeller Tuxedo

Rent or purchase men's formalwear here from a good selection of designer names. Oscar de la Renta and Loro Piana are available for rentals, and you can buy such well-known high-profile lines as Calvin Klein and Joseph Abboud, as well as less expensive brands. Rental prices start at $135, while buying runs from $400 to $1,000. Shirts and black tie accessories available. *zellertuxedo.com*

Moderate to expensive *Amex/MC/V*

Upper East Side   **(212) 688-0100**
1010 Third Avenue (2nd floor)   btw 60/61st St
NYC 10021   Mon-Fri 9-6:30, Sat 10-5:30, Sun 11-4

Midtown East   **(212) 286-9786**
459 Lexington Avenue   at 45th St
NYC 10017   Mon-Fri 9-6:30, Sat 10-5:30

Midtown West   **(212) 290-0217**
421 Seventh Avenue   at 33rd St
NYC 10001   Mon-Fri 9-7, Sat 10-6

Flatiron   **(212) 532-7320**
201 East 23rd Street (2nd floor)   at Third Ave
NYC 10010   Mon-Sat 9-6:30, Sat 10-5

Zero/Maria Cornejo

Actresses, models (lots of models), 20-year-olds and, yes, 60-year-olds are all among the women who shop here. Designer Maria Cornejo's strength is in subtle, geometric clothes. Case in point: the bubble dress, in lace or viscose jersey, which echoes the spirit of the op-art Sixties and could be carried off by the right playful fashion plate either downtown or at the beach – it's a little bit young Cher with a twist of St Tropez. The sophisticated silk charmeuse Oyebo dress was made for tangoing, with the fabric forming most tasteful and sexy cutouts surrounding the bust and swishing seductively below the knee.   *mariacornejo.com*

Moderate   *Amex/MC/V*

Nolita   **(212) 925-3849**
225 Mott Street   btw Prince/Spring
NYC 10012   Daily 12:30-7:30

Zion

Sylvia Lee Zion's wonderful little shop is filled with sophisticated apparel for women, including a wide range of sharp suits and dresses. Attentive shoppers will appreciate the delicate tailoring, colors and patterns helping to build Zion's burgeoning following.   *zionny.com*

Moderate   *Amex/MC/V*

SoHo   **(212) 226-7917**
93 Grand Street   btw Greene/Mercer
NYC 10013   Mon-Sat 11-7

Zitomer

A mini department store—with crazy themed windows—boasting three floors of shopping for everything from beauty to toys. The main floor is home to every beauty, bath and health product imaginable. The second and third have the children's clothing and the toy department. And they will even cater to your pet's needs with their pet shop one door down.   *zitomer.com*

Affordable to expensive   *Amex/MC/V*

Upper East Side   **(212) 737-4480**
969 Madison Avenue   btw 75/76th St
NYC 10021   Mon-Fri 9-8, Sat 9-7, Sun 10-6

Midtown West
40 West 57th Street
NYC 10019

(212) 956-6000
btw Fifth/Sixth Ave
Mon-Fri 8-8, Sat 9-7, Sun 10-6

Zora

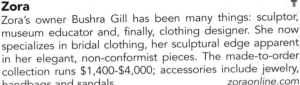

Zora's owner Bushra Gill has been many things: sculptor, museum educator and, finally, clothing designer. She now specializes in bridal clothing, her sculptural edge apparent in her elegant, non-conformist pieces. The made-to-order collection runs $1,400-$4,000; accessories include jewelry, handbags and sandals. *zoraonline.com*

Expensive   *Amex/MC/V*

Midtown West
55 West 45th Street (4th floor)
NYC 10036   Tues-Fri 10-6, Sat 12-4 (by appointment only)

(212) 840-7040
btw Fifth/Sixth Ave

Stores by Neighborhood

Harlem

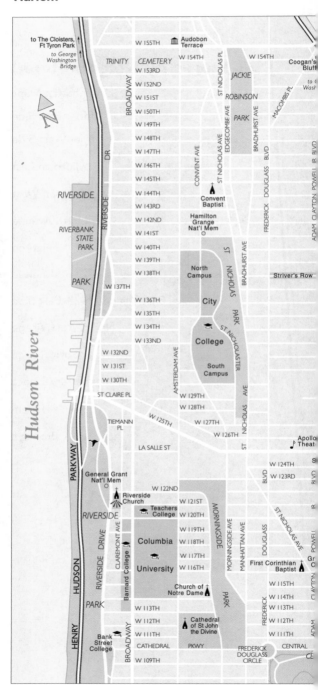

to The Cloisters, Ft Tyron Park

to George Washington Bridge

TRINITY CEMETERY

W 155TH
W 154TH
W 153RD
W 152ND
W 151ST
W 150TH
W 149TH
W 148TH
W 147TH
W 146TH
W 145TH
W 144TH
W 143RD
W 142ND
W 141ST
W 140TH
W 139TH
W 138TH
W 137TH
W 136TH
W 135TH
W 134TH
W 133RD
W 132ND
W 131ST
W 130TH

Audobon Terrace

W 154TH

JACKIE ROBINSON PARK

Coogan's Bluff

to Wash

BROADWAY

DR

RIVERSIDE

RIVERSIDE

RIVERBANK STATE PARK

PARK

Hudson River

CONVENT AVE

ST NICHOLAS PL

EDGECOMBE AVE

BRADHURST AVE

MACOMBS PL

FREDERICK DOUGLASS BLVD

ADAM CLAYTON POWELL JR BLVD

Convent Baptist

Hamilton Grange Nat'l Mem

North Campus

City

College

South Campus

ST NICHOLAS PARK

BRADHURST AVE

Striver's Row

AMSTERDAM AVE

ST NICHOLAS AVE

ST CLAIRE PL

TIEMANN PL

W 125TH

LA SALLE ST

PARKWAY

General Grant Nat'l Mem

Riverside Church

Teachers College

RIVERSIDE

CLAREMONT AVE

Barnard College

RIVERSIDE DRIVE

Columbia

University

W 129TH
W 128TH
W 127TH
W 126TH

W 124TH
W 123RD

Apollo Theat

BLVD

DOUGLASS

ST NICHOLAS AVE

POWELL

First Corinthian Baptist

W 122ND
W 121ST
W 120TH
W 119TH
W 118TH
W 117TH
W 116TH
W 115TH
W 114TH
W 113TH
W 112TH
W 111TH

MORNINGSIDE AVE

MANHATTAN AVE

MORNINGSIDE PARK

FREDERICK DOUGLASS

ADAM CLAYTON

CENTRAL

Church of Notre Dame

Cathedral of St John the Divine

Bank Street College

HUDSON

HENRY

PARK

BROADWAY

CATHEDRAL

CATHEDRAL PKWY

W 109TH

FREDERICK DOUGLASS CIRCLE

Gr

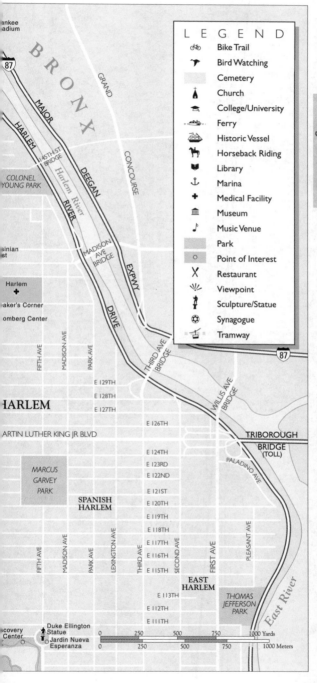

East Harlem, Spanish Harlem

L E G E N D

- Bike Trail
- Bird Watching
- Cemetery
- Church
- College/University
- Ferry
- Historic Vessel
- Horseback Riding
- Library
- Marina
- Medical Facility
- Museum
- Music Venue
- Park
- Point of Interest
- Restaurant
- Viewpoint
- Sculpture/Statue
- Synagogue
- Tramway

Neighborhoods

Yankee Stadium

BRONX

87

MAJOR

HARLEM

145TH ST BRIDGE

GRAND

CONCOURSE

Harlem River

DEEGAN

COLONEL YOUNG PARK

MADISON AVE BRIDGE

EXPWY

DRIVE

sinian st

Harlem

aker's Corner

omberg Center

FIFTH AVE

MADISON AVE

PARK AVE

THIRD AVE BRIDGE

87

HARLEM

E 129TH

E 128TH

E 127TH

WILLIS AVE BRIDGE

E 126TH

TRIBOROUGH

ARTIN LUTHER KING JR BLVD

BRIDGE (TOLL)

E 124TH

PALADINO AVE

MARCUS GARVEY PARK

E 123RD

E 122ND

SPANISH HARLEM

E 121ST

E 120TH

E 119TH

E 118TH

FIFTH AVE

MADISON AVE

PARK AVE

LEXINGTON AVE

THIRD AVE

SECOND AVE

FIRST AVE

PLEASANT AVE

E 117TH

E 116TH

E 115TH

EAST HARLEM

E 113TH

THOMAS JEFFERSON PARK

East River

E 112TH

E 111TH

scovery Center

Duke Ellington Statue

Jardin Nueva Esperanza

| 0 | 250 | 500 | 750 | 1000 Yards |
| 0 | 250 | 500 | 750 | 1000 Meters |

299

Upper West Side

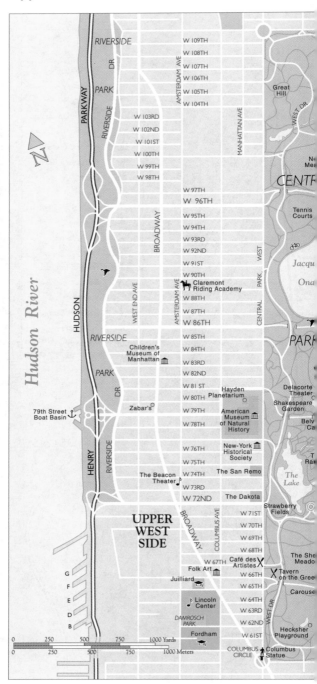

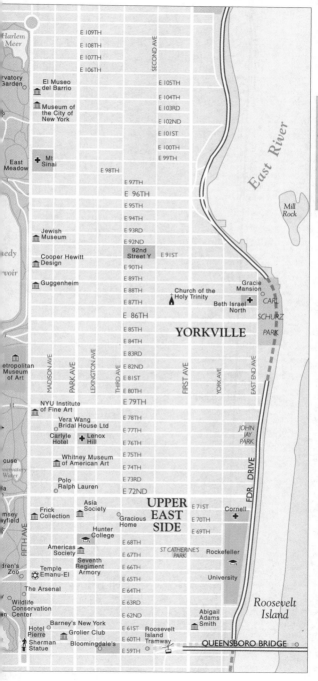

Midtown West, Chelsea

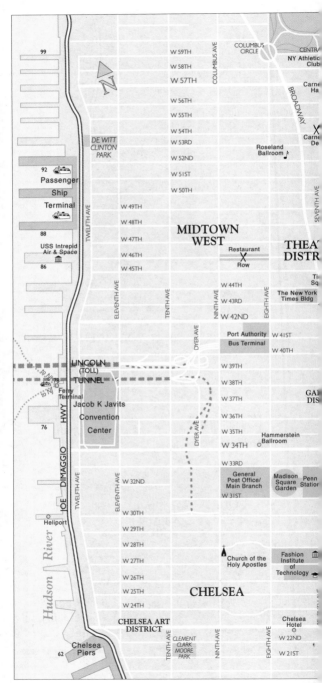

Midtown East, Fifth Avenue

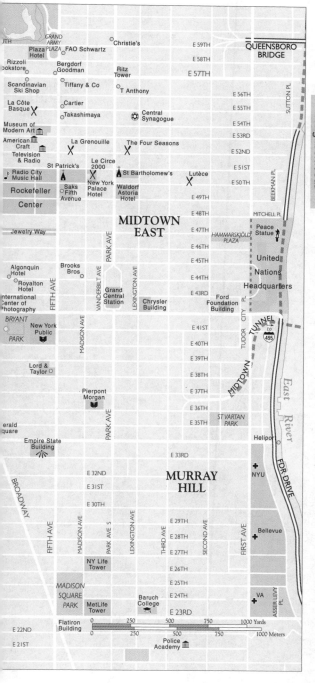

Plaza Hotel
GRAND ARMY PLAZA
FAO Schwartz
Christie's
E 59TH
QUEENSBORO BRIDGE

Rizzoli Bookstore
Bergdorf Goodman
E 58TH

Scandinavian Ski Shop
Tiffany & Co
Ritz Tower
E 57TH

La Côte Basque
Cartier
T Anthony
E 56TH

SUTTON PL

Museum of Modern Art
Takashimaya
Central Synagogue
E 55TH

American Craft
E 54TH

Television & Radio
La Grenouille
The Four Seasons
E 53RD

Radio City Music Hall
St Patrick's
Le Circe 2000
E 52ND

Rockefeller
Saks Fifth Avenue
New York Palace Hotel
St Bartholomew's
Lutèce
E 51ST

Center
Waldorf Astoria Hotel
E 50TH

BEEKMAN PL

E 49TH

MITCHELL PL

MIDTOWN EAST
E 48TH
Peace Statue

Jewelry Way
E 47TH
HAMMARSKJOLD PLAZA
United

PARK AVE
E 46TH

E 45TH
Nations

Algonquin Hotel
Brooks Bros
E 44TH
Headquarters

VANDERBILT AVE

LEXINGTON AVE

Royalton Hotel
E 43RD
Ford Foundation Building

International Center of Photography
Grand Central Station
Chrysler Building

FIFTH AVE

TUDOR CITY PL

BRYANT
New York Public
E 41ST
TUNNEL to 495

PARK
LIBRARY
E 40TH
MIDTOWN

MADISON AVE
E 39TH

Lord & Taylor
E 38TH

East River

Pierpont Morgan
E 37TH

E 36TH

Gerald Square
E 35TH
ST VARTAN PARK

Empire State Building
Heliport

E 33RD

FDR DRIVE

E 32ND
MURRAY HILL
NYU

E 31ST

BROADWAY
E 30TH

FIFTH AVE

MADISON AVE

PARK AVE S

LEXINGTON AVE

THIRD AVE

E 29TH

SECOND AVE

FIRST AVE

E 28TH
Bellevue

E 27TH

E 26TH

NY Life Tower
E 25TH

MADISON SQUARE
E 24TH
VA

PARK
MetLife Tower
Baruch College
E 23RD
ASSER LEVY PL

Flatiron Building
250   500   750   1000 Yards
0   250   500   750   1000 Meters

E 22ND
Police Academy

E 21ST

Chelsea, Flatiron, West Village, SoHo

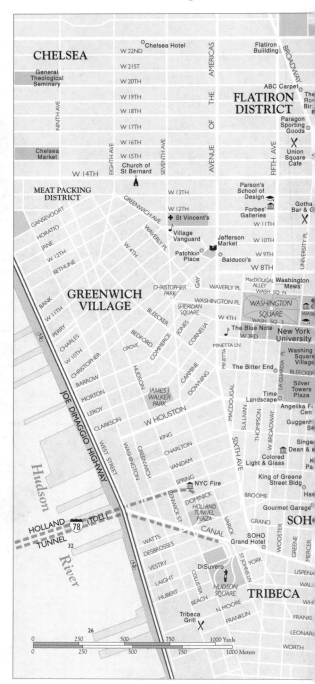

CHELSEA

General Theological Seminary

Chelsea Market

W 22ND
W 21ST
W 20TH
W 19TH
W 18TH
W 17TH
W 16TH
W 15TH
W 14TH

NINTH AVE
EIGHTH AVE
SEVENTH AVE

Chelsea Hotel

Church of St Bernard

AVENUE OF THE AMERICAS

Flatiron Buiilding

BROADWAY

ABC Carpet

FLATIRON DISTRICT

The Ro
Bir

Paragon Sporting Goods

Union Square Cafe

FIFTH AVE

MEAT PACKING DISTRICT

GANSEVOORT
HORATIO
JANE
W 12TH
BETHUNE

GREENWICH AVE

WAVERLY PL

W 13TH
W 12TH
St Vincent's
Village Vanguard
Patchin Place

W 4TH

W 11TH
W 10TH
W 9TH
W 8TH

Jefferson Market
Balducci's

Parson's School of Design
Forbes Galleries

Gotha
Bar & G

UNIVERSITY PL

GREENWICH VILLAGE

BANK
W 11TH
PERRY
CHARLES
W 10TH
CHRISTOPHER
BARROW
MORTON
LEROY
CLARKSON

CHRISTOPHER PARK
SHERIDAN SQUARE

BLEECKER

BEDFORD
GROVE
COMMERCE

HUDSON

JAMES J WALKER PARK

GAY

WAVERLY PL
WASHINGTON PL
W 4TH
W 3RD

JONES
CORNELIA
CARMINE
DOWNING

MINETTA LN
MINETTA

MacDOUGAL ALLEY
WASH SQ N
WASHINGTON SQUARE
WASH SQ S

The Blue Note
The Bitter End

Washington Mews

WASH

New York University

Washington Square Village

BLEECKER

MACDOUGAL
SULLIVAN
THOMPSON

W BROADWAY

LA GUARDIA

Silver Towers Plaza

Time Landscape

Angelika Fi
Cen

Guggenh
Se

W HOUSTON
KING
CHARLTON
VANDAM
SPRING
DOMINICK

GREENWICH
WASHINGTON
WEST STREET

Singe
Dean & S

Colored Light & Glass

King of Greene Street Bldg

NYC Fire

HOLLAND TUNNEL PLAZA

CANAL

BROOME
GRAND

SOHO Grand Hotel

VARICK

SIXTH AVE

Ka
Pa

Gourmet Garage

SOH

WOOSTER
GREENE
MERCER

HOLLAND TUNNEL
32

78 TOLL

JOE DIMAGGIO HIGHWAY

RENWICK ST

WATTS
DESBROSSES
VESTRY
LAIGHT
HUBERT

COLLISTER

ST JOHN'S

DiSuvero

HUDSON SQUARE

BEACH
N MOORE
FRANKLIN

YORK

LISPENA
WAL
WH
FRANKL
LEONAR

Tribeca Grill

TRIBECA

Hudson River

26

0   250   500   750   1000 Yards
0   250   500   750   1000 Meters

WORTH

East Village, NoHo, NoLiTa, Lower East Side

TriBeCa

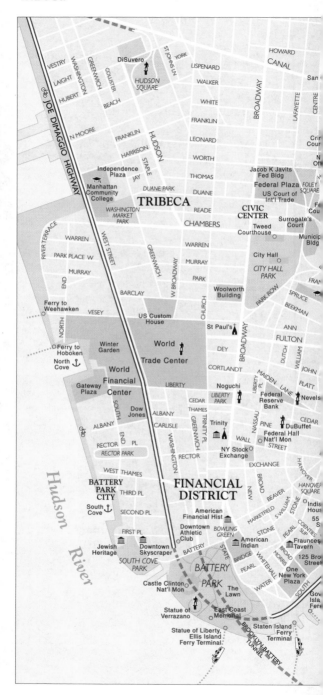

LOWER
EAST SIDE

CHINATOWN

SEWARD
PARK

LaGuardia
Houses

Asian
American
Arts Center

Chinatown History

BAYARD

Buddhist
Temple

Confucious
Plaza

PELL

Church
of the
Transfiguration

Edward
Mooney
House

CHATHAM
SQUARE

Rutgers
Houses

SMITH
MEMORIAL
PARK

Governor
Alfred E Smith
Houses

FDR DRIVE

MANHATTAN BRIDGE

36

to LaGuardia Airport

BROOKLYN BRIDGE
Pedestrian Walkway

EMPIRE-
FULTON FERRY
STATE PARK

BROOKLYN

Grimaldi's

DOVER

PECK SLIP

FRONT

SOUTH

Fulton
Market

South
Street
Seaport

Pier 16

to Fulton Landing Brooklyn

East River

BROOKLYN – QUEENS EXPWY

Plymouth
Church
of the
Pilgrims

ORANGE

BROOKLYN

BROOKLYN
HEIGHTS

HEIGHTS

Pier 13

9

PROMENADE

Downtown
Heliport

6

278

VAN
VOORHEES
PARK

STATE

250	500	750	1000 Yards
250	500	750	1000 Meters

Upper East Side

See map page 301

EAST 90s

Bonpoint	1269 Madison at 91st
Capezio	1651 Third btw 92/93rd
Catimini	1284 Madison btw 91/92nd
Diana & Jeffries	1310 Madison btw 92/93rd
East Side Kids	1298 Madison btw 92/93rd
Jacadi	1296 Madison at 92nd
J.McLaughlin	1311 Madison btw 92/93rd
Nocturne	1744 First btw 90/91st
René Collections	1325 Madison btw 93/94th
Veronique Maternity	1321 Madison at 93rd
The Wicker Garden	1300 Madison btw 92/93rd

EAST 80s

agnès b.	1063 Madison btw 80/81st
Aldo	157 East 86th btw Lexington/Third
Allure Lingerie	1324 Lexington btw 88/89th
Anik	1122 Madison btw 83/84th
Ann Taylor	1055 Madison at 80th
Ann Taylor Loft	1492 Third at 84th
Banana Republic	1136 Madison btw 84/85th
Banana Republic	1529 Third at 86th
Barbour by Peter Elliot	1047 Madison btw 79/80th
Betsey Johnson	1060 Madison btw 80/81st
Bis Designer Resale	1134 Madison btw 84/85th
Bonne Nuit	1193 Lexington at 81st
Cashmere New York	1100 Madison btw 82/83rd
Catimini	1125 Madison at 84th
Chuckies	1159 Madison btw 85/86th
Coach	35 East 85th at Madison
Cose Belle	7 East 81st btw Fifth/Madison
Easy Spirit	1518 Third btw 85/86th
Encore	1132 Madison btw 84/85th
Eric Shoes	1222 Madison at 88th
Foot Locker	159 East 86th btw Lexington/Third
Gap	1511 Third at 85th
Gap Kids & Baby Gap	1535 Third at 87th
G.C.William	1137 Madison btw 84/85th
Great Feet	1241 Lexington at 84th
Greenstones & Cie	1184 Madison btw 86/87th
Gymboree	1120 Madison btw 83/84th
Infinity	1116 Madison at 83rd
Jonathan Adler	1097 Madison at 83rd
Karen's for People & Pets	1195 Lexington btw 81/82nd
LeSportSac	1065 Madison btw 80/81st
Lester's	1534 Second at 80th
Little Eric Shoes	1118 Madison btw 83/84th
Magic Windows	1186 Madison btw 86/87th
Marsha D.D.	342 Lexington btw 88/89th

Modell's	1535 Third btw 86/87th
Montmartre	1157 Madison btw 85/86th
Nancy & Co	1242 Madison at 89th
Nellie M. Boutique	1309 Lexington at 88th
Original Leather	1100 Madison btw 82/83rd
Orva	155 East 86th btw Lexington/Third
Peter Elliot	1070 Madison at 81st
Peter Elliot (kids & outlet)	1067 Madison btw 80/81st
Peter Elliot Women	1071 Madison btw 80/81st
Petit Bateau	1100 Madison at 82nd
Planet Kids	247 East 86th btw Third/Fourth
Rapax	1100 Madison btw 82/83rd
Searle	1124 Madison at 84th
Seigo	1248 Madison btw 89/90th
Spence-Chapin Thrift Shops	1850 Second btw 95/96th
Spence-Chapin Thrift Shops	1473 Third btw 83/84th
Steve Madden	150 East 86th btw Lexington/Third
Super Runners Shop	1337 Lexington at 89th
Victoria's Secret	165 East 86th btw Lexington/Third
Vilebrequin	1070 Madison at 81st

EAST 70s

A Pea in the Pod	860 Madison at 70th
ABH Design	401 East 76th at First
Alexandre de Paris	971 Madison btw 75/76th
Alicia Mugetti	999 Madison btw 77/78th
Anik	1355 Third btw 77/78th
Ann Taylor	1320 Third btw 75/76th
Annika Inez	243 East 78th btw Second/Third
Arche	995 Madison at 77th
Bambini	1367 Third at 78th
Barami	1404 Second at 73rd
Berluti	971 Madison at 76th
Betsey Bunky Nini	980 Lexington btw 71/72nd
Big Drop	1321 Third btw 75/76th
Big Drop	1044 Madison btw 79/80th
Bra Smyth	905 Madison btw 72/73rd
Calypso St Barths	935 Madison btw 74/75th
Cantaloup	1036 Lexington at 74th
Cantaloup	1359 Second btw 71/72nd
Carolina Herrera	954 Madison at 75th
Che Che	1045a Lexington btw 73/74th
Chloé	850 Madison at 70th
Christian Louboutin	941 Madison btw 74/75th
Clea Colet	960 Madison at 71st
Delfino	1351a Third btw 76/77th
Eileen Fisher	1039 Madison btw 79/80th
Eric Shoes	1333 Third btw 76/77th
FM Allen	962 Madison btw 75/76th
Forreal	1335 Third btw 76/77th

Neighborhoods

Forreal Basics	1375 Third btw 78/79th
Fragments	997 Madison btw 76/77th
French Sole	985 Lexington btw 71/72nd
Galo	895 Madison at 72nd
Gamine	1322 Third btw 75/76th
Gianfranco Ferré	845 Madison btw 70/71st
Gymboree	1332 Third at 76th
Hoofbeats	232 East 78th btw Second/Third
Intermix	1003 Madison btw 77/78th
Issey Miyake	992 Madison at 77th
Jacadi	1260 Third at 72nd
Jackie Rogers	1034½ Lexington at 74th
Jane	1025 Lexington btw 73/74th
Jay Kos	986 Lexington btw 71/72nd
K.C.Thompson	987 Madison btw 76/77th
Liz Lange Maternity	958 Madison btw 75/76th
Luca Luca	1011 Madison at 78th
Make 10	1227 Third btw 70/71st
Makola	1045 Madison btw 79/80th
Malia Mills	960 Madison btw 75/76th
Malia Mills	1031 Lexington at 74th
Mariko	998 Madison btw 77/78th
Mary Efron	308 East 78th at Second
Michael Kors	974 Madison at 76th
Michael's The Consignment Shop for Women	
	1041 Madison btw 79/80th
Missoni	1009 Madison at 78th
Miu Miu	831 Madison btw 69/70th
Mom's Night Out	147 East 72nd btw Lexington/Third
Pat Areias	966 Madison btw 75/76th
Pelle Via Roma	1322 Third btw 75/76th
Pelle Via Roma	234 East 75th btw Second/Third
Peter Elliot	997 Lexington at 72nd
Pookie & Sebastian	249 East 77th btw Second/Third
Prada	841 Madison at 70th
Precision	1310 Third at 75th
Ralph Lauren	867 Madison at 72nd
Ralph Lauren	888 Madison at 72nd
Ralph Lauren Baby	872 Madison btw 71/72nd
René Collections	1007 Madison btw 77/78th
Ricky's	1380 Third btw 78/79th
Ricky's	1372 First btw 73/74th
Roberta Freymann	153 East 70th at Lexington
Santoni	864 Madison btw 70/71st
Scoop	1275 Third btw 73/74th
Searle	1296 Third at 74th
Searle	1035 Madison at 79th
Selima Optique	899 Madison btw 72/73rd

Shen	1005 Madison btw 77/78th
Shen	990 Lexington at 72nd
The Shoe Box	1349 Third at 77th
Small Change	964 Lexington btw 70/71st
Sonia Rykiel	849 Madison btw 70/71st
Spring Flowers	905 Madison btw 72/73rd
Super Runners Shop	1244 Third btw 71/72nd
Talbots	1251 Third at 72nd
Talbots Kids	1523 Second at 79th
VBH Gallery	940 Madison btw 74/75th
Vera Wang Bridal Salon	991 Madison at 77th
Vera Wang Maids on Madison	980 Madison btw 76/77th
Victoria's Secret	1240 Third at 72nd
Vincent & Edgar	972 Lexington at 71st
Wolford Boutique	996 Madison btw 77/78th
Yves Saint Laurent Rive Gauche	855 Madison btw 70/71st
Z' Baby	996 Lexington at 72nd
Zitomer	969 Madison btw 75/76th

EAST 60s

Aerosoles	1555 Second at 61st
American Apparel	1090 Third btw 63/64th
Anne Fontaine	687 Madison btw 61/62nd
Ann Taylor	645 Madison at 60th
Ann Taylor Loft	1155 Third btw 67/68th
Anya Hindmarch	29 East 60th btw Madison/Park
Arche	1045 Third btw 61/62nd
Arden B.	1130 Third btw 66/67th
Baby Gap	1131-49 Third at 66th
Banana Republic	1110 Third at 65th
Barneys New York	660 Madison at 61st
Barry Kieselstein-Cord	810 Madison at 68th
BCBG by Max Azria	770 Madison at 66th
Bebe	1127 Third at 66th
Beretta	718 Madison btw 63/64th
Betsey Johnson	251 East 60th btw Second/Third
Billy Martins	220 East 60th btw Second/Third
Bonpoint	811 Madison at 68th
Borrelli	16 East 60th btw Fifth/Madison
Boyd's Madison Avenue	655 Madison btw 60/61st
Brioni	57 & 67 East 57th btw Madison/Park
Calvin Klein	654 Madison at 60th
Canyon Beachwear	1136 Third btw 66/67th
Capezio	136 East 61st btw Park/Lexington
Celine	667 Madison at 61st
Cesare Paciotti	833 Madison btw 69/70th
Chuckies	1073 Third btw 63/64th
Church's English Shoes	689 Madison at 62nd
Clifford Michael Design	45 East 60th btw Madison/Park
Club Monaco	1111 Third at 65th

Neighborhoods

Cole Haan	667 Madison at 61st
Davide Cenci	801 Madison btw 67/68th
Diesel	770 Lexington at 60th
DKNY	655 Madison at 60th
Dolce & Gabbana	825 Madison btw 68/69th
Donna Karan New York	819 Madison btw 68/69th
Dooney & Bourke	28 East 60th btw Madison/Park
Eddie Bauer	1172 Third at 68th
Emanuel Ungaro	792 Madison at 67th
Entre Nous	1124 Third btw 65/66th
Etro	720 Madison btw 63/64th
Fendi	755 Madison btw 65/66th
Furla	727 Madison btw 63/64th
Gallery of Wearable Art	34 East 67th btw Madison/Park
Galo	825 Lexington at 63rd
Gap	1131-49 Third at 66th
Gi Gi	1173 Second at 62nd
Giordano's	1150 Second btw 60/61st
Giorgio Armani	760 Madison at 65th
Giuseppe Zanotti Design	806 Madison btw 67/68th
Givenchy	710 Madison at 63rd
Gymboree	1049 Third at 62nd
Hermès	691 Madison at 62nd
Hervé Léger	744 Madison btw 64/65th
Jacadi	787 Madison at 67th
Jean Paul Gaultier	759 Madison btw 65/66th
Jimmy Choo	716 Madison at 63rd
J.Mendel	723 Madison btw 63/64th
J.M.Weston	812 Madison at 68th
John Lobb	680 Madison btw 61/62nd
Joseph	816 Madison btw 68/69th
Judith Leiber	680 Madison at 61st
Julie Artisan's Gallery	762 Madison btw 65/66th
Krizia	769 Madison btw 65/66th
Lai	35 East 65th btw Madison/Park
Laila Rowe	1031 Third at 61st
La Layette et Plus	170 East 61st btw Lexington/Third
La Perla	777 Madison btw 66/67th
Lara Hélène Bridal Atelier	13 East 69th btw Fifth/Madison
Lee Anderson	23 East 67th btw Fifth/Madison
Leggiadro	680 Madison btw 61/62nd
Legs Beautiful	1025 Third at 61st
Les Copains	807 Madison btw 67/68th
Lingerie on Lex	831 Lexington btw 63/64th
Longchamp	713 Madison at 63rd
Loro Piana	821 Madison btw 68/69th
Luca Luca	690 Madison at 62nd
Lucky Brand Jeans	1151 Third at 67th
m0851	748 Madison btw 64/65th

Malo	814 Madison at 68th
Marina Rinaldi	800 Madison btw 67/68th
Martier	1010 Third at 60th
Martier	827 Lexington btw 63/64th
Martinez Valero	1029 Third at 61st
MaxMara	813 Madison at 68th
Mimi Maternity	1021 Third btw 60/61st
Morgane Le Fay	746 Madison btw 64/65th
Myla	20 East 60th at Madison
Nicole Farhi	10 East 60th btw Fifth/Madison
Nicole Miller	780 Madison btw 66/67th
Oilily	820 Madison btw 68/69th
Oilily For Women	820 Madison btw 68/69th
Olive & Bette's	1070 Madison btw 80/81st
Orva	782 Lexington btw 60/61st
Oscar de la Renta	772 Madison at 66th
Pan American Phoenix	857 Lexington btw 64/65th
Paul & Shark	772 Madison btw 66/67th
Pilar Rossi	784 Madison btw 66/67th
Porthault	11 East 69th btw Fifth/Madison
Pucci	24 East 64th btw Fifth/Madison
Reem Acra	14 East 60th btw Fifth/Madison
Ricky's	1189 First at 64th
Robert Clergerie	681 Madison btw 61/62nd
Roberto Cavalli	711 Madison at 63rd
Robert Talbott	680 Madison btw 61/62nd
Saada	1159 Second btw 60/61st
Searle	805 Madison btw 67/68th
Searle	1051 Third at 62nd
Searle	635 Madison at 60th
Selma & Sid	220 East 60th btw Second/Third
Shanghai Tang	714 Madison btw 63/64th
Spring Flowers	1050 Third at 62nd
Stephane Kélian	717 Madison btw 63/64th
Suzanne Couture Millinery	27 East 61st btw Madison/Park
Tanino Crisci	795 Madison btw 67/68th
Timberland	709 Madison at 63rd
Tse	827 Madison at 69th
Tupli	780 Madison btw 66/67th
Unisa	701 Madison btw 62/63rd
Valentino	747 Madison at 65th
Vanessa Noel Boutique	158 East 64th btw Lexington/Third
Varda	786 Madison btw 66/67th
Versace	815 Madison at 68th
Via Spiga	692 Madison btw 62/63rd
Warren Edwards	107 East 60th btw Park/Lexington
Yurman	729 Madison at 64th
Zeller Tuxedo	1010 Third btw 60/61st

Neighborhoods

Upper West Side   *See map page 300*

Aerosoles	310 Columbus btw 74/75th
Allan & Suzi	416 Amsterdam at 80th
Alskling	228 Columbus btw 70/71st
Ann Taylor	2380 Broadway at 87th
Ann Taylor	2015-17 Broadway at 69th
April Cornell	487 Columbus btw 83/84th
Assets London	464 Columbus btw 82/83rd
A.Tempo	290 Columbus btw 73/74th
Banana Republic	215 Columbus btw 69/70th
Banana Republic	2360 Broadway at 86th
Barneys Co-op	2151 Broadway btw 75/76th
Bati	2151 Broadway btw 75/76th
Betsey Johnson	248 Columbus btw 71/72nd
Blades Board & Skate	120 West 72nd btw Amsterdam/Columbus
Bloch	304 Columbus btw 74/75th
Boyd's	309 Columbus btw 74/75th
Brief Encounters	239 Columbus at 71st
Central Park West	495 Amsterdam at 84th
Club Monaco	2376 Broadway at 87th
Coach	2321 Broadway at 84th
CPW	495 Amsterdam at 84th
Crunch	162 West 83rd btw Amsterdam/Columbus
Danskin	159 Columbus btw 67/68th
Daphne	467 Amsterdam btw 82/83rd
Darryl's	492 Amsterdam btw 83/84th
Diana & Jeffries	2062 Broadway btw 70/71st
Eastern Mountain Sports	20 West 61st at Broadway
Easy Spirit	2251 Broadway at 81st
Eddie Bauer	1976 Broadway at 67th
Eileen Fisher	341 Columbus btw 76/77th
Express	321 Columbus at 75th
Filene's Basement	2222 Broadway at 79th
Foot Locker	1530 Broadway btw 44/45th
Frank Stella	440 Columbus at 81st
French Connection	304 Columbus btw 74/75th
Gap	1988 Broadway at 67th
Gap	2373 Broadway at 86th
Gap Kids	1988 Broadway at 67th
Gap Kids	2300 Broadway at 83rd
G.C.William	111 West 72nd btw Amsterdam/Columbus
Granny-Made	381 Amsterdam btw 78/79th
Greenstones & Cie	442 Columbus btw 81/82nd
Gymboree	2271 Broadway at 81/82nd
Gymboree	2015 Broadway btw 68/69th
Intermix	210 Columbus at 69th
Jacadi	1841 Broadway at 60th

Karen Alexis	490 Amsterdam btw 83/84th
Kenneth Cole	353 Columbus at 77th
Laila Rowe	2190 Broadway at 78th
Laila Rowe	253 Columbus at 72nd
Laina Jane Lingerie	416 Amsterdam at 80th
Liana	324 Columbus btw 75/76th
Liberty House	2389 Broadway btw 87/88th
Liberty House	2878 Broadway at 112th
Lord of the Fleas	2142 Broadway btw 75/76th
Lucky Brand Jeans	216 Columbus at 70th
Malia Mills	220 Columbus at 70th
Medici	420 Columbus btw 80/81st
Mimi Maternity	2005 Broadway btw 68/69th
Montmartre	2212 Broadway btw 78/79th
Morris Bros	2322 Broadway at 84th
The New York Look	30 Lincoln Plaza btw 62/63rd
The New York Look	2030 Broadway btw 69/70th
Nine West	2305 Broadway btw 83/84th
Off Broadway	139 West 72nd btw Broadway/Columbus
Olive & Bette's	252 Columbus btw 71/72nd
Only Hearts	386 Columbus btw 78/79th
Patagonia	426 Columbus btw 80/81st
Planet Kids	2688 Broadway at 103rd
Purdy Girl	464 Columbus at 82nd
Really Great Things	284a Columbus btw 73/74th
Really Great Things	300 Columbus at 74th
Reebok	160 Columbus btw 67/68th
Ricky's	112 West 72nd btw Broadway/Columbus
Roberto Vascon	140 West 72nd btw Broadway/Columbus
Rockport	160 Columbus btw 67/68th
Roslyn	276 Columbus at 73rd
Sacco	324 Columbus btw 75/76th
Scarpe Diem	2286 Broadway btw 81/82nd
Sean	224 Columbus btw 70/71st
Shen	311 Columbus btw 74/75th
Steven Alan	465 Amsterdam at 82nd
Super Runners Shop	360 Amsterdam btw 77/78th
Talbots	2289-2291 Broadway btw 82/83rd
Tani	2020 Broadway btw 69/70th
Tani	131 West 72nd btw Broadway/Columbus
Theory	230 Columbus btw 70/71st
Tibet Bazaar	473 Amsterdam btw 82/83rd
Tip Top Kids	149 West 72nd btw Amsterdam/Columbus
Varda	2080 Broadway btw 71/72nd
Variazioni	2389 Broadway btw 87/88th
Variazioni	2395 Broadway at 88th
Victoria's Secret	1981 Broadway at 67th
Z' Baby	100 West 72nd at Columbus
Zan	2394 Broadway btw 87/88th

Midtown East

See map page 303

Addison On Madison	29 West 57th btw Fifth/Sixth
Aldo	730 Lexington btw 58/59th
Aldo	139 East 42nd btw Lexington/Third
Alexandros	5 East 59th btw Fifth/Madison
Alfred Dunhill	711 Fifth btw 55/56th
Allen Edmonds	551 Madison btw 55/56th
Allen Edmonds	24 East 44th btw Fifth/Madison
Amsale	625 Madison at 58th
Ann Taylor	850 Third at 52nd
Ann Taylor	330 Madison at 43rd
Ann Taylor Loft	150 East 42nd at Lexington
Ann Taylor Loft	488 Madison at 52nd
A.T.Harris Formalwear	11 East 44th btw Fifth/Madison
Bally	628 Madison at 59th
Banana Republic	130 East 59th at Lexington
Barami	136 East 57th at Lexington
Barami	375 Lexington at 41st
Bebe	805 Third at 50th
Belgian Shoes	110 East 55th btw Park/Lexington
Bloomingdale's	1000 Third btw 59/60th
Bottega Veneta	635 Madison btw 59/60th
Boyd's Madison Avenue	968 Third at 58th
Bric's	535 Madison at 53rd
Bridal Atelier	127 East 56th btw Park/Lexington
Brioni	57 East 57th btw Madison/Park
Brioni	55 East 52nd btw Madison/Park
Brooks Brothers	346 Madison btw 44/45th
Caché	805 Third btw 49/50th
Chanel	15 East 57th btw Fifth/Madison
Charles Tyrwhitt	377 Madison btw 46/47th
Christian Dior	21 East 57th btw Fifth/Madison
Citishoes	445 Park btw 56/57th
Clarks/Bostonian	363 Madison at 45th
Coach	342 Madison at 44th
Coach	595 Madison at 57th
Crouch & Fitzgerald	400 Madison btw 47/48th
Crunch	1109 Second btw 58/59th
Crunch	554 Second at 31st
Daffy's	335 Madison at 44th
Daffy's	125 East 57th btw Park/Lexington
Dana Buchman	65 East 57th btw Madison/Park
Denimaxx	444 Madison btw 49/50th
Dior Homme	19 East 57th btw Fifth/Madison
Domenico Spano	611 Fifth at 50th
Easy Spirit	555 Madison btw 55/56th
Eddie Bauer	711 Third at 45th
Eileen Fisher	521 Madison btw 53/54th
Elleven Up	12 West 57th at Fifth

Emporio Armani	601 Madison btw 57/58th
Enzo Angiolini	551 Madison at 55th
Eredi Pisan	522 Madison btw 53/54th
Eres	621 Madison btw 58/59th
Express	477 Madison at 51st
Express	722-728 Lexington at 58th
Fila	340 Madison at 43rd
Fogal	510 Madison at 53rd
Forman's	145 East 42nd btw Lexington/Third
Frank Shattuck	510 Madison at 53rd
Fratelli Rossetti	625 Madison at 58th
Furla	598 Madison at 57th
Gap	657 Third at 42nd
Gap	734 Lexington btw 58/59th
Gap Kids	545 Madison at 55th
Gap Kids	657 Third at 42nd
Geox	575 Madison at 57th
Ghurka	683 Madison btw 61/62nd
H.Herzfeld	507 Madison btw 52/53rd
Jay Kos	475 Park btw 57/58th
Johnston & Murphy	520 Madison at 54th
Johnston & Murphy	345 Madison btw 44/45th
Jos. A. Bank	366 Madison at 45th
J.Press	7 East 44th btw Fifth/Madison
Kavanagh's Designer Resale Shop	146 East 49th btw Lexington/Third
Kenneth Cole	107 East 42nd at Park
Kenneth Cole	130 East 57th at Lexington
Kiton	4 East 54th btw Fifth/Madison
Lacoste	575 Madison at 57th
Laila Rowe	8 East 42nd at Fifth
Lana Marks	645 Madison btw 59/60th
The Leather & Suede Workshop	107 East 59th btw Park/Lexington
Lederer	457 Madison at 51st
Legs Beautiful	200 Park btw 44/45th
Leonard Logsdail	9 East 53rd btw Fifth/Madison
Linda Dresner	484 Park btw 58/59th
Mason's Tennis Mart	56 East 53rd btw Madison/Park
Men's Wearhouse	380 Madison at 46th
Men's Wearhouse	350 Fifth at 34th
Mimi Maternity	360 Madison at 45th
Modell's	51 East 42nd btw Madison/Vanderbilt
Moreschi	515 Madison at 53rd
Natalie & Friends	205 East 60th at Third
Naturalizer	712 Lexington btw 57/58th
New Balance New York	821 Third btw 50/51st
Niketown	6 East 57th btw Fifth/Madison
Nine West	750 Lexington btw 58/59th
Nine West	757 Third btw 47/48th

Neighborhoods

Nine West   331 Madison at 43rd
Noriko Maeda   598 Madison btw 57/58th
The Original Levi's Store   750 Lexington btw 59/60th
Otto Tootsi Plohound   38 East 57th btw Madison/Park

Oxxford Couture Collection   36 East 57th
                                          btw Madison/Park
Paul Stuart   Madison at 45th
Pookie & Sebastian   541 Third at 36th

Prada (shoes only)   45 East 57th btw Madison/Park
Precision   522 Third at 35th
René Mancini   470 Park at 58th
Richard Metzger   325 West 38th btw Eighth/Ninth

Ricky's   509 Fifth btw 42/43rd
Ricky's   383 Fifth btw 34/35th
Sacco   118 East 59th btw Park/Lexington
Saint Laurie Merchant Tailors   22 West 32nd
                                       btw Broadway/Fifth

Sean John   475 Fifth at 41st
The Shirt Store   51 East 44th at Vanderbilt
Skechers USA   3 Times Square at 42nd/Seventh
Sports Authority   845 Third at 51st

Spring Flowers   538 Madison btw 54/55th
Stuart Weitzman   625 Madison btw 58/59th
Suarez   450 Park btw 56/57th
Super Runners Shop   Grand Central Terminal
                                      (main concourse)

Talbots   525 Madison btw 53/54th
Talbot Kids   527 Madison at 54th
T.Anthony   445 Park at 56th
Taryn Rose   30 East 60th btw Madison/Park

Thomas Pink   520 Madison at 53rd
Tod's   650 Madison btw 59/60th
Tumi   64 Grand Central Terminal (Lexington Passage)
Tumi   520 Madison at 54th

Turnbull & Asser   42 East 57th btw Madison/Park
Vertigo and Friends/Magaschoni   36 East 60th
                                          btw Park/Madison
Victoria's Secret   34 East 57th btw Madison/Park

Vincent Nicolosi   510 Madison at 53rd
Walter Steiger   417 Park at 55th
Western Spirit   686 Lexington at 56th
Wolford Boutique   619 Madison btw 58/59th

World of Golf   147 East 47th btw Lexington/Third
Yves Saint Laurent Rive Gauche   3 East 57th
                                          btw Fifth/Madison
Zara   750 Lexington at 59th

Midtown West   *See map page 302*

Abercrombie & Fitch   720 Fifth at 56th

Aldo	15 West 34th btw Fifth/Sixth
Alixandre	150 West 30th btw Sixth/Seventh
Ann Taylor	1166 Sixth at 46th
Ann Taylor Loft	1290 Sixth at 52nd
Arche	128 West 57th btw Sixth/Seventh
Arthur Gluck Shirtmakers	47 West 57th btw Fifth/Sixth
Ascot Chang	7 West 57th btw Fifth/Sixth
A/X Armani Exchange	Time Warner Mall at Columbus Circle
Baldwin Formalwear	1156 Sixth at 45th
Banana Republic	17 West 34th btw Fifth/Sixth
Barami	485 Seventh btw 36/37th
Behrle	440 West 34th btw Ninth/Tenth
Beverly Feldman Shoes	7 West 56th at Fifth
Billabong	1515 Broadway btw 44/45th
Blades Board & Skate	at Manhattan Mall 901 Sixth at 33rd
Blair Delmonico	Time Warner Mall at Columbus Circle
Burberry	9 East 57th btw Fifth/Madison
Caché	Time Warner Mall at Columbus Circle
Capezio	1776 Broadway at 57th
Capezio	1650 Broadway at 51st
Christie Brothers Furs	150 West 30th btw Sixth/Seventh
Clea Colet	589 Eighth at 39th
Club Monaco	8 West 57th btw Fifth/Sixth
Coach	Time Warner Mall at Columbus Circle
Cole Haan	Time Warner Mall at Columbus Circle
Crunch	144 West 38th btw Broadway/Seventh
Crunch	555 West 42nd at Eleventh
Daffy's	1311 Broadway btw 33/34th
Daffy's	1775 Broadway at 57th
Delfino	56 West 50th at Rockefeller Center
Designer Loft	226 West 37th btw Seventh/Eighth
Duty Free Apparel	204 West 35th at Seventh
Easy Spirit	1166 Sixth at 46th
Eileen Fisher	Time Warner Mall at Columbus Circle
Enzo Angiolini	at Manhattan Mall, 901 Sixth btw Broadway/33rd
Esprit	Time Warner Mall at Columbus Circle
Express	7 West 34th btw Fifth/Sixth
Express	at Manhattan Mall, 901 Sixth btw Broadway/33rd
Fame	512 Seventh btw 37/38th
Foot Locker	at Manhattan Mall, 901 Sixth at 33rd
Foot Locker	120 West 34th btw Sixth/Seventh
Foot Locker	43 West 34th btw Fifth/Sixth
Forever 21	50 West 34th btw Fifth/Sixth
Frank Stella	921 Seventh at 58th
French Connection	1270 Sixth at 51st
Gap	60 West 34th at Broadway
Gap	1212 Sixth btw 47/48th

Gap	1466 Broadway at 42nd
Gap	250 West 57th btw Broadway/Eighth
Gap Kids	1212 Sixth btw 47/48th
Gap Kids & Baby Gap	1466 Broadway at 42nd
Gerry Cosby & Co	3 Penn Plaza at MSG
H&M	1328 Broadway at 34th
H&M	731 Lexington btw 58/59th
Jack Silver Formal Wear	1780 Broadway btw 57/58th
John Anthony	130 West 57th btw Sixth/Seventh
Keni Valenti	247 West 30th btw Seventh/Eighth
Lady Foot Locker	120 West 34th at Sixth
Lane Bryant	7 West 34th btw Fifth/Sixth
Le Chateau	34 West 34th btw Fifth/Sixth
Macy's	Broadway at 34th
Maggie Norris Couture	494 Eighth at 35th
Make 10	1386 Sixth btw 56/57th
Make 10	44 West 39th btw Fifth/Sixth
Manolo Blahnik	31 West 54th btw Fifth/Sixth
Maternity Works	16 West 57th btw Fifth/Sixth
Michelle Roth Design Studio	24 West 57th btw Fifth/Sixth
Modell's	1293 Broadway at 34th
Montmartre	Time Warner Mall at Columbus Circle
Motherhood Maternity	at Manhattan Mall
	901 Sixth at 33rd
Motherhood Maternity (outlet)	16 West 57th btw Fifth/Sixth
Motherhood Maternity	36 West 34th btw Fifth/Sixth
New Balance	51 West 42nd btw Fifth/Sixth
New Balance	745 Seventh at 49th
New York Golf Center	131 West 35th btw Broadway/Seventh
The New York Look	570 Seventh at 41st
Norma Kamali	11 West 56th btw Fifth/Sixth
Old Navy Clothing Co	150 West 34th btw Sixth/Seventh
Piccione	7 West 56th btw Fifth/Sixth
Quiksilver	3 Times Square at 42nd/Seventh
Ricky's	988 Eighth at 58th
Ricky's	332 West 57th at Columbus Circle
Ricky's	728 Ninth btw 49/50th
Ricky's	1412 Broadway btw 39/40th
Ritz Furs	107 West 57th btw Sixth/Seventh
Rochester Big & Tall	1301 Sixth at 52nd
Rosa Custom Ties	30 West 57th btw Fifth/Sixth
Scandinavian Ski Shop	16 East 55th btw Fifth/Madison
Sisley	Time Warner Mall at Columbus Circle
Skechers	140 West 34th btw Sixth/Seventh
Soho Woman	32 West 40th btw Fifth/Sixth
Sports Authority	57 West 57th at Sixth
Steve Madden	41 West 34th btw Fifth/Sixth

Stuart Weitzman	Time Warner Mall at Columbus Circle
Thomas Pink	1155 Sixth at 44th
Thomas Pink	Time Warner Mall at Columbus Circle
Training Camp	25 West 45th btw Fifth/Sixth
Training Camp	1079 Sixth at 41st
Tristan & America	1230 Sixth at 49th
Victoria's Secret	at Manhattan Mall, 901 Sixth at 33rd
Victoria's Secret	Herald Square at 34th
Wet Seal	at Manhattan Mall, 901 Sixth at 33rd
William Fioravanti	45 West 57th btw Fifth/Sixth
Zan 1666	Broadway btw 51/52nd
Zara	39 West 34th btw Fifth/Sixth
Zitomer	40 West 57th btw Fifth/Sixth
Zora	55 West 45th btw Fifth/Sixth

Fifth Avenue

See map page 303

Alfred Dunhill	711 Fifth btw 55/56th
Ann Taylor	575 Fifth btw 46/47th
Asprey	723 Fifth at 56th
A.Testoni	665 Fifth btw 52/53rd
A/X Armani Exchange	645 Fifth at 51st
Banana Republic	626 Fifth at Rockefeller Center
Barami	535 Fifth at 45th
Benetton	597 Fifth btw 48/49th
Bergdorf Goodman	754 Fifth at 58th
Bergdorf Goodman The Men's Store	745 Fifth at 58th
Best of Scotland	581 Fifth btw 47/48th
Bottega Veneta	699 Fifth btw 54th/55th
Botticelli	666 Fifth btw Fifth/Sixth (enter on 53rd)
Botticelli	522 Fifth btw 43/44th
Botticelli (women)	620 Fifth at Rockefeller Center
Brooks Brothers	666 Fifth btw 52/53rd
Coach	620 Fifth at Rockefeller Center
Cole Haan	620 Fifth at 50th
Domenico Spano	611 Fifth at 50th
Domenico Vacca	781 Fifth btw 59/60th
Ermenegildo Zegna	743 Fifth btw 57/58th
Escada	715 Fifth at 56th
Façonnable	689 Fifth at Rockefeller Center
Fendi	677 Fifth btw 53/54th
Forman's	560 Fifth at 46th
The Fur Salon at Saks Fifth Avenue	611 Fifth at 49th
Gant	645 Fifth btw 51/52nd
Gap	680 Fifth at 54th
Gucci	685 Fifth at 54th
H&M	640 Fifth at 51st
Helen Yarmak	730 Fifth btw 56/57th
Henri Bendel	712 Fifth btw 55/56th
Hickey Freeman	666 Fifth btw 52/53rd

Hugo Boss	717 Fifth at 56th
Jimmy Choo	645 Fifth at 51st
Kenneth Cole	610 Fifth at Rockefeller Center
Lacoste	608 Fifth at 49th
Lord & Taylor	424 Fifth btw 38/39th
Louis Vuitton	1 East 57th at Fifth
Maggie Norris Couture	754 Fifth at Bergdorf Goodman
Make 10	366 Fifth btw 34/35th
MEXX	650 Fifth btw 51/52nd
The New York Look	551 Fifth at 45th
Nine West	675 Fifth at 53rd
Oshkosh B'Gosh	586 Fifth btw 47/48th
Prada	724 Fifth btw 56/57th
Pucci	701 Fifth btw 54/55th
Ripplu	575 Fifth btw 46/47th
Saks Fifth Avenue	611 Fifth btw 49/50th
Salvatore Ferragamo	661 Fifth btw 52/53rd
Sisley	133 Fifth at 20th
St John	665 Fifth at 53rd
Takashimaya	693 Fifth btw 54/55th
Versace	647 Fifth btw 51/52nd

Flatiron

See map pages 304–305

agnès b.	13 East 16th btw Fifth/Union Square West
Ann Taylor	149 Fifth at 21st
Anthropologie	85 Fifth at 16th
Arden B.	104 Fifth btw 15/16th
Banana Republic (women)	89 Fifth at 16th
Banana Republic (men)	114 Fifth at 17th
Bebe	100 Fifth at 15th
Club Monaco	160 Fifth at 21st
Couture by Jennifer Dule	89 Fifth at 16th
Crunch	54 East 13th btw Broadway/University Place
Daffy's	111 Fifth at 18th
Eileen Fisher	116 Fifth btw 21/22nd
Esprit	110 Fifth at 16th
Express	130 Fifth at 18th
Gap	122 Fifth at 18th
Gap Kids & Baby Gap	122 Fifth at 18th
Harry Rothman's	200 Park South at 17th
Intermix	125 Fifth btw 19/20th
J.Crew	91 Fifth btw 16/17th
Kenneth Cole	95 Fifth at 17th
Laila Rowe	2 West 14th at Fifth
Laila Rowe	600 Sixth btw 17/18th
Lucky Brand Jeans	172 Fifth at 22nd
Manhattan Saddlery	117 East 24th btw Park/Lexington
Nine West	115 Fifth at 19th

Otto Tootsi Plohound	137 Fifth btw 20/21st
Paragon Sporting Goods	867 Broadway at 18th
Paul Smith	108 Fifth at 16th
Princeton Ski Shop	21 East 22nd btw Broadway/Park South
Runway	12 West 23rd btw Fifth/Sixth
Sacco	14 East 17th btw Fifth/Union Square West
Searle	156 Fifth at 20th
Skechers	150 Fifth btw 19/20th
Space Kiddets	46 East 21st btw Broadway/Park
Thread	26 West 17th btw Fifth/Sixth
Victoria's Secret	115 Fifth btw 19/20th
Zara	101 Fifth btw 17/18th

Chelsea

See map pages 302, 304

See map pages 302, 304

Alexander McQueen	417 West 14th btw Ninth/Washington
Alexandros Furs	213 West 28th btw Seventh/Eighth
An Earnest Cut & Sew	821 Washington btw Little West 12th/Gansevoort
Balenciaga	542 West 22nd btw Tenth/Eleventh
Banana Republic	111 Eighth btw 15/16th
Barney's Co-op	236 West 18th btw Seventh/Eighth
Benetton	120 Seventh at 17th
Ben Thylan Furs	150 West 30th btw Sixth/Seventh
Blades Board & Skate	23rd and West Side Highway at Chelsea Pier 62
Burlington Coat Factory	707 Sixth at 23rd
Camouflage	139/141 Eighth at 17th
Carlos Miele	408 West 14th btw Ninth/Tenth
Catriona MacKechnie	400 West 14th at Ninth
Charles Nolan	30 Gansevoort btw Hudson/Ninth
Comme des Garçons	520 West 22nd btw Tenth/Eleventh
Destination	32-36 Little West 12th btw Washington/Ninth
Eisenberg & Eisenberg	16 West 17th btw Fifth/Sixth
Ellen Christine Millinery	255 West 18th btw Seventh/Eighth
Elizabeth Charles	639½ Hudson at Ninth
The Family Jewels	130 West 23rd btw Sixth/Seventh
Filene's Basement	620 Sixth at 18th
Find Outlet	361 West 17th btw Eighth/Ninth
Fisch for the Hip	153 West 18th btw Sixth/Seventh
Gap	277 West 23rd btw Seventh/Eighth
Gerry's	110 & 112 Eighth btw 15/16th
Giraudon	152 Eighth btw 17/18th
Henry Beguelin	18 Ninth at 13th
James Perse	411 Bleeker at West 11th
Jeffrey	449 West 14th btw Ninth/Tenth
Jim Smiley Vintage	128 West 23rd btw Sixth/Seventh
Kleinfeld	110 West 20th at Sixth

LaCrasia Gloves	15 West 28th btw Fifth/Broadway
La Perla	425 West 14th btw Ninth/Tenth
Lingo	257 West 19th btw Seventh/Eighth
Loehmann's	101 Seventh btw 16/17th
Lost Art	515 West 29th btw Tenth/Eleventh
Lucy Barnes	320 West 14th btw Eighth/Ninth
Medici	24 West 23rd btw Fifth/Sixth
Men's Wearhouse	655 Sixth at 20th
Motherhood Maternity	641 Sixth at 20th
Nicole Farhi	75 Ninth at 16th
Old Navy Clothing Co	610 Sixth btw 17/18th
Parke & Ronen	176 Ninth btw 20/21st
Powers Court Tennis Outlet	1321/2 West 24th btw Sixth/Seventh
The Puma Store	421 West 14th btw Ninth/Tenth
Reminiscence	50 West 23rd btw Fifth/Sixth
Ricky's	267 West 23rd btw Seventh/Eighth
Sacco	94 Seventh btw 15/16th
Selima Optique	888 Broadway at 19th
Shelly Steffee	34 Gansevoort at Hudson
Sports Authority	636 Sixth at 19th
Stella McCartney	429 West 14th btw Ninth/Washington
Theory	40 Gansevoort at Hudson
T.J.Maxx	620 Sixth btw 18/19th
Urban Outfitters	526 Sixth at 14th
Utowa	17 West 18th btw Fifth/Sixth
Yigal Azrouel	408 West 14th btw Ninth/Tenth

East Village/Lower East Side   *See map page 305*

99X	84 East 10th btw Third/Fourth
AB Apollo Braun	193 Orchard at Houston
A.Cheng	443 East 9th btw First/Avenue A
Alife	178 Orchard btw Houston/Stanton
Alife Rivington Club	158 Rivington btw Clinton/Suffolk
Alpana Bawa (outlet)	70 East 1st btw First/Second
Amarcord Vintage Fashion	84 East 7th btw First/Second
American Apparel	183 East Houston at Orchard
Amy Downs Hats at YU	151 Ludlow btw Stanton/Rivington
Angelo Lambrou	96 East 7th btw First/Avenue A
Anna	150 East 3rd btw Avenue A/B
Atomic Passion	430 East 9th btw First/Avenue A
Azaleas	223 East 10th btw First/Second
Barbara Feinman Millinery	66 East 7th btw First/Second
Barbara Shaum	60 East 4th btw Bowery/Second
D/L Cerney	13 East 7th btw Second/Third
Do Kham	304 East 5th btw First/Second
Doyle & Doyle	189 Orchard btw Houston/Stanton
Edith & Daha	104 Rivington btw Ludlow/Essex
Eileen Fisher (outlet)	314 East 9th btw First/Second

Neighborhoods

Ellen	122 Ludlow btw Rivington/Delancey
Enerla Lingerie	48½ East 7th btw First/Second
Eugenia Kim	203 East 4th btw Avenue A/B
Fabulous Fanny's	335 East 9th btw First/Second
Foley & Corinna	114 Stanton btw Ludlow/Essex
Foley & Corinna (men)	143 Ludlow btw Stanton/Rivington
Foot Locker	252 First at 15th
Foot Locker	94 Delancey btw Ludlow/Orchard
Foot Locker	58 West 14th at Sixth
Forman's	82 Orchard btw Broome/Grand
Frock	148 Orchard btw Stanton/Rivington
Gabay's Outlet	225 First btw 13/14th
Gap (men)	750 Broadway at 8th
Gap (women)	1 Astor Place at Broadway
The Gown Company	333 East 9th btw First/Second
Hello Sari	261 Broome btw Allen/Orchard
Huminska New York	315 East 9th btw First/Second
Jill Anderson	331 East 9th btw First/Second
Jivamukti	404 Lafayette btw Astor/East 4th
Johnson	179 Orchard btw Houston/Stanton
Jutta Neumann	158 Allen btw Stanton/Rivington
Laila Rowe	55c East 8th btw Mercer/University
Lord of the Fleas	305 East 9th btw First/Second
Love Saves the Day	119 Second at 7th
Love Shine	543½ East 6th btw Avenue A/B
Manhattan Portage	333 East 9th btw First/Second
Marmalade	172 Ludlow btw Houston/Stanton
Mary Adams	138 Ludlow btw Stanton/Rivington
Mavi	832 Broadway btw 12/13th
Meg	312 East 9th btw First/Second
Metropolis	43 Third btw 9/10th
miks	100 Stanton btw Ludlow/Orchard
Missbehave	231 Eldridge btw Stanton/Houston
Mod World	85 First btw 5/6th
MoMo FaLana	43 Avenue A at 3rd
New York Om Yoga	826 Broadway at 12th
Nort 235	235 Eldridge btw Houston/Stanton
The Open Door Gallery	77 East 4th btw Second/Bowery
Outlet 7	117 East 7th btw First/Avenue A
Peacock NYC	440 East 9th btw First/Avenue A
Peggy Pardon	153 Ludlow btw Stanton/Rivington
Pippin	72 Orchard btw Broome/Grand
Plum	124 Ludlow btw Rivington/Delancey
Project	175 Orchard at Stanton
Ricky's	278 Third at 22nd
Ricky's	7 East 14th btw Fifth/University
Ricky's	111 Third at 13th
Rue St Denis	170 Avenue B btw 10/11th
Selia Yang	328 East 9th btw First/Second

Selima Optique	7 Bond btw Broadway/Lafayette
Selima Optique	84 East 7th btw First/Second
Shop	105 Stanton at Ludlow
Some Odd Rubies	151 Ludlow btw Stanton/Rivington

Suzette Sundae	182 Avenue B btw 11/12th
Tahir	412 East 9th btw First/Avenue A
Tees.com	147 Avenue A btw 9/10th
TG-170	170 Ludlow btw Houston/Stanton

Three Turtle Doves	201 East 2nd btw Avenue A/B
Tokio 7	64 East 7th btw First/Second
Tokyo Joe	334 East 11th btw First/Second
Urban Outfitters	162 Second btw 10/11th

The Village Scandal	19 East 7th btw Second/Third
Vlada	101 Stanton at Ludlow
Western Spirit	803 Broadway at 11th

NoHo/West Village   *See map pages 304–305*

Aerosoles	63 East 8th btw Broadway/University Place
Albertine	13 Christopher btw Greenwich/Waverly
Aldo	700 Broadway at East 4th
American Apparel	712 Broadway at Washington Place

American Apparel	373 Sixth at Waverly
Andy's Chee Pees	691 Broadway btw 3/4th
Annelore	636 Hudson at Horatio
Ann Taylor Loft	770 Broadway btw 8/9th

Arche	10 Astor Place btw Lafayette/Broadway
Arleen Bowman	353 Bleecker btw West 10th/Charles
Athlete's Foot	60 East 8th at Broadway
Atrium	644 Broadway at Bleecker

B8 Couture	27 Little West 12th at Ninth
Banana Republic	205 Bleecker at Sixth
Basic Basic	710 Broadway btw Washington Place/4th
Benetton	749 Broadway btw 8th/Astor Place

Betwixt	245 West 10th btw Bleecker/Hudson
Blades Board & Skate	659 Broadway btw West 3rd/Bleecker
Bond 07	7 Bond btw Broadway/Lafayette

Buckler	13 Gansevoort btw Eighth/Ninth
Butik	605 Hudson at Eighth
Calypso	654 Hudson at 14th
Cherry	19 Eighth btw West 12th/Jane

Cherry	17 Eighth at West 12th
Christian Louboutin	59 Horatio at Greenwich
Classic Kicks	298 Elizabeth btw Houston/Bleecker
Claudine	19 Christopher btw Greenwich/Waverly

Constanca Basto	573 Hudson btw West 11th/Bank
Crunch	404 Lafayette btw Astor Place/East 4th
Crunch	152 Christopher at Greenwich

Crunch	623 Broadway at Houston
Darling	1 Horatio at Eighth
Diane von Furstenberg The Shop	385 West 12th
	btw Washington/West Side Highway
Diesel	1 Union Square West at 14th
Eye Candy	329 Lafayette btw Bleecker/Houston
Flight 001	96 Greenwich btw West 12th/Jane
Foot Locker	734 Broadway at 8th
French Connection	700 Broadway btw Astor Place/4th
Geminola	41 Perry btw Seventh Ave South/West 4th
Gerry's	353 Bleecker btw West 10th/Charles
Ghost	28 Bond btw Lafayette/Bowery
Girlshop	819 Washington btw Ninth/Tenth
Handmade NYC	150 West 10th btw Greenwich/Seventh
Jean Shop	435 West 14th btw Ninth/Tenth
Joyce Leslie	20 University Place at Eighth
Jungle Planet	175 West 4th btw Sixth/Seventh
KD Dance	339 Lafayette at Bleecker
Laila Rowe	649 Broadway at Bleecker
Laina Jane Lingerie	45 Christopher btw Sixth/Seventh
La Petite Coquette	51 University Place btw Ninth/Tenth
The Leather Man	111 Christopher btw Bleecker/Hudson
Le Chateau	704 Broadway
	btw Washington Place/West 4th
Lucien Pellat-Finet	14 Christopher btw Sixth/Seventh
Lulu Guinness	394 Bleecker btw 11th/Perry
Magic Shoes	178 Bleecker btw MacDougal/Sullivan
Make 10	49 West 8th btw Fifth/Sixth
Marc Jacobs	403 Bleecker btw West 11th/Hudson
Marc Jacobs (accessories)	385 Bleecker
	btw West 11th/Perry
Massimo Bizzocchi	433 West 14th btw Ninth/Tenth
Memes	3 Great Jones btw Lafayette/Broadway
Nalu NYC	10 Little West 12th btw Seventh/Washington
Nom De Guerre	640 Broadway at Bleecker
Olive & Bette's	384 Bleecker at Perry
Otte	121 Greenwich at 13th
Peanutbutter & Jane	617 Hudson btw Jane/12th
Petit Peton	27 West 8th btw Fifth/Sixth
Polo Ralph Lauren	381 Bleecker btw Perry/Charles
Project 159	159 Seventh Ave South btw Perry/Waverly
Purdy Girl	220 Thompson btw Bleecker/West 3rd
Purdy Girl	540 LaGuardia Pl at Bleecker
Rafé New York	1 Bleecker at Bowery
Rags A Go Go	218 West 14th btw Seventh/Eighth
Rebecca & Drew Manufacturing	342 West 13th at Hudson
Ricky's	718 Broadway btw Astor Place/4th
Ricky's	44 East Eighth at Greene

Neighborhoods

Ruben Chappelle	410 West 14th btw Ninth/Tenth
Ruehl	370 Bleecker btw Charles/Perry
Scoop	861 & 873 & 875 Washington at 14th
Screaming Mimi's	382 Lafayette btw Great Jones/4th
Sisley	753 Broadway at 8th
Spatial etc	19 Christopher at Gay
Thom Browne	17 Little West 12th btw Ninth/Washington
Tibetan Arts & Crafts	197 Bleecker btw MacDougal/Sixth
Tina Tang	49 Greenwich btw Charles/Perry
Tina Tang Too	48 Greenwich btw Charles/Perry
Transit	665 Broadway at Bond
Untitled	26 West 8th btw Fifth/Sixth
Urban Outfitters	374 6th btw Waverly/Washington Place
Urban Outfitters	628 Broadway btw Houston/Bleecker
Verve Shoes	105 Christopher btw Bleecker/Hudson
Viv Pickle	238 West 10th btw Bleecker/Hudson
Wet Seal	670 Broadway at Bond
Whiskey Dust	526 Hudson btw 10th/Charles
Yoya	636 Hudson at Horatio
Yoya	15 Gansevoort at Hudson

SoHo/Nolita
See map pages 304–305

37=1	37 Crosby btw Broome/Grand
30 Vandam	30 Vandam btw Sixth/Varick
A Bathing Ape (BAPE)	91 Greene btw Prince/Spring
Active Wearhouse	580 Broadway btw Broome/Spring
Add accessories	461 West Broadway btw Houston/Prince
A Détacher	262 Mott btw Houston/Prince
Adidas	136 Wooster btw Houston/Prince
Adidas Performance Store	610 Broadway at Houston
agnès b.	103 Greene btw Prince/Spring
agnès b. homme	79 Greene btw Spring/Broome
Alex	268 Elizabeth btw Houston/Prince
Alpana Bawa	41 Grand btw West Broadway/Thompson
American Apparel	121 Spring at Greene
Anna Sui	113 Greene btw Prince/Spring
Anne Fontaine	93 Greene btw Prince/Spring
Anne Klein	417 West Broadway btw Prince/Spring
Anthropologie	375 West Broadway btw Spring/Broome
A.P.C.	131 Mercer btw Prince/Spring
Arden B	532 Broadway btw Prince/Spring
Art Fiend Foundation	123 Ludlow btw Rivington/Delancey
Ashley Tyler	112 Greene btw Prince/Spring
Atelier	125 Crosby at Prince
Avirex	652 Broadway btw Bleecker/Bond
A/X Armani Exchange	568 Broadway at Prince
Bagutta Life	76 Greene btw Broome/Spring
Banana Republic (men)	528 Broadway at Spring
Banana Republic (women)	550 Broadway btw Prince/Spring

Barbara Bui 117 Wooster btw Prince/Spring
Barneys Co-op 116 Wooster btw Prince/Spring
Barry Kieselstein Cord 454 West Broadway
btw Houston/Prince

BBL (Baby Blue Line) 238 Mott btw Prince/Spring
BCBG Max Azria 120 Wooster btw Prince/Spring
Benetton 555 Broadway btw Prince/Spring
Betsey Johnson 138 Wooster btw Houston/Prince

Big Drop 174 Spring btw Thompson/West Broadway
Big Drop 425 West Broadway btw Prince/Spring
Bio 29 Prince btw Elizabeth/Mott
Bloomingdale's SoHo 504 Broadway btw Spring/Broome

Blue Bag 266 Elizabeth btw Houston/Prince
Bonaparte 154 Spring btw West Broadway/Wooster
Brooklyn Industries 286 Lafayette btw Prince/Houston
Built by Wendy 7 Center Market Place
` btw Broome/Grand

Cadeau 254 Elizabeth btw Houston/Prince
Calvin Klein Underwear 104 Prince btw Greene/Mercer
Calvin Tran 115 Grand btw Mercer/Broadway
Calypso Bijoux 252 Mott btw Houston/Prince

Calypso 280 Mott btw Houston/Prince
Calypso 424 Broome btw Crosby/Lafayette
Calypso Enfant 426 Broome btw Crosby/Lafayette
Calypso Outlet 405 Broome btw Centre/Lafayette

Catherine Malandrino 468 Broome at Greene
Cath Kidston 201 Mulberry btw Spring/Kenmare
Chanel 139 Spring at Wooster
Chelsea Girl 63 Thompson btw Spring/Broome

Christopher Fischer 80 Wooster at Spring
Christopher Totman 262 Mott btw Houston/Prince
Club Monaco 121 Prince btw Wooster/Greene
Club Monaco 520 Broadway btw Spring/Broome

Coach 143 Prince at West Broadway
C.P.Shades 154 Spring btw Wooster/West Broadway
C.Ronson 269 Elizabeth btw Houston/Prince
Cynthia Rowley 112 Wooster btw Prince/Spring

D&G 434 West Broadway btw Prince/Spring
Debra Rodman 49 Prince at Mulberry
Deco Jewels 131 Thompson btw Houston/Prince

Diesel Children's Boutique 414-416 West Broadway
btw Prince/Spring
Domenico Vacca 367 West Broadway at Broome
Design in Textiles by Mary Jaeger 51 Spring
btw Lafayette/Mulberry
Detour 421 West Broadway at Prince

Dinosaur Designs 250 Mott btw Houston/Prince
DKNY 420 West Broadway btw Prince/Spring
Dosa 107 Thompson btw Prince/Spring

Neighborhoods

Duncan Quinn	8 Spring btw Bowery/Elizabeth
Dusica Dusica	67 Prince at Crosby
Earl Jean	160 Mercer btw Houston/Prince
Easy Spirit	182 Broadway at John
Eastern Mountain Sports	591 Broadway btw Houston/Prince
Eddie Bauer	578 Broadway btw Houston/Prince
Eleni Lambros	591 Broadway btw Houston/Prince
Elie Tahari	417 West Broadway btw Prince/Spring
Emporio Armani	410 West Broadway btw Prince/Spring
Eres	98 Wooster at Spring
Eskandar	33 East 10th btw University/Broadway
Flying A	169 Spring btw West Broadway/Thompson
Foot Locker	523 Broadway btw Spring/Broome
Forever 21	40 East 14th at Fifth
Fossil	541 Broadway btw Prince/Spring
Fragments	116 Prince at Greene
French Connection	435 West Broadway at Prince
Gas Bijoux	238 Mott btw Prince/Spring
Gi Gi	217 Mulberry btw Prince/Spring
Girl Cat	167 Elizabeth btw Spring/Kenmare
Girlprops.com	153 Prince at West Broadway
Guess?	537 Broadway btw Prince/Spring
H&M	588 Broadway btw Prince/Spring
H&M	515 Broadway btw Spring/Broome
Hans Koch	174 Prince btw Sullivan/Thompson
The Hat Shop	120 Thompson btw Prince/Spring
Helen Mariën	250 Mott btw Houston/Prince
Henry Lehr	232 Elizabeth btw Prince/Lafayette
Henry Lehr	9 Prince btw Elizabeth/Bowery
Highway	238 Mott btw Prince/Spring
Hogan	134 Spring btw Greene/Wooster
Hollywould	198 Elizabeth btw Prince/Spring
Hotel Venus	382 West Broadway btw Spring/Broome
Hugo Boss	132 Greene btw Houston/Prince
Hunting World	118 Greene btw Prince/Spring
ICB	159 Mercer btw West Houston/Prince
If	94 Grand btw Mercer/Greene
i Heart	262 Mott btw Houston/Prince
Il Bisonte	120 Sullivan btw Prince/Spring
Ina	101 Thompson btw Prince/Spring
Institut	97 Spring btw Mercer/Broadway
Intermix	98 Prince at Mercer
Jack Gomme	252 Elizabeth btw Houston/Prince
J.Crew	99 Prince at Mercer
Jenne Maag	29 Spring at Mott
Jill Stuart	100 Greene btw Prince/Spring
J.Lindeberg	126 Spring at Greene
John Fluevog Shoes	250 Mulberry at Prince

John Varvatos	122 Spring Street
Jonathan Adler	130 West 57th btw Sixth/Seventh
Joseph	106 Greene btw Prince/Spring
Julian & Sara	103 Mercer btw Prince/Spring
Juno	543 Broadway btw Prince/Spring
Just for Tykes	83 Mercer btw Spring/Broome
Kate Spade	454 Broome at Mercer
Kazuyo Nakano	117 Crosby btw Houston/Prince
Keiko	62 Greene btw Spring/Broome
Kelly Christy	(new location n/a at press time)
Kenneth Cole	597 Broadway btw Houston/Prince
Kinnu	43 Spring btw Mulberry/Mott
Kirna Zabête	96 Greene btw Prince/Spring
Klurk	360 Broome btw Mott/Elizabeth
Label	265 Lafayette btw Houston/Prince
Lace	223 Mott btw Prince/Spring
Lacoste	134 Prince btw Wooster/West Broadway
Laila Rowe	424 West Broadway btw Prince/Spring
Laila Rowe	199 Prince btw Sullivan/Macdougal
La Perla	93 Greene btw Prince/Spring
Laundry by Shelli Segal	97 Wooster btw Prince/Spring
Le Corset	80 Thompson btw Spring/Broome
Legacy	109 Thompson btw Prince/Spring
Les Petits Chapelais	142 Sullivan btw Houston/Prince
LeSportSac	176 Spring btw West Broadway/Thompson
Lilliput/SoHo Kids	265 Lafayette btw Prince/Spring
Lilliput/SoHo Kids	240 Lafayatte btw Prince/Spring
Linda's	462 West Broadway btw Prince/Houston
Liora Manné	91 Grand btw Mercer/Greene
Lisa Shaub	232 Mulberry btw Prince/Spring
Living Doll	280 Lafayette btw Houston/Prince
Louis Vuitton	116 Greene btw Prince/Spring
The Lounge	593 Broadway btw Prince/Houston
Lucky Brand Jeans	38 Greene at Grand
Lunettes et Chocolat	25 Prince btw Mott/Elizabeth
Lyell	173 Elizabeth at Delancey
Lynn Park NY	51 Wooster at Broome
m0851	106 Wooster btw Prince/Spring
Makie	109 Thompson btw Prince/Spring
Malia Mills	199 Mulberry btw Spring/Kenmare
Malo	125 Wooster btw Prince/Spring
Manhattan Portage	301 West Broadway btw Canal/Grand
Mankind	8 Greene btw Grand/Canal
Marc Jacobs	163 Mercer btw Houston/Prince
Mare	426 West Broadway btw Prince/Spring
Marni	161 Mercer btw Houston/Prince
Mary Efron	68 Thompson btw Spring/Broome
Mat Mercer	49 Mercer btw Grand/Broome
Matta	115 Grand btw Broadway/Mercer

Neighborhoods

Mavi	510 Broome btw Thompson/West Broadway
MaxMara	450 West Broadway btw Prince/Houston
Max Studio	426 West Broadway btw Prince/Spring
Mayle	242 Elizabeth btw Prince/Houston
Me & Ro	241 Elizabeth btw Houston/Prince
Mexx	500 Broadway btw Prince/Spring
Michael K	512 Broadway btw Spring/Broome
Min-K	219 Mott btw Prince/Spring
Miss Sixty	386 West Broadway btw Spring/Broome
Miu Miu	100 Prince btw Greene/Mercer
Mixona	262 Mott btw Houston/Prince
Morgane Le Fay	67 Wooster btw Spring/Broome
MZ Wallace	93 Crosby btw Prince/Spring
Nancy Geist	107 Spring at Mercer
Nanette Lepore	423 Broome btw Lafayette/Crosby
New & Almost New	65 Mercer btw Spring/Kenmare
Nine West	577 Broadway at Prince
Objets du Desir	241 Mulberry btw Prince/Spring
Old Navy Clothing Co	503 Broadway btw Spring/Broome
Olive & Bette's	158 Spring btw Wooster/West Broadway
Only Hearts	230 Mott btw Prince/Spring
Onward SoHo	159 Mercer btw Prince/Houston
Opening Ceremony	35 Howard btw Broadway/Lafayette
Operations	60 Mercer at Broome
The Original Levi's Store	536 Broadway btw Prince/Spring
Ottiva	192 Spring btw Thompson/Sullivan
Otto Tootsi Plohound	413 West Broadway btw Prince/Spring
Otto Tootsi Plohound	273 Lafayette btw Houston/Prince
Patagonia	101 Wooster btw Prince/Spring
Patina	451 Broome btw Broadway/Mercer
Pearl River Mart	477 Broadway btw Broome/Grand
Peter Fox Shoes	105 Thompson btw Prince/Spring
Peter Hermann	118 Thompson btw Prince/Spring
Phat Farm	129 Prince btw West Broadway/Wooster
Phi	71 Greene btw Spring/Broome
Philosophy di Alberta Ferretti	452 West Broadway btw Houston/Prince
Pipsqueak	248 Mott btw Houston/Prince
Pleats Please, Issey Miyake	128 Wooster at Prince
Polo Ralph Lauren	379 West Broadway btw Spring/Broome
Poppy W	281 Mott btw Houston/Prince
Project 234	234 Mulberry btw Prince/Spring
Push	240 Mulberry btw Prince/Spring
Prada	575 Broadway at Prince
The Puma Store	521 Broadway btw Spring/Broome
Quiksilver	109 Spring btw Mercer/Greene
Ralph Lauren	381 West Broadway btw Broome/Spring
Rampage	127 Prince at Wooster

R by 45rpm	169 Mercer at Houston
Rebecca Taylor	260 Mott btw Houston/Prince
Red Wong	181 Mulberry btw Kenmare/Broome
Reiss	387 West Broadway Spring/Broome
Replay Store	109 Prince at Greene
Resurrection Vintage	217 Mott btw Prince/Spring
Ricky's	590 Broadway btw Houston/Prince
Ricky's	235 Mulberry btw Prince/Spring
Sacco	111 Thompson btw Prince/Spring
Saeyoung Vu Couture	214 Mulberry btw Prince/Spring
Sample	268 Elizabeth btw Houston/Prince
Scoop	532 Broadway btw Prince/Spring
Scott Mallory	155 Spring btw West Broadway/Wooster
Sean	132 Thompson btw Houston/Prince
Seize sur Vingt	243 Elizabeth btw Houston/Prince
Selvedge	250 Mulberry btw Prince/Spring
Seven New York	110 Mercer btw Prince/Spring
Sharagano	529 Broadway btw Prince/Spring
Shin Choi	119 Mercer btw Prince/Spring
Shoe	197 Mulberry btw Spring/Kenmare
Sigerson Morrison	242 Mott btw Houston/Prince
Sigerson Morrison	28 Prince btw Mott/Elizabeth
Skechers	530 Broadway at Spring
SoHo Baby	247 Elizabeth btw Houston/Prince
Sol	6 Prince btw Bowery/Elizabeth
Stackhouse	276 Lafayette btw Houston/Prince
Stackhouse	325 Lafayette btw Houston/Bleecker
Steve Madden	540 Broadway btw Prince/Spring
Steven	529 Broadway btw Prince/Spring
Steven Alan	60 Wooster btw Spring/Broome
Stüssy	140 Wooster btw Houston/Prince
Supreme	274 Lafayette btw Houston/Prince
Swiss Army	136 Prince btw West Broadway/Wooster
Ted Baker London	107 Grand btw Mercer/Broadway
Temperley	453-455 Broome at Mercer
T'Frisson	77 Greene btw Spring/Broome
Tina Tang	230 Mulberry btw Prince/Spring
Togs	68 Spring btw Crosby/Lafayette
Tommy Hilfiger	372 West Broadway btw Spring/Broome
Tory by TRB	257 Elizabeth btw Houston/Prince
Tracy Feith	209 Mulberry btw Spring/Kenmare
Triple Five Soul	290 Lafayette btw Houston/Prince
Tsubi	219c Mulberry btw Prince/Spring
Union	172 Spring btw West Broadway/Thompson
Unis	226 Elizabeth btw Houston/Prince
United Nude Terra Plana	260 Elizabeth btw Houston/Prince
Varda	147 Spring btw Wooster/West Broadway
Via Bus Stop	172 Mercer at East Houston

Neighborhoods

Vice	252 Lafayette btw Prince/Spring
Victoria Keen	357 Lafayette btw Bond/Bleecker
Victoria's Secret	565 Broadway at Prince
Vilebrequin	436 West Broadway btw Prince/Spring
Vitraux	72 Thompson btw Spring/Broome
Vivienne Tam	99 Greene btw Prince/Spring
Warehouse	581 Broadway btw Houston/Prince
Western Spirit	395 Broadway at Walker
What Comes Around Goes Around	351 West Broadway btw Broome/Grand
Wolford Boutique	122 Greene at Prince
Work in Progress	513 Broadway btw Broome/Spring
Work in Progress	481 Broadway btw Broome/Grand
X Girl	265 Lafayette btw Prince/Spring
Y & Kei water the earth	125 Greene btw Prince/Spring
Yaso	62 Grand btw West Broadway/Wooster
Yellow Rat Bastard	478 Broadway btw Broome/Grand
Yohji Yamamoto	103 Grand at Mercer
Yvone Christa	107 Mercer btw Prince/Spring
Zabari	506 Broadway btw Spring/Broome
Zabari	542 Broadway btw Prince/Spring
Zara	580 Broadway at Prince
Zero/Maria Cornejo	225 Mott btw Prince/Spring
Zion	93 Grand btw Greene/Mercer

Lower Manhattan/Tribeca *See map pages 306–307*

Abercrombie & Fitch	119 Water at S.S.S.
Aerosoles	18 John btw Broadway/Nassau
Assets London	152 Franklin btw Hudson/Varick
Banana Republic	200 Vesley at the World Financial Center
Benetton	10 Fulton at S.S.S.
Century 21	22 Cortland btw Church/Broadway
Champs	89 South at S.S.S.
Crunch	25 Broadway at Morris
Daffy's	50 Broadway at Exchange Pl
Foot Locker	89 South at S.S.S.
Gap	225 Liberty btw West Side Highway and South End Ave
Gap Kids & Baby Gap	11 Fulton at S.S.S.
Garde Robe	(no published address for security reasons)
Guess?	23-25 Fulton at S.S.S.
Issey Miyake	119 Hudson at North Moore
J.Crew	203 Front at S.S.S.
Koh's Kids	311 Greenwich btw Chambers/Reade
Loftworks@Lafayette	100 Lafayette btw White/Walker
Men's Wearhouse	115 Broadway at Cedar
Miao	176 Hester btw Mott/Mulberry
Mika Inatome	93 Reade btw Church/West Broadway
Modell's	200 Broadway btw Fulton/John
Modell's	55 Chambers at Broadway

Montmartre   at the World Financial Center
Nikki B   20 Harrison btw Greenwich/Hudson
Nine West   2 Broadway btw Beaver/Whitehall
Samuel's Hats   74 Nassau btw Fulton/John

Shack Inc   137 West Broadway btw Thomas/Duane
Shoofly   42 Hudson btw Thomas/Duane
Sorelle Firenze   (new private showroom, n/a at press time)
Talbots   189-191 Front at S.S.S.

Victoria's Secret   19 Fulton at S.S.S.
Young's Hat Corner   139 Nassau at Beekman

Harlem   *See map pages 298–299*

Aerosoles   2913 Broadway btw 113/114th
Champs   208 West 125th at Seventh
Foot Locker   268 West 125th at Eighth
H&M   125 West 125th at Lenox

Lane Bryant   222 West 125th btw Seventh/Eighth
Modell's   300 West 125th btw Frederick Douglass Blvd/
                                               St Nicholas Blvd
Motherhood Maternity 163 East 125th btw Lexington/Third

Brooklyn

Aerosoles   100C Seventh Ave
Amarcord Vintage Fashion   223 Bedford Ave
                                 btw North 4th/North 5th
American Apparel   104 North 6th btw Wythe/Berry

American Apparel   112 Court at State
B2Gear   777 Fulton btw South Oxford/South Portland
Baby Bird   428 7th Ave btw 14/15th
Beacon's Closet   220 5th Ave btw President/Union

Beacon's Closet   88 North 11th btw Berry/Wythe
Blueberi   143 Front btw Pearl/Jay
Brooklyn Industries   184 Broadway at Drakes
Brooklyn Industries   206 5th Ave at Union

Brooklyn Industries   162 Bedford Ave at North 8th
Brooklyn Industries   100 Smith at Atlantic
Built by Wendy Outlet   46 North 6th btw Wythe/Kent
Calliope   135 Grand btw Berry/Bedford

Castor & Pollux   671/2 6th Ave at Bergen
Catbird   390 Metropolitan Ave at Havemeyer
Diana Kane   229b 5th Ave btw Carroll/President
Diane T   174 Court btw Amity/Congress

Flirt   252 Smith btw Douglas/DeGraw
Flirt   93 5th Ave btw Warren/Baltic
Fortuna   370 Metropolitan at Havemeyer
Frida's Closet   296 Smith btw Union/Sackett

Gureje   886 Pacific at Washington
Hootie Couture   321 Flatbush Ave at 7th
Hot Toddie   741 Fulton btw South Portland/South Elliot

In God We Trust	135 Wythe Ave btw North 7th/North 8th
Isa	88 North 6th at Wythe
Lily	209 Court btw Warren/Wyckoff
Love Shine	249 Grand btw Driggs/Roebling
Neda	413a 7th Ave btw 13/14th
Otte	132 North 5th at Bedford Ave
Pieces	671 Vanderbilt Ave at Park Place
Premium Goods	347 5th btw 4th/5th St
Redberi	339 Flatbush Ave btw Park/Prospect
Slang Betty	172 5th Ave btw Lincoln/Berkeley
Sleep	110 North Sixth at Berry
Soda Fine	246 DeKalb Ave btw Clermont/Vanderbilt
Watts	248 Smith btw Douglass/Degraw

Stores by Category

Women's Accessories

AB Apollo Braun
Add Accessories
Alexandre de Paris
Alexia Crawford Accessories
Annika Inez
Anthropologie
Azaleas
Barneys New York
Barry Kieselstein Cord
Bergdorf Goodman
Bess
Beverly Feldman
Blair Delmonico
Bloomingdale's
Borealis
Boucher Jewelry
Boyd's Pharmacy
Butik
Calypso St Barths
Castor & Pollux
Catbird
Catherine
Chanel
Che Che
Claudine
David Yurman
Destination
Dinosaur Designs
Doo.ri
Doyle & Doyle
Dressing Room
Edith & Daha
Ellen Christine Millinery
En Soie
Eye Candy
Fabulous Fanny's
Flight 001
Forever 21
Fortuna
Fragments
Frock
Gamine
Gas
Girl Cat
Girlprops.com
Girlshop
The Good, The Bad
  & The Ugly
Handmade NYC
Helen Mariën
Henri Bendel
Henry Beguelin

Hermès
Highway
Hollywould
In God We Trust
It's a Mod Mod World
Kors Michael Kors
LaCrasia Gloves
LAI
Laila Rowe
Lingo
Lord & Taylor
Love Shine
Lunettes et Chocolat
Lynn Park
Macy's
Marc Jacobs
Massimo Bizzocchi
Max Studio
Me & Ro
Miao
Miss Sixty
Objets du Desir
Orva
Pat Areias
Peacock
Pearl Daddy
Pearl River
Pippin
Precision
Project 159
The Puma Store
Purdy Girl
Push
Rampage
Redberi
Reminiscence
Roslyn
Scarpe Diem
Selima Optique
Slang Betty
Spatial Etc
Soda Fine
Sonia Rykiel
Steven Vaughan
Suzette Sundae
Tahir
Three Turtledoves
Tommy Hilfiger
Toto
Variazioni
VBH Gallery
Verve

Women's Accessories (continued)

Via Bus Stop
Vitraux
XGirl

Yvone Christa
Zitomer

Women's Ballet, Dance & Work-Out

Adidas
Adidas Performance Store
Athlete's Foot
Bloch
Capezio
Champs
Crunch
Daffy's

Danskin
Equinox
Fila
KD Dance
Lady Foot Locker
New York Om Yoga
Niketown
The Puma Store

Bridal

Amsale
Angelo Lambrou
Barney's New York
Bergdorf Goodman
Blair Delmonico
Bloomingdale's
Blue
Bonaparte
Bridal Atelier
Carolina Herrera
Century 21
Clea Colet
Clifford Michael Design
Cose Belle
Couture by Jennifer Dule
Designer Loft
Eleni Lambros
Emanuel Ungaro
Eric Shoes
Escada
The Gown Company
Jackie Rogers (mother of
  the bride)
J.Crew
Jimmy Choo (shoes only)
Kenneth Cole (shoes only)
Kleinfeld
Lara Hélène Bridal Atelier
Lucy Barnes

Macy's
Maggie Norris Couture
Manolo Blahnik (shoes only)
Mary Adams
Michael's, The Consignment
  Shop for Women
Michelle Roth Design
  Studio
Mika Inatome
Mom's Night Out
Morgane Le Fay
Nicole Miller
Norma Kamali
Oscar de la Renta
Peter Fox (shoes only)
Pilar Rossi
Reem Acra
Saeyoung Vu Couture
Saks Fifth Avenue
Selia Yang
Stuart Weitzman (shoes
  only)
Thread (bridesmaids only)
Tupli
Vanessa Noel (shoes only)
Vera Wang Bridal Salon
Vera Wang Maids on
  Madison (bridesmaids)
Zora

Women's Consignment

Alice Underground
Allan & Suzi
Bis Designer Resale
Encore
Fisch for the Hip
Fortuna
Ina

Kavanagh's Designer
Resale
Michael's, The Consignment
Shop for Women
Project 159
Tokio 7
Tokyo Joe

Women's Contemporary

AB Apollo Braun
ABH Design
A.Cheng
A Détacher
agnès b.
Albertine
Alpana Bawa
Alskling
American Apparel
Amy Chan
Anastasia Holland
Anik
Anna
Anthropologie
The Apartment
A.P.C.
Arden B
Ashley Tyler
Assets London
Atrium
BBL (Baby Blue Line)
Bagutta
Barneys New York
Basiques
BCBG by Max Azria
Bebe
Believe It
Bergdorf Goodman
Berkley Girl
Betsey Bunky Nini
Big Drop
Bloomingdale's
Bond 07
Boudoir
Brooklyn Industries
Built by Wendy Outlet
Calypso St Barths
Cantaloup
Carlos Miele
Catbird

Catherine Malandrino
Central Park West
Christopher Fischer
Christopher Totman
Claudine
Club Monaco
C.P.Shades
CPW
C.Ronson
Crush
Darling
Darryl's
Debra Rodman
Detour
Diana & Jeffries
Diane T
DKNY
D/L Cerney
Doo.ri
Dosa
Dressing Room
Eileen Fisher
Elizabeth Charles
Emporio Armani
Epperson Studio
Erica Tanov
Fame
Find Outlet
Flirt
Foley & Corinna
Forreal
French Connection
Galo
Gamine
Ghost
Gi Gi
Girlshop
H&M
Henri Bendel
Henry Beguelin

Women's Contemporary *(continued)*

Highway
Hugo Boss
Huminska New York
ICB
If
i heart
In God We Trust
Institut
Intermix
Jeffrey New York
Jenne Maag
Jill Anderson
J.Lindeberg
Johnson
Joseph
Kirna Zabête
Label
La La
Language
Laundry by Shelli Segal
Le Chateau
Liana
Lily
Linda Dresner
Loftworks @ Lafayette
Lucy Barnes
Lynn Park NY
Mark Montano
Marni
Martier
Max Studio
Mayle
Meg
Miks
Min-K
Min Lee
Missbehave
Miss Sixty
MoMo FaLana
Montmartre
Nalu NYC
Nancy & Co
Nanette Lepore
Nellie M
Oilily for Women
Olive & Bette's
Onward Soho
The Open Door Gallery
Opening Ceremony
The Original Levi's Store
Otte
Outlet 7

Parke & Ronen
Peacock NYC
Phi
Pleats Please, Issey Miyake
Plum
Project 159
Pookie & Sebastian
Precision
Purdy Girl
Quiksilver
Rampage
Really Great Things
Redberri
Red Wong
Reiss
Roberta Freymann
Robert Danes
Rubin Chappelle
Runway
Saada
Sac Boutique
Saks Fifth Avenue
Scoop
Searle
Selia Yang
Shack Inc
Shanghai Tang
Sharagano
Shin Choi
Shop
Sisley
Sorelle Firenze
Spatial Etc
Steven Alan
Suzette Sundae
Tahir
Tees.com
T'Frisson
TG-170
Theory
Togs
Tracy Feith
Trash & Vaudeville
Tsubi
Untitled
Variazioni
Vertigo
Vertigo &
Friends/Magaschoni
Via Bus Stop
Vice
Vlada

Women's Contemporary *(continued)*

Warehouse
Xgirl
Yaso
Yellow Rat Bastard
Yigal Azrouel

Zabari
Zan
Zara
Zero/Maria Cornejo
Zora

Women's Custom Tailoring

Arthur Gluck Shirtmakers
Couture by Jennifer Dule
Domenico Spana
Domenico Vacca
Frank Shattuck
Frida's Closet
John Anthony
Jussara Lee
Keiko (swimwear)
The Leather & Suede
  Workshop
Lee Anderson
Lucy Barnes
Maggie Norris
Mary Adams

Meg
Mika Inatome (bridal)
Mom's Night Out
New York City Custom
  Leather
Piccione
Pierre Garroudi
Pilar Rossi
Reva Mivasagar
Ripplu (undergarments)
Seize sur Vingt
Sylvia Heisel
Thread
Vincent Nicolosi

Women's Designer

Alexander McQueen
Anna Sui
Anne Klein
Balenciaga
Barbara Bui
Betsey Johnson
Blair Delmonico
Calvin Klein
Carolina Herrera
Catherine Malandrino
Celine
Chanel
Chloé
Christian Dior
Comme des Garçons
Costume National
Cynthia Rowley
D&G
Diane von Furstenberg
Dolce & Gabbana
Donna Karan New York
Eleni Lambros
Elie Tahari

Emanuel Ungaro
Escada
Fendi
Geoffrey Beene
Gianfranco Ferré
Giorgio Armani
Givenchy
Gucci
Hervé Léger
Hugo Boss
Issey Miyake
Jean Paul Gaultier
Jill Stuart
Kenzo
Kors Michael Kors
Krizia
Les Copains
Louis Vuitton
Lucien Pellat-Finet
Lucy Barnes
Maggie Norris Couture
Marc Jacobs
MaxMara

Women's Contemporary (continued)

Huminska New York
ICB
If
i heart
In God We Trust
Institut
Intermix
Jeffrey New York
Jenne Maag
Jill Anderson
J.Lindeberg
Johnson
Joseph
Kirna Zabête
Label
La La
Language
Laundry by Shelli Segal
Le Chateau
Liana
Lily
Linda Dresner
Loftworks @ Lafayette
Lucy Barnes
Lynn Park NY
Mark Montano
Marni
Martier
Max Studio
Mayle
Meg
Miks
Min-K
Min Lee
Missbehave
Miss Sixty
MoMo FaLana
Montmartre
Nalu NYC
Nancy & Co
Nanette Lepore
Nellie M
Oilily for Women
Olive & Bette's
Onward Soho
The Open Door Gallery
Opening Ceremony
The Original Levi's Store
Otte
Outlet 7
Parke & Ronen
Peacock NYC

Phi
Pleats Please, Issey Miyake
Plum
Project 159
Pookie & Sebastian
Precision
Purdy Girl
Quiksilver
Rampage
Really Great Things
Redberri
Red Wong
Reiss
Roberta Freymann
Rubin Chappelle
Runway
Saada
Sac Boutique
Saks Fifth Avenue
Scoop
Searle
Selia Yang
Shack Inc
Shanghai Tang
Sharagano
Shin Choi
Shop
Sisley
Sorelle Firenze
Spatial Etc
Steven Alan
Suzette Sundae
Tahir
Tees.com
Tehen
T'Frisson
TG-170
Theory
Togs
Tracy Feith
Trash & Vaudeville
Tsubi
Untitled
Variazioni
Vertigo &
   Friends/Magaschoni
Via Bus Stop
Vice
Vlada
Warehouse
Xgirl
Yaso

Women's Contemporary *(continued)*

Yellow Rat Bastard
Yigal Azrouel
Zabari
Zan

Zara
Zero/Maria Cornejo
Zora

Women's Custom Tailoring

Arthur Gluck Shirtmakers
Couture by Jennifer Dule
Domenico Spana
Domenico Vacca
Frank Shattuck
Frida's Closet
John Anthony
Jussara Lee
Keiko (swimwear)
The Leather & Suede
  Workshop
Lee Anderson
Lucy Barnes
Maggie Norris
Mary Adams

Meg
Mika Inatome (bridal)
Mom's Night Out
New York City Custom
  Leather
Piccione
Pierre Garroudi
Pilar Rossi
Reva Mivasagar
Ripplu (undergarments)
Seize sur Vingt
Sylvia Heisel
Thread
Vincent Nicolosi

Women's Designer

Alexander McQueen
Anna Sui
Anne Klein
Balenciaga
Barbara Bui
Betsey Johnson
Blair Delmonico
Calvin Klein
Carolina Herrera
Catherine Malandrino
Celine
Chanel
Chloé
Christian Dior
Comme des Garçons
Costume National
Cynthia Rowley
D&G
Diane von Furstenberg
Dolce & Gabbana
Donna Karan New York
Eleni Lambros
Elie Tahari

Emanuel Ungaro
Escada
Fendi
Geoffrey Beene
Gianfranco Ferré
Giorgio Armani
Givenchy
Gucci
Hervé Léger
Hugo Boss
Issey Miyake
Jean Paul Gaultier
Jill Stuart
Kenzo
Kors Michael Kors
Krizia
Les Copains
Louis Vuitton
Lucien Pellat-Finet
Lucy Barnes
Maggie Norris Couture
Marc Jacobs
MaxMara

Women's Designer *(continued)*

Michael Kors
Missoni
Miu Miu
Morgane Le Fay
Net-a-Porter
Nicole Farhi
Nicole Miller
Norma Kamali
Oscar de la Renta
Philosophy by Alberta
Ferretti
Prada
Pucci
Ralph Lauren
Roberto Cavalli

Salvatore Ferragamo
Shelly Steffee
Sonia Rykiel
Stella McCartney
Temperley
Tory by TRB
Valentino
Vera Wang
Versace
Vivienne Tam
Y & Kei water the earth
Yohji Yamamoto
Yves Saint Laurent
  Rive Gauche

Women's Discount

Burlington Coat Factory
Century 21
Daffy's
Filene's Basement
Find Outlet

Forman's
Gabay's Outlet
Loehmann's
Loftworks @ Lafayette
TJ Maxx

Women's Ethnic

Bokhee
Christopher Totman
Craft Caravan
Do Kham
Frida's Closet
Gureje
Hello Sari
Himalayan Crafts
Jungle Planet
Kenzo

Kinnu
Love Shine
Matta
Neda
Pan American Phoenix
Pearl River Mart
Roberta Freymann
Tibet Arts & Crafts
Tibet Bazaar
Toto

Women's Evening & Special Occasion

37=1
Alicia Mugetti
Amsale
Angelo Lambrou
Ann Taylor
A.Tempo
BBL (Baby Blue Line)
BCBG Max Azria
Betsey Bunky Nini
Betsey Johnson
Bergdorf Goodman
Bloomingdale's
Bonaparte
Caché
Calvin Klein
Carolina Herrera
Cashmere New York
Celine
Chanel
Cheap Jack's
Christian Dior
Circle
Clea Colet
Clifford Michael Design
Cose Belle
Costume National
Couture by Jennifer Dule
D&G
David Yurman (jewelry)
Darryl's
DKNY
Donna Karan New York
Eleni Lambros
Elizabeth Charles
Emporio Armani
Entre Nous
Escada
Eva
Fendi
Fragments (jewelry)
Gallery of Wearable Art
Geoffrey Beene
Gianfranco Ferré
Giorgio Armani
Gucci
Hervé Léger
Jackie Rogers
Jane
Jill Stuart
John Anthony

Jussara Lee
Keni Valenti
Krizia
Lara Hélène Bridal Atelier
Lee Anderson
Liana
Linda Dresner
Liz Lange Maternity
Lord & Taylor
Luca Luca
Lucy Barnes
Maggie Norris Couture
Makola
Mary Adams
Mary Efron
Max Studio
Michael Kors
Michelle Roth & Co
Mom's Night Out
Oscar de la Renta
Montmartre
Morgane Le Fay
Nellie M.
Net-a-Porter
The New York Look
Nicole Miller
Norma Kamali
Phi
Pierre Garroudi
Pilar Rossi
Ralph Lauren
Reva Mivasagar
Richard Metzger
Roberta Freymann
Roberto Cavalli
Saeyoung Vu Couture
Saks Fifth Avenue
Steven Stolman
St John
Sylvia Heisel
T'Frisson
Thread
Untitled
Valentino
Variazioni
Vera Wang Bridal Salon
Versace
Via Bus Stop
Vivaldi Boutique
Yigal Azrouel

Women's Furriers

Alexandros
Alixandre
Basso Furs
Ben Thylan Furs
Bergdorf Goodman
Bloomingdale's
Christie Brothers Furs
Denimax

Fendi
The Fur Salon
  at Saks Fifth Avenue
Helen Yarmak
J.Mendel
Ritz Furs
Saks Fifth Avenue

Women's Handbags & Leather Goods

Add Accessories
A Détacher
Alexia Crawford
Anya Hindmarch
A.Testoni
Baghouse
Barneys New York
Bergdorf Goodman
Beverly Feldman
Bloomingdale's
Blue Bag
Bond 07
Bottega Veneta
Bric's
Brooklyn Industries
Bruno Magli
Burberry
Calypso St Barths
Castor & Pollux
Celine
Chanel
Che Che
Christian Dior
Christopher Fischer
Coach
Cole Haan
Crouch & Fitzgerald
Crush
Cynthia Rowley
Davide Cenci
Deco Jewels
Delfino
Denimaxx
Dernier Cri
Destination
Dior
Dolce & Gabbana
Dooney & Bourke
Doo.ri
Dressing Room

Edith & Daha
Elaine Arsanault
Eye Candy
Fendi
Fisch for the Hip
Forward
Frida's Closet
Frock
Furla
Gabay's Outlet
Gap
Ghurka
Girl Cat
Girlshop
Gucci
Guess?
Hans Koch
Helen Mariën
Helen Yarmak
Henri Bendel
Henry Beguelin
Hermès
Highway
Hogan
Hollywould
Hunting World
Il Bisonte
Ina
Issey Miyake
Jack Gomme
Jamin Puech
Jonathan Adler
Judith Leiber
Jutta Neumann
Kate Spade
Kazuyo Nakano
Kenneth Cole
LAI
Laila Rowe
Lana Marks

Categories

347

Women's Handbags & Leather Goods *(continued)*

Lederer
LeSportSac
Lingo
Longchamp
Lord & Taylor
Louis Vuitton
Love Shine
Lulu Guinness
Lunettes et Chocolat
Lynn Park
m0851
Macy's
Manhattan Portage
Marc Jacobs
Massimo Bizzocchi
Max Studio
Minette by Blue Bag
Miss Sixty
MZ Wallace
Peacock NYC
Peggy Pardon
Pelle Via Roma
Peter Hermann
Plum

Prada
Project 159
Rafé New York
René Collections
Roberto Vascon
Roslyn
Ruehl
Saks Fifth Avenue
Salvatore Ferragamo
Scarpe Diem
Scoop
Scott Mallory (belts)
Searle
Sigerson Morrison
Spatial Etc
Suarez
Suzette Sundae
T.Anthony
Tod's
Verve
Via Bus Stop
Viv Pickle
Yvone Christa

Women's Hats

Add Accessories
Amy Downs Hats at YU
Barbara Feinman Millinery
Barneys New York
Bergdorf Goodman
Bloomingdale's
Bond 07
Calypso St Barths
Cheap Jack's
Denimaxx
Destination
Doo.ri
Ellen Christine Millinery
Eugenia Kim
Forward
The Hat Shop
Henri Bendel

Huminska New York
Kelly Christy
Kirna Zabête
Lisa Shaub
Lord & Taylor
Macy's
Precision
Rampage
Roslyn
Saks Fifth Avenue
Samuel's Hats
Shoofly
Suzanne Couture Millinery
Temperley
Verve
Village Scandal

Women's Hosiery

Allure Lingerie
Ann Taylor Loft
Assets London
Barneys New York
Bergdorf Goodman
Bloomingdale's
Capezio
Enerla Lingerie
Eres
Fogal
Henri Bendel

Laina Jane Lingerie
Legs Beautiful
Lingerie on Lex
Lord & Taylor
Macy's
Orva
Ricky's
Saks Fifth Avenue
Victoria's Secret
Wolford Boutique

Women's Juniors

Abercrombie & Fitch
American Apparel
American Eagle Outfitters
A.Tempo
B2Gear
Basic Basic
Betwixt
Billabong
Bloomingdale's
Century 21
Crush
Express
Forreal Basics
Gap
H&M
i heart
Infinity
Le Chateau
Lester's
Lord of the Fleas

Macy's
Magic Windows
Marsha D.D.
Miss Sixty
The New York Look
Old Navy Clothing Co
The Original Levi's Store
Orva
Peter Elliot Junior
Quiksilver
Ralph Lauren
Reminiscence
Sean John
Space Kiddets
Tommy Hilfiger
Wet Seal
X Girl
XLarge
Zabari
Z' Girl

Categories

Women's Leather

Avirex
Behrle
Bric's
Chanel
Chrome Hearts
Clifford Michael Design
Denimaxx
Dior
Fendi
Gucci
Henry Beguelin

Jack Gomme
The Jean Shop
Kenneth Cole
Leather Corner
The Leather & Suede
   Workshop
Lost Art
m0851
New York City Custom
   Leather
Tahir

Women's Lingerie & Sleepwear

37=1
Agent Provocateur
Allure Lingerie
Azaleas
Barneys New York
Bergdorf Goodman
Bloomers
Bloomingdale's
Bonne Nuit
Bra Smyth
Brief Encounters
Catriona MacKechnie
Darling
Diane Kane
Enerla Lingerie
Eres
Erica Tanov
Fogal
Gap
Henri Bendel
Hotel Venus
J.Crew
Joyce Leslie
Laina Jane Lingerie
La Perla
La Petite Coquette
Le Corset
Legs Beautiful
Linda's
Lingerie on Lex
Lord & Taylor
Lyell
Macy's
Makie
Martier
Mixona
Motherhood Maternity
Myla
Nocturne
Old Navy Clothing Co
Only Hearts
Peggy Pardon
Petit Bateau
Porthault
Purdy Girl
Ripplu
Roberto Cavalli
Saks Fifth Avenue
Sleep
Takashimaya
Victoria's Secret
Wet Seal

Maternity

A Pea in the Pod
Barneys New York
Burlington Coat Factory
Cadeau
Liz Lange Maternity
Lucy Barnes
Maternity Works
Mimi Maternity
Mom's Night Out
Motherhood Maternity
Veronique Maternity

Women's Petite Size

Ann Taylor
Bloomingdale's
Dana Buchman
Forman's
Loehmann's
Lord & Taylor
Macy's
Saks Fifth Avenue
Talbots

Women's Plus Size

Bloomingdale's
Burlington Coat Factory
Daphne
Elleven Up (shoes)
Forman's
H&M
Lane Bryant

Lord & Taylor
Macy's
Marina Rinaldi
Old Navy Clothing Co
Richard Metzger
Saks Fifth Avenue
SoHo Woman

Women's Shirts

A.Cheng
agnès b.
Anne Fontaine
Ann Taylor
A.P.C.
Banana Republic
Barami
Barneys New York
Bergdorf Goodman
Bloomingdale's
Borrelli
Brioni
Brooks Brothers
Charles Tyrwhitt
Davide Cenci
D/L Cerney
Duncan Quinn
Elie Tahari
Eredi Pisan
Eskandar
Gap
Jackie Rogers
J.Crew
J.Lindeberg
J.McLaughlin

Joseph
Leggiadro
Lyell
Massimo Bizzocchi
Miks
Paul Smith
Paul Stuart
Peter Elliot Women
Phi
Ralph Lauren
Rebecca & Drew
Reiss
Rubin Chappelle
Saks Fifth Avenue
Scoop
Seize sur Vingt
Shin Choi
Talbots
Temperley
Theory
Thomas Pink
Turnbull & Asser
Vertigo &
   Friends/Magaschoni

Women's Shoes

Aerosoles
Aldo
Anthony T. Kirby
Arche
A.Testoni
Avitto
Banana Republic
Barbara Shaum
Barneys Co-op
Barneys New York
Bati
Belgian Shoes

Bergdorf Goodman
Beverly Feldman
Bloomingdale's
Bottega Veneta
Botticelli
Bruno Magli
Calliope
Camper
Capezio
Celine
Cesare Paciotti
Chanel

Women's Shoes *(continued)*

Cherry
Chloé
Christian Louboutin
Chuckies
Cole Haan
Constanca Basto
Costume National
Dusica Dusica
East Side Kids
Easy Spirit
Edith & Daha
Elleven Up
Emanuel Ungaro
Enzo Angiolini
Eric Shoes
Fratelli Rossetti
French Sole
Frock
Gabay's Outlet
Galo
Geox
Giordano's
Giraudon
Girl Cat
Giuseppe Zanotti Design
Gucci
Harry's Shoes
Henry Beguelin
Hogan
Hollywould
Iramo
Jaime Mascaro
Jeffrey New York
Jimmy Choo
J.M.Weston
John Fluevog Shoes
Juno
Jutta Neumann
Kenneth Cole
Lace
Lord & Taylor
Macy's
Magic Shoes
Make 10
Manolo Blahnik
Marc Jacobs
Mare
Martinez Valero
Maud Frizon
Medici
Michel Perry

Miss Sixty
Miu Miu
Nancy Geist
New York Look
Nine West
Orva
Oscar de la Renta
Ottiva
Otto Tootsi Plohound
Peter Fox Shoes
Petit Peton
Prada
Project 159
Rapax
Really Great Things
René Mancini
Robert Clergerie
Rockport
Sacco
Saks Fifth Avenue
Salvatore Ferragamo
Santoni
Scarpe Diem
Searle
Shoe
The Shoe Box
Sigerson Morrison
Skechers
Sonia Rykiel
Stephane Kélian
Steve Madden
Stuart Weitzman
Stubbs & Wootton
Suzette Sundae
Tahir
Tani
Tanino Crisci
Timberland
Tod's
Trash & Vaudeville
Tupli
Unisa
United Nude Terra Plana
Vanessa Noel
Varda
Verve Shoes
Via Bus Stop
Via Spiga
Vincent & Edgar
Walter Steiger
Warren Edwards

Women's Swimwear

Adidas Performance Store
Azaleas
Barneys New York
BCBG Max Azria
Believe It NYC
Benetton
Bergdorf Goodman
Billabong
Bloomingdale's
Blue Bag
Bra Smyth
Calypso St Barths
Canyon Beachwear
Enerla Lingerie
Eres
J.Crew
Keiko
La Perla
Leggiadro
Linda's

Lord & Taylor
Macy's
Malia Mills
Martier
Missoni
Miss Sixty
Modell's
Norma Kamali
Old Navy Clothing Co
Paul & Shark
Pucci
Quiksilver
Ralph Lauren
Redberi
Saks Fifth Avenue
Scandinavian Ski Shop
Sol
Sonia Rykiel
Speedo Authentic Fitness
Wolford Boutique

Women's Vintage & Retro

99X
Albertine
Alice Underground
Allan & Suzi
Amarcord Vintage Fashion
Andy's Chee-pees
Anna
Atomic Passion
Barneys New York
Beacon's Closet
Bond 07
Butik
Calliope
Cheap Jack's
Chelsea Girl
Cherry
Crush
DKNY
Dressing Room
Edith & Daha
Ellen
Eye Candy
Fabulous Fanny's
The Family Jewels
Fisch for the Hip
Flying A
Foley & Corinna

Fortuna
Frock
Gabay's Outlet
Hootie Couture
In God We Trust
Jill Stuart
Jim Smiley Vintage
Keni Valenti
Le Corset
Legacy
Love Saves the Day
Lunettes et Chocolat
Lyell
Marmalade
Mary Efron
Norma Kamali
Patina
Peggy Pardon
Pippin (jewelry)
Project 159
Rags A Go Go
Reminiscence
Resurrection Vintage
Rue St Denis
Screaming Mimi's
Slang Betty
Soda Fine

Categories

Women's Vintage & Retro *(continued)*

Some Odd Rubies
Suzette Sundae
Tahir
Three Turtle Doves

Tokio 7
The Village Scandal
What Comes Around
    Goes Around

Women's Wearable Art

Design in Textiles
  by Mary Jaeger

Gallery of Wearable Art
Julie Artisan's Gallery

Women's Young & Trendy

99X
Alife
Assets London
B2 Gear
Barney's Co-op
Barneys New York
Beacon's Closet
Berkley Girl
Big Drop
Billabong
Bloomingdale's
Bloomingdale's SoHo
Built by Wendy
Built by Wendy Outlet
Calliope
Claudine
DDC Lab
Debra Rodman
Detour
Diesel
Elizabeth Charles
Forever 21
Forward
French Connection
G.C.William
Girlshop
H&M
Hotel Venus
i heart

In God We Trust
Le Chateau
Lily
Lord of the Fleas
Luca Luca
Lyell
Macy's
Operations
Otte
Plum
Project 159
Rampage
Reiss
Scoop
Soda Fine
Spatial Etc
Steven Alan
Suzette Sundae
Tahir
TG-170
Tsubi
Unis
Urban Outfitters
Vertigo &
  Friends/Magaschoni
Via Bus Stop
Warehouse
Zara
Z' Girl

Men's Business Apparel—European

agnes b. Homme
Barneys New York
Bergdorf Goodman (men)
Bloomingdale's
Borrelli
Brioni
Davide Cenci
Domenico Spanno
Domenico Vacca
Duncan Quinn
Emporio Armani
Eredi Pisan
Ermenegildo Zegna
Etro
Façonnable
Frank Stella

Giorgio Armani
Henry Beguelin
Hugo Boss
Jay Kos
Jeffrey New York
Kiton
Leonard Logsdail
Massimo Bizzocchi
Paul Smith
Reiss
Rochester Big & Tall
Saks Fifth Avenue
Salvatore Ferragamo
Sean
Seize sur Vingt
Thomas Pink

Men's Business Apparel—Discount

Century 21
Eisenberg & Eisenberg
Harry Rothman's

Loftworks @ Lafayette
Men's Wearhouse

Men's Business Apparel—Traditional

Addison on Madison
Alfred Dunhill
Anthony T. Kirby
Barneys New York
Bergdorf Goodman (men)
Bloomingdale's
Brooks Brothers
Burberry
H.Herzfeld
Hickey Freeman
Jay Kos

Jos. A. Bank
J.Press
Oxxford Clothes
Paul Stuart
Peter Elliot
Ralph Lauren
Saint Laurie
Saks Fifth Avenue
Sean John
Thom Browne
Turnbull & Asser

Men's Cashmere/Knitwear

Barneys New York
Bergdorf Goodman (men)
Berk
Best of Scotland
Bloomingdale's
Borrelli
Cashmere New York
Christopher Fischer
Eskandar

Henry Beguelin
Loro Piana
Lucien Pellat-Finet
Malo
Massimo Bizzocchi
Micheal Kors
Ralph Lauren
Saks Fifth Avenue
Tse

Men's Casual

A Bathing Ape (BAPE)	James Perse
Abercrombie & Fitch	The Jean Shop
American Apparel	Lacoste
American Eagle Outfitters	Lord & Taylor
Avirex	Lucky Brand Dungarees
A/X Armani Exchange	m0851
B8 Couture	Macy's
Banana Republic	Mexx
Barneys New York	Old Navy Clothing Co
Benetton	Operations
Bloomingdale's	The Original Levi's Store
Buckler	Original Penguin
Christopher Fischer	Phat Farm
Diesel	Quiksilver
Eddie Bauer	Ralph Lauren
Eskandar	Reiss
Fossil	Replay Store
Gant	Sean John
Gap	Tahir
Guess?	Tommy Hilfiger
H&M	Tsubi
In God We Trust	Watts
J.Crew	Yellow Rat Bastard

Men's Custom Tailoring

Addison on Madison	Frank Shattuck
An Earnest Cut & Sew	H.Herzfeld
Anthony T. Kirby	Hickey Freeman
Arthur Gluck Shirtmakers	Jay Kos
Ascot Chang	Kiton
Bironi	Leonard Logsdail
Borrelli	Massimo Bizzocchi
Domenico Spano	Rosa Custom Ties
Domenico Vacca	Vincent Nicolosi
Etro	William Fioravanti

Men's Designer

Burberry	Hugo Boss
Calvin Klein	Issey Miyake
Comme des Garçons	Jean Paul Gaultier
Costume National	John Varvatos
D&G	Kenzo
Dior Homme	Krizia
Dolce & Gabbana	Louis Vuitton
Donna Karan	Marc Jacobs
Fendi	Missoni
Gianfranco Ferré	Nicole Farhi
Giorgio Armani	Prada
Gucci	Paul Smith

Men's Designer *(continued)*

Roberto Cavalli
Ralph Lauren
Salvatore Ferragamo
Valentino

Versace
Yohji Yamamoto
Yves Saint Laurent

Men's Discount

Burlington Coat Factory
Century 21
Daffy's
Filene's Basement

Forman's
Loehmann's
TJ Maxx

Men's Ethnic

Eskandar
Henry Beguelin
Men's Wearhouse

Pan American Phoenix
Shanghai Tang

Men's Formal Wear & Tuxedos

A.T.Harris Formalwear
Baldwin Formalwear
Barney's New York
Bloomingdale's
David Yurman (cufflinks)
Domenico Spano
Duncan Quinn
Eisenberg & Eisenberg

Giorgio Armani
Hickey Freeman
J.Press
Jack Silver Formal Wear
Turnbull & Asser
Valentino
Zeller Tuxedo

Men's Hats

Barneys New York
Bergdorf Goodman
Bloomingdale's
Brooks Brothers
Cheap Jacks
Foley & Corrina Men
The Hat Shop
H.Herzfeld
Lord & Taylor

Jay Kos
Kelly Christy
Lisa Shaub
Macy's
Paul Stuart
Saks Fifth Avenue
Samuel's Hats
Young's Hat Corner

Men's Juniors

Abercrombie & Fitch
American Apparel
American Eagle Outfitters
Billabong
Blades Board & Skate
Bloomingdale's
Brooks Brothers
Century 21
Diesel
Gant
Gap
H&M

Lester's
Lord & Taylor
Lord of the Fleas
Macy's
Old Navy Clothing Co
The Original Levi's Store
Patagonia
Peter Elliot
Quiksilver
Sean John
XLarge

Men's Large Sizes

Harry's Shoes
Rochester Big & Tall

Men's Leather

Averix
Behrle
Burberry
Chrome Hearts
Denimaxx
Leather Corner

The Leather Man
Lost Art
m0851
New York City
   Custom Leather

Men's Leathergoods

Bally
Barneys New York
Bergdorf Goodman (men)
Bloomingdale's
Bottega Veneta
Coach
Crouch & Fitzgerald
Dooney & Burke
Fendi
Ghurka
Gucci
Henry Beguelin
Hermès
Hunting World
Il Bisonte
Jack Gomme

Jack Spade
The Jean Shop
LAI
Lederer
Longchamp
Lord & Taylor
Louis Vuitton
m0851
Macy's
Massimo Bizzocchi
Peter Hermann
Prada
Saks Fifth Avenue
Salvatore Ferragamo
Scott Mallory
T.Anthony

Men's Shirts

Addison On Madison
Alfred Dunhill
Ascot Chang
Barneys New York
Bergdorf Goodman (men)
Bloomingdale's
Borrelli
Brooks Brothers
Burberry
Charles Tyrwhitt
Christopher Fischer
Davide Cenci
Domenico Vacca
Duncan Quinn
Eskandar
Façonnable
Frank Stella
Henry Beguelin
H.Herzfeld

Hickey Freeman
Hugo Boss
Jay Kos
Lord & Taylor
Macy's
Men's Wearhouse
Operations
Paul Stuart
Reiss
Robert Talbott
Saks Fifth Avenue
Sean
Sean John
Seize sur Vingt
The Shirt Store
Thomas Pink
Thom Browne
Turnbull & Asser

Men's Shoes

99X
A Bathing Ape (BAPE)
Aerosoles
Aldo
Alife Rivington Club
Allen Edmonds
Anthony Kirby
A.Testoni
Avitto
Bally
Barbara Shaum
Barneys New York
Belgian Shoes
Bergdorf Goodman (men)
Berluti
Bloomingdale's
Bottega Veneta
Botticelli
Bruno Magli
Camper
Cesare Paciotti
Church's English Shoes
Citishoes
Clarks/Bostonian
Classic Kicks
Cole Haan
Duncan Quinn
Fratelli Rossetti
Gabay's Outlet
Giraudon

Gucci
Henry Beguelin
Hogan
Iramo
Jaime Mascaro
J.M.Weston
John Fluevog
John Lobb
Johnston & Murphy
Juno
Jutta Neumann
Kenneth Cole
Lord & Taylor
Macy's
Magic Shoes
Make 10
Mare
Massimo Bizzocchi
Nort 235
Ottiva
Otto Tootsi Plohound
Petit Peton
Prada
Premium Goods
Reiss
Robert Clergerie
Rockport
Saks Fifth Avenue
Salvatore Ferragamo
Santoni

Men's Shoes (continued)

Shoe
Sigerson Morrison
Skechers
Stephane Kélian
Steve Madden
Stubbs & Wootton
Tanino Crisci
Timberland

Training Camp
Tod's
United Nude Terra Plana
Varda
Via Spiga
Vincent & Edgar
Walter Steiger
Warren Edwards

Men's Sportswear—Contemporary

A Bathing Ape (BAPE)
Adidas
Adidas Performance Store
agnès b. homme
A.P.C.
Atrium
Banana Republic
Billabong
Buckler
Camouflage
Club Monaco
Dior Homme
DKNY
D/L Cerney
Emporio Armani
Equinox
Fila
Flying A
French Connection
H&M
Hugo Boss

If
J.Lindeberg
Joseph
Lynn Park NY
m0851
Mankind
Operations
Parke & Ronen
Reiss
Sean John
Sisley
Swiss Army
Ted Baker London
Tommy Hilfiger
Triple Five Soul
Tristan & America
Tsubi
Union
Untitled
Unis
Zara

Men's Sportswear—Traditional

Bally
Barneys New York
Bergdorf Goodman (men)
Beretta
Billabong
Borrelli
Brioni
Brooks Brothers
Burberry
Davide Cenci
Domenico Vacca
Dunhill
Ermenegildo Zegna
Etro
H.Herzfeld

Hermès
Hickey Freeman
Holland & Holland
Hunting World
Jay Kos
J.McLaughlin
Joseph A. Bank
Lord & Taylor
Loro Piana
Paul & Shark
Paul Stuart
Peter Elliot
Ralph Lauren
Saks Fifth Avenue
Turnbull & Asser

Men's Swimwear

Barneys New York
Bergdorf Goodman
Bloomingdale's
J.Crew
Lord & Taylor
Macy's

Polo Sport
Prada Sport
Quiksilver
Saks Fifth Avenue
Speedo Authentic Fitness
Vilebrequin

Men's Ties

Addison on Madison
Anthony T. Kirby
Alfred Dunhill
Barneys New York
Bergdorf Goodman
Bloomingdale's
Borrelli
Brioni
Brooks Brothers
Burberry
Charles Tyrwhitt
Domenico Vacca
Duncan Quinn
Ermenegildo Zegna
Etro
Façonnable
Hermès
Hugo Boss
Jay Kos

Jos. A. Bank
J.Press
Lord & Taylor
Macy's
Massimo Bizzocchi
Men's Wearhouse
Paul Stuart
Ralph Lauren
Reiss
Robert Talbott
Rosa Custom Ties
Saks Fifth Avenue
Salvatore Ferragamo
Sean John
Seigo
Thomas Pink
Today's Man
Turnbull & Asser

Categories

Men's Vintage & Retro (& consignment)

99X
Alice Underground
Amarcord Vintage Fashion
Andy's Chee Pees
Atomic Passion
Beacon's Closet
Cherry
Duncan Quinn
The Family Jewels
Fisch for the Hip
Foley & Corinna Men
Ina

In God We Trust
Jim Smiley's Vintage
Original Penguin
Reminiscence
Resurrection Vintage
Screaming Mimi's
Tahir
Tokio 7
Tokyo Joe
The Village Scandal
What Comes Around
  Goes Around

Men's Young & Trendy

99X
A Bathing Ape (BAPE)
Alife
Amarcord Vintage Fashion
American Apparel
An Earnest Cut & Sew

B8 Couture
Beacon's Closet
Billabong
Bloomingdale's
Brooklyn Industries
Buckler

Men's Young & Trendy *(continued)*

DDC Lab
Diesel
Foley & Corinna Men
H&M
Hotel Venus
In God We Trust
Isa
Klurk
Lord of the Fleas
Macy's
Mexx
Operations
Original Penguin

Reiss
Sean John
Stackhouse
Stussy
Supreme
Tahir
Transit
Tsubi
Union
Unis
Urban Outfitters
Watts

Unisex Athletic

Adidas
Adidas Performance Store
Athlete's Foot
Blades Board & Skate
Champs
Crunch
Equinox
Fila
Foot Locker
Modell's

New Balance
Niketown
Paragon
The Puma Store
Reebok
Speedo Authentic Fitness
Sports Authority
Super Runners Shop
Training Camp

Unisex Department Stores

Barneys New York
Bergdorf Goodman
Bergdorf Goodman (men)
Bloomingdale's
Brooks Brothers

Loftworks @ Lafayette
Lord & Taylor
Macy's
Saks Fifth Avenue
Takashimaya

Unisex Golf

Adidas Performance Store
Champs
Equinox
Fila
Hugo Boss
J.Lindeberg
Lacoste

LAI (golf bags)
New York Golf Center
Niketown
Paragon
Ralph Lauren
Walter Steiger (shoes only)
World of Golf

Unisex Jeans

Abercrombie & Fitch
An Earnest Cut & Sew
A/X Armani Exchange
Barneys New York
Bloomingdale's
Diesel
Earl Jean
Gap
Guess?

Henry Lehr
The Jean Shop
Lucky Brand Dungarees
Old Navy Clothing Co
The Original Levi's Store
R by 45rpm
Replay Store
Selvedge
Tsubi

Unisex Outdoor Sports (clothes & equipment)

Adidas
Adidas Performance Store
Athlete's Foot (shoes only)
Blades Board & Skate
Champs
Diesel
Eastern Mountain Sports
Equinox
Fila
Gerry Cosby & Co
Lacoste
Lady Foot Locker
Manhattan Saddlery
Mason's Tennis Mart

Modell's
Niketown
Orvis
Paragon Sporting Goods
Patagonia
Powers Court Tennis Outlet
Princeton Ski Shop
The Puma Store
Reebok
Scandinavian Ski Shop
Speedo Authentic Fitness
Sports Authority
Training Camp

Unisex Outerwear

Barneys New York
Bergdorf Goodman
Bloomingdale's
Brooks Brothers
Burberry
Davide Cenci

Denimaxx
Lord & Taylor
Macy's
Paul Stuart
Saks Fifth Avenue
Searle

Unisex Tennis

Adidas Performance Store
Champs
Equinox
Fila
Foot Locker
Lacoste
Mason's Tennis Mart
Modell's

New Balance
Niketown
Paragon Sporting Goods
Powers Court Tennis Outlet
Ralph Lauren
Reebok
Sports Authority

Unisex Western

Billy Martins
Henry Beguelin

Western Spirit
Whiskey Dust

Children's Clothing

April Cornell
Baby Bird
Bambini
Barneys New York
Bloomingdale's
Bombalulus
Bonpoint
Bu & the Duck
Burberry
Calypso Enfant
Catimini
Christopher Fischer

City Cricket
Design in Textiles
Diesel Children's Boutique
Erica Tanov
Gap Kids & Baby Gap
Granny-Made
Greenstones & Cie
Gymboree
Hoofbeats
Hot Toddie
Ibiza/Ibiza Kids
Jacadi

Children's Clothing *(continued)*

Jay Kos
Julian & Sara
Just for Tykes
Koh's Kids
La Layette et Plus
Les Petit Chapelais
Lester's
Lilliput/SoHo Kids
Lord & Taylor
Macy's
Magic Windows
Makie
Morris Bros
Natalie & Friends
Oilily
Old Navy Clothing Co
OshKosh B'Gosh
Patagonia
Peanutbutter & Jane

Peter Elliot Kids
Petit Bateau
Pipsqueak
Planet Kids
Quiksilver
Ralph Lauren Baby
Saks Fifth Avenue
Shanghai Tang
Small Change
SoHo Baby
Space Kiddets
Spring Flowers
Talbots Kids
Vilebrequin
The Wicker Garden
Yoya
Z' Baby Company
Zitomer

Children's Discount

Century 21
Daffy's

TJ Maxx

Children's Shoes

Bambini
East Side Kids
Galo
Great Feet
Hogan
Jacadi
Juno
Kids Foot Locker
Lester's

Little Eric Shoes
Shoofly
Skechers
Spring Flowers
Timberland
Tip Top Kids
Tod's
Training Camp

Tweens

Abercrombie & Fitch
Basic Basic
Berkley Girl
Betwixt
Bloomingdale's
Crush
Forreal Basics
Gap
i Heart
Infinity
Lester's

Le Petit Bateau
Lord of the Fleas
Macy's
Magic Windows
Marsha D.D.
Old Navy Clothing Co
Petit Bateau
Space Kiddets
Wet Seal
Zabari

Restaurants

In-Store Restaurants

American Café @ Lord & Taylor   **(212) 391-3344 (ext 5068)**
424 Fifth Avenue   btw 38/39th St

Auntie Anne's @ Macy's   **(212) 695-4400**
Broadway @ Herald Square   btw Broadway/34th St

Blanche's Organic Café @ DKNY   **(212) 223-3569**
655 Madison Avenue   at 60th St

Café SFA @ Saks Fifth Avenue   **(212) 753-4000 (ext 4080)**
611 Fifth Avenue   btw 49/50th St

745 Café @ Bergdorf Goodman   **(212) 339-3326**
The Men's Store 745 Fifth Avenue   btw 57/58th St

Café On Five @ Bergdorf Goodman   **(212) 872-8843**
754 Fifth Avenue   btw 57/58th St

40 Carrots @ Bloomingdale's   **(212) 705-3085**
1000 Third Avenue   btw 59/60th St

Cucina & Co @ Macy's   **(212) 695-4400**
Broadway @ Herald Square   btw Broadway/34th St

Fred's @ Barneys   **(212) 833-2200**
10 East 61st Street   btw Fifth/Madison Ave

Jimmy's Pizza @ Macy's   **(212) 695-4400**
Broadway @ Herald Square   btw Broadway/34th St

Le Train Bleu @ Bloomingdale's   **(212) 705-2100**
1000 Third Avenue   btw 59/60th St

Macy's Cellar Bar & Grill @ Macy's   **(212) 695-4400**
Broadway @ Herald Square   btw Broadway/34th St

Nicole's @ Nicole Farhi   **(212) 223-2288**
10 East 60th Street   btw Fifth/Madison Ave

Showtime Café @ Bloomingdale's   **(212) 705-2155**
1000 Third Avenue   btw 59/60th St

The Tea Box @ Takashimaya   **(212) 350-0180**
693 Fifth Avenue   btw 54/55th St

Restaurants

Shop till you drop…then drop into a comfortable chair for lunch. Here is a select list of restaurants perfect for your shopping spree.

UPPER EAST SIDE (61ST-96TH)

EAST 60s

Aureole *(New American)*
34 East 61st Street

(212) 319-1660
btw Madison/Park Ave

Jackson Hole *(hamburgers)*
232 East 64th Street

(212) 371-7187
btw Second/Third Ave

La Goulue *(French bistro)*
746 Madison Avenue

(212) 988-8169
btw 64/65th St

Le Bilboquet *(French bistro)*
25 East 63rd Street

(212) 751-3036
btw Madison/Park Ave

Le Charlot *(French bistro)*
19 East 69th Street

(212) 794-1628
btw Madison/Park Ave

Lexington R.S.V.P. Café *(American)*
1007 Lexington Avenue

(212) 535-6000
btw 72/73rd St

Maya *(haute Mexican)*
1191 First Avenue

(212) 585-1818
btw 64/65th St

Nello *(Italian bistro)*
696 Madison Avenue

(212) 980-9099
btw 62/63rd St

Park Avenue Café *(New American)*
100 East 63rd Street

(212) 644-1900
at Park Ave

Serafina *(Italian pizzeria)*
29 East 61st Street

(212) 702-9898
btw Madison/Park Ave

EAST 70s

Atlantic Grill *(Asian)*
1341 Third Avenue

(212) 988-9200
btw 76/77th St

Bid *(American)*
1334 York Avenue

(212) 988-7730
at 71st St

Cafe Boulud *(French)*
20 East 76th Street

(212) 772-2600
btw Fifth/Madison Ave

EJ's Luncheonette *(glorified diner)*
1271 Third Avenue

(212) 472-0600
at 73rd St

The Gallery @ the Carlyle Hotel
(omelettes, salads, sandwiches)
35 East 76th Street

(212) 744-1600

at Madison Ave

Ikeno Hana *(Japanese)*
1016 Lexington Avenue

(212) 737-6639
btw 72/73rd St

J.G.Melon *(hamburgers)*
1291 Third Avenue

(212) 744-0585
at 74th St

Mezzaluna *(pizzas, pasta)*
1295 Third Avenue

(212) 535-9600
btw 74/75th St

Orsay *(bistro)*   **(212) 517-6400**
1057 Lexington Avenue   at 75th St

The Sultan *(Turkish)*   **(212) 861-0200**
1435 Second Avenue   btw 74/75th St

Swifty's *(American bistro)*   **(212) 535-6000**
1007 Lexington Avenue   btw 72/73rd St

Via Quadronno *(Italian)*   **(212) 650-9880**
25 East 73rd Street   btw Fifth/Madison Ave

EAST 80s & 90s

Brasserie Julien *(French)*   **(212) 744-6327**
1422 Third Avenue   btw 80/81st St

Cafe Sabarsky *(Austrian)*   **(212) 288-0665**
1048 Fifth Avenue   at 86th St

E.A.T. *(gourmet sandwiches and salads)*   **(212) 772-0022**
1064 Madison Avenue   btw 80/81st St

Island (Italian bistro)   **(212) 996-1200**
1305 Madison Avenue   btw 92/93rd St

Jackson Hole *(hamburgers)*   **(212) 427-2820**
1270 Madison Avenue   at 91st St

Luca *(Italian)*   **(212) 987-9260**
1712 First Avenue   btw 88/89th St

Pio Pio *(South American)*   **(212) 426-5800**
1746 First Avenue   btw 90/91st St

Sarabeth's *(tea room)*   **(212) 410-7335**
1295 Madison Avenue   btw 92/93rd St

Taste *(American)*   **(212) 717-8100**
1411 Third Avenue   btw 80/81st St

UPPER WEST SIDE

Café Arte *(Italian)*   **(212) 501-7014**
106 West 73rd Street   btw Amsterdam/Columbus Ave

Café Luxembourg *(French bistro)*   **(212) 873-7411**
200 West 70th Street   btw Amsterdam/West End Ave

The Great Burrito *(Mexican)*   **(212) 724-5151**
405 Amsterdam Avenue   btw 79/80th St

Isabella's *(Mediterranean)*   **(212) 724-2100**
359 Columbus Avenue   at 77th St

Jean Georges *(French)*   **(212) 299-3900**
1 Central Park West   at 60th St

Nick & Toni's *(Mediterranean)*   **(212) 496-4000**
100 West 67th Street   btw Broadway/Columbus Ave

Ouest *(French)*   **(212) 580-8700**
2315 Broadway   at 84th St

Ruby Foo's *(Chinese)*   **(212) 724-6700**
2182 Broadway   at 77th St

Sarabeth's *(tea room)*   **(212) 496-6280**
423 Amsterdam Avenue   btw 80/81st St

Shun Lee Café *(Chinese)*   **(212) 769-3888**
43 West 65th Street   btw Columbus Ave/Central Park West

Time Café *(brunch, salads, sandwiches)*   **(212) 579-5100**
2330 Broadway   at 85th St

Vince and Eddie's *(American bistro)*   **(212) 721-0068**
70 West 68th Street   btw Columbus Ave/Central Park West

MIDTOWN/FIFTH AVENUE (42ND-61ST)

Atelier *(French)*   **(212) 521-6125**
50 Central Park South   btw Fifth/Sixth Ave

Azaza *(Chinese)*   **(212) 751-0700**
891 First Avenue   at 50th St

Bice *(northern Italian)*   **(212) 688-1999**
7 East 54th Street   btw Fifth/Madison Ave

Blue Fin *(seafood)*   **(212) 918-1400**
1567 Broadway   btw 46/47th St

Bricco *(Italian)*   **(212) 245-7160**
304 West 56th Street   btw Eighth/Ninth Ave

Burger Joint @ the Parker Meridien hotel   **(212) 245-5000**
118 West 57th Street   btw Sixth/Seventh Ave

California Pizza Kitchen *(pizza, pasta, salads)* **(212) 755-7773**
201 East 60th Street   btw Second/Third Ave

Carnegie Deli   **(212) 757-2245**
854 Seventh Avenue   at 55th St

Chola *(Indian)*   **(212) 688-4619**
232 East 58th Street   btw Second/Third Ave

DB Bistro Moderne *(French bistro)*   **(212) 391-2400**
55 West 44th Street   btw Fifth/Sixth Ave

The Four Seasons *(New American)*   **(212) 754-9494**
99 East 52nd Street   btw Park/Lexington Ave

Fresco by Scotto on the Go *(Italian)*   **(212) 754-2700**
40 East 52nd Street   btw Madison/Park Ave

Koi *(Japanese)*   **(212) 921-3330**
40 West 40th Street   btw Fifth/Sixth Ave

Le Bernardin *(French)*   **(212) 489-1515**
155 West 51st Street   btw Sixth/Seventh Ave

Norma's *(breakfast)*   **(212) 708-7460**
18 West 57th Street   at Sixth Ave

Per Se *(New American)*   **(212) 823-9335**
10 Columbus Circus   btw 58/59th St

Rue 57 Brasserie *(French bistro)*   **(212) 307-5656**
60 West 57th Street   at Sixth Ave

San Domenico *(Italian)*   **(212) 265-5959**
240 Central Park South   btw Broadway/Seventh Ave

Restaurants

FLATIRON/NOHO/CENTRAL VILLAGE

Artisanal (fromagerie/French bistro) (212) 725-8585
2 Park Avenue at 32nd St

Blue Smoke (BBQ) (212) 447-7733
116 East 27th Street btw Park/Lexington Ave

Borgo Antico (Tuscan) (212) 807-1313
22 East 13th Street btw Fifth/University Place

Craft (American) (212) 780-0880
43 East 19th Street btw Broadway/Park Ave

Gramercy Tavern (American) (212) 477-0777
42 East 20th Street btw Broadway/Park Ave South

Indochine (French/Vietnamese) (212) 505-5111
430 Lafayette Street btw Astor Place/4th St

Marquet Patisserie (bistro) (212) 229-9313
15 East 12th Street btw Fifth/University Place

Thé Adore (pastries, salads, sandwiches) (212) 243-8742
17 East 13th Street btw Fifth/University Place

Time Café (brunch, salads, sandwiches) (212) 533-7000
380 Lafayette Street at Great Jones

T Salon (soups, salads, sandwiches) (212) 358-0506
11 East 20th Street btw Broadway/Fifth Ave

Union Square Café (New American) (212) 243-4020
21 East 16th Street btw Fifth/Union Square West

Wichcraft (American, sandwiches) (212) 780-0577
49 East 19th Street btw Broadway/Park Ave

CHELSEA/WEST VILLAGE

Amy's Bread (sandwiches) (212) 462-4338
75 Ninth Avenue btw 15/16th St (Chelsea Market)

Barbuto (Italian) (212) 924-9700
775 Washington Street btw West 12th/Jane

Blue Ribbon Bakery (American) (212) 337-0404
35 Downing Street at Bedford

Chelsea Bistro & Bar (French bistro) (212) 727-2026
358 West 23rd Street btw Eighth/Ninth Ave

Corner Bistro (hamburgers) (212) 242-9502
331 West 4th Street at Jane

Diner 24 (212) 242-7773
102 Eighth Avenue at 15th St

EJ's Luncheonette (diner) (212) 473-5555
432 Sixth Avenue btw 9/10th St

Florent (diner) (212) 989-5779
69 Gansevoort Street btw Washington/Greenwich

Havana Chelsea Restaurant (Cuban) (212) 243-9421
190 Eighth Avenue btw 19/20th St

'ino *(panini)*　　　　　　　　**(212) 989-5769**
21 Bedford Street　　　　btw Sixth Ave/Downing

La Bottega *(Italian)*　　　　**(212) 243-8400**
88 Ninth Avenue　　　　　　　　at 16th St

Le Madri *(Italian)*　　　　　**(212) 727-8022**
168 West 18th Street　　btw Sixth/Seventh Ave

Markt *(Belgian brasserie)*　　**(212) 727-3314**
401 West 14th Street　　　　　at Ninth Ave

Otto Enoteca Pizzeria　　　**(212) 995-9559**
1 Fifth Avenue　　　　　　　　at 8th St

Pastis *(French bistro)*　　　**(212) 929-4844**
9 Ninth Avenue　　　　at Little West 12th St

The Park *(American/lounge)*　**(212) 352-3313**
118 Tenth Avenue　　　　　btw 17/18th St

Petite Abeille *(soups, waffles, sandwiches)*　**(212) 604-9350**
107 West 18th Street　　btw Sixth/Seventh Ave

Pintxos *(tapas)*　　　　　　**(212) 343-9923**
510 Greenwich Street　　　btw Canal/Spring

Rickshaw Dumpling Spot *(Chinese)*　**(212) 924-9220**
61 West 23rd Street　　　btw Fifth/Sixth Ave

Son Cubano *(Cuban)*　　　　**(212) 366-1640**
405 West 14th Street　　btw Ninth/Tenth Ave

Spice Market *(Asian)*　　　**(212) 675-2322**
29-35 Ninth Avenue　　　　　at 13th St

Tartine *(French bistro)*　　**(212) 229-2611**
253 West 11th Street　　　　at West 4th St

Vento *(Italian)*　　　　　　**(212) 699-2400**
675 Hudson Street　　　　　　at 13th St

SOHO/NOLITA/LOWER EAST SIDE

AKA Café *(American)*　　　　**(212) 979-6096**
49 Clinton Street　　　btw Stanton/Rivington

Balthazar *(French bistro)*　　**(212) 965-1414**
80 Spring Street　　　btw Broadway/Crosby

Boom *(Italian)*　　　　　　　**(212) 431-3663**
152 Spring Street　　btw Wooster/West Broadway

Bread *(Italian)*　　　　　　　**(212) 334-1015**
20 Spring Street　　　　btw Elizabeth/Mott

Butter *(New American)*　　　**(212) 253-2828**
415 Lafayette Street　　btw West 4th St/Astor Place

Café Colonial *(Brazilian, South American)*　**(212) 274-0044**
276 Elizabeth Street　　　　btw Houston/Prince

Café El Portal *(Mexican)*　　**(212) 226-4642**
174 Elizabeth Street　　　btw Kenmare/Spring

Café Gitane *(French bistro)*　**(212) 334-9552**
242 Mott Street　　　　　btw Houston/Prince

Café Habana (Cuban) **(212) 625-2001**
17 Prince Street at Elizabeth

Cipriani Downtown (Italian) **(212) 343-0999**
376 West Broadway btw Spring/Broome

Congee Village (Chinese) **(212) 941-1818**
100 Allen Street at Delancey

Cornershop (sandwiches) **(212) 253-7467**
643 Broadway at Bleecker

Eight Mile Creek (Australian) **(212) 226-4642**
240 Mulberry Street btw Prince/Spring

Fanelli's Café (hamburgers) **(212) 226-9412**
94 Prince Street at Mercer

Felix (French bistro) **(212) 431-0021**
340 West Broadway at Grand

Hampton Chutney Company (Indian) **(212) 226-9996**
68 Prince Street at Crosby

Inoteca (panini) **(212) 614-0473**
98 Rivington Street at Ludlow

Katz's Deli **(212) 254-2246**
205 East Houston Street at Ludlow

Kuma Inn (Asian small plates) **(212) 353-8866**
113 Ludlow Street (2nd floor) btw Rivington/Delancey

Lil' Frankie's Pizza **(212) 420-4900**
19 First Avenue btw East 1/2nd St

Lombardi's (pizza) **(212) 941-7994**
32 Spring Street btw Mulberry/Mott

Lovely Day (pan-Asian) **(212) 925-3310**
196 Elizabeth Street btw Prince/Spring

Mercer Kitchen (French/Mediterranean) **(212) 966-5454**
99 Prince Street at Mercer

Mezzogiorno (Italian) **(212) 334-2112**
195 Spring Street at Sullivan

Rialto (French American) **(212) 334-7900**
265 Elizabeth Street btw Houston/Prince

Rice (Thai/Asian) **(212) 226-5775**
227 Mott Street btw Prince/Spring

Schiller's Liquor Bar (American traditional) **(212) 375-0010**
131 Rivington Street at Norfolk

Teany (vegetarian) **(212) 475-9190**
90 Rivington Street btw Orchard/Ludlow

Thom @ the Thompson Hotel **(212) 219-2000**
(modern American)
60 Thompson Street btw Spring/Broome

TRIBECA/LOWER MANHATTAN

Bouley *(modern French)*
120 West Broadway

(212) 964-2525
at Duane

Bubby's
(soups, burgers, salads, sandwiches)
120 Hudson Street

(212) 219-0666
at North Moore

Franklin Station Café *(Malaysian)*
222 West Broadway

(212) 274-8525
btw West Broadway/Varick

Next Door Nobu *(Japanese)*
105 Hudson Street

(212) 334-4445
btw Franklin/North Moore

The Odeon *(bistro)*
145 West Broadway

(212) 233-0507
btw Duane/Thomas

66 *(Chinese)*
241 Church Street

(212) 925-0202
btw Worth/Leonard

Tribeca Grill *(modern American)*
375 Greenwich Street

(212) 941-3900
at Franklin

BROOKLYN

Aurora *(Italian/Mediterranean)*
70 Grand Street

(718) 388-5100
at Wythe Ave

Bacchus *(French)*
409 Atlantic Avenue

(718) 852-1572
btw Nevins/Bond

Bar Tabac *(bistro)*
128 Smith Street

(718) 923-0918
at Dean

Biscuit *(BBQ)*
367 Flatbush Avenue

(718) 398-2227
btw Sterling Place/Carlton Ave

ChipShop *(fish and chips)*
383 5th Avenue

(718) 244-7746
at 6th St

Diner
85 Broadway

(718) 486-3077
at Berry

Faan *(Pan-Asian)*
209 Smith Street

(718) 694-2277
btw Baltic/Butler

Peter Luger *(steakhouse)*
178 Broadway

(718) 387-7400
btw Bedford/Driggs

Schnäck *(hamburgers, hot dogs)*
122 Union Street

(718) 855-2879
near Columbia

Thai Sky
386 5th Avenue

(718) 788-7889
at 7th St

Verb Café *(soup, sandwiches)*
218 Bedford Avenue

(718) 599-0977
btw North 4/5th St

Restaurants

Health & Beauty

Barbers

Haircuts—Unisex

Haircuts—Children

Hair Salons

Hair Removal

Beauty Treatments

Eyebrow Grooming

Manicures/Pedicures

Day Spas

Gyms

Pilates/Mat Classes

Yoga

Massage Therapists

Tanning

Make-up Artists

Personal Shoppers

Bridal Consultants

Barbers

Chelsea Barbers
465 West 23rd Street
NYC 10011

(212) 741-2254
btw Ninth/Tenth
Mon-Fri 9-7, Sat 9-6

Delta Men's Hairstylists
992 Lexington Avenue
NYC 10021

(212) 628-5723/650-9055
btw 71/72nd
Mon-Fri 8:30-7, Sat 8:30-6

La Boite a Coupe
18 West 55th Street
NYC 10019

(212) 246-2097
btw Fifth/Sixth
Mon-Thurs 9-7, Fri 9-5

Paul Mole Barber Shop
1031 Lexington Avenue
NYC 10021

(212) 535-8461
btw 73/74th
Mon-Sat 7:30-6:30, Sun 9-3:30

York Barber
981 Lexington Avenue
NYC 10021

(212) 988-6136
btw 70/71st
Mon-Fri 8-7, Sat 8-6

Haircuts—Unisex

Astor Place Hair
2 Astor Place
NYC 10003

(212) 475-9854
at Broadway
Mon, Sat 8-8, Tues-Fri 8-10, Sun 9-6

Jean Louis David
2146 Broadway
NYC 10023

(212) 873-1850
at 75th
Mon-Fri 9-7:30, Sat 9-7, Sun 11-5

Jean Louis David
783 Lexington Avenue
NYC 10021

(212) 838-7372
at 61st
Mon-Fri 8-8, Sat 10-7, Sun 11-5

Jean Louis David
1180 Sixth Avenue
NYC 10011

(212) 944-7389
at 46th
Mon-Sat 10-7, Sun 11-5

You Hairdressing
644 Driggs Avenue
Brooklyn 11211

(718) 599-0220
at Metropolitan
Tues-Sat 11-8

Haircuts—Children

Cozy's Cuts for Kids
1125 Madison Avenue
NYC 10028

(212) 744-1716
at 84/85th
Mon-Fri 10-6, Sat 9-5

Cozy's Cuts for Kids
448 Amsterdam Avenue
NYC 10024

(212) 579-2600
btw 81/82nd
Mon-Fri 10-6, Sat 9-5

Kids Cuts
201 East 31st Street
NYC 10016

(212) 684-5252
btw Second/Third
Mon-Sat 10-6

Lulu's Cuts and Toys
310 Fifth Avenue
Brooklyn 11215

(718) 832-3732
btw 2/3rd
Mon-Sat 10-6, Sun 11-5

Hair Salons

Antonio Prieto Salon **(212) 255-3741**
127 West 20th Street btw Sixth/Seventh
NYC 10011 Tues-Fri 12-8, Sat 10-6

April Barton's Suite 303 **(212) 633-1011**
@ the Chelsea Hotel
222 West 23rd Street btw Seventh/Eighth
NYC 10011 Tues-Sat 12-7

Armando Corral Salon **(212) 206-7712**
12 Little West 12th Street btw Ninth/Washington
NYC 10014 Tues-Sat 11-7, Sat 11-5

Arte Salon **(212) 941-5932**
294 Elizabeth Street btw Bleecker/Houston
NYC 10012 Mon-Fri 11-8, Sat 10-6

Blow Styling Salon **(212) 989-6282**
342 West 14th Street at Ninth
NYC 10014 Mon-Fri 8-8, Sat 10-8, Sun 12-6

Bollei **(212) 759-7985**
115 East 57th Street btw Park/Lexington
NYC 10022 Mon-Fri 9-6:30 (Thurs 10-7:30), Sat 9-5:30

Bumble & Bumble **(212) 521-6500**
415 West 13th Street btw Ninth/Washington
NYC 10014 Tues-Sat 10-7

Charles Worthington Salon **(212) 941-9696**
568 Broadway (suite 101) at Prince
NYC 10012 Mon-Wed 10-7, Thurs-Fri 10-8, Sat 9:30-6

Cutler Hair Salon **(212) 308-3838**
115 East 57th Street btw Park/Lexington
NYC 10022 Mon-Sat 10-6 (Thurs 10-7), Sat 9-4

Cutler Hair Salon **(212) 308-3838**
465 West Broadway btw Houston/Prince
NYC 10012 Tues-Fri 10-7, Sat 9-5, Sun 10-5

Devachan Hair Salon **(212) 274-8686**
560 Broadway btw Prince/Spring
NYC 10012 Tues-Fri 11-7, Sat 10-5

Donsuki **(212) 826-3397**
19 East 62nd Street btw Fifth/Madison
NYC 10021 Tues-Sat 9-5, Sun 9-6:30

Dop Dop Salon **(212) 965-9540**
170 Mercer Street btw Houston/Prince
NYC 10012 Mon 12-6, Tues, Thurs-Sat 11-7:30
  Wed 11-5, Sun 11-6

Edris Salon **(212) 989-6800**
430 West 14th Street btw Ninth/Tenth
NYC 10014 Tues-Wed 10-7, Thurs 10-8, Fri 11-8, Sat 9-6

Eiji **(212) 838-3454**
601 Madison Avenue (5th floor) btw 57/58th
NYC 10022 Mon-Sat 9-7

EM Studio Salon　　　　　　　**(212) 472-3440**
762 Madison Avenue　　　　　　　btw 65/66th
NYC 10021　　　Mon 9-5, Tues 7:30-6, Thurs 8:30-8
　　　　　　　　　　　　　　　Fri 7:30-5, Sat 9-5

Frédéric Fekkai　　　　　　　**(212) 753-9500**
New salon @ Bendel's in 2006　(info n/a at press time)

Gemini Salon & Spa　　　　　**(212) 675-4546**
547 Hudson Street　　　　　　　btw Charles/Perry
NYC 10014　　Mon-Wed 9:30-7:30, Thurs-Fri 9:30-8:30
　　　　　　　　　　　　　　Sat 9:30-6:30, Sun 11-5

John Barrett Salon　　　　　　**(212) 872-2700**
754 Fifth Avenue (9th floor)　　@ Bergdorf Goodman
NYC 10019　　　　Mon-Fri 8:30-7 (Thurs 8:30-8)
　　　　　　　　　　　　　　　Sat 9-6, Sun 12-6

John Frieda　　　　　　　　　**(212) 879-1000**
797 Madison Avenue (2nd floor)　　btw 67/68th
NYC 10021　　Mon-Sat 8:30-6:30 (Thurs 8:30-7:30)

John Masters Organic Haircare　**(212) 343-9590**
77 Sullivan Street　　　　　　　btw Spring/Broome
NYC 10012　　Mon-Fri 11-6:30, Sat 10-6:30

John Sahag　　　　　　　　　**(212) 750-7772**
425 Madison Avenue (2nd floor)　　at 49th
NYC 10017　　Mon 8:30-5:30, Tues-Sat 8:30-7:30

Joseph Valery　　　　　　　　**(212) 517-2333**
1044 Madison Avenue　　　　　　btw 79/80th
NYC 10021　　　　Mon-Sat 9-6, Sun 12-5

Joseph Valery　　　　　　　　**(212) 517-7377**
820 Madison Avenue　　　　　　btw 68/69th
NYC 10021　　Mon-Sat 9-6 (Tues, Thurs 9-7)

Josephine Beauty Retreat　　　**(212) 223-7157**
200 East 62nd Street　　　　　　btw Second/Third
NYC 10021　　　　Mon-Fri 10-7, Sat 10-5

Julien Farel　　　　　　　　　**(212) 888-8988**
605 Madison Avenue　　　　　　btw 57-58th
NYC 10022　　　　Mon-Sat 9-6 (Thurs 9-7)

Julius Caruso Salon　　　　　**(212) 759-7574**
22 East 62nd Street　　　　　　btw Fifth/Madison
NYC 10021　　　　　　　　　　Mon-Sat 9-5

Kenneth Salon　　　　　　　　**(212) 752-1800**
301 Park Avenue　　　　@ the Waldorf Astoria Hotel
NYC 10022　　　　Mon-Sat 9-6 (Wed 9-8)

Louis Licari Color Group　　　**(212) 758-2090**
693 Fifth Avenue　　　@ Takashimaya btw 53/54th
NYC 10021　　Mon 7:30-7, Tues, Thurs-Fri 7:30-9
　　　　　　　　　　　　　　Wed, Sat 7:30-5:30

Luis Canas @ Equinox　　　　**(212) 750-4671**
140 East 63rd Street　　　　　　at Lexington
NYC 10021　　Mon-Fri 9-9, Sat-Sun 9-8

Miano Viel
16 East 52nd Street
NYC 10022
(212) 980-3222
btw Fifth/Madison
Tues 9-6, Wed, Sat 9-5, Thurs-Fri 9-7

Minardi Salon
29 East 61st Street (5th floor)
NYC 10021
(212) 308-1711
btw Madison/Park
Tues-Thurs 9-9, Fri-Sat 9-7

Mudhoney
148 Sullivan Street
NYC 10012
(212) 533-1160
btw Houston/Prince
Tues-Fri 12-8, Sat 12-6

Orlo
34 Gansevoort Street
NYC 10014
(212) 242-3266
btw Hudson/Greenwich
Tues-Sat 10-7

Oscar Blandi
746 Madison Avenue
NYC 10021
(212) 988-9404
btw 64/65th
Mon-Fri 9-5

Oscar Bond
42 Wooster Street
NYC 10013
(212) 334-3777
btw Broome/Grand
Tues-Wed 10-7, Thurs-Fri 11-8
Sat 10-5, Sun 11-5

Paul LeBrecque Salon and Spa
171 East 65th Street
NYC 10021
(212) 988-7815
btw Lexington/Third
Mon-Fri 8-9, Sat 9-8, Sun 10-8

Pierre Michel
131 East 57th Street
NYC 10022
(212) 593-1460
btw Park/Lexington
Mon-Fri 8:30-6 (Thurs 8:30-7), Sat 8:30-5:30

Prive @ the Soho Grand
310 West Broadway
NYC 10013
(212) 274-8888
btw Grand/Canal
Mon 11-6, Tues-Fri 10-7 (Thurs 10-9)
Sat 10-6, Sun 12-6

Q Hair
19 Bleecker Street
NYC 10012
(212) 614 8729
btw Lafayette/Bowery
Tues-Fri 11-8, Sat 10-8

Red Salon
323 West 11th Street
NYC 10014
(212) 924-1444
btw Greenwich/Washington
Tues-Fri 12-7, Sat 10-5

Robert Kree Salon
375 Bleecker Street
NYC 10014
(212) 989-9547
btw Charles/Perry
Sun-Mon 12-7, Tues-Fri 11-8
Sat 10-6:30

Salon 74 (men)
30 East 74th Street
NYC 10021
(212) 988-7400
btw Madison/Park
Mon-Sat 9-5 (Tues, Thurs 9-7)

Salon à Deux
1117 Madison Avenue
NYC 10021
(212) 628-7505
btw 83/84th
Mon-Fri 8-6, Sat 8-4, Sun 11-5

Salon A.K.S.
694 Madison Avenue
NYC 10021
(212) 888-0707
btw 62/63rd
Mon-Sat 9-6 (Thurs 9-8)

Salon A.K.S. Fifth **(212) 888-0707**
689 Fifth Avenue at 54th
NYC 10022 Mon-Sat 9-6 (Wed-Thurs 9-8)

Salon Ishi **(212) 888-4744**
70 East 55th Street btw Park/Madison
NYC 10022 Mon-Wed 9-5, Thurs-Fri 8-7, Sat 8-5

Sally Herschberger **(212) 206-8700**
425 West 14th Street btw Ninth/Tenth
NYC 10014 Mon-Sat 9-5

Signorelli's Hair Color Consultant **(212) 734-6098**
60 East 66th Street (suite 1B) btw Fifth/Madison
NYC 10021 (by appointment only)

Simadi Salon **(917) 528-4531**
154 East 64th Street at Lexington
NYC 10021 Daily 10-6

Soon Beauty Lab **(212) 260-4423**
318 East 11th Street btw First/Second
NYC 10003 Mon-Fri 11-9, Sat-Sun 10-6

Space **(212) 647-8588**
155 Sixth Avenue at Spring
NYC 10013 Mon 12-5, Tues-Fri 11-8:30, Sat 10-6

Sparkle Beauty Studio **(212) 645-4745**
3 Charles Street at Greenwich
NYC 10014 Tues-Fri 12-8, Sat 10-5

Thomas Morrissey Salon **(212) 772-1111**
787 Madison Avenue btw 66/67th
NYC 10021 Mon-Fri 9-5 (Thurs 9-7:30), Sat 9-4

Tricia's Place **(212) 226-3319**
171 Elizabeth Street at Spring
NYC 10012 Mon-11-7, Sat 10-5, Sun 12-6

Ultra **(212) 677-4380**
233 East 4th Street btw Avenue A/B
NYC 10009 Tues-Wed, Fri 11-8, Thurs 12-9, Sat 10-5

Woon **(212) 608-2272**
6 Spring Street btw Elizabeth/Bowery
NYC Mon-Sat 12-last appt. (no set closing times)

Yann Varin **(212) 734-9055**
142 East 73rd Street btw Park/Lexington
NYC 10021 Mon, Wed 10-5, Tues, Thurs, Fri 10-7, Sat 9-6

Younghee Salon **(212) 334-3770**
64 North Moore Street btw Hudson/Greenwich
NYC 10013 Tues-Fri 10:30-6:30, Sat 9-4:30

Hair Removal

Bernice Electrolysis & Beauty Center **(212) 355-7055**
29 East 61st Street (2nd floor) btw Madison/Park
NYC 10021 Mon-Sat 8-6

Completely Bare
764 Madison Avenue
NYC 10021

(212) 717-9300
btw 65/66th
Mon-Thurs 10-9, Fri 10-7
Sat 10-6, Sun 10-5

Expert Electrolysis Inc.
57 West 57th Street (suite 810)
NYC 10022

(212) 755-0671
btw Fifth/Sixth
(by appointment)

Haven
150 Mercer Street
NYC 10012

(212) 343-3515
btw Houston/Prince
Mon-Fri 11-7, Sat-Sun 10-6

Isabella Electrolysis
794 Lexington Avenue
NYC 10021

(212) 832-0431
btw 61/62nd
Mon 10-7, Tues-Fri 10-7:30, Thurs 10-8
Sat 10-6

J. Sisters International
35 West 57th Street
NYC 10019

(212) 750-2485
btw Fifth/Sixth
Tues, Fri-Sat 8:30-5:30
Wed-Thurs 8:30-7:30

Maksim Skincare
80 Fifth Avenue
NYC 10011

(212) 414-9434
at 14th
Tues-Thurs 11-8, Fri 9:30-8, Sat 9-5:30

Miriam Vasicka
897 Park Avenue
NYC 10021

(212) 734-1017
at 79th
Mon-Fri 8-6 (by appointment)

Red Market Salon & Lounge
32 Gansevoort Street (3rd floor)
NYC 10014

(212) 929-9600
btw Hudson/Ninth
Mon-Wed 4-11, Thurs-Sat 4-12:30am
Sun 2-10

Smooth
133 East 58th Street (suite 507)
NYC 10022

(212) 759-6997
btw Park/Lexington
Mon-Fri 12-7, Sat 1-4

Victor Orris Dermatology
30 East 76th Street (suite 6)
NYC 10021

(212) 249-3050
btw Madison/Park
(by appointment)

Beauty Treatments

Bernice Electrolysis & Beauty Center
29 East 61st Street (2nd floor)
NYC 10021

(212) 355-7055
btw Madison/Park
Mon-Sat 8-6

Carlos Araque Essential Therapy
122 East 25th Street
NYC 10010   Mon-Fri 10-10, Sat-Sun 10-8 (by appointment)

(212) 777-2325
at Park Ave South

Dashing Diva Nail Spa & Boutique
41 East 8th Street
NYC 10003

(212) 673-9000
at Broadway
Sun-Wed 10-8, Thurs-Sat 9-9

Diane Young Anti-Aging Salon
38 East 57th Street (8th floor)
NYC 10022

(212) 753-1200
btw Madison/Park
Mon-Thurs 10-8, Fri 10-6, Sat 9-5

Eastside Massage Therapy Center　　**(212) 249-2927**
351 East 78th Street　　btw First/Second
NYC 10021　　Mon-Fri 10-9:30, Sat-Sun 10-8

Norclaire Spa　　**(212) 754-9866**
815 Fifth Avenue　　btw 62/63rd
NYC 10021　　Tues-Sat 9-5 (by appointment)

Elizabeth Arden　　**(212) 546-0200**
691 Fifth Avenue　　btw 54/55th
NYC 10022　　Mon, Tues, Sat 8-6:30
Wed 8-7:30, Thurs-Fri 8-8, Sun 9-6

Erbe　　**(212) 966-1445**
196 Prince Street　　btw MacDougal/Sullivan
NYC 10012　　Daily 11-7

Firozé　　**(212) 249-5445**
manicure/pedicure/house calls　　(by appointment)

Gemayel Salon　　**(212) 787-5555**
2030 Broadway　　at 70th
NYC 10023　　Mon-Fri 10-8, Sat 9-7, Sun 10-6

Janet Sartin　　**(212) 751-5858**
500 Park Avenue　　btw 58/59th
NYC 10022　　Mon-Fri 9:30-7, Sat 9:30-6

Lia Schorr Skin Care　　**(212) 486-9670**
686 Lexington Avenue (4th floor)　　btw 56/57th
NYC 10022　　Mon-Fri 11-6, Sat 9-5

Ling Skin Care　　**(212) 989-8833**
12 East 16th Street　　btw Fifth/Union Square
NYC 10003　　Mon-Thurs 10-9, Fri-Sun 11-7 (Sat 9:30-8)

Mario Badescu　　**(212) 758-1065**
320 East 52nd Street　　btw First/Second
NYC 10022　　Mon-Tues, Fri 8:30-6
Wed-Thurs 8:30-8:30, Sat 9-5, Sun 10-5:30

The Mezzanine Spa　　**(212) 431-1600**
62 Crosby Street　　btw Spring/Broome
NYC 10012　　Tues-Wed 12-8, Thurs-Fri 9-8
Sat-Sun 10-6

Miano Viel　　**(212) 980-3222**
16 East 52nd Street　　btw Fifth/Madison
NYC 10022　　Tues 9-6, Wed 9-5, Thurs-Fri 9-7, Sat 9-3

Oasis Day Spa　　**(212) 254-7722**
108 East 16th Street　　btw Irving Place/Union Square
NYC 10003　　Mon-Fri 10-10, Sat-Sun 9-9

Skinklinic　　**(212) 521-3100**
800b Fifth Avenue　　at 61st
NYC 10021　　Mon 11-7, Tues-Thurs 8-8
Fri 8-7, Sat 9-3

Soho Sanctuary　　**(212) 334-5550**
119 Mercer Street (3rd floor)　　btw Prince/Spring
NYC 10012　　Mon 3-9, Tues-Fri 10-9, Sat 10-5, Sun 12-6

Steven Knoll Salon   **(212) 421-0100**
625 Madison Avenue   btw 58/59th
NYC 10022   Tues-Wed, Fri 10-5, Thurs 11-6, Sat 10-4

Tracie Martyn   **(212) 206-9333**
59 Fifth Avenue   btw 12/13th
NYC 10003   Mon-Sat 8:30-7 (by appointment)

The Wellpath   **(212) 737-9604**
1100 Madison Avenue   at 83rd
NYC 10028   Mon-Sat 9-5 (Tues-Thurs 9-7)
    (and by appointment)

Yasmine Djerradine   **(212) 588-1771**
30 East 60th Street   btw Madison/Park
NYC 10022   Mon-Sat 9-8

Eyebrow Grooming

Ramy Beauty Therapy   **(212) 684-9500**
39 East 31st Street   btw Madison/Park
NYC 10016   Tues-Sat 10-7 (by appointment only)

Eliza's Eyes @ Avon Salon & Spa   **(212) 755-2866**
725 Fifth Avenue   btw 56/57th
NYC 10022   Mon, Sat 8-6, Tues-Fri 7:30-8, Sun 11-6

John Barrett   **(212) 872-2700**
754 Fifth Avenue (9th floor)   @ Bergdorf Goodman
NYC 10019   Mon-Fri 8:30-7 (Thurs 8:30-8)
    Sat 9-6, Sun 12-6

Maksim Skincare   **(212) 414-9434**
80 Fifth Avenue   at 14th
NYC 10011   Tues-Thurs 11-8, Fri 9:30-8, Sat 9-5:30

Oama @ Pierre Michel   **(212) 593-1460**
131 East 57th Street   btw Park/Lexington
NYC 10022   Mon-Sat 8:30-7

Warren Tricomi @ Sports Club/LA   **(212) 218-8650**
45 Rockefeller Plaza   at 50th
NYC 10111   Mon 9-6, Tues-Fri 9-8, Sat 9-3
    (except in summer)

Manicures/Pedicures

Acqua Beauty Bar   **(212) 620-4329**
7 East 14th Street   btw Fifth/Union Square
NYC 10003   Mon, Thurs 10-9, Tues-Wed
    Fri 10-8, Sat-Sun 10-7

Barbara Mutnick   **(917) 788-0932**
In-home service   (by appointment only)
Buff Spa @ Bergdorf Goodman   **(212) 872-8624**
754 Fifth Avenue   at 58th
NYC 10019   Mon-Sat 10-7 (Thurs 10-8), Sun 12-6

Four Seasons   **(212) 350-6420**
57 East 57th Street   btw Madison/Park
NYC 10022   Daily 8-9

Josephine Beauty Treatment
(212) 223-7157
200 East 62nd Street
btw Second/Third
NYC 10021
Mon-Fri 10-7 (Thurs 10-8), Sat 10-5

Just Calm Down
(212) 337-0032
32 West 22nd Street
btw Fifth/Sixth
NYC 10010   Mon-Wed 11-8, Thurs-Fri 12-9, Sat-Sun 10-6

Nails Niche
(212) 288-9100
741 Madison Avenue
btw 64/65th
NYC 10021
Mon-Sat 9:30-7

Paul Lebrecque @ Reebok Sports Club/NY
(212) 595-0099
160 Columbus Avenue
btw 68/69th
NYC 10023
Mon-Fri 8-11, Sat 9-8, Sun 10-8

Ramy Spa
(212) 684-9500
39 East 31st Street
btw Madison/Park
NYC 10016
Tues-Sat 10-7 (by appointment only)

Rescue Beauty Lounge
(212) 431-0449
8 Center Market Place
btw Broome/Grand
NYC 10012
Mon-Fri 11-8, Sat-Sun 10-6

Robin Narvaez @ Borja Color Studio
(212) 308-3232
118 East 57th Street
btw Park/Lexington
NYC 10022
Tues-Fri 11-7, Sat 10-4

Shobha
(212) 931-8363
594 Broadway (suite 403)
btw Houston/Prince
NYC 10012   Tues-Fri 11-7 (Thurs 11-8), Sat 10-6, Sun 11-5

Shobha
(212) 223-2872
595 Madison (suite 1403)
at 57th
NYC 10022
Tues-Fri 11-7 (Thurs 11-8), Sat 10-6

Sweet Lily Natural Nail Spa
(212) 925-5441
222 West Broadway
btw White/Leonard
NYC 10013
Mon-Fri 11-8, Sat 10-6

Warren-Tricomi
(212) 262-8899
16 West 57th Street (4th floor)
btw Fifth/Sixth
NYC 10019
Mon-Sat 9-7

Day Spas—Women

Ajune
(212) 628-0044
1294 Third Avenue
at 74/75th
NYC 10021
Mon 9-6, Tues-Fri 9-8, Sat 9-6, Sun 10-6

Allure Day Spa
(212) 644-5500
139 East 55th Street
btw Third/Lexington
NYC 10022
Mon-Fri 10:30-7:30, Sat-Sun 10-6

Amorepacific
(212) 966-0400
114 Spring Street
btw Greene/Mercer
NYC 10012
Mon-Sat 11-7 (Thurs 11-8), Sun 12-6

Anushka Day Spa & Cellulite Clinic
(212) 355-6404
501 Madison Avenue
btw 52/53rd
NYC 10022
Mon, Sat 10-6, Tues, Thurs 10-8
Wed, Fri 10-7

Athena Spa
32 East 31 Street
NYC 10016

(212) 683-4484
btw Park/Madison
Daily 8-12

The Avon Center
725 Fifth Avenue
NYC 10022

(212) 755-2866
btw 56/57th
Mon, Sat 8-6, Tues-Fri 8-8, Sun 11-6

be mini spa
173 Ludlow Street
NYC 10002

(212) 253-5665
btw Houston/Stanton
Mon-Fri 12-7:30, Sat-Sun 11-7:30

Bliss Spa
19 East 57th Street (3rd floor)
NYC 10022

(212) 219-8970
btw Fifth/Madison
Mon-Fri 9:30-8:30
(Wed 12:30-8:30), Sat 9:30-6:30

Bliss Spa
568 Broadway (2nd floor)
NYC 10012

(212) 219-8970
at Prince
(opening hours as above)

Body Central
99 University Place (5th floor)
NYC 10003

(212) 677-5633
btw 11/12th
Mon, Wed 12-9, Tues, Thurs 8:30-9
Fri 8:30-4, Sat 10-4

Buff Spa in Bergdorf Goodman
754 Fifth Avenue
NYC 10019

(212) 872-8624
at 57th
Mon-Fri 10-7

Butterfly Studio
149 Fifth Avenue
NYC 10010
Sat 9-5

(212) 253-2100
at 21st
Mon, Wed, Fri 10-6, Tues 11-8, Thurs 12-10,

D'Mai Urban Spa
157 Fifth Avenue
NYC 11217

(718) 398-2100
btw Lincoln/St John's Place
Mon-Fri 11-7 (Thurs 11-8), Sat-Sun 10-7

Dorit Baxter Day Spa
47 West 57th Street (3rd floor)
NYC 10019

(212) 371-4542
btw Fifth/Sixth
Mon-Sat 9-8, Sun 10-6

Eden Day Spa
388 Broadway
NYC 10013

(212) 226-0515
btw Walker/White
Mon-Sat 10-9, Sun 10-7

Elemur Day Spa
940 Third Avenue
NYC 10022

(212) 588-8895
66/67th
Mon-Fri 11-8, Sat-Sun 11-7

Elle Bache Spa
8 West 36th Street
NYC 10018

(212) 279-8562
btw Fifth/Sixth
Tues, Fri 10-6, Wed-Thurs 10-7, Sat 10-5

Exhale
150 Central Park South
NYC 10019

(212) 249-3000
btw Sixth/Seventh
Daily 6:30-9:30 (Sun 8-8)

Faina European Spa
315 West 57th Street (suite 402)
NYC 10019

(212) 245-6557
btw Eighth/Ninth
Mon-Fri 10-8, Sat 9-7, Sun 10-6

Health & Beauty

Gemayel Salon & Spa
2030 Broadway
NYC 10023
(212) 787-5555
at 70th
Daily 10-8

Georgette Klinger
501 Madison Avenue
NYC 10022
(212) 838-3200
btw 52/53rd
Mon, Fri 9-6, Tues-Thurs 9-7, Sat-Sun 9-5

Glow Skin Spa
30 East 60th (8th floor)
NYC 10022
(212) 319-6654
btw Madison/Park
(by appointment)

Gloss Day Spa
51 East 73rd Street
NYC 10021
(212) 249-2100
btw Madison/Park
Mon-Fri 10-7, Sat 11-5

Great Jones Spa
29 Great Jones Street
NYC 10012
(212) 505-3185
at Lafayette
Tues-Sun 9:30-10

The Greenhouse Day Spa
127 East 57th Street
NYC 10022
(212) 644-4449
btw Park/Lexington
Mon-Fri 9-8, Sat 10-6, Sun 12-6

Hair Fashion East
411 Park Avenue South
NYC 10016
(212) 686-7524
btw 28/29th
Tues-Fri 10-7:30, Sat 9-3:30

Haven
150 Mercer Street
NYC 10012
(212) 343-3515
btw Houston/Prince
Mon-Fri 11-7, Sat-Sun 10-6

Jin Soon Natural Hand & Foot Spa
56 East 4th Street
NYC 10003
(212) 473-2047
btw Bowery/Second
Daily 11-8

Max Day Spa & Laser Center
181 Seventh Avenue
NYC 10011
(212) 989-6555
btw 20/21st
Mon-Fri 10-8, Sat 10-7, Sun 12-7

Karen Wu Beauty & Wellness Spa
1377 Third Avenue
NYC 10021
(212) 585-2044
btw 78/79th
Mon-Fri 10-9, Sat 10-8, Sun 10-7

La Prairie Spa @ the Ritz-Carlton
50 Central Park South (2nd floor)
NYC 10022
(212) 521-6135
at Sixth
Daily 8-9:30

Le Spa Naturale
269 West 72nd Street
NYC 10023
(212) 580-3333
at West End Ave
Daily 8-8 (by appointment)

Lush Essential Hand & Foot Spa
98 Thompson Street
NYC 10012
(212) 625-1839
btw Prince/Spring
Mon-Fri 11-8, Sat-Sun 12-7

Mark Joseph
147 West 40th Street
NYC 10018
(212) 391-6699
btw Seventh/Broadway
Mon-Fri 8-7:30

Maximus
15 Mercer Street
NYC 10013
(212) 431-3333
btw Grand/Canal
Tues 11-7, Wed-Fri 11-8, Sat 10-6

The Mezzanine Spa **(212) 431-1600**
62 Crosby Street btw Spring/Broome
NYC 10012   Tues-Wed 12-8, Thurs-Fri 9-8, Sat-Sun 10-6

Nicole Summers **(212) 734-8348**
300 East 75th Street (suite 3H) at Second
NYC 10021   (by appointment; home/office visits available)

Oasis Day Spa **(212) 254-7722**
108 East 16th Street   btw Irving Place/Union Square East
NYC 10003 Mon-Fri 10-10, Sat-Sun 9-9

OC Salon & Spa **(212) 935-6201**
33 East 61st Street btw Madison/Park
NYC 10021 Mon-Sat 9-6 (Thurs 9-7)

The Peninsula Spa **(212) 903-3910**
700 Fifth Avenue (21st floor) at 55th
NYC 10022 Mon-Fri 8:30-10, Sat 8:30-7:30

Pharma **(212) 505-3505**
17 Clinton Street btw Houston/Stanton
NYC 10002 Tues-Sat 1-7, Sun 1-6

Repechage Spa de Beaute **(212) 751-2500**
115 East 57th Street btw Park/Lexington
NYC 10022 Mon, Thurs 10-8
Tues-Wed, Fri 10-6:30, Sat 10-6

Shija Day Spa **(212) 366-0706**
37 Union Square West btw 16/17th
NYC 10003 Tues-Sun 10-8

Silk Day Spa **(212) 255-6457**
47 West 13th Street btw Fifth/Sixth
NYC 10011 Mon-Fri 10:30-9, Sat 9:30-9, Sun 11-7

Skin Care Lab **(212) 334-3142**
568 Broadway btw Prince/Houston
NYC 10012 Mon-Fri 11-8, Sat 10-7, Sun 12-6

Sole **(212) 420-SOLE**
227 East 14th Street btw Second/Third
NYC 10003 Wed-Fri 12-8, Sat-Sun 10-6

Susan Ciminelli Day Spa **(212) 872-2650**
754 Fifth Avenue @ Bergdorf Goodman btw 57/58th
NYC 10019 Mon-Sat 9-7 (Thurs 9-8), Sun 12-6

Ula Day Spa **(212) 343-2376**
8 Harrison Street btw Greenwich/Hudson
NYC 10013 Tues-Fri 11-7, Sat 10-6, Sun 12-6

Yin Beauty & Arts Spa **(212) 879-5040**
22 East 66th Street btw Fifth/Madison
NYC 10021 Mon-Fri 10-8, Sat 10-6

Day Spas—Men

Bliss Spa **(212) 219-8970**
19 East 57th Street (3rd floor) btw Fifth/Madison
NYC 10022 Mon-Fri 9:30-8:30
(Wed 12:30-8:30), Sat 9:30-6:30

Bliss Spa   **(212) 219-8970**
568 Broadway (2nd floor)   at Prince
NYC 10012   (opening hours as above)

Eden Day Spa   **(212) 226-0515**
388 Broadway   btw Walker/White
NYC 10013   Mon-Sat 10-9, Sun 10-7

Equinox Spa   **(212) 396-9611**
205 East 85th Street   at Third
NYC 10028   Mon-Thurs 9-10, Fri 9-9, Sat-Sun 9-8

Equinox Spa   **(212) 750-4671**
140 East 63rd Street   at Lexington
NYC 10021   Mon-Fri 9-9, Sat-Sun 9-8

Glow Skin Spa   **(212) 319-6654**
30 East 60th (8th floor)   btw Madison/Park
NYC 10022   (by appointment)

John Allan's Club   **(212) 922-0361**
46 East 46th Street   btw Madison/Park
NYC 10017   Mon-Fri 11-7 (Thurs 11-7:30)

Nickel Day Spa   **(212) 242-3203**
77 Eighth Avenue   at 14th
NYC 10014   Sun, Mon 1-9, Tues-Fri 11-9, Sat 10-9

Paul Lebrecque @ Reebok Sports Club/NY   **(212) 595-0099**
160 Columbus Avenue   btw 68/69th
NYC 10023   Mon-Fri 8-11, Sat 9-8, Sun 10-8

SkinCareLab   **(212) 334-3142**
568 Broadway   btw Houston/Prince
NYC 10012   Mon-Fri 11-8, Sat 10-7, Sun 12-6

Gyms

Aerospace   **(212) 929-1640**
332 West 13th Street   btw Eighth/Ninth
NYC 10014   Mon-Fri 7-9, Sat 10-1

Casa Fitness (personal training only)   **(212) 223-9280**
540 Park Avenue   at 51st (in Regency Hotel)
NYC 10021   (by appointment)

Classic Bodies   **(212) 737-8440**
189 East 79th Street   btw Second/Third
NYC 10021   (call for class hours)

Clay   **(212) 206-9200**
25 West 14th Street   btw Fifth/Sixth
NYC 10011   Mon-Thurs 5:30-11, Fri 5:30-10, Sat-Sun 8-9

Crunch   **(212) 875-1902**
162 West 83rd Street   btw Amsterdam/Columbus
NYC 10024   Mon-Fri 5:30-11, Sat-Sun 8-9

Crunch   **(212) 758-3434**
1109 Second Avenue   btw 58/59th
NYC 10022   Mon-Thurs 5-11, Fri 5-10, Sat-Sun 8-9

Crunch
555 West 42nd Street
NYC 10036

(212) 594-8050
at Eleventh
Mon-Fri 6-10, Sat-Sun 9-7

Crunch
144 West 38th Street
NYC 10018

(212) 869-7788
btw Broadway/Seventh
Mon-Fri 5:30-10, Sat-Sun 8-6

Crunch
54 East 13th Street
NYC 10003

(212) 475-2018
btw Broadway/University Place
Mon-Fri 6-10, Sat-Sun 8-8

Crunch
404 Lafayette Street
NYC 10003

(212) 614-0120
btw Astor Place/East 4th
Mon-Fri open 24 hrs, Sat-Sun 8-9

Crunch
623 Broadway
NYC 10012

(212) 420-0507
btw Houston/Bleecker
Mon-Fri 6-11, Sat-Sun 6-8

Crunch
152 Christopher Street
NYC 10014

(212) 366-3725
btw Washington/Greenwich
Mon-Fri 6-11, Sat-Sun 8-9

David Barton Gym
30 East 85th Street
NYC 10028

(212) 517-7577
btw Fifth/Madison
Mon-Fri 5:30-11, Sat-Sun 8-9

The Equinox
2465 Broadway
NYC 10025

(212) 799-1818
btw 91/92nd
Mon-Thurs 5:30-11, Fri 5:30-10
Sat-Sun 7:30-9

The Equinox
344 Amsterdam Avenue
NYC 10024

(212) 721-4200
at 76th
(opening hours as above)

The Equinox
897 Broadway
NYC 10003

(212) 780-9300
btw 19/20th
(opening hours as above)

The Equinox
97 Greenwich Avenue
NYC 10012

(212) 620-0103
at West 12th
(opening hours as above)

The Equinox
140 East 63rd Street
NYC 10021

(212) 750-4900
at Lexington
(opening hours as above)

The Equinox
205 East 85th Street
NYC 10028

(212) 439-8500
btw Second/Third
Mon-Thurs 5:30-10:30
Fri 5:30-10, Sat-Sun 8-9

The Equinox
250 East 54th Street
NYC 10022

(212) 277-5400
at Second
Mon-Thurs 5:30-11
Fri 5:30-9, Sat 8-9, Sun 8-8

The Equinox
10 Columbus Circle
NYC 10019

(212) 871-0425
at 60th
Mon-Thurs 5:30-11, Fri 5:30-10; Sat-Sun 8-9

Health & Beauty

The Equinox   **(212) 541-7000**
1633 Broadway   at 50th
NYC 10019   Mon-Thurs 5:30-10, Fri 5:30-9, Sat 9-6

The Equinox   **(212) 953-2499**
420 Lexington Avenue   at 44th
NYC 10070   Mon-Thurs 5:30-10, Fri 5:30-8, Sat 9-4

The Equinox   **(212) 972-8000**
521 Fifth Avenue   at 43rd
NYC 10175   Mon-Thurs 5:30-10, Fri 5:30-8

The Equinox   **(212) 566-6555**
54 Murray Street   at West Broadway
NYC 10007   Mon-Thurs 5:40-11, Fri 5:30-10
Sat-Sun 8-8

The Equinox   **(212) 964-6688**
14 Wall Street   at Nassau
NYC 10005   Mon-Thurs 5:30-10, Fri 5:30-8, Sat 9-6

New York Sports Club   **(212) 768-3535**
19 West 44th Street   btw Fifth/Sixth
NYC 10036   Mon-Thurs 6-10, Fri 6-9, Sat-Sun 9-5

Radu   **(212) 581-1995**
25 West 57th Street (2nd floor)   at Fifth
NYC 10019   Mon-Fri 7-7, Sat 10-12
(by appointment only)

Reebok Sports Club/NY   **(212) 362-6800**
160 Columbus Avenue   at 67th
NYC 10023   Mon-Thurs 5-11, Fri 5-10, Sat-Sun 7-9

Soho Dance Studio   **(212) 226-6767**
598 Broadway   at Houston
NYC 10012   Daily 11-9:30

The Sports Club/LA   **(212) 355-5100**
330 East 61st Street   btw First/Second
NYC 10021   Mon-Fri 5-11, Sat-Sun 7-9

The Sports Center @ Chelsea Piers   **(212) 336-6000**
Pier 60, West Side Highway   at West 23rd
NYC 10011   Mon-Fri 6-11, Sat-Sun 8-9

Studio Uma   **(212) 249-7979**
20 East 68th Street   btw Fifth/Madison
NYC 10021   Mon-Fri 6-9, Sat 7-9, Sun 9-6

Synergy Fitness Center   **(212) 879-6013**
1438 Third Avenue   btw 81/82nd
NYC 10028   Mon-Fri 5:30-11, Sat-Sun 8-8

Synergy Fitness Center   **(212) 545-9590**
4 Park Avenue   btw 33/34th
NYC 10016   Mon-Fri 5:30-11, Sat-Sun 8-7

Threshold   **(212) 868-2837**
521 West 26th Street   btw Tenth/Eleventh
NYC 10001   (by appointment only)

Pilates/Mat Classes

Pilates on Fifth   **(212) 687-8885**
501 Fifth Avenue (suite 22)   at 42nd
NYC 10017   Mon-Fri 7-9, Sat-Sun 9-2

Drago's Gymnasium   **(212) 757-0724**
50 West 57th Street (6th floor)   btw Fifth/Sixth
NYC 10019   Mon-Fri 7-8, Sat 8-2

InForm Fitness   **(212) 755-9895**
201 East 56th Street   btw Second/Third
NYC 10022   Mon-Fri 6:30-8, Sat-Sun 8-2
(by appointment only)

The Kane School of Core Integration   **(212) 463-8308**
151 West 19th (2nd floor)   btw Sixth/Seventh
NYC 10011   Mon-Fri 9-8

Power Pilates   **(212) 627-5852**
49 West 23rd Street (10th floor)   btw Fifth/Sixth
NYC 10011   Mon-Fri 7-8, Sat 9-6, Sun 10-4

re:AB   **(212) 420-9111**
33 Bleecker Street   btw Lafayette/Bowery
NYC 10012   Mon-Fri 7-9, Sat 9-2, Sun 10-4

Real Pilates   **(212) 625-0777**
177 Duane Street   btw Greenwich/Hudson
NYC 10013   Mon-Thurs 7-9, Fri 7-8, Sat 9-3, Sun 10-3

Yoga

Atmananda Yoga and Holistic Center   **(212) 625-1511**
324 Lafayette Street   btw Bleecker/West Houston
NYC 10012   Mon-Fri 6-10, Sat 10:30-730, Sun 12:15-7:30

Be Yoga (formerly Yoga Zone)   **(212) 650-9642**
1319 Third Avenue   btw 74/75
NYC 10021   (call for class schedule)

Be Yoga (formerly Yoga Zone)   **(212) 935-9642**
160 East 56th Street   btw Lexington/Third
NYC 10011   (call for class schedule)

Integral Yoga Institute   **(212) 721-4000**
200 West 72nd Street   at Broadway
NYC 10023   (call for class schedule)

Integral Yoga Institute   **(212) 929-0586**
227 West 13th Street   btw Seventh/Eighth
NYC 10011   (call for class schedule)

Jivamukti Yoga Center   **(212) 353-0214**
404 Lafayette Street   btw East 4th/Astor Place
NYC 10003   Mon-Fri 11:30-7, Sat-Sun 9:30-6

New York Yoga   **(212) 717-9642**
1629 York Avenue   at 86th
NYC 10028   (call for class schedule)

Soho Sanctuary   **(212) 334-5550**
119 Mercer Street (3rd floor)   btw Prince/Spring
NYC 10012   (by appointment only)

Massage Therapists

Carlos Araque Essential Therapy   **(212) 777-2325**
122 East 25th Street   at Park Ave South
NYC 10010   Mon-Fri 10-10, Sat-Sun 10-8 (by appointment)

Ease Salon & Massage   **(212) 661-5151**
51 East 42nd Street (Suite 1406)   btw Madison/Vanderbilt
NYC 10017   Mon-Fri 12-8:30, Sat-Sun 12-6

Eastside Massage Therapy Center   **(212) 249-2927**
351 East 78th Street   btw First/Second
NYC 10021   Mon-Fri 10-9:30, Sat-Sun 10-8

Lisa Smith   **(212) 969-8718**

Massage Massage   **(212) 696-9069**

Marcelo Coutinho (Rolfing)   **(212) 924-3741**

New York Massage Company   **(212) 427-8175**

Osaka   **(212) 956-3422**
50 West 56th Street (2nd floor)   btw Fifth/Sixth
NYC 10019   Mon-Sat 10-2

Physical Advantage   **(212) 460-1879**

Salon de Tokyo   **(212) 757-2187**
200 West 57th Street (suite 1308)   at Seventh
NYC 10019   Mon-Sat 11-12

Tui Na   **(212) 387-0733**

Tanning Salons

Portofino Sun Center   **(212) 988-6300**
1300 Third Avenue   at 75th
NYC 10021   Mon-Fri 9-10, Sat 9-9, Sun 10-7

Portofino Sun Center   **(212) 769-0200**
104 West 73rd Street   at Columbus
NYC 10023   Mon-Fri 9-9, Sat 9-8, Sun 10-6

Portofino Sun Center   **(212) 355-2772**
38 East 58th Street   btw Park/Madison
NYC 10022   Mon-Tues 9-8:15, Wed-Fri 9-9:15
Sat 9-8:15, Sun 10-6:15

Portofino Sun Center   **(212) 473-7600**
462 West Broadway   btw Houston/Prince
NYC 10012   Mon-Fri 9-8, Sat 9-7, Sun 11-6

Portofino Sun Center   **(212) 627-4775**
64 Greenwich Avenue   at Perry
NYC 10011   Mon-Fri 9-10, Sat 9-9, Sun 11-7

Self-tanning

Completely Bare Downtown
103 Fifth Avenue
NYC 10003

(212) 366-6060
btw 17/18th
Tues-Wed 12-8, Thurs 12-9
Fri 10-7, Sat 10-6

Completely Bare @ Barneys
660 Madison Avenue
NYC 10021

(212) 366-6060
btw 60/61st
Mon-Sat 10-7, Sun 11-6

Paul Lebrecque @ Reebok Sports Club/NY
171 East 65th Street
NYC 10021

(212) 595-0099
btw Lexington/Third
Mon-Fri 8-9, Sat 9-8, Sun 10-8

Bridal Consultants

Ober, Onet & Associates
9 East 97th Street
NYC 10128

(212) 876-6775
btw Fifth/Madison
Contact: Polly Onet

Marcy Blum Associates
259 West 11th Street
NYC 10014

(212) 929-9814
at Fourth
Contact: Marcy Blum

Saved by the Bell
11 Riverside Drive
NYC 10023

(212) 874-5457
btw 73/74th
Contact: Susan Bell

Make-up Artists

Carlos Solano

(917) 447-5197

Kimara Ahnert
1113 Madison Avenue
NYC 10028

(212) 452-4252
btw 83/84th
(by appointment)

Rochelle Weithorn
431 East 73rd Street
NYC 10021

(212) 472-8668
btw York/First
(also does hair; by appointment)

Personal Shoppers

Barbara Sussberg
youvegotstyleonline.com

(917) 213-7436

Barneys New York
660 Madison Avenue (3rd floor)
NYC 10021

(212) 826-8900
btw 60/61st
Mon-Sat 10-6

Bergdorf Goodman
754 Fifth Avenue
NYC 10019

(212) 872-8772
btw 57/58th
Mon-Fri 9:30-5:30
Contact: 'Solutions' by Betty Halbreich

Bloomingdale's
1000 Third Avenue
NYC 10022

(212) 705-2000
at 59/60th
Mon-Fri 10-8:30, Sat 10-7, Sun 11-7

Health & Beauty

Dorian May (for secondhand clothes)   **(212) 249-8378**
(by appointment)

Go Lightly   **(212) 352-1153**
95 Horatio Street (suite 432)   at Washington
NYC 10014   *Contact: Jenny Gerin*
golight@go-lightly.com

Lord & Taylor   **(212) 391-3344**
424 Fifth Avenue   btw 38/39th
NYC 10018   Mon-Sat 10-8:30, Sun 11-7

Macy's   **(212) 494-4181**
151 West 34th Street   at Herald Square
NYC 10001   Mon-Sat 10-7:30, Sun 11-6
Contact: Linda Lee

Paul Stuart   **(212) 682-0320**
Madison Avenue   at 45th
NYC 10017   Tues-Sat 8:30-5:30 (by appointment)

NYC General Store Vintage Shopping Package
nycgeneralstore.com   **(212) 961-1111**

One on One @ Saks Fifth Avenue   **(212) 940-4145**
611 Fifth Avenue   btw 49/50th
NYC 10022   Mon-Sat 10-7 (Thurs 10-8), Sun 11-7

Sak Fifth Avenue   **(212) 753-4000**
611 Fifth Avenue   at 50th
NYC 10022   Mon-Sat 10-7 (Thurs 10-8), Sun 12-6
Contact: Susan Shebarro

Visual Therapy   **(212) 315-2233**
24 West 57th Street (suite 502)   btw Fifth/Sixth
NYC 10019   Mon-Fri 9-6
Contact: Jesse Garza, Joe Lupo, Lani Rosenstock

Repairs & Services

Dry Cleaners

Mending & Alterations

Custom Design Tailors

Shoe Repair

Leather Repair (Handbags & Luggage)

Trimmings (Ribbons, Buttons, etc.)

Thrift Shops

Dry Cleaners—Haute Couture & Bridal

Fashion Award Cleaners   **(212) 289-5623**
2205 Broadway   btw 78/79th
NYC 10024   Mon-Fri 730-6:30, Sat 9-3 (except in summer)

Hallak Cleaners   **(212) 879-4694**
1232 Second Avenue   btw 64/65th
NYC 10021   Mon-Fri 7-6:30, Sat 8-4

Jeeves of Belgravia   **(212) 570-9130**
39 East 65th Street   btw Madison/Park
NYC 10021   Mon-Fri 8-6, Sat 10-4 (10-2 in summer)

Madame Paulette   **(212) 838-6827**
1255 Second Avenue   btw 65/66th
NYC 10021   Mon-Fri 7:30-7, Sat 8-5

Montclair   **(212) 289-2070**
1331 Lexington Avenue   btw 88/89th
NYC 10128   Mon-Fri 7-7, Sat 8-6

Dry Cleaners—All-Purpose

Anita Cleaners   **(212) 717-6602**
1380 First Avenue   btw 73/74th
NYC 10021   Mon-Fri 8-6

Meurice Garment Care   **(212) 475-2778**
31 University Place   btw 8/9th
NYC 10003   Mon-Fri 7:30-6 (Wed 7:30-7)
    Sat 9-3, Sun 10-3

Meurice Garment Care & Tiecrafters   **(212) 759-9057**
245 East 57th Street   btw Second/Third
NYC 10022   Mon-Fri 7:30-6 (Wed 7:30-7), Sat 9-3

Montclair   **(212) 289-2070**
1331 Lexington Avenue   btw 88/89th
NYC 10128   Mon-Fri 7-7, Sat 8-5

New York's Finest French Cleaners   **(212) 431-4010**
154 Reade Street   btw Hudson/Greenwich
NYC 10013   Mon-Fri 7-7, Sat 8-5

Perry Process   **(212) 628-8300**
427 East 74th Street   btw First/York
NYC 10021   Mon-Fri 8-6, Sat 8:30-2:30

Tiecrafters   **(212) 629-5800**
252 West 29th Street   btw Seventh/Eighth
NYC 10001   Mon-Fri 8:30-5, Sat 9-2

Torpe   **(212) 734-1342**
30 East 71st Street   btw Madison/Park
NYC 10021   Mon-Fri 9-5

Young's Cleaners and Launderers   **(212) 473-6154**
188 Third Avenue   at 17th
NYC 10003   Mon-Fri 7-7, Sat 8-5

Mending & Alterations

Bhambi Custom Tailors
14 East 60th Street (room 610)
NYC 10022
(212) 935-5379
btw Fifth/Madison
Mon-Sat 9:30-7

Eddie Ugras
125 West 72nd Street (3rd floor)
NYC 10023
(212) 595-1596
btw Columbus/Broadway
Mon-Sat 9:30-7

Fine Alterations & Sewing
240 East 6th Street
NYC 10003
(212) 253-2022
at Second
(by appointment)

French American Weaving Co
119 West 57th Street (room 1406)
NYC 10019
(212) 765-4670
btw Sixth/Seventh
Mon-Fri 10:30-5:30, Sat 11-2
(except in summer)

John's European Boutique & Tailoring
118 East 59th Street (2nd floor)
NYC 10022
(212) 752-2239
btw Park/Lexington
Mon-Fri 9-6:15, Sat 10-1
(by appointment)

Nelson Ferri
766 Madison Avenue (4th floor)
NYC 10021
(212) 988-5085
btw 65/66th
Mon-Fri 9-6, Sat 10-5
(except in summer)

Sebastian Tailors
767 Lexington Avenue (room 404)
NYC 10021
(212) 688-1244
btw 60/61st
Tues-Fri 8:30-5, Sat 9-4

Superior Repair Center (leather)
141 Lexington Avenue
NYC 10016
(212) 889-7211
btw 29/30th
Mon-Fri 10-6, Sat 10-3 (except in summer)

Three Star Leather Custom Tailors
790 Madison Avenue (room 507)
NYC 10021
(212) 879-4200
at 67th
Mon-Sat 10-6 (except in summer)

Custom Tailoring

Alan Flusser Shop
3 East 48th Street (4th floor)
NYC 10017
(212) 265-4591
btw Fifth/Madison
Mon-Fri 10-6 (Sat by appointment)

Albert Sakhai (bridal)
albertsakhaidesigns.com
(212) 397-7883
(by appointment only)

Dynasty Custom Tailoring
6 East 38th Street
NYC 10016
(212) 679-1075
btw Fifth/Madison
Mon-Fri 9-6:30, Sat 10-3

Eva Devecsery
201 East 61st Street
NYC 10021
(212) 751-6091
at Third
Mon-Fri 9-6:30, Sat 10-4

Eva Dressmaker
675 Madison Avenue
NYC 10021
(212) 753-4922
at 61st
(by appointment)

Guillermo Couture **(212) 366-6965**
153 West 27th Street, suite 301 btw Sixth/Seventh
NYC 10001 (by appointment)

Hong Kong Tailor Jack **(212) 675-0818**
136 Waverly Place at Sixth
NYC 10014 Mon-Sat 10-7

Judy's Fancies (children) **(212) 689-8663**
home/office consultations (by appointment only)

L&S Custom Tailors **(212) 752-1638**
138 East 61st Street at Lexington
NYC 10021   Mon-8:30-5:30, Sat 8:30-4 (except in summer)

Leonard Logsdail **(212) 752-5030**
9 East 53rd Street (4th floor) btw Fifth/Madison
NYC 10022   Mon-Fri 8:30-5 (and by appointment)

Leung's Professional Tailors **(212) 860-6617**
1386 Lexington Avenue btw 91/92nd
NYC 10128 Mon-Fri 8:30-6, Sat 8:30-5

Mandana **(212) 988-0800**
1175 Lexington Avenue btw 80/81st
NYC10028   Mon-Fri 9-1, 2-5, Sat 10-4 (except in summer)

Mr. Ned's **(212) 924-5042**
137 Fifth Avenue at 20th
NYC 10010 Mon-Fri 8-5, Sat 8-3 (summer Sat 8-1)

Boutique Clothing Storage

Garde Robe **(212) 227-7554**
P.O. Box 746 (no published address, for security)
NYC 10159 (by appointment)
garderobeonline.com

Shoe Repair

Andrade Boot and Shoe Repair **(212) 787-0465**
379 Amsterdam Avenue btw 78/79th
NYC 10024 Mon-Fri 8-7, Sat 9-6:30

Andrade Shoe Repair **(212) 529-3541**
103 University Place btw 12/13th
NYC 10003 Mon-Fri 7:30-7, Sat 9-6

Angelo Shoe Repair **(212) 757-6364**
666 Fifth Avenue (lower level) at 53rd
NYC 10136 Mon-Fri 7-6:30, Sat 10-5

B.Nelson **(212) 869-3552**
1221 Sixth Avenue btw 48/49th
NYC 10020 (level C2) Mon-Fri 7:30-5

Empire Shoe Repair **(212) 744-1257**
991 Lexington Avenue 71/72nd
NYC 10021 Mon-Fri 7-7, Sat 8-6

Hector's Shoe Repair
11 Greenwich Avenue
NYC 10014

(212) 727 1237
btw Christopher/10th
Mon-Fri 7:30-7, Sat 9:30-6

Jim's Shoe Repair
50 East 59th Street
NYC 10022

(212) 355-8259
btw Madison/Park
Mon-Fri 8-6, Sat 9-4 (except in summer)

Shoe Service Plus
15 West 55th Street
NYC 10019

(212) 262-4823
btw Fifth/Sixth
Mon-Fri 7-7, Sat 10-5

T.O. Dey
9 East 38th Street (7th floor)
NYC 10016

(212) 683-6300
btw Fifth/Madison
Mon-Fri 9-5, Sat 9-1 (except in summer)

Top Service
845 Seventh Avenue
NYC 10019

(212) 765-3190
btw 54/55th
Mon-Fri 8-6, Sat 9-3

Leather Repair (handbags & luggage)

Art Bag
1130 Madison Avenue
NYC 10028

(212) 744-2720
at 84th
Mon-Fri 9:30-5, Sat 10-4

Modern Leather
2 West 32nd Street (4th floor)
NYC 10001

(212) 947-7770
btw Fifth/Broadway
Mon-Fri 8:30-4:45
Sat 8:30-1 (except in summer)

Superior Leather Repair Center
141 Lexington Avenue
NYC 10016

(212) 889-7211
at 29th
Mon-Fri 10-6, Sat 10-3
(except in summer)

Trimmings (ribbons, buttons, feathers, odds & ends)

Greenberg & Hammer
24 West 57th Street
NYC 10019
(trims, notions, buttons, zippers etc)

(212) 246-2836
btw Fifth/Sixth
Mon-Fri 9-6, Sat 10-5

Hyman Hendler & Sons
67 West 38th Street
NYC 10018
(the highest quality ribbons from around the world)

(212) 840-8393
btw Fifth/Sixth
Mon-Fri 9-5

M&J Trimming Co
1000-1008 Sixth Avenue
NYC 10018
(ribbons, trimmings, buttons, rhinestones etc)

(212) 391-9072
btw 37/38th
Mon-Fri 9-6, Sat 10-5

Margola
48 West 37th Street
NYC 10018
(feather trimmings, silk flowers, ribbons, veiling
and netting, beading and stones)

(212) 564-2929
btw Fifth/Sixth
Mon-Fri 8:30-6, Sat 10-4

Repairs & Services

Mokuba
55 West 39th Street
NYC 10018
(212) 869-8900
btw Fifth/Sixth
Mon-Fri 9-5
(super-fancy ribbons in silk, velvet, chiffon, fake fur)

Tender Buttons
143 East 62nd Street
NYC 10021
(212) 758-7004
btw Lexington/Third
Mon-Fri 10:30-6, Sat 10:30-5:30
(an exquisite collection of buttons, modern and antique)

Tinsel Trading
47 West 38th Street
NYC 10018
(212) 730-1030
btw Fifth/Sixth
Mon-Fri 10-5:30, Sat 11-3
(call to confirm Saturday hours)
(flowers, fringes, ribbons, cords, tassels;
specialist in 1920s metallics)

Thrift Shops

Cancer Care Thrift Shop
1480 Third Avenue
NYC 10028
(212) 879-9868
btw 83/84th
Mon-Tues, Fri 11-6, Wed-Thurs 11-7
Sat 11-4:30, Sun 12:30-5

Housing Works Thrift Shop
202 East 77th Street
NYC 10021
(212) 772-8461
btw Second/Third
Mon-Fri 11-7, Sun 12-5

Housing Works Thrift Shop
306 Columbus Avenue
NYC 10023
(212) 579-7566
btw 74/75th
Mon-Fri 11-7, Sat 10-6, Sun 12-5

Housing Works Thrift Shop
157 East 23rd Street
NYC 10004
(212) 529-5955
btw Lexington/Third
Mon-Sat 10-6, Sun 12-5

Housing Works Thrift Shop
143 West 17th Street
NYC 10004
(212) 366-0820
btw Sixth/Seventh
(opening hours as above)

Memorial Sloan-Kettering Thrift Shop
1440 Third Avenue
NYC 10028
(212) 535-1250
btw 81/82nd
Mon-Fri 10-5:30, Sat 11-5

Spence-Chapin Thrift Shop
1850 Second Avenue
NYC 10128
(212) 426-7643
btw 95/96th
Mon-Sat 10-5, Sun 12-5

Spence-Chapin Thrift Shop
1473 Third Avenue
NYC 10128
(212) 737-8448
btw 83/84th
Mon-Fri 11-6:15, Sat 11-5:15, Sun 12-4:30

5 very good reasons why you should become a *Where to Wear* online subscriber

1. Access the guide online from wherever you are.

2. Take the guide on a laptop or CD ROM.

3. Find a particular designer, type of clothing or boutique easily by just typing in what you want and seeing the result.

4. Results printed out to show information and location, member concessions, special offers and promotions from stores.

5. Exclusive seasonal offers available to *Where to Wear* members only from selected stores.

Visit our new exclusive members website at
www.wheretowear.com/member.htm

How to order *Where to Wear*

Where to Wear publishes guides to the following cities: *London*, *New York*, *Paris*, *Los Angeles*, *San Francisco*, *Italy* (which includes Florence, Milan and Rome), *Australia* (which includes Sydney, Melbourne, Adelaide), *Las Vegas* and *Florida*. Each edition retails at £9.99 or $14.95.

There is also a gift box set, *Shopping Guides to the World's Fashion Capitals*, available for £29.99 or $49.99 which includes the *London*, *New York*, *Paris* and *Italy (Milan, Florence, and Rome)* guides (four books for the price of three).

If you live in the UK or Europe, you can order your copies of *Where to Wear* by contacting our London office at:

10 Cinnamon Row
Plantation Wharf
London SW11 3TW
TEL: 020 7801 1381
EMAIL: uk@wheretowear.com

If you live in the USA, you can order your copies of *Where to Wear* by contacting our New York office at:

666 Fifth Avenue
PMB 377
New York, NY 10103
TEL: 212-969-0138
TOLL-FREE: 1-877-714-SHOP (7467)
EMAIL: usa@wheretowear.com

Or simply log on to our website: www.wheretowear.com
Where to Wear delivers worldwide.

Where to Wear

NEW YORK

PLACE YOUR
CORPORATE LOGO
HERE

FASHION SHOPPING FROM A-Z

CUSTOMIZE TO MEET YOUR OBJECTIVES

Where to Wear, the only recognized brand name in fashion shopping guides, is an effective marketing tool for your business. *Where to Wear* can customize any of its city guides to reflect your company's brand identity. Our corporate clients have used *Where to Wear* in a variety of different ways: subscription renewals, hotel in-room gift, magazine cover mount, event or holiday gift, or a much needed thank-you to key clients.

Where to Wear has its own in-house design team who will work with you to co-brand our guides:

- Stamp your corporate logo onto the *Where to Wear* front cover
- Create co-branded covers with additional pages detailing your important information
- Offer mini guides with specially selected stores to your demographic profile
- Design leather pocket-size agenda books for men and women
- Cover full-size editions of *Where to Wear* in beautiful leather or suede in a variety of colors
- Create a box set, including different cities, with a co-branded cover